William Ramsey

The Mostellaria of Plautus with Notes Critical and Explanatory

William Ramsey

The Mostellaria of Plautus with Notes Critical and Explanatory

ISBN/EAN: 9783741158223

Manufactured in Europe, USA, Canada, Australia, Japa

Cover: Foto ©Thomas Meinert / pixelio.de

Manufactured and distributed by brebook publishing software
(www.brebook.com)

William Ramsey

The Mostellaria of Plautus with Notes Critical and Explanatory

Ext. fcap. 8vo. cloth, price 5s. 6d.

O V I D

SELECTIONS FOR THE USE OF SCHOOLS

WITH INTRODUCTIONS AND NOTES

AND AN APPENDIX ON THE ROMAN CALENDAR

BY

WILLIAM RAMSAY, M.A.

FORMERLY PROFESSOR OF HUMANITY IN THE UNIVERSITY OF GLASGOW
AUTHOR OF 'MANUAL OF ROMAN ANTIQUITIES,' ETC.

EDITED BY

GEORGE G. RAMSAY, M.A.

TRIN. COLL. OXON.

PROFESSOR OF HUMANITY IN THE UNIVERSITY OF GLASGOW

OXFORD, printed at the CLARENDON PRESS
and Published by
MACMILLAN AND CO., LONDON
Publishers to the University

.

THE

MOSTELLARIA OF PLAUTUS.

RAMSAY.

THE

MOSTELLARIA OF PLAUTUS

WITH NOTES CRITICAL AND EXPLANATORY

PROLEGOMENA AND EXCURSUS

BY

WILLIAM RAMSAY, M.A.

FORMERLY PROFESSOR OF HUMANITY IN THE UNIVERSITY OF GLASGOW
AUTHOR OF 'MANUAL OF ROMAN ANTIQUITIES' ETC

EDITED BY

GEORGE G. RAMSAY, M.A.

TRIN. COLL. OXON.

PROFESSOR OF HUMANITY IN THE UNIVERSITY OF GLASGOW

London:

MACMILLAN AND CO.

1869.

CONTENTS.

CONTENTS.

PREFACE.

THE materials for the present edition of the Mostellaria were left incomplete and unarranged by the late Professor William Ramsay at the time of his death in 1865. It had long been his intention to prepare a complete edition of several of the plays of Plautus; and the appearance of the work was expected with much interest by many scholars in this country, not only amongst those who as students in his class had enjoyed the privilege of listening to his scholarlike and animated expositions of his favourite author, but also by those who hoped to see preserved in an important work the fruits of his mature scholarship, and of that leisure which after a long life of devoted and unremitting toil he had at length been enabled to secure. But unhappily he did not live to complete the task; the strength which had been severely tested by a life of incessant work, and for twelve years overstrained by a constant battle with failing health, gave way at length almost as soon as he had resigned his office; and it was left to me to put together as best I could the unfinished work of the truest and dearest of friends, one of the most accomplished scholars, and certainly one of the most distinguished and successful Professors, that Scotland ever produced.

Anxious as I was to preserve the remains of his rare and learned scholarship, I was keenly alive to the responsibility which attaches to a man who undertakes to give to the world the work of another; and in the papers as I received them

b

there was much that was perplexing and that could only have
been explained by the writer himself. Hardly any part of the
work was absolutely complete; I could not tell what portions
had been finally revised, or at what period the different portions
had been written; and in some particulars, trifling in themselves no doubt, I found just so much inconsistency as would
spring from a gradual ripening of opinion, and would seem
to shew that while each portion of the subject had been
minutely studied in itself, there was wanting that larger and
fuller review which gathers together the various fragments of
a subject in a single grasp, and gives them the unity of a
whole.   At the same time, the MS. contained so much that
was valuable in itself, so much on which heavy labour had
been bestowed, and I was so strongly encouraged to publish
it by several of my uncle's intimate friends, amongst whom
I may mention, with the warmest acknowledgments for the
assistance they have rendered me, Professor Lushington of
this University, and Professor Lewis Campbell of the University of St. Andrew, that I could have no hesitation in under-
taking the task.   And though I cannot presume that the work
as now published is as perfect as he intended it to be, though
it may omit much that he would have included, and include
what he might have excluded, it contains nothing but what
he wrote; and my work has been almost entirely limited to
that of an editor in the strictest sense.

I have arranged and put together the various fragments of
the work, including everything which I thought of value, and
omitting whatever was manifestly incomplete, or seemed to require more revision than the mere correction of inaccuracy.   In
many cases I have found it necessary to supply the phraseology:
in others I have had to supply the connection. Where it has
been necessary to fill up a gap in the sense, or to indicate
more fully the line of an argument, I have enclosed my own
additions within brackets.   And as there are some points, as
to which, not having enough to guide me as to the author's

intention, I have had to follow my own judgment, I will describe more particularly the condition of some portions of the MS. as I found it.

The text, fortunately, was left in a completed state. It is founded almost entirely, as the reader will perceive, upon the readings of the Vatican MSS., and especially B, with such assistance as can be obtained from A, whose authority is of course paramount in all those cases where its evidence is available.

The critical apparatus has been derived partly from printed editions, but also in part from an original edition of the MSS. themselves; and the chief value of this collation, in a critical point of view, will be found in the circumstance that in the winter of 1863-4, Mr. Ramsay spent several months in making a careful collation of the Vatican MSS., more particularly of B, having previously on his way to Rome examined the celebrated Milan Palimpsest. The result of these labours is to be found partly in the Prolegomena, partly in the critical notes, which embrace a considerable number of readings not recorded by Ritschl, and in some few instances correct his errors. These additions and corrections, not included in the copy of the text as I found it, have been incorporated by myself; and in several cases, where I felt uncertain as to the exact meaning or reference of the MS. notes in my hands, I was enabled to set doubt at rest by a careful personal examination of the Vatican MSS. in June, 1867, when I had the satisfaction of testing the perfect accuracy of every statement made in this edition as to the readings and condition of those MSS.

In the matter of orthography, I found myself placed in a considerable difficulty. It will be observed that in the Prolegomena the more important points of doubt in connection with this subject are discussed at length, and in many cases a decision arrived at as to the modes of spelling particular forms and words, which we may, from the evidence of inscriptions, believe to have been prevalent at the time when Plautus wrote, and which we may therefore presume to have been actually employed by him. From the manner in which these conclusions are stated, it would seem that the author had intended to adopt such modes of spelling in his text, and I attempted accordingly to carry that idea into effect.

But I soon found that the attempt involved inconsistencies. The number of cases as to which the inscriptions referred to can be regarded as affording any clear evidence is extremely small; and however strongly we may be satisfied that in such cases Plautus probably did make use of some particular mode of spelling, in the vast majority of cases we have no evidence from inscriptions at all, and we are obliged to fall back upon that afforded by the best MSS. Now, although it is doubtless true that in the case of Plautus the authority of MSS. is of less value on points of orthography than in the case of later writers, inasmuch as during the two succeeding centuries little interest was felt in orthographical and grammatical questions, while a respect for the antique as such was almost entirely wanting; still, since the evidence of inscriptions is so meagre, and fails to afford materials for a complete orthography, I have thought it more consistent and uniform to adopt an orthography based wholly upon the best MS. evidence, than one based partly on the inscriptions of one age and partly on the MSS. of another—an orthography which, as the author remarks in the Prolegomena, might preserve a flavour of the antique, but which could not be regarded as representing the practice of any particular author or of any particular time. And it is obvious that if there is no distinct object to be gained by the adoption of a peculiar mode of spelling, it is undesirable to deface a text with forms which shock the eye of all but the scientific scholar, and throw a needless difficulty in the way of the young student.

I have refrained therefore from adopting in the text those modes of spelling for which we have no sufficient MS. authority, but which, from the evidence of inscriptions, Mr. Ramsay held himself entitled to conclude were in all probability actually employed by Plautus himself. I have preferred to exhibit an orthography all but identical with that presented by the most distinguished of the recent critics, especially Ritschl and Fleckeisen, and which, so far as the Mostellaria is concerned, is to be found in an excellent form in the edition of that play by Aug. Lorenz (1866), forming part of the Haupt and Sauppe classics. Almost all the peculiarities which distinguish that orthography have been sanctioned by Mr. Ramsay, and have been therefore incorporated in the text. Thus *p* has been uniformly substituted for *b* before *s* or *t*, as in *apstinere, optinere*, and the like; *uo* (*vo*) is uniformly written for *uu* (*vu*), except in the words *tuum* and *suum*, where, in deference to the authority of Ritschl, I have retained the familiar mode of spelling: *o* is written for *e* in *vorter, vorto* and its compounds; *oplumus, maxumus, carnufex*, etc. is written for *optimus*, etc.; *p* is in all cases inserted between *m* and either *s* or *t* following, while the spellings *faenus, caenum, adulescens, gnatus* (the noun), and others for which there is good MS. authority, are adopted throughout.

But, for the reasons above stated, I have refrained from substituting *eis* for *is* in datives and ablatives plural of the first and second declensions, and from writing uniformly *es* in all plural cases of the third, although Mr. Ramsay holds it to be an older form than either *is* or *ns*; nor have I ventured to write *quei, sei, quasei, ibei, ubei, ceivis, deico*, etc., though in all those cases it can be shewn from inscriptions that the longer form was that more commonly employed in the time of Plautus.

It will be seen from the Prolegomena that the evidence of inscriptions proves as certainly as that of MSS., that in many cases uniformity of spelling did not prevail until a comparatively late period; we see the rival forms side by side in the same inscriptions, and we cannot doubt that in such cases both forms were in use together, and that it was only gradually and after a long conflict that the older forms gave

way to the more recent. Such being the case, it is obviously
not worth while to disfigure a text for the sake of what is
only a greater probability on one side ; the evidence shews
that Plautus probably wrote *es* in nominatives and accusatives
plural, *eis* in datives and ablatives, more often than *is;* but it
is still more probable that he employed both forms; and in a
case like this, where the MSS. actually do preserve traces of
variety, it is better to follow that variety implicitly, whenever
we have confidence in the MS. reading, than to adopt a rigid
uniformity which we can assert with something approaching to
confidence was not observed by our author. I have therefore
endeavoured in all such cases to reproduce the best MS.
reading; the critical notes will almost always indicate the
authority followed.

Next, as regards that part of the Prolegomena which deals
with the metres and prosody of Plautus. The MS. of this
portion of the work was in much confusion, had evidently
undergone little or no revision, and had apparently been
written at different times. The examples had not been finally
selected or arranged; the connection was often imperfectly
traced, and some lines of argument will be found to be hinted
at rather than followed out. The greater part seems to have
been written not very recently, and without any reference to the
labours of those more recent German critics who have been
waging so fierce a battle as to the true principles of Plautine
prosody, amongst whom I may mention Fleckeisen, Corssen,
Studemund, Spengel, Ritschl (so far as concerns his later views,
which present some important modifications from those expressed in his earlier writings), and in our own country
Dr. W. Wagner, who in the Prolegomena to his valuable
edition of the Aulularia has laid before English readers a clear
and powerful statement of the view of Plautine prosody opposed
to that adopted by Mr. Ramsay and by the bulk of English
scholars. And this is the more to be regretted, as Mr. Ramsay
had devoted much attention to the subject of Latin prosody,

and is well known as the author of the most complete and
systematic Manual of Latin Prosody in the English language.
To the latest edition of that Manual he added an acute and
learned appendix on the so-called Saturnian verse, from which
it will be seen in how critical and sceptical a spirit he was
prepared to deal with the various metrical fancies of modern
German scholars, while the critical notes of this edition will
shew how rigorous he was in the demand for definite evidence
before admitting an emendation of the text on the ground of
metre only.

In the present work, the great difficulties which beset the
prosody of Plautus, and especially the great question whether
the anomalies of Plautine metre are to be explained by some
kind of contraction, or running together of syllables in quick
pronunciation, according to the view adopted by Mr. Ramsay,
or by supposing a wholesale violation of the ordinary laws of
Latin prosody, as these were observed by the later poets, cannot
be said to be either fully discussed or finally solved; yet the
authority of a scholar who had made the subject of prosody
his peculiar study, will have some value; the view adopted is
stated with some important modifications, and supported by
a large number of examples, many of them included amongst
those which have been brought forward by Dr. Wagner and
others in support of the rival theory, and which are here shewn
to be capable of an easy explanation other than that advanced
by them as part of their case. It is pointed out how few are
the words which can with any confidence be asserted to have
been used by Plautus with a quantity different from that observed by later writers; and the impression is left, that a critical examination into the objections commonly brought forward
to the theory of contraction or 'correption,' will be found to
have but little solid foundation; that the proof on the other
side is negative rather than positive; while in proportion as
the difficulties attending that theory are removed, the argument

from the general analogy of the Latin language, and the languages derived from it, will have the greater weight.

The Notes and the Excursus speak for themselves; the latter, it will be observed, as well as the Prolegomena, refer to the plays of Plautus generally, and have no special application to the Mostellaria. Whether either are as full as they were intended ultimately to be, I have no means of judging.

In conclusion, I have only to say that by the most careful verification of references throughout, I have done everything in my power to ensure accuracy in points of detail. The edition to which the references have been uniformly made to apply is the Vulgate, as represented in the Delphin edition. In the case of the Mostellaria, the reference to the text of the present edition, where it differs from the Vulgate, is appended within brackets.

GEORGE G. RAMSAY.

Glasgow College,
Dec. 8, 1868.

PROLEGOMENA.

I.—THE TEXT.

At the period of the revival of letters eight only of the Comedies of Plautus were known to the learned, viz. the *Amphitruo, Asinaria, Aulularia, Captivi, Casina, Cistellaria, Curculio,* and the *Epidicus.* The first announcement of the existence of a MS. containing the whole of the twenty which we now possess is made in a letter written from Rome about the beginning of 1429, by Poggio Bracciolini, at that time Apostolic Secretary to Pope Martin V, in which he informs his friend Niccolo Niccoli at Florence that Nicolas of Treves had discovered in Germany several classical works, and among others a volume containing twenty plays of Plautus, and Poggio gives the titles of all the new pieces. In reality the MS. was found to comprise sixteen only, but of these twelve were previously unknown, the *Casina, Cistellaria, Curculio,* and *Epidicus* being omitted. About the close of the year Nicolas arrived in Rome with his treasures, which were delivered to Cardinal Giordano Orsini, as we learn from another letter of Poggio written on December 27, 1429, and his words are so important that they deserve to be transcribed—

"Nicolaus Trevirensis huc venit afferens secum sexdecim Plauti comoedias in uno volumine, in quibus quatuor sunt ex iis quas habemus; scilicet Amphitruo, Asinaria, Aulularia, Captivi; duodecim autem ex lucro; hae sunt: Bacchides, Mustellaria, Menaechmi, Miles Gloriosus, Mercator, Pseudolus, Poenulus, Persa, Rudens, Stichus, Trinummus, Truculentus. Has nondum aliquis transcripsit, neque enim earum copiam nobis facit Cardinalis: tamen adhuc nullus praeter me petiit. Liber est illis litteris antiquis corruptis, quales sunt Quintiliani, et multa in multis desunt. Non faciam transcribi, nisi prius illas legero, atque emendavero: nam nisi viri eruditi manu scribantur, inutilis erit labor." And again, in another letter, January 6, 1431—

"Nullus, mihi crede, Plautum bene transcribet, nisi is sit doctissimus:

b

est eis litteris, quibus multi libri ex antiquis, quos a mulieribus
conscriptos arbitror, nulla verborum distinctione, ut persaepe divi-
nandum sit."

Difficulties and jealousies regarding the use of this MS. seem to
have arisen between the Cardinal and Poggio, whose letters are filled
with complaints, and we know not precisely at what period it was
placed at his disposal. A copy, however, made by some one, was
sent to the Duke of Milan in 1431, and the MS. itself was sent to
Florence at the request of Lorenzo de Medici, and there a copy of
the last twelve plays was made by Niccolo Niccoli with his own hand,
and this very copy is known to have existed at a comparatively
recent period in the Library of St. Mark at Florence, but it is not
certain where it is now to be found.

For a long period the MS. brought to Italy by Nicolas of Treves
was the only source from which the twelve plays were derived.
Merula, in his preface to the Editio Princeps (1472), speaks of the
last twelve Comedies as having been discovered forty years before
the time when he was writing, and adds that there was but one MS.
from which, as from an archetype, all the copies in circulation had
been derived; and again, Ugoletus, in 1515, employs the same
language.

It appears, from what has been said above, that the MS. of Nicolas
of Treves was copied at least twice within two years from its arrival
at Rome, and these copies, and probably the original MS. also, would
be transcribed and retranscribed until the twelve new plays became
generally known to the literary men of Italy and Germany. But we
must not suppose that the whole or even the greater number of these
copies corresponded with each other, and were faithful representatives
of the MS. from which they were derived. That original, as described by Poggio, is written in a character hard to be decyphered,
the words are not properly divided, and it abounds in corruptions
of every kind. Moreover the archaic forms, strange words, and
colloquial phrases which abound in Plautus, even when represented
correctly in the MS., would in many cases be unintelligible to the
scholars of that day, and would by them be regarded as corruptions.
Hence all who applied themselves to these pursuits would endeavour
to reduce their author into an intelligible form by correcting as they
went, a practice almost universal at that period, and Poggio, in one
of the passages quoted above, speaks of this process as essential, and
evidently intended, when he gained possession of the MS., not to
make a faithful transcript, but to present a text elaborated by his own

ingenuity. This system was encouraged by those who lectured publicly on Plautus, and who were compelled to submit him to their auditors in a shape which could be understood. Hence each play became encumbered with a mass of conjectural emendations and arbitrary changes, many of them ingenious, some probably true, but the greater number altogether preposterous. The object in view was, however, accomplished, and editions of the different pieces were circulated, readable indeed, but in which the genuine text was, in innumerable passages, recklessly sacrificed. Whether this work was performed by many hands, as is most probable, or by one individual, possibly Poggio himself, as Ritschl believes, we are unable to determine, but the corrected pieces were certainly collected, arranged, and combined before the end of the fifteenth century, and thus arose a family of interpolated MSS., which became largely multiplied, of which specimens are to be found in most of the great libraries of Europe, and which, although differing in details, all bear a general and even close resemblance to each other.

The Editio Princeps of the whole twenty plays was printed, as noticed above, at Venice in 1472, the editor being Georgius Merula. In his preface he repeatedly complains of the numerous corruptions which had been introduced by the perversity of ignorant or half-learned grammarians, and of the difficulty of procuring a faithful transcript of the original MS. from which the last twelve plays had been derived; and it would appear that in so far as the *Bacchides*, the *Mostellaria*, the *Menaechmi*, the *Miles*, and the *Mercator* were concerned, he had been obliged to content himself with interpolated copies, and that, in consequence, these plays were exhibited under a worse aspect than the remainder.

For eighty years after the appearance of the Editio Princeps, which was reprinted at Treviso in 1482, the text of Plautus underwent little or no improvement. Editions were published by Scutarius of Vercelli (1490), by Saracenus (Venice, 1499), by Io. Baptista Pius (Milan, 1500), by Ph. Beroaldus (Bologna, 1500), by Pylades (Brescia, 1506, reprinted at Venice, 1511), by Ugoletus (Parma, 1510), and the two editions of Simon Charpentarius (Lyons probably, 1513, and Paris), and many others of inferior note. Numerous changes were introduced by the whole of these, especially by Pylades, who may be said to have remodelled the existing text, but although some or all of them may have had access to a correct copy of D, and may have compared it with various interpolated MSS., no new source of information had become available during the period

b 2

above named; and although many of the conjectural emendations were in themselves ingenious and plausible, yet on the whole the text of Plautus was more encumbered with a load of foreign matter and more deformed than even in the Editio Princeps.

But a new era dawned in 1552, when a complete edition of the twenty plays was published at Leipsic by Joachim Camerarius, who had previously published (Lips. 1545) five pieces, and subsequently (Lips. 1549) six more.

Camerarius had obtained possession of two MSS. unknown to previous editors.

One of these contained the whole twenty plays, and is generally known among critics as the *Vetus Codex Camerarii*, in consequence of being older than any then known.

The other is very frequently referred to as the *Codex Decurtatus*, because although it had originally contained the whole twenty, the first eight had been torn off and had disappeared before it came into the hands of Camerarius. Both of these, the first especially, proved of the highest value, and by their aid, combined with his own remarkable acuteness and good sense, Camerarius, who thoroughly understood his author, and was deeply imbued with his spirit and phraseology, was enabled to elaborate a text immeasurably superior to any that had been previously given to the world. He could say with justice when he entered upon his task—" Si ullum cuiusquam opus miserabiliter depravatum et corruptum scelerate fuit, hoc profecto fuit optimum et praestantissimum Plautinarum comoediarum. Correctiones autem comprobaverunt proverbium vetus et ipsae, multorum medicorum curationibus aegrotos plerumque perdi;" and again, " nostra diligentia et industria etiam quadam permulta de nostro illo veteri libro in Plautinis comoediis restituta sibi fuerunt, tam in verbis quam numeris versuum, de quorum integritate nihil etiam dubii iam nobis relinquitur. Ac possem annumerare non δεκάδας neque ἑκατοντάδας, sed plane χιλιάδας, si ostentare operam nostram vellemus, sed pauperis est numerare pecus;" and when it was completed he was able to boast without vainglory—" vere ac simpliciter affirmare possum vix ullum versum, de quo non aliquid, certe paginam nullam esse, de qua non plurimum mendorum sublatum sit."

Not only did Camerarius collate these MSS. with so much care and accuracy that when eagerly scrutinized by subsequent scholars wonderfully few mistakes were detected and omissions supplied, but in consequence of his natural acuteness and his thorough acquaintance with the spirit and phraseology of Plautus, the greater number of his

numerous conjectural emendations carry conviction to our minds,
and have in the great majority of cases been acquiesced in as
certain, or at least acknowledged to be superior to those proceeding
from any other source. Although many of the best scholars of the
sixteenth and seventeenth centuries busied themselves with Plautus,
and several examined again and again his MSS. with the most
anxious care—among whom we may name Fabricius, Lambinus,
Donsa, Taubmannus, Pareus, Gruterus, and Guyetus—and although
doubtless not a few alterations and improvements were introduced
by these eminent men, still the result of their exertions, in comparison with those of Camerarius, may be regarded as insignificant,
and the text as presented by him is essentially the same with that
exhibited in the Vulgate or Standard Recension, which was worked
up by Gronovius, and appears under its best form in the edition
printed at Leyden in 1684.

[At this point, after remarking that little was done for our author
during the seventeenth century, the author had intended to insert a
general criticism of the editions of Bothe, Weise, and Ritschl, and it
is much to be regretted that this portion of his task, like so many
others, was left uncompleted. It will be seen abundantly from the
critical notes how often and how strongly he dissents from the arbitrary changes introduced into the text by Ritschl, and especially those
introduced for supposed metrical reasons.—ED.]

MANUSCRIPTS OF PLAUTUS.

The most important of the existing manuscripts of Plautus
are—

A. The Milan Palimpsest.

This MS. was transferred from the celebrated monastery of
St. Columbanus at Bobbio to the Ambrosian Library about the
beginning of the seventeenth century. An account of it was first
published by Angelo Mai, in 1815, in his "*M. Accii Plauti frag-
menta inedita*," and it has since been carefully scrutinized by Ritschl,
Schwartzmann, and others. The original writing was believed by
Mai to belong to the age of the Antonines, but may with greater
probability be ascribed to the fifth or sixth century, and it must
be regarded as one of the oldest, if not the very oldest, specimen
in existence of any Latin classical author. The superimposed writing
belongs to the ninth century, and consists of a portion of the Old

Testament in an exceedingly coarse and ill-executed character. The MS. in its primitive state contained the whole twenty plays, and was bound up in "fasciculi" or "quaterniones," each fasciculus being composed of four sheets of parchment laid one above another and then doubled so as to form eight leaves of parchment (membranae) and sixteen pages, and these fasciculi were distinguished by numerals placed at the bottom, just as a printer distinguishes his sheets by the letters called 'signatures.' The volume, when required for a second writing, had been taken to pieces, the doubled parchments had been washed and scraped separately, and when rebound, as might have been expected, no attention was paid to the original arrangement. Hence many of the sheets which formed the fasciculi have altogether disappeared, some have been torn and mutilated, in others the original writing has been wholly or partially obliterated by the cleansing process, and in others the same result has been produced by damp and neglect. Thus in a very few instances only is a whole page legible, more commonly a few lines or portions of lines, but frequently a few straggling letters only, or mere traces of letters. Enough however remains to enable us to introduce many important changes and improvements, and to prove that the MS., if it had been preserved entire, would have been worthy to rank with the Vatican Virgil and the Bembine Terence.

But this is not the whole. Although we talk of certain portions of the MS. being legible, it must not be understood that what remains is in all cases legible by ordinary inexperienced scholars. Notwithstanding the ingenious chemical contrivances which have been applied for the purpose of reviving the faded characters, these are in numerous instances so indistinct and evanescent that it is only by dint of the most laborious and painful efforts, efforts laborious and painful alike to the mind and to the eye, that they can be decyphered at all. Sometimes the MS., when held in a particular light, will present glimpses of marks before invisible; from these marks we must endeavour to restore the letters which they indicate, and then to combine them into syllables and words. It is manifest that a process of this nature will often yield different results in different hands. Consequently some individuals have succeeded, or believed that they have succeeded, in recovering much that is invisible or unintelligible to others, and there is always the danger of an enthusiastic student being carried away by a zealous fancy, and then making discoveries which exist in his imagination only.

The *Mostellaria* in the original MS. seems to have occupied those

fasciculi or quaterniones, described above, which were numbered
XL, XLI, XLII, XLIII, and a few pages of XLIV. Of XL, XLI, no portion
remains, and the Palimpsest does not become available for this play
until we reach the second leaf of XLII (III. l. 45). Altogether eight
leaves or sixteen pages remain of XLII, XLIII (i. e. one-half of XLII
and one-half of XLIII), more or less legible, but the leaves of XLIV,
which contained the continuation of the play from V. ii. 11 to the end,
are lost. The MS. was written, like all those belonging to an early
period, in large, distinct, well-executed capitals; the lines in the
Iambic Senarians and Septenarians were correctly divided, but the
Trochaic and Iambic words which make up a line are not divided,
the letters being written continuously. When the dialogue passes
from one character to another at the beginning of a line, there is no
mark to indicate this, but when such a change takes place in the
middle of a line, then a blank space, such as would be occupied by
two letters, is left, which it was probably intended to fill up with the
initial of the name in red ink. In like manner the scenes are divided
from each other by a blank space sufficient to contain two lines of
writing, and this in like manner it was intended should be filled up
with the names of the personages who took part in the action of
the scene in question.

B. *The Vetus Codex Camerarii.* *

From the hands of Camerarius this MS. passed into the Palatine
Library at the beginning of the seventeenth century, was conveyed to
Rome in the year 1622, and is still preserved in the library of the
Vatican among the Palatine MSS. and numbered 1615.

The writing belongs to the eleventh century, and extends over
213 sheets of vellum in moderate-sized folio. It contains the whole
of the twenty extant plays of Plautus, together with the title of the
Vidularia subjoined to the Truculentus, while prefixed to the Amphitruo we find the *Querolus.*

The work, which for the most part is coarse and irregular, appears
to have been executed by a number of different hands, and in ink of
different colours. Not unfrequently the scribe has been changed more
than once in the course of a single play. This is especially conspicuous
in the case of the *Persa,* where we can distinctly trace five, if not six,
different hands, several leaves being written in ink which has faded to

---

* All that is known of the previous history of B will be found in Ritschl,
Rhein. Mus. (Welck. and Naek.) vol. iv., p. 311 sqq. and p. 339 sqq.

a very pale brown, while the ink of others is unusually black. Again,
in the same play, portions of several pages have been left blank, and
as these blanks do not indicate any gap in the sense, and occur before a change in the hand, it seems reasonable to infer that different
scribes had different portions of the play allotted to them, without
any nice calculation as to the accurate union of the portions.

The MS. has been ruled throughout, generally with some blunt-
pointed instrument which marked the vellum without ruffling the
surface. The lines however are in many cases irregular, being
closer to each other in some parts of the same page than in others,
while the number of lines in different pages varies much, the general
number however contained in one page being fifty-one or fifty-two.
In some cases, e. g. in portions of the *Rudens*, the pages are written
in double columns. Irregular as is the execution of the work, the
writing is notwithstanding legible throughout, the contractions are
few and for the most part simple.

As to the division of the words, the statement of Ritschl, "Verborum
distinctio aut nulla est aut prava," is not borne out, at least as far as
the *Mostellaria* is concerned, as in this play the words are for the
most part correctly divided in the MS. There is no division into
acts; but in some plays the different scenes are distinguished, a space
being left at the end of each in which are inserted in red ink the
names of the persons who take part in the following scene. In like
manner, the changes of person in the dialogue are carefully indicated
by the insertion of the speaker's name in red ink, either at the beginning of the line or in a space left for the purpose in the middle
of the line as the case may be. This however does not apply to all
the plays, in some of which great irregularity prevails. In the *Persa*,
for example, although spaces have been left marking the divisions
of the scenes, the names of the characters have been inserted in five
or six cases only, while, although spaces are left to indicate the
transition from one speaker to another in the dialogue, the names
have in no case been inserted. In all probability the names of the
characters were added after the plays were transcribed, and by a
different hand; a view which derives confirmation from the fact that
while in some plays they are written in red ink, in others, e. g. the
Curculio, Casina, Epidicus, in black, which in some cases has been
written or painted over with red; in some cases, e. g. conspicuously
in the *Persa*, the blanks have never been filled up at all, and while
Roman characters are generally employed in some plays, Greek
characters have been made use of in others.

Some plays, amongst which is the *Mostellaria*, have been very carefully corrected, and by different hands, in others the corrections are few and insignificant, in others wanting altogether.

Such then being the state of the MS. as a whole, it will be evidently necessary to describe the portion of the MS. which applies to each play separately, as the remarks which apply to one portion will obviously not necessarily hold good of another.

The *Mostellaria* is written upon twelve sheets, of which ten are complete, eight lines at the beginning of the first being occupied with the conclusion of the *Bacchides*, and twenty-five at the close of the twelfth being devoted to the commencement of the *Menechmus*. Each complete page contains, as a rule, fifty-two lines, but two or three have only fifty-one, one or two fifty-three. We have first of all the title, INCIP PLAUTI MUSTELLARIA, in red capitals; then we have the acrostic argument in eleven lines, which reads *Mostellaria*, and then without a break

    GRUMIO—TRANIO. SERVI II in red-ink capitals.

At the top of each left-hand page we have *Plauti*, at the top of each right-hand page *Mustellaria*, each in a large cursive hand. At the conclusion,

PLAUTI MUSTELLARIA EXPLICIT

INCIPIT MENECHMUS . ARGUMEŇ MENECHMI

all in red capitals.

The play seems to be written from beginning to end in the same hand, though it is impossible to assert this positively, as in several places the size of the hand is suddenly enlarged (e. g. I. ii. 21-29, III. ii. 69-73), the original size being resumed after a few lines, while the last leaf, especially where it joins the *Menechmus*, is written in ink of a darker shade, and very probably by a different hand, from the rest. The changes in the size of hand may possibly have arisen from blanks having been left when the MS. was first transcribed, which were subsequently filled up from other sources.

Corrections.

These are by many different hands.

1. Corrections evidently made by the first hand on casual slips, the colour of the ink being the same as that of the original writing.

2. Corrections made over an erasure, where the colour of the ink having been changed by the roughened surface, it is extremely difficult to determine whether they proceeded from the first or from

a later hand. To the same class belong erasures made we cannot tell by whom, as in I. i. 42,

Non omnes possunt olere unguenta exotica,

which was originally written in B,

Non omnes possunt tolere unguenta exotica,

but the *t* has been erased, leaving only a faint trace, and this erasure may or may not have been the work of the first hand. Ritschl therefore is hardly justified in giving *tolere* as the reading of Ba without remark.*

3. Corrections in ink which is perfectly black, and which must proceed from a late hand. Most of the stops and marks of interrogation have been added by this hand. These corrections in black ink are made in two ways, either in the word, or over the word. Thus in I. i. 15 the writing in the original brown ink has

Rus mihi tu obiceta sane^b credo tranio,

but an *s* is added in black ink at the end of *obicta;* or has been added to the *h* in ink darker than the original,† but this may arise from an erasure made between *sane* and *credo,* some wrong word having stood there. A point has been added in red ink after *obicetas,* so that the whole now stands,

Rus mihi tu obiectas. sane^{hoc} credo tranio.

Again, I. i. 31 was written originally in B,

Ante hoc est habitus pacus nec magis contineas,

but an *r* has been inserted in black ink after *a* in *pacus,* and an *n* also in black written over the *a* in *contineas,* so that the line now appears in the MS.

Ante hac est habitus pár^{r}cus nec magis continú^{n}s.

This hand is called Bb by Ritschl.

4. Corrections on the margin, written in a particularly neat, small hand with a fine-pointed pen, and preceded by a *t.* The ink of this hand is intermediate in colour between the brown of the original MS. and the jet-black of the last corrector. This hand is called Dc by Ritschl. We have a good example of the correction of this hand in I. i. 5,

Exi inquam . nidore cupinam quid tales$^{t culim}$.

---

* [My opinion is that the *t* is by the first hand. The ink is of the same colour, and the correction appears to have been made at once.—Ed.]

† [I cannot agree with the author in thinking the ink of this correction darker than that of the original writing. It appears to me to be, if anything, somewhat fainter than the average.—Ed.]

So also I. i. 12 was originally written

Sine modo venire salvos quem absentem comes,

but has been changed by correction into

Sine modo venire salvos quem absentem comes i comœdis,

where the correction of *salvos* into *salvum* is from Db and the marginal *comœdis* from Bc. The corrections of b are frequently rough and coarse.

5. Occasionally stops are inserted in red ink.

6. Occasionally a black line is drawn under a word, as if to call attention to something doubtful or erroneous, as in I. i. 52, which appears in B

O carnificum cribrum . quod credo fore,

where the line under *carnificum* is in ink blacker than that of the first hand. Moreover there is a mark over the first *i*, *carnificum*, as if the first hand had wished to substitute a *u* for the *i*, but it is by no means distinct.

So again, II. i. 70 is written,

Neque quicquam nobis pariant excisin commodi,

the line being in black ink.

So II. ii. 68 was written,

Quia premature vita care operfidem,

the *e* at the end of *premature*, the whole of the word *vita*, and the *e* following, being written over an erasure, and being much blacker than the rest. Then some reader was startled by the combination *operfidem*, and drew a line under it, and then lines were drawn to separate the *o* from *perfidum*, so that the whole now appears as

Quia premature vita care o,'perfidem.

These lines occur very frequently in several plays (e. g. the *Rudens*), and more or less in all, or nearly all.

7. But there is another class of corrections in B to which special attention must be directed. These are inserted in small spaces left blank in the MS., in a small, scratchy hand in red ink, and are intended to complete imperfect lines. These are conjectural emendations by Camerarius, and written in his own hand, and therefore of no value except as specimens of ingenuity. Several examples will be found in III. i., e. g. v. 6, *argentum fenori; v. 7, opus in sumptus fuit; v. 21, atque; v. 23, TH. Negat inquam. TR. Perii oppido; v. 24, Non confitetur*, and many others.

c 2

There is one correction, probably of a late date, in the margin
of III. ii. 5,

      alq*nam*   *Non mihi forte visum ilico fuit,*

i. e. *aliqui legunt nam.* This appears to be the only example of a
correction in this hand in this play, and it is impossible to assign
a date to it either positive or relative: the ink is rather pale.

Finally, there are here and there, especially towards the end of
the play, some corrections and remarks written in black ink in a
hand strongly resembling that of Camerarius, and which have been
ascribed to him. Thus, in I. iii. 93, which appears in B,

       Mulier quae suamq̃ ætatem sperniit speculo elusa est,

where the *a* in *elusa* is written over an erasure, we find in the margin
in the hand spoken of, *ei usus est.* These notes, by whomsoever
written, are evidently modern, and may be safely neglected by any
collator, however scrupulous. They are most numerous in III. ii,
and sometimes are a sort of explanatory commentary, as in *v.* 26,

       Hoc habet repperi qui senem ducerem,

where we find, interlined above *repperi*, *astutiam;* and so in *v.* 51,
above *qui* is written *quomodo* as an explanation.

The following is a list of the interpolations in red ink by Camerarius in the *Mostellaria :*

III. i. 6, 7, stands in B,

       Danista adest qui dedit,

       Qui amica dat empta quq'

Camer. completes the lines with *argenti fenori* Δ and *opus in sūptus
fuit.* Δ

v. 21 stands in B,

            Tr. (so written above)

       Dixtin quæso . dixi inquam ordine omnia.

Camer. has *atque* interlined above the words *inquam ordine.**

v. 23 stands in B,

       N̄egat.   *quom cogita.*

Camer. corrects, *Tn. N̄egat inquam. Tn. perii oppido,* and an *o* in
red ink over the *a* in *cogita.*

v. 24 stands in B [with some scratches below and above the
syllables *si con.*—Ed.],

       dicam si confessus sit

Camer. has *Non confitetur ?* and then some scratches [the first being
apparently an erasure of the name *Thra.* or *Tra.*—Ed.].

       * [Or rather between the two.—Ed.]

In *v.* 36, at the beginning of the line, B has *Tra.* in red ink from the old hand. Camer. has erased this, and has written in his own hand *Tr.* above, thus, *hilarus.*

vv. 43, 44, and 45, stand in B,

> *Magius oportunus adven*   *advenis*
> *Quid est.~ concede huc*   *ditur*
> *Scio te bona īe na*

Camer. *v.* 43, has *ire quam* and Δ at the end of the line.

v. 44, *D. Quin mihi argentum red*

v. 45, he adds at the end of the line *clama nimis*

v. 64 stands in D,

> *Ferre hoc potis an*   *quo habeat foras*

where Camer. has filled up the blank with

> *mavis ut aliquo.*

v. 65 stands in B,

> *Vrbem exsul*   *hic causa tui,*

where Camer. [after an erasure of parts of two or three words in his own hand, as if in some other conjecture had occurred to him first.—ED.] supplies the blank with

> *linquat factus.*

v. 66 stands in D,

> *Quoi sortem*   *cebit. DA. Quin non peto.*

Camer. supplies *vix dare li* [and places a circumflex over *quō.* —ED.].

It may be remarked that in these two lines the spaces left are much larger than would be required for the words supplied by Camerarius.

At the end of each line, where he has inserted a correction, Camer. affixes the mark Δ in red ink. There are in other places here and there a few marks and scratches in the red ink of Camer., but nothing of any importance.

[The only other insertion in the hand of Camerarius that I was able to discover, was after the line (*v.* 78 of same scene),

> *Quod illuc est fenus obsecro quod illic petii,*

where he has written on the margin in the same line, at a short interval, the words *eia mastigia* and something like *&c.* after them, so ᔆ.—ED.]

C. The *Codex alter* of Camerarius, frequently designated, since the time of Pareus, as the *Codex Decurtatus*.

On the death of Camerarius this MS. was purchased, along with the *Vetus Codex*, and deposited in the Palatine Library; from thence it was transferred to the Vatican; in 1797 it was carried to Paris, and in 1815 restored to the Library at Heidelberg, where it now remains.

It belongs to the twelfth century, and is written on 238 leaves of parchment in quarto. It originally contained the whole twenty plays, but the first eight have been torn off, and the last twelve alone remain. It was executed by various hands, and the writing is by no means elegant. The division into words is more corrupt than in D; there is no separation into lines except in a few cases in the Senarians. The names of the characters are generally inserted both at the commencement of the scenes and in the changes in the dialogue, and when omitted a space is usually left blank for their insertion.

The arrangement of the plays is the same as in D.

D. The *Codex Vaticanus*, numbered 3870.

This has been proved to be the identical MS. brought to Italy in 1429 by Nicolas of Treves from Germany, and delivered to Cardinal Orsini,* concerning which we have spoken at length above.

It contains, in 308 sheets of parchment, the *Amphitruo*, *Asinaria*, *Aulularia*, about one-half of the *Captivi*, and the twelve last plays entire.

It bears a very close resemblance to C, both in age, shape, writing, and perverse distribution of the metrical lines, but was written uniformly by a single hand, and is somewhat less faulty in the division of the words.

F. The *Codex Lipsiensis*, belonging to the Bibliotheca Senatoria. It belongs to the fourteenth century, is written beautifully on 314 sheets of parchment in folio, and contains the whole twenty plays. It is sometimes designated as the *Codex Suritanus*, in consequence of having, during a portion of the sixteenth century, been in the possession of Hieronymus Surita, of Saragossa. It is regarded by R. as presenting the interpolated text under its best form.

Lastly, we may mention Z, the *Editio Princeps*, edited by George Merula, and printed at Venice in 1472.

[Hence called by R. 'Ursinianum.'—ED.]

It will be readily inferred, from what has been already stated, that the constitution of the text in the twelve last plays of Plautus depends entirely on B, C, D, together with such aid as we occasionally derive from A, whose authority, when distinctly available, is almost paramount. The readings of F are curious, as in them we trace the process by which so many of the Latin classics became corrupted in the fifteenth and sixteenth centuries, while Z, the value of which has frequently been greatly over-estimated, must be regarded as an attempt to return more nearly to the genuine text by rejecting several of the more flagrant interpolations.

Moreover, there is such a close general resemblance between B, C, D, that it is evident that they belong to one family; that is to say, that they were all three derived from the same archetype without passing through many intermediate stages; but it is certain that no one of these three was copied from either of the two others, although, as noticed above, the connection between C and D is more close than that between B and either of them.

B, C, D, have all been frequently collated since the time of Camerarius, and it may be proper to notice the manner in which they have been variously designated.

B and C are generally distinguished, since the time of Pareus, as *Cod. Vet.* and *Cod. Decurt.*, and, when spoken of jointly, as the *Codd. Palatt.*

Until the time of Ritschl, D was not sharply distinguished from the three other MSS. in the Vatican (which he calls G, H, K), all of which were written in the fifteenth century, and all belong to the interpolated family, and as such are of little or no value, the whole being frequently referred to vaguely as *Codd. Vatic.*

c

II.—THE ORTHOGRAPHY OF PLAUTUS.

Every one who is familiar with the text of Plautus, as presented
in the printed copies, must be struck by the differences which it
exhibits in orthography. Not only does he detect these discrepancies
in the more important editions, when compared with each other, but
he often finds the same word appear under a different form in the
same edition, in the same play, and even in lines almost consecutive.
Nor will he be able to discover any fixed principle by which editors
have been guided. They seem to have followed at one time one
guide, at another time another, and not unfrequently to have partially
adopted some system founded upon their own individual views of
grammar and etymology. This is most perplexing to a young scholar.
It seriously embarrasses and retards his progress, and the labour
necessary to master the difficulties, when unattended by any sure
result, proves most irksome, because his memory is severely tasked
without the conviction that his mind has been beneficially exercised.
It is clearly desirable to put an end to this state of things. More
than one method may be pursued.

1. We may endeavour to restore the orthography of the Latin
language as it existed during the third century B.C., and to reproduce
the lines of Plautus exactly as we may suppose them to have proceeded from the pen of the author. Every one acquainted with the
subject will at once admit that this is simply impossible; that we
have no means at our disposal which would enable us to accomplish
such an object.

2. We may content ourselves with adopting what may be called
the standard orthography of Latin, which, although varying slightly
according to the views of scholars upon particular points, is sub-
stantially the same in all the leading editions of the classics, and was
probably formally adjusted during the first century of the Empire.
This is perhaps the most simple plan, and is open to fewer objections.
The learner is not discouraged by encountering unnecessary obstacles,
and he can investigate the questions connected with the early history
and orthography of the language when he has advanced farther in
his studies. Moreover, this is the course which we here ourselves
have adopted with regard to our own Shakespeare.

3. There is however yet another path open, a sort of *via media*,
and this is the one which I feel inclined to follow. It can be proved

by very satisfactory evidence that certain modes of spelling, not only
particular words, but whole classes of words, were not introduced
until long after the death of Plautus, and therefore could not possibly
have been employed by him. Everything leads to the conclusion
that a gradual change took place in orthography from the time of
Ennius down to the first century of the Empire; that for a considerable period a struggle took place between some of the old and
of the new forms, and hence we find them frequently side by side;
that several of the former were quickly superseded, while not a few
of the latter were not admitted at all until a comparatively late period.
It is to those old forms—which kept their ground steadily, and were
still in general use when Cicero, Pompeius, and Caesar were born,
when not a little of the roughness of the olden time still lingered—
that we desire chiefly to direct attention.   They are not very
numerous; they are easily learned; and they will serve to give an
antique flavour at least to the language of one of Rome's earlier
writers.

It was probably something of this sort that Ritschl intended to
effect when he says, " id agamus ut, qualem aliquanto politior aetas
Plautum legisse videatur, quoad eius fieri possit, recuperemus." But
in carrying out this intention it appears to me that he very frequently
neglects the best testimony and puts faith in the worst—that he is
inconsistent, arbitrary, fanciful, and not seldom positively wrong, so
that we can in no way accept his conclusions as authoritative.

Before going farther, it will be necessary to state and examine the
sources from which our information upon questions of orthography
is derived.   These are three in number—I. The Grammarians;
II. Manuscripts; III. Inscriptions.

1. *The Grammarians.*

Any one who should attempt to ascertain the ancient orthography
of the Latin language, or even the orthography of any particular
period, by relying on the statements of the ancient grammarians,
would speedily find himself involved in inextricable confusion. He
will discover that they frequently contradict not only each other, but
also themselves: they frequently declare, in treating of such matters,
that a word ought to be spelled in a certain manner, in accordance
with their own theories, without referring to the actual usage of any
particular period, and not seldom present their own theories, fancies
and conjectures as if they were real facts. Moreover, the text of these

writers is frequently so corrupt that it is impossible to determine their actual meaning. Of this we have a conspicuous example in the earliest grammatical essay which has come down to us, viz. the lines of Lucilius upon the termination EI, which are in such confusion that it is impossible to elicit any satisfactory signification from them without having recourse to a number of conjectural emendations. Not that we would reject the evidence of the grammarians in a mass. All that we find in Quintilian is worthy of the most serious attention, and may for the most part be accepted without hesitation. The authority of Priscian also is considerable, although he is by no means a guide that can be entirely depended upon; but the lower we descend the less trustworthy do the authorities become, and their evidence cannot be accepted except when corroborated by other sources of information.

In order to give an idea of the small reliance that can be placed upon the statements of the ancient grammarians in matters of orthography, we may briefly examine their assertions with regard to the doubling of consonants.

In cases where the same word occurs written sometimes with a single, sometimes with a double consonant, it may be difficult to decide with certainty which is the original form, but the presumption will always be that the more simple form is also the most ancient. Since no word or syllable can either begin or end with a doubled consonant, it follows that wherever doubled consonants occur they must stand between two vowels, except in the case of certain compound words. But some of the old grammarians maintained that a doubled consonant could not be admitted except after a short vowel. Thus Cornut. ap. Cass. p. 2283 (ed. Putsch.):

"*Causa* per unam S, nec quemquam moveat antiqua scriptura, nam et *accussare* per duo SS scripserunt, sicut *fuisse, divisisse, esse* et *caussasse* per duo SS scriptum invenio. In qua enuntiatione quomodo duarum consonantium sonus exaudiatur, non invenio." He then goes on to give *vostra, advorsum, pervorsum, rotare* (vetare), *vortex, convolvere, amplectere,* as examples of archaic spelling out of date in his time.

Compare with this Mar. Victorin. p. 2456: "Est itaque in principio dicendum quemadmodum antiqui scripserint, dehinc quid nunc debeamus observare. Consonantes literas non geminabant ut in his *Annius, Lucullus, Memmius,* et cetera his similia, sed supra literam quam geminari oportebat scilicet Siciliaum imponebant cuius figura haec est,   quod erat signum geminandi, sicut apparet in multis adhuc veteribus ita scriptis libris. Iidem (sc. antiqui) voces quae pressiore sono eduntur, *aurus, causa, fusus, odiosus* per duo S scribebant, *aussus*" etc. Compare further *Terent. Scaur.* p. 2257. "*Causam* item multis scio per duo S scribi ut non attendentibus hanc literam, ut etiam cognatam illius R, nisi correpta vocali praecedente, non solere geminari" etc.

The passage from Velius Longus, pp. 2237, 2238, must be read carefully, but is too long to quote. From it we find, 1. That Nisus wrote *comess* and *asusse* (i.e. apparently *comedisse* and *assuevisse*, for the words are corrupt) with one *s*, giving two reasons for so doing; (1) because a consonant cannot be doubled after a long vowel; (2) because the '*antiqui*' did not double a consonant at all, but instead of doubling placed a mark over the single consonant. 2. Velius Longus contradicts Nisus on two grounds; (1) the unquestionable usus of doubling a consonant after a long vowel in such words as *errasse, saltasse, abiecisse, calcasse;* (2) that there is no real difference between writing a doubled consonant and placing a mark over it to point out that it was to be pronounced as doubled. He goes on to remark that the reason why we write *narare* with one R is that it is derived from *gnarus*.

Again, he questions the propriety of spelling *paullum* with two Ls, which was done by some because *pullus* has two Ls, and then adds, "Hic (i.e. the word *paullum*) autem in longitudine syllabae antecedentis huic literae (i.e. *l*) obstatur. Est enim (i.e. syllaba antecedens) quam Graeci dicunt δίφθογγος, iuxta quam omnino geminari consonans non potest."

That the earliest Latins did not double the semivowels is distinctly asserted also by Quintilian, I. 7, § 14:

"Semivocales non geminare diu fuit usitatissimi moris;" and the same statement is made repeatedly by Festus, who however extends the rule to mutes also. Thus, s.v. *anus*, p. 6, ed. Müll, he says, "antiqui eam literam non geminabant," s. v. *aulas*, "antiqui .. nullam literam geminabant;" and again, "antiqui non geminabant consonantes;" and s.v. *solitaurilia*, p. 293, he ascribes the practice of doubling consonants to Ennius, who adopted in this, as in other things, the Greek fashion.

But if we return to Quintilian, I. 7, § 20, we find a passage specially worthy of notice: "Quid? quod Ciceronis temporibus, paulumque infra fere quoties S litera media vocalium longarum vel subiecta longis esset, geminabatur? ut *caussae, cassus, divisiones,* quomodo et ipsum (et) Virgilium quoque scripsisse, manus eorum docent.

d 2

Atqui paulum superiores etiam illud quod nos gemina S dicimus
iussi, una dixerunt."

From these passages then we see that Nisus, as quoted by Velius
Longus, maintained that a consonant could not be doubled after
a long vowel. Velius Longus controverts this doctrine when stated
generally, but in discussing the orthography of the word *paullum*
denies that it can be written with a double L, because the preceding
syllable is a diphthong, "iuxta quam omnino geminari consonans non
potest." Priscian expressly asserts, "*au* dipthongus post se geminari
consonantem prohibet;" and Terent. Scaur., when controverting the
opinion of those who would spell *causa* with a double S, declares that,
"S—ut etiam cognatam illius R—nisi correpta vocali praecedenti
non solere geminari." But when we turn to Quintilian, we learn from
him that in the age of Cicero, and for some time after, wherever
S occurred between two long vowels, or after a long vowel, it
was always doubled, and that MSS. still extant in the hand-
writing of Cicero and Virgil proved that they wrote *caussae*, *caussus*,
divissiones.

Fresh complications arise from the loose manner in which the
grammarians employ the words *antiqui* and *antiqua scriptura*. Thus,
when Paul. Diac. p. 6, s.v. *anus*, says, "*Anus* dicta est ab annorum
multitudine quoniam antiqui non geminabant consonantes;" and
again, s.v. *aulas*, p. 23, "*Aulas* antiqui dicebant quas nos dicimus ollas
quia nullam literam geminabant;" and s.v. *folium*, p. 83, "*Folium*
a Graeco venit quod illi dicunt φύλλον, sed ideo per unum L quia
antiqui non geminabant consonantes;" and again, when Festus, s.v.
porigam, p. 218, ed. Müll, says, "*Porigam* dixisse antiqui videntur
pro *porrigam* propter morem non ingeminandarum literarum;" and
again, p. 358, ed. Müll., "*Torum* ut significet torridum, aridum, per
unum R antiqua consuetudine scribitur; sed quasi per duo R scri-
batur pronuntiari oportet: nam antiqui nec mutas nec semivocales
litteras geminabant ut fit in *Ennio*, *Arrio*, *Annio*," we might entertain
doubts as to the limits of the term *antiqui*, but these are removed by
what he says when discussing the etymology of *solitaurilia*, p. 293,
ed. Müll., "Quod si a *sollo* et *tauris* earum hostiarum ductum est
nomen antiquae consuetudinis, per unum L enuntiari non est mirum,
quia nulla tunc geminabatur littera in scribendo: quam consuetudinem
Ennius mutavisse fertur, ut pote Graecus Graeco more usus, quod illi
scribentes ac legentes duplicabant mutas semi (vocales) et liquidas,"
which passage proves most satisfactorily that when he speaks of the
practice of the *antiqui* he means those who preceded Ennius.

But when Cornutus, in the passage quoted above, enjoins us to write *causa*, and adds, "nec quemquam moveat antiqua scriptura nam et *accussare* per duo SS scripserunt," and when Mar. Vict. asserts that the *antiqui* wrote such words as *ausus, causa, fusus, odiosus*, with a double S, *ausrus*, &c., we infer from the passage in Quintilian, quoted above, that *antiqua scriptura* and *antiqui* indicate not the predecessors of Ennius, but the cotemporaries of Cicero and Virgil.

The passage from Mar. Vict. on the same topic is such a curious mass of confusion and contradiction, that we have quoted it at length above, to avoid the suspicion of misrepresenting his meaning. From this it will be seen that he enunciates three propositions : (1) that the *antiqui* did not double consonants at all; (2) that when it was necessary (*oportebat*) to double a consonant, they placed a mark called a Sicilicus over the consonant to be doubled; (3) that the *antiqui* did double the consonants in words *quae pressiore tono eduntur*, such as *ausas, causa*, &c. Nisus says the same thing with regard to the *Sicilicus*, but is very properly censured by *Velius Longus*, who remarks that there is in reality no difference between doubling a consonant and placing a mark over a single consonant, to point out that it was to be pronounced as double. But the curious circumstance connected with these statements is, that among all the inscriptions preserved, no trace of any mark corresponding to what is called the Sicilicus can be discovered.

Moreover, the ancient grammarians frequently state their own fancies and conjectures and theories as if they were acknowledged facts. Thus Cornutus, in the passage already quoted, partially leads us to infer that the use of the double S in such words as *fuisse, divisisse, esse*, and *causasse*, was an *antiqua scriptura* as much as *accussare*, whereas in point of fact these words were uniformly written with a double S, except in the very earliest times. With equal recklessness Velius Longus, l.c., asserts that the verb *narro* ought to be spelled with a single R, because it is derived from *gnarus !*

II. *Manuscripts.*

The authority of MSS. must be considered inferior to that of
the grammarians. Many of them were written at a late period (the
oldest MSS. of Plautus belong to the tenth century); they passed
through the hands of a series of transcribers, many of whom were
ignorant, and many careless; and so little attention was paid to such
matters, that we repeatedly find the orthography of the same word
varying in the same MS.; and hence not only particular words but
the forms of particular inflexions present the same variations (e. g. in
the case of plural terminations in *is* or *es*). It may indeed be urged
that where we meet with an archaic word in the MSS. of Plautus,
even although that form is not uniformly observed, we may conclude
that it is an archaism which has been transmitted from a remote
period and preserved by the hand of the faithful copyist, and ought
therefore at once to be admitted and adopted universally. But this
is by no means a safe principle. Thus, although in the earliest
Palimpsests we find uniformly *adulescens* and *epistula*, we have no
right to infer that this is actually the archaic form, which would
naturally accord more closely with the Greek, but, on the contrary,
may only be the mode of spelling which became fashionable in the
fourth or fifth centuries. Again, although we find in the best MSS.
of Plautus the word *herus* in the great majority of cases written *erus*
without the aspirate, yet when we remember the variations which
took place in the use of the aspirate at different epochs, it is just
as likely that *erus* may be a modern as an ancient form. Where
the archaism is undoubted, we know it to be such only from
inscriptions, and in certain cases from the testimony of the grammarians. We ought therefore in all cases to betake ourselves at
once to the best evidence, where we have it at our command. I
conceive that it would be just as reasonable to attempt to establish
the orthography of the English language in the age of Queen
Elizabeth by the aid of the text of Shakespeare, as exhibited in the
edition of Johnson and Malone, as to ascertain the orthography
of the Latin language in the sixth century of the city by the aid of
the existing MSS. of Plautus. In either case the old form would
be preserved here and there, while the great mass would be completely modernised.

III. *Inscriptions.*

By far the most reliable and authoritative evidence on questions of early Latin orthography is afforded by inscriptions.   The only sources of fallacy, in so far as inscriptions are concerned, may be classed under four heads :

1. The mistakes made by the original engravers on the stone or metal.

2. The mistakes made by the scholars who have transcribed them.

3. The difficulty of ascertaining the exact period at which they were engraved.

4. The genuineness of the inscriptions themselves.

The mistakes made by the engravers are for the most part obvious, are not numerous, and but few of them affect the questions under consideration.

The great care taken and exertions made by modern scholars to arrive at perfect accuracy in representing the originals, has in a great measure removed any difficulties which might have embarrassed one from this quarter.   Still the necessity of care is rendered obvious by the errors pointed out, and the corrections introduced by each new copyist, and the difficulty of arriving at absolute accuracy is proved by the variations—trifling it is true, but still variations—presented in almost all the different editions of the Inscription on the tomb of the Scipios.   So also in transcribing from the original capitals into ordinary type, the eye and hand, however practised, will sometimes fail.

In the case of almost all the inscriptions we have selected and enumerated below, the date is clearly ascertained, within very narrow limits, by internal evidence.

The genuineness of only one of the series has been seriously impugned by Maffei, but the concurrent testimony of scholars is in its favour.

[To the evidence of inscriptions, therefore, so far as these will serve us, we must betake ourselves in the first instance, if we desire to arrive at any certain knowledge as to those archaic forms by which we must suppose the spelling of Plautus to have differed from that of the later writers.   In all cases where we can collect from genuine inscriptions a sufficient number of undoubted instances to justify the inference that a particular mode of spelling either a single word, or a whole class of words, was prevalent up to and for some time after the time of our poet, and that the more modern forms did not come into general use till after his time, we must consider this evidence to be conclusive, and might without scruple, and even in defiance of MS. authority, employ that mode of spelling in the text of our poet. In other cases, where usage even in early times seems to have varied, or where the number of instances in inscriptions is so small as not to warrant us in arriving at any general conclusion, or, lastly, where inscriptions afford no evidence at all, we must be content to follow the method adopted with regard to the orthography of the later writers by our most distinguished modern scholars, and follow implicitly, in variety as well as in uniformity, the evidence afforded by our best MSS. Lachmann, Ritschl, Fleckeisen, and others in Germany, Mr. Munro in this country, have done vast service by pointing out how tenacious the best MSS. are of particular modes of spelling, and how great a mistake it is to suppose that in ancient spelling uniformity rather than variety was the rule.

For the purpose of enabling us to decide, so far as the evidence of extant inscriptions will permit, what are those archaic forms of spelling which it is most probable that Plautus actually employed, we have selected for special examination twenty of the most important and reliable of the early inscriptions from the Corpus of Mommsen, and, with a view to facilitating reference, have numbered them, as in the annexed table, from 1 up to 20, by which numbers they will be referred to in the course of the following remarks.—Ed.]

TABLE OF INSCRIPTIONS TO BE REFERRED TO IN THE TEXT.

No. as referred to in Text.	No. in Mommsen.	
1	29, 30	L. Cornelius Scipio Barbatus, Cos. B.C. 298.
2	39	Cornelia Hispalli, date uncertain.
3	31, 32	L. Corn. Scipio, Cos. B.C. 259.
4	33	P. Corn. Scip. Africanus, Augur B.C. 180.
5	34	Epitaphs of { L. Corn. Scipio, son of Hispallus, Cos. B.C. 176.
6	35	L. Corn. Scipio, Quaestor B.C. 167, son of *Asiagenus* or *Asiaticus*, Cos. B.C. 190.
7	38	Cn. Corn. Scip. Hispanus, Praetor B.C. 139.
8	36	— Corn. Scip. Asiag., son of 6, died at age of XVI.
9	37	Fragment containing PIONEM AD VEIXEI
10	196	Epistula Consulum ad Teuranos de Baccanalibus, B.C. 186.
11	197	Tabula Bantina, B.C. 133–118.
12	198	Lex Repetundarum, B.C. 123–122.
13	199	Sententia Q. M. Minuciorum inter Genuates et Viturios, B.C. 117.
14	200	Lex Agraria, B.C. 111.
15	201	Epistula Praetoris ad Tiburtes, circ. B.C. 90.
16	202	Lex Cornelia de XX. Quaestoribus, B.C. 81.
17	203	S. C. de Asclepiade Polystrato Menisco in amicorum formulam referendis, B.C. 78.
18	204	Lex Antonia de Termessibus, B.C. 71.
19	205	Lex Rubria de civitate Galliae Cisalpinae, B.C. 49.
20	206	Lex Iulia Municipalis, B.C. 45.

Orthography of Long Vowels.

Quintilian and some of the later grammarians explicitly state that in the earliest times long syllables were distinguished in writing by doubling the vowel. Thus I. O. I. vii. 14:

"Semivocales non geminare diu fuit usitatissimi moris: atque e contrario usque ad Accium et ultra, porrectas syllabas geminis, ut dixi, vocalibus scripserunt. Diutius duravit, ut *e, i,* iungendis, eadem ratione qua Graeci *ei,* uterentur. Ea casibus numerisque discreta est, ut Lucilius praecipit" &c.

And Mar. Victor. p. 2456, "Naevius et Livius, cum longa syllaba scribenda esset, duas vocales ponebant, praeterquam quae in I literam inciderant, hanc enim per E et I scribebant."

Acting upon this principle, Düntzer, who published an edition of the fragments of Livius Andronicus (Berol. 1835), represents them in the following fashion:

> "In seedeis collocat see reegiaas
> Clutaimneestra iuxtim, tertiaas naatai occupant
>   .   .   .   .
>
> Quin, quod paareere voos maaiestaas mea
> Procat, toleraatis, templooque hanc deeduucitis."

But in so far as the doubling of vowels is concerned, it seems certain that no such system prevailed generally at the period when our oldest inscriptions were engraved, and these belong to an epoch as remote as Livius, and much more remote than Pacuvius, Accius, and Ennius. Thus on the tombs of Scipio Barbatus and his son we have CORNĒLIVS, BARBĀTVS, PROGNĀTVS, DVO-NŌRVM, VIRTŪTEI, VŌS, OPSIDĒS.

The practice was not altogether unknown, for we find a few examples here and there, but these are so rare that we might almost ascribe them to ignorance or accident. In the whole of the twenty inscriptions we have enumerated above there are only seven in-stances, and the whole of these are found in 10 (No. 202 Momm.), which is as late as B.C. 81, viz. HAACE LEGE, HOICE LEEGEI, SEESE twice, LVVCI (from LVX), and PEGVLATVV * twice, while in the same inscription LEGE or LEGEM occur three times, and LVCI twice.

* Observe that both *hvci* and *pegulatvv* are anomalous on other con-siderations.

In point of fact, as far as we can learn from inscriptions, there was no method in general use, in the earliest period of Roman literature, by which the vowels *ā*, *ē*, *ō*, when pronounced long, were distinguished in orthography from the same vowels when pronounced short. We have seen that there is no trace of anything of the kind in the very oldest inscriptions, and although we find occasionally in some inscriptions engraved before the downfall of the Republic such forms as FAATO, MAANIVM, NAATAM, PAASTORES, SEEDES, REE, and the proper names, MAARCVS, MAAR-CIVS, STAATIVS, VAARVS, VAARIVS, FEELIX, and a few others, which are collected in the Index to Mommsen, these are for the most part solitary examples scattered over a wide area.

With regard to those words which in later times were written with long *u*, we find the long vowel represented sometimes by the diphthong *oi*, as in OINO, PLOIRVME [2], COMOINEM, OINVORSEI [10], MOINICIPIVM *quater*, OINA [14], OITI-LE [15], less frequently by *œ*, as POENICIO, OETVNTVR [14], but often by *ou*, as ABDOVCIT, LOVCANAM [1], IN-DOVCERE, INDOVCIMVS, INDOVCEBAMVS [15], IOVBEA-TIS [10], IOVSERVNT [13], IOVSERIT [12], IOVSISET [10], IOVS [12, 14, 18], IOVDEX [11, 12], IOVDICO [11, 13, 14], ADIOVDICARI [14], IOVDICIVM [11, 12], IOVDICATIO [12], IOVRO [11, 12], CONIOVRASE, NOVNDINVM, PLOVS [10].

On the other hand, we have VIRTṼTEI [1], VIRTṼTES, VIRTṼTEI [8].

The uncertainty that prevailed in the early part of the seventh century with regard to such words* is well illustrated by the Tables of the Lex Servilia, in which we find IOVS, IOVDEX, IOVDICES, IOVDICIVM, IOVDICIO, IOVDICATO, IOVDICET, IOVDI-CA(TA), IOVDICANDAM, intermingled freely with IVDEX, IVDICEI, IVDICEM, IVDICES, IVDICVM, IVDICIBVS,

---

* Great uncertainty prevails also in the Inscriptions anterior to the death of Cæsar, with regard to the orthography of the perfect tense of the verb CVRO. Not only do we find CVRAVERVNT, CVRAVERE, but more frequently COIRAVIT, COIRAVERVNT, COIRARVNT, COIRAVERE or COERAVIT, COERARVNT, COERAVERINT, COERAVERE; in one instance, CORAVERONT (n. 61); and in one, QVRAVERVNT (n. 1428). In fact, in inscriptions commemorating the erection of some monument, the expression FACIVNDVM COIRAVIT (AVERVNT) or COERAVIT (AVERVNT) seem to have been the established forms.

IVDICIVM, IVDICIO, IVDICET, IVDICARE, IVDICETVR, IVDICATA, also IOVSERIT and IVSERIT; IOVRET, IOV-RENT, IOVRATO, and IVRATO, IVRARIT.

The case of long *i* deserves particular consideration. We find a multitude of examples from the earliest inscriptions downwards, in which it is represented by *ei*, and this both in terminations and roots. Thus, VIRTVTEI, QVEI [1], QVEI, GESISTEI, SEI [4], QVOIEI, VIRTVTEI, QVEI [8], PETIEI, SIBEI [7], QVEI, FOIDERATEI, EXDEICENDVM, NEIQVIS, SEI, QVEI, SIBEI, DEICERENT, VTEI, VBEI, IBEI, CEIVIS, NISEI, OINVORSEI VIREI, NISEI, INCEIDERE-TIS, PREIVATOD [10].

But this mode of representing long *i* was not observed with anything approaching to uniformity even in our most ancient authorities: thus, AIDILIS [1], AIDILES, AIDILIS, BAR-BATI [3], PVBLI, CORNELI [4], ACCVMVLAVI, GENVI, OPTENVI [7], but in the same inscription PETIEI [7], VENIRENT, AVDITA, VRBANI, COVENTIONID, SACRI [10].

The absolute uncertainty which prevailed upon this point is proved by the Lex Thoria, in which we find not only FRVEI and FRVI, HEREDEI and HEREDI, DEICITO and EDICITO, AGREI and AGRI, both in the genitive, but such combinations as POPVLEI ROMANEI, POPVLI ROMANEI, POPVLI ROMANI; AGREI LOCEI, AGRI LOCEI, AGRI LOCI; POPVLI LEIBEREI, and many others.*

This uncertainty seems to have disturbed literary men, for Lucilius endeavoured to lay down rules which might determine the cases in which *ei* should be employed to denote the long vowel, and those in which the simple *i* should be used. Quintilian,† Velius Longus,‡ and Terentius Scaurus § all refer to the principles which he sought to establish, and quote his words, but the passages are so obscure and corrupt that it is very difficult to ascertain what his views really were. It would seem that in nouns of the second declension he wished to distinguish the numbers by writing *puri*, *viri* in the genitive singular and *purei*, *virei* in the nominative plural, while in nouns of the third declension he wrote *ei* in the dative singular, as

---

* So in the Lex Servilia, LEITIS and LITIS; DEIXERIT and DICAT.
† I. vii. 15.   ‡ p. 2220, ed. P.   § p. 2255, ed. P.

furti mendacei, perhaps to distinguish it from the ablative *mendaci*.*
There is no reason to suppose that the proposals of Lucilius were
ever accepted and recognised in practice; the use of *ei* for *i* gradually, although slowly, fell into disuse, and to the last we find no
consistency.

There are however a few words in which, for a long period, *ei*
was uniformly employed.

Foremost among these is the relative *Qui*, which, both in the nom.
sing. and nom. pl., appears almost invariably as *Quei* down to the
beginning of the eighth century.

QVEI in the nom. sing. occurs upwards of two hundred times in
the inscriptions 1-19; QVI once only, viz. in 13 (B.C. 117). In
20 QVEI occurs about fifty times, QVI twice.

QVEI in the nom. pl. occurs about sixty times in 1-20, QVI once
only, viz. in 13. QVEIQVOMQVE (sing. and pl.) appears first in
11, and in inscriptions 11-20 about twenty-six times without variation.
SEI for SI occurs upwards of seventy times in 1-20; SI once only,
viz. in 14. QVASEI is found in 11, 12, 16, in all seven times;
QVANSEI, apparently a blunder,† in 14; QVASI never. VTEI
appears first in 10, and in the inscriptions 10-20 upwards of ninety
times; VTI occurs five times, commencing with 11. In the inscriptions 10-20, IBEI, VBEI, NEI, NEIVE, occur more frequently than IBI, VBI, NE, NEVE, but IBI, NE, NEVE are by
no means uncommon.

CEIVIS seems to have long maintained its ground. It is found
in 10, and in the inscriptions 10-14 CEIVIS and its cases, spelled
with *ei* in first syllable, occur about fourteen times; CIVES appears
for the first time in 16.‡ CEIVITATE occurs four times in 12.
So in the inscriptions 11-19 DEICO occurs nearly thirty times:
viz. DEICAT three times, DEICERENT once, DEICET eight
times, DEICITO eleven times, DEICVNTO twice, DEICERE
once, DEICEI twice, DEICVNDO once. DICERE, DICITO
appear first in 20; the forms DIXI and DEIXI, with their
derivatives, were used indifferently.

* Varro also appears to have attempted to lay down rules upon the
same subject (Terent. Scaur. l. c.), but the words of Scaurus are very
obscure.

† [Does not this spelling rather afford a trace of the original form
of the word, *quam si*?—ED.]

‡ CIVIBVS is quoted from 14, but there is a flaw in the tablet at the
commencement of the word.

Diphthongs.

Considerable uncertainty prevailed in the use of diphthongs.
Originally *ai* seems to have been used in preference to *ae*. Thus,
GNAIVOD, AIDILIS [1], AIDILES, AIDILIS, AIDE(M) [3],
QVAIRATIS [6], QVAIS(*ter*) [6], AID. CVR. [7], AEDEM,
AIQVOM, TABELAI DATAI (*nom.*) [10]. So PRAIDAD, n. 63,
64; QVAISTORES, n. 181, 185 (also QVEISTORES, n. 183);
AIRE, n. 181. So in many proper names, especially in AIMILIVS.

Again, we have *oi* used for *oe*: as FOIDERATEI [10], and
FOIDERE [20].

Less frequent is the use of a simple vowel for a diphthong, as
FORTVNE, n. 64; FRVDE [12], which may be an accidental
blunder, since we have FRAVDE a few lines lower down in the
same inscription.

EIS for IS in Datives and Ablatives Plural of the First and Second Declensions.

The practice in this case was similar to what took place in the use
of *ei* for long *i*. In all probability the longer form was universal at first,
prevailed for a considerable time, and by degrees fell altogether into
disuse. It maintained its ground however more firmly and for a
longer period than *ei*. All the examples in the earliest inscriptions
uniformly exhibit *eis*. Thus FACTEI(S) [4], MIFIS [7], EEIS
three times, and VOBEIS [10], PROXSVMEIS [11 *ter*], TABO-
LEIS [11 *bis*], EIS [11]. When we come down to 12 we find the first
indications of uncertainty; although the examples of *eis* are numerous, we find ROSTREIS and ROSTRIS, AESTVMANDEIS and
AESTVMANDIS, LEGVNDEIS and LEGVNDIS, and the combination TABOLEIS PVPLICIS, although TABOLEIS POPLI-
CEIS occurs also. We have three examples of PRIMIS in 12,
in 16 three examples of PRIMEIS, and, generally speaking, down to
20, and even later, the form *eis* will be found greatly to preponderate,
so that we may without scruple employ it in the text of Plautus.*

Plural Cases of the Third Declension in EIS, ES, IS.

It is well known that nominatives, and especially accusatives

* [It would appear from this expression that the author had contemplated employing in his text the form *eis* in the cases specified above. It
will be seen from the Preface on what grounds I have thought it advisable
to retain the more familiar orthography.—ED.]

plural of masculine and feminine nouns of the third declension, have the terminations in *eis* and *is* as well as *es*.

Thus we have the nominatives CEIVEIS in 12, FINEIS twice in 13, and IOVDICIS in 12, FINIS in 13; the accusatives FINEIS [13 *bis*, 18 *quinquies*], GENVATEIS [13], OMNEIS [13, 16 *bis*], CALLEIS [14], DECEMBREIS [16 *sexies*], CIVEIS [18 *bis*], ALPEIS [19 *bis*], and LITIS [12], SEXTILIS [13], OMNIS [12 *ter*], OCTOBRIS [14], MVNICIPIS [20 *bis*]. It is reasonable to suppose that *eis* was the original form, and that the two forms in *es* and *is* arose from some dropping out one vowel and some the other.

In some of the oldest MSS. of the Latin classics, the Medicean Virgil for example, the form in *is*, especially in accusatives, is much more common than that in *es*, although the latter is by no means excluded. Hence a conclusion has been drawn that the form in *is* is the more ancient, and therefore ought to be introduced in all cases into the text of Plautus in preference to *es*, at all events in accusatives.

But setting aside the consideration that the practice of the fifth century after Christ cannot be accepted as any evidence of the practice of the second or third century before Christ, we can prove that the termination in *es* was in use from the earliest period to which our knowledge extends, and appears even before *eis*: thus we have OPSIDES, acc. [1]; VIRTVTES, acc. [5]; VIRTVTES, acc. [7]; HOMINES, nom., MVLIERES, nom. [10]; RE-CVPERATORES, acc. [11]; while we have no trace of *is* in the nominative or accusative until we come down to 11 and 12; we have given all the examples of *is* which are to be found in 12-20, amounting to eight * in all, while the termination *es* recurs much more frequently.

Curiously enough, in the Polla inscription,† although extending to a few lines only, we have examples of all the three forms: PON-TEIS OMNEIS, HOMINES, FORVM AEDISQVE POPLICAS, all in the accusative, and PAASTORES in the nominative.

O for V.

Priscian (p. 653) tells us, on the authority of Pliny, that some states of Italy, especially the Umbrians and the Etruscans, had not the vowel *o*, but employed the vowel *v* instead; and this assertion

---

* [Besides these there is one instance in the Carmen Arvale, and in the Duilian Column four more, making thirteen in all.—Ed.]

† Momm. No. 551, B.C. 132.

is fully confirmed by the inscriptions in those languages. Again (p. 554) he says—

"V quoque multis Italiae populis in usu non erat, sed e contrario O, unde Romanorum quoque vetustissimi in multis dictionibus loco eius O posuisse inveniuntur, *poblicum* pro *publicum*, quod testatur Papirianus de Orthographia, *polchrum* pro *pulchrum*, *colpam* pro *culpam* dicentes et *Hercolem* pro *Herculem*: et maxime digamma antecedente hoc faciebant, ut *servos* pro *servus*, *volgus* pro *vulgus*, *Davos* pro *Davus*."

This statement is borne out by existing inscriptions, and the further · back we go the more general do we find the use of *o* for *v*. Thus, CONSOL [1], COSOL, HONC, OINO (*unum*), COSENTIONT, DVONOVO (*bonorum*), LVCIOM, FILIOS, CONSOL [2], ANTIOCO (*Antiochum*) [6], CONSOLVERVNT, COSOLERE-TVR *ter*, SENATVOS* *ter*, OQVOLTOD (*occulto*), TABO-LAM, POPLICVS [10], HOICE, NONDIN (*um*), POPOLVM, POPLICVS *quater*, TABOLEIS *bis*, (*De*) NONTIARI [11], CONCILIABOLEIS *bis*, DETOLERIT *ter*, HOIVSCE, PRO-NONTIARE *ter*, POPLICVS *quater*, SINGOLOS *bis*, TABO-LEIS *quater* [12], CONSOL, POPLICVS [14], POPLICAE, NONTIATA [16], CONSOLIBVS [18]; and in the Tituli Con-sulares (Momm. 350 sq.), from B.C. 211-155, we have CONSOL three times. Many more examples may be collected from inscrip-tions belonging to the Republican period, but of which the precise period is uncertain. But although *o* seems to have lingered in some forms, especially in CONSOL, CONSOLO, the practice was not maintained steadily or long.

With regard however to the second case mentioned by Priscian, when in the later orthography of the language the Digamma, that is *v* employed as a consonant, preceded *v* employed as a vowel, the use of *o* instead of the latter remained invariable down to the youth of Quintilian: "Nostri praeceptores CERVVM SERVVM-QVE, V et O literis scripserunt" (i. e. CERVOM—SERVOM) "quia subiecta sibi vocalis in unum sonum coalescere et confundi nequiret: nunc V gemina scribuntur, ea ratione, quam reddidi: neutro sane modo vox, quam sentimus, efficitur. Nec inutiliter Claudius Aeolicam illam ad hos usus literam adiecerat. Illud nunc melius, quod *cui*, tribus, quas proposui, literis enotamus: in quo, pueris nobis, ad pinguem sane sonum, *qu* et *oi* utebantur, tantum ut ab illo *qui* distingueretur;" I. O. I. vii. § 26.

---

* *Senatus* is perhaps for *Senatuis*.

But we may go farther, and lay it down as a general rule, that down to B.C. 100, or even later, the combination *vv* (*uu*) was unknown, whether the first *v* had the force of a vowel or of a consonant. Thus not only did the ancients write *volnus, volgus, cervos, servos,* but also *mortuos, compascuos, aequom, quom,* and the like invariably, and I know not why Ritschl and others should have made an exception and written *tuus* and *suus* instead of *tuos, suos.*[*] Thus MORTVOS [6], AIQVOM [10], EQVOM, MORTVOS, PERPETVOM, SVOS *ter* [12], COMFLVONT, FLOVIOM, FLOVIVM *septies,* FLOVIO *quater,* FLOVI, INIQVOM, IOVENTIO, RIVOM [18], AEQVOM [18, 17, 18]. So with *quom, quiquomque,* &c.: QVOM [6, 10 *bis,* 12 *quinquies,* 14, 15 *bis,* 19 *quater*], QVEI-QVOMQVE [11, 12 *sexies,* 14 *octies,* 16, 17, 19 *sexies,* 20 *sexies*], QVOIA [12, 18 *bis*], QVOIVM [12 *bis,* 14 *bis*], QVOIVS [1, 12], QVOIVSQVE [12, 14, 20 *quater*], QVOI [12], QVOIQVE [20 *bis*], QVOIEI [6, 12, 14], QVOIEIQVE [14 *quinquies*].

O for E.

There are two words which, during the period of the Republic, so far as our evidence extends, were invariably written with *o,* although *e* afterwards prevailed. These are *Voster,* and *Vorto*[†] with its derivatives and compounds: thus VOSTRAE, VOSTRVM, VOSTRA [18], ARVORSVM [10], VORSVS, ADVORSVS, ADVORSVM [11], AVORSVM *bis,* ADVORSVS, ADVOR-SARIVM, ARVORSARIO *ter* [12], CONTROVORSIEIS, CONTROVORSIAS, CONTROVOSIAS, SVRSVMVORSVM, SVRSVORSVM, SVSO VORSVM [18], ADVORTIT [18], ADVORSVS [18 *bis*].

There was a tradition in the time of Quintilian that the change from *o* to *e* in *vertices, versus,* and such like words, was first introduced by Scipio Africanus: "Quid dicam *vortices* et *vorsus,* ceteraque ad eundem modum, quae primo Scipio Africanus in E literam secundam vertisse dicitur?" But if we can put faith in the grammarians, many words in addition to the above were written with *e,*

---

[*] [Here too, as in some other cases, I have thought it best to retain in the text the spelling sanctioned by Ritschl, Fleckeisen, and the Plautine critics, and have written uniformly *tuus, suus, tuom, suom,* &c., notwithstanding the opinion here expressed.—ED.]

[†] VERSVS occurs in n. 603, an inscription which professes to belong to B.C. 58, but which is attended with so many suspicious circumstances that it cannot be regarded as possessing any authority.

f

in which it was eventually superseded by *e*. Among these we find *Tonores* for *Tenores*, Quintil. I. v. 22; *Amplocti* for *Amplecti*, Prisc. p. 552, Cassiodor. p. 2283. The latter gives *Amploctere*, *Vortere*, *Advorsum*, and *Convollere*, *Votare* for *Convellere*, *Vetare*. Charis. p. 174, gives *Voturios* for *Veturios*, and this receives some support from the inscriptions, nn. 1029, 1057, 1082, in which the letters VOT. are usually interpreted to refer to the *Tribus Veturia*. *Votitam* for *Vetitam* is quoted from Plaut. As. IV. L 44 by Nonius, p. 45; *Volim* for *Velim*, Prisc. p. 848.

V for E.

Judging from the examples preserved, the form *undus* instead of *endus* was general in gerundives of the third and fourth conjugations until towards the close of the Republic. Thus we find DE-FERVNDO, DEICVNDO, FACIVNDVM *bis*, LEGVNDEIS, LEGVNDIS, QVAERVNDAI, SCRIBVNDI [12], VENDVN-DEIS [14 *bis*], LEGVNDEIS [10 *bis*], REFERVNDVM [17], CAPIVNDEIS [18 *ter*], DEIVIDVNDA *bis*, ERCEISCVNDA *bis* [19], REFERVNDVM *sexies*, REFICIVNDVM, FACIVN-DVM [20]; SAEPIVNDVM, n. 1419; VENIVNDVM, n. 1431, and so in many other inscriptions, which may be fairly reckoned as falling within the above limit.

This form however did not prevail to the exclusion of that in *endus*, for we find FACIENDAM, EXDEICENDVM, as early as 10, and COLENDI [13]. Observe also that *endus* is employed uniformly in those verbs where the use of the termination *undus* would have involved the introduction of *uu* : thus TRIBVENDEI [12], FRVENDVS, FRVENDVM, FRVENDA *quinquies*, FRVENDEIS [14], FRVENDEIS [20].

V for I.

"Etiam *optimus*, *maximus*, ut mediam I literam, quae veteribus V fuerat, acciperent, C. primum Caesaris inscriptione traditur factum." Quintil. L O. I. vii. 21. This mode of spelling was not however confined to *optumus*, *maxumus*, but extended to all super-latives which in later times were written with *imus*. Thus PARI-SVMA [1], PLOIRVME, OPTVMO [3], FACILVMED [10], PROXSVMVS [11 *ter*], PLVRVMAE, PROXVMVS, PROX-SVMVS *quater* [12], PROXVMVS *bis*, INFVMVM *ter* [13], OPTVMVS, PROXVMVS, PROXSVMVS *octies* [14].

There are scarcely any exceptions but INFIMO [13], while INFVMVM, INFVMO occur in the same inscription. PLVRIMIS is quoted from 13, but the only portion of the word extant on the tablet is VR. PROXSIMVM is found on a stone, n. 1291, Momm., but although there are some archaisms in the inscription, there is nothing to fix the date even approximately.

But the use of *v* for *i* in the older forms of the language was by no means restricted to these superlatives: thus Cornutus ap. Cassiodor. p. 2284, "*Lacrumae* an *Lacrimae, Maxumus* an *Maximus*, et si quae similia sunt, scribi debeant, quaesitum est. Terentius Varro tradidit Caesarem per I eius modi verba solitum esse enuntiare et scribere, inde propter auctoritatem tanti viri consuetudinem factam. Sed ego in antiquiorum multo libris quam C. Caesar est, per V pleraque scripta invenio, *optumus, intumus, pulcherrumus, lubido, dicundum, faciundum, maxumae, monumentum, contumelia, minumas.* Melius tamen est et ad enuntiandum et ad scribendum, I literam pro V ponere, in quod iam consuetudo inclinavit."

So also Velius Longus, p. 2228, "Antiquis varie etiam scriptitatum est *mancupium, aucupium, manubiae* : siquidem C. Caesar per I scripsit, ut apparet ex titulis ipsius, at Augustus I per V, ut testes sunt eius inscriptiones."

In so far as the words enumerated above, and not already discussed, are concerned, we have the authority of early inscriptions for LACRVMAS, n. 1008; LVBENS [4], but LIBENS in n. 190, which Mommsen places among the "antiquissima," without however any very satisfactory reason, except the presence of the *d* in *merited;* LVBENS in n. 1448; LVB(*ns*), n. 1469; LVBE(N)TES, n. 1175; (LVBS, n. 183; LIBS, n. 182). MONVMENTVM occurs frequently; MONIMENTVM and MONEMENTVM are rare; MANCVPVM [14 *bis*]. There seems little or no evidence to determine whether the early writers used *finitumus, maritumus, legitumus,* and the like, or *finitimus, maritimus, legitimus;* AVRVFEX is found in an inscription, n. 1310, whence it has been inferred that *carnufex* is an older form than *carnifex.*

There can be little doubt that in many of these words the sound of the vowel was something intermediate between *i* and *v* : "medius est quidam V et I literae sonus, non enim sic *optimum* dicimus ut *opimum;*"* and hence the Emperor Claudius endeavoured to introduce a new character into the Roman alphabet, which should

---

* Quintil. I. O. I. iv. 7; Diomed. p. 416; Priscian, p. 539; Donat. p. 1735; Serg. 1817; Cledon. 1883.

represent this middle sound.   He selected Ⱶ, the mark of aspiration
in ancient Greek inscriptions, and hence, according to this proposal,
we should write MAXⱵMVS, OPTⱵMVS, and the like.*

E for I.

In some of the oldest inscriptions *e* frequently holds the place sub-
sequently occupied by *i;* thus, PLOIRVME, FVET, DEDET [3],
n. 63, 64, MERETO, TEMPESTATEBVS, AIDILES, but AIDI-
LIS in same inscription; TIDE [4], VELET, nine times, VELENT,
COMPROMESISE [10].   We have also in the Col. Rost. *Exomet,
Ornavet, En, Navebos;* so *Minerva, Magester, Leber,* Quint. I. iv. § 17;
and *Amecus, Ameca, Lepareses (Liparenses),* Fest. s. vv. *Amicus,
Lepareses.*

H.

The ancient Romans employed the aspirate more sparingly than
their descendants.   They did not employ it before a vowel at the
beginning of many words in which it was afterwards generally
adopted, and they excluded it altogether from those syllables in
which it was afterwards placed after a consonant.   Thus Quintil. I.O.
I. v. 7, "Parcissime ea veteres usi sunt etiam in vocalibus, quum
ædos, ircosque dicebant.   Diu deinde servatum ne consonantibus
aspiraretur, ut in *Graccis* et *triumpis.*   Erupit brevi tempore nimius
usus, ut *choronae, chenturionus, pracchonus,* adhuc quibusdam inscrip-
tionibus maneant: qua de re Catulli nobile epigramma est."   And
Cicero, Orat. XLVIII. § 160, confirms the statement of Quintilian,
"Quin ego ipse, quum scirem ita maiores locutos esse ut nusquam
nisi in vocali aspiratione uterentur, loquebar sic ut *pulcros, Cetegos,
triumpos, Kartaginem,* dicerem," &c.

Although the use of the aspirate became more common in the age
of Cicero and of Augustus, it was again dropped to a considerable
extent in the decline of the language: thus Marius Victorinus (fourth
or fifth century), p. 2466, when speaking of the use of *h* in certain
words, "Sed credo vos antiquitatem sequi, sed quum asperitas vetus
illa paulatim ad elegantioris vitæ sermonisque est limam perpolita,
sic vos quoque has voces sine H secundum consuetudinem nostri
seculi scribite;" where, when speaking of *antiquitas* and *vetus illa
asperitas,* he must be understood to refer to the Augustan age.
Hence, in a matter of this sort, the testimony of MSS. is absolutely

* On this see Tacit. Ann. XI. 14; Suet. Claud. 41; Vel. Long. 2233.

worthless, because the writers would in most cases represent the orthography prevalent in their own day.

Where the question arises as to the insertion or omission of an aspirate at the beginning of a word, or between two vowels, we have absolutely nothing to guide us; but in so far as Plautus is concerned, we might be safe in omitting it after a mute, and in writing *Corintus*, *Cartago*, *Antiocus*, *Agatocles*, BACANAE [10 *quater*], *Pulcer*, BRACIVM [12], *Arcitectus*, *sepulcrum*, *tratrum*, *triumpus*; although we could scarcely bring ourselves to adopt the form *Pilipus*, which is found on a coin, especially as *Philippus* appears on other pieces belonging apparently to the same epoch; and, generally speaking, in proper names, and especially those of foreign origin and rare occurrence, we cannot look for accuracy, or adhere to Latin rules; and hence we may retain the Greek spelling, and adopt *Philolaches*, *Philematium*, and *Theuropides*, instead of *Pilolaces*, *Pilematium*, *Teuropides*.

In so far as the rule of Quintilian is concerned, it is closely observed in inscriptions. We have indeed an aspirate before a vowel at the commencement of a few words which discarded the aspirate at a later period, such as HARENATO, n. 557, HOLITOR, n. 1057, HERVCINA, n. 1495; on the other hand, it does not appear in EREDES, n. 1034, OSTIA, n. 819, ARRESPEX, n. 1348, ERCEISCVNDA [19 *bis*]. The only violation of the precept which forbids the use of the aspirate after a consonant, in a word not a proper name, is SEPVLCHR(*um*) in n. 1107 (but there is nothing to fix the date of this inscription with certainty), and the proper name, PHISIDAE, which occurs in 18, B.C. 71, but which is evidently a mere blunder, since the word (PISIDAE) appears in its correct form repeatedly in the same inscription. PVLCHER, as a proper name, appears on a Denarius minted in all probability towards the close of the Republic, on some coins struck in Asia, and on a fragment of sculpture found at Eleusis.

Q.

Although *q* was never extensively employed by the Romans, it certainly was employed commonly, at an early period, in certain words in which it was afterwards supplanted by *c*. Foremost among these is PEQVNIA, which is written with a *q* in the great majority of cases in the oldest inscriptions, although, curiously enough, the first example of the word is in 10, where it appears as PECVNIAM. Thus PECVNIA and its cases take a Q about twenty-six times in 11,

12, 13, 14, but in 14 we have also PECVNIAE once. So we have OQVOLTOD in 10, PEQVS *bis*, PEQVDES, but also PECVDES. PERSEQVTIO, OQVPATAM, all in 14; PEQVLAT(V) in 12, and the blunder PEQVLATVV twice in 16. To these we may add QVR, n. 1454, QVRA, n. 1006, QVRAVERVNT, n. 1428, PEQVARIORV, n. 1130.

It has been proposed to write the adjective *reliquus*, where it occurs in Plautus, as *relicuos*, because it is in many cases a quadrisyllable; but this idea receives no support from inscriptions, in which we find RELIQVEI [20], RELIQVIAE, n. 1009, 1016, RELLIQVIAE, n. 1051, and different parts of the verb *relinquo*, *q* being uniform in all cases.

The letter X.

X, the last letter in the Latin alphabet, was, according to Isidorus (I. 4) and Petrus Diaconus (p. 1582), not introduced until the age of Augustus. But this is an absolute mistake, for we find SAXSVM [5], ADVEIXI [9], EXDEICENDVM, EXDEICATIS, EX-STRAD [10]. Much confusion however appears to have existed with regard to the exact power of *x*, and hence we find a great many examples of PROXSVMVS, MAXSVMVS, VIXSI, DEIXSI, VXSOR, ALEXSANDER, and the like; and so SAXSVM and EXSTRAD in the examples quoted above.

The question as to the orthography of *Exsilium* or *Exilium* depends of course on considerations altogether different.

Y.

Y did not properly belong to the Latin alphabet, but was introduced at a comparatively late period to represent Υ in words transplanted directly from the Greek. We cannot fix with precision the period when it was first employed in writing, but there is scarcely a single trustworthy example of it to be found in inscriptions anterior to the death of Caesar, but the Υ in Greek proper names, and the like, is represented generally by *u*, and more rarely by *i*, as in AMVCES, ERVCINA or HERVCINA, GLVCERA, LVCIOS, ILLVRICVM, PVLADES, SIBVLLA, SVRVS, &c., CRISIDA, HIMINIS, SISIPVS. The name HYPOLITVS, n. 741, Momma., belongs to an inscription certainly not older than B.C. 21.

There is no reason to believe that such a character was known in the age of Plautus, and therefore we may safely eject it wherever it occurs in the text, and write *Suracusae, Gunacarum, Suria*, and the like, instead of *Syracusae, Gynacarum, Syria*, &c.

Assimilation.

It is natural to conclude that the softening of prepositions in composition by assimilation should have become more and more general as the cultivation of the language advanced, but it is a decided mistake to suppose that the practice was altogether unknown in early times. The statement of *Pierius*, in his note on the line (Virg. Aen. IV. 175), *Mobilitate viget viresque adquirit eundo*, "Antiqua pene omnia exemplaria integras servant praepositiones in compositis, ut *adquirit*: et ita scribi solitum usque ad Aurelii Antonini Pii tempora, publica declarant monumenta," can be at once disproved by many of the "publica monumenta" to which he appeals. Setting aside the change of *ab, ob*, into *ap, op*, &c., of which we shall speak below, and which may depend upon different considerations, we find in 7 ACCVMVLAVI; ACCIPIO and its tenses are used in early inscriptions to the exclusion of the harder *adripio*, and occur in 11, 12, 14, 18 *quater*, 19 *quinquies*, 20 *bis*, and also in n. 818 *bis* and 819; so ACCVSASSE [20], ATINGAT, ATTIGAT, ATTINGAT, ATTIGERET [12], AVFERATVR [18 *bis*], COMVOVISSE [10], COMVALEM [13], COMPORTENT [14].

These examples are quite sufficient to disprove the broad assertion that assimilation was unknown until the time of Antoninus Pius, but on the other hand it is unquestionable that in early inscriptions, in the great majority of cases, prepositions in composition undergo no change. Thus we have ADFERATVR, ADSIGNARE, ADSIDVO, ADTRIBVERE, CONLATA, CONLEGA, CONLEGIVM, CONLEIBERTVS, CONLOCARE, CONPLVRIBVS, CONPROMESISE, CONRIGI, DISMOTA, EXDEICENDVM, INGNOMINIAE, INMITTERE, INMORTALIVM, INPEDITVS, INPONITO, INPROBARINT, INPROBVM, INPVLSVM, INROGARE, and others.

In a few cases there seems to have been uncertainty; thus we find CONFLOVONT and COMFLVONT both in 13, INPERIVM* and its cases in 11, 12, 14, IMPERIO [19], INPERARE [14], INPERATO [18], IMPERATOR [20], and uniformly in all

[* See Munro's Lucretius, vol. II. p. 26, where the want of uniformity in the spelling of this word and its compounds is dwelt upon and an explanation suggested.—ED.]

inscriptions before the death of Caesar; PERLEGE, n. 1009; PER-
LIGE, n. 1306; PELLIGE, n. 1007; SVFRAGIVM [11, 12],
SVFRAGIO [12, 20]; SVBFRAGIA, n. 1492. We find in inscriptions ADSIENT, ADFVERIT, ADFVERINT, but there is a
line in Plautus, Poen. l. ii. 67. *Ao. Milphio, heus! Milphio, ubi es?
M. Assum apud te, eccum! A. Ego elixus sis volo:* where the pun
would be destroyed if we were to read *Adsum* instead of *Assum.*

There is a remarkable softening of the preposition *ad* into *ar,* of
which we have a few examples: thus ARFVISE, ARF(*uersus*),
ARVORSVM, all in 10, and ARVORSARIO three times in 12.

Generally speaking, therefore, in printing the text of Plautus it will
be safe to retain the prepositions in composition unchanged, except
in such cases as *accipio,* where our authorities are all opposed to the
harder form.

Doubling of Semivowels and Mutes.

That the earliest Latin writers did not double the semivowels is
asserted by Quintilian, 1. O. 1. vii. 14, " Semivocales non geminare
diu fuit usitatissimi moris," words which however do not necessarily
imply that they *never* doubled them. The same statement is made
more broadly by Festus and his abbreviator Paulus, and they in
several passages extend it to consonants in general, e. g. Fest. s. v.
solitauriba, p. 293, ed. Müll. "quod si a *sollo* et *tauris* earum
hostiarum ductum est nomen antiquae consuetudinis, per unam L
enuntiari non est mirum, quia nulla nunc geminabatur litera in scribendo; quam consuetudinem Ennius mutavisse fertur, ut pote Graecus
Graeco more usus, quod illi aeque scribentes ac legentes duplicabant
mutas semi (*vocales et liquidas*);" and again, s. v. *porigam,* p. 218,
" *Porigam* dixisse antiqui videntur pro *Porrigam* propter morem non
ingeminandarum literarum;" s. v. *polel,* p. 205. "*Polel, pollel,* quia
nondum geminabant antiqui consonantes." So also s.v. *torum,* p. 355,
and Paul. Diac. a. vv. *anus,* p. 6; *ab olors,* p. 19; *aulas,* p. 23.

We have already had occasion to advert to the contradictions and
confusion which prevail among the later grammarians upon this
subject, and therefore we need not now examine their discussions.

Our most ancient inscriptions fully bear out the statement of
Quintilian, provided we admit that the words *usitatissimi moris* denote
that the practice, although general, was not invariable. Thus in 1
we have PARISVMA; in 2 we have AVLLA and HISPALLI, but
the date of this is by no means certain; in 4. GESISTEI, LICV-
(I)SET, SVPERASES, but in the same inscription ESSENT and

TERRA; in 5, POSIDET, but also ANNOS; in 6, ANNOS; in
7, ACCVMVLAVI, but the two Cs may here be regarded as
belonging to separate words. In 10 (the S.C. de Bacchanalibus)
the rule is most strictly adhered to; there is no example of a consonant doubled, and between thirty and forty words written with
single consonants where double consonants would have been used
at a later period, e.g. BACANALIBVS, HABVISE, ESENT,
NECESVS, ADIESE, IOVSISET, FECISE, CONPROMESISE,
CONIOVRASE, COMVOVISE, &c.

The same holds good of the Polla inscription (B.C. 132), but the
examples are less numerous: MILIARIOS, TABELARIOS, MEI-
LIA *bis*, SVMA, REDIDEI. In 11, probably a few years later
than the preceding, we find SVFRAGIVM, INTER(C)ESVRVM;
but on the other hand, FERRE, (G)ESSERIT, POSSIDEANTVR.
In 13, IVSERVNT, IOVSERVNT, CASTELI, CASTELVM,
CASTELANOS, APENINVM *bis*, ANOS, ACIPIANT, CAVSA,
INTRO MITAT, COMVALEM, POSEDET, POSEDENT, PO-
SIDENT *ter*, POSIDEBIT, POSIDEBVNT *ter*, POSIDETO,
POSIDERE, PO(SI)DERE; but on the other hand, ANNOS,
ANNI, INMITTERE, ESSENT, ESSE. The name of a place
appears as MANICELVM, MANICEIO, and also as MANNI-
CELO; MALENT may stand for MALLENT or MALINT. In
12 the preponderance is very decidedly in favour of the doubled
consonant: ATINGAT *bis*, NECESITVDINE, IVSEI ERVNT,
DIMITERE; but on the other hand, ANNVM *quater*, ANNOS *bis*,
(A)NNOS, ANNEIS *bis*, ANNIS, CAVSSA *bis*, ESSE *quinquies*,
ADESSE *ter*, ADESSINT, PRAESSE, ATTIGERET, ATTIN-
GAT, OPPEDEIS, POSSIDEANTVR, PROFERRE, SITELLAM,
POSSITVR, INTERROGET; and so also in 13. Throughout 13
we have various forms of the verb *Possidere*: POSEDET, POSIDENT,
POSSIDERENT, POSIDEBIT, POSIDEBVNT *bis*, POSEDEIT,
POSIDETO, POSIDERE *bis*. In 14, uniformly, POSSESIO and
POSSESOR; POSSIDEAT, POSSIDEANT, POSSIDEBIT *quin-
quies*, POSIDEBVNT, POSSEDERIT, POSSIDERE.

Words ending in B.

It would appear that the letter *p* approached very closely in sound
to *b*, especially when the latter stood before *s* or *t*, and hence the
orthography of words in which such a combination occurs became
a matter of doubt and controversy. This is exactly what we might

g

have anticipated from the close, natural relation which subsists between these two labial mutes, in virtue of which they are constantly interchanged, not only in cognate languages but in different dialects of the same language, and even in different parts of the same word in the same dialect, as, for instance, in *nubo, nupsi; scribo, scripsi; labor, lapsus,* and the like. The only Latin words which end in *b* are the prepositions *ab, ob, sub.* The connection of two of these with ἀπό and ὑπό is obvious, and although no trustworthy examples of *ap, op,* or *sup* are supplied by inscriptions, it is certain that they frequently took this sound in composition when prefixed to words commencing with *s* or *t.*

Thus Quintil. I. O. I. vii. 7 : "Quaeri solet, in scribendo praepositiones, sonum, quem iunctae efficiunt, an, quem separatae, observare conveniat ; ut quum dico *obtinuit,* secundam enim B literam ratio poscit, aures magis audiunt P."

As might have been expected, in the earlier forms of the language the ear exercised greater influence than etymological considerations, and we find in the inscriptions which we have enumerated above, *ap, op,* and *sup,* for *ab, ob, sub,* when these prepositions are compounded with words beginning with *s* or *t.* Thus APSOLVTVS [13 *bis*], OPSIDES [1], OPSIGNETVR [12], OPTINENT [17], OPTINEBIT [12, 14, 16 *bis*], OPTENVI [7], SVPSIGNET, SVPSIGNENT, SVPSIGNATO, SVPSIG(*netur*), SVPSIGNA-TVM, SVPSIAVO [14]. These instances are not very numerous, but they are all in the same direction, and we find no example of any of these prepositions retaining its proper shape before *s* or *t* until we reach 19, B.C. 49, which contains ABSOLVITO thrice; and 20, B.C. 45, which has OPTEMPERETVR, and therefore we may feel justified in assuming that the practice prevailed during the age of Plautus and long afterwards. We may safely extend the rule to those cases in which the preposition *abs* enters into composition, for we find in inscriptions of a comparatively late date such forms as APSTINERE, APSTINENTI, APSTVLIT, APSTVLERIT, APSENS, APSENTI.

Numerous passages are to be found in the old grammarians bearing upon the relation subsisting between *bs, ps,* and the Greek ψ, the sound of the latter not being accurately represented by either of the two former,* so that Claudius, among other grammatical

----
* Thus Priscian, p. 557, "multo molliorem et volubiliorem sonum habet ψ quam ps vel bs . . . sicut ergo ψ melius sonat (quam ps vel bs) sic x etiam quam gs vel cs: et x quidem assumpsimus, ψ autem non."

reforms, proposed to introduce a new character into the Latin alphabet, the Antisigma)(, which might serve as the representative of ψ. See especially Priscian. pp. 557, 566; Vel. Long. pp. 2224, 2233; Terent Scaur. pp. 2252, 2261; Curt. Valerian. ap. Cassiodor. pp. 2289, 2290; Papirian. ap. Cassiodor. p. 2291; Mar. Victorin. pp. 2465, 2466.

Before quitting this subject, we may notice that the preposition *ab*, occasionally, although rarely, appears under the form of *af:* thus in 18, AF VOBIS; in the Polla inscription, AF CAPVA, but in the same, AB REGIO; n. 1143, AF MVRO; n. 1161, AF SOLO; see also nn. 551, 587, which are less satisfactory.

Words ending in D.

Ten Latin words end with the letter *d*—*Ad, Aliud, Apud, Haud, Id, Illud, Istud, Quid. Quod, Sed.* It seems certain that, in later times at least, the sound of *d* in these words could not be distinguished from that of *t*, and that, in writing them, *t* was frequently substituted for *d.* Thus Quintil. I. O. I. vii. 5, " Illa quoque servata est a multis differentia, ut *ad*, quum esset praepositio, D literam, quum autem coniunctio, T acciperet." These words clearly indicate that, whichever letter was employed, the sound must have been the same, and seems to imply that many persons, and probably Quintilian himself, employed *d* and *t* indifferently in writing the words in question.

In the testimony of the later grammarians, fact and opinion, theory and practice, are, as is usual with them, mixed up together. Terent. Scaurus (p. 2250) considers it a mistake to write the preposition with a *t*, or the conjunction with a *d*, proving that the interchange was not uncommon. Velius Longus (pp. 2230, 2287) tells us that to avoid confusion we *ought* to write the preposition *ad* and the pronouns *id, quid, quod*, all with a *d*, in order to distinguish them from the conjunction *at*, the verbs *it* and *quit*, and the adverb *quot;* he maintains that *apud* ought to be written with a *d, because* no preposition ends with *t*, and because it sounds better " propter nimiam T literae exilitatem." On the other hand, he holds that *sed* ought to be written with a *t, because* no conjunction ends with *d*, but admits that in pronunciation the sound of the final letter was that of *d* rather than of *t*, and that therefore the question was whether we should write it as it was pronounced, or pronounce it as it was written.

In direct opposition to this, Charisius (p. 87), Scaurus (p. 2251), and Marius Victorin. (p. 2458), agree that we ought to write *sed* and not *set*, because the word is an abbreviation of the ancient *sedum*. The words of Victorinus are, "Antiqui pro *sed*, *sedum* scribebant, sed quum nostra aetas partem literarum in eo reservarit, partem, brevitatis causa, ex eo detraxerit, nonnullam immutarit, et nos per *sed* quam per *set* scribamus;" where observe that he says *scribamus*, not *scribimus*: a few lines before he had observed, "sed nos nunc et *adventum* et *apud* per D potius quam per T scribamus, *atventum* et *aput*." Again, the same Victorinus (p. 2462) derives *haud* from *ou*, and lays it down as a rule that it ought to be written *haud* when the word following begins with a vowel, as *haud equidem*, but *haut* when the word following begins with a consonant, as *haut placitura*; but this must be regarded as an opinion of what ought to be done, not as the record of an established usage. The forms *haud* and *haut* were probably both in common use when Victorinus composed his treatise; and he sought to establish a distinction as to their use. Ritschl (Proleg. XCIX, C.), who has a pet theory of his own with regard to the form *hau*, which may or may not have been occasionally employed,[*] reconstructs the above passage, and endeavours to convince us that the precept which Victorinus intended to inculcate was that we ought to write *haud* before a vowel and *hau* before a consonant.

But without attempting to penetrate farther into the thorny thicket of these grammatical speculations, it may be stated as a fact that the forms *At*, *Aput*, *Set*, *Aliut*, *Haut*, for *Ad*, *Apud*, *Sed*, *Aliud*, *Haud*, and also *It*, *Quit*, *Quot*, for *Id*, *Quid*, *Quod*, occur not unfrequently in inscriptions and the oldest MSS., and hence Bentley has admitted *Aput*, *Set*, *Haut*, into the text of his Terence, while Ritschl adopts these and also *aliut* and *illut*. But although it is certain that in later times *t* was frequently substituted for *d* in many, if not all, of the ten words above enumerated, the real question which we have now to consider is whether there is any evidence to prove that this was the case in the earlier period of the language. If we examine the whole of the twenty inscriptions on which we chiefly rely, and even extend our researches into the whole of those which are ranked in the great work of Mommsen as belonging to an epoch anterior to the death of Caesar, we shall arrive at the following result:

AD occurs upwards of ninety times;

AT, never in the inscriptions 1-20, but once in n. 1252, an

---

[*] We find HAV in an inscription, n. 1007, Mommsen, but the original tablet has long since disappeared, and the reading of the word is by no means certain.

inscription found at Pompeii, and ascribed by Mommsen to the age
of Augustus.

ALIVD, twice in 19, once in 20;
ALIVT, never.

APVD, 1, 3, 10, 11 *quater*, 12 *sexies*, 17, 19 *sexies*, 20;
APVT, three times in 20, the last of the series, belonging to B.C. 45.

HAVD, no example in 1-20, but one in n. 1306. For HAV,
see above.

ID, nom. and. acc., 1-20, about thirty-six times;
IT, never.

ILLVD, no example.

ISTVD, no example.

QVOD, nom. and acc., 1-20, upwards of ninety times;
QVOT, never;
QVOD, conj., 1-20, about sixteen times.

QVID, nom. and acc., 1-20, about twenty-eight times;
QVIT, never.

Sed, the conjunction, is not found in 1-20; it occurs on one of
the curious brazen "sortes," n. 1442, and a reference is made in
the index to *Sed*, in n. 1270; but there must be some mistake in the
number, for *Sed* is certainly not found in that inscription.[*]

Under these circumstances there would appear to be no pretext
for departing from the ordinary orthography of any one of the ten
words in question.

D Paragogicum.

It is well known that in the earlier stages of the Latin language
we find many words ending with a *d*, which was entirely dropped
at a later period. Grammarians have given to the letter thus

---

[*] To prevent mistakes we must call the attention of the young scholar
to the fact that in the older forms of the language he will find two words,
Sed, distinct from the conjunction and from each other. 1. *Sed*, which is
equivalent to *Sine*, and which enters into some ancient legal forms; the expression *se fraude* being introduced to declare that the doer of certain acts,
performed ministerially, should be relieved from responsibility. Thus, in fragment of the Laws of the XII. Tables, preserved by Aul. Gell. XX. 1, § 49,
" Tertiis . Nundinis . Partis . Secanto . Si . Plus . Minus . Ve . Secuerunt .
Se . Fraude . Esto;" and in the Lex Servilia (12), " Eam . Pequniam .
Eis . Se . Frude . Solvito;" and again in the same Law, " Id . Quaestor .
. . . . Sed . Fraude . Sua . Extra . Ordinem . Dato . Solvitoque." See
Paul. Diac. s. v. p. 336, ed. Müll. 2. *Sed*, the accusative of *Sui*, with
what is called the *D paragogicum*. See next section.

employed the designation of *D paragogicum*, a term as irrational as that of ἐφελκυστικόν in Greek.

It appears chiefly in datives and ablatives, but by no means exclusively, and Charisius goes so far as to assert that in ancient times it was attached to all words ending with a vowel. Thus, in 1 we have GNAIVOD; and in n. 63, 64, DE PRAIDAD; n. 181, AIRE MOLTATICOD; n. 190, MERITOD; 10 abounds in examples, such as SENTENTIAD *ter*, OQVOLTOD, POPLICOD, PREIVATOD, CONVENTIONID. These are all ablatives, but we have in the same inscription, EAD, acc. pl., EXTRAD, FACILVMED, SED for SE (the pronoun), SVPRAD *ter*. Charisius, p. 87, specially quotes *ted* from Plautus, and the forms *med* and *ted* occur repeatedly in the MSS. of the plays. Indeed, some scholars have imagined that by a free introduction of *d* at the end of words ending with a vowel, we might escape from the embarrassment felt by metrical scholars on account of the constant recurrence of hiatus.

It is evident however, from our oldest inscriptions, that in the early part of the sixth century, although the use of the *D paragogicum* had not fallen entirely into disuse, it was not generally employed, and hence any attempt to introduce it on an extensive scale into the text of Plautus would be unjustifiable.

Final M and Final S.

That final *m* was but faintly pronounced is evident from the fact that a final syllable ending in *m* was elided before a word beginning with a vowel in all ages of Latin poetry. The same took place frequently in words ending in *us* or *is*, in the earlier ages of Latin poetry; the practice was still common in the age of Lucretius, but afterwards fell into disuse. Hence it is not surprising that, in the older class of inscriptions, final *m* is frequently omitted; and the same holds good, but to a smaller extent, in final *s* also.

As instances of the dropping of final *m* we have OMNE(*m*) [1], OINO(*m*), DVONORO(*m*), OPTVMO(*m*), VIRO(*m*), SCIPIONE(*m*), CORSICA(*m*), ALERIA(*m*)*que*, VRBE(*m*), AIDE(*m*) [3], APICE(*m*), INSIGNE(*m*), GREMIV(*m*) [4], HONORE(*m*) [5], ANTIOCO(*m*) [6], ANNORV(*m*) [9]. As we advance, the practice becomes more and more rare, and finally disappears. From the first, however, it was by no means uniformly observed: thus, OMNE LOVCANAM [1], LVCIOM SCIPIONE [3], REGEM ANTIOCO [6], INGENIVM, GLORIAM, MAIORVM,

PROGNATVM [4], SAXSVM [5], PROGENIEM, MAIORVM, LAVDEM, CREATVM, STIRPEM [7]. From the above examples it would be impossible to deduce any rule or principle by which writers were guided as to the insertion or omission of the letter.

As to the omission of final *s*, we have ANTIOCV, n. 1095, LECTV, n. 1313 *bis*, PATRONV, n. 1033: and in combination with *est*, SATIVST, n. 1444, SITVST, n. 1397, VOCITATVST [13]. A few more examples will be found in the index to Mommsen, but they are by no means numerous.

M, N.

In derivatives and compounds *m* had a tendency to pass into *n* before the letters *c, q, d, t*. Thus we have uniformly before *c*, *Clanculum, Nuncubi, Sinciput, Princeps*, but *horumce* or *horunce*; before *d, Tantundem, Tandem, quondam, Quando, Nundinae, Clandestinus*; before *t, Identidem*, &c. Before *q*, however, there seems to have been a diversity of practice with regard to the manner of writing the same words, depending probably upon individual taste: thus in MSS. we find indifferently *umquam, numquam* and *unquam, nunquam; tamquam, quamquam* and *tanquam, quanquam; utrimque, utcumque, quicumque* and *utrimque, utcunque, quicunque*. On the other hand, *m* is almost always retained in *numquis, quamquam, namque, plerumque, utrumque, quemque, usquequamque*. As a solitary example of *m* into *n* before *t*, we have *quoniam = quom iam*.

The passages in the grammarians, with regard to *m* into *n*, are, Priscian, p. 555, who, after giving as examples, *tandem, tantundem, identidem, muncubi*, adds, "et, ut Plinio placet, *nunquis, nunquam :*" Priscian, p. 945, gives *eundem, eandem, quendam, quandam, quorundam, quarundam*, all of which however he adds *may* be written by simple composition, i. e. by *m :* Priscian, p. 958, gives as examples of *m* passing into *n* before *c, hunc, hanc, horunce, harunce*. Compare Vel. Long. p. 2236; Beda, pp. 2337, 2344; Martian. Capell. Lib. III. p. 65. Marius Victorinus, p. 2462, seems to say that we may at pleasure unite *nonnunquam, nunquam, nunquid, quanquam, unquam*, or substitute *m* for *n*.

As an example of the care which it is necessary to exercise in reading the grammarians, in distinguishing an opinion from a fact, we may take the following statement of Cornutus ap. Cassiodorum, p. 2286 : "*Tantus* et *Quantus* in medio *m* habere debent: *quam* enim et *tam* est unde *quamtitas, quamtus, tamtus*, nec quosdam moveat ti *m* non sonat: iam enim supra docui non sonare debere tametsi in scriptura *m* posita sit." Cf. Caesell. ap. Cassiodor. p. 2314, and Isidor. Origg. 1, 26 post med. But although it is here said that we ought to write *iambus* and *quamtus*, we have no reason to believe that these words ever were written under that form, and therefore we must regard this as merely a theoretical speculation as to what ought to have been, not what actually was.

N is occasionally omitted, in old inscriptions, in the middle of a word, but not apparently upon any fixed principle: thus in 2, COSOL, CESOR, COSENTIONT, but we have CONSOL, CENSOR, in another part of the same inscription, and also in 1; in 10, COSOLORETVR thrice, but also CONSOLVERVNT, COVENTIONID. The abbreviations *Cos.* and *Coss.* for *Consule*, *Consulibus*, seem to have originated in the use of *Cosol* for *Consul*.

Insertion of P between M and S or T following.

There exists great diversity of opinion upon this point among ancient grammarians. Priscian, pp. 551, 564, 854, 897, 898, 931, writes *hiems, dempsi, compsi, prompsi, sumpsi* and *demptus, comptus, promptus, sumptus, temptsi, ademptus, redemptus,* and also *emptus.* Terent. Scaur., pp. 2256, 2261, admits that it was common to write *sumptus, demptus, comptus,* but calls *p* in this case "supervacua," and argues that the introduction of it is irrational. At the same time he tells us that there was a dispute whether *hiems* or *hiemps* was the correct orthography, and decides in favour of the former. Papirian. ap. Cassiodor., p. 2292, rejects *hiemps,* but says that *sumpsi, sumptus, sumpturus,* must be written with a *p.* Beda, pp. 2337, 2346, rejects *hiemps,* but adopts *sumpsi, sumpturus.* Mar. Victorin., p. 2466, insists upon writing *hiems, sumsit, insumsit, demsit,* and utterly rejects such forms as *consumptum, emptum, temptat, attemptat.*

Thus we see that while Priscian, Terentianus Scaurus, Papirianus, and Beda agree in writing *sumpsi, sumptus, dempsi, demptus, compsi comptus, emptus,* and the like, Marius Victorinus rejects the *p* in each case. All seem to agree in preferring *hiems* to *hiemps.*[*]

Setting aside *hiems,* inscriptions insert the *p* in the above words and their derivatives more frequently than they omit it. But a good many examples of both occur.

---

[*] Compare *Thomson* and *Thompson, Simson* and *Simpson,* in English, which is Σαμψών in Greek, and *Samson* in Latin.

Some forms of orthography seem to have been adopted by the very earliest Roman writers, which, like the duplication of the vowel, passed away at once: thus Priscian, p. 556, tells us on the authority of Varro, "de origine Linguae Latinae," that the "vetustissimi auctores Romanorum" wrote *Agchises, agceps, aggulus, aggens, agguilla, iggeruni,* for *Anchises, anceps, angulus, angens, anguilla, ingeruni,* as the Greeks wrote ἄγγελος, Ἀγχίσης: see also p. 569, and Mar. Victorin. pp. 2462, 2465.

III.—THE METRES AND PROSODY OF PLAUTUS.

Comic Metres. *

There is no topic connected with classical literature which, generally speaking, proves so repulsive to a young scholar as an inquiry into the metres of Plautus and Terence. This arises not so much from the difficulties which the subject presents, although these are unquestionably numerous and perplexing, as from the manner in which the subject has been handled. He will find himself called upon to peruse a series of disquisitions by different authors who accord with each other neither in principles nor details, but, on the contrary, exhibit for the most part fierce antagonism, agreeing in this only, that each propounds his ideas with dogmatic confidence, and assumes a contemptuous and insolent tone towards those whose views differ from his own.

The extreme positions in the controversy are held by two parties. The followers of the one, whenever they encounter a difficulty, are satisfied with calling it a 'licence'—a term which, if used freely and without discrimination, suffices to abrogate all metrical laws.

Those who adhere to the other have persuaded themselves that the verses of Plautus and Terence were constructed with the same delicate care, precision, and strictness which characterise those of the best Greek models, and that wherever we meet with any combination inconsistent with this doctrine we must at once pronounce the passage corrupt, and proceed to correct it. If we adopt this view to its full extent, we shall be called upon to re-write at least one-fourth of the plays now extant.

The ample space between these two poles has been occupied by those who entertain more moderate opinions, and who by their researches have done much to throw light upon what is obscure. But almost every one of these has some favourite hypothesis applicable to a particular class of cases; these hypotheses are for the most part founded on a very limited and imperfect induction, and

---

* Throughout this chapter it is taken for granted that the reader is familiar with Latin prosody and versification, as exhibited in the works of the Latin poets from Lucretius and Catullus downwards.

wherever any obstacle presents itself, a process literally Procrustean is forthwith resorted to, and short limbs are pulled out and long limbs cut short without compunction.

If, before going further, we endeavour to ascertain what the ancients thought on this matter, we shall find that those who were best qualified to judge were blind to the extreme skill and grace which some modern critics have discovered in the Iambic Trimeter of the comic writers, and it is amusing to contrast the expressions of Cicero and Ritschl.

The former, Orat. LV. § 184—"At comicorum propter similitudinem sermonis sic saepe sunt abiecti senarii, ut nonnumquam vix in eis numerus et versus intelligi possit."

The latter, when arguing against the admission of the hiatus under certain circumstances, exclaims indignantly, "Et hoc ut artis fuerit? et Plautinae artis, cuius tantam in reliquis partibus senariorum septenariorumque condendorum omnibus elegantiam merito admiramur?" And yet Cicero was certainly familiar with, and greatly admired, the early literature of his own country, and was moreover an accomplished Greek scholar.

Again, Horace, although jealous perhaps of the blind admiration evinced by some of his contemporaries for the older Latin writers, would scarcely have ventured to attack the 'numeri' of Plautus so decidedly had they in reality been regarded generally as faultless. See Ep. II. i. 58, 170 sqq., A. P. 54, 270.

From Priscian we learn that even in his time there were persons, we must suppose with some pretensions to learning, who asserted that there were no metres at all in Terence, while others pretended that they were of a mysterious, recondite character, and known to themselves alone. In the MSS. much confusion prevails as to the arrangement of lines, and the editor of the *Editio Princeps* seems to have been almost completely ignorant of the subject, and in many cases to have made scarcely an attempt to distribute the words into verses.

Now although many difficulties present themselves when we proceed to scan particular lines, and although much diversity of opinion exists with regard to the precise laws which the dramatists imposed upon themselves in constructing their verse, it must be observed that, except in some particular cases to be noticed below, there is no more difficulty in determining the classes and species of verse employed than in the works of Virgil and Horace. We can assert with absolute certainty that, for the most part, the ordinary

dialogue is carried on either in the Iambic Trimeter Acat. or in
Trochaic Tetrameter Cat.; that the Iambic Tetrameter Cat., the
measure of which Aristophanes was so fond, is occasionally
employed, and also, although more sparingly, Trochaic and Iambic
Tetrameters Acatalectic. Moreover, Bacchiac and Cretic Tetrameters are so frequently introduced that they can be easily recognised, and also, although with less certainty, the shorter species
and varieties of verses belonging to the whole of the four classes
specified.

But, in so far as the *Cantica* are concerned, the case is altogether
different. Some of these present little or no difficulty, in others all
is doubt, uncertainty, and confusion. Metrical scholars have accordingly here given free rein to their imaginations, and, as might have
been anticipated, have arrived at the most discordant results. We
have excellent examples of both kinds of Cantica in the Mostellaria.
The Canticum with which the Second Act commences can be
arranged in a satisfactory manner with little difficulty, and without
any important changes in the text, and we shall take an opportunity
below of reviewing it in detail. But the Canticum with which the
Fourth Act commences presents a different aspect. In B, the most
trustworthy of our MSS., the monologue is divided into twenty-five
lines, of which four in succession (6, 7, 8, 9) are mutilated, exhibiting lacunae to the extent of about two words in each, and *v.* 15
is evidently very corrupt. Hermann (Lib. II. c. xxiii.) distributes
the words into twenty-six lines, leaves many blanks, and introduces
several conjectural changes. Ritschl distributes the words into
twenty-seven lines, introducing a set of changes different from those
of Hermann, and agreeing with him as to the structure of seven or
eight lines only. Weise distributes the words into thirty-seven lines,
differing totally from those of Hermann and Ritschl. The remainder
of the scene, in which a second speaker is introduced, is distributed
in B into seventeen lines, and by Hermann into the same number,
but his arrangement is totally different. Some critics had supposed that they were Irregular Cretics, but Hermann has convinced
himself that they may be divided into Iambic Tetrameters Cat., but
admits that numerous alterations are necessary.* Ritschl adopts
this theory and most of Hermann's emendations in so far as the
first eleven lines are concerned, but the remainder he supposes to
consist of a compound measure, made up of an Iambic Dimeter

---

* "Bin ich völlig überzeugt, dass diese Verse *iambici septenarii* sind, die
aber freilich mancher Veränderung bedürfen."

and a Trochaic Dipodia. Weise distributes the seventeen lines into twenty-one, differing *toto caelo* from both H. and R. Thus, altogether, Weise distributes the forty-two lines, as they stand in B, into fifty-eight, in the course of which he supposes the measure to change thirty times. Moreover, he is obliged to imagine all sorts of strange combinations; thus two of the lines are described as consisting of *Dipod. Cret. cum Choriambo;* two more as *Cretic. monom. cum Choriambis;* another, a single *Anapaestus;* another as *Trispondacus;* another, *Creticus cum anacrusi;* four are *Troch. Tetram. partim pleni, partim Catal. partim etiam imminuti;* five are *Dimetr. Anap. cum Iambis.* It is hard to see how any one would suppose that any rhythm whatever could be detected by the nicest ear in such a heterogenous combination, where no attempt is made to discover a system of Strophes and Antistrophes, as in a Greek Chorus. Indeed it must be evident that any page in a prose author might, without violence, be cut up into fragments of varying length, each of which might receive a metrical title.

The same Weise boasts that he has discovered and arranged upwards of seventy 'Saturnian Verses' in Plautus, and has expounded his doctrine fully in a short treatise. But some scholars have as yet been unable to settle what Saturnian verse really was, since these so-called Saturnian verses, detected by Weise, differ widely from each other in structure, without being connected by any common bond; and since they are, according to his own admission, altogether distinct from the verses described as Saturnian by Terentianus Maurus and other ancient grammarians, we feel ourselves relieved from the necessity of investigating his arguments.*

The truth is, however unwilling scholars may be to admit their own ignorance, that the metrical arrangement of many of the Cantica is altogether obscure, and they may be regarded as affording exercises for the ingenuity of those who love to speculate on such subjects. Regarded merely as problems of doubtful solution, they would not be without their use; but unfortunately many persons become so wedded to their fancies, and persuade themselves so firmly of the reality of the visionary children of their imagination, that they become not only violent and abusive towards those who venture to express doubts, but scruple not recklessly to mutilate the text of the poet.

* See the 'Chapter on Saturnian Verses' appended to the author's 'Manual of Latin Prosody,' Griffin and Co., 1859, in which the whole subject is carefully and critically discussed.

What we propose at present is to examine—

I. Those kinds of verse employed by the dramatists, with regard to the existence and general structure of which no reasonable doubts can be entertained.

II. The prosody of Plautus and Terence, in so far as it is really or apparently at variance with that with which we are familiar in the works of the Latin poets from Lucretius downwards.

It may be urged that this is not the natural and logical arrangement of the subject—that a knowledge of the prosody ought to precede an inquiry into the versification. But in practice the plan we have indicated will prove the more convenient. We can find numerous examples which will enable those acquainted with the prosody of the Augustan age to comprehend the structure of the different verses of which we treat; and when we have acquired a general knowledge of these, we shall be enabled to discuss those particular cases in which the scansion is apparently difficult or anomalous.

The Iambic Trimeter Acatalectic

is the principle vehicle for the dialogue of Latin comedy, when it is carried on in a calm, unimpassioned tone. Priscian, in his treatise *De metris Comicis*, asserts that the Iambus, the Tribrach, the Spondee, the Anapaest, and the Dactyl, are employed "indifferenter" in all the places of the Comic Iambic Trimeter except the last, which is reserved for the Iambus exclusively, and this statement is fully borne out by the works of Plautus and Terence. It must not however be supposed that such lines as

Tityre tu patulae recubans sub tegmine pini,
Castaneasque nuces mea quas Amaryllis habuit,
Huic coniux Sychaeus erat ditissimus agri

could be recognised, although not directly incompatible with the above rule, any more than that

Κατάβα, κατάβα, κατάβα, κατάβα, καταβήσομαι,

could be accepted as a fair specimen of an Aristophanic Trimeter. The Latin poets always contrive to preserve the Iambic rhythm, and although Anapaests and Dactyls are not excluded from any one of the first five places, they are used more sparingly than Spondees, and not strung together in an unbroken series in the same line. The Dactyl especially is comparatively rare in the 5th place, although many examples may be quoted, as Most. I. i. 23,

Parasitos opsonate polluctibiliter ;

and III. i. 40,

D. Hic homo est inanis. Tr. Hic homo certe est ariolus ;

and in I. i. 69 we have two Dactyls consecutively in the 4th and 5th places. Lines however constantly recur which contain no Iambus, except in the last place, e. g. Most. I. i. 4,

Ego pol te ruri si vivam ulciscar probe,

where we have an Anapaest in the 1st place, followed by four Spondees; in v. 18,

Augebis ruri numerum genu' ferratile,

we have Spondees in the 1st, 2nd, and 5th, and Dactyls in the 3rd and 4th; in v. 16,

Quod te in pistrinum scis actutum tradier,

we have five Spondees in succession.

The penthemimeral caesura is preserved with considerable regularity, although, as might have been expected, it is frequently neglected.

The Iambic Tetrameter Catalectic,

called by the Latin grammarians *Septenarius* and *Comicus Quadratus,* was formed, according to the views of Varro, by the addition of three syllables to the Iambic Trimeter.[*]

It consists of seven and a-half feet, and admits the same feet as the Trimeter, viz., the Iambus, Tribrach, Spondee, Anapaest, and Dactyl.[†]

There is a division of the verse at the end of the 4th foot, which thus ought to end with a word, and this rule, although occasionally violated by the Latin writers, is observed by them more strictly than by the Greeks.

All the above-named feet are admissible in any place of the verse, but the Spondee and the Anapaest are rarely found in the 4th, and the Dactyl is still more uncommon. Bentley would exclude both the

---

[*] Varro, quoted by Diomedes, p. 514, and by Rufinus, pp. 2706, 2707.
[†] Bentley and Hermann add to these the Proceleusmaticus (i. e. ◡◡◡◡), but I believe that all the passages quoted in support of this opinion are either manifestly corrupt, or may be scanned so as to get rid of such an intruder.

Spondee and the Anapaest from the 4th place, but Hermann, while he admits the canon when the division of the verse is observed, considers that when the division is not observed, the Spondee, the Anapaest, and even the Dactyl, are all admissible.

In so far as the 7th foot is concerned, the Latins admit freely the proper foot, the Tribrach, the Spondee, and the Dactyl, the Anapaest more rarely, and generally include it in a single word.

Finally, this verse is Asynartete, and therefore the last syllable of the 4th foot may be either long or short, and the hiatus in this place is freely permitted.

According to what has been said above, the scheme of the Iambic Tetr. Cat. will be as follows :—

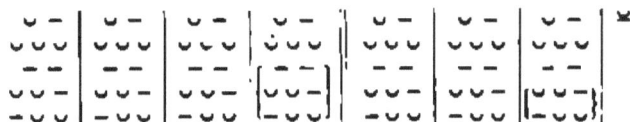

We shall give a few specimens to illustrate the varieties of structure indicated above, selecting our examples from the Mostellaria, in which the lines at the commencement of I. iii. (1–90) are composed in this measure :—

I. iii. 1, regular,

    Iampridem ecastor frigida | non lavi magi' lubenter.

v. 2, Asynartete, and Spondee in 7th,

    Nec quom me melius, mea Scapha, || rear esse defaecatam.

v. 3, Spondee in 7th, but not necessarily,

    Eventus rebus omnibus, | velut horno messis magna.

v. 6, Asynartete,

    Haec illa est tempestas mea, || mihi quae modestiam omnem.

v. 7, regular,

    Deterxit lectus qua fui, | quam mihi Amor et Cupido.

v. 8, regular,

    In pectus perpluit meum, | neque iam umquam optegere possum.

v. 9, regular,

    Madent iam in corde parietes | : periere haec oppido aedes.

v. 10, Asynartete and Dactyl in 7th,

    Contempla amabo, mea Scapha, || satin haec me vestis deceat.

v. 12, regular,

> *Qui tu te exornas moribus* | *lepidis quom lepida tute es.*

v. 13, *milyert'*, Spondee in 7th, but not necessarily,

> *Non vestem amatores amant* | *mulieris sed vesti' fartum.*

v. 14, Asynartete,

> *Ita me di' ament, lepida est Scapha :* || *sapit scelesta multum.*

v. 15, regular,

> *Vt lepide res omnes tenet* | *sententiasque amantum.*

v. 16, Dactyl in 7th,

> *Quid nunc ? S. Quid est ? P. Quin me aspice et* | *contempla ut haec me deceat.*

v. 17, Tribrach in 7th,

> *Virtute formae id evenit* | *te ut deceat quidquid habeas.*

v. 18, Asynartete,

> *Ergo hoc ob verbum te, Scapha,* || *donabo ego hodie aliqui.*

v. 19, regular,

> *Neque patiar te istanc gratiis* | *laudasse quae placet mi.*

v. 21, Spondee in 7th,

> *Eho mavis vituperarier* | *falso quam vero extolli.*

v. 22, Spondee in 7th,

> *Equidem pol vel falso tamen* | *laudari multo malo.*

The Trochaic Tetrameter Catalectic,

called *Septenarius* by Cicero (Tuscul. I. 44), and *Versus Quadratus* by Aulus Gellius (N. A. II. 29), is used very frequently by the Latin dramatists, especially in those portions of the dialogue which are characterised by unusual animation, bustle, or excitement.

The line consists, as the name implies, of seven and a-half feet, and, in addition to the Trochee and Tribrach, admits the Spondee, the Dactyl, and the Anapaest in any place except the 7th, where the Trochee and Tribrach alone are found.

There is a division of the verse at the end of the 4th foot, which ought thus to end with a vowel, but the Romans observe this rule much less strictly than in the case of the Iambic Tetr. Cat.

Like the Iambic Tetr. Cat. the verse is Asynartete, and therefore the last syllable of the 4th foot may be long or short, and hiatus is neglected.

According to what we have said above, the scheme of the Troch.
Tetr. Cat. will be as follows:—

$$
\begin{array}{ccc|ccc|ccc|ccc||ccc|ccc|ccc}
- \cup & - \cup & - \cup & - \cup \,\|\, - \cup & - \cup & - \cup & \square \\
\cup\cup\cup & \cup\cup\cup & \cup\cup\cup & \cup\cup\cup \,\|\, \cup\cup\cup & \cup\cup\cup & \cup\cup\cup & ! \\
-- & -- & -- & -- \,\|\, -- & -- \\
- \cup\cup & - \cup\cup & - \cup\cup & - \cup\cup \,\|\, - \cup\cup & - \cup\cup \\
\cup\cup- & \cup\cup- & \cup\cup- & \cup\cup- \,\|\, \cup\cup- & \cup\cup- \\
\end{array}
$$

Bacchiac Verses.

It is doubtful whether Bacchiac Verses were ever employed by the
Greeks, for the few examples quoted are all susceptible of a different
mode of scansion. They are common in the fragments of the Latin
dramatists, and specimens are to be found in most of the plays of
Plautus.

The species which occurs most frequently is the Bacchiac Tetrameter Acatalectic, which is found sometimes in a system, sometimes
combined with other species, and sometimes interspersed among
verses belonging to other classes, especially Cretica. Bacchiac
Tetrameters Catalectic, Trimeters Acat. and Cat., and also Dimeters,
are met with occasionally, but they are comparatively rare.

The proper foot is, as the name implies, the Bacchius ($\cup - -$), and
the following is a pure Tetrameter:—

> Sibi quisque ruri metit si male emplae.

The Molossus ($- - -$) is used freely, and is admissible in every
place, frequently in the 1st and 3rd, less frequently in the 2nd
and 4th.

In 1st,

> Quid nunc, vise, specta, tuo usque arbitratu.

In 2nd,

> Recordatus multum et diu cogitavi.

In 3rd,

> Ego esse autumo quando dicta audietis.

In 1st and 3rd,

> Quando hic nutus est, ei rei argumenta dicam.

In 2nd and 4th,

> Simul gnaruris vos volo esse hanc rem mirum.

In 1st, 2nd, and 4th, in Amph. II. ii. 22,

> Forti atque obfirmato: id modo si mercedis.

Nay, examples such as the following, if genuine, would go to prove that a whole Tetrameter might be made up of Molossi alone :—
Amph. II. ii. 20,

Et patria ti * prognati, tutantur, servantur.

and Poen. I. ii. 9,

Postquam aurora illuxit, numquam concessamus.†

In addition to the Bacchius and the Molossus this verse permits of the resolution of the first syllable of the Molossus, and thus the Ionic a minore ($\cup \cup - -$) finds a place, but is used much more sparingly than either the Bacchius or the Molossus :—

In 1st,

Mērito hōc nōbis fit qui quidem huc venerimus.

In 2nd,

Soror, cogita, amabō, item nos perhiberi.

In 3rd,

Quamquam haud falsa sum nos ŏdiŏsŭs haberi
Nam multum loquaces mērito ŏmnēs habemus.

In 4th,

Tun me, verbero, audes herum ludĭfĭcāri.

Lastly, either of the long syllables of the Bacchius may be resolved, and then we shall obtain the fourth Paeon ($\cup \cup \cup -$) and the second Paeon ($\cup - \cup \cup$) as feet available in any place except the 4th, from which the second Paeon is excluded : thus—

Quam si salsa mărĭatica esse autumantur.
Neque eis ulla ornandi satis satietas est.
Notarum aedium esse arbĭtrŏr similem ego hŏmĭnēm.

According to what has been said above the scheme of the Bacchiac Tetrameter will be as follows :—

$$
\begin{array}{llll}
\cup - - & \cup - - & \cup - - & \cup - - \\
- - - & - - - & - - - & - - - \\
\cup \cup - - & \cup \cup - - & \cup \cup - - & \cup \cup - - \\
\cup \cup \cup - & \cup \cup \cup - & \cup \cup \cup - & \cup \cup \cup - \\
\cup - \cup \cup & \cup - \cup \cup & \cup - \cup \cup & \quad \ddagger
\end{array}
$$

---

* To be scanned *Et patry' et.*
† So Hermann, but the text is very doubtful.
‡ This is the doctrine of Hermann, which has generally been adopted by metrical scholars, but I have serious doubts as to the admissibility of the fourth and second Paeon. In the first of the examples given above, *mariatica* might be pronounced *miryatica*, and this actually takes place some lines lower down—so, *satietas* may become *satjetas*, *similem* may become *similem*, and *hŏmĭnēm* may be *hŏmnēm*.

i 2

There is usually a division of the verse at the end of the second
foot, as in

    Recordatus multum et || *diu cogitavi*,

but this is not strictly observed, as,

    Ausculta argumenta dum dico ad hanc rem.

The following passage will afford a good example of a system of
Bacchiac Tetrameters. It is from Poen. I. ii. 1, and we have for
the most part preserved the Vulgate text. Some of the lines have
been differently arranged by Hermann in his Elementa D. M. Lib. II.
cap. 23—

    Negoti sibi qui volet vim parare,
    Navem et mulierem* haec duo sibi comparato,
    Nam nullae magis res duae plus negoti
    Habent, forte si occeperis exornare,
    Neque umquam sat istae† duae res ornantur,
    Neque eis ulla ornandi satis satietas‡ est.
    Atque haec ut loquor nunc domi§ docta dico,
    Nam nos usque ab aurora ad hoc quod diei est
    Ex industria ambae numquam concessamus ||
    Lavari aut fricari aut tergeri aut ornari
    Poliri, expoliri, pingi, fingi, et una
    Binae singulis quae datas nobis ancill(ae)¶
    Eas nos lavando, eluendo,** operam dedere (Ad-)
    -gerundaque aqua sunt viri duo defessi.
    Apagesis†† negoti quantum in muliere‡‡ una est;
    Sed vero duae, sat scio, maximo uni
    Populo quoi§§ lubet plus satis dare||||| potis sunt,
    Quae noctes diesque omni in aetate semper
    Ornantur, lavantur, tergentur, poliuntur.¶¶

---

* *Mulierem*, pronounced *mulyerem; duo,* a monosyllable here and below
in *v.* 11; *sibi,* inserted by Hermann.
† *Sat istae,* Herm. The MSS. have *satisbae.*
‡ Second Paeon in third place, unless we pronounce *satyetas.*
§ The MSS. have *modo* for *domi.* || Contraction for *concessavimus.*
¶ Last syllable of *ancillae* cut off before *eas.* See also next line.
** *Eluendo,* pronounced as a trisyllable, *eluendo,* and then we have a
second Paeon in the third place, unless we pronounce *operam.*
†† Ionic a minore.   ‡‡ Pronounce *mulyere.*
§§ Ionic a minore, unless we read *poplo.*
|||| Second Paeon in third place.
¶¶ Ionic a minore in the fourth place, unless we pronounce *polyuntur.*

There is a system of Tetrameters Acat. and Tetrameters Cat. in Men. V. vi. 1—

> *Spectamen bono servo id est, qui rem herilem*
> *Procurat, videt, collocat, cogitat,*
> *Ut absente hero suo* rem heri diligenter*
> *Tuetur, quam si ipse assit, aut rectius :*
> *Tergum, quam gulam, crura, quam ventrem, oportet*
> *Potiora esse,† quoi cor modeste situm est.*
> *Recordetur id, qui nihili sunt,‡ quid illis*
> *Preti datur ab suis heris, improbis*
> *Ignavis viris, verbera et compedes,*
> *Molae [magna] lassitudo, fames, frigus durum.*

It will be observed that in these Catalectic lines the third and fourth feet are uniformly Bacchii.

The following are regarded by Hermann as Bacchiac Dimeters Catalectic, while by Weise they are scanned as Dochmiacs : Pers. V. ii. 28—

> *Perge ut coeperas*
> *Hoc leno tibi*
> . . .
> *Deinde ut lubet*
> *Herus dum hinc abest*
> . . .
> *Videsne ut tuis*
> *Dictis pareo.*

Bentley detected, or believed that he had detected, a few Bacchiacs in the Andria, III. ii. 1—

> *Adhuc, Archylis, quae adsolent quaeque oportet*
> *Signa esse ad salutem, omnia huic esse video.*
> *Nunc primum fac istaec laves : post deinde*
> *Quod iussi ei dari bibere, et quantum imperavi*
> *Date, mox ego huc revertor.§*

The first line presents no difficulty; in the second we must scan *es|sē video* | as a Bacchius; in the third, *deinde* must be a trisyllable; in the fourth we have the second Paeon in the 2nd place.‖ But

---

* *Suo*, a monosyllable.
† Ionic a minore in first place, unless we pronounce *pŏtyŭra*.
‡ Ionic a minore in third place, unless we read *nili*.
§ If the lines are really Bacchiacs, it is the only example of this class of verses to be found in Terence.
‖ Bentley seems to have supposed that any one of the Paeons was admissible in the 2nd, 3rd, and 4th places, v. l. s. c.

Priscian (p. 1326) takes a totally different view of these verses; "Terentius trochaico mixto vel confuso cum iambico utitur in sermone personarum, quibus maxime imperitior hic convenit, quem puto ut imitetur hanc confusionem rhythmorum facere. Sunt autem trimetri ac plus minusque, et habent penultimam versus syllabam in quibusdam longam, et in quibusdam breve, ut in Andria." He then quotes the first four lines quoted above, and then goes on, "Haec sequitur dimeter catalecticus finiendi sermonis causa, quem ad Archillida habuit;

> *Dabo, mox ego huc revertor.*

Similiter Plautus in Truculento eodem metro usus est in sermone ancillae Astaphii;

> *Ad fores auscultate, atque asservate aedis,*
> *Ne quis adventor gravior abeat atque adveniat,*
> *Neu quis manus attulerit steriles intro ad nos,*
> *Gravidas fores exportet, novi ego hominum mores."*

The lines to which he refers in Plautus (Truc. I. ii. seqq.) are called by Weise *Saturnian!*

We may now proceed to discuss in detail all the Bacchiac Verses in the Mostellaria. The peculiarities which these exhibit in their structure will, when explained, be sufficient to enable the intelligent student to examine for himself those which appear in other plays.

A number of Bacchiacs occur in Act I. ii. 1 seqq., and these we shall give according to the arrangement of Hermann, noting the changes which he has introduced into the text, which are neither numerous nor important. It is to be understood that the whole of these lines are Tetrameters Acatalectic, except such as are specially noted as belonging to a different species—

v. 1. Molossus in 2nd place.

v. 2. Molossus in 1st and 3rd. *Instítui*, the reading of the MSS., was changed by Reizius into *instítiri*, a form analogous to *posívi*, from *pono*.

v. 3. Pure.

v. 4. Pure, but the MSS. have *eam rem volutari*, which scans equally well if we pronounce *diu* as a monosyllable, and make a Molossus in the 4th place: hence any change seems quite unnecessary.

v. 5. A Trimeter Acat. with Ionic a minore in 1st, followed by two Molossi.

v. 6. Ionic a minore in 1st and 3rd.

r. 7. Iambic Dim. Cat.

v. 8. Here we must pronounce *similem, hominem*, as *sīmlem, kōm̄-nem*, the last syllable in *similem* being elided, and thus we shall have a pure Bacchiac Tetr.

v. 9. Molossus in 3rd.

v. 10. Molossus in 1st and 3rd, *simile* being pronounced as *sīmĭle*.

r. 11. A Trimeter Acat., with an Ionic in the 1st, Bacchius in the 2nd, and Molossus in the 3rd. *Faciam* is pronounced as *făcyam*, and the last syllable elided; moreover, the MSS. have *esse ita*.

v. 12. Pure; the MSS. have *ita esse*.

v. 13. Molossus in 1st.

v. 14. Molossus in 3rd.

v. 15. Iambic Dim. Cat., *Mea* being entirely elided before *aliter*. It will be observed that the arrangement of the words in lines 13, 14, 15 is different from that found in B, as exhibited in our text of the play, but no change has been introduced in the words themselves.

v. 16 (15). Molossi in 1st and 2nd.

r. 17 (16). Molossi in 2nd and 4th.

v. 18 (17). Molossi in 1st and 2nd.

v. 19 (18). Iambic Dim. Cat.　　$- - \mid \cup - \mid \cup - \mid -$

Then follow some Iambic, Cretic, and Trochaic lines, the Bacchiac measure being revived in

v. 37 (36). Molossus in 1st.

r. 38 (37). Molossus in 1st and 2nd.

v. 39 (38). Molossus in 1st, *et* being placed at the end of this line instead of at the beginning of the next, as in B.

r. 40 (39). Ionic in 1st, *speciem* pronounced *spēcyrm* and *populo* as a dissyllable, *poplo*.

v. 41 (40). Molossi in 2nd, 3rd, and 4th, *materias* being pronounced *matēryas*.

r. 42 (41). Iambic Dim. Cat.

v. 43 (42). Molossus in 1st, *expoliunt* being pronounced *expōlyunt*.

v. 44 (43). Iambic Dim. Cat., followed by Iambic, Cretic, and Trochaic lines to the end of the scene. The lines 39–44 are arranged differently from B, but no change has been made in the words, except that Hermann has *tibi sumptui esse ducunt* instead of *tibi sumptui esse ducunt*, and *sumptu suo* instead of *suo sumptu*.

We find another series of Bacchiac Tetrameter lines in III. ii., extending from *v*. 94 to the end of *v*. 112 (in Vulg. 96–114), but several of these cannot be scanned without conjectural emendations more or less violent—

v. 94. Molossus followed by two Bacchii, but unless we pronounce the word *congrediar* as a trisyllable, and regard the line as Catalectic, we must have recourse to some such conjectural emendation as that proposed by W. and R., who read *congredibor*.

v. 95. Molossus in 1st.

v. 96. As it stands the line is Catalectic, but the MSS. are in some confusion.

v. 97. Molossus in 1st.

v. 98. Considering the first syllable in *Utic* as short (of this we shall treat below), we have here the first Paeon followed by three Bacchii.

v. 99. Pure, but in that case we must lengthen the second syllable in *eral*.

v. 100. Molossus in 1st.

v. 101. Molossus in 1st. To avoid the hiatus R. reads *hoc verbum*.

v. 102. The text rests upon the authority of A, C, and D. To scan we must pronounce *facient*, and then we have three Bacchii followed by a Molossus.

v. 103. This line is quite refractory, even if we read *potivi*. R. corrects it thus—

> *Ego hic esse et illi similis haud potivi.*

v. 104. Molossus in 1st.

v. 105. Cannot be scanned without correction; the most simple is—

> *Age i duce me—Num moror—Subsequor te.*

v. 106. Molossus in 2nd.

v. 107. Cannot be scanned without corrections; the most simple are—

> *Sed is maestus est te hasce vendidisse,*

or—

> *Sed ut maestus est te hasce vendidisse.*

v. 108. Molossus in 1st. *Philolacheti* pronounced *Philolacheti.*

v. 109. Pure. There is an hiatus between *tibi* and *haud*, but this can scarcely be objected to by the most fastidious, since there is a change of person.

v. 110. Pure.

v. 111. Pure, the first syllable in *redhibere* being regarded as long.

v. 112. Can only be scanned by resolving the last syllable of the Molossus in the 3rd place, *domum traher'* ($\cup - \cup \cup$), or contracting

traker into one long syllable. The lines which immediately follow
are confessedly in a mutilated state. At *v.* 119 a series of Troch.
Tetr. Cat. commence.

The Catalectic Tetrameter is sometimes found subjoined to the
Acatalectic, as in Men. V. vi. 1,

> *Spectamen bono servo id est qui rem herilem,*

and so on to the end of *v.* 10.

The following four lines, at the commencement of the fourth scene
of the first Act, are set down by Weise as ' Bacchiaci,'

> *Advorsum venire mihi ad Philolachem*
> *Volo temperi : audi : hem, tibi imperatum est.*
> *Nam illi, ubi fui, effugi foras :*
> *Ita me ibi male convivii sermonisque taesum est.*

The first presents no difficulty if we change *venire* into *veniri* and
Philolachem into *Philolachrem*, pronouncing *Philo* as one long syllable, *Philo*.

In the second line we can make out two Bacchii at the commencement and one at the end, but it is hard to squeeze *Hem tibi imp*
into anything, unless we avoid elision, contract *tibi* into one long
syllable, and call the result a Molossus.

The third line has confessedly a Catalectic ending, and is mutilated
in the middle.

The fourth line presents us with six short syllables at the beginning, which may be conceived to result from the resolution of a
Molossus, and then follow two Molossi and a Bacchius.

Cretic Verses.

The Cretic measure was extensively used by the Roman tragic
and comic poets. The species generally employed was the Tetrameter Acatalectic, but specimens of the Catalectic variety occur here
and there, and Dimeters are not uncommon.

The proper foot, as the name implies, is the Pes Creticus ($-\cup-$),
and the following are pure Tetrameters—

> *Ilico res foras libitur liguitur.*
> *Ne arbitri ducta nostra arbitrari queant.*
> *Num doli non doli sunt nisi astu colas.*
> *Sed malum maximum, si id palam provenit.*

Either of the long syllables of the Cretic may be resolved, and in this way the fourth Paeon ($\cup \cup \cup -$) and the first Paeon ($- \cup \cup \cup$) become admissible, thus—

Fourth Paeon in 2nd,

Musice hercle ágilis aetatem ita ut vos decet.

Fourth Paeon in 3rd,

Nos profecto probe ut voluimus riximus.

Fourth Paeon in 1st and first Paeon in 3rd,

Dominus indiligens reddere alias nevolt.

But, in addition to these feet, the Romans (not the Greeks) admit the Molossus. This doctrine was first distinctly laid down by Bentley, in his notes on Cic. Tusc. III. 19, and Terent. Adel. IV. iv. 2.*

Examples are common—

In 1st and 2nd,

Vino et victu piscatu probo electili.

In 1st and 3rd,

Processerunt ita ut dicis facta haud nego.

In 1st, 2nd, and 3rd,

Venti navis nostrae mira quae frangat ratem,

where *navis* is to be pronounced as a monosyllable.

Generally speaking, the Cretic vindicates to itself the 4th place, but even into this the Molossus and the fourth Paeon occasionally intrude, but not the first Paeon.

According to what has been said the scheme of the Cretic Tetrameter Acat. will be—

$$
\begin{array}{c|c|c|c}
- \cup - & - \cup - & - \cup - & - \cup - \\
\cup \cup \cup - & \cup \cup \cup - & \cup \cup \cup - & \left(\cup \cup \cup - \right. \\
- \cup \cup \cup & - \cup \cup \cup & - \cup \cup \cup & \left. - \, - \, - \right) \\
- \, - \, - & - \, - \, - & - \, - \, -
\end{array}
$$

There is another point connected with the scansion of Cretic Tetrameters which deserves special attention, viz., that the two halves are Asynartete, and thus the last syllable of the second foot may

---

* It is admitted, somewhat grudgingly, by Hermann, with a qualification not very precise nor easily applied—"qui pes tamen ita temperari solet, ut aut propter ambiguitatem mensurae non sit molossus, ut in Plauti Captivis II. L. 11 ; aut solutos sinat, quos argento emerit, vel ubi *concede huc, secede huc*, et similia retracto in primam syllabam accentu dicuntur ; aut a pronuntiatione accentum solum sequente obscuretur, ut in Rudente I. v. 15, 19,

Quaene cierior e mari ambae sumus, te opsecro
Ut tuo recipias tecto, servesque nos."

be long or short at pleasure, and a hiatus may be freely admitted; thus Cas. II. ii. 29,

> Quin viro aut suptrahat ‖ aut stupro intemerit;

and v. 16,

> Nec mihi ius meum ‖ optineadi optio est;

and Rud. IV. iii. 12,

> Sed boni consili ‖ ecquid in te mihi est;

where suptrahat, ius meum, and consili, although each is followed by a vowel, stand for Cretics. In so far as the hiatus is concerned, we may remark that it is not unfrequently neglected in other parts of the verse.

The following passage will afford a good example of the Cretic Tetrameter Acat.; it is from Cas. III. v. 1—

> Nulla sum, nulla sum ! Tota, tota occidi !
> Cor metu mortuom est : membra miserae* tremunt,
> Nescio unde auxili, praesidi, perfugi
> Mi, aut opum copiam comparem aut expetam :
> Tanta factis modo mira miris modis
> Intus vidi, novam atque integram audaciam.
> Cave† tibi, Cleostrata :‡ apscede ab ista, opsecro,
> Ne quid in te mali faxit ita§ percita.

The Cretic Tetrameter Catalectic occurs here and there in detached lines. Hermann arranges seven in succession in Trin. II. i. 17-23, but several of these cannot be scanned without conjectural emendations; one presents no difficulty, and may serve as an example—

> Da mihi hoc, mel meum, si me amas, si audes;

see also what is said below on Most. I. iv.

Cretics combined with Trochees.

Lines are occasionally found in Plautus which belong unquestionably to the class of Cretics, but which terminate in a peculiar manner.

---

* Fourth Paeon in 3rd place, unless we pronounce misrae.
† Cave, a monosyllable, pronounced Cau.
‡ Cleostrata, a trisyllable, pronounced Cleostrata.
§ Fourth Paeon in 3rd place. Ita is a conjectural emendation, for the MSS. have ira, but it is not satisfactory. The next line, which concludes the speech of Pardalisca, seems to be a Choriambic Tetrameter Acat.,—

> Eripite isti gladium quae sui est impos animi.

The best example of a measure of this sort is to be found in
Most. III. ii., where there is a system extending from the commencement of the scene down to the end of *v.* 37. Take the first
half-dozen lines as a specimen—

> *Melius anno hoc mihi non fuit domi,*
> *Nec quod una esca me iuverit magis.*
> *Prandium uxor mihi perbonum dedit;*
> *Nunc dormitum iubet me ire. Minume !*
> *Non mihi forte visum ilico fuit,*
> *Melius quom prandium, quam solet, dedit.*

According to Hermann the lines consist of a Cretic Dimeter Acat.,
to which is subjoined a Trochaic Monometer Hypercat. These
we should scan—

> *Mḗlĭŭs ắnn' | hŏc mĭhĭ || nŏn fŭ|ĭt dŏm|ĭ*
> *Nēc qŭŏd ŭn' | ēscā mē || iūvĕr|ĭt māg|ĭs*
> *Prāndĭ' ŭx|ŏr mĭhĭ || pērbŏn|ŭm dēd|ĭt,*

and so on. There is a passage in the Bacchides, IV. iv. 4, where
those verses which Hermann believes to be Trochaic Monom. Hyperc.
are interspersed among Cretic Tetrameters Acat.—

> *v.* 1.   *Callidum senem.*
> *v.* 2.   *Callidis dolis.*
> *v.* 3.   *Compuli et perpuli mi omnia ut crederet.*
> *v.* 4.   *Nunc amanti hero.*
> *v.* 5.   *Filio senis.*
> *v.* 6.   *Quicum ego bibo.*
> *v.* 7.   *Quicum edo et amo.*
> *v.* 8.   *Regias copias aureasque optuli.*
> *v.* 9.   *Vt domo sumeret, neu foris quaereret.*
> *v.* 10.   *Non mihi isti placent Parmenones Syri.*
> *v.* 11.   *Qui duas tres minas auferunt heris.*

where *vv.* 1, 2, 4, 5, 6, 7 are Trochaic Monom. Hyperc.; *vv.* 3, 8,
9, 10 are pure Cretic Tetram. Acat.; and *v.* 11, after which the
measure changes, is composed of the Cretic Dim. with the Trochaic
Monom. Hyperc. subjoined, and may be considered as a *Clausula.*
Others do not recognise any admixture of Trochees, but hold that
such lines as

> *Melius anno hoc mihi non fuit domi*

are complete Cretic Trimeters, followed by a Pyrrhich (the last
syllable of the verse being common), which arises from the resolution

of the first long syllable of the Cretic, and thus the scientific name
would be Cretic Tetrameter Brachycatalectic, while such lines as

Callidis dolis

are in like manner Cretic Dimeter Brachycatalectic.

Although Cretic verses are extremely common in Plautus, they
are very rare in Terence. An isolated line may here and there be
picked out, as in Adel. IV. iv. 1,

Discrucior animi
Hoccine ex improviso mali mihi obici,

where Bentley has substituted *ex* for the MS. reading *de*. The only
example of a continuous series is to be found in Andr. IV. l. 1,
which are thus arranged by Bentley, the first being a pure Dactylic
Tetram. Acat., and the nine following Cretic Tetram. Acat.—

Hoccine credibile aut memorabile,
Tanta vecordia innata cuiquam ut siet,
Vt malis gaudeant atque ex incommodis
Alterius sua ut comparent commoda? ah
Idne est verum? imo id est genus hominum pessumum in
Denegando, modo quis pudor paullum adest:
Post, ubi tempus promissa iam perfici,
Tum coacti necessario se aperiunt,
Et timent: et tamen res premit denega—
—Re, ibi tum eorum impudentissima oratio est.

Hiatus.

It is well known that the Hiatus is occasionally, although sparingly,
admitted by the epic and lyric poets. We might have anticipated,
a priori, that it would take place more frequently in familiar dialogue,
and we are positively assured by Cicero that such was the practice
of the older poets. When speaking of the tendency of the speech of
the Romans to run together vowels, opposed to the practice of many
among the Greeks, he goes on (Orator. c. 45), ' Sed Graeci viderint :
nobis ne si cupiamus quidem distrahere voces conceditur. Indicant
orationes illae ipsae horridulae Catonis, indicant omnes poetae praeter
eos qui ut versum facerent saepe hiabant, ut Naevius,

Vos qui accolitis Histrum flumen, atque algidam

Et ibidem

Quom numquam vobis Graii atque Barbari

At Ennius semel
   Scipio invicte . .
Et quidem nos
   Hoc motu radiantis Etesiae in vada ponti.' *

There is no controversy that, in so far as the text of Plautus and
Terence depends upon MS. authority, there is an immense number
of cases in which elision is altogether neglected, that is, in which the
last syllable of a word ending in a long or in a short vowel, in a
diphthong or in the letter *m*, is not elided before a word beginning
with a vowel, a diphthong, or the letter *h*. Weise refers to sixty-six
"indubitata exempla" in the Amphitruo alone, and every play will
furnish a large number. But notwithstanding this, not a few of the
editors of Plautus, by changing the order of the words, by inserting
or omitting monosyllables and ejaculations, or, when the more simple
means fail, by bad and arbitrary conjectural changes, have considered themselves entitled, at any cost, to force the verses of Plautus
into accordance with the metrical rules observed by poets whose
compositions are of a character totally different, and who flourished
at a period when the language and the laws of versification had
reached their highest point of cultivation and stringency. The first
who undertook to satisfy the conditions of this self-imposed law was
Pylades, of Brescia, who considered the simple explanation, "metri
causa," a justification for any change he thought fit to introduce
into the text, and many of his interpolations were adopted by his
successors, and long maintained their ground. Others followed in
the same direction until the work of destruction and reconstruction
seems to have been pushed to its extreme limit by Bothe and Ritschl.

Bentley, while admitting that the licence was frequently resorted
to by Terence, endeavoured to establish a code of rules by which
he supposed it to be defined and limited. These were—"In his
autem aliisque similibus tria sunt observanda; numquam hoc fieri
nisi in verbo monosyllabo; quod verbum si in vocalem exit, oportet
syllabam esse longam; ictum denique habere in prima syllaba
Anapaesti. Harum vero conditionum ignorantia quot nuper peperit
errores? dum et in polysyllabis verbis, et in syllabis brevibus, et in
aliena sede, posse fieri hoc existimabant."

It was soon perceived however by all who took an unprejudiced
view of the subject that the boundaries here marked out were far

---

* [See Ritschl, Proleg. p. cxcviii., who vainly attempts to get rid of the
evidence afforded by this passage.—Ed.]

too confined. In 1819 a tract was published by Lingius, afterwards Rector of the Gymnasium of Hirschberg, in Silesia, entitled *De Hiatu in Versibus Plautinis*, written with great good sense and moderation, in which, after a careful examination, he endeavours to classify the different examples of hiatus found in Plautus, and to distinguish those which are common from those which are more rare, and to specify cases in which, according to his views, hiatus is altogether inadmissible. Although the limits which he assigns are so wide as to comprehend a vast number of examples, and practically it will be found very difficult, if not impossible, to fix upon any limits at all, yet we shall have no difficulty in enumerating the different cases in which the licence, if we can call it so, is most common, and in which there is no reasonable ground for altering the text on this account alone.

1. *Long Monosyllables.* In these elision is freely neglected. The long monosyllable may remain long, or may be shortened, as in the familiar Virgilian lines,

Ecl. VIII. 108,

   Credimus? an qui amant ipsi sibi somnia fingunt.

Aen. VI. 507,

   Nomen et arma locum servant, të, amice, nequiri.

Thus Most. I. i. 42, 71,

   Si tú ‖ oles: neque superior quam herus accumbere,
   Molestus ne sis: modo iam i rus, te ‖ amove.

Mil. II. vi. 88,

   Nae tu hercle, si te dî ‖ amant, linguam comprimes.

Eun. V. viii. 50,

   Neque istum metuas nê ‖ amet mulier: facile pellas, ubi velis.

Phorm. Prol. 27,

   Quia primas partes qui ‖ aget, is erit Phormio.

Mil. IV. viii. 4,

  P. Quid vis? Pr. Quin (tu) iubes referri omnia quae ‖ isti dedi.

2. The *Penthemimeral Caesura* in Iambic Trimeters. Hiatus is exceeding common in this place: thus Pseud. I. i. 24,

   Interpretari ‖ alium posse neminem,

which is the reading of all the MSS., including A.

Rud. Prol. 7,

   Inter mortales ambulo ‖ interdius.

Most. I. i. 80,

   Video corruptum ‖ ex adulescente optumo;

so all the MSS. Such III. ii. 7,

> *Mustela murem* || *apstulit praeter pedes;*

so all the MSS., including A.

3. The *Hepthemimeral Caesura* in Iambic Trim. Hiatus is less common in this than in the Penthemimeral, but is by no means rare. Most. I. i. 38,

> *Dique omnes perdant : oboluisti* || *allium.*

Men. III. ii. 11,

> *Prandi, potavi, scortum accubui,* || *apstuli.*

Sometimes we find a hiatus both in the Penth. and the Hepth. in the same line, e.g., Most. I. i. 20,

> *Corrumpe herilem* || *adulescentem* || *optumum,*

where Pylades foisted in *filium*, and Ritschl *nostrum* after *herilem*, in order to bolster up the metre. Rud. III. vi. 21,

> *Ego hunc scelestum* || *in ius rapiam* || *exulem.*

So also Merc. IV. iv. 15,

> *Videre, amplecti* || *osculari* || *adloqui,*

where, if it were worth while, we might avoid the hiatus by writing *amplectier* and *oscularier.*

We find in Trin. II. iv. 138, 139, two lines in succession which appear in all the best MSS. under the form—

> *Nam fulguritae sunt alternae* || *arbores*
> *Sues moriuntur angina* || *acerrume.*

In the former Camer. inserts *hic* after *sunt*, and is followed by W., while R. foists in *ibi;* in the second, Hermann has *hic* after *angina*, R. has *illi*, Lind. transposes and reads—

> *Sues angina moriuntur acerruma,*

leaving the last syllable in *moriuntir* long, and in his preface quotes this as an example of this peculiar prosody.

4. *Wherever there is a distinct pause in the sense.* Even Virgil thought himself justified in writing, Ecl. II. 53,

> *Addam cerea pruna :* || *honos erit huic quoque pomo.*
> *Et vera incessu patuit Dea.* || *Ille ubi matrem.*

Thus Capt. III. iii. 17,

> *Nugas ineptiasque incepso.* || *— Haereo.*

Cist. II. iii. 12,

> *Age, perge, quaeso :* || *animus audire expetit.*

5. *A fortiori when there is a transition in the middle of a verse from one speaker to another :* thus Merc. I. ii. 74,

> *C. Qui potuit videre ?* || *A. Oculis. C. Quo pacto ?* || *A. Hiantibus;*

and Most. III. i. 55,

> *D. Iam hercle ego illunc nominabo.* || *T. Euge! strenue;*

and again, ii. 111 (109), in a Bacchiac Tetr.,

> *Ut istas remittat tibi.* || *Tu. Haud opinor.*

6. *All exclamations, interjections, imprecations, and the like*, are exempted from elision, as they are indeed from all the ordinary rules of prosody. Aul. II. viii. 22,

> *Perii hercle!* || *aurum rapitur! aula quaeritur.*

Mil. IV. viii. 20,

> *O mi oculi! O mi anime! P. Opsecro, tene mulierem.*

Most. III. i. 156, 153,

> *Euge, optume, eccum, aedium dominus foras;*

so in I. i. 1,

> *Quid tibi, malum, hic ante aedis clamatio est?*

Bothe, by a slight change, *est clamatio*, gets rid of the hiatus after *malum*, but it is clearly unnecessary to introduce any change.

7. We have already pointed out that Iambic, Trochaic, and Cretic Tetrameters must be regarded as Asynartete verses, and therefore it is unnecessary to notice the hiatus which occurs again and again at the end of the 4th foot in these measures.

We must repeat, however, that we would not confine the neglect of elision to the particular cases specified above. We would merely point out that it occurs frequently under these circumstances, and when encountered need excite no suspicion with regard to the genuineness of the text.

Rule of Position.

But after these obstacles have been cleared away, the chief difficulty remains untouched. As soon as scholars began to turn their attention to the metres of Plautus and Terence, they found a great number of lines which apparently could not be scanned at all without violating the Rule of Position, which may be said to lie at the very foundation of Latin prosody. We shall quote several of these lines, selecting as examples those which belong to the kinds of verse whose structure is well ascertained, and in which there is no evident corruption of the text.

Bentley, in his celebrated *Schediasma de Metris Terentianis*, admits the facts as in many cases indisputable, and points out that his predecessors had endeavoured to escape from the difficulty by following one of two paths—

1. Either by correcting every passage in which they discovered a violation of their own metrical canons, and in this way—to use his own vigorous words—"singulos fere versus miseris modis, addendo, mutilando, invertendo, contra Codicum fidem, lugulant et trucidant"—a description which applies very closely, not only to the persons indicated by Bentley, but to many modern editors, conspicuously to Bothe and Ritschl.

2. Or else they lay down the broad principle that wherever a word occurs in Plautus and Terence, in which the quantity differs from that exhibited by the same word in the epic and lyric writers, it must be held that the dramatists merely represented the ordinary pronunciation of these words at the time when they wrote. If this doctrine be accepted in its full extent, it will supersede the necessity for all further inquiry, and we may freely make long syllables short, and short syllables long, and at pleasure extend or curtail the natural dimensions of words. Bentley, while rejecting this hypothesis as untenable and even ridiculous, urges that if it were true we should find at all events uniformity of practice with regard to the same words, while, on the contrary, it is notorious that the dramatists sometimes observe the ordinary prosody, and sometimes deviate from it, in the same word. Thus *Ille, Esse, Propter*, have the first syllable invariably long in the later poets; in Plautus and Terence they are apparently sometimes long and sometimes short.

Bentley then proceeds to propound his own views. He admits that these departures from the ordinary rule must be regarded as a licence—"Licentia certe erat; et *indigna* forte, cui Romuli nepotes indulgerent"—but a licence restricted within well-defined and narrow limits:—

1. That vowels naturally long are never shortened, but those only which being naturally short become long by their position before two consonants. According to this view, although *mātris* from *māter* could never have the first syllable short, *simillimus* from *similis* might have the second short. This rule may be true, but the number of examples is too limited to enable us to speak positively.

2. The number of words which admit of such licences is small, and they are for the most part monosyllables, dissyllables, or compounds of these with prepositions.

There is much truth in this observation, but the statement is not sufficiently qualified. It will be seen, from the instances given, that several words which are not comprehended in the definition appear to violate the Law of Position.

3. This we shall give in the words of Bentley, as he claims the doctrine as original: "Illud tantum monebo, quod ante me opinor nemo—In primo fere versuum pede, et parcius alias, Licentiam hanc exercuisse Nostrum:* idque rectissimo iudicio: cum Actor, in fine prioris versus anima recepta, plenum rapidumque spiritum posset effundere." He then quotes thirty-eight examples from Terence.

Here again the observation, although just to a certain extent, is stated too strongly. There are many examples of this licence at the beginning of a line, but we cannot say that they are even comparatively rare in other parts of the verse. The explanation seems altogether fanciful.

We may now consider the opinion of Hermann, and this is deserving of the most careful study and the greatest respect on account of his profound scholarship, singular acuteness, and the special attention which he devoted throughout his long life to metrical topics. His views may be gathered from a number of passages in his great work, the *Elementa Doctrinae Metricae*, but they are distinctly and tersely enunciated in his *Epitome Doctrinae Metricae*, and seem to have undergone no change during the long period which elapsed between the publication of the first edition and the appearance of the third in 1852, the words in both (§ 79) being the same:—

"Apud Latinos duplex recitatio in usu fuit, una accentum maxime vocabulorum et vulgarem pronuntiationem sequens, qua scenici veteres usi sunt, altera ad Graecorum exemplum conformata, quae ab Ennio primum in epicam poesin, Augusti aevo in omnia fere genera poeseos introducta est. Scenica illa recitatio abundat correptionibus, neque curat positionem, unde *ille, atque, Philippi, iuventutis* et alia plurima correptis ante duplicem consonantem vocalibus pronuntiantur. Quin etiam vocales longas corripiunt, ubi ultima eliditur ut *concede huc, sicede huc.*"

It will be observed that in the above passage a fact is stated and an explanation given. It is stated as a fact that the dramatists neglect the Rule of Position (this without limitation), and that they moreover in certain cases shorten vowels naturally long. The explanation proposed is that there were two modes of pronouncing Latin; the one natural, national, and familiar to all; the other

* Sc. Terentium.

foreign, artificial, and known only to the learned, introduced first
by Ennius along with the Greek epic measure, and gradually adopted
in poetical compositions until it became universal in the time of
Augustus. Even if we accept this hypothesis it is clear that we do
not advance one step in our inquiry, for the result is merely this—
Certain syllables are long in the epic poets because they pronounced
them as long, and the same syllables are found short in the dramatic
poets because they pronounced them as short. But the objections
to the hypothesis are so numerous and so obvious, that we feel surprised that it should have been seriously propounded by Hermann
as affording a general solution of the difficulties encountered. In
the first place, if there had been two distinct styles, the differences
between them must have been much more numerous and more
serious than anything we can infer from the prosody of the dramatists. Secondly, since the supposition that a new pronunciation
was introduced by Ennius must rest upon the belief that such a
change was necessary to give effect to the Dactylic Hexameter and
other metres which he borrowed from the Greeks, it is inconceivable
that the dramatists should, like him, have borrowed all their metres,
or at least all their chief metres, the Iambic and the Trochaic, from
the Greeks and adopted the Greek mode of scanning, while at the
same time they retained a pronunciation which would have destroyed
their rhythmical effect. Lastly, had there been a marked and well-
defined distinction between the popular and what we may call the
epical pronunciation, the dramatists would have adhered steadily to
the former, and not, as is really the case, have resorted to it only
occasionally, while in the great majority of cases they adopted the
latter.

It will be seen that Hermann, in the passage quoted above,
mentions cursorily the "accentum vocabulorum" as combined with
and, we must suppose, forming part of the "vulgarem pronuntiationem." This leads us to say a few words upon the Latin accent,
in which not a few scholars imagine that they have discovered the
true key to the metrical anomalies in the dramatists. Foremost
among these is Lindemann, who, in an elaborate treatise, *De
Prosodia Plauti*, prefixed to his very useful edition of the Captivi,
Miles, and Trinummus, after adopting in a somewhat modified
shape the views of Hermann with regard to a change in the popular
pronunciation which, if not absolutely introduced by Ennius, was by
him first fully established, thus goes on—"Igitur Graeci sermonis
et graecissandi consuetudo, quamquam eius non sunt immunes

scriptores antiquiores, tamen magis structuram occupat, quam pronuntiationem et quae ei est coniunctissima, prosodiam; minime vero in
vulgus transierat, sed doctiorum hominum erat propria. Quapropter
peculiarem quandam et litterarum appellationem et prosodiam re-
perimus apud scenicos Romanorum poetas, quippe qui, tametsi
ingruente iam Graeca consuetudine scripserint, ad volgi tamen aures
se componere et communi sermone uti deberent." *

Now I would earnestly impress upon the young scholar, that the
belief that we can employ the knowledge which we possess with regard
to the accentuation of Latin words in any way whatsoever so as to
explain or illustrate questions with regard to quantity, is an absolute
delusion, and is moreover a mischievous delusion, because it is not
only erroneous itself but tends to divert us away from a path which,
although intricate, may possibly be threaded, into an inextricable
labyrinth of fanciful conjectures. Although from the language held
in the passage quoted above and adopted by others, we should be
led to suppose that we were handling something real and substantial,
a very few words will suffice to show that in following such researches
we are in reality striving to grasp an airy nothing.

1. Anything which we know with regard to the accentuation of
Latin words is derived from the old grammarians, who state in
the most specific terms that Accent and Quantity are perfectly
distinct.

2. The rules which they give for the determination of the accent †
in each word are founded on the *previously ascertained quantity* of
certain syllables in the word. To determine the position of the
accent therefore from the quantity of certain syllables, and then to
employ the accent as an instrument for determining the quantity of
the same, or of other syllables in the same word, is altogether
illogical, and in many cases amounts to a circular argument.

3. Among much confusion and many discrepancies our ancient
authorities are unanimous upon one point, that the accent in polysyllables can fall only on the penultimate and antepenultimate. But
Lindemann is obliged at the very outset to throw this canon over-
board, and to carry back the accent in many words to the fourth
syllable from the end of the word.

4. In reality all the mistakes with regard to this matter have
arisen from the loose manner in which the word "Accent" is

* But see what Ritschl says on this subject, Prol. p. ecvii.
† When we speak of accent we must be understood to mean the acute
accent, for it is to this alone that any power is ascribed.

employed in our own language, and the corresponding Latin term
Accentus by several continental writers.   In popular language the
terms *Quantity*, *Accent*, and *Emphasis*, although perfectly distinct,
are frequently confounded, but all who employ precise and scientific
language understand that *Accent* applies only to that elevation or
depression of tone which correspond to what are termed high and
low notes in music.   It is by the proper application of accent that
we prevent reading or recitation from becoming monotonous, but
this has no necessary connection whatever with the quantity of a
syllable, which depends solely on the time that the voice dwells
upon it in comparison with other syllables.

   But while several modern grammarians have vainly imagined that
the quantity of a syllable might be influenced by the accent, Bentley
introduced fresh complications and fell into the strange mistake of
confounding the Acute Accent with the Ictus Metrius, which has by
some writers been most unfortunately termed the *Metrical Accent*.
This phrase, *Ictus Metricus*, it is now universally admitted, was employed by grammarians to denote the stress which must be laid upon
certain syllables in repeating verse in order that the rhythm of the
measure may be made perceptible to the ear.   In Dactylic verse
the Ictus falls upon the first syllable of the Dactyl and of the Spondee;
in Iambic verse, on the long syllable of the Iambus and the second
syllable of the Spondee; in Trochaic verse, on the long syllable of
the Trochee and the first syllable of the Spondee.   When feet are
resolved, the Ictus maintains its place, and hence in Iambic verse the
Ictus falls on the second syllable of the Tribrach, the second syllable
of the Dactyl, and the last syllable of the Anapaest; in Trochaic verse,
on the first syllable of the Tribrach, the Dactyl, and the Anapaest.
That the Ictus Metricus has not in itself any connection with quantity
is evident from what has been stated above, that it falls according to
the verse, sometimes upon the first and sometimes on the second
syllable of the Spondee, on the first or second of the Dactyl, and on
the first or second of the Tribrach.   Of the two syllables of the
Spondee, which are, in so far as quantity is concerned, equally long,
the first receives the Ictus in Dactylic verse, and the second in Iambic
verse, while one of the short syllables of the Dactyl has the Ictus in
Iambics, and one of the short syllables of the Anapaest in Trochaics.
That it has no connection with the Acute Accent or Accent proper
is equally evident from the fact that in polysyllables the Acute Accent
can fall only on the penultimate or antepenultimate, while in innumerable instances the Ictus must fall upon the last syllable.   Bentley

saw this difficulty very clearly,* and was obliged to have recourse to
the strange and gratuitous hypothesis that this rule, with regard to the
accentuation of the last syllable, was enforced in the second dipode
of an Iambic Trimeter, but might be freely neglected in the first and
third dipode, but he is obliged to admit that even these limits, wide
as they are, will not embrace every case, and that examples occur,
even in the second dipode of a Senarian, where the last syllable of
a polysyllable must receive the Ictus.

To show that we are not misrepresenting the views of this great
but rash scholar, we give his very words:—

"Totum autem hoc, quod de Ictu in ultimis syllabis cantum fuisse
diximus, de secunda tantum Trimetri διποδία capiendum; nam in
prima et tertia semper licuit; siquidem ista sine venia conclamatum
actumque erat de Comoedia Tragoediaque Latina. Cum igitur hunc
versum similesque apud nostrum videris,

Malúm quod isti di deaeque omnés duint,

cave vitio id poetae verteris; etsi *Malum* illud et *Omnes* si in
communi quis sermone sic acuisset, deridiculo fuisset. Nimirum
aures vel invitae patienter id ferebant, sine quo ne una quidem
in fabula scaena poterat edolari. * * * * In secunda igitur
Trimetri διποδία hoc de quo agimus non licebat. * * * *
Rarissime igitur, semel atque iterum, sed magno sententiae lucro,
admisit hoc in Trimetris Terentius;

Persuasit nox amor vinum, adolescentia
Scelesta cum lupo commisi, dispudet.

Nam illud

Nosse omnia haec salus est adolescentibus

in hac editione *Salute* est."

Hence we find, in every page, *soló, ductarúm, habét, homini,
corrumpi, cómmutaturús,* or the like. It must be understood therefore that these marks, which distinguish Bentley's edition, and which
have been adopted by several recent editors of Plautus and Terence,

---

* Indeed, he himself quotes the leading passages from the ancient
grammarians in which it is laid down, as a positive law, that in polysyllables the penultimate and antepenultimate alone admit the acute
accent—"Illud sane in lingua Latina notabile, ne unum quidem verbum
praeter Monosyllaba tonum in ultima habuisse. *Deúm* igitur, *Virúm Meúm
Tuúm* priore licet brevi pronuntiabant, numquam nisi in Versu *Deám,
Virúm, Meúm, Tuúm.*" It is to be observed that in not one of the passages
referred to by Bentley is there the slightest indication of the limitation
he would insist upon.

indicate nothing except that the syllables over which they are placed
receive the Ictus Metricus or are *In Arsi;* and there can be no
objection to their use, since they frequently guide a young scholar
to the proper scansion of the line, although the object would be more
fully attained if the quantity of each syllable were marked according
to the practice followed in some editions of Caesar and other 'First
Reading Books,' for the use of those commencing the study of the
language.

But although we must regard the views of Bentley, of Hermann,
of Lindemann, and their followers, as untenable, taken as a whole,
it by no means follows that we must give up the inquiry in despair.
Many of their remarks are most just and valuable, and will prove
of the greatest service, if we pursue the investigation according to
a rational system. Two things are essential—

1. We must not form a theory founded upon a limited induction,
and then insist upon forcing reluctant facts into accordance with it;
but,

2. We must carefully collect all those words which present anomalies in quantity, and then endeavour to ascertain whether they
form an incongruous heap, or whether they admit of being, to a
certain extent at least, grouped and classified. If we succeed in
classifying them, we may, lastly, proceed to inquire whether there
is any principle which will serve to explain our difficulties.

We may begin by what may be called a natural arrangement;

1. Words in which the vowel is apparently shortened before a
consonant at the end of the word followed by a consonant at the
beginning of the next word.

2. Words in which a vowel is apparently shortened before two
consonants in the same word.

3. Lastly, we may consider the case of those vowels or syllables
which, although not affected by the Rule of Position, exhibit in the
dramatists a quantity different from that assigned to them by the
practice of later writers.

To class 1 belong the following words, the last syllables of which
seem to be occasionally, many of them frequently, left short before
a word beginning with a consonant: *Apud, Amor, Bonus, Caput,
Canum, Colas, Domus, Enim, Fores, Foras, Herus, Manus, Malus,
Minas, Miser, Modus, Nimis, Pater, Potest, Quidem, Senex, Simul,
Soror, Tamen, Volunt.*

Under class 2 are ranked the following words, the last syllables
of which seem to be occasionally, many of them frequently, left short

before two consonants which follow in the same word: *est, esse, eccum, Ule, Ule, Ipse, Inde, inde, Intus, Inter, nempe, Umnis,* and some others.

In the above and other words of a similar character many metrical scholars have maintained that there was an evident violation of the Rule of Position, and scanned lines in which those words occur, as if the last syllables in *apud, amor,* &c., were short, and so also the first syllables in *esse, eccum,* &c.

But another solution of the difficulty has been proposed, which we have no hesitation in adopting, viz., that all the words given above were occasionally, in familiar conversation, pronounced '*correptim;*' that is, the first syllable was almost entirely suppressed in enunciating the word, and thus the dissyllables were transformed into mono-syllables. Much may be said in favour of this view.

1. It will be seen that, with very few trifling exceptions, all the changes made by the Roman poets upon words are *in the direction of contraction.*

2. It will be observed that all the words enumerated in class 1 are dissyllables, having the first short, and that in the greater number the short vowel is followed by a liquid, so that there would be little difficulty in pronouncing them in a syncopated form without de-stroying the sound of the word. Some of these words must be pronounced '*correptim,*' even when position is not involved.

3. Those in class 2 are all words which recur perpetually in dialogue, and are exactly the kind of words which would be abbreviated in conversation.

4. We can find abundance of analogies in our own language, some of them completely in point.

5. If we pass to foreign languages we shall find that the same holds good with respect to them.

6. If we trace the passage of certain of these words into the Romance language we shall perceive that many of them were adopted in an abbreviated form, thus affording an indication at least that in the popular dialect such abbreviations were common.

Now before proceeding to give and discuss examples of the two classes of metrical anomalies we have just mentioned, it is necessary to call attention to the fact that even the epic and lyric writers of the Augustan age assumed the right of modifying the form or pronun-ciation of certain words which must otherwise have been altogether excluded from their measures, or which, in their ordinary shape, would have been productive of embarrassment. These changes have

m

been comprehended by grammarians under the general title of
Poetical Licences. Without stopping to inquire into the strict propriety of this term, we should expect that all the 'licences' found
in the epic and lyric poets would present themselves in the dramatists, and we need feel no surprise if they exceed those of the
later writers both in number and boldness.

  1. *The letter I.* Since the character *i* was employed to denote
both a vowel and also a consonant, which, it is probable, had the
sound of an English *y*, the Augustan poets permitted themselves
occasionally to give it the force of a consonant in certain words in
which it properly represented a vowel. Thus the words, *abietibus,
parietibus,* which as quinquesyllables, with the first four short, would
be inadmissible in Dactylic verse, were pronounced and scanned
as quadrisyllables, *abyetibus, paryetibus,* the first syllable being now
made long by position. So also, without the plea of absolute
necessity, we find *fluryorum, abyegnas,* as trisyllables, and such
combinations as *consily'et* (for *consilium et*), *principy'huc* (for *principium huc*), and a few others.

  In the same way in Plautus we have such contractions as
diu, Most. I. ii. 4 (Bacch. Tetr.),

            Eam rem volutavi, et dīu disputavi,

(but *diu* in v. 1), and in Epid. II. iii. 40; *dīes,* Trin. II. iv. 180
(Senar.),

         Dies constituatur; eadem haec confirmabimus;

dīe (dat. for *diei*), in IV. ii. 1 (Troch. Tetr. Cat.),

    Huic ego dīe nomen Trinumo faciam, nam ego operam meam;

dīe totally elided in Truc. V. 15 (Troch. Tetr. Cat.),

    Numquam hoc uno dīe efficiatur opus quin opus semper siet;

hōdie in Stich. V. ii. 6 (Senar.),

      Me hōdie venturum ut cenam coquerem temperi;

and so Pers. II. v. 13; *quoiusmodi,* Most. III. 1. 110 (106) (Senar.),

     Ain tu aedes? Aedes inquam, sed scin quoiusmodi;

iis, Capt. III. iv. 23 (Troch. Tetr. Cat.),

      Quibus insputari saluti fuit atque iis profuit;

alios, Most. I. iii. 23 (Troch. Tetr. Cat.),

      Quam vero culpari aut meam speciem alios inridere

(so the MSS.; Pylad. has *alios meam speciem*); *mulieris* is a trisyllable (= *mulyěris*) in Most. I. iii. 13 (Troch. Tetr. Cat.), where all the MSS. have,

Non vestem amatores amant mulieris sed vestis fartum.

Pylad., Bothe, and R. have re-written the line in various ways: I would scan it,

Non vest|em ama|tores | amant ‖ mulyěri' | sed ves|ti' far|tum.

In verbs, Ritschl allows that *scio* in all its parts, and also *nescio*, &c., admit synizesis freely; *ais* and *ait* may be monosyllables, and *aibam* in all its persons a dissyllable. Such forms as *audibam*, &c., he regards as grammatical rather than metrical, and with these exceptions he lays down a canon that, in the case of verbs (as in the case of nouns, with the exception of *diu*, *dies*, and *trium*), the letter *i* never forms a synizesis with any vowel following it in the more regular metres, but only in Octonarians and Anapaests. But we have an undoubted instance of *sarriunt* in Capt. III. v. 5 (Senar.),

Nam semper occant priusquam sarriunt rustici,

which R. would attempt violently to get rid of by substituting *sariunt*, a form unheard of elsewhere. So *ambiunt*, Mil. I. 69 (Senar.), where all the MSS. have,

Molestiae sunt, orant, ambiunt, opsecrant.

In the same manner R. vainly endeavours to get rid of *eveniat*, Trin. I. ii. 3; *eveniant*, Most. II. i. 48; *proveniant*, v. 67; substituting the forms *evenat*, *evenant*, *provenant*, for what is in each case the reading of all the MSS. *Expoliunt* occurs Most. I. ii. 42.

2. *The letter V.* In like manner the character *v* being employed to denote a vowel and also a consonant, which, it is probable, had the sound of the English *w*, we find *tenuia*, *tenuius*, converted into *tenuvia*, *tenuvius*, and, without the plea of necessity, *genua*, *curruum*, *tenues*, &c., become *genuva*, *curruvum*, *tenuves*, &c.

Again, without any reference to the exigencies of verse-making, there was a tendency in the language to drop altogether the *v* when it occurred between two vowels, and to contract the vowels into one syllable; thus instead of *movibilis*, *movimentum*, *iuvenior*, *noviter*, *providens*, we have *mobilis*, *momentum*, *iunior*, *nuper*, *prudens*, &c.; while in verbs the double forms *amaverunt*, *amarunt*; *amaveram*, *amaram*; *audivi*, *audii*, and the like, are employed indifferently.

Thus in the dramatists, wherever *v* is found between two vowels

in such words as *anus, avis, ovis, navis, novus,* &c , the two syllables
may be contracted into one: thus Bac. IV. vi. 27 (Senar.),

   Bene navis agitatur, pulcre haec confertur ratis;

Aul. IV. vii. 3 (Senar.),

   Fac mentionem cum avonculo, mater mea;

Asin. I. iii. 65 (Troch. Tetr. Cat.),

   Aves adsuescunt. Necesse est facere sumptum qui quaerit lucrum,

where *aves* is a monosyllable and *necesse est* a dissyllable; II. ii. 105
(Troch. Tetr. Cat.),

   Mox quom Saurean imitabor cavelo ne succenseas,

where *cavelo* is pronounced *caulo.*

There is a curious passage in the Truculentus, III. ii. 15, where
Stratilax enunciates *cavillator* as *caullator,* and Astaphium ridicules
him for his pronunciation,

   S.   *Heus tu, iam postquam in urbem crebro commeo,*
   Dicax sum factus: iam sum cavillator (i. e. *caullator*) *probus.*
   A.   *Quid id est, amabo? Istaecce ridicularia*
   Cavillationes vis fortasse dicere.
   S.   *Ita, ut pauxillum differant a cavillulis* (i. e. *caululis* or
   caulibus, 'cabbages').

The well-known story in Cic. Div. II. 40 serves to illustrate the
popular pronunciation of *cave.* There was a town in Caria called
Caunus, famous for its figs, which were imported into Italy and
hawked about, the cry used by the vendors being *Caunas !* When
Crassus was embarking his troops at Brundusium, previous to his
fatal campaign against the Parthians, he encountered one of these
itinerant dealers, and Cicero says it might be urged by the super-
stitious that if he had been warned by the omen he might have
escaped destruction; *Caunas* and *Cave ne eas* being, it would appear,
identical in pronunciation.

So with the word *iuventus;* Amph. I. i. 2 (Iamb. Tetr. Acat.),

   Iuventutis mores qui sciam, qui hoc noctis solus ambulem,

where we must pronounce *Iventutis* or *Iuntutis,* not, as some would
have, *Iuventutis;* In Curc. I. i. 38 (Senar.),

   Iuventute et pueris liberis; ama quid lubet,

Iuventute is a trisyllable, *ama* a monosyllable; in Most. I. i. 29
(Senar.),

Quo nemo adaeque iuventute ex omni Attica,

there is no correption, as indicated by Weise, but an Anapaest in the 3rd place.

Obliviscendi is a quadrisyllable in Mil. IV. viii. 49 (Troch. Tetr. Cat.),

Muliebres mores discendi obliviscendi stratiotici;

divitias a trisyllable in Rud. II. vi. 58 (Senar.),

Ibi me corruere posse aiebas divitias.

With regard to the line Merc. Prol. 29,

Inhaeret etiam aviditas, desidia, iniuria,

which is sometimes referred to as an example of *v* dropped, it is scarcely possible to scan it as it stands, and Pareus is probably right when he proposes to omit *etiam* altogether.

The example of *avo* contracted, quoted from Aul. Prol. 5, depends upon an unnecessary change in the reading of the best MSS. In Amph. IV. iii. 16 (Troch. Tetr. Cat.),

Seu patrem sive avom videbo || optruncabo in aedibus,

we may either consider *avom* as a monosyllable, or *sive* as a monosyllable and totally elided. A good example of *avos* as a monosyllable occurs in Men. Prol. 44 (Senar.),

Et ipsus eodem est āvos vocatus nomine.

3. But this shortening or contraction takes place in the middle of many words without the presence of the letter *v*. Thus *aspero, circulus, manipulus, gubernaculo, oracula, saecula, pericula, vincula, laminae,* and many others become *aspro, circlos, maniplos, gubernaclo, oracla, saecla, pericla, vincla, lamnae.* This takes place most frequently when a short vowel in the middle of a word is separated from another vowel by a liquid, as in the above examples; but this is by no means a necessary condition, for we find *caldior* for *calidior, puertia* for *pueritia, universum* for *universum, calfacit* for *calefacit,* and Quintilian I. 6, tells us that in his time *calfacit* was more common than *calefacit.*

4. *Other contractions.* When *e* is followed by another vowel in the same word, it frequently coalesces with it in dactylic verse, generally, though not uniformly, from necessity. Thus we have *aurēā, alvēāria, eadem, eaedem, respondeāmus, acrei, aranēi, ferrei, alvēō, aurēō, eodem, eosdem.*

So also *oo* is contracted in such words as *coöluerint, coöperiant.*

Those cases in which *i* precedes a vowel, *vindemiator, omnia, denariis, connubio, omnium, inferius,* &c., may be regarded as provided for in the remarks made above on the letter *i*.

The following words in the comic writers always appear under a contracted form: as monosyllables, *dein, dehinc, proin, praeut, quoi;* as dissyllables, *antehac, anteit, coire, deinde,* (deinceps,) *deorsum, proinde, quoniam, seorsum;* as trisyllables, *introire, praeoptare.*

As examples of the letter *e* coalescing with a vowel following, we may take the various cases and genders of *is, meus, idem:* thus we have *ea* in Poen. Prol. 2 (Senar.),

> *Inde mi principium capiam ex ea tragœdia;*

is, Trin. Prol. 14 (Senar.),

> *Quoniam īi, qui me aleret, nil video esse relicui*

(where A and all the MSS. have *reliqui*); and *v.* 15,

> *Dedi īi meam gnatam quicum aetatem exigat;*

and again, I. ii. 138 (Senar.),

> *Utrum indicare me īi thesaurum aequom fuit;*

ēum, v. 81 (Senar.),

> *Quin ēum restituis, quin ad frugem corrigis;*

eae, Most. III. i. 157 (148) (Senar.),

> *Videndumst primum utrum eae velintne an non velint;*

eorum, Trin. I. ii. 178 (Senar.),

> *Ego de ēorum verbis famigeratorum inscius;*

eas and *duas,* III. iii. 45 (Senar.),

> *Duas eas nos consignemus quasi sint a patre;*

eodem, Mil. III. i. 18 (Troch. Tetr. Cat.),

> *Sed volo scire eodem consilio quod intus meditati sumus;*

eadem and *dies,* Trin. II. iv. 180 (Senar.),

> *Dies constituatur, eadem haec confirmabimus;*

meam, I. ii. 127 (Senar.),

> *Et meam fidelitatem et celata omnia;*

meum, v. 137 (Senar.),

> *Quod fuit officium meum me facere, fac sciam;*

and Most. III. i. 60 (56) (Senar.),

> *Beatus vero es nunc quom clamas. Meum peto;*

m̄ĕŏ, Trin. I. ii. 44 (Senar.),

> *Ne admittam culpam ego m̄ĕŏ sum promus pectori;*

and Mil. I. 1 (Senar.),

> *Curate ut splendor m̄ĕŏ sit clupeo clarior;*

m̄ĕae, Most. III. i. 23 (19) (Senar.),

> *Metllŏ | nĕ tĕch|nāe meae | pĕrpĕtĭ|ŏ pĕrĭ|ĕrīnt.*

Deus also occurs as a monosyllable: Trin. I. ii. 19 (Senar.),

> *Deus oro ut vitae tūāe superstes suppetat;*

Asin. IV. i. 37 (Senar.),

> *Dēŭm nullum: si magi' religiosa fuerit;*

Most. III. i. 154 (Senar.),

> *Di te deāeque omnes funditus perdant, senex.*

Rei is a monosyllable, Trin. I. i. 16 (Senar.),

> *Remoramque faciunt r̄ei privatae et publicae.*

The possessive pronouns *tuus, suus*, are frequently contracted by the dramatists: thus we have *tūās* and *suās* in Mil. I. 12 (Senar.),

> *Neque aequiperare tūās virtutes ad suās;*

tuō is entirely elided, and *sui* a dissyllable, in Aul. IV. iv. 27 (Troch. Tetr. Cat.),

> *Tuō arbitratu nequi sui me quicquam invenisti penes;*

tuos, Mil. I. 40 (Senar.),

> *Novisse mores tuōs me meditate decet;*

suum, entirely elided, Trin. III. ii. 49 (Troch. Tetr. Cat.),

> *Si istuc conare ut nunc facis indicium tuum incendes genus;*

tuos, tui, Stich. II. ii. 4 (Troch. Tetr. Acat.),

> *Tuōs inclama tu delinquont: ego quid me velles viscebam;*

suam, suam, Trin. I. ii. 73, 74 (Senar.),

> *Suāmque filiam esse adultam virginem*
> *Simul eius matrem suāmque uxorem mortuam;*

tuae, v. 80 (Senar.),

> *Qui tuae mandatus est fidei et fiduciae;*

suō, v. 117 (Senar.),

> *Flens me opsecravit suō ne gnato crederem;*

suum, v. 119,

> *Nunc si ille huc salvos revenit reddam suum sibi.*

The letter *u* coalesces occasionally with the vowel following in the words *duo quatuor;* both forms, *dúos* and *duos*, occur in the same passage in Most. III. ii. 147 (145) and 149 (147) (Troch. Tetr. Cat.),

> *Viden pictum ubi ludificatur cornix una volturios dúós?*
> *Cornix astat, ea volturios duos vicissim vellicat;*

so Trin. III. iii. 46 (Senar.),

> *Duas tas nos consignemus quasi sint a patre;*

Truc. II. ii. 52 (Troch. Tetr. Cat.),

> *Quisquam homo mortalis posthac duarum rerum creduit;*

Poen. IV. ii. 75 (Troch. Tetr. Cat.),

> *De praedone Siculo. M. Quanti? S. Duodeviginti minis.*
> *M. Duas illas duodeviginti? S. Et nutricem earum tertiam,*

where we must pronounce *duas* as a monosyllable: *duodeviginti* may in each line be regarded either as a sexsyllabic or quinquesyllabic word: in the one case the first three syllables will form an Anapaest, in the other a Spondee; Most. III. i. 121 (117) (Senar.),

> *Quatuor quadraginta illi debentur minae.*

In Men. I. iii. 22, 23 (Troch. Tetr. Cat.),

> *Quatuor minis ego emi istanc anno uxori meae*
> *Quatuor minae perúrunt plane, ut ratio redditur,*

it will be observed that *quatuor* is a trisyllable with the first syllable long.

Fuit is a monosyllable Truc. II. i. 7 (Iamb. Tetr. Cat.),

> *Dum fuit, dedit: nunc nihil habet: quod habebat, nos habemus.*

We have thus seen that the principle of synizesis, of which we find occasional examples in the writings of the Augustan poets, was employed to a far greater extent, and in a much bolder manner, by the early dramatists. But Ritschl, while in his eagerness to establish the purity and correctness of the metres of Plautus he would deprive him of those licences in which the most fastidious versifiers have indulged, is in some particulars willing to grant him an amount of license from which the most careless would have shrunk. In support of the theory that the dramatists were in many cases indifferent to the Rule of Position, he adduces a number of examples to prove that such words as *peristromata, expapillato, sat illius, supellex, trapezita,*

Philippus, and others, must be considered to afford instances of the violation of that rule. We shall examine in detail the most remarkable of these examples, and show how insufficient is the evidence they afford to support the theory that has been built upon them.

The word *peristromata* occurs twice :

1. In Stich. II. ii. 54, upon which nothing can be founded, for the MSS., including the Palimpsest, are in the greatest confusion. The Vulgate, which is due to Camerarius,

Tum Babulonica peristromata, consutaque tapetia,

may be readily scanned as a Troch. Tetr. Cat. without doing violence to the obvious quantity of *peristromata*. Weise has—

Tum Babulonica peristromata, conchuliata tapetia,

which may also be scanned as a Troch. Tetr. Cat. by pronouncing *conchylyata*. Ritschl has—

Tum Babylonica peristromatia conchyliata tapetia,

which is less plausible than either of the preceding.

2. The second example is in Pseud. I. ii. 13,

Vi me peristromata quidem aequa picta sint Campanica.

Here the MSS. present no important variation, and the Vulgate, W., and R. acquiesce in the same reading. Editors have regarded this as a Troch. Tetr. Cat., in which case it is impossible to scan it without considering that the three first syllables of *peristromata* form an Anapaest; but the line may be scanned without difficulty and without violating the ordinary rules of quantity as an *Iambic Tetrameter Acatalectic*, and it cannot be objected that an Iambic verse is here intruded into a series of Trochaics, for the measure in this passage changes in almost every line, and Iambic Tetrameters immediately follow the verse in question. According to the arrangement of W., we have from the commencement of the scene—

v. 1-5. Tetr. Spondiaci Acat.

6. Dimeter Creticus.

7-9. Cretici Tetram.

10. Iamb. Tetr. Hyperm.

11, 12. Troch. Tetr. Acat.

13, 14. Troch. Tetr. Cat.

15-29. Tetram. Iamb. partim Acat. partim Cat. partim Hypercat.

There is nothing therefore startling or unnatural in supposing that *v.* 14 is an Iamb. Tetr. Acat. instead of Troch. Tetr. Cat.

Another example quoted is the word *expāpillāto*, found in Mil. IV. iv. 44,

Id connexum in humero laevo expapillato brachia,

D

where it is to be observed that elision is neglected in the division of
the verse after *laevo*. Nonius, p. 103, refers to this very line : " *Expapillato* brachio, quasi usque ad papillam renudato. Plautus Milite
glorioso : *id, connexum in numero laevo, expapillato brachio;*" and the
expression *expapillato brachio* is acknowledged by Paul. Diac., p. 79 :
" *Expapillato* brachio, exserto : quod quum fit, papilla nudatur."
But on the other hand *expapillato* appears in not one of the best
MSS., all of which seem to have had *exfafillato brachio*, and this in
one of the interpolated family appears as *expalliato brachio*. Moreover, Paul. Diac., p. 83, has, " *Effafilatum,* exsertum, quod scilicet
omnes exserto brachio sint *exfilati*, id est, extra vestimentum filo
contextum."

Now while we are free to repudiate the etymological explanation,
we can scarcely avoid the conclusion that there existed a phrase,
effafilato brachio, which was equivalent to *exserto brachio*, and it seems
highly probable that the word *effafilato*, having become obsolete at
an early period, was explained by grammarians by the more obviously
intelligible *expapillato*, and thus the latter found its way into the text.
It would be contrary to the natural and usual process to suppose
that *expapillato*, with regard to the force of which there would be no
doubt, would be changed into the forgotten *effafilato*. The conjecture
of O. Müller, that *fafila* in old Latin was equivalent to *fibula*, is very
plausible; reading therefore,

> *Id connexum in humero laevo effafilato brachio,*

we can scan the line without difficulty, supposing the quantity of the
verb to be either *fűfilo* or *fafilo;* the meaning will clearly be, ' The
arm being thrust out beyond (or below) the buckle.'

Again, with the word *satellites.* This word is found in Mil. I. 78,
with its proper quantity,

> *Age eamus ergo—Sequimini, satellites,*

but R. is disposed to allow the second vowel to remain short before
the double *ll*, and pronounce *satéllites*, relying on Trin. IV. i. 14,
one of a series of Trochaic Tetrameters Acatalectic. He prints—

> *Distraxissent disque tulissent satéllites tui miserum foede,*

whereas all the MSS. have—

> *Distraxissent disque tulissent satellites tui me miserum foede,*

and *me* seems to be required by the idiom of the language. Under
this shape the line is impracticable, and hence Hermann reads—

> *Distraxissent disque tulissent tui satellites me foede,*

transposing *tui* and omitting *miserum*, which will make all smooth.
Moreover, it will be found that much confusion prevails in this portion of the scene, and that various violent changes and transpositions
are necessary in order to maintain the system in its integrity. Hence
obviously we may pronounce that there is in reality no authority for
satellites. In Weise's text we find the reading of the MSS., and he
calls the line a Troch. Tetr. Cat., but how he proposes to scan it
I cannot tell.

The word *supellex* in the nominative occurs in Aul. II. v. 17,
Men. II. iii. 53, V. ix. 96, Pers. IV. viii. 2, Poen. V. iii. 27, In all
of which we may adhere to the quantity of *supellex*, as found in
Virgil, Propertius, Horace, and Juvenal, although some of the MSS.
and earlier editions, including the Vulgate, uniformly write *supellex*.
But two passages, in which the word appears in oblique cases,
present a difficulty. In Poen. V. iii. 26 (Senar.) we have—

> *Tace atque parce muliebri supellectili;*

and in Stich. I. ii. 5 (Troch. Tetr. Cat.),

> *Iam quidem in suo quidque loco nisi erit mihi situm supellectilis,*

where the Palimpsest and the Vet. Cod. Camer. have *quicque;* the
Cod. Decurt. and the best Vatic., *quique;* the Cod. Lips., *quoque;*
the Ed. Princ., *quarque;* the Cod. Lips., *sita;* the Palimps., the Cod.
Lips., and the Ed. Princ., *supellectilis;* the two Pall. and the Vat.,
suppellectilis. Moreover, Festus (p. 294) and other grammarians
recognise *supellectilis* as a form of the nominative.

This being premised, if the two lines as given above exhibit the
genuine text, then the word *supellectilis* must undergo some modification. According to the views of R. it will belong to the same
category as that in which he has placed *expapillato* and *satellites*,
and may be scanned as *supellectilis;* a less violent mode of escaping
from the difficulty would be to sink the second syllable and to pronounce *suplectilis.* But neither expedient is necessary. As to the
first example (Poen. V. iii. 26), we may avoid all embarrassment
by a simple transposition—

> *Tace atque muliebri parce supellectili;*

in the second (Stich. I. ii. 5), the rhythm of which is so harsh that
R. proposes to re-write the line, we may, without violence to the MSS.,
consider *supellectilis* as a nominative, and write—

> *Iam quidem in suo quaeque loco nisi erit mihi sita supellectilis,*

the corruption having in all probability originated in some early

transcriber, who was not acquainted with *supellectilis* as a form of
the nominative.

Trapezita. Goeller, Lindemann, and Ritschl would allow the
second syllable in *Trapezita* to be short, on the authority of Trin. II.
iv. 23 (Senar.),

Trapezitae mille drachumarum Olympicum,

in which they suppose the first foot to be an Anapaest. B has
drachumarum; C, D, E, *drahcumarum;* but A has the common
form *drachmarum.* But although the first syllable in *drachma* must
be long, it by no means follows that the first syllable in *drachuma*
is also long; on the contrary, we should be justified in asserting
that it *must* be short, for the Greek δραχμή is naturally short, and
accordingly being followed by the aspirated mute χ and the liquid μ
appears as short in Aristop. Plut., 884,

Τὸν δακτύλιον τονδί παρ' Εὐδάμου δράχμης.

Hence all difficulty as to the scansion of the above line vanishes, and
it is unnecessary to have recourse to the expedient of pronouncing
mille as a monosyllable. In other passages of Plautus *trapezita* has
uniformly its proper quantity, e. g. Asin. II. iv. 32, Capt. I. II. 90,
II. iii. 89, Curc. II. iii. 62, 66, III. 36, 50, IV. iv. 3, V. ii. 20,
iii. 34, 43, Pseud. II. iv. 67.

Philippus, Philippeus, Philippicus. The case of these words is
peculiar, and demands special notice. They occur upwards of
thirty times in Plautus with reference to gold coin, and in every
instance, except perhaps one, to be noticed below, the two first
syllables are to be pronounced as one—*Phlippus, Phlippeus. (Philippus* however does not occur in nominative sing.) This cannot
be accidental, but must have resulted from the ordinary pronunciation of the word, for the form *Philippus* would be quite as serviceable in an Iambic or Trochaic line as *Phlippus.* Again, *Philippeus,
Philippeo, Philippei,* &c., seem sometimes pronounced as trisyllables,
Phlippeus, &c., but more frequently as dissyllables, *Phlippeis,* &c.,
never as tetrasyllables, *Philippeus. Philippicum* occurs once only,
and must be pronounced *Phlippicum.* Thus Poen. I. iii. 6 (Senar.),

Trecentos Philippos Collubisco villico;

Bac. IV. ix. 83 (Senar.),

*Pol haud derides, nam ducentis aureis
Philippis redemi vitam ex flagitio tuam;*

viii. 27 (Senar.),

Nunc nisi ducenti Philippi redduntur mihi;

Poen. I. i. 38 (Senar.),

> *Trecenti nummi Philippei—Sexcenti quoque,*

where *Philippei* is a dissyllable; Curc. III. 70 (Senar.),

> *Solidam, faciundam, ex auro Philippeo, quae siet,*

where *Philippeo* is a dissyllable; Trin. IV. ii. 113 (Troch. Tetr. Cat.),

> *An ille tam esset stultus, qui mihi mille nummum crederet*
> *Philippium, quod me aurum deferre iussit ad gnatum suum,*

where *Philippum* is a dissyllable; Asin. I. iii. 1 (Troch. Tetr. Cat.),

> *Vnumquodque istorum verbum nummis Philippeis aureis,*

where *Philippeis* is a dissyllable. But on the other hand, Poen. III.
iv. 4 (Senar.),

> *Trecenti nummi qui vocantur Philippei,*

where *Philippei* is a trisyllable; Trin. I. ii. 115 (Senar.),

> *Nemo est—Numorum Philippeum ad tria millia,*

where *Philippeum* is a trisyllable. We find *Philippicum* in Truc. V.
60 (Troch. Tetr. Cat.),

> *Hem tibi talentum argenti! Philippicum est, tene tibi,*

where *Philippicum* must be pronounced *Phlippicum.* The only
example of the word *Philippus,* employed to denote a piece of
money, being a trisyllable, is in Poen. III. v. 36 (Senar.),

> *Qui ad te trecentos modo Philippos detulit,*

but the word *modo* is wanting in some of the MSS., and is probably
the interpolation of a transcriber to complete an imperfect line.

But when *Philippus* or *Philippa* are proper names, either the full
or the contracted forms may be employed. Thus in Aul. IV. viii. 4
(Senar.), it is a trisyllable,

> *Ego sum ille rex Philippus! O lepidum diem ;*

but in I. iii. 8 (Senar.), it is a dissyllable,

> *Philippum regem aut Darium, trivenefica ;*

and also in Pers. III. i. 11 (Senar.),

> *Mirum quin regis Philippi causa aut Attali.*

Philippa is found in Epid. V. i. 29 (Troch. Tetr. Cat.),

> *E Philippa matre natam ac Thebis, Epidauri satam.*

For other examples of *Philippus,* &c., as a coin, see Bac. II. ii. 52,
IV. ii. 8, viii. 38, 41, 78, ix. 10, 74, 103, 127, Trin. IV. ii. 117, 123.

V. ii. 34, Poen. III. ii. 22, iii. 57, iv. 22, v. 26, V. vi. 26. The following are in Anapaestic lines: Bac. V. ii. 64, Mil. IV. ii. 69 (72). The line, Bac. II. iii. 38, cannot be scanned as it appears in the MSS. The reading of Rud. V. ii. 27 is very doubtful.

Ex. There are some passages quoted from Plautus in which the syllable *ex* appears to be short in the words *exemplum, exigere,* and *exercitus.*

For *Exemplum* we are referred to Rud. II. iii. 40 (Iamb. Tetr. Cat.),

Iactamur exemplis plurimis miserae perpetuam noctem.

But *iactamur* is an unskilful conjecture by Scheider; all the MSS. have—

Iactatae exemplis plurimis miserae perpetuam noctem,

which presents no difficulty either in metre or construction, for *iactatae* is here equivalent to *iactatae sumus.*

Exigere is quoted from Trin. IV. iii. 46 (Troch. Tetr. Cat.),

Si mage exigere cupias duarum rerum exoritur optio.

All the MSS. have *si mage;* A, F, have *exigere;* B, C, D, E, have *ex genere;* A has *roapiat-duarum;* all the rest of the MSS. *cupias duarum.* Since the verb *exigere* and its tenses occur in at least twenty passages in Plautus with the *ex* long, and this is a solitary example on the other side, this is precisely one of those cases in which a slight transposition may fairly be resorted to, and all difficulty removed by reading—

Mage si exigere cupias duarum rerum exoritur optio.

There is yet another method of avoiding the supposition that *ex* is shortened. *Magis* being one of those words which may be pronounced as a monosyllable, *mage* may be altogether absorbed, as not unfrequently takes place in *sibi, tibi, scio, mea, eum,* &c.

Exercere and its tenses, *exercitus* and its cases, occur nearly forty times in Plautus, and in three of these *exercitum* and *exercitu* appear to have the first short. It is to be remarked that the whole of these examples are in the Amphitruo, and two of them within a few lines of each other in the Prologue—a portion of the play which contains a number of metrical licences within a short compass, and with regard to the genuineness of which some good scholars have entertained grave doubts. The passages are as follows:—

Exercitus. 1. Amph. Prol. 125 (Senar.),

Qui cum Amphitruone abiit hinc in exercitum,

where the difficulty may at once be removed by introducing, as proposed by Bothe, *indu*, the old form of *in*.

2. *v.* 140 (Senar.),

Nunc hodie Amphitruo veniet huc ab exercitu.

Bothe maintains that as *hic* and *hoc* pronouns are of doubtful quantity, the same holds good in the earlier poets with regard to *hic* and *huc* adverbs, although this is opposed to the dictum of the grammarians. If we have a choice of difficulties, few will hesitate to make *huc* short rather than *exercitu.*

3. I. iii. 6 (Troch. Tetr. Cat.),

Sed ubi summus imperator non adest ad exercitum.

W. gets rid of the difficulty by proposing to read *exercitu*, but unfortunately there seems to be no authority for this form. I would suggest that the true reading is—

Sed ubi summus imperator non adest exercitu,

where *exercitu* is the dative. Some half-learned transcriber mistook this for *exercitû*, i.e. *exercitum*, and then the *ad* was inserted to complete the construction.

Weise, in his Index (first edition), gives four additional examples of *exercitus* with the *ex* short, all of them from the Amphitruo.

1. Prol. 102 (Senar.),

Is priusquam hinc abiit ipsemet in exercitum,

where the line scans perfectly with a Spondee in the fifth place and a Tribrach in the fourth.

2. I. i. 245 (Troch. Tetr. Cat.),

Qui cum Amphitruone hinc una iveram in exercitum,

where W. leaves the last syllable in *iveram* unelided, and supposes the first in *exercitum* to be short. It is quite as simple to suppose that *cum* is not elided, in which case the line scans easily with an Anapaest in the sixth place.

3. II. ii. 101 (Troch. Tetr. Cat.),

Neque meum pedem huc intuli etiam in aedis, ut cum exercitu.

There are several ways in which the line may be scanned without shortening the first in *exercitu*: *pedem* may be pronounced as a monosyllable, and then totally elided; or *huc* may be taken as short; or we may leave *cum* unelided; or we may resort to a simple transposition, and read *Neque pedem meum.*

4. V. ii. 7 (Senar.),

> *Tu gravidam item fecisti, quom in exercitum,*

where *quom* is not elided, and then the fourth foot is a Dactyl.
Accepisti seems to occur in Trin. IV. ii. 122 (Troch. Tetr. Cat.),

> *Vel trecentis—Haben tu id aurum quod accepisti a Charmide?*

This seems to be the reading of the MSS., and if retained would involve the shortening of *accepisti;* but a case of this sort fully justifies a simple transposition; read therefore with Hermann—

> *Vel trecentis—Haben tu aurum id quod accepisti a Charmide?*

which is more natural and obvious than the emendation of R. W. retains the Vulgate without remark.

Gubernabunt is quoted from Mil. IV. ii. 99. Even supposing the line to form one of an Anapaestic system, the measure is avowedly loose and irregular. W. says, in his Index, ' *gubernabunt* correptim.'

Argenti is quoted from Capt. Cat. 3 (Troch. Tetr. Cat.),

> *Nec pueri suppositio neque argenti circumductio,*

which I would scan by pronouncing *neque* as a monosyllable, and then eliding it altogether; again, in Curc. V. ii. 15 (Troch. Tetr. Cat.),

> *Quod argentum, quas tu mihi trias narras? quam tu virginem?*

quod, like *quid,* must be suppressed.* See other examples in the Index of W. under *quod etc.*

Astutia, apparently in Capt. II. i. 63,

> *Memoriter meminisse, inest spes nobis in hac astutia.*

So the Vulgate. There is a difficulty in the scansion, which Lindemann removes by reading *hac in astutia.* Bothe has *nobis huic astutiae.* [If for *inest* we substitute *est,* there would be no difficulty. —Ed.]

Fenestra seems to occur in the following passages: Rud. I. i. 6 (Senar.),

> *Illustriores fecit fenestrasque indidit;*

Cas. I. 44 (Senar.),

> *Quid facis?—Concludere in fenestram firmiter;*

---

* [Would not this line be scanned more simply by transposing *tu,* and reading—
> *Quod tu argentum, quas mibi trias narras? quam tu virginem!*
—Ed.]

Mil. II. iv. 26 (Iamb. Tetr. Cat.),

> *Nec fenestra nisi clatrata.—Nam certo ego te his intus vidi,*

where W. reads *nec*, R. *neque*, without remark; Ba has *fenetra*, A and all the rest, *fenestra*. *Clatrata* or *clathrata* is a conjectural emendation; A has *neque clarata;* all the rest, *nisi clarata*. We learn however from Macrobius, S. III. 12, that there was an old Latin word *festra* used by Ennius, the precise meaning of which was a subject of discussion in the age of Cicero, and which was interpreted to signify *astium minusculum*, while Paul. Diac. p. 91, ed. Müll., says expressly, "*Festram* antiqui dicebant quam nos *fenestram;*" Müller in his note says, "Corrupte Placidus, p. 464: *Frestram*, fenestram," and refers to Doederlein, Syn. et Etym., Tom. VI., p. 127, q. v. *Festram* is quoted from Petronius also, Frag. xxi. 6, but there it is a conjectural emendation for *festam* of the MSS. There can be little doubt therefore that Bothe was fully justified in substituting *festra* for *fenestra* in the passages quoted above. The word *festra* or *fenestra* does not, apparently, occur elsewhere in Plautus.

Invidia, Ingenium. We have a line in Terent. Andr. I. i. 39 (Senar.),

> *Sine invidia laudem invenias, et amicos pares,*

where D. "Ceterum *invidia* primam hic corripit ut pote positione tantum longam : sono literae *I* hic exili : adde quod in primo versus pede maior concessa sit licentia. Sic *ingenium* primam corripit, III. i. 8" (Senar.),

> *Bonum ingenium narras adulescentis—Optumum.*

The true explanation is the same in both cases; *sine* and *bonum* being words which may be pronounced as monosyllables, are in these passages altogether elided.

Intro. The following examples of *Intro* have been quoted: Aul. III. iii. 3 (Troch. Tetr. Cat.),

> *Tu tam nunc iam intro omnes et coci et tibicinae,*

but it is much more simple to regard *iam* as a monosyllable elided before *intro;* II. viii. 22 (Senar.),

> *Nimirum occidor nisi ego intro huc propero currere,*

but even thus the line will not scan unless we read *ni* for *nisi* or sink *ego* altogether. Gulielmus and others, relying upon a MS., insert *propere* before *propero*, thus transforming the line into a Troch. Tetr. Cat., but the whole of this scene is composed of Senarians. Stich. IV. i. 29 (Troch. Tetr. Cat.),

> *Deos salutatum atque uxorem modo intro devortor domum.*

So the MSS. Guyetus and R. get rid of the difficulty by transposing, and have *intro modo*.

We occasionally find violent transgressions of quantity depending upon a single example; thus Aul. III. v. 42,

Strophiarii adstant, adstant semisonarii,

where, if we retain the Vulgate, we must shorten the two first syllables in *sēmīsonarii*. Nothing is more likely than that a corruption should be found in this passage, where there is a long string of strange words invented apparently for the nonce. Bothe has proposed a simple emendation—

Strophiarii stant, stant semisonarii,

but the word *semisonarii* itself is very doubtful.

[Having thus shown that little or no reliance can be placed on the above examples as affording evidence that the early dramatists had no scruple in violating the Rule of Position, wherever it suited the exigencies of their verse to do so, we will proceed to give a few examples of lines containing one or other of the two classes of anomalies referred to above, p. lxx, and which we have sufficiently indicated are in our opinion to be scanned by the process called 'correption,' that is, by slurring over and running together two syllables into one, rather than by an indiscriminate neglect of the fundamental Law of Position.—Ed.]

I. Under class 1, consisting chiefly of dissyllables with a short penultimate, we may instance the following :—

Apud must be pronounced as a monosyllable in Epid. III. iv. 14 (Senar.),

Memorant apud reges armis arte duellica,

where it will be observed that the two first syllables of *duellica* suffer synizesis; again, in Amph. III. ii. 66 (Senar.),

Ut quos apud legionem vota voti si domum.

Other instances will be found in Capt. I. ii. 90, Curc. II. iii. 66, Most. I. iii. 141.

Enim is a monosyllable Trin. I. ii. 23 (Senar.),

Namque enim tu credo mihi imprudenti obrepseris.

So the MSS.; Camer. has *numquam enim*, and R. corrects *nempe enim*. In Trin. I. iii. 77 (Senar.) we have both *enim* and *nimis* as monosyllables,

Ita faciam—At enim nimis longo sermone utimur.

Magis occurs as a monosyllable in Capt. IV. ii. 1 (Bacch. Tetr. Acat.),

Quanto in pectore hanc rem meo magis voluto;

and in the same manner we have *magistratus* as a trisyllable in Rud. II. v. 20 (Senar.),

Magistratus si quis me hanc habere viderit.

Cf. Amph. Prol. 74. Epid. IV. ii. 22 (Troch. Tetr. Cat.) has been quoted as an instance of *magister* as a dissyllable,

Epidicus mihi fuvit magister. Perii, plaustrum perculi;

but observe that if we read *fuit* and pronounce it as a monosyllable, there will be no necessity for pronouncing *magister* 'correptim.'

Manus seems to be a monosyllable in Truc. V. 9 (Troch. Tetr. Cat.),

Manus vetat priusquam penes sese habeat quicquam credere;

while in Trin. II. ii. 10 (Troch. Tetr. Cat.) we have *manu, manus,* and *habent* all as monosyllables,

Quod manu nequeunt tangere tantum fas habent quo manus
apstineant.

Tamen is shortened in Stich. V. iv. 20 (Troch. Tetr. Cat.),

Tamen ludere inter nos strategum te facio huic convivio.

Potest also occurs as a monosyllable; Pseud. II. ii. 38 (Troch. Tetr. Cat.),

Potest ut alii ita arbitrentur, et ego ut ne credam tibi;

so all the MSS., including A; R. has *potis ut.* Bac. III. iii. 75 (Troch. Tetr. Cat.),

Nullon pacto ris mandata potest agi nisi identidem;

so W. and R. accent it, but if we have a Dactyl in 4th and neglect the division we may give to *potest* its usual form. Truc. IV. ii. 42 (Troch. Tetr. Cat.),

Redin An non? A. Reduem, sed vocat me, quae in me plus potest
quam potes,

where we have *vocat* as well. Trin. III. iii. 2 (Senar.),

Potest fieri prorsus quin dos detur virgini;

so the MSS.; B. and R. have *pote.* Stich. I. ii. 64 (Troch. Tetr. Cat.),

Qui potest mulieres vitare, vitet, ut quotidie;

so A and the MSS.; D. and R. have *pote*, Scalig. *potis*.   Trin. II.
ii. 71,

> *Quandoquidem nec tibi bene esse $\overline{potes}$ pati neque alteri;*

here, according to R., A has *pote;* the rest of the MSS., *potes*.   In
Poen. I. iii. 35 the Vulgate has—

> *Opus est coniectore qui Sphingi interpres fuit,*

in which case *opus est* must be a pyrrich; but the old reading is the
true one,

> *Opus coniectore est qui Sphingi interpres fuit,*

i. e. *opu' coniectore.*

Of *senex* as a monosyllable we may quote the following examples:—Aul. II. iv. 16 (Senar.),

> *$\overline{Senex}$ opsonari filiai in nuptiis;*

Epid. I. ix. 3 (Troch. Tetr. Cat.),

> *Animi causa.   Corium perdidi: nam $\overline{senex}$ ubi senserit;*

Cas. Prol. 35 (Senar.),

> *$\overline{Senex}$ hic maritus habitat: eii est filius;*

IV. i. 4 (Senar.),

> *$\overline{Seni}$ nostro et nostro Olumpioni villico;*

v. 6 (Senar.),

> *$\overline{Senex}$ in culina clamat, hortatur cocos;*

Rud. Prol. 35 (Senar.),

> *$\overline{Senex}$ qui huc Athenis exul venit haud malus;*

while *senectus* and *senecta* are dissyllables in the following:—Trin.
II. iii. 7 (Senar.),

> *Suae $\overline{senectuti}$ is acriorem hiemem parat;*

Most. I. iii. 60 (Iamb. Tetr. Cat.),

> *Dum tibi nunc hace aetatula est, in $\overline{senecta}$ male quaerere.*

Sedens is shortened into one syllable in Bac. I. i. 14 (Troch. Tetr.
Cat.),

> *Poteris agere: atque, is dum veniat, $\overline{sedens}$ ibi opperibere,*

where the MSS. vary between *sedens ibi* and *sedens hic;* we have
also *sedentarii*, Aul. III. v. 39,

> *$\overline{Sedentarii}$ sutores, diabathrarii;*

and *vetustab*, Poen. III. iii. 87,

> *Vetustate vino edentulo aetatem irriges.*

Of *volo* and its derivatives we have *volunt*, Pseud. IV. i. 2 (Troch. Tetr. Acat.),

> *Tum me et Calidorum serratum volunt esse et lenonem extinctum ;*

so all the best MSS., except that D. has *serrtum ;* R. and others ' correct' it. *Voles*, Cist. I. i. 48 (Iamb. Tetr. Cat.),

> *Necesse est, quo tu me modo voles esse, ita esse, mater ;*

Both. ' corrects' by transposition. *Voluntate*, Trin. V. ii. 42 (Troch. Tetr. Cat.),

> *Si id mea voluntate factum est, est quod mihi succenseas.*

The second *est*, which is required both by the metre and the idiom, is wanting in the MSS. and was supplied by Camer.; R. and W. both read as above. Stich. I. ii. 2 (Troch. Tetr. Cat.),

> *Nec voluntate id facere meminit, servos is habitu haud probust,*

where there is no important variation in the MSS. *Voluptabilem*, Epid. I. i. 19 (Iamb. Tetr. Acat.),

> *Voluptabilem mihi tuo adventu attulisti nuncium.*

The Vulgate is different, but so the best MSS. *Voluptariis*, Mil. III. i. 46 (Troch. Tetr. Cat.),

> *Neque dum exarui ex amoenis rebus et voluptariis.*

Voluptarii, Men. II. i. 34 (Senar.),

> *Voluptarii atque potatores maxumi.*

Voluptarios, Rud. Prol. 54 (Senar.),

> *Eat in Siciliam: ibi esse homines voluptarios.*

Voluptarium, Poen. III. ii. 25 (Troch. Tetr. Cat.),

> *Liberum ut commonstraremus tibi locum et voluptarium.*

Voluptas, Most. I. iii. 92 (Troch. Tetr. Cat.),

> *Ornata ut siem quom huc veniat Philolaches voluptas mea ;*

Mil. IV. viii. 36 (Troch. Tetr. Cat.),

> *Hominem, perii, sumne apud me ? Ne time, voluptas mea.*

Voluptatum, Pseud. I. i. 67 (Senar.),

> *Harum voluptatum mi omnium atque itidem tibi.*

Examples abound. The word however is found under its natural form also, e.g. *vŏlŭptŭs*, Men. II. i. 1,

> *Vŏlŭptăs nulla est navitis, Messenio.*

Tĭbĭ and *sĭbĭ* are occasionally pronounced as monosyllables and altogether absorbed before a word beginning with a vowel: Amph. II. ii. 86 (Troch. Tetr. Cat.),

> *Amphitruo, speravi ego istanc tĭbi parituram filium,*

where Lind. reads *parturam;* V. i. 36 (Troch. Tetr. Cat.),

> *Omnium primum tibi Alcumena geminos peperit filios;*

ii. 1 (Senar.),

> *Bono animo es: adsum auxilio Amphitruo tibi et tuis;*

Bac. II. ii. 10 (Senar.),

> *Salutem tibi ab sodali solidam nuntio;*

Mil. III. iii. 15 (Troch. Tetr. Cat.),

> *Ea sibi inmortalis memoria est meminisse et sempiterna;*

Aul. Prol. 32 (Senar.),

> *Sibi uxorem poscit: id ea faciam gratia.*

II. Next, we shall give a few examples of lines containing words ranked under class 2, in which a vowel appears to be shortened before two consonants in the same word, but which are in our opinion to be scanned by the method of correption above explained.

Esse seems to be a monosyllable in the following: Bac. IV. ix. 144 (Senar.),

> *Curatum est esse te tenerum omnium miserrimum.*

So all the MSS.: R. has *Curatumst esse te.* Asin. V. i. 10 (Troch. Tetr. Cat.),

> *Credam istuc si esse te hilarum videro. A. An tu esse me*
> *tristem putas?*

ii. 5 (Troch. Tetr. Cat.),

> *Artemona si huius rei med esse mendacem inveneris;*

Aul. II. iv. 36 (Senar.),

> *Crasen vero adeo esse parcum et misere vivere;*

Mil. IV. iii. 25 (Senar.),

> *Dicas uxorem tibi necessum esse ducere,*

where *esse* may be considered equivalent to '*ss;* Truc. I. i. 65 (Senar.),

Quem infestum ac odiosum tibi esse memorabat mala,

where *sibi* is elided altogether.

Inest is a monosyllable in Mil. III. i. 38 (Troch. Tetr. Cat.),

Inest in hoc annutilata sua sibi ingenua indoles,

where there is no doubt as to the reading. So *is est*, Trin. III. ii. 71 (Troch. Tetr. Cat.),

Is est honos homini pudico meminisse officium suum,

where however we might get rid of the difficulty by a simple transposition, *Is honos est;* II. iii. 73 (Troch. Tetr. Cat.),

Is est immunis quoi nihil est qui munus fungatur suum.

This line occurs in a long unbroken system of Troch. Tetrameters, and so there can be little doubt as to the measure. Observe however that the line might be scanned as an Iamb. Tetr. Acat., and the same remark applies to the preceding line.

Adest (according to the other view, *adest*) is quoted from Trin. Prol. 3,

Adest, en, illae sunt aedes. I intro nunc iam.

So Hermann; but as the MSS., including A, have *hem* for *en*, the example is not satisfactory. Bac. IV. ix. 63 (Iamb. Tetr. Acat.),

Nunc superum limen scinditur! nunc adest exitium Ilio.

Weise quotes Truc. V. 28 and Cas. II. iii. 30 as instances of *adest*, but neither example is satisfactory.

Quid est must be pronounced as a monosyllable in Rud. IV. iv. 16 (Troch. Tetr. Cat.),

Quid est de qua re litigatis nunc inter vos? T. Eloquar.

In Most. I. i. 66 (Senar.),

Quid est? quid tu me nunc opturre, furcifer?

if we pronounced *opturre*, then *quid est* must be a monosyllable; but if we take the form *opturre*, *quid est* will form an Iambus. Cist. V. 1 (Troch. Tetr. Cat.),

Quid hoc negoti est quod omnes homines fabulantur per viam?

Quid is absorbed in Most. IV. iii. 20 (iv. 20), where the Iamb. Trim. begins with—

Quid a Tranione servo?

so Trin. II. ii. 36 (Troch. Tetr. Cat.),

Quid exprobras? bene quod fecisti; tibi fecisti non mihi.

So all the MSS., including A; B. omits *quid.* Curc. I. iii. 10 (Troch. Tetr. Cat.),

> *Palinure, Palinure. P. Eloquere, quid est quod Palinurum voces?*

Epid. IV. ii. 1 (Troch. Tetr. Cat.),

> *Quid est, pater, quod me excivisti ante aedes? P. Vt matrem tuam.*

Of *inde* as a monosyllable we may give the following examples: Amph. I. i. 4 (Iamb. Tetr. Acat.),

> *Inde eras e promptuaria cella depromar ad flagrum;*

Aul. II. vii. 4 (Senar.),

> *Inde coctum sursum subducemus corbulis;*

Pers. III. i. 66,

> *Dabuntur dotis tibi inde sexcenti logi,*

where we have the choice of absorbing *tibi* or of making *inde* a long monosyllable; Capt. I. ii. 25 (Senar.),

> *Inde me continuo recipiam rursus domum;*

Poen. Prol. 2 (Senar.),

> *Inde mi principium capiam ex ia tragoedia;*

V. iii. 34 (Senar.),

> *Inde porro ad puteum, atque ad robustum codicem.*

So *unde*, Cist. II. iii. 19 (Senar.),

> *Vnde tibi talenta magna viginti pater;*

Trin. I. ii. 182 (Senar.),

> *Vnde quidque auditum dicant: nisi id appareat;*

Poen. Prol. 109 (Senar.),

> *Vnde sit, quoiatis, captane an surrepta sit;*

V. ii. 95 (Senar.),

> *Vnde sum oriundus. H. Di dent tibi omnes quae velis.*

Three examples are quoted of *perinde* with the penultimate syllable short: Pseud. II. i. 4, where the metre is very doubtful; Stich. I. ii. 43,

> *Perinde habetis quasi praesentes sint. P. Pudicitia est, pater,*

where A has *proinde*, although the rest of the MSS. have *perinde;* Heaut I. ii. 21,

> *Atque haec perinde sunt ut illius animus qui ea possidet,*

which is to be scanned as an Iamb. Tetr. Acat., and presents no difficulty. It is not pretended that any example can be found of *exinde*.

Inter must be pronounced as *'nter* in Amph. IV. iii. 1 (Troch. Tetr. Cat.),

> *Vas inter vos istoc partile: ego abeo: mihi negotium est;*

Capt. III. iv. 84 (Troch. Tetr. Cat.),

> *Nunc ego inter sacrum saxumque sto, nec quid faciam scio;*

Cist. I. i. 54 (Iamb. Tetr. Cat.),

> *Equidem hercle addam operam sedulo, sed quid tu inter istaec verba,*

where we have a choice between *'nter* and *'staec.*

So *interim*, Curc. IV. i. 25 (Troch. Tetr. Cat.),

> *Sed interim fores crepuere: linguae moderandum est mihi;*

Stich. V. iv. 23 (Troch. Tetr. Cat.),

> *Sed interim, stratege noster, cur hic cessat cantharus?*

Most. V. i. 45 (ii. 30) (Troch. Tetr. Cat.),

> *Ego interim hanc aram occupabo. T. Quid ita? Ta. Nullam*
> *rem sapis.*

Ille is a monosyllable, Trin. I. ii. 100 (Senar.),

> *Ille qui mandavit cum exturbasti ex aedibus;*

and so *illic* and *illuc*, III. I. 82 (78) (Senar.),

> *Quod illuc est facinus, opsecro, quod illic petit?*

and v. 87 (83) (Senar.),

> *Quid ais tu? quid vis? quis illuc est? quid illic petit?*

and again below, *Quod illuc argentumst.*

Ipse as a monosyllable occurs rarely; we have in Curc. I. iii. 14 (Troch. Tetr. Cat.),

> *Ipse se excruciat, qui homo quod amat, videt, nec potitur dum licet;*

Epid. I. i. 45 (Senar.),

> *Ipse mihi mandavit, ab lenone ut fidicina,*

where the MSS. vary, but all give at the beginning either *Ipse mandavit* or *Ipse mihi;* Amph. I. i. 259 (Troch. Tetr. Cat.),

> *Et ipsus Amphitruo optruncavit regem Pterelam in praelio,*

where *ipsus = 'psus.*

Nempe occurs as a monosyllable, Pseud. I. iii. 124 (Troch. Tetr. Cat.),

> B. *Fateor*. C. *Nempe conceptis verbis*. B. *Etiam consultis quoque ;*

IV. vii. 92 (Troch. Tetr. Cat.),

> *Meo peculio empta*. B. *Nempe quod femina nomma sustinet ;*

Mil. II. iii. 66 (Troch. Tetr. Cat.),

> *Nempe tu istic ais esse herilem concubinam ?* S. *Atque arguo ;*

III. iii. 32 (Iamb. Tetr. Cat.),

> *Nempe ludificari militem tuum herum vis*. P. *Elocuta es ;*

v. 48, (Iamb. Tetr. Cat.),

> *Nempe tu novisti militem, meum herum ?* A. *Rogare mirum est.*

Other examples may be found in Cas. III. iv. 9, Aul. II. iv. 15, Epid. III. iv. 13, Trin. II. ii. 51, iv. 25.

> *Eccum* is found, Rud. III. v. 25 (Senar.),

> *Ehem, optume edepol, eccum, clavator advenit ;*

Stich. IV. i. 71 (Troch. Tetr. Cat.),

> *Atque eccum tibi lupum in sermone ! praesens esuriens adest.*

Sed eccum forms a Spondee, Pers. I. iii. 3 (Senar.),

> *Sed eccum parasitum quoius mihi auxilio est opus :*

Pseud. IV. ii. 10 (Troch. Tetr. Cat.),

> *Sed eccum, qui ex incerto faciet mihi quod quaero certius.*

Omnis and its cases seem to be monosyllables (='*unis*) in the following : Mil. I. 55 (Senar.),

> *Quid tibi' ego dicam quod omnes mortales sciunt ?*

Trin. I. ii. 41 (Senar.),

> *Quia omnes bonos bonasque adcurare addecet,*

but here, as elsewhere, *quia* may be *unk* ; III. i. 20 (Troch. Tetr. Cat.),

> *Quoi tuam quom rem credideris sine omni cura dormias ;*

Rud. I. i. 5 (Senar.),

> *Ita omnes de lecto deturbavit tegulas ;*

V. i. 5 (Iamb. Tetr. Cat.),

> *Ita omnes mortales si quid est mali lenoni gaudent ;*

Mil. III. l. 66 (Troch. Tetr. Cat.),

Lepidiorem ad omnes res, nec qui amicus amico sit magis;

Cist. V. 1 (Troch. Tetr. Cat.),

Quid hoc negoti est quod omnes homines fabulantur per viam,

where *quid hoc* also is a monosyllable.

Ergo. Autem. Quippe. But although the principle of shortening certain common words in pronunciation may be fairly admitted in the words enumerated above, it has been extended to others upon very feeble and imperfect evidence. Such are *ergo, autem, quippe,* and perhaps some others, but we shall be content with examining these.

Autem is one of the words which it was held might be pronounced as a pyrrich, *autem*, with the first short, as if it were *dtem*, or 'correptim,' that is, as a monosyllable; but although Lindemann seems to acquiesce in this (Ad Trin. II. ll. 52), he admits elsewhere (De Prosodia Pl. p. xxiv.) that only one satisfactory example can be adduced: Stich. L iii. 60 (Senar.),

Quot potiones mulsi : quot autem prandia,

a reading which is retained by W., who remarks, "Luculentum hoc exemplum correpti *autem* ab initio. Cf. et Amph. Prol. 36, Merc. II. iii. 85, Mil. III. l. 84, Pers. V. i. 11." There is no doubt that in the above passage all the MSS., including A, have *autem ;* Brixius, who is followed by R., corrects *item*. In Mil. III. l. 84 the MSS. are corrupt and the reading is very uncertain. In Amph. Prol. 36, W. has got into confusion, for while in his note he speaks of *autem* as pronounced 'correptim,' his text (which is here the Vulgate) presents no difficulty—

Iusta autem ab iniustis petere insipientia est,

although he says that *petere* is not to be elided. In fact, he seems to have forgotten that the last syllable of *autem* is elided before *ab*. See his accentuation. Merc. II. iii. 85 (Troch. Tetr. Cat.),

Litigare nolo ego vos, neque tuam autem accusari fidem,

is another of the examples given by W., but surely the simple way to scan the line is to sink *tuam*—

Lītĭ|gārĕ | nōlŏ ĕgŏ | vōs nĕ|quĕ || tŭ' aŭt' | ăc|cūsă|rī fĭd|ēm.

Nothing can be asserted positively as to the measure of Pers. V. l. 11. On the whole, as Lindemann observes, the whole doctrine of *autem,*

with the first short, or pronounced 'correptim,' seems to rest upon
Stich. I. iii. 60. The following are additional examples from the
index of W.: Merc. I. ii. 9 (Troch. Tetr. Cat.), a line which in the
MSS. is corrupt; Men. V. ix. 31, where also the reading is uncertain, but without departing a hair-breadth from the MSS. we have—

> *Quam hic tui est, tuque huius autem; postea eandem patriam*
> *ac patrem.*

R. has *pork*, but *postya eam* forms a Spondee. The last example
quoted is from Rud. III. iv. 22,

> *Hae autem Veneri complacuerunt—Habeat, si argentum dabit,*

on which W. has the note, "*Hae* non elidendum, *autem* vero corri-
piendum priori syllaba, quasi *Hae diem*." It seems positively perverse
to go out of the straight path in search, as it were, of a difficulty.
Elide *hae* before *autem*, and the scansion is simple and obvious.

Ergo is another of those words in which it is supposed that we
may occasionally pronounce the first syllable short, or the whole
word 'correptim.' Lind. says, "De *ergo* correptim pronunciata non
dubitatum est, quamquam rara sunt exempla, veluti Mil. IV. ii. 17."
The following are quoted as examples: Mil IV. ii. 17 (Troch. Tetr.
Cat.),

> *Ego hanc continuo uxorem ducam—Quid ergo hanc dubitas*
> *conloqui?*

So the MSS., except that B has *Quid ergo hae*, which would make
no difference in the scansion. The difficulty here however is not
confined to *ergo*, but we must make either a Trochee or a Spondee
out of *Ego hanc con|tinuo.* R. corrects—

> *Ego continuo uxorem hanc ducam—Ergo hanc quid, &c.*

Again, *quid ergo* at the commencement of a Troch. Tetr. Cat.,
Men. II. iii. 79, occurs in a corrupt passage. *Ergo* is not found in
any of the best MSS., and in any case the *quid* is probably the
word curtailed in the pronunciation. So Trin. IV. ii. 81 (Troch.
Tetr. Cat.),

> *Ne male loquere apsenti amico—Quid ergo ille ignavissumus.*

So the MSS.; Reiz and R., *Quid ille ergo.* Pers. I. i. 26 is called
a Troch. Tetr. Cat., but it cannot be scanned as such without the
omission of a word, and here again we have *quid ergo.* In Pers. II.
ii. 3 (Troch. Tetr. Cat.), we have again *quid ergo.* Stich. V. iv. 45
(Troch. Tetr. Cat.),

Age ergo, opserva ! Si peccassis, multam hic retinebo ilico.

So the MSS.; R. omits *age*, but *age ergo* may be regarded as a short, sharp, colloquial expression, and, as such, liable to be curtailed when enunciated. Poen. IV. ii. 71 (Troch. Tetr. Cat.),

Facile—Fac ergo id facile noscam, ut ille possit nascere,

where *fac ergo id* must form a Spondee, or, as W. seems to think, an Anapaest. It will be observed that *quid ergo, age ergo, fac ergo,* are expressions all belonging to the same class.

With regard to *quippe,* Lind. says, " *Quippe* duobus locis Plauti correptum reperitur, quare de eius correptione dubitatur." The passages to which he refers are probably—As. I. i. 51 (Senar.),

Quippe qui mage amico utantur grato et benevolo,

a line which Fleck. brackets as spurious ; Epid. V. i. 12 (Troch. Tetr. Cat.),

Habe bonum animum—Quippe ego quoi libertas in mundo
                              sita est,

which is referred to in the Index of W., but erroneously, for the line scans perfectly without altering the natural form of *quippe;* and Men. IV. ii. 17 (Senar.),

Quippe qui pro illis loquantur, male quae fecerint.

This is in a Canticum, where W. has picked out a couple of Senarians from the midst of a number of Bacchiacs and Cretics of varying dimensions. The distribution is most uncertain.

III. We now come to the consideration of those words, the quantity of which, as used by Plautus, differs from that observed by later writers. Considering that quantity depends upon pronunciation, we might have expected to find a number of words, the pronunciation, and therefore the quantity, of which had undergone a change during the 150 years which elapsed from the period when Plautus flourished to the last days of the Republic. But these are in fact very few.

Acheron, or, according to the earlier orthography, *Acheruns,* and its derivatives, have the first uniformly short in Lucretius and Virgil: Lucret. I. 120,

Et si praeterea tamen esse Acherusia templa;

III. 37,

Et metus ille foras praeceps Acheruntis agundus;

Virg. Aen. VII. 312,

Flectere si nequeo superos, Acheronta movebo;

while in Plautus they have the first syllable generally long, e.g. Most.
II. ii. 67 (Senar.),

> *Nam me Acheruntem recipere Orcus noluit;*

Mil. III. i. 32 (Troch. Tetr. Cat.),

> *Quid ais tu? itane tibi ego videor oppido Acheruntidus?*

Trin. II. iv. 93 (Senar.),

> *Censetur censu ad Acheruntem mortuos.*

See also Amph. IV. ii. 9, V. 1. 29, Capt. III. v. 31, V. iv. 1, 2,
Cas. II. vill. 12, Bac. II. ii. 21, Merc. II. ii. 19, III. iv. 21, Trin. II.
iv. 124, Poen. I. iii. 22, Truc. IV. ii. 40.

We have said that the first syllable is generally long in Plautus,
for two or three examples are quoted in which it is said to be short.
But of these there is only one which will not bear examination.
This is Most. II. ii. 76,

> *Vivom me arcessunt ad Acheruntem mortui;*

where all the best MSS. have the *ad*, which however might very
readily have been interpolated by a transcriber, and be omitted
without injury to the construction, and it is singular that the poet
should have made the first syllable of *Acheruntem* long in *v.* 67
and short in *v.* 76. Three other examples are quoted from the
Poenulus—Prol. 71 (Senar.), I. ii. 131 (Troch. Tetr. Cat.), IV. ii. 9
(Troch. Tetr. Cat.),

1. *Ipse abiit ad Acheruntem sine viatico.*
2. *Quo die Orcus ab Acherunte mortuos amiserit.*
3. *Quodvis genus ibi hominum videas, quasi Acheruntem veneris.*

But in the first example, an Anapaest in the second place of the
Senarian is perfectly admissible;[a] in the second, we may consider
the 2nd foot to be a Dactyl; in the third, *quasi*, as elsewhere, may
be pronounced as a monosyllable and totally elided. And yet the
evidence afforded of the quantity of *Acheruns* in these three lines
is considered by Weise sufficient to prove that the whole play is
spurious! The evidence therefore for *Acheruns* in Plautus rests on
the line of the Mostellaria alone, which, as we have pointed out
above, is suspicious and easily corrected.

---

[a] [Is an Anapaest admissible in the second place after a Dactyl? Would
it not be simpler to omit the *ad*, as suggested in reference to the passage
quoted from Most. II. II. 76? Spengel would read *abit* for *abiit.*—ED.]

Tabernaculum. This word appears twice in the syncopated form, *tabernaclo*, in Amph. I. L 270, 272 (Troch. Tetr. Cat.),

In tabernaclo, id quidem hodie numquam poterit dicere,

and—

Quid in tabernaclo fecisti ? Victus sum si dixeris.

In the second of these lines $\overline{quid\ in}$ must be pronounced as one long syllable, but neither of them decide the quantity of the first syllable in *tabernaculo*, which does not, as far as I know, occur in any of the poets of the Augustan age. *Taberna* is found in several passages in Plautus, but not one of these decides the quantity of the first syllable, which is however unquestionably short in the Augustan poets. Terence affords no example. But in Trin. III. ii. 100 (Troch. Tetr. Cat.), we find—

Cassidem in caput, dormibo placide in tabernaculo,

and this is the reading of all the MSS. Now this line, as it stands, cannot be scanned unless upon the supposition that *tabernaculo* has the first long. Hermann proposes to substitute *contubernio*, while R. changes *placide* into *placidule*, and thus scans *in tăbĕrn|ăcŭl|o*. We must therefore either adhere to the MSS. and suppose that *tabernaculum* has the first long; or, adopt *contubernio*, as proposed by Herm.; or else adopt the conj. emend., *placidule*, and suppose that *tabernaculo* has the second short. Few will hesitate to conclude that whatever the difficulties of the case may be, the remedy proposed by R. is much more violent than the disease, and that therefore we have no evidence whatever of a violation of the Rule of Position in this case.

Taberna occurs six times in Plautus. In five of these passages the first syllable may be long or short without affecting the verse. The sixth instance is Pseud. IV. vii. 14 (Cret. Tetr. ?),

Nam me in taberna usque adhuc siverat Surus.

If the line is, as W. sets it down, a Cretic Tetrameter, *tăbĕrna* would seem to be required. I cannot however scan it comfortably as such, but both the text and the arrangement of lines are very uncertain. R. gives an unexceptionable Tetr.,

Nam in taberna usque adhuc siverat [me] Surus,

but *me* is not found in the MSS.; and even admitting this reading, the 1st foot might be a Molossus.

Somewhat analogous, at first sight, to the case of *tabernaculum* is *volentarius.* Curc. II. iii. 16 (Troch. Tetr. Cat.),

Ex unoquoque eorum excutiam crepitum polentarium,

where the word must be scanned *polentarium*, although *polenta* has the first short in Ovid and Persius. But here we may observe that *polentarius* is a word apparently coined by Plautus himself, and found in this passage only, nor is it used by any other author until we come down to Apuleius, and there is no reason why we should not connect it with the kindred *pollen*. In so far as the unsavoury joke is concerned, the readers of Rabelais will at once perceive that it will lose nothing of its force if we derive the word directly from *pollen*, and not through the medium of *polenta*.

Suspicio, the substantive, with the second long, is frequently quoted as an example of an anomalous quantity, because *suspicio*, the verb, has the second short. But *suspicio*, the noun, occurs frequently in Plautus and Terence, and has the second syllable uniformly long; it has the same syllable long in Martial and the later poets; and, as far as I know, no example of this word, with the second short, can be quoted from any classical writer.

So also *Rubidus* (from *rubeo*?) occurs twice, Cas. I. v. 2, Stich. L. iii. 77; *coquinatum* (from *coquinus*), Aul. III. i. 3, Pseud. III. ii. 64; and *coquinare*, v. 85; but these words occur in verse in Plautus only, and therefore we cannot compare his practice with that of other poets. Moreover, with regard to the first, the derivation of *rubidus* from *rubeo* is by no means certain; and with regard to the second, we might be led to believe, from a passage in Paul. Diac. (p. 61, ed. Müll.), that the form used by Plautus was *coquitare*, and not *coquinare*.

Protervus and its derivatives have the first syllable short in the Augustan writers, as in the Horatian Choriambic,

Vrit grata protervitas,

and the Ovidian pentameter,

Damnaret nati facta proterva pater,

while in Plautus, Bac. IV. iii. 1 (Troch. Tetr. Acat.),

Petulans protervo iracundo animo, indomito, incogitato,

and Amph. II. ii. 207 (Troch. Tetr. Cat.),

Audacem esse, et confidenter pro se et protervo loqui,

protervo and *proterve* must have the first long. When however we remember the uncertainty and inconsistency which prevails in the best writers as to the quantity of the first syllable of words compounded with *pro*, we need feel no surprise with regard to *protervus*.

Rudens has the first syllable short in Virgil—

> *Exoritur clamorque virum stridorque rudentum;*

but in the following line of Plautus the first syllable must be long, Rud. IV. iii. 76 (Troch. Tetr. Cat.),

> *Mitte rudentem, scelus ! —Mittam, omitte vidulum.*

The word occurs again *v.* 1 (Troch. Tetr. Cat.), and *v.* 92 (Troch. Tetr. Cat.), but these passages do not decide the quantity of the first syllable.

Nebula, which has the first short in the Augustan writers, is said to have the first sometimes long and sometimes short in Plautus. It occurs four times: In Pseud. I. v. 48 (Senar.), where, according to the received reading, it has the first short; in Poen. I. ii. 62 (Troch. Tetr. Cat.), where the reading is very doubtful, but that adopted by the best editors admits of *nebulae* having the first short; in Cas. IV. iv. 21, where the distribution of the lines is entirely arbitrary and uncertain; and lastly, in Capt. V. iv. 26,

> *Nunc edepol demum in memoriam regredior, quom cogito*
> *Quasi per nebulam, Hegionem patrem meum vocarier,*

where the speech of Tyndarus is slow and hesitating, as he strives to recall the impressions of his childhood. An actor therefore would probably make a considerable pause after *Quasi per nebulam*, which is itself a sort of parenthetic clause, and as even the most fastidious could scarcely insist upon the elision of the last syllable in *nebulam*, it may therefore be regarded as a Tribrach.

Neutiquam. Neuter. Lindemann says that *neutiquam* is always a Tribrach, and *neuter* a pyrrich, by which he means, I presume, that *neutiquam* is always a quadrisyllable with the first three short, and *neuter* a trisyllable with the first two short. The examples which I find of these words are, Capt. III. iv. 54 (Troch. Tetr. Cat.),

> *Filium tuum quod redimere se ait, id neutiquam mihi placet,*

where *neutiquam*, according to my scansion, is *neutiquam*; Mil. III. i. 37 (Troch. Tetr. Cat.),

> *Si albicapillus hic videtur neutiquam ab ingeniosi senex.*

Here also *neutiquam ab* form a Trochee. B. has *albus capillus*, C. *albi capillus*, but this makes no difference. Merc. III. iv. 14 (Troch. Tetr. Cat.),

> *Nunc quid restat, heri, disperii, volhus neutiquam huius placet.*

Here, if we consider *huius* as a monosyllable, we might scan *neutiquam*,

q

but it is more simple to make *neutiquam hui* a Spondee. The best
MSS. have *et ei* instead of *hei*, but this does not affect the scansion.
Poen. I. i. 71 (Senar.),

> *Sine damno magno quae elui neutiquam potest,*

where *neutiquam* must be a dissyllable. These are the whole of the
examples in the Delphin index, and the same are given in the index
of W., preceded by the remark "*neutiquam* prima correpta." I think
I am justified in asserting that *neutiquam* is uniformly a dissyllable.
     Now for *neuter*. Merc. III. i. 40 (Iamb. Tetr. Cat.),

> *Neuter strupri causa caput limaret—Di inmortales!*

where *neuter* is a Spondee. *Neuter* is found also in Cas. V. iv. 32
and Stich. V. iv. 51, but in both these passages the text is so
uncertain that nothing can be founded on it. In Stich. I. ii. 84
(Troch. Tetr. Cat.),

> *Certumne est, neutram vostrarum persequi imperium patris?*

neutram is a Spondee; so also in Mil. II. v. 18 (Troch. Tetr. Cat.),

> *Et tu et hic—Non nos novisti?—Neutram—Metuo maxume;*

Rud. III. vi. 16 (Senar.),

> *Utrum vis, opta, dum licet?—Neutrum volo;*

and Frag. Vidular. 6 (apparently Iamb. Tetr. Acat.),

> *Ego servabo, quasi sequestro detis: neutri reddibo dominum.*

In Aul. II. ii. 56 (Troch. Tetr. Cat.),

> *Neutrubi habeam stabile stabulum, si quid divorti fuat,*

neutrub' is a Trochee, as also in Men. V. ii. 35 (Troch. Tetr. Cat.),

> *Ut caveres neuter ad me iretis cum querimonia.*

In every case, therefore, in which *neuter* occurs, *neuter* may be
naturally scanned as a dissyllable and Spondee.
     Amator. Weise quotes as examples of *āmator* with the first long,
Cas. III. iii. 2 (Senar.),

> *Hominem amatorem ullum ad forum procedere,*

where surely it is quite as good to make the 1st foot a Tribrach as
an Anapaest; again, Epid. II. ii. 30 (Troch. Tetr. Cat.),

> *Obviam ornatae occurrebant, suis quaeque amatoribus,*

where it is better to leave a hiatus after *quaeque* than to lengthen *ām.*
(It will be observed that *suis* must be pronounced as a monosyllable.)
So in Merc. Prol. 4 (Senar.),

Vidi facere amatores, qui aut nocti aut die,

the 2nd foot is a Tribrach. More difficult is Pseud. L v. 1 (Senar.).

Si de damnosis aut de amatoribus;

since this is the reading of the Palatine MSS., but here the Palimpsest comes to our rescue—

Si de damnosis aut si de amatoribus.

All the other examples quoted by W. as instances of the lengthening of the first syllable of *amo* and its compounds, can be disposed of as easily as the above. He refers to other passages where the first syllable of *amo*, &c., suffers contraction; but of these only one is at all satisfactory—Curc. L i. 38,

Iuventute et pueris liberis āmā quid lubet.

The pronunciation and orthography of the word *iacio* and its compounds deserve especial notice. Of the compounds of *iacio* the forms *abicio, adicio, eicio, inicio, obicio, reicio, subicio*, alone are in use, never *abiicio, adiicio*, &c. Men. III. iii. 31 (Senar.),

Demam coronam, atque abiciam ad laevam manum;

Merc. II. iv. 23 (Troch. Tetr. Cat.),

Adicito vel mille numum plus quam poscet—Iam tace;

Pers. L ii. 18, 19 (Senar.),

Vbi quadruplator quoipiam iniexit manum,
Tantidem illa illi inicial manum,

where *iniexit* is a conj. of Camer. for the *inlexit* of the MSS.; Trin. V. i. 8 (Troch. Tetr. Cat.),

Hae sonitu suo mihi moram obiciunt incommode;

As. IV. ii. 5 (Senar.),

Praeripias scortum amanti, atque argentum obicias;

I. ii. 1 (Cret. Tetr. Acat.),

Siccine hoc fit? foras aedibus me eici;

Mil. III. ii. 31 (Senar.),

Poste sagina ego eiciar cellaria;

Truc. III. i. 14 (Senar.),

Hoc ictu exponam atque omnes eiciam foras;

ēicis, As. I. iii. 9; *ēicite*, Cas. Prol. 23; *ēiēci*, Pers. V. ii. 5; *ēiēcit*, Rud. I. ii. 80, 82; *eiectas*, v. 14; *eiectam*, iii. 4, metre uncertain;

iiectas (tris.), II. iii. 78, vii. 4; *ciecti* (tria.), Prol. 73, I. ii. 66. In
Pers. II. v. 18, 19 (Iamb. Tetr. Cat.),

> *Enim metuo ut possim in bubilem reicere ne vagentur.*
> *Ego reiciam: habe animum bonum—Creditur, commodabo,*

the reading of the first line is doubtful, but it may be scanned by
omitting the elision of *possim;* thus *reicere* and *reiciam* will both be
quadrisyllables. Merc. V. ii. 69 (Troch. Tetr. Cat.),

> *Sed quin ornatum hunc reicio? heus aliquis actutum foras.*

The MSS. have *aliquis est*, in which case we must drop *heus* in the
scansion; either way, *reicio* is a quadrisyllable. As. II. i. 6 (Troch.
Tetr. Cat.),

> *Quin tu aps te socordiam omnem reicis, segnitiem amoves.*

The best MSS. seem to have *reice*, W. has *reicis*. If we read *reice*,
the word may be either a Trochee or a Tribrach; if *reicis*, either
a Spondee or an Anapaest.

T. MACCI PLAVTI MOSTELLARIA.

GRAECA PHASMA.

ARGVMENTVM.

Manumisit emptos suos amores Philolaches,
Omnemque apsente rem suo apsumit patre.
Senem, ut revenit, ludificatur Tranio :
Terrifica monstra dicit fieri in aedibus,
Et inde primum emigratum. Intervenit
Lucripeta faenus faenerator postulans,
Ludusque rursum fit senex : nam mutuom
Acceptum dicit pignus emptis aedibus.
Requirit, quae sint. Ait, vicini proxumi.
Inspectat illas ; post se derisum dolet ;
Ab sui sodale gnati exoratur tamen.

PERSONAE.

TRANIO SERVOS.

GRVNIO SERVOS.

PHILOLACHES ADVLESCENS.

PHILEMATIVM MERETRIX.

SCAPHA ANCILLA.

CALLIDAMATES ADVLESCENS.

DELPHIVM MERETRIX.

PVER.

THEVROPIDES SENEX.

MISARGVRIDES DANISTA.

SIMO SENEX.

PHANISCVS ADVORSITOR.

ADVORSITOR.

LORARII.

ACTVS I.   SCENA I.

GRVMIO. TRANIO.

Exi e culina, sis, foras, mastigia,
Qui mi inter patinas exhibes argutias.
Egredere, herilis pernicies, ex aedibus.
Ego pol te ruri, si vivam, ulciscar probe.
Exi, inquam, nidor, e culina. Quid lates?   5
  TR. Quid tibi, malum, hic ante aedis clamatio est?
An ruri censes te esse? Apscede ab aedibus!
Abi rus! abi dierecte! apscede ab ianua!
En, hocine volebas?   *GR.* Perii, cur me verberas?
  TR. Quia tu vis.   *GR.* Patiar. Sine modo adveniat
      senex: 10
Sine modo venire salvom, quem apsentem comes.

            .

1. *culina* R, following Nonius (p. 55), who quotes this and the following
line, observing, COLINAM *veteres coquinam dixerunt;* but he again quotes
these lines (p. 239), retaining the ordinary orthography.
2. *exibes* BD.
3. *herilis* BFZ. *heriles* C. *herilés* D, *raro exemplo addito b litera,*
says R. *pernities* B. *pernities* CD and R, who quotes Koch Exerc.
Crit. in priac. poet. Rom. In the former plays R left the *n.* *pernicies*
FZ. *edibus* BCD.
5. *nidor e culina*; this reading was introduced by Pylades, " *e priuis
codd.*" *nidore supinam* BCFZ. *nidore copiná* D. R has remodelled
the line upon conj.,—
            Eal inquam, nidoricape, nam quid hic lates.
6. *ardis* all the MSS. See v. 44.   *clamatio est,* so Camer., and this
appears in reality to be the reading of the MSS. *clamat iasi* (a slight
corruption of *clamatiast*) BCD, with the letters *l, as* written over *clamat*
in B by the first hand. *clamitatio est* Acidal. Vulg. RW.   *est clamatio*
Both., which will remove any difficulty as to the metre.
7. *abcede* C.   *edibus* BC.
8. *dirrecte* BaDF.   *directe* BbC. R, on conj., has admitted *abi biae*
dirrecte.   *inua* Ba.   *inua* Bc.
9. *En* BDFZ. *In* C. Donsa introduced *Hem* and so Vulg. W.
En is not included in the scansion of 9.   *hocine* BD. *hocciae* CFZ.
par B.   *cur* the rest of the MSS.   *quor* R.
10. *tu vis,* so Camer. *vivis* BFZ.   *vivas* C.   *tui vis* D.   *tu vis* is
not satisfactory.
11. *salvom*; Nonius (p. 81) has *salvum.* The MSS. have either *salvus*
or *salvas.*

TR. Nec veri simile loquere nec verum, frutex,
Comesse quemquam ut quisquam apsentem possiet.
GR. Tu, urbanus vero scurra, deliciae popli,
Rus mihi tu obiectas? Sane credo, Tranio,   15
Quod te in pistrinum scis actutum tradier.
Cis, hercle, paucas tempestates, Tranio,
Augebis ruri numerum, genus ferratile.
*Nunc dum tibi lubet licetque, pota, perde rem,
Corrumpe herilem [filium], adulescentem optumum: 20
Dies noctesque bibite, pergraecamini;
Amicas emlte, liberate: pascite
Parasitos: opsonate pollucibiliter!
Haecine mandavit tibi, quom peregre hinc iit, senex?
Hocine modo hic rem curatam offendet suam?   25
Hocine boni esse officium servi existumas,
Vt heri sui corrumpat et rem et filium?
Nam ego illum corruptum duco, quom his factis studet;

12. *frutex*, so the MSS. Guyetus conj. *rupex*, and so R.
13. *passiet*, so Pylad. *possiet* BaC. *passi,t* Bb. *possit* DFZ.
14. *rura* Ba. *scura* Bb. *delitiae* BD. *popli* B. The rest
of the MSS. *populi*.
15. *obiectis* Ba, an obvious blunder. *sane credo* B, with the erasure
of two letters after b. *sane erdo* Bb. *sane erdo* the rest of the MSS.
16. *scis* FZ. *sis* BCD, an obvious blunder. R most perversely
reads *hac scis*.
17. *tempestates*, so apparently all the MSS.
18. *numerum*, so the MSS. Some edd., among whom is W, following
Muretus and Lambinus, have, without any good reason, introduced *numero*.
ferratile Z.
19. The MSS. have *Nunc dum tibi ...*, which cannot be scanned.
Hence some editors omit *nunc*, and some *tibi*.
20. *herilem* [*filium*]. The MSS. have *herilem* alone without *filium*,
which was introduced by Pylades, and has been adopted by most editors.
R has *herilem nostrum*, a conj. In every way inferior.   *adolescentem* C.
optimum B, the *m* over being by Bb.   *optimum* FZ.   *optumum* C.
21. *noctes*, all the MSS.   *pergrecamini* BCD. (*pergrecamini* BCD
in line 61).   *pergraecamini* FZ.
22. *emica emnite* Ba.
23. *Pol lautibiliter* B.
24. *Haecine* BCD.   *iit*, so the MSS.   *it* Both. R.
25. *Hocine* Ba.
26. *Hocine* B.   *officium* D.
27. *rem et* B. The rest of the MSS. have *semet*, an evident corruption.

Quo nemo adaeque iuventute ex omni Attica
Antehac est habitus parcus nec magis continens,   30
Is nunc in aliam partem palmam possidet.
Virtute id factum tua et magisterio tuo.
  TR. Quid tibi, malum, me, aut quid ego agam, curatio est?
An ruri, quaeso, non sunt, quos cures, bovis?
Lubet potare, amare, scorta ducere :   35
Mei tergi facio haec, non tui, fiducia.
  GR. Quam confidenter loquitur! fue! TR. At te Iupiter
Dique omnes perdant : oboluisti allium,
Germana inluvies, rusticus, hircus, hara suis,
Canes capra commixta!   GR. Quid vis fieri?   40
Non omnes possunt olere unguenta exotica,
Si tu oles ; neque superior quam herus accumbere,

29. *ad arquet* Ba.   *ad arquæ* Bb.   *æqæ* F.
30. *parus* Ba.   *parus* Bb.   *parrus* Da.   *continens* Ba.   *continens* Bb.
31. *posidet* Da.
33. *tua et*, so the MSS.   R has introduced *tuast* (*tua est*).
33. *me aut*, so Muret.   The MSS. have *mea ut*, which serves to
exemplify the kind of mistakes which constantly arise from an erroneous
distribution of the letters copied from a MS. written continuously.
34. *quess* BC.   *bovis*, so the MSS. except Da, which has *bovri*.
36. *fatio* B.   *facro* Da.   *fiducia* B.
37. *fue* BD.   *fut* C.   FZ carry on the corruption still farther, by
writing *loquitur fue*.   R omits *fue* in this place, and inserts *fu* after
perdant in the next line.
38. *alium* Ba.   *alium* Bb.   *allium* CDF.   *allium* Z.   *oboluisti* Ba.
oboluisti Bb.
39. *inluvies* B.   *rusticus*, so the MSS.   R proposes to substitute
rus merum, regarding *rusticus* as a gloss.   *hara suis* Z and the MSS. of
Pylades.   The rest of the MSS. have *hara sui*.
40. *canes capra commixta*.   This reading has been generally adopted,
although unsupported by the MSS.   *canem capris commixtā* B.   *cant
caprJ cōmixtān* CDF.   Scaliger conj. *capro*, and so Vulg. R.   *quid
vis* ; the Vulg. has *quid tu vis*, but *tu* is an addition by Pylad.
41. *tolere* B.   The word was originally written *tolerr*, but the *r* is
erased, leaving only a faint trace ; but by whom the erasure was made we
cannot tell.   R therefore is hardly justified in giving *tolere* as the reading
of Ba without remark.   This line is quoted by Nonius (p. 108), and
twice by Priscian (pp. 818, 866).
42. *sit toles (si tu ales)* C.   The words *quam herus* are found in B
only (*quamerus*).   The Vulg. omits them, thus leaving the line mutilated.
R supposes that portions of two lines have been lost, and prints—

           Si tu oles . . . .
           . . . . neque superior cum ero accumbere.

Neque tam facetis, quam tu vivis, victibus.
Tu tibi istos habeas turtures, piscis, avis;
Sine me alliato fungi fortunas meas.   45
Tu fortunatus; ego miser. Patiunda sunt.
Meum bonum me, te tuum maneat malum.
TR. Quasi invidere mihi hoc videre, Grumio,
Quia mihi bene est, et tibi male est. Dignissumum est.
Decet me amare, et te bubulcitarier;   50
Me victitare pulcre, te miseris modis.
GR. O carnuficium cribrum, quod credo fore:
Ita te forabunt patibulatum per vias
Stimulis, si huc reveniat [quam primum] senex.
  TR. Qui scis, an tibi istuc eveniat prius quam mihi? 55
  GR. Quia numquam merui: tu meruisti, et nunc meres.
  TR. Orationis operam compendiface,
Nisi te mala re magna mactari cupis.

43. R supposes that a line has dropped out between 43 and 44.
44. *turtures* all the MSS. apparently.   *piscis* BC.   *pisces* the rest of
the MSS.   *avis* B, as originally written, corrected into *avis*.   *avis*
the rest.   The first five words of this line are quoted by Serv. Virg.,
Ecl. I. 59.
45. *me alliato* F.   *me alcato* BCD.   *me alleato* Z.   R has *aliatum*, a
conj. of Saracenus, who, however, writes *alliatum*.
46. *fortunatus*.   R prints *fortunate's*.   *patiunda* Da, also DbF,
attributing the words to Tranio.   *patiunda* C.   *patienda* B.
48. *mihi hoc*, so the MSS.   *hoc mihi* R.
49. *bene est—male est*, so the MSS.   *dignissimum est* DFZ.
dignis sumust B.   *dignis sumist* Bb.   *dignissimumist* C.
50. *Decet* B and Non., p. 79.   All the rest of the MSS. *Eect.*
bubulcitarier BC.   *bubaltitarier* D.   *bubultuarier* Z.   *bubucbuarier* F.
51. *pulcre* Ba.   *pulcbre* Bb and the rest.
52. *carnuficium*, a conj. of Pylad. The MSS. and Vulg. have *carnificum*.
54. The MSS. have
                    Stimulis si huc reveniat senex
(except that Ba has *stimuliis*), thus presenting an imperfect line. Some
of the earlier edd. have
                    Stimulis si huc reveniat quam primum senex.
R has printed
                    Stimuleis [terebris] huc si reveniat senex.
55. *eveniat prius*, so the MSS.   *prius eveniat* Camer., RW.   *eveniat
prius* Both.
58. *magnam actari* B (*magna mactari*).

GR. Ervom daturin' estis, bubus quod feram?
Date aes si non estis. Agite, porro pergite,   60
Quoniam occepistis! bibite! pergraecamini!
Este! effercite vos! saginam caedite!
     TR. Tace atque abi rus: ego ire in Piraeum volo,
In vesperum parare piscatum mihi.
Ervom tibi aliquis cras faxo ad villam adferat.   65
Quid est? quid tu me nunc optuere, furcifer?
     GR. Pol tibi istuc credo nomen actutum fore.
     TR. Dum interea sic sit, istuc "actutum" sino.
     GR. Ita est; sed unum hoc scito, nimio celerius
Venire quod molestum est, quam illud quod *cupide petas.   70
     TR. Molestus ne sis: nunc iam i rus, te amove.
Ne tu erres, hercle, praeterhac mihi non facies moram.

59. *ervom* B. *ervum* BbFZ. *servom* Ba. *servum* CD. *daturis'*,
so Pylad. The MSS. have *daturi*. *Bubus* B. *Bobus* the rest.
60. *Date aes si non estis*, so Vulg. The MSS. are all corrupt here.
Data es inonestis B, and so Bb with an *b* above the *o*. *Datae si non estis*
Bc. *Date es inhoneste* C. *Dataesinhonestis* D. *Date aes inhonestis* FZ.
R has remodelled the line—
     Date, si non estis: [ceterum] agite pergite—
where he considers *estis* as equivalent to *editis*. W has *Date aes, si ne
estis*. We have retained the Vulgate, but the text must be regarded as
quite uncertain. W. places a comma after *agite*, the Vulg. after *porro*.
61. *Quoniam* B. *qd* a contraction for *quoniam* in CD. *Quomodo* F.
Vulg. *Quo* ZW. *occepisti* CD. *bibite* Bc. *bibi* BaCD.
62. *effercite*, so Camer. The MSS. are very corrupt. *et ferite* B.
efferute CDa. *efferite* Db. *at ferite* FZ. R writes *exfercite*. *eardite*
B. *cedite* the rest of the MSS. The reading is not satisfactory.
63. *abi rus* BC. *abiturus* (i.e. *abi tu rus*) D. *rus abi* Camer., Vulg.
66. *quid tu* CDZ. Vulg. W. *quod tu* BFR. *optuere* B.
68. *interea sic*, so Muret. and Lamb. *intereas sic* BCD.
69. *Ita est*, so the MSS. *Ita fit* R, without reason.
70. The MSS. have
     Venire quod moleste quam illud quod cupide petas,
(*illut quo* Ba. *illuc quod* C.) *Venire quod molestum est quam id quod cupide
petas* Pylad. Vulg. W. has
     Venire, quod molestum est, quam illud quod petas.
R, as usual, makes more violent changes,—
     Venire quod tu nolis, quam illut quod petas.
71. So the MSS. *nunc iam rus te amove* R. *nunc iam i rus teque
amove* Camer. Vulg. W.
72. So the MSS., except that B has *preterhac* and *facies*. *facias* C.
facias F. W leaves out *hercle*, which may be omitted in scanning. R has
     Ne tu erres, non mihi praeterhac facies moram.

GR. Satin' abiit, neque, quod dixi, flocci existumat?
Proh di inmortales, opsecro vostram fidem,
Facite, huc ut redeat noster quam primum senex,   75
Triennium qui iam hinc abest, priusquam omnia
Perdere, et aedis et ager. Qui nisi huc redit,
Paucorum mensum sunt relictae reliquiae.
Nunc rus abibo : nam eccum herilem filium
Video, corruptum ex adulescente optumo.   Ho

ACTVS I. SCENA II.

PHILOLACHES.

Recordatus multum et diu cogitavi,
Argumentaque in pectus multa institui
Ego, atque in meo corde, si est quod mihi cor,
Eam rem volutavi et diu disputavi,
Hominem quoius rei, quando natus est,   5
Similem esse arbitrarer simulacrumque habere.
Id repperi iam exemplum.
Novarum aedium esse arbitror similem ego hominem,

---

74. *inmortales* C.
77. *rdis* (nom.) BCFZ.   *huc redit* the MSS.   *nunc redit* R.
R supposes that a line has fallen out between 77 and 78.
78. *mensum* Lamb.   *mensum* BCD.   *mensium* FZ. Vulg.   *relicte*
reliquiae BaC.
79. *eccum* CDFZ.   *equum* B.   *hic quom* R.
80. *corruptum ex,* so the MSS.   *corruptum hic ex* Pylad.   *corruptum*
ita ex R.   *adulescente* BZ. The rest *adolescente.*   R supposes
that a line has dropped out after 80.

In distributing the following Scene into lines, we have adhered closely
to the arrangement of B. Hermann, Ritschl, Weise, and others, have
their own metrical views, upon which it is quite unnecessary to enlarge.
  1. *multum iam et* R, without any MS. authority.
  2. C omits *in pectus.*   The MSS. have *institui.* Reizius, R, W,
and others, have adopted *institui* for the sake of the metre.
  3, 4. These two lines are bracketed by R as interpolations.
  4. W, following Hermann, has *volutavi eam rem.*
  5, 6. So the MSS. R is dissatisfied, and thus remodels them—
    Hominem quoius rei similem esse arbitrarer [simulacrumque habere].
  8. *edium* B.

Quando hic natus est.   Ei rei argumenta dicam.

Atque hoc haud videtur veri simile vobis?   10

At ego id faciam esse ita ut credatis,

Profecto, ita esse ut praedico vera, vincam: atque hoc
        vosmet ipsi,

Scio, proinde uti nunc ego esse autumo,

Quando dicta audietis mea, haud aliter id dicetis.

Auscultate, argumenta dum dico ad hanc rem: 15

Simul gnarures vos volo esse hanc rem mecum.

Aedes quom extemplo sunt paratae, expolitae,

Factae probe, examussim:

Laudant fabrum atque aedes probant; sibi quisque inde
        exemplum expetunt.

Sibi quisque simile, suo usque sumptu; operam non parcunt
        suam.   20

Atque ubi illo inmigrat nequam homo indiligensque

10–12. R brackets these three lines.   W brackets line 11 only.

11. *eur ita*, so the MSS.   In B *ita* appears erased either by the first
hand or by b.   Possibly, however, it is only the stroke of the *i* exaggerated.
ita esse R, following Hermann.

12. *ita esse*, so the MSS.   *esse ita*, RW, following Hermann.   *praedico*
B.   *vera*, so the MSS.   *vero*, Vulg., following Pylad.

12–14. There can be no objection to arrange these lines as Hermann
has done,—

        Profecto ita esse ut praedico vera vincam
        Atque hoc vosmet ipsi, scio, proinde uti nunc
        Ego esse autumo quando dicta audietis.

14. *mea . . . dicetis* BC.   *dicrates* Da.   *mea, aliter ban dicetis* R.

15, 16. R brackets these lines.

16. *Simul gnarures vos*, so Lamb. on conj.   The MSS. are corrupt.
Simul gna ruri suo B.   *Simul gnaruriuus* CD.   C omits *hanc*.

17. *quom* for *cum* BF.   *parate* (*paratae*) B.

18. *examussim* B, the *u* being a correction by c.

19. *ardes* BZ.   *rdes* CDF (accusative).

20. R brackets this line, and so also W.   *simile suo usque sumptu*, a
conj. emend. due to Camer.   The MSS. are corrupt.   BCD have *simile
suo is sua sumptu*, except that D has *issua* and CD *sumptu*.   *simile suis
suo sumptu* F.   *similis suis sumptu suo* Z.   *similis volt suo sumptu* R.
operam non parcunt suam, so Hermann on conj.   *operam parcunt suam* B.
opera parcunt sui CDFZ (*sua* C).   *operae ne parcunt suae*, Camer. on conj.,
and so Vulg. W.

21. *inmigrat* C.   *indiligensque*, so the MSS.   Pylad. omits *que*, and
is followed by RW.

Cum pigra familia, inmundus, instrenuus:
Hic iam aedibus vitium additur, bonae quom curantur male.
Atque illud saepe fit: tempestas venit,
Confringit tegulas imbricesque: ibi   25
Dominus indiligens reddere alias nevolt.
Venit imber, lavit parietes: perpluont
Tigna; putrefacit aer operam fabri:
Nequior factus iam est usus aedium;
Atque haud est fabri culpa. Sed magna pars   30
Moram hanc induxerunt: si quid numo sarciri potest,
Vsque mantant, neque id faciunt, donicum
Parietes ruont: aedificantur aedes totae denuo.
Haec argumenta ego aedificiis dixi; nunc etiam volo
Dicere, ut hominis aedium esse similis arbitremini.   35
Primumdum parentes fabri liberum sunt
Et fundamentum supstruont liberorum;

22. The following nine lines are written in B in a larger hand than
the rest, but in the same character and with ink of the same colour;
but the *a* in *pigra* and the *f* in *familia* are written in the black ink of c.
inmundus BCD.   *instrenuus* FZ.   *strenuus* BCD.
23. *aedibus* C.   *vitium* BC.   *bonae (bonae)* C.
24. *saepe* BC.   *tempestas . . . nevolt.* These words are quoted by
Nonius, p. 381.
27. *Venit,* so the MSS. *Venint* W, following Both.   *lavit,* so the
MSS. *periavit* R.
28. *putrefacit,* so the MSS. *putefacit* R.   *aer operam,* a conj. of
Camer.   *per operam* B.   *popera* CDF, with a stroke through the tail of
the first *p.*
29. So the MSS. *iam usus est* W.   *edium* B.
30. *Atque haud,* so the MSS.   *Atque ea haud* Herm. RW.
31. *Moram hanc,* so the MSS., except Ba, which has *hauc* (with an *a,*
however, written over by c), whence Lamb. and R read *Moram hunc.*
nummos arciri Ba, corrected by last hand into *sarciri.*   *nummos arciri* D.
32. Hermann, to suit his views of the metre, supposes some words to
have dropped out between *id* and *faciunt,* and so W.
33. *Parietes ruont* the MSS. *Parietes ruont* R.   *Ruunt parietes* W.
aedificantur aedes totae, so the MSS. except that B has *edificatur edes totae*
denuo, corrected by c *edificatur.*   R has *tam aedificant aedis totas.*
34. *edificiis* BC.
35. *Dicere,* so the MSS.   *Dccere* W, following Herm. and Relz.
hominis BCDF (acc). R has *homines.*
36. *parentes,* so all.
37. *Et,* so the MSS.   *Ei* R, following Gulielmus.

Extollunt, parant sedulo in firmitatem
Et ut in usum boni et in speciem
Populo sint, sibique aut materiae ne parcunt,   40
Nec sumptus ibi sumptui esse ducunt.
Expoliunt, docent literas, iura, leges, suo sumptu et labore.
Nituntur ut alii sibi esse illorum similis expetant.
Ad legionem quom itum, adminiculum eis danunt
Tum iam aliquem cognatum suum :   45
Eatenus abeunt a fabris. Vbi unum emeritum est stipen-
    dium,
Igitur tum specimen cernitur, quo eveniat aedificatio.
Nam ego ad illud frugi usque et probus fui, in fabrorum
Potestate dum ful.
Posteaquam inmigravi in ingenium meum,   50
Perdidi operam fabrorum ilico oppido.
Venit ignavia, ea mihi tempestas fuit,
Mi adventu suo grandinem, imbremque attulit;
Haec verecundiam mi et virtutis modum
Deturbavit *texit detexitque a me ilico.   55

39. *Et ut in*, so the MSS. R omits *Et*. W places *Et* at the end of
the preceding line. W puts a comma after *parunt*.   *sue* B.   *boni*
et in speciem populo sint, so the MSS.   *boni sint et in speciem populo* RW.
speciem B.
    40. *ne parcunt*, a conj. of Camer.   *reparcunt* BaCD.   *reparcunt* Bb.
    41. *ibi sumtui* BCDZ.   *sibi sumtui* FR.
    42. *leges* (acc.) all apparently.   This line is divided into two by
RW, and bracketed by the former.   W has *sumto suo*.
    43. *similis* (acc.) all apparently.
    44. *quom itum* Z (*ra itum*), W. The MSS. are corrupt.   *comita* B,
the correction being by c.   *comita* C.   *clida* D.   *quom itur* FR.
quom itant Camer. Vulg.
    46. *Eatenus*, so the MSS.   *Protenus* R.   *babrant* (*abeunt*) BaCD.
Vbi unum, so the MSS.   W omits *Vbi*.   R omits *unum*.
    48. *illud*, so the MSS.   *id* W.   *fabrorum*, so the MSS.   *fabrum* W.
    50. *Posteaquam*, so the MSS.   *Postea quom* R following Guyetus.
imigravi Ba.   *in ingenium*, so the MSS.   *ingenium in* R following
Both.
    51. *opido* BF.
    51, 52. B includes these in a single line.
    53. *Mi adventu*, so the MSS.   *Ea mi* Pylad. Vulg. W.   *Quae mi* R.
imbremque, so the MSS.   Herm. Both. RW omit *que*.
    55. *Deturbavit texit detexitque a me*, so the MSS., where *texit* is mani-
festly corrupt.   *Deturbavit detexitque de me* R.   *Deturbavit detexitque*
a med W.

Postilla optigere eam neglegens fui.
Continuo pro imbre amor advenit in cor meum ;
Is usque in pectus permanavit, permadefecit cor meum.
Nunc simul res, fides, fama, virtus, decusque
Deseruerunt : ego sum in usu factus nimio nequior :   60
Atque edepol (ita haec tigna humide putent) non videor
    mihi
Sarcire posse aedes meas, quin totae perpetuae ruant,
Quin cum fundamento perierint, nec quisquam esse auxilio
    queat.
Cor dolet, quom scio, ut nunc sum, atque ut fui.
Quo neque industrior de iuventute erat,   65
Arte gumnastica, disco, hastis, pila,
Cursu, armis, equo ; victitabam volupe ;
Parsimonia et duritia disciplinae aliis eram :
Optumi quique expetebant a me doctrinam sibi.
Nunc postquam nihili sum, id vero meopte ingenio repperi.   70

56. *Postilla* BCD. *Post illam* FZW.   *obtigere* Camer. , *opti-
ere* BCD. *obtexere* FZW. *optigere* R. B has on the margin *optinere*.
W omits *eam*.
57. *advenit in cor meum* BCDF.   R has a blank after *advenit*,
supposing that the words *in cor meum* crept in from the following line.
59. *virtus decusque*, so the MSS. except C, which has *virtusque decus*.
Herm. Both. RW have *virtus decus*.
60. *usu*, so the MSS.   *usum* Lamb. W.
61. *ita haec tigna humide putens*, so Camer.   *ita haec tigna umide
putent* D.   *putent* is from a correction in Bb.   *ita haec . tingna umide
putan* Ba.   *ita hec ita tigna umida putant* C.   W has *ita tigna hace h. p.*
R has *ita tigna umide hace p.*   *videor*, so Camer.   *videor* BC.   *vidio* D.
62. *aedes* (acc.) BZ.   *edes* CDF.   *perpetue* (*perpetuae*) BDF.
63. *Quin* *non* the MSS.   R omits *Quin*.   W brackets *cum*.
64. *eom* (*quom*) BCDZ.   *ut nunc sum*, so the MSS.   *nunc ut sum* W.
66. *Arte gumnastica* ; R brackets these words.   *pila* ; BCDF have
alia.   *pila* appears in the margin of B and in Z.
67. R believes that some words have dropped out after *equo*, and reads
victitabat against all the MSS.   *volup* BR.   *volupe* BcCDFZ.
68. *Parsimonia et duritia* F.   *Parsimonias eduritia* B,   *Parsimonia
eduricia* CD ; the latter has *i* for *e*.   *Per simonia et duricia* Z.   *discipline aliis* BbFZ.   *discip li-meali is* B.   *discipuli nealiis* Ba.   *discipuli
nealiis* CD. The Vulg. has *disciplinae*, and so W.
69. R brackets this line.   *expetebant a me doctrinam* Bb.   *expetebant
iam edoctrinam* BaC.   *expetebant am edoctrinam* D.   *expetebant eam
doctrinam* F.

C 2

ACTVS I.   SCENA III.

PHILEMATIVM. SCAPHA. PHILOLACHES.

PH. Iampridem ecastor frigida non lavi magis lubenter;
Nec, quom me melius, mea Scapha, rear esse defaecatam.
Sc. Eventus rebus omnibus, velut horno messis magna
Fuit.   *PH.* Quid ea messis attinet ad meam lavationem?
Sc. Nihilo plus, quam lavatio tua ad messim.   *PHIL.* O
   Venus venusta,   5
Haec illa est tempestas mea, mihi quae modestiam omnem
Detexit, tectus qua ful, quam mihi Amor et Cupido
In pectus perpluit meum; neque iam umquam optigere
   possum.
Madent iam in corde parietes: periere haec oppido aedes.
   PH. Contempla, amabo, mea Scapha, satin' haec me
     vestis deceat.   10
Volo meo placere Philolachi, meo ocello, meo patrono.
   Sc. Quid tu te exornas, moribus lepidis quom lepida
     tute es?
Non vestem amatores amant mulieris sed vestis fartum.

2. *quom me* the MSS.   *quod me* R.   *rear esse defaecatam*, so
Camer.   *rea res . . de . ficatam* Ba.   *rear . esse de . ficatam* Bb.   *defecatā* in
marg. of B.   *reares edificatam* CD.   *reris edificatam* F.   *reres edificatā* Z.
3.   *velud* C.
3, 4.   So the MSS.   R has
    Sc. Eventus rebus omnibust, velut horno messis magnast.
    Ph. Quid ea nam messis attinet ad meam lavationem?
W, following Saracenus, has
    Sc. Eventus rebus omnibus velut horna messis magna
    Fuit.   *Ph.* Quid ea messis attinet ad meam lavationem?
7. *tectus qua* Z.   *tectusq'* CDF.   *tectus quā* B.   *quam mihi*, so the
MSS.   *quom mihi* R.
8. *umquam*, so B.   *unquam* or *ūquam* the rest.   *usquam* R, following
Acidal.   *obtegere* RW.   *optingere* B.   *obtingere* CDF.   *obtigere* Z
Vulg.
9. *haec* Camer.   *hec* B, so v. 41.   *hac* the rest of the MSS. Vulg.
11. *mero placere*, so the MSS.   *me placere* RW, following Both.
Philolachi, so Camer.   The MSS. have *Philolacheti*.
13. *amatores amant mulieris*, so the MSS.   *amatores mulieris amant*

PHIL. Ita me di ament, lepida est Scapha: sapit scelesta
  multum.

Vt lepide res omnes tenet, sententiasque amantum !   15
  PH. Quid nunc? Sc. Quid est? PH. Quin me aspice
  et contempla, ut haec me deceat.
  Sc. Virtute formae id evenit, te ut deceat, quidquid
  habeas.
  PHIL. Ergo hoc ob verbum te, Scapha, donabo ego hodie
  aliqui,
Neque patiar, te istanc gratiis laudasse, quae placet mi.
  PH. Nolo ego, te adsentari mihi.   Sc. Nimis tu
  quidem stulta es mulier.   20
Eho mavis vituperarier falso, quam vero extolli ?
Equidem pol vel falso tamen laudari multo malo,
Quam vero culpari aut meam speciem alios inridere.
  PH. Ego verum amo ; verum volo dici mihi, mendacem
  odi.
  Sc. Ita tu me ames, ita Philolaches tuus te amet, ut
  venusta es.   25
  PHIL. Quid ais, scelesta ? quomodo adiurasti ? " ita ego
  istam amarem ?"

Pylad. Vulg.   R following Lachm. gives *amantes mulieris amant.* W,
following Both., has *amator mulieris amat.*   *fartum* is a conj. of the
early edd.   *fartim* BCD.   *partum* FZ.
   14. *dii* FZ 35, 49.   *lepida est,* so Gruter.   The MSS. omit *est.*
   15. *res omnes* Camer.   *omnes res* the MSS.   *lepide eo omnis res* R
on conj.
   16. *haec me deceat,* so Camer.   *haec me decet* is the reading of the MSS.
haec decet me W, following Both.
   17. *forma* Ba.
   18. *Ergo hoc ob,* so Camer.   The MSS. have *Ergo ab hoc.*   R has
Hercle ego ab hoc.   *ergo hodie aliqui,* so the MSS.   *ego hoc die aliqui*
Both. W.   *ego profecto hodie aliqui* Camer. Vulg.   *donabo hodie aliqui*
[*merito*] R.
   19. *patiar* C.   *istanc* B.   *hanc* the rest of the MSS.   *gratiis*
. . . *mi ;* the MSS. have *gratiis . . . mihi.*
   20. *adsentari* B.
   21. *Eho mavis,* so the MSS.   *Eho an mavis* R, excluding *eho* from the
scansion.   *vituperarier* Both. RW.   *vituperari* the MSS.
   22. *spetiem* Codd. Pll.   *inridere* BZ.   *irridere* the rest.
   24. *dici mihi* BCDZ.   *mihi dici* FWR.
   25. *me ames ita.* These words are thus derived in B—*mea me sita.*
   26. *amarem* the MSS.   *amarim* Guyet. RW.   No correction required.

Quid ? "istaec me" id cur non additum est ? Infecta dona
    facio.
Periisti : quod promiseram tibi dono, perdidisti.
  Sc. Equidem pol miror, tam catam, tam doctam te et
    bene eductam,
Non stultam stulte facere.   *PH.* Quin mone, quaeso, si
    quid erro.   30
  Sc. Tu ecastor erras, quae quidem illum expectes unum,
    atque illi
Morem praecipue sic geras, atque alios asperneris.
Matronae, non meretricium est, unum inservire amantem.
  PHIL. Proh Iupiter, nam quod malum vorsatur meae
    domi illud ?
Di deaeque omnes me pessumis exemplis interficiant,   35
Nisi ego illam anum interfecero siti, fameque, atque
    algu.

27. The best MSS. exhibit this line under a corrupt form. *Quid ista
bare me cura* B. *Quid ista bre me id cura* CD. *Quid lsta . . . er me
cur* Bb. *Quid istec me id cura* F. We have retained the Vulg. which
approaches closely to Bb. R gives *Quid "ita haec me" quor non additum st.*
W has *Quid " ita haec me" id cur non additum est.*
   28. So the MSS., except that B has *Per . . . sti* with an erasure, and
CD have *dona*, while Ba has *dona*, the correction being from the first hand.
R brackets the line as an Interpolation. W has
        Periit quod iam promiseram tibi, dona perdidisti,
which is a conj. of Merula.
   29. *catam* is the correction of Plus. The MSS. have *captam.*   *tam
doctam. tam docta* Ba.   *te et bene eductam,* so Camer.   The MSS.
have *te et bene doctam.* R gives *doctam et bene te eductam.*
   30. *Non stultam.* This reading is found in the margin of B, and was
adopted by Camer. *Non staitam* B.   *nonsta Tam* C.   *nonsta itd* D.
Nosti id tam F. *Non scire te stulte* Z.   *Nunc stultam stulte* Both. R.
Non scire stulte W.
   31. *expectes* BCDZ.   *exoptes* is a conj. of Acidal., and has been
adopted by R.
   32. *praecipue* BC.   *aspernaris* BbFZ.   *aspernaris* BaCD.   *asperne-
re* R.
   33. *matrone* Bb.   *meretricion* BaZ.   *meretritium* Da.   *meretricium* C. *meretricum* BbF. *meretricis* Guyet. R.
   34. *vorsatur* all the MSS.   *meae domi illud,* so Camer. The MSS.
have *mea edomilli.*
   35. *omnes me,* so the MSS., except Ba, which omits *me.*   *me omnes* R.
pessimis all the MSS.
   36. *algu* B.   The rest of the MSS. have *gelu.*

PH. Nolo ego mihi male te, Scapha, praecipere.

   Sc. Stulta es plane,

Quae illum tibi aeternum putes fore amicum et benevol-
   entem.

Moneo ego te : te ille deseret aetate et satietate.

PH. Non spero. *Sc.* Insperata accidunt magis saepe,

   quam, quae speres.   40

Postremo, si dictis nequis perduci, ut vera haec credas,

Mea dicta ex factis nosce; rem vides, quae sim et quae
   fui ante.

Nihilo ego, quam nunc tu, sum amata atque uni modo
   gessi morem,

Qui pol me, ubi aetate hoc caput colorem commutavit,

Reliquit deseruitque me. Tibi idem futurum credo. 45

   PHIL. Vix comprimor, quin involem illi in oculos stimul-
     atrici.

   PH. Solam illi me soli censeo esse oportere opse-
     quentem,

Solam ille me soli sibi suo [argento] liberavit.

   PHIL. Proh di immortales, mulierem lepidam et pudico
     ingenio !

Bene hercle factum, et gaudeo, mihi nihil esse huius
   causa.   50

---

37. *mihi* Z. *mei* BaCDF. *mei* Bb. *mi* R.   *te scapha,* so the
MSS. *te mea Scapha* R.   *praecipere* B.
38. *putes* B. The rest of the MSS. have *putas*.
39. *deseret ille* Pylad. Vulg. *satietate* BC.
40. *sepe* BC. *que* C.
42. *vides,* so the MSS. *vide* W. R thus remodels the line—
   Ex factis nosce rem : vide, ego quae sim et quae fui ante.
43. So the MSS. *amata sum* W. R thus remodels the line—
   Nihilo ego sum amata tetlus, atque uni gessi morem.
45. *credo,* so the MSS. *crede* Acidal. Vulg. R.
47. *Solam illi me soli,* so Camer. Vulg. W. *Solam illi meo soli* BD.
Solam illi meo soli illi C. *Solam me soli* R. *opsequentem* B.
48. R places 48 before 47. Not so the MSS. *suo* [*argento*]
liberavit. The MSS. have simply *suo liberavit.* Some word, such as
argento, sumptu, aere, is required to complete the line, and edd. have
adopted one or other of these according to their fancy.

Sc. Inscita ecastor tu quidem es. *Ph.* Quapropter?

Sc. Quae istuc cures,

Vt te ille amet. *Ph.* Cur, opsecro, non curem? *Sc.* Libera

es iam.

Tu iam, quod quaerebas, habes: ille te nisi amabit ultro,

Id, pro capite tuo quod dedit, perdiderit tantum argenti.

Phil. Perii hercle, ni ego illam pessumis exemplis

enicasso.   55

Illa hanc corrumpit mulierem malesuada vitilena.

Ph. Numquam ego illi possum gratiam referre, ut meritus

est de me,

Scapha: id tu mihi ne suadeas, ut illum minoris pendam.

Sc. At hoc unum facito cogites, si illum inservibis

solum,

Dum tibi nunc haec aetatula est, in senecta male querere. 60

Phil. In anginam ego nunc me velim vorti, ut vene-

ficae illi

Fauces prebendam, atque enicem scelestam stimulatricem.

Ph. Eundem animum oportet nunc mihi esse gratum,

ut impetravi,

Atque olim, priusquam id extudi, quom illi subblandiebar.

---

51. *Inscita ecastor* FZ. *Inciste ceastor* B. *inciste eastor* C. *incistecastor* D. The correction of these corrupt forms is easy and certain.

51, 52. . . . *istuc cures* = *Vt te ille*, so Pylad. *cures* is omitted in BCD.

53. *querebas* BaC.

54. *Id pro capite tuo*, so the MSS. *Id pro tuo capite* W. R thus reconstructs the line—

        Pro capite tuo quantum dedit . . . . .

56. *corrumpit*, so the MSS. *corrumpt* R.   *malesuada vitilena.* This is the exact reading of D. *malesuadam vitilena* B. *malesuada Vitilena* C. *malesuada Vii lena* F. R has *malesuada invitam lena*, which is more plausible than his conjectures usually are. *vitii lena* W, following Lamb.

59. *inserviis* Ba. *inservius* Bb.

60. *aetatulest* B. *aetatula est* the rest.

61. *aginam* Ba. *me velim*, so the MSS. *me* is omitted in Vulg. *vorti* B. *verti* DFZ. *benefice* Ba.

62. *fauas* all the MSS. *enicem* Ba. *enicem* Bb. *enicem* the rest.

63. *impetravi* Z. *impetravit* BDF. *imperavit* C.

64. *extudi*, so B. The rest of the MSS. have *extuli*.

PHIL. Divi me faciant, quod volunt, ni ob istam
    orationem   65
Te liberasso denuo, et ni Scapham enicasso.
Sc. Si tibi sat acceptum est, fore tibi victum semp-
    iternum,
Atque illum amatorem tibi proprium futurum in vita:
Soli gerundum censeo morem, et capiundos crines.
PH. Vt fama est homini, exin solet pecuniam invenire; 70
Ego si bonam famam mihi servasso, sat ero dives.
PHIL. Siquidem hercle vendundum est, pater venibit
    multo potius,
Quam te, me vivo, umquam sinam egere aut mendicare.
Sc. Quid illis futurum est ceteris, qui te amant?
    PH. Magis amabunt,
Quom videbunt gratiam referri.   75
PHIL. Vtinam meus nunc mortuos pater ad me nuntietur:

65. *Divi* Both. W.   The MSS. have *Di*.   R has *Di pol*.   *volunt*,
so the MSS.   *volunt* R.
66. *ni Scapham* F.   *nicaspam* BCD.   *nisi Scapham* Camer. Vulg.
enecasso Bb.
67. *sat*, so B.   The rest of the MSS. omit *sat*.   *acceptum* C.
tibi victum CD.   *tibi .. ctum* with an erasure Ba.   *tibi vi ctum* Bb.
victum tibi Gruter. Vulg.
69. So the MSS., except that Ba has *capiundas*.   R perversely insists
upon reconstructing the line by the aid of an imperfect quotation in
Nonius (p. 202)—
    Morem gerundum censeo tibi et capiundas crinis.
70. *exin solet* B.   CD have corruptly *exin sole*, whence *ex insole* F.
ex in sole Z.
72. *vendundum est*, so Camer.   *vendundum si* BCDF, a slight corruption of *vendundumst*, whence *vendundum sit* Z.   R has *vendundust*
pater, which destroys the force of the passage.
73. *quom* BF.   *cum* CDZ, and again v. 93.   This line is imperfect
in the MSS.   B has
    Quom videbunt gratiam referr .. i,
with an erasure, while CD have *referrui* instead of *referri*.   Camerarius
thus restores the line—
    Quando videbunt gratiam bene merenti referri.
R has—
    Quom me videbunt gratiam referre bene merenti.
W has—
    Quom me videbunt gratiam referentem rem ferenti.
76. *meus nunc* B.   The rest of the MSS. have *nunc meus*.   *mortuos*
the MSS.

Vt ego exheredem meis bonis me faciam, atque haec sit
heres.

Sc. Iam ista quidem apsumpta res erit: dies noctesque ·
estur, bibitur,

Neque quisquam parsimoniam adhibet; sagina plane est.

PHIL. In te hercle certum est principium, ut sim parcus,
experiri;   8o

Nam neque edes quicquam, neque bibes apud me his decem
diebus.

PH. Si quid tu in illum bene voles loqui, id loqui licebit;

Nec recte si illi dixeris, iam ecastor vapulabis.

PHIL. Edepol si summo Iovi vivo argento sacruficassem,

Pro illius capite quod dedi: numquam aeque id bene
locassem.   85

Vt videas eam medullitus me amare! Oh, probus homo
sum:

Quae pro me causam diceret, patronum liberavi.

Sc. Video, te nibili pendere prae Philolache omnes
homines:

77. *bonis me faciam* Camer. *me bonis fatiam* B. *me bonis fariam* D.
me fariam bonis C. *sit heres,* so B. *sit res* CD.

78. *quidem absumta res* Z. The MSS. erroneously repeat *quidem* after
absumpta. *dies noctesque* all the MSS. (acc.)

79. Camer. places *bibitur* at the commencement of this line, and so
Vulg. *Neque quisquam* BCD. *Nec quisquam* W.

8o. *certumst* CD. *certum est* B and the rest. *principium,* so the
MSS. *principe* Both. RW, which may be right.

81. *me hic decem,* a conj. of Both., followed by RW. *me isdec* B.
mris Da. *me isdem* CDb. *me hisce* Lamb. Vulg.

84, 85, 86, 87, are arranged by R in the following order:—86, 87, 84, 85.
He, moreover, assigns the words *ut videas . . . amare* to Philemathium, and
changes *eam* into *eum* against the MSS.

84. *si summo Iovi vivo argento* BbDFZ, *si summo iovi bo agend o . . . .*
with an erasure Ba. *si summo iovi . bo agent-o . . . . .* Bb. *si summo iovi
iovi argento* C, which is manifestly corrupt. *summo ego Iovi illac argento*
Camer. W, while R has—

Edepol si vel summo Iovi eo argento sacruficassem.

85. *locassem* is a conj. of Guyet, adopted by RW. The MSS. have
collocassem.

87. *Quae* (*quae*) B and rv. 94, 121.

88. *omnes,* so the MSS. Varro LL. ix. 54, p. 494, *omnis.*

Nunc, ne eius causa vapulem, tibi potius adsentabor,
Si acceptum sat habes, tibi fore illum amicum semp-
iternum. 90
PH. Cedo mihi speculum et cum ornamentis arculam
actutum, Scapha,
Ornata ut siem, quom huc veniat Philolaches, voluptas mea.
SC. Mulier, quae se suamque aetatem spernit, speculo ei
usus est :
Quid opus est speculo tibi, quae tute speculo speculum es
maxumum ?
PHIL. Ob istuc verbum, ne nequiquam, Scapha, tam
lepide dixeris, 95
Dabo aliquid hodie peculi tibi, Philematium mea.
PH. Suo quique loco viden' capillus satis compositus est
commode ?
SC. Vbi tu commoda es, capillum commodum esse credito.
PHIL. Vah, quid illa pote peius quicquam muliere
memorarier ?
Nunc adsentatrix scelesta est ; dudum advorsatrix erat. 100
PH. Cedo cerussam. SC. Quid cerussa opus nam ?
PH. Qui malas oblinam.

PLAVTI MOSTELLARIA.

Sc. Vna opera ebur atramento candefacere postules.
Phil. Lepide dictum de atramento atque ebore! Euge,
plaudo Scaphae.
Ph. Tum tu igitur cedo purpurissum.   Sc. Non do:
scita es tu quidem;
Nova pictura interpolare vis opus lepidissumum?   105
Non istanc aetatem oportet pigmentum ullum attingere,
Neque cerussam, neque melinum, neque aliam ullam
offuciam.
Cape igitur speculum.   Phil. Hei mihi misero: savium
speculo dedit.
Nimis velim lapidem, qui ego illi speculo diminuam
caput.
Sc. Linteum cape atque exterge tibi manus.   Ph. Quid
ita, opsecro?   110
Sc. Vt speculum tenuisti, metuo, ne oleant argentum
manus:
Ne usquam argentum te accepisse suspicetur Philolaches.
Phil. Non videor vidisse lenam callidiorem ullam
alteram.
Vt lepide atque astute in mentem venit de speculo malae!
Ph. Etiamne unguentis unguendam censes?   Sc. Min-
ume feceris.   115
Ph. Quapropter?   Sc. Quia ecastor mulier recte olet,
ubi nihil olet.

103. R inserts *brevie* after *ebur* against the MSS.
104. *ebure* B.   *Euge plaudo*, so the MSS.   *Euge adplaudo, Scapha.*
Both. R.
105. *leppidissimum* C.   *lepidissimum* the rest.
107. *neque melinum*, so the MSS.   *melinumve* R.   *ullam aliam*
Camer. Vulg. W.   The MSS. have *aliam ullam.*   *offuciam* Dc.
offugiam BCDa.
109. *speculo diminuam*, so Camer.   *speculum dim minuat* Ba.   *speculum
dimminuat* Bb.   *speculo imminuat* CDa.   R retains the orthography
dimminuam.
111. *oleant*, so the MSS.   *olent* R.
113. *alteras* BaC.   *alterās* D.
114. *speculo male* B, which in CD is corrupted into *speculo mane.*
115. *minime* the MSS.

Nam istae veteres, quae se unguentis unctitant, interpoles,
Vetulae, edentulae, quae vitia corporis fuco occulunt,
Vbi sese sudor cum unguentis consociavit, ilico
Itidem olent, quasi quom una multa iura confudit cocus: 120
Quid oleant, nescias, nisi id unum, ut male olere intellegas.
   PHIL. Vt perdocte cuncta callet! nihil hac docta doctius!
Verum illud esse maxuma adeo pars vostrorum intellegit,
Quibus anus domi sunt uxores, quae vos dote meruerunt.
   PH. Agedum, contempla aurum et pallam, satin' haec
   me deceat, Scapha.   125
   Sc. Non me curare istuc oportet. PH. Quem, opsecro,
   igitur?   Sc. Eloquar.
Philolachem: is ne quid emat nisi quod tibi placere
   censeat.
Nam amator meretricis mores sibi emit auro et purpura:
Quid opus est, quod suum esse nolit, ei ultro ostentarier?
Purpura aetas occultanda est; aurum turpe mulieri,   130
Pulcra mulier nuda erit, quam purpurata, pulcrior:
Postea nequiquam exornata est bene, si morata est male:
Pulcrum ornatum turpes mores peius caeno conlinunt.

117. *istae*. *iste* the MSS.—*istaec* Vulg. R, which is probably right.
118. *viria* B.   *occultant*, so Camer.   *occultans* the MSS.
120. *unam* BaC.
121. *oleant*, so Lamb.   *oleas* the MSS.   *olant* R.   *ut male*, so
Camer. The MSS. have *ni male*, which might, perhaps, be retained.
male ut R.
122. *doctius*, so the MSS.   *doctiust* R.
123. *illud esse maxuma adeo*, so Aul. Gell., xx. 6.   *illud est* BCDFZ.
maxima adeo with a space after *maxima* B, and hence Camer. corrects
maximaque. The rest of the MSS. have *maximi adeo*.   *maxumum* F.
vestrorum B.
125. *me deceat*, so Camer. The MSS. omit *me*.
126. *curare istuc*, so the MSS.   *istuc curare* R.
127. R supposes a gap to exist after *nisi*, extending to the end of the
line, and as far as *quod* in the line following. This imaginary blank he fills
up from his own fancy.
128. R brackets this line.
129. *nolit ei*, so Pylad.   *nollite* B.   *nolit te* CDFZ.   *nolit id ei* R.
130. *aetas* is found in the margin of B. The MSS. have *artate*.
turpe B.   *turpi* CD.   *turpeit* R.
131. *pulchra* the MSS., and so in the following lines.
132, 133. Are bracketed by R, who reads *Poste* instead of *Postea*.
nequicquam the MSS.

Nam si pulcra est, nimis ornata est.   *Phil.* Nimis diu
   apstineo manum.
Quid hic vos duae agitis?   *Ph.* Tibi me exorno ut
   placeam.   *Phil.* Ornata es satis.   135
Abi tu hinc Intro, atque ornamenta haec aufer.—Sed,
   voluptas mea,
Mea Philematium, potare tecum conlubitum est mihi.
   Ph. Lubet et edepol mihi tecum : nam quod tibi lubet,
   Idem mihi lubet,
Mea voluptas.   *Phil.* Hem, istuc verbum vile est viginti
   minis.
   Ph. Cedo, amabo, decem : bene emptum tibi dare hoc
   verbum volo.   140
   Phil. Etiam nunc decem minae apud te sunt : vel
   rationem puta :
Triginta minas pro capite tuo dedi . . . .   *Ph.* Cur ex-
   probras ?
   Phil. Egone id exprobrem ?   Qui mihimet cupio id
   opprobrarier ;
Nec quicquam argenti locavi iam diu usquam aeque bene.

133. *erao* the MSS. *carao* Z, *carao* R,   *conliumal*—BCD have
contionvnl, an obvious corruption of *conlimeui*. Baracenus first introduced
collimeui, and so Vulg. W.
134. *Nam si*, so Camer. *Nam nisi* Ba. *Nam nisi* Bb. *Nam m si*
CDFZ.   *manum* FZ.   *manu* BCD.
135. *Quid*, so the MSS. *Nam quid* R.   *vos duae*, so Camer.
vos dae Bb. *vos diu* BaCDZ. *vos dui* F.   *duae* is omitted by RW.
exorno ut placeam, so the MSS. R omits *ut placeam* as a gloss.
136. *tu hinc* BCD. *tu*, omitting *hinc*, FZ. *hinc tu*, Camer. Vulg. W.
137. *conlibitum* BD.
138. *Lubet et edepol* BCDF. *Lubet* is probably a gloss, and is omitted
by RW.   All the MSS. have *lubet* twice.
139. *Hem istuc*, so Camer. *em istuc* Bb. *eam istuc* BaCD. Ba
and Db assign the words *Mea voluptas* to Philolaches. Hence R arranges
the words thus—

   Phil. Hem, istuc verbum, mea voluptas, vilest viginti minis.

140. *decem bene*, so Acidal. *decom bene* BaD. *decumbe ne* BbCF.
142. *quor* F.
143. *qui mihimet*, so the MSS. *quin mibimet* Vulg. W.   *oprobarier*
Ba. *abprobarier* F. *opr.* Bb. *oprobarier* CD.
144. *iam diu*, so Camer. The MSS. have *tam diu*.

PH. Certe ego, quod te amo, operam nusquam melius
potui ponere.   145

PHIL. Bene igitur ratio accepti atque expensi inter
nos convenit:

Tu me amas, ego te amo; merito id fieri uterque existumat.

Haec qui gaudent, gaudeant perpetuo suo semper bono;

Qui invident, ne umquam eorum quisquam invideat prosus
commodis.

PH. Age, accumbe igitur.—Cedo aquam manibus, puer.

Appone hic mensulam.   150

Vide, tali ubi sint.—Vin' unguenta?   *PHIL.* Quid opus
est?   Cum stacta accubo.

Sed estne hic meus sodalis, qui huc incedit cum amica
sua?

Is est Callidamates; cum amica, eccum, incedit.   Euge,
oculus meus,

Conveniunt manuplares, eccos; praedam participes petunt.

143. *certe;* R has *certo.*   *operam nusquam* BbZ.   *opera manus*
quam BaCDF.

147. *existimat* all the MSS.

149, 150. In the MSS. v. 150 is placed before 149. Acidal. first restored
the true arrangement.

149. *ne nusquam* or *nusquid* the MSS.   *nusquam* R.   *prorsus* BbFZ.
prorsu BaCDR.

150. *puer,* so the MSS. R following Priscian (p. 618) has *puerr.*
mensulam, so Priscian l. c.   *mensam* BCFZ.   *mesam* Da.   *mèam* Db.

151. *Vide tali ubi sint, vin' unguenta.* This is the reading of the best
MSS., although the words are erroneously divided, thus in B—
> Vide tali ubi sintu in unguenta,

and in C—
> Videt aliubis intu inunguenta,

and in D—
> Videt aliubi sio tu in unguenta.

153. The MSS. have—
> Is est Callidamates cum amica cum incedit euge oculus meus,

but D omits *est,* and Bb corrects *cum incedit* into *eccum incedit,* and so Volg.,
which we have retained. W has—
> Is est: est Gallidamates: eccum incedit: Euge oculus meus.

R has—
> Is est [profecto]: Callidamates eccumst: euge, oculus meus.

154. *manuplares* B.

ACTVS I. SCENA IV.

CALLIDAMATES. DELPHIVM. PHILOLACHES.
PHILEMATIVM.

CA. Advorsum venire mihi ad Philolachem
Volo temperi : audi : hem, tibi imperatum est.
Nam illi, ubi fui, inde effugi foras :
Ita me ibi male convivii sermonisque taesum est.
Nunc commissatum ibo ad Philolachetem,   5
Vbi nos hilari ingenio et lepide accipiet.
Ecquid tibi videor, ma-ma-madere ?

In the following Scene, more than the usual amount of confusion exists
in the different MSS. and edd. In regard to the distribution of the dialogue
among the characters. We have, for the most part, adhered to the
Vulgate. Hermann, Ritschl, and Weise, differ as to the metrical constitution of the passage, and each introduces changes in order to suit his
own views. We have closely followed the division into lines found in B,
except in one instance, and have adhered to the text of that MS., except
where it was obviously corrupt.

1. *venire*, so the MSS. *veniri* RW and others. The *i* in *venire* a
correction of *e*. The fourth letter corrected and blurred.

2. *temperi*, so the MSS. *tempori* Vulg. *audi hem—audicm* CD.
In Ba very doubtful. The word is corrected and blurred in the fourth
letter. *audi em* Bb. Apparently in B the *em* was placed at first too near
to the *audi* and a mark was made by the first hand thus, *audi.em*, to shew
they were distinct words. *tibi imperatum est* the MSS. *tibist imperatum* R.

3. *illi*, so the MSS. *illis* Camer. Vulg. W. *fui*, so Camer. *fuit*
the MSS.

4. *me ibi male* CDFZ. *ibi* is omitted in B, being written above by c
or a late hand. *taesum est*, so Pareus. *tesunt* D. In B there is a
sort of dash or stroke at the end of the word, so, *Tesum*; it is probably
intended for *Tesum*. In iv. 1. 17 (873) the *m* is written in exactly the
same way, where R reads *non—sunt* seems better. *te sunt* C. *tesunt* FZ.

5. *Philolachem* R against the MSS.

6. *hilari*, so the MSS. *hilaro* W. *et lepide*, so Camer. The line
appears thus in B—

     Vbi nos ilari ingenio elepida accipia.

The *s* in red ink. *elepida* CDa. R has *et lepide [victu] accipiet*.

7, 8. In B these two form a single line.

7. *Ecquid* FZ. *Hecquid* BD, so *nequis*, v. 36. *Hec quid* C. *Ecquid*
Bb. In B the first letter is erased, probably N or H. *ma-ma-madere*,
so Both. R. The MSS. have *mammam adire*. Scaliger introduced
mamma madere, and so Vulg. W.

DE. Semper istoc modo moratus, vita, debebas——
CA. Visne ego te ac tu me amplectere?
DE. Si tibi cordi est facere, licet.   *CA.* Lepida es.   10
Duce me, amabo.   *DE.* Cave ne cadas.   Asta.
  CA. Oh! oh! ocellus es meus; tuus sum alumnus, mel
    meum.
DE. Cave modo, ne prius in via accumbas,
Quam Illi, ubi lectus est stratus, coimus.
  CA. Sine sine cadere me.   *DE.* Sino.   *CA.* Sed et hoc,
    quod mihi in manu est.   15
DE. Si cades, non cades, quin cadam tecum.
Iacentis tollet postea nos ambos aliquis.
Madet homo.   *CA.* Tun' me ais ma-ma-madere?

---

8. So the MSS., except that they have *vite*, whence *vivere debebas* Camer. Vulg. W.   R has—
      Semper istoc modo (tute) moratu's
      · · · · vita, debebas.
9. So the MSS. Camer. has *tute* instead of *tu amplectare* Pylad. *tute me amplexare* Vulg.   R has—
      Visne ego te ac tu med amplectare.
10. *cordi* Z. *corde* the MSS. *facere cordi est* Herm. R.
11. *Duce* the MSS. B has no blank at the beginning as R gives, but *Duce* probably after an erasure of *Dkt.* inserted by mistake. *Duc* Herm. R.
12. This appears thus in B:—*D.be* . *ocellus*, etc., the letter *D* written on an erasure, the second letter erased; after *D.be* an erasure with faint traces of an *l* or *b*. Two dots under the second *u* in *suum*, so, *suum*. *Obl ob! ocellus* FZ. *O be bverlls* D. *Obabocellus* D.   W brackets *mel meum*.
13. B has a red line over the *u* in *accibas*.
14. *illi* CD. *illi'* B. The *c* added by first hand. *illic* FZ Vulg. W. *lectus est*; the MSS. have *lectus es*, unless there is a misprint in R, who does not notice the variation. *stratus coimus* BC. *catmus* Da. *stratus nos coimus* Herm. on conj. R prints *stratus [nos] coimus*.
15. *Sine sine*, so the MSS. W omits the second *sine*. *Sino sed et hoc*, so Camer. B has *sino*, then a letter (probably *s*) obliterated, then *sei*. *Sinas & hoc* C. *Sin. sey hoc* D.   R has—
    Call. Sine sine cadere me. *Del.* Sino. *Call.* Set [ne sine] hoc
      quod mi in manust.
manu FZ. *manus* BCD.
16. *non cades quin* FZ. *non clades quin* B. *non dades quin* C. *non clades que in* D.
17. So the MSS. *jacentis* (acc.) B and the rest. *ambo* Herm R. *Tollet iacentes post* W.
18. *Tun me ais*, so Scaliger. *Tun mei . is* B. *Tun mei vis* Bb. The

DE. Cedo manum: nolo equidem te adfligi.

CA. Hem, tene.   *DE.* Age, i i simul.   *CA.* Quo ego

    eam, an scis?   20

DE. Scio.   *CA.* In mentem venit modo: nempe domum eo

Commissatum.   *DE.* Imo.   *CA.* Istuc quidem iam memini.

PHIL. Num non vis me obviam his ire, anime mi?

Illi ego ex omnibus optume volo.

Iam revortar.   *PH.* Diu " iam" id mihi.   25

    CA. Ecquis hic est?   *PH.* Adest.   *CA.* Eu, Philolaches,

Salve, amicissume mihi omnium hominum.

PHIL. Di te ament.   Accuba, Callidamates.

Vnde agis te?   *CA.* Vnde homo ebrius.

PHIL. Probe.   Quin amabo accubas, Delphium mea?   30

CA. Da illi, quod bibat; dormiam ego iam.

PHIL. Num mirum aut novom quippiam facit?

---

first letter of *vis* written over an erasure, but apparently by first hand; the
correction *aderv* also apparently by first hand.   The line is evidently—
    Madet homo—tuo meam vis mammam adire,
and the meaning is obvious.   *Tun mea bis* CD.   *ma-ma-madere*, so
Both. R, see v. 7.   *mammam adere* B.   *mammam adere* C.   *mammadere*
D.   *mammam adbere* F.
   19.   W supposes that a word has dropped out after *te*.   *adfigi* B.
affigi DFZ.
   20.   *Age i i simul.*   *Age ii simul* B.   *Ageu simul* C.   *Age simul* FZ.
Age i simul Camer. Vulg. W.   *Quo ego eam an scis*, so Both. Herm.
RW.   *Quod ego* Ba, with a dot in black ink under the *d*.   *Quod ego eam
an scis* CD.   *Quo eam an scis* FZ.
   21.   *domum eo* CDFZ.   *domú meo* B.
   22.   R has *Immo* [*bur*].
   23.   *me obviam*, so the MSS.   *obviam me* Camer. Vulg.   *obviam med* W.
his ire Bb.   *bis . . re* Ba.   *bis ei re* C.   *iscire* Da.   *is ire* Db.   *bisre ire*
FZ, Vulg., which is perhaps right.
   24.   *Illi ego*, so Camer.   *Ilico* the MSS.   *optume*, so the MSS.
   25.   *revortar*, so the MSS.   R has *Diust iam* [*tuum*] *id mibi.*
   26.   *Ecquis* FZ.   B has *ecquis* with an erasure before the *e*.   *Hecquis* D.
Hec quis C.   See v. 7.   *Adest*, so the MSS.   *Is est* ZW.   *Eu*, so
the MSS.   *Eugr* R.
   27.   *amicissime* the MSS.   *omnium hominum*, so the MSS.   *hominum
omnium* Pylad. R.
   28.   R has [*mi*] *Callidamates.*
   30.   R connects *probe* with *ebrius*, and assigns it to Callid.
   31.   *Da*, so the MSS.   *Date* Camer. W.   W brackets *iam.*
   32.   *Num*, so the MSS.   *Non* Camer. RW.   *quippiam* the MSS.
R has *quippiam* [*nunc*] *facit.*

Quid ego hoc faciam postea, mea? *DE.* Sic sine eumpse.
PHIL. Age tu, interim da ab Delphio cito cantharum
circum.

ACTVS II.   SCENA I.

TRANIO.   PHILOLACHES.   CALLIDAMATES.
DELPHIVM.   PHILEMATIVM.   PVER.

TR. Iuppiter supremus summis opibus atque industriis
Me perisse et Philolachetem cupit, herilem filium.
Occidit spes nostra: nusquam stabulum est confidentiae,
Nec Salus nobis saluti iam esse, si cupiat, potest:
Ita mali maeroris montem maxumum ad portum modo   5
Conspicatus sum: herus advenit peregre: periit Tranio.
Ecquis homo est, qui facere argenti cupiat aliquantum lucri,
Qui hodie sese excruciari meam vicem possit pati?
Vbi sunt isti plagipatidae, ferritribaces viri,
Vel isti, qui *hastis trium numorum causa subeunt sub
    falas,   10
Vbi aliqui quindenis hastis corpus transfigi solent?
Ego dabo et talentum, primus qui in crucem excucurrerit;

---

11. *fatiam* B. *faciam* CDFZ.   *eumpse,* so Gruter.   *eum ipse*
the MSS.
14. *ab Delphio cito,* so the MSS.   *cito ab Delphio* Herm. RW.

---

1. *Iuppiter* seems to be the reading of the MSS., and in v. 51.   *Iupiter*
FZ in Both.
2. *herilem* FZ.
5. *Ita mali maeroris* Bb.   *Itam aliam erroris* BaC.   *Itaaliaerroris* D.
Ita alium erroris FZ.   *Ita altum erroris* Pylad.   *maximum* BC.
8. *meam vicem,* so Pylad.   *meamvi* BaD.   *mea vice* Bb.   *me amice* C.
9. *plagi patidae* BC.
10. *qui hastis trium.* The MSS. all have *hastis,* but it looks like a gloss,
and destroys the metre.   It is omitted in most edd., but retained in Vulg.
falas a very ingenious conj. of Camer.   *falia* BCDF.   *hasta* Z.
11. *Vbi aliqui quindenis,* so Camer.   *Vel aliqui quiq' denis* Ba.   *Vbi*
aliqui quiq' denis BbCDZ.   *Vbi aliqui quinque denis* F.   *Vel ubiquaeque*
denis R.   *solent* BbFZ.   *solet* BaCDR.

E 2

Sed ea lege, ut offigantur bis pedes, bis brachia.

Vbi id erit factum, a me argentum petito' praesentarium.

Sed ego sumne ille infelix, qui non curro curriculo
　　　domum?　　　　　　　　　　　　　　　　　　　15

PHIL. Adest opsonium: eccum, Tranio a portu redit.

TR. Philolaches!　*PHIL.* Quid est?　*TR.* [Et] ego et
　　　tu ...　*PHIL.* Quid " et ego et tu"?　*TR.* Perimus!

PHIL. Quid ita?　*TR.* Pater adest.　*PHIL.* Quid ego
　　　ex ted audio?　*TR.* Apsumpti sumus.

Pater, inquam, tuus venit.　*PH.* Vbi is est, opsecro [te?]

TR. Adest.　*PHIL.* [Adest?]

Quis id ait? quis vidit?　*TR.* Egomet, inquam, vidi.

PHIL. Vae mihi!　　　　　　　　　　　　　　　　20

Quid ego ago?　*TR.* Nam quid tu, malum, me rogitas,
　　　quid agas? Accubas.

PHIL. Tun' vidisti?　*TR.* Egomet, inquam.　*PHIL.* Certe?

TR. [Certe], inquam.　*PHIL.* Occidi,

Si tu vera memoras.　*TR.* Quid mihi sit boni, si men-
　　　tiar?

13. *offigantur* BCDZ.　*obfringantur* F.　*affigantur* Camer. Vulg.

14. *praecautarium* B.

15. *sumne ille infelix*, so the MSS. Most edd., following Pylad., omit
ille. It is retained in Vulg.

16. *Adest ... Tranio*, so the MSS.　*Adest adest* Gruter.　*Tandem adest*
Herm.　*En adest* R.　*Adest ... Tranionem* W.　*redit* Bb.　*ardit*
BaC.　*edit* D.　*adit* FZ.　*venit* codd. Pylad.

17. *Quid est? et ego et tu*, so Dousa. The MSS. omit *et* before *ego.
perimus*, so all the MSS., which creates a difficulty in the metre.　*periimus*
RW. See v. 28.

18. *adest* BbFZ.　*adatest* Ba.　*adat est* C.　*adatt* Da.　*a'. att* Db.
ex ted, so Both.　*cte* BCD.　*ex te* FZ.

19. *Vbi is est obsecro*.　*Adest*, so the MSS.　*Vbi est is obsecro te.*
TR. *Adest* Camer. Vulg.　*Vbi is est obsecro te.* TR. *Adest.* PHIL. *Adest?*
W.　*Vbi is est obsecro.* TR. [*In portu iam*] *adest* R.
Ve BC.

20. *Ve* BC.

21. *ago*, so Dousa.　*agam* BCDFZ.　*Nam quid*, so Dousa. *Nam
quid* BCDFZ.　*rogitas* B.　*rogitet* CD.　*Accubas*, so Camer.
Accubeas BCD.

22. *Tun' vidisti* Dc Camer.　*Tu vidisti* B, which is in reality the
same. The rest of the MSS. are more wide of the mark.　*Tui innuti* C.
Tuvn vidisti D.　*Tu en vidisti* FZ.　*Certe certe.* The MSS. omit the
second *certe*, which was supplied by Camer., and has been generally received.

23. *mentiar*, so Pylad. The MSS. have *mentirrr.*

PHIL. Quid ego nunc faciam? *TR.* Iube haec hinc
  omnia amolirier.
Quis istic dormit? *PHIL.* Callidamates. *TR.* Suscita
  istum, Delphium.   25
DE. Callidamates, Callidamates, vigila! *CA.* Vigilo:
  cedo ut bibam.
DE. Vigila: pater advenit peregre Philolachae. *CA.* Val-
  eat pater.
PHIL. Valet ille quidem; atque [ego] disperi. *CA.* Dis-
  peristi? qui potest?
PHIL. Quaeso edepol, exsurge: pater advenit. *CA.* Tuus
  venit pater?
Iube abire rursum. Quid illi reditio huc etiam fuit?   30
  PHIL. Quid ego agam? Pater iam hic me offendet
  miserum adveniens ebrium,
Aedis plenas convivarum et mulierum. Miserum est opus,
Igitur demum fodere puteum, ubi sitis fauces tenet;
Sicut ego adventu patris nunc quaero, quid faciam miser.
  TR. Ecce autem, hic deposivit caput, et dormit.
  Suscita.   35
  PHIL. Etiam vigilas? Pater, inquam, aderit iam hic
  meus. *CA.* Ain' tu? pater?

24. *bre* C.
25. *Quid* B. *Quis* FZ. *Quid* CD.   *istum,* so the MSS. *istunc* W.
26. *cedo ut,* so the MSS.   R omits *ut.*
28. W has *illic,* a conj. of Both., and *at* (for *atque*), a conj. of Dousa.
ego was inserted by Pylad., but is not found in the MSS.   *disperi*
BaCD.   *Disperisti* FZ.   *Bis peristi* B.   *Bisperisti* CD.
29. *Quaeso edepol exsurge,* so the MSS., except that B has *Queso.
Quaeso edepol te exsurge* R.
30. *Iube abire,* so the MSS.   *Iube cum abire* R.   *reditio* D.
huc etiam, so Camer.   *etiam huc* BFZ.   *etiam huc* D.   *et etiam huc* C.
31. *Pater iam hic me offendet miserum,* so the MSS., except that BCD
have *offendit,* which is corrected in FZ.   W omits *me,* and, following
Both., has *misere.*   R has *nam iam hic offendet miserum.*
33. This line is found in B, but omitted in CDFZ.
34. *quero* BC.   *faciam* B.
35. *deposivit,* so Camer.   *deposuit* the MSS.   *Ecere autem hic deposivit* R.   *Suscita* BbFZ.   *Suscitat* BaCD.
36. *aderit* BbFZ.   *adberit* BaCD.

Cedo soleas mihi, ut arma capiam! iam pol ego occidam
 patrem.

  PHIL. Perdis rem : tace.   Amabo, abripite hunc intro
  actutum inter manus.

    CA. Iam hercle ego vos pro matula habebo, nisi mihi
    matulam datis.

  PHIL. Perii!   *TR.* Habe bonum animum : ego istum
  lepide medicabo metum.   40

  PHIL. Nullus sum!   *TR.* Taceas : ego, qui istaec sedem,
  meditabor, tibi.

Satin' habes, si ego advenientem ita patrem faciam
 tuum,

Non modo ne intro eat, verum etiam ut fugiat longe ab
 aedibus ?

Vos modo hinc abite intro atque haec hinc propere amolimini.

  PHIL. Vbi ego ero ?   *TR.* Vbi maxume esse vis : cum
  hac, cum istac eris.   45

  DE. Quid est igitur ? abeamus hinc nos ?   *TR.* Non hoc
  longe, Delphium.

Nam intus potate haud tantillo hac quidem causa
 minus.

---

37. *Cedo soleas mibi ut arma,* so the MSS.   *Soleas cedo mi ut arma* R.
39. *nisi mibi* B. The rest of the MSS. omit *mibi.*
40. *medicabo* DaFZR. *meditabor* B. *meditabo* C. *medicabor* Db.
Pylad. Vulg. W.
41. *Nullus* BbFZ. *Nullum* BaCD.   *ista bet* BCD and v. 48.
42. There is some confusion here in the MSS., arising, probably, from
a portion of the two following lines having been copied twice over.
43. *intro at* BaCD. *intro'at* Bb. *introeat* FZ.
44. *babite* D. *bac* C.   *bine propere,* so the MSS. *propere
bine* R.
45. So the MSS. *maxime* the MSS.   *vis esse* Both. R.   *cum
bac : ta cum istac eris* W. W believes this line and all which follow
to the end of the scene to be spurious. He brackets, however, only
[45-53].
46. *Quid est igitur,* so the MSS. *Quid si igitur* Both. *Quid igitur si*
R. *Quid igitur* W.   *babeamus* BCD.
47. *Nå intus* B. *Namentus* C. *Nimentus* D. *Nam metuis potare* Z.
Nam metuis potare F. *Namque intus* Vulg. W.   *bautantillo* BaD.
bautantillo Bb. *baud tantillo* F. *baut ancillo* C.

PHIL. Ei mihi, quam, istaec blanda dicta quo eveniant,
madeo metu!

TR. Potin', animo ut sies quieto et facias, quod iubeo?

PHIL. Potest.

TR. Omnium primum Philematium, intro abi, et tu,
 Delphium.   50

DE. Morigerae tibi erimus ambae.   *TR.* Ita ille faxit
Iuppiter!

Animum advorte nunc tu iam, quae volo accurarier.

Omnium primumdum aedes iam face occlusae sient.

Intus cave muttire quemquam siveris.   *PHIL.* Curabitur.

TR. Tamquam si intus natus nemo in aedibus habitet.

PHIL. Licet.   55

TR. Neu quisquam responset, quando hasce aedis pul-
tabit senex.

PHIL. Numquid aliud?   *TR.* Clavem mi harunce aedium
Laconicam

Iam iube efferri Intus: hasce ego aedis occludam hinc
foris.

PHIL. In tuam custodiam meque et spes meas trado,
Tranio.

48. *Ei* BCD.   *Hei* FZ.   *quam istarr*, so Camer.   *quom ista brr*
BaD.   *quom ista . re* Bb.   *qnomista barr* C.   *commixta* F.   *commista*
brr Z.   *eveniant*, so the MSS.   *evvnant* Both. R.

49. *animo ut sies*, so Camer.   The MSS. have *animo at siu — ut animo sis*
Both. Herm. R.   *fatias* B, v. 80.   *fatiam* Ba.

50. *babi* D.

51. *Morigera et ibi* BaCD.

52. *advorte*, so the MSS.   *advortito* W.   *tu iam* BFZ.   *tulam*
CD.   *iam tu* Both. R.   *que* C, and in v. 65 BC.   *adcurarier* Z.

53. R inserts *barr* before *ardes*.   B appears to have had *face*—the
rest *far.*

54. *mutire* the MSS.

55. *si intus* Vulg.   *stintus* BaCD.   *natus nemo*, so apparently
all the MSS.   *nemo natus* Vulg.   *edibus* B, and *edium* v. 57 in
several.

56. *putabit* BaD, an obvious blunder.

57. *bartoite aedium*, so Camer.   *barunerdium* Ba.   *barunredium* D.
barä cediä C.   *barou aedium* R.   *laconicam* B.   *ioronicam* CD.
aunc iam Z.

59. *custodiam meque et spes meas*, so the MSS.   *custodiant me et meas*
spes Pylad. W.   *custodelant meque et spes meas* Both. R.

Tr. Pluma haud interest, patronus an cluens proprior
     siet   60
Homini, quoi nulla in pectore est audacia.
Nam quoivis homini, vel optumo vel pessumo,
Quamvis desubito facile est facere nequiter;
Verum id videndum est, id viri docti est opus,
Quae designata sint et facta nequitia,   65
Ni quid patiatur, quamobrem pigeat vivere :
Tranquille cuncta et ut proveniant sine malo :
Sicut ego efficiam, quae facta hic turbabimus,
Profecto ut liqueant omnia et tranquilla sint,
Nec quicquam nobis pariant ex se incommodi.   70
Sed quid tu egrederis? Perii! o, iamiam optume
Praeceptis paruisti! *Pv.* [Herus] iussit maxumo

60. *an tlicus* BbDFZ.   *ar tlicus* Ba.   *addirus* C.   *proprior* BaCDF.
propior BbZW.   *probior* Sciopp. Vulg.   *probrior* R.   *siet* BbF.
siet BaCD.   R supposes that a line has fallen out after v. 60, and
says that space for a line appears in BCD.
  61. *cui* all the MSS.   *in pertore est,* so Pylad.   *est in pectore* the
MSS.   *audatia* BC.
  62. This verse is bracketed by R.   *cuivis* BbDcFZ.   *cuius* BaCDa.
bomine BaC.   *hominis* Da.   *pessimo* BCD.
  63. After this line we find in the MSS. and Vulg. the verse which occurs
again below, apparently in its proper place as v. 77—*Clavim credo,* &c.
  64. *docti est* BbFZ.   *docte est* BaCD.
  65. *designata* Z.   *dissignata* BaF.   *dissignita* BbCD.   *nequitia,*
so the MSS.   *nequiter* Dousa R.
  66, 67.   These lines follow each other thus in the MSS.   Acidal. places
67 before 66, and is followed by RW.
  66. *Ni* BaDR.   *Ne* BbCFZW.   *patiatur* Bb.   *potiatur* BaCD.
ponatur FZ.
  67. *et ut proveniant,* so the MSS.   *ut proveuant et* R.   *sine malo,*
there can be no doubt that this is the true reading, but the words are
curiously blundered in the MSS.   *sinemo malo* Ba.   *sine mo malo* Bb.
sine mamalo C.   *sine morolo* D.   *sine modo* FZ.
  68. *turbabimus,* so the MSS.   *turbavimus* Lamb. R.
  69. *liqueant,* so Vulg.   BCDa have *linquant.*
  70. *ex se incommodi,* so Camer.   *exsiincommodi* B.   *exri incommodi* C.
ex si incommodi D.   *ex eo incommodi* F (*exco* Z).
  71. *egrederis: perii,e* so Gruter.   *egrederes perio* BaCD.   *egrederes*
perio Bb.   *egredere perii ebo* R.
  72. So Camer.   *praeceptis* BC.   The MSS. omit *Herus.*   R has—
          Praeceptis pares.   *Pv.* Erus te iussit maxumo.
maximo or *maxima* the MSS.

Opere orare, ut patrem aliquo apsterreres modo,
Ne introiret aedis. *TR.* Quin etiam illi hoc dicito,
Facturum, ut ne etiam aspicere aedis audeat,   75
Capite obvoluto ut fugiat, cum summo metu.
Clavim cedo atque abi hinc intro, atque occlude ostium,
Et ego hinc occludam.—Iube venire nunc iam!
Ludos ego hodie vivo praesenti hic seni
Faciam, quod credo mortuo numquam fore.   80
Concedam a foribus huc; hinc speculabor procul,
Vnde advenienti sarcinam inponam seni.

ACTVS II.   SCENA II.

THEVROPIDES.   TRANIO.

TH. Habeo, Neptune, gratiam magnam tibi,
Quom me amisisti a te vix vivom modo!
Verum si posthac me pedem latum modo
Scies inposisse in undam: haud causa ilico est,
Quod nunc voluisti facere, quin facias mihi.   5

---

73. *opere* DeFZ.   *opere* BCDa.
74. [Fleck., and R (in his later volumes), Lor., and others, write *intro
ire* in two words. Ed.]   *aedis* Camer.   *adest* BCD.
75. *haut aedis* R, against the MSS.   *audiat* Ba.
76. *cum summo*, so the MSS.   *summo cum* ZW.
77. So the MSS.   *abi hinc intro: occlude* R.   W omits *hinc*.
78. *nuntiam* C, for *nunc iam*, and again v. 43 in BaCD.
79. *presenti* BC.   *hic*, so the MSS.   *huic* R, following Bentley and
others.   *seni* Bb.   *sene* BaCD.
80. *quod credo* B after correction, FZ.   *quo do edo* C.   *quodceda* D.
82. *inponam*, so B.

---

1. *Quom me*, so the MSS.   *Quoniam* Gruter. R.   *amisisti me* R.
a te vix, so Vulg.   *ad te vix* BCD.   *vix a te* Pylad. W.   *vivom*, so B.
3. *Verum*, so Vulg.   *Virum* BCD.
4. *Scies* DeFZ.   *Sies* BaCD.   *Sines* Bb.   *inposisse* or *impoisisse*
BCDZ.   *impoisisse* FW.   *hau* for *haud* BaCDa.   *ilico est* the
MSS.   *est ilico* R.   *est illico* W.
5. *facias* Ba.

F

Apage, apage te a me nunc iam post hunc diem;
Quod crediturus tibi fui, omne credidi.
TR. Edepol, Neptune, peccavisti largiter,
Qui occasionem hanc amisisti tam bonam.
TH. Triennio post Aegupto advenio domum.   10
Credo, exspectatus veniam familiaribus.
TR. Nimio edepol ille potuit exspectatior
Venire, qui te nuntiaret mortuom.
TH. Sed quid hoc? Occlusa ianua est interdius?
Pultabo. Heus, ecquis istas aperit mihi fores?   15
TR. Quis homo est, qui nostras aedes accessit prope?
TH. Meus servos hic quidem est Tranio.   *TR.* O Theu-
ropides,
Here, salve: salvom te advenisse gaudeo.
Vsque invaluisti?   *TH.* Vsque, ut vides.   *TR.* Factum
optume.
TH. Quid vos? insanin' est?   *TR.* Quidum?   *TH.* Sic: quia   20
Foris ambulatis; natus nemo in aedibus
Servat, neque qui recludat, neque qui respondeat.
Pultando pedibus pene confregi hasce ambas.*

6. *apage ac age* CD2, an obvious blunder, and so *omei* in v. 7.
8. *largiter* BC. *lägiter* D. *ingiter* FZ.
9. *boccasiomem* D.
13. *mortuom* the MSS.
15. *ras brepuis* BaCD. *istas aperit* BbDcFZ. *istaperit* BaCDa.
mibi, so Camer. *in* BCDa. The word is omitted in DcFZ. *fores*
(acc.) the MSS.
16. *ardes* or *edes* BCD.
17. *servus* B.
18. *Here salus*, so the MSS. of Pylad. *Errgahv* BaCDa. *salvom*
B. *salvum* DbFZ. *salvm* CDa.
19. *Vsque invaluisti*, so the MSS. *Vsqune valuisti* Camer. *Vsqune
valuisti* W. *Vsquin valuisti* R. *optime* BCD.
21. *edibus* C.
22. *neque qui respondent* FZW. *neque quis respondeat* BCD. Both.
omits *quis*, and is followed by R, who, however, endeavours to rewrite
the line.
23. Such is the reading of B, with which the rest of the MSS. agree
closely. The line is evidently imperfect. R has—
          Pultando paene confregi hasce foris;
which is very reasonable, and not unlikely to be true. W has—
          Pultando pedibus pene confregi assulas.

Tr. Eho an tu tetigisti has aedis? *Th.* Cur non
tangerem?
Quin pultando, inquam, pene confregi foris.   25
Tr. Tetigistin'? *Th.* Tetigi, inquam, et pultavi.
Tr. Vah! *Th.* Quid est?
Tr. Male hercle factum! *Th.* Quid est negoti? *Tr.* Non
potest
Dici, quam indignum facinus fecisti et malum.
Th. Quid iam? *Tr.* Fuge, opsecro, atque apscede ab
aedibus.
Fuge huc, fuge ad me propius! Tetigistin' fores?   30
Th. Quomodo pultare potui, si non tangerem?
Tr. Occidisti hercle. *Th.* Quem mortalem? *Tr.* Omnis
tuos.
Th. Di te deaeque omnis faxint cum isto omine.
Tr. Metuo, te atque istos expiare ut possies.
Th. Quamobrem, aut quam subito rem mihi adportas
novam?   35
Tr. Et, heus, iube illos illinc, amabo, apscedere.
Th. Apscedite. *Tr.* Aedes ne attigatis! Tangite
Vos quoque terram! *Th.* Opsecro hercle, quin eloquere
[iam].

24. *Eho* F. The rest have *Eo.*   *an tu* FZ.   *ante te* BaC.   *an tu
te* BbD.   *edes* DFZ.   *quor* F.
25. *confregi* Ba.   *confrigi* CDa.
26. R here changes the order of the ten following lines, and arranges
them thus:—26, 31, 27, 28, 39, 32, 33, 34, 29, 30, 36.
30. *Tetigistin' fores*, so the MSS. R considers this to be a repetition of
v. 26, and therefore prints—
    Fuge huc, fuge ad me propius [tene terram manu].
32. *mis* C.   *ellis* B.   *omnes* DFZ.
33. *omnis* (nom. plur.) BCDZ.   *omnes* FR.   *faxint* B.   *axint*
CDa.   *axint* Db, and hence *perduassint* F.   *perduaxint* Z.   *perduint* W.
isto omine BbF.   *isto homine* BaC.   *istoc omine* ZR.
36. *illinc*, so the MSS.   *illim* Both. R.
37. *edis* (acc.) Diomedes, p. 378.   *edes* the MSS.   *attigatis*, so
Diomedes lb.   *atigate* BaCD.   *attingite* BbFZ.
38. *quin eloquere iam* Pylad. W.   *quin eloquere* the MSS. R conj.
quin [intro imus huc], supposing *eloquere* to have been derived from
v. 41.

TR. Quia septem menses sunt, quom in hasce aedis
pedem

Nemo intro tetulit, semel ut emigravimus.   40

TH. Eloquere, quid ita?   *TR.* Circumspicedum, num
quis est,

Sermonem nostrum qui aucupet.   *TH.* Tutum probe est.

TR. Circumspice etiam.   *TH.* Nemo est: loquere nunc
iam.

TR. Capitalis caedis facta est.   *TH.* *Quid est? non
intellego.

TR. Scelus, inquam, factum est iamdiu, antiquom et
vetus.   45

Antiquom. Id adeo nos nunc factum invenimus.

TH. Quid istuc est, *sceleste, aut quis id fecit? cedo.

TR. Hospes necavit hospitem captum manu;
Iste, ut ego opinor, qui has tibi aedis vendidit.

TH. Necavit?   *TR.* Aurumque ei ademit hospiti,   50
Eumque hic defodit hospitem ibidem in aedibus.

TH. Quapropter id vos factum suspicamini?

TR. Ego dicam: ausculta.   Vt foris cenaverat
Tuus gnatus, postquam redit a cena domum:

---

39. *menus* (nom. plur.) D.   *ardis*, so apparently BCD (acc. plur.)
ædis FZ.

42. *Sermonem* BaCDa, an obvious blunder.   *probest* BCDF.
43. *nunc iam*, so Vulg.   *nuntiam* BaCDa, an obvious blunder.
44. *Capitalis caedis facta est*. This is the true reading of the MSS.,
thus—*Capitali sedis* BaC.   *Capitali sedis* Bb.   *capitalis cedis* DF.
Capitalis aedis ZW.   *Caputale factumest* R.   *Quid est*, so the MSS.
Camer. omits the words, and so W.   *Quid id est* Both. R.

45. *antiquom* the MSS.
46. *Antiquom*, so the MSS.   R conj. [*Capatale*].   FW give the word
Antiquom to Theuropides.
47. *est sceleste*, so the MSS.   *scelus est* R, Scaliger having previously
proposed *est scelus*.   *sceleste est* W.
48. *necavit*, so Vulg.   *negavit* BaCDa.
49. *has tibi* BbDcFZ.   *astib* .. with erasure B.   *hastibus* CDa.
ædis BC.   *aedes* DFZ.
50. *ei ademit*, an early correction.   *et ademit* BCDF.   *eidem ademit* R.
eii ademit Vulg.   *ipsi ademit* Pylad.
54. *gnatus* the MSS. here and v. 58.   *redit* the MSS.   *rediit*
Dousa.

Abimus omnes cubitum, condormivimus.   55
Lucernam forte oblitus fueram extinguere:
Atque ille exclamat derepente maxumum.
   TH. Quis homo? an gnatus meus?   *TR.* Si tace;
   ausculta modo.
Ait, venisse illum in somnis ad se mortuom.
   TH. Nempe ergo in somnis?   *TR.* Ita. Sed ausculta
   modo.   60
Ait illum hoc pacto sibi dixisse mortuom . . . .
   TH. In somnis?   *TR.* Mirum, quin vigilanti diceret,
Qui abhinc sexaginta annis occisus foret.
Interdum inepte stultus es.   *TH.* Taceo.   *TR.* Sed ecce,
   quae ille inquit:
" Ego transmarinus hospes sum Diapontius;   65
Hic habito; haec mihi dedita est habitatio:
Nam me Acheruntem recipere Orcus noluit,
Quia praemature vita careo. Per fidem
Deceptus sum: hospes me hic necavit, isque me

----

55. *Abimus,* so the MSS.   *Abiimus* W, which is unnecessary,
gubitum the MSS.
   57. *maximum* the MSS.
   58. *gnatus meus* the MSS. *meus gnatus* Both. R.   *Si tace,* so
Camer. *Sitace* Ba. *Si tace* CD. *Sed tace* Bb. *Si taces* De, *sic
tace* FZ.
   59, 61. *mortuom* the MSS. In both.
   62. *quin* Pylad. *qui* the MSS., which may be defended.   *dicerit*
CDa. *dixerit* De.
   64. This verse, unless we suppose an interruption in the versification,
is obviously corrupt. B divides it into two lines—
       Interdum inepte stultus es
       Th. Taceo. *Tr.* Sed ecce quae ille inquit.
CD include the whole in a single line, and have *Interdum inepte stultus es
taceo sed ecce que illum* (*imptae* C. *ecce* D.) W thus rewrites it—
       Interdum inepte stultus's. Sed ecce quae ille ait,
while R, with some ingenuity, restores two complete lines—
       Interdum inepte stultus es, [Theuropides].
       Th. Taceo. *Tr.* Set ecce quae illi ille inquit [mortuos].
   66. *haec mihi dedita est,* so the MSS. *dedita haec mihi est* Both. R.
habitacio Da.
   67. *Nam me* BDa. *Nam me* C. *Nam me in* DbFZ.   *orcus*
BCD. *borcus* Z.
   69. *me hic* RW. *hic me* the MSS.

Defodit insepultum clam *ibidem in hisce aedibus,   70
Scelestus, auri causa. Nunc tu hinc emigra :
Scelestae hae sunt aedes, impia est habitatio."
Quae hic monstra fiunt, anno vix possum eloqui.
St, st I *Th.* Quid, opsecro, hercle, factum est ? *Tr.* Con-
crepuit foris.
Hicine percussit ?   *Th.* Guttam haud habeo sanguinis.   75
Vivom me arcessunt ad Acheruntem mortui.
  Tr. Perii! illisce hodie hanc conturbabunt fabulam.
Nimis quam formido, ne manufesto hic me opprimat.
  Th. Quid tute tecum loquere ?   *Tr.* Apscede ab ianua.
Fuge, opsecro hercle!   *Th.* Quo fugiam ? Etiam tu fugis. 80
  Tr. Nil ego formido : pax mihi est cum mortuis.—
  Th. Heus, Tranio!   *Tr.* Non me appellabis, si sapis :
Nihil ego commerui, neque istas percussi fores.
  * *Th.* Quaeso, quid aegre est ? quae res te agitat, Tranio ?

---

70. *ibidem* is found in the MSS., but is probably a gloss, omitted by R
and bracketed by W.
72. *hae sunt aedes impia est* Ba. *hae sunt aede simpla est* C. *brde
simpla est* Da. Plus first made the obvious correction *impia.* *Scelesta
haec ardis* W. *Scelestae haec ardes* R.
73. *que* C. *monstra,* so Vulg. *monitra* BaCDa, an obvious
blunder.
74. *St st,* so Gruter. *Sedet* BCD. *Secede* FZ. *hercle ;* W
brackets this word without necessity. *forts* B. *farts* C. *foraes* D.
foris FZ.
75. *Hiscine percussit,* so the MSS. *Haccine perrussast* R.
76. *vivum* BC. *accersunt* C, which is, perhaps, the true orthography. *ad* is found in all the MSS. (*adcherantem* CDa), but is
omitted for the sake of the metre by Herm., R, and others.
77. *Perii illisce,* so Camer. *Per illisce* BCDa. *Peri illis te* De.
illise W, following Dousa, which may be right.
78. *manifesto* the MSS. *oppriment* CDFZ.
79. *Quid tute tecum* Vulg. *Quit te tu cum* BaCDa (*Quitte* D. *turum*
CD). *Quid tu tecum* BbDcF.
80. *Qua,* so the MSS. *Quor* Both. R. *fugis,* so Camer. *fugis*
B. *fuges* the rest of the MSS. *fuge* W.
81. *commerui* Vulg. *quom merui* B. *quomwerui* CDa. *fores,* so
the MSS. (acc.) and again v. 87.
84. This line as it stands in the text is a conj. of Camer., being made
up from the fragments of two lines, of which the traces, as found in BCD,
are these—

Queso . . . . Quid segreges
. . . . este agitat Tranio

Quicum istaec loquere? *TR.* An, quaeso, tu appella-
veras? 85
Ita me di amabunt, mortuom illum credidi
Expostulare, quia percussisses fores.
Sed tu etiamne astas, nec, quae dico, optemperas?
TH. Quid faciam? *TR.* Cave respexis, fuge, operi
*atque caput!
TH. Cur non fugis tu? *TR.* Pax mihi est cum
mortuis. 90
TH. Scio. Quid? modo igitur cur tanto opere ex-
timueras?
TR. Nil me curassis, inquam: ego mihi providero;
Tu, ut occepisti, tantum quantum quis, fuge;
Atque Herculem invocabis. *TH.* Hercules, te invoco!
TR. Et ego, tibi hodie ut det, senex, magnum malum. 95
Proh di immortales, opsecro vostram fidem,
Quid ego hodie negoti confeci, malum!

(*Quaeso* and *e grege* in D). In FZ we find the single line—
　　Th. Quaeso. Tr. Quid e grege es? Th. Quis te agitat, Tranio.
The two lines are restored by R, but this is merely a work of fancy.
85. *ista brt* BaCDF. *queso* BC.
86. *amabunt* Vulg. *amabant* BCDa.
87. *percussisses* BDcFZ. *percusserises* Da. *petes isses* C. *percussissem* Acidal. R. *forts* the MSS. *foris* R.
88. *astas,* to ZR. *astias* B. *astras* CD. *adstas* F. *optemperas* BCD. *quae dico* BCD. *quod dico* FZW.
89. *fatiam* B. *fuge operi atque,* so the MSS. *fuge atque operi* Vulg. Most edd. omit *atque.*
90, 91. So BCD. R, without any plausible reason, rewrites these lines.
92. *providro* C.
93. *fuge* FZ. *furis* B. *fui* CD. *fugias* Camer. Vulg.
94. *invocabis* BbFZ. *invocabi* BaCDa. *invora* R.
95. *tibi hodie ut* FZ. *ut ibi hodie ut* BaCD. *ut'ibi hodie ut* Bb.
96. *Dii* BC. *Di* D. *vostram* the MSS.
97. W, following Pareus, prints *hodie* [*hic*]. *argotii* BD. *argoti* C. *argotii* FZ. *malum,* so the MSS. *malus* Acidal. *mali* Guyet. R.

ACTVS III.   SCENA I.

DANISTA.   THEVROPIDES.   TRANIO.

DA. Scelestiorem ego annum argento faenori
Numquam ullum vidi, quam hic mihi annus optigit.
A mane ad noctem usque in foro dego diem ;
Locare argenti nemini numum queo.

TR. Nunc pol ego perii plane in perpetuom modum :   5
Danista adest qui dedit [argentum faenori]
Qui amica est empta, quoque [opus in sumptus fuit]
Manufesta res est, nisi quod occurro prius,
Ne hoc [nunc] senex resciscat. Ibo huic obviam.
Sed quidnam hic sese tam cito recipit domum ?   10
Metuo, ne de hac re quidpiam indaudiverit.
Accedam atque adpellabo. Hei, quam timeo miser !
Nihil est miserius, quam animus hominis conscius,
Sicut me habet. Verum utut res sese habet,

---

1. *faenori* BC, but both have *fenus* vv. 30 and 49. We may notice a
disposition in these MSS. to sink diphthongs. A has uniformly *faenus*
wherever the word can be read. A has, however, *Torterrone* for
teterrone, and *tartriorem* for *tetriorem* v. 74.

2. *optigit* BCDa.

3. *mane*, so the MSS.   *mani* R.   See III. ii. 80.

5. *perpetuum* all.

6, 7.   B has preserved here the fragments only of two lines—

> Danista adest qui dedit . . . .
> Qui amica est empta quoque . . . . .

which the rest of the MSS. present as a single verse. Z omits *quoque*.
The words within brackets are ingenious conjectures by Camer., adopted
in the Vulg. W has concocted the following—

> Danista adest, qui amica est emta, qui dedit.

8. *manifesta* the MSS.   *quod*, so the MSS.   *quid* an early correction adopted by RW.

9. *Ne hoc* [*nunc*]. The MSS. omit *nunc*, which was added on conj.
by Camer., and has been adopted by RW.   *resciscat* Vulg.   *resciscat*
BCDa.

11. *indaudiverit* a conj. of Both., adopted by RW. The MSS. have
inaudiverit.

12. *Hei*, so Taubman.   *ei* BCDF.   *ei* R.   *ai* Pylad. W.

14. *me*, so the MSS.   *mi* Both. R.   *utut res sese*, so De Camer.
utut res esse se BaCDa.   *utut res . sse se* Bb.   *ut res bare seae* FZ.   *utut
res sese haec* W.   *ututi seae res* R.

Pergam turbare porro: ita haec res postulat.   15
Vnde is? *TH.* Conveni illum, unde hasce aedis emeram.
   TR. Numquid dixisti de illo, quod dixi tibi?
TH. Dixi hercle vero [illi] omnia.   *TR.* Vae misero
   mihi!
Metuo, ne technae meae perpetuo perierint!
   TH. Quid tute tecum?   *TR.* Nihil enim. Sed dic
   mihi: 20
Dixtine, quaeso? *TH.* Dixi, inquam, ordine omnia.
   TR. Etiam fatetur de hospite? *TH.* Imo pernegat.
   TR. Negat? [*TH.* Negat, inquam. *TR.* Perii oppido]
   quom cogito.
[Non confitetur].   *TH.* Dicam si confessus sit.
Quid nunc faciundum censes? *TR.* Egon' quid censeam? 25
Cape, opsecro hercle [te], cum eo una iudicem;
Sed cum videto ut capias, qui credat mihi:
Tam facile vinces, quam pirum volpes comest.

                                        G

DA. Sed Philolachetis servom eccum Tranium;
Qui mihi neque faenus neque sortem argenti danunt.   30
  TH. Quo te agis?   *TR.* Nec quoquam abeo. Nam ego
    sum miser,
Scelestus, natus dis inimicis omnibus.
Iam illo praesente adibit. Nae ego homo sum miser :
Ita et hinc et illinc mi exhibent negotium.
Sed occupabo adire.   *DA.* Hic ad me it : salvos sum :   35
Spes est de argento.   *TR.* Hilarus est. Frustra est homo.
Salvere iubeo te, Misargurides, bene.
  DA. Salve et tu. Quid de argento est ?   *TR.* Abi, sis,
  belua!
Continuo adveniens pilum iniecisti mihi.
  DA. Hic homo est inanis.   *TR.* Hic homo certe est
  hariolus.   40
  DA. Quin tu istas mittis tricas? *TR.* Quin, quid vis, cedo.
  DA. Vbi Philolaches est?   *TR.* Numquam potuisti mihi
Magis opportunus adven[ire, quam] advenis.

29. *eccum servom* Pylad.   *servom eccum* BbDc.   *servom eccum* BaDa. *servo merum* C.
30. *neque . . . neque,* so the MSS.   *nec . . . . nec* Both. R.
31. *Nec quoquam,* BbDF. *Nec quoquam* BaC. *Nequoquam* RZ.
32. *dis,* so Vulg.   *debis* the MSS.
33. *praesente* BC.   *ego homo,* so the MSS.   *homo* is omitted by Herm. R.
34. *exibent* BaCDa.
35. *me it* FZ.   *me is* CDb.   *meis* or *meas* B.   *merbis* Da.   *salvus* BbFZ.   *salus* BaCD.
36. W and others give *Hilarus est* to the Danista.
37. *Misargurides.* This is derived from Donat. in Terent. Adelph. l. l. The MSS. exhibit a variety of forms all, apparently, corrupt. *mi sartiretes* B. *misartirites* C. *mi sartiretes* DF. *mi saturites* Z. *mi Saturides* is a conj. of Camer., adopted by W.
38. *Salve et tu,* so the MSS. *Salveto* Lachm. R.   *Quid,* so Vulg. *Qui* BaCD.   *argento est—argent . est,* with the erasure of one letter, B. *argentos* CD.   *argento* FZ Vulg. W.
39. *Continuo,* so Vulg. *Continuo* Ba., an evident blunder. *Continu* CDa.
40. *est inanis* Pylad. Vulg. RW.   *inanis est* the MSS.   *certe est* RW.   *est certe* the MSS. Vulg.
41. *mittis* B.   *mittistis* CD.   *mittisti* FZ.
43. *Magis* FZ.   *Magius* B.   *Maius* or *Mavis* CD.   *oportunus* BCD.   *adven[ire quam].* There is a blank after *adven* in BCD. *adventare quam nunc advenis* F.   *advenire quam nunc advenis* Z. The reading in the text was introduced by Camer., and adopted in Vulg. RW.

DA. Quid est? TR. Concede huc. [DA. Quin mihi
argentum red]ditur?

TR. Scio te bona esse voce: [ne clama nimis]. 45

DA. Ego hercle vero clamo. TR. Ah, gere morem mihi.

DA. Quid tibi ego morem vis geram? TR. Abi, quaeso,
hinc domum.

DA. Abeam? TR. Redito huc circiter meridiem.

DA. Reddeturne igitur faenus? TR. Reddetur. *Nunc
abi.

DA. Quid ego huc recursem, aut operam sumam aut
conteram? 50

Quid si hic manebo potius ad meridiem?

TR. *Imo abi domum. Verum hercle dico. Abi *modo
domum!

DA. Quin vos mihi faenus date. Quid hic nugamini?

TR. Eu hercle!—Nae tu abi modo; ausculta mihi.

DA. Iam hercle ego illunc nominabo. TR. Euge
strenue! 55

Beatus vero es nunc, quom clamas. DA. Meum peto.

---

44. [DA. *Quin mibi argentum red*]*ditur*; the words within brackets are
blank in BCD. The text as it stands is the reading of FZ, and has been
generally adopted. R changes *argentum* into *faenus*; W *mihi* into *mi*.

45. *ne* [*clama nimis*]. There is a blank after *ne* in BCD. *ne clama*
FZ. *ne clama nimis* Camer., and this, according to Schwartzmann, is the
reading of A, which now becomes available for this play.

46. *clamo* B. The rest of the MSS. have *clamabo*. *gere morem*
mihi BbF. *gerem morem mihi* Ba. *cherem morem mibi* CD. A is said
to have MIHIMOREM.

47. *ceram* for *geram* BaCD. *bine*, so Vulg. *huoc* BaCDa, an
evident blunder.

48. *meridiem* FZRW. *meridie* BCD, but the letter M is visible at the
end of the line in A.

49. *Nunc abi*, so the MSS. W omits *nunc*. R has *Reddetur tibi*.

50. *summam* for *sumam* BcDZ, an obvious blunder. *conteram*; A
appears to have CONTERO.

52. *Abi modo domum*. A is said to have ABIMODODOMUM. The rest of
the MSS. omit *domum*, and so Vulg. W. There are said to be traces
of a line in A, wanting in all other MSS., between 52 and 53.

54. *Eu* BCD. *Tu* FZ. *Heu* R, following Schneid. *Nae*, so
Vulg. *Ne* the MSS. *Nunc* R. *abi*. It is said that A has ADI.
modo, so the MSS. *modo domum* R.

55. *illunc* BCD. *illum* FZ, and according to some, ILLUM is the
reading in A. R supposes that a line has dropped out after v. 55.

56. *Meum peto* B. *Meum puto* CD.

Multos me hoc pacto iam dies frustramini.
Molestus si sum, reddite argentum: abiero.
Responsiones omnes hoc verbo eripis.
    TR. Sortem accipe. *DA.* Imo faenus: id primum volo.   60
    TR. Quid ais tu? omnium hominum teterrume,
Venisti huc te extentatum? Agas, quod in manu est.
Non dat: non debet.   *DA.* Non debet?   *TR.* Ne γρυ
    quidem.
Ferre hoc potes? an [mavis ut ali] quo abeat foras
Vrbem exul [linquat factus] hic causa tui?   65
Quoi sortem [vix dare] licebit?   *DA.* Quin non peto.
Mihi faenus *reddunt, faenus actutum mihi.
Molestus ne sis; nemo dat; age, quod lubet.
Tu solus, credo, faenore argentum datas?

59. *omnes* (acc.) all the MSS. *omnis* R.   VERBOERIPIS A. *verbo eripit* BaCDFZ. *verbo eripite* Bb Camer. *verbum eripit* Rost. W.
61. QVIDAISTVOMNIPMHOMINVMTAETERR . . . so A.   *Quid tu hominem omnium* BaCD, where Bb has *hominum*. *teterrime* BCDb. *terrime* Da. *deterrime* FZ.   *Quid ais tu? tun', hominum omnium teaterrume* R.   *Quid? tu, ted, homo hominum omnium teterrume* W.
62. *te extentatum* BCD. *tu extentatum* F. *te* omitted by ZW.
63. *Ne gru quidem*, an Ingenious conj. of Acidal. The MSS. have *Nec erit quidem.*
64, 65, 66. So BCD, excluding the words and letters within brackets, which are blank in the MSS., and were supplied on conj. by Camer. Moreover, in v. 64 all have *habeat*, and in v. 65, B has *bis*, and not *hic*, as in CD. It is to be observed, that some scholars affirm that they have succeeded in deciphering v. 65 in A, and that it stands thus—

            VRBEEXOLATVMFACIATHICCAVSATVA.

It is quite unnecessary to enumerate the conj. of different scholars, as they are mere works of imagination.
67. This line is altogether wanting in BCDFZ. Traces of it are certainly to be found in A, and some scholars have professed to decypher it as follows, although the commencement, at all events, is very doubtful—

            MIHIFAENVSREDDVNTFAENVSACTVTVMMIHI,

where REDDVNT is evidently corrupt, but may be easily corrected REDDANT, or, as R proposes, REDDAT.   Instead of this line we find from the time of Camerarius the verse—

            Ela, mastigia, ad me redi!   *Tr.* Iam istic ero,

which is placed more properly at v. 32 of the next scene.
68. *quod lubet* Ba. *quid lubet* the rest of the MSS. W.
68, 69. Both., who is followed by W, would place these lines after v. 77.

DA. Cedo faenus! redde faenus! faenus reddite! 70
Daturin' estis faenus actutum mihi?
Date mihi faenus! *TR.* Faenus illic, faenus hic!
Nescit quidem nisi faenus fabularier
Veterator, neque ego tetriorem beluam
Vidisse me umquam quemquam, quam te, censeo. 75
DA. Non edepol nunc me tu istis verbis territas.
Calidum hoc est; etsi procul abest, urit male.
    TII. Quod illuc est faenus, upsecro, quod illic petit?
    TR. Pater eccum advenit peregre non multo prius
Illius; is tibi et faenus et sortem dabit : 80
Ne inconciliare quid nos porro postules.
Vide, num moratur? *DA.* Quin feram, si quid datur.
    TII. Quid ais tu? *TR.* Quid vis? *TII.* Quis illic est?
    quid illic petit?
Quid Philolachetem gnatum compellat [meum]
Sic, et praesenti tibi facit convicium 85
Quid illi debetur? *TR.* Opsecro hercle iube

71. *Daturin' estis,* so Vulg. *Datur inestis* B.
72. *Date mibi fenus* BC. According to some, A has DATVRIN-
FAENVSMIHI, according to others, DATVR . . . . . . SMIHI. *Daturus fenus* R.
74. *Veterator neque;* this is a conj. of Camerarius, Ingenious, but not
certain. *Vetro tene que* B. *Vetro te neque* C. *Vetrote neque* D. In A
we read UNO . . NEQVE, or, according to others, VETOTENEQVE, neither of
which is intelligible. *beluam* BbF. *belum* BaCDb. *bellum* DaZ.
75. *me umquam quemquam quam te* B. MEUMQUAMQUEMQUAMTE A.
CD are in confusion.
76. *me tu istis* CDF. *me tu tuis* B. MEISTIS A. *tu me istis* R.
77. *abest urit male,* so Plus. *babes turitamale* B. *babes turita male*
CD. This line is found in this place in all the MSS., including A, but R,
following Acidal., places it after v. 132, and brackets it. W inserts after
v. 77 the two lines given above as 68, 69.
78. ILLVC A. The rest of the MSS. *illud.* *quod illic petit* AB.
et sortem (sorte D) *dabis* CD. .
79. W brackets [79 . . . 85].
80. *tibi et,* so the MSS. R omits *et.*
81. *quad* B.
84. *[meum.]* This word is not found in the MSS., and was supplied by
Camer. Other edd. propose *feras,* and so W.
85. *presenti* B. *convitium* BbCDF. *contium* Ba.
86. *errk* CD.
86, 87. The MSS. here are corrupt. BCD have—
        . . . hercle iubi ꝗ Obi argentum,

Obici argentum ob os impurae beluae.

TH. Iubeam?   TR. Iube homini argento os verberarier.

DA. Perfacile ego ictus perpetior argenteos.

TH. Quod illud argentum est?   TR. Est—huic debet

     Philolaches   90

Paulum.   TH. Quantillum?   TR. Quasi quadraginta minas.

    DA. Ne sane id multum censeas; paulum id quidem est.

    TR. Audin? videtur, opsecro hercle, idoneus,

Danista qui sit, genus quod improbissumum est?

    TH. Non ego [nunc] istuc curo, qui sit, unde sit :   95

Id volo mihi dici, id me scire expeto :

Adeo etiam argenti faenus creditum audio.

for which we find in F—

          . . . hercle iube ‖ Obiici argentum.

and so Vulg.   W has—

          . . . iube obiici ‖ Argentum,

R has—

          . . . hercle, te obici ‖ Iube huic argentum.

Camer. conj.—

          . . . hercle te iube ‖ Obici argentum huic.

87. *ob os impurae beluae*—*obusim purae beluae* B. *obos impura ebrlue* CD, *buir ob as* Camer. Vulg.

88. *Iubeam!* T R. *Iube homini*, so Pylad. from his MSS. Vulg. W. *Iubeam*. T R. *Iube in homine* Ba (*iuben homini* Bb). *Iubeam? Iube in homini* CDa. R has *Quid iubeam?* T R. *Huic homini argento os verberarier*. *argento os*, so Pius. *argentos* B. *argentos* the rest of the MSS.

90. R changes the ordinary arrangement of the lines after 89, and places them as follows:—93, 94, 95, 96, 90, 91, 92, 97, 98, 118, 119, 99. *argentum est*. T R. *Est huic* BCD. The Vulg. omits the second *est*, and so RW, the former writing *huice*, the latter *huiis*.

91. *Paululum* B.

92. *paulum id quidem est*, BCD give this to Tranio. Camer. Vulg. W assign the whole verse to the Danista. R has—

     Th. Paulum id quidem est?   *Tr*. Ne sane id multum censeas.

93. *Audin videtur* BCDFZ (*Audi invidetur* C).   *Audin videturus* Camer. Vulg. RW.

94. *qui sit* FZ. *quid sit* BCD.   *improbissumum* B. *improbissimum* the rest.

95. *ego* [*nunc*], so R.   *nunc* is omitted in the MSS.   *nunc ego* Both. W.

96. *Id volo mibi dici* the MSS. and Vulg., except that C omits *mibi*. W has *Illud volo dici mihi*. R rewrites the line, *Id volo mi actutum dici*.

97. *Adeo* seems to be the reading of BCD. *Ab* ∾ FZW.   *argenti faenus creditum* FZ. *argenti faenus credit* BCD, with a small space after *credit* in B. *faenus creditum argenti* R.

TR. Quatuor quadraginta illi debentur minae.
Dic te daturum, ut abeat.   *TH.* Ego dicam dare?
   TR. Dic. *TH.* Egone?   *TR.* Tu ipsus. Dic modo!
   ausculta mihi!   100
Promitte! age, inquam: ego iubeo.   *TH.* Responde
   mihi :
Quid eo est argento factum? *TR.* Salvom est. *TH.* Sol-
   vite
Vosmet igitur, si salvom est.   *TR.* Aedes filius
Tuus emit.   *TH.* Aedis?   *TR.* Aedis.   *TH.* Euge,
   Philolaches
Patrissat! iam homo in mercatum vortitur.   105
Ain' tu? aedis? *TR.* Aedis, inquam. Sed scin', quoius-
   modi?
   TH. Qui scire possim?   *TR.* Vah!   *TH.* Quid est?
   TR. Ne me roga.
   TH. Nam quid ita?   *TR.* Specula claras, clarorem
   merum.
   TH. Bene hercle factum! Quid? eas quanti destinat?
   TR. Talentis magnis totidem, quot ego et tu
   sumus.   110
Sed arraboni has dedit quadraginta minas.

98. *quatuor* AC. *quatuor* BD and the rest.
101, 103. *Salvom* all apparently.
103. *aedes* (acc.) all the MSS.
104. *aedis* (acc.) twice in all the MSS.
105. *Patrissat iam* Dc. *Patrissat inm* Da. *Patrissatiam* Ba. *Patri-*
iatim Bb. *Patris etia* C. *in mercatura vortitur*, so Camer., this being
in reality the reading of the MSS. *inmercatur avortitur* B, and so CD
employing contractions.
106. *An tu* Ba. *aedis* (acc.) twice in all. So *aedis* (nom.) v. 113,
and (acc.) v. 114. In v. 141 we have *aedis* and *fores*. *Sed scin* Bb.
Sed sint Ba. *Sed in* CD. *quoiusmodi* the MSS.
107. *possum*, so the MSS. *possim* Camer. Vulg. W.
108. So the MSS., except that they have *canorem*, which Camer.
changed into *clarorem*. R supposes that the line is made up of the
mutilated fragments of two lines.
110. *magnis* Bb. *amagnis* BaCD. *a magnis* FZ. *quot* BbZ.
quod BaCDF.
111. *Sed* BC. *Si* DFZ. *arraboni*, so the MSS., without the *b*.
R supposes that a line has fallen out after v. 111.

Hinc sumpsit, quas ei dedimus. Satin' intellegis?
Nam postquam haece aedis ita erant, ut dixi tibi,
Continuo est alias aedis mercatus sibi.

TH. Bene hercle factum l DA. Heus, iam adpetit
    meridies. 115

TR. Apsolve hunc, quaeso, vomitum; ne hic nos
    enecet.

Quatuor quadraginta illi debentur minae,
Et sors et faenus. DA. Tantum est; nihilo plus peto.

TR. Velim quidem hercle, ut uno numo plus petas.

TH. Adulescens, mecum rem habe. DA. Nempe aps
    te petam? 120

TH. Petito cras. DA. Abeo: sat habeo, si cras fero.

TR. Malum—quod isti di deaeque omnes duint:
Ita mea consilia perturbat penissume.
Nullum edepol hodie genus est hominum tetrius
Nec minus bono cum iure, quam danisticum. 125

TH. Qua in regione istas aedis emit filius?

TR. Ecce autem perii! TH. Dicisne hoc, quod te
    rogo?

TR. Dicam; sed nomen domini quaero quid siet.

TH. Age, comminiscere ergo. TR. Quid ego nunc
    agam,

112. *Hinc*, so Pylad. *Hic* the MSS. *quas ei* B. *quasi* the rest
of the MSS.
113. *haec cedis* B. *haec cedis* C. *haecredis* D. *hic aedis* F Z.
ita erant Camer. *iterant* BC. *iterant* D. *viderat* F Z.
115. *adpetit* BaCD. *meridies*, so Saracen. *meridie* the MSS.
116. *quaeso* BC. *vomitum*, so the MSS. *quaeso: vomitu ne* Both. R.
enecet all the MSS.: comp. *intellego*.
120. *babe* B. *babri* CDFZ.
121. *abeo sat* Bb. *babeo sat* BaCD.
122. *di dcaeque* Bb. *de deaq* .. Ba. *de deaeque* CDa. *dii deaeque* F Z.
123. *penissume*, so Priscian, pp. 608, 1008. *plenissime* BCDF. *plan-
issime* Z. Priscian, in quoting this line, has *pervertit* for *perturbat*.
124. *hodie genus est.* A is said to have GENVSESTHODIE. *tetrius*
the MSS.
126. *aedis* or *edis* (acc.) the MSS., and so v. 131.
128. *quid* the MSS. *quod* Z W. *siet* Vulg. *sciet* BaCZ. *sciaet*
D, evident blunders.

Nisi ut in vicinum hunc proxumum mendacium? 130
Eas emisse aedis huius dicam filium.
Calidum hercle audivi esse optumum mendacium;
[Calidum hoc est: etsi procul abest, urit male.]
Quidquid dei dicunt, id rectum est dicere.
   TH. Quid igitur? iam commentus?   *TR.* Di istum
      perduint!   135
—Imo istunc potius!—De vicino hoc proxumo
Tuus emit aedis filius.   *TH.* Bonan' fide?
   TR. Si quidem es argentum redditurus, tum bona;
Si redditurus non es, non emit bona.
   TH. Non in loco emit perbono.   *TR.* Imo in
      optumo.   140
   TH. Cupio hercle inspicere hasce aedis: pultadum fores
Atque evoca aliquem intus ad te, Tranio.
   TR. Ecce autem iterum nunc, quid dicam, nescio.
Iterum iam ad unum saxum me fluctus ferunt.
Quid nunc? Non hercle, quid nunc faciam, reperio;   145

---

130. *Nisi ut* BC. *ut* is omitted in DFZ, and so W. *proximum*
BCDZ. So *proximo* Bc, v. 136. *mendacium*, so the MSS., except B,
which has *mendatium*. *proximum [rem conferam]* R.
131. *Eas* the MSS. *Eius* R.
133. See above, v. 77 of this scene.
134. *id rectum est* B. *id decretum est* CDW. R partly following
Acidal. thus rewrites the line—
    Quicquid dehinc dicam, nunc id certum est dicere.
135. *commentus*, so the MSS., but this is probably a contraction for
commentu's, and so R prints it. *Di istum* D. *diis tuum* B. *Dristum*
C. *perdunt* D. *perdivnt* FZ.
136. *istunc* FZ. *istuc* BCD. *pocius* C.
140. PERBONO IMMOIN A. *in* is omitted in BCDFZ. *perbono bas.
Immo* Vulg. W.
141. *hasce aedis* the MSS., including A. *has aedis* Vulg. W. *fores*
all the MSS.
142. *evoca*, so the MSS., including A. *evocato* Pylad. Vulg. W.
aliquem intus, so the MSS., including A. *aliquem huc intus* R.
ADTETRANIO A. *ut te terum* BaCDF. Pius arrived at the true reading
by conj.
143. *autem iterum nunc quid dicam*, so the MSS. *quid ego* Camer.
Vulg. R has *perii* instead of *iterum*. AUTEM . . . . NVNCQVID A.
144. *unum*, so the MSS., including A. *ferunt* ABC. *eferunt* Da.
efferunt FZ.
145. REPERIO A. *reterio* BCD. Camer. arrived at the true reading
by conj.

H

Manufesto teneor. *TH.* Evocadum aliquem ocius :
Roga, circumducat. *TR.* Heus tu! At hic sunt mulieres :
Videndum est primum, utrum eae velintne, an non velint.
   TH. Bonum aequomque oras : percontare et roga.
Ego hic tantisper, dum exis, te opperiar foris.   150
   TR. Di te deaeque omnis funditus perdant, senex :
Ita mea consilia undique oppugnas male.
Euge, optume, eccum, aedium dominus foras
Simo progreditur ipsus. Huc concessero,
Dum mihi senatum consilii in cor convoco :   155
Igitur tum accedam hunc, quando quid agam invenero.

ACTVS III. SCENA II.

SIMO. THEVROPIDES. TRANIO.

   SI. Melius anno hoc mihi non fuit domi,
Nec quod una esca me iuverit magis.

146. *manufesto* ABCD.   ocivs, so A.   *foras* the rest of the MSS.
and edd., except R.
   147. *At hic* ABF.   *At hinc* CDZ.
   148. VIDENDVMST A.   *velintne an non* BCDFZ. According to
some, A has VELINTAVTNON, according to others, VELINTNEAVTNON.
   149. *aequom* B.   *oras,* so the MSS., but according to some, A has
ROGAS.   *percontare,* so the MSS. (PERCVNCTARE A). *percontare dum*
Both. W. *i percontare* R.
   151. DITE AD.   *Dite* B.   *De te* C.   *Dii te* FZ.   *omnis* (nom.
plur.) BCD.
   152. *consilia undique,* so the MSS., including A.   *consilia tu undique* R.
MALE A. *male* the rest of the MSS.
   153. EVGAE A. *Fuge* the rest of the MSS. Camer. conjectured *Euge.*
obtume CD.   *eccum aedium,* so the MSS. *eccum huc aedium* R.
   155. MIHI A.   *mi* the rest of the MSS.   *consilii,* so the MSS.
consili RW.
   156. *Igitur* AB.   *Itur* CD.   *tum,* so the MSS., including A.
dum Vulg.   *hunc* B.   *huc* the rest of the MSS., including A.
invenero, so Vulg. *invenero* BaDb. *invenero* C. *invero* Da.

In the Canticum which follows, we have adhered to the distribution of
lines presented in AB.
   2. NECQVODVNAESCAMEIVVERIT A, it being doubtful whether we
should read *me iuverit* or *meruerit*. *Nequadeit caussa meruerit* B. *Ne
quod est caussam eruerit* C. *Nec quod est caussa meruerit* D. *Nec quando
una esca meruerit magis* Vulg. W, but the latter has *me* before *meruerit*.

Prandium uxor mihi perbonum dedit ;
Nunc dormitum iubet me ire. Minume!
Non mihi forte visum ilico fuit,   5
Melius quom prandium, quam solet, dedit :
Voluit in cubiculum abducere me anus.
Non bonum est somnium de prandio; apage!
Clanculum ex aedibus me edidi foras.
Tota turget mihi uxor scio [nunc], domi.   10
  TR. Res parata est mala in vesperum huic seni :
Nam et cenandum ei et cubandum est male.
  ST. Quom magis cogito cum meo animo :
Si quis dotatam uxorem atque anum habet

1. PRANDIUM AFZ.   *Peronium* BC, but with *prandium* written above
in B by an old hand.   *Peronnium* D.
4. MEIRE A.   *mirire* BaCDa,   *me ire* BbDbFZ.   *ire me* W.
minime the MSS.
5. *iliro* ABDc.   *iloco* Da.   *in loco* CFZ.
6. QVAMPRANDIUMQUAMSOLET A.   *quam prandium quam solum* BaCD.
(*quom solum* Bb.)   *quom prandium quam solitum* Vulg.   We have exhibited
in the text the reading of A, with the slight change of *quam* into *quom*,
and so R.
7. *abducere me anus*, so A and B.   *abducerem eamus* CD, whence
abducere : eamus FZ.
8. BONVMSTSOMNIVM A, or, according to others, BONVMESTOMNVM.
bonus somnus est BCD Vulg.   *bonust somnus* R.   *bonus somnus de prandio
est* W.
9. *me edidi*, so the MSS., including A,   *me dedi* R.
10. *scio* [*nunc*].   A omits *nunc*, which is found in the rest of the MSS.
nunc scio Camer. Vulg. W.
11. *parata est* A and the rest of the MSS.   *mala* the MSS., except
A, which has MALE.
12. *cenandum* ABCD.   CENANDVMEIETCVBANDVMSTMALE, so A,
except that there is some doubt with regard to the letters that make up *ei
et*, for one critic decyphers CENANDVMSTETCVBANDVMESTMALE.   *cenandum
et cubandumst ui trabis male* BD (*uitrabis* D).   *cenandum et cubandum
sunt uitra bis male* C, whence *cenandum et cubandum est intus male*
Camer. Vulg. W. (*intus est* W).   R has *cenandum et cubandumst ei
male*.
13. *cum* A.   *quom* the rest.   *cogito*, so the MSS., including A.
cogito ego Pylad. Camer. Vulg.
14. VKOREMATQVEANVMHABET, this is said to be the reading of A.
In BCD there is a blank between *uxorem* and *habet*.   FZ and the Vulg.
have *uxorem habet* without making any blank.   *uxorem atque anum homo
habet* R.   W presents the line thus—

Si quis dotatam habet, neminem sopor] Sollicitat.

Neminem sollicitat sopor: ibi omnibus   15
Ire dormitum odio est, velut nunc mihi.
Exsequi certa res est, ut abeam
Potius hinc ad forum, quam domi cubem.
Atque pol nescio ut moribus sient
Vostrae: haec, sat scio, quam me habeat male;   20
Peius posthac fore, quam fuit, mihi.
   TR. [Si] abitus tuus tibi, senex, fecerit male,
Nihil erit, quod deorum ullum accusites;
Te ipse iure optumo merito incuses licet.
Tempus nunc est senem hunc adloqui mihi.   25
Hoc habet! repperi, qui senem ducerem,
Quo dolo a me dolorem procul pellerem.
Accedam. Di te ament plurumum, Simo.
   SI. Salvos sis, Tranio.   *TR.* Vt vales?   *SI.* Non male.
Quid agis?   *TR.* Hominem optumum teneo.   *SI.* Amice
   facis,   30

15. *Neminem*, so the MSS., including A. *Eum bominem* R, which destroys the sense.   SOPORIBIOMNIBUS is said to be the reading of A. The rest of the MSS. have *sopo* or *sopor*, omitting *ibi omnibus*, and so Vulg. W.
16. ODIOESTVELUTNUNCMIHI is said to be the reading of A. The rest of the MSS. omit the words *velut nunc mibi. adio estue* BaD (*est ve* C). *adio est urro* Bb.   *ire dormitum mibi adio est* W.   *veluti* R.
17. *abeam* Vulg.   *babeam* BaCD.   *ut ego abeam* W.
20. *Vostrae: bare*, so the MSS., including A.   *Vastrae: at bare* R. *me babeat*, so the MSS. (B omits *me*).   *babet* Herm. W (*quae* Herm.)
21. *Peius* ABbDbFZ.   *Pelius* BaCDa.   *Priusque* Camer. Vulg.
22. [*Si*] *abitus*. The MSS. omit *Si*. It was suggested by Camer., and has been admitted by most edd.
23. *ullum* AFZ.   *nullum* B.   *nullum* CD.
24. *Te ipse*. A is said to have TEIPSUM.   *optimo* BCDZ.   v. 29 *plurimum* all; v. 63 *maximo* all; v. 86 *maximas* all; and v. 138 *infimo* all.   *merito incuses* BbFZ.   *merito incusis* BaCD.   *incusites* omitting *merito* R.
25. *alloqui mibi* Camer. A is said to have ADLOQUIMIHI.   *adloqui-mini* BCD.   *alloqui me* FZ.
26. *repperi* ABCD.   *senem* B. Both here and in the preceding line CDa have *semen*, an evident blunder.
27. *Quo* Vulg.   *Quod* BaCD, an evident blunder.
28. R has *accedam bus*, but *bus* is not found in the MSS.
29. *saltus*, so B, but corrupted.
30. *teneo amice* FZ.   *te acotamice* Ba.   *teneo va mice* C.   *teneo vamice* BbDa.   *teneo vab amice* Dc.

Quom me laudas.   *Tr.* Decet certe.   *Si.* Hercle, *te habeo hau
Bonum teneo servom.
  Th. Heia, mastigia, ad me redi!   *Tr.* Iam istic ero.
  Si. Quid nunc? quam mox?   *Tr.* Quid est?   *Si.* Quod
    solet fieri.
  Tr. Dic [igitur, quod solet fieri], quid id est?   35
  [*Si.* Quid facitis vos?   Sed ut verum, Tranio], loquar,
Sic decet, [ut homines sunt], ita morem geras,
Vita quam sit brevis, simul cogita ... Quid?
  Tr. Ehem, vix tandem percepi, super his rebus nostris
    te loqui.
  Si. Musice hercle agitis aetatem ita, ut vos decet: 40

31, 32. We have printed these two lines in the corrupt and mutilated
form in which they appear in BCD. In B there are several corrections
by a late hand.   In v. 31 C has *mel audis* for *me laudas*, and D has *diret*
for *decet*, while the words *Haudbonumteneoservvom* are said to be legible in A.
Camer. thus remodels the lines—

  Quom me laudas.   *Tr.* Decet certe.   *Si.* Certe hercle; at ego te
  Haud bonum teneo servom.   *Tr.* Quid ita vero, Simo

It is unnecessary to enumerate the conjectures of other scholars, all being
alike mere flights of imagination.
  33. This line appears in a corrupt form in the MSS.   A is said to have
HEIAMASTIGIAADMEREDICUMERO, the three letters below which we have
placed dots being very doubtful.   B has *Eia mastigia ad me redieram
istic ero*   C has *Etiam astigia admere die amistierro*.   D has *Eia mastigia
ad me redic*.   *am istierro*, with a space.   Combining these we form the
Vulg. which is given in the text, and probably approximates to the true
reading.   It has been adopted by RW, who, however, have *isti* instead
of *istic*.   In the Vulg. the line is placed at v. 71 of the preceding scene.
R places it at v. 52 of this scene.
  34, 35, 36, 37, 38, 39, 40.   Here again the MSS. are sadly mutilated.
The words which appear in the text within brackets are the conjectures
by which Camer. endeavoured to fill up the blanks.   In v. 34 A is said to
exhibit QUODSOLETFIERIHIC, and another line appears which has been
thus deciphered—

    INTVSQUIDIDESTSCISTIBIQUOD .... SOLETFIERI.

BCDF agree, except that in v. 35 *Ibi* is found in Bb only.   B has *Lis*.
CDF have *His*, and in v. 38 CD have *brevi*, and CDF *simul*, while *simul* is
added as a correction in B.   Camer. Vulg. W. print v. 40 as two lines—

    Tr. Quid? ehem uix tandem
    Percepi super his rebus nostris te loqui.

The last line is quoted by Festus (p. 305, ed. Müll.), where we read
percipio and *loqui te*, omitting *his*.
  40. *statrm* BaC.

Vino et victu, piscatu probo, electili,
Vitam colitis. *TR.* Imo vita antehac erat ;
Nunc nobis omnia haec exciderunt.
  SI. Quidum? *TR.* Ita oppido occidimus omnes, Simo.
  SI. Non taces ? Prospere vobis cuncta usque adhuc
    processerunt.   45
  TR. Ita ut dicis, facta haud nego : nos
Profecto probe, ut voluimus, viximus ;
Sed, Simo, ita nunc ventus navem
Deseruit. *SI.* Quid est ? Quo modo ? *TR.* Pessumo.
  SI. Quaene subducta erat tuto in terra ?   50
  TR. Hei ! *SI.* Quid est ? *TR.* Me miserum! occidi !
  SI. Qui ? *TR.* Quia
Venit navis, nostrae navi quae frangat ratem.
  SI. Velim, ut tu velles, Tranio. Sed quid est negoti ?
    TR. Eloquar.
Herus peregre venit.   *SI.* Tunc [tibi actutum] chor [da]
  tenditur,

---

41. *Vino et victu*, so the MSS. W omits *et*.
42. *Immo vita* FZ. *Immovit* BaCDa. *Immo ut* BbDb. *Immo ita ea quidem* W.
43. *nobis omnia*, so Pylad. Camer. *nobis communia* the MSS. *nobis simitu omnia* Herm. R. *nobis omnia haec exciderunt simul* W.
44. *hic oppido* Herm R, but *hic* is not in the MSS.
45, 46, 47. We have arranged these lines exactly as they appear in B. Camer. places *processerunt* at the commencement of v. 47, and *nos* at the commencement of v. 48, and is followed by Vulg. RW.
48, 49, 50, 51, 52. Here again we have followed the arrangement of D. W places *navem* at the beginning of v. 50. R departs much more widely from the distribution of B.
48. *ventus navem*, so the MSS. *ventus navem nostram* R.
50. *Quaene*, so Pylad. Vulg. RW. *Quae nec* BCD.
51. *ni* BCD. *Me miserum*, so the MSS. *Heu me miserum* R.
52. *nostre* C.
53. *Velim*, so the MSS. *Vellem* Both. R. *ut tu velles*, so the MSS. *tu* omitted in Vulg. W. *Tranio sed quid est* FZ. *Trannios est* Ba. *Trannius est* with a space CD. *negoii* BFZ. *negoti* CD. *Eloquar* BbCDFZ. *Eloqurre* Ba. R has *Ego eloquar.*
54. 55. These lines appear in a mutilated form in BCD; in B they stand thus —

    Erus venit peregre venit. Si. Tunc . . . . . Cor tenditur

    Inde ferriterium postea . . . . . enus obscuro,

Inde ferriterium; postea—[*Tr.* Pol per tua te g]enua
    opsecro   55
Ne indicium hero facias meo. *Si.* E me, ne quid metuas,
    nil sciet.
  Tr. Patrone, salve.   *Si.* Nil moror mi istiusmodi
    cluentis.
  Tr. Nunc hoc, quod ad te noster me misit senex . . . .
  Si. Hoc mihi responde primum, quod ego te rogo:
Iam de istis rebus voster quid sensit senex ?   60
  Tr. Nihil quicquam. *Si.* Numquid increpavit filium ?
  Tr. Tam liquidus est, quam liquida esse tempestas
    solet.
Nunc te hoc orare iussit opere maxumo,
Vt sibi liceret inspicere has aedis tuas.
  Si. Non sunt venales.   *Tr.* Scio equidem istuc ; sed
    senex   65
Gunaeceum aedificare volt hic in suis,
Et balineas et ambulacrum et porticum.
  Si. Quid [ille] consomniavit ?   *Tr.* Ego dicam tibi.
Dare volt uxorem filio, quantum potest :
Ad eam rem facere volt novom gunaeceum.   70

and so CD, except that they omit the first *venit*, and D has *omnia*. In FZ
they are thus corrected—

        Herus peregre venit. *Si.* Tuus ne. *Tr.* Cor tenditur
        Inde ferit iterum . postea hem obsecro.

The supplements given in the text are those of Ritschl, and are less
violent than those suggested by Camer., and those adopted in the Vulg.
and W.
  56. *inditium* CDF.   *sciet* BbF.   *sciat* BaCD.   *siet* Z.
  57. *clientis* (acc.) all except Ba, which has *clientes*.
  58. *me misit*, so Vulg.   *meme misit* BCD.   R believes that
something has fallen out after v. 59.
  61. *Nihil quicquam . Numquid* FZ.   *Nihil quicquam unum quid* BD.
unum quid C, omitting *nihil quicquam* here, and inserting it at the end
of the following line.
  62. *liquidus est*, so Camer.   *liquidum est* the MSS.   *quam nihil
quicquam* C at the end of the line.
  64. *has* B.   *hauce* CDFZ.   *edis* (acc.) BD.
  66. *Gineceum* Ba.   *Gyneceum* Bb and the rest of the MSS.   *edi-
ficare* CZ.
  68. *Quid [ille]*, so Camer.   The MSS. omit *ille*.   *Hem quid* R.
  70. *novum gynecium* the MSS.   *gynaeceum novom* Both. W.

Nam sibi laudasse hasce ait architectonem
Nescio quem, esse aedificatas has sane bene :
Nunc hinc exemplum capere volt, nisi tu nevis ....
*Nam ille eo malum hinc opere exemplum petit.
*Quia est auditum esse aestate ibidem victum perbonum;   75
*Te sub sole (diu ?) col [ere] usque perpetuom diem.
   Si. Imo edepol vero, quom usquequaque umbra est,
     tamen
Sol semper hic est usque a mani ad vesperum;
Quasi flagitator astat usque ad ostium;
Nec mihi umbra usquam est, nisi si in puteo quaepiam
     est.   80

71. *laudavisse* R. *hasce* B. The rest of the MSS. omit the word.
architectonem B. *architectorem* BbDFZ. *architectetorem* C.
72. *esse aedificatas* B. A is said to have AEDIFICATASESSE. The rest
of the MSS. omit *esse*.
74, 75, 76. The MSS. here are miserably mutilated. The reading in
A, as far as it can be decyphered, is the following, dots being placed under
those letters which are doubtful :—

    NAMILLEEOMALUMHINCOPERE . . . .

    QVIAESTAUDITUMESSEAESTATEIBIDEMVICTUMPERBONUM

    TESUBSOLECOLUMEMUSQUEPERPETUUMDIEM.

B has—

   Nam ille eo mal . no   . . .   opere exte exemplum petit

   Quia hic. . . . . Et est ate perbonam

   Subdiu col . . . . perpetuum diem.

In v. 74 CD *eo malo* distinctly, and omit *exte*. In v. 75 *esse estate perbonam*
CD (*aestate* C). In v. 76 C has *col perpetuum diem*, without any mark of
a blank. FZ contract the three lines into two, as follows :—

   Nam ille malo quidem ab opere exemplum petit
   Quia hic esse estate perbonam subdiu sol perpetuű diem.

F, however, omits *quidem*. R has—

   Si. Ne ille ex malo malum hinc opere exemplum petit.
   Tr. Quin aestu audivit esse sibi victum perbonum
     Subdiu colere te usque perpetuam diem.

W has—

   Si. Nae ille malo quidem ab opere sibi exemplum petit.
   Tr. Quia hic audivit esse aestatem perbonam
     Subdiu coll has solere perpetuum diem,

which approaches closely to the Vulg.

78. *mani*, so Serv. ad. Virg. Æn. I. 19. *mane* BCDFZ.
79. *bastion* CDFZ, and v. 106 DFZ. *astat*, so the MSS.,
except FZ.

TR. Quid? Sarsinatis ecqua est, si Vmbram non
   habes?
St. Molestus ne sis. Haec sunt sicut praedico.
TR. Attamen inspicere volt.   *St.* Inspiciat, si lubet.
Si quid erit, quod illi placeat, de exemplo meo
Ipse aedificato.   *TR.* Eon'? voco huc hominem?   *St.* [I,]
   voca.   85
   TR. Alexandrum   magnum   atque   Agathoclem   aiunt
   maxumas
Duo res gessisse: quid mihi fiet tertio,
Qui solus facio facinora inmortalia?
Vehit hic clitellas, vehit hic autem alter senex.
Novitium mihi quaestum institui non malum: 90
Nam muliones mulos clitellarios
Habent; ego habeo homines clitellarios.
Magni sunt oneris; quidquid inponas, vehunt.
Nunc hunc haud scio an conloquar. Congrediar.
Heus, Theuropides!   *Th.* Hem, quis hic nominat me?   95
   TR. Hero servos multum suo fidelis.

80. *mibi ambra usquam est* BCD.   MIHIVMBRA .. VSQVAMST A,
whence R *ner mi umbra ibi usquamst*, but As ESTVSQUAM.   *nisi si*
ABCDF.   *si* is omitted in Z Vulg.
81. QUIDARSINATIS A.   *ecqua est* FZ.   *ecquam est* B.   *et
qud* CD.
82. *predico* Bc.
85. *I vera*, so Acidal.   The MSS. omit *I*, which may have been
swallowed up in the last letter of *St.*, the name of the speaker.
87. *tercio* C.
88. *facio* Ba.   *inmortalia*, so BD.
89. *Vehit clitellas* Bb.   Ba and the rest of the MSS. omit *hic*.
90. *novicium* C.   *questum* all.
92. *habeo homines*, so the MSS., including A.   *homines habeo* Pylad.
homines (acc.) all.
93. *buerris* BA.
94. *baucio* in B.   *baudirio* in A.   *conloquar* AB.
94,95. These two lines are somewhat confused in BCD, but are
distinctly legible in A, as given in the text.   *Congredibar* RW.   *quis
me nominat* W.   *quis nominat me*, omitting *hic*, Vulg.
96. *servos* B.   *servus* A and the rest.   *multum suo fidelis*, so B.
There is a space in CD after *suo*, and *fidelis* is omitted.   A appears
to have—
                MVLTIMODISFILIVS VNVSEST,

1

Quo me miseras, adfero omne impetratum.
Th. Quid illic, opsecro, tam diu restitisti?
Tr. Seni non erat otium: id sum opperitus.
Th. Antiquom optines hoc tuum, tardus ut sis.   100
Tr. Heus tu, si voles verbum hoc cogitare,
Simul flare sorbereque haud factu facile est:
Ego hic esse et illi simul haud potui.
Th. Quid nunc? *Tr.* Vise, specta, tuo usque arbitratu.
Th. Age, duc me. *Tr.* Num moror? *Th.* Supse-
quor te.   105
Tr. Senex ipsus te ante ostium, eccum, opperitur.
Sed [is] maestus est, se hasce vendidisse.
Th. Quid tandem? *Tr.* Orat, ut suadeam Philolacheti,
Vt istas remittat sibi. *Th.* Haud opinor.

whence R—
          Tr. Ero servos multimodis suo fidus.   *Tb.* Vnde is?
W has—
          Hero servos multum fidelis suo.
97. *Qmd* Ba.   *Qmd* Bb.   *Qm* the rest of the MSS.   MISSERAS
A, and so R.   *misras* the rest of the MSS.   *adfero* AB.   *affero*
the rest.   *impetratum*, so BD.
98. *dstitisti*, so all MSS., including A.   *restitisti* has been adopted by
almost all edd. since Lambinus.
99. ERATOTIUM A.   The rest of the MSS. have *otium erat*, and so
Vulg.
100. *obtines hoc* the MSS.   *hoc obtines* Camer. Vulg.   SIES A.
101. *verbum hoc*, so the MSS., including A.   *hoc verbum* R.
102. HAUDFACTUFACILEST A, and so with *facile est* CDFZ.   *aut factu*
facile est Ba (*aut* Bb).   *haud facile est* Camer. Vulg., omitting *factu*
and *est*.
103. *illi simul haut potui* B.   *illic simul et haud potui* CDFZ.   *illi*
similtu hau potivi R.
104. *Quid nunc*   *vise specta* BCD.   QVIDNUNVIS VISAS A.   TUO-
USQARBITRATU A.   *usque* is omitted in all other MSS., and in all edd.
before R.
105. *Age duc me*, so the MSS., including A.   *Age, i, duc me* RW.
Num Bb.   *Nunc* BaCD.
106. IPSUS A.   *ipse* the rest of the MSS. and the edd. before R.
te ante B.   The rest of the MSS. omit *te*.   *eccum*, so the
MSS., except A, which has ILLUD.   *opperitur* CDF.   *opperibitur* B.
opperitur AZ.
107. *Sed* [is] *maestus est*.   The word *is* is not found in the MSS., but
in A we read SE . . . MAESTUSEST, with space for three letters, hence R
supplies *ut*.   W proposes *is*.   *mestus* BD.   *mustus* C.   *se hasce*, so
all the MSS., including A.   *hasce se* RW.
109. *Haus* Ba.   *Haud opinor*, so the MSS.   *Haud hercle opinor* R.

Sibi quisque ruri metit. Si male emptae   110
Forent, nobis has redhibere haud liceret.
Lucri quidquid est, id domum trahere oportet.
Misericordias [iam habere haud] hominem oportet.
    TR. Morare hercle [quom verba] facis; supsequere.
    TH. Fiat.
    TR. Do tibi ego operam. Senex illic est.—Hem, tibi
    adduxi hominem.   115
    SI. Salvom te advenisse peregre gaudeo, Theuropides.
    TH. Di te ament. *SI.* Inspicere hic aedis te has velle
    aiebat mihi.
    TH. Nisi tibi incommodum est. *SI.* Imo commodum.
    I intro atque inspice.
    TR. At enim mulieres. *SI.* Cave tu ullam floccifaxis
    mulierem.
Qualibet perambula aedis oppido tamquam tuas.   120
    TH. Tamquam? *TR.* Ah, cave tu illi obiectes nunc in
    aegritudine,
Te has emisse. Non tu vides hunc, voltu ut tristi est
    senex?
    TH. Video. *TR.* Ergo inridere ne videare et gestire
    admodum,

110. *ruri metit* B. *ruri metuit* CD. *iure melior* F. *iure metuit* Z.
111. *liceret* B. *placeret* the rest of the MSS.
113, 114. These lines appear in a mutilated form in the MSS., the
words within brackets being supplied on conj. by Camer. BCD agree,
except that *fiat* is wanting in B.
115. *Do tibi ego.* Ba has *Do tibi senex.* *illic est hem* B. *illi
est* C. *illic est em* D. *ille eccumst, em* R. *tibi adduxi hominem,*
so the MSS. *adduxi tibi hominem* Camer. W. *adduxi hominem tibi* Ald.
Both. R. *hominem adduxi tibi* Guyet.
117. *Inspicere hic aedis te,* so Camer. *Inspicere te , aedis te* B, with
an erasure. *Inspicerent aedis te* CD. *velle,* so Vulg. *belle* BD.
belle C.
118. *incommodum est,* so the MSS. *est incommodum* Both. RW.
I intro CDFZ. *I* is omitted in B.
121. *in illi* BCD. *in id illi* R. *egritudine* BC.
122. *tu vides,* so the MSS. *vides tu* Guyet. R. *ut tristi est,* so
the MSS. *uti tristis* R.
123. B omits *et.* *inridere* BbD. *irridere* Ba and the rest.

Noli facere mentionem, te [has] emisse. *TH.* Intellego,
Et bene monitum duco atque te existumo humano ingenio. 125
Quid nunc? *ST.* Quin tu is intro? atque otiose perspecta,
  ut lubet.
 TH. Bene benigneque arbitror te facere. *ST.* Factum
  edepol volo.
Vin' qui perductet?   *TH.* Apage istum perductorem.
Non placet.
 ST. Quid? [quid] est?   *TH.* Errabo potius, quam per-
  ductet quispiam.
 TR. Viden', vestibulum ante aedis hoc, et ambulacrum,
  quoiusmodi?   130
 TH. Luculentum edepol profecto!   *TR.* Age specta,
  postes quoiusmodi,
Quanta firmitate facti, et quanta crassitudine!
 TH. Non videor vidisse postis pulcriores. *ST.* Pol mihi
Eo pretio empti fuerant olim.   *TR.* Audin' "Fuerant"
  dicere?
Vix videtur continere lacrumas.   *TH.* Quanti hosce
  emeras?   135
 ST. Tris minas pro istis duobus praeter vecturam dedi.

124. *te [has] emisse* Guyet. The MSS. omit *has.* R has *te
emisse bas.*
125. *atque te existumo humani ingenio* B, the corrections being in the
original hand. *atque te existumo humani ingenio* CD. *et te esse humano
ingenio existumo* R, *atque esse existumo humani ingeni* W.
126. *ii intro atque otiose perspecta ut,* so the MSS. *i intro atiose perspecta
aedis ut* R,
127. *benigneque,* so Camer. *benique* BaCDF, *denique* Bb. *beniquu* Z.
128, 129. These lines are bracketed by W, and omitted by R, since
they occur again, with some changes, after v. 161.   In v. 129 Camer. has
Quid, quid est? but the second *quid* is not in the MSS.
130. *Viden vestibulum ante aedis hoc,* so the MSS., except that B has
aedes. *Viden hoc ante aedis vestibulum* R.   *ambulacrum* BbFZ
amplatrum BaCD.
131. *cuiusmodi* the MSS.
132. *Quanta* CDFZ. *Quam* Ba. *Qua* Bb. *Qua sint* Camer. W.
133. *pulcbriores* the MSS.
134. *pretio* C.   *Audin fuerant* F. *Audnfuerat* Ba.   *Audenfuerat*
Bb. *Autin fuerat* D.   *aut infuerat* C.
136. *tris* all.   *duobus* Z, *dubus* the MSS., an evident blunder.
preter BC.

TH. Hercle quin multum inprobiores sunt, quam a
primo credidi.
TR. Quapropter? *TH.* Quia edepol ambo ab infumo
tarmes secat.
TR. Intempestivos excisos credo; id eis vitium nocet.
Atque etiam nunc satis boni sunt, si sunt inducti
pice. 140
Non enim haec pultiphagus opifex opera fecit barbarus.
Viden' coagmenta in foribus? *TH.* Video. *TR.* Specta,
quam arte dormiunt.
TH. Dormiunt? *TR.* Illud quidem, ut conivent, volui
dicere.
Satin' habes? *TH.* Vt quicquid magis contemplor, tanto
magis placet.
TR. Viden' pictum, ubi ludificatur cornix una volturios
duos? 145
TH. Non edepol video. *TR.* At ego video *eam inter*
volturios duos
Cornix astat; ea volturios duos vicissim vellicat.
Quaeso, huc ad me specta, cornicem ut conspicere
possies.

137. *quin* Pylad. *qui* the MSS. *multum* BCD. *multo* Lamb. R.
138. *tarmes secat*, a happy conj. of Scalig. *tramisecat* B. *trami secat*
CD. *terram secant* FZ. *trames secat* Camer.
139. *vitium* D.
140. *si sunt*, so the MSS., including A. *si sint* Camer.
141. So the MSS. Vulg. R. W omits *boni*, and has *operam*. A is
said to have PULTUFAGIS.
142. *arte* ABCDR. *dormiunt*, so Vulg. *dormunt* BaCD, an
evident blunder.
143. *ubi ludificatur cornix una volturios*, such is the reading of the MSS.,
including, perhaps, A. *ut ludificat una cornix volturios* R. *ubi ludificat
cornix una volturios* W. *duos* Dc and, perhaps, A. The rest have *duo*.
146. This line is altogether wanting in BCDFZ, and was discovered
in A. The eight or nine letters between *video* and *volturios* are, however,
altogether uncertain. Schwarzmann at first believed that he could read
CORNICEMAT, and then, upon closer inspection, thought that he made out
TUMONIER. R inserts *eam inter* on conj.
147. DUOS ADc. The rest of the MSS. *duo*, and so W. *vellicat*
Bb. *vellitat* BaCDZ. *velitat* F.
148. *quaeso* BC. POSSIES A, and so Camer. The rest of the
MSS. *possis*.

Iam vides? *TH.* Profecto nullam equidem illic cornicem
intuor.

TR. At tu isto ad vos optuere, quoniam cornicem
nequis   150
Conspicari, si volturios forte possis contui.
Iam vides? *TH.* Non edepol video. *TR.* At ego volturios
duos.

TH. Omnino, ut te apsolvam, nullam pictam conspicio
hic avem.

TR. Age, iam mitto. Ignosco: aetate non quis optuerier.

TH. Haec, quae possum, ea mihi profecto cuncta vehementer placent.   155

SI. Latius demum est operae pretium ivisse. *TH.* Recte
edepol mones.

SI. Eho, istum, puer, circumduce has aedis et con-
clavia.

Nam egomet ductarem, nisi mi esset ad forum negotium.

TH. Apage istum [a] me [perductorem]: nihil moror
ductarier.

Quidquid est, [errabo potius, quam] perductet quispiam. 160

149. *cornicem intuor* Z. CORNICVMINTVOR A. *cornicem intueor* BF.
cornicem intues D.
150. *isto* ABCD. *istor* FZW. *istae* R (B has *istô*, which may
indicate *istor*).
152. This line is omitted by R. See note of W.
153. *conspitio* B.
154. *optuerier* BC, and so in reality D.
155. *Hic qur* C. *placent* BZ. *iacent* CDF.
156. *est opere tretium* Ba (*pretium* Bb). *est operae pretium* D. *est
opere precium* CFZ. *operae est pretium* Both. RW.
157. *purr,* so the MSS. *purre* Both. R. *HAS* A. *hasce* the rest
of the MSS. and most edd.
159, 160, 161. These lines appear in a very mutilated form in BCD,
and apparently in A also. We have given in the text the reading of B,
the words within brackets being the conjectures by which Camer. filled
up the blanks. BCD agree closely. All have *adis dico,* but CD place
these words at the end of v. 159 (Bb has *adis,* i. e. *adi*). All, including A,
have *igitur* after *intro eo.* Camer. supplies *a* before *me,* but there is no
blank here in the MSS., and in v. 159 he reads *Quid, quid est?* which is in
no way better than *Quidquid est,* as in BCD. These is a blank in B after
Adis dico, but none in CD). In Ca *perducet.*

Si. Aedis dico. *Th.* Ergo intro eo *igitur sine per-
    ductore? *Si.* I, licet.

Th. Ibo intro igitur. *Tr.* Mane, sis: videam, ne
    canis.... *Th.* Agedum, vide.

Tr. Est. Abi. Canis est. Abi dierecta! St! Abin'
    hinc, in malam crucem?

At etiam restas? St! abi istinc! *Si.* Nihil pericli est.
    Age.

Tam placida est, quam est aqua, vise: ire intro audacter
    licet.   165

Eo ego hinc ad forum. *Th.* Fecisti commode. Bene
    ambula.—

Tranio, age, canem istam a foribus [aliquis] abducat face,

Etsi non metuenda est. *Tr.* Quin tu illam aspice, ut
    placide accubat!

Nisi molestum vis videri te atque ignavom.... *Th.* Iam,
    ut lubet.

Tr. Sequere hac me igitur. *Th.* Equidem haud usquam
    a pedibus apscedam tuis.   170

---

162. *igitur est* BCD, but Bb has *est.* *Mane sis ut videam* C.
vide Z. The MSS. have *unde.*

163. *Est abi canis est abi* BaCDF, but variously divided as to the
speakers. *Est ubi* Bb. Hence, Tr. *Est.* Th. *Vbi canis est?* Tr. *Abi*
Camer. Vulg. Tr. *Est.* Th. *Vbi est?* Tr. *Abi* RW. *dierecta . st!*
abin Gruter., and so Vulg. *dierecta est abin* Ba. *dierecta est abin* Bb.
dierecte est abin CD. *hinc dierecte abin* R. *dierecta abin* W. *in* BZ.
The word is omitted in CDF.

164. *restas abi istinc* Bb Camer. *restat est abistinc* Ba. *restas est abi*
istinc CD. *restas! st! abi istinc* Gruter. W, and this we have adopted.
age modo R, without any authority.

165. *quam est aqua: vise: ire,* so Camer. The true reading is very
doubtful. *quam .. a qua . vis . ire,* with erasures Ba. *qu? aqua vise ire*
Bb. *quam feta qua vis ire* C. *quam feta quavisire* D. *quam feta:*
qua vis ire F. *quam feta qua visere* Z. *quam placidast aqua: vise:*
ire R. *quam feta: quavis ire* W.

166. *Eo ego hinc ad* B. *Et ego hinc ad* CD, an evident slip. *Ego eo*
hinc R. A is said to have EGOAD.

167. *foribus abducat face* BCDFZ. *foribus abducas face* Camer.
foribus aliquis abducat face R. *foribus [intus] abducat face* W.

170. *a pedibus* B. *ab edibus* CDFZ. *apscedam* B.

ACTVS IV.   SCENA I.

PHANISCVS.

Servi qui quom culpa carint tamen malum metuont
Hi solent esse heris utibiles.
Nam illi qui nihil metuont postquam sunt malum meriti
Stulta sibi expetunt consilia.
Exercent sese ad cursuram: fugiunt. Sed hi si reprehensi
    sunt   5
Faciunt a malo peculium quod nequeunt [a bono].
Augent ex pauxillo [thesaurum in] de parant.
Mihi in pectore consilii [quod est, lubet cavere] malam
    rem prius

The following scene appears under a very mutilated form in the MSS. In order to elicit any sense, a few additions and changes must be made upon conjecture, but these are, with one or two exceptions, not very serious. Hermann, Ritchl, and some other modern editors, following the *ignis fatuus* of metrical systems, have made alterations which are altogether unjustifiable, and do not deserve to be noticed, except as ingenious flights of imagination. We have taken the text as it appears in B as the groundwork; this has been occasionally improved by comparing it with CD, but in several instances the corruptions affect all alike. The words within brackets are supplements introduced by various scholars to supply the blanks which occur in the MSS.
The names of persons prefixed to this scene in B are—TRANIO, THEVROPIDES, SIMO, DANISTA.
1. *quom* CF. *qn̄* B.
2. There is a blank in B after *solent*, as if one or two words had dropped out, but this does not appear in CDFZ, and the sense seems to be complete without any addition. *eris* all the MSS. *ero* vv. 18 and 21. *erus* vv. 22 and 35.
3. *metuont* CDFZ. *metiont* B. The correction apparently by the first hand.
5. *reprehensi* CDF. *reprehensis* B, with a dot under the *s* in black ink.
6. *faciunt* B. *facious* CDFZ. v. 38 *fatiam* all, at least B. *peculium* is a conj. of Pylades. The MSS. have *peculio*, but the transition from *peculio* (i. e. *peculiom*) to *peculio* is so slight and so common, that the correction may be regarded as certain. [*a bono*], so W. This seems to be more simple than the Vulg. *aequirou* [*facere de suo*], which was introduced by Acidalius.
7. [*thesaurum in*], the blank was thus filled by Camerarius, and so the Vulg. WR.
8. *consilii* B. *consili* CD. [*quod est, lubet cavere*], this also is a guess of Camerarius, adopted in the Vulg.

Quam ut meum [tergum doleat]
Vt adhuc fuit mihi corium esse oportet, 10
Sincerum, atque ut votem verberari.
Si huic imperabo probe tectum habebo.
Malum quom inpluit ceteros ne inpluat mihi.
Nam ut servi volunt esse herum ita solet.
Boni cum probis sunt, [improbi qui] malus fuit : 15
Nam nunc domi nostrae tot pessumi vivont,
Peculi sui prodigi, plagigeruli : ubi advorsum ut eant
Vocantur hero—Non eo, molestus ne sis,
Scio quo properas, gestis aliquo iam hercle ire, vis, mula,
    foras pastum.
Bene merens hoc pretium inde apstuli : abii foras : 20
Solus nunc eo advorsum hero ex plurimis servis.
Hoc die crastini quom herus resciverit,
Mane castigabit eos bubulis exuviis.
Postremo minoris pendo tergum illorum quam meum,
Illi erunt bucaedae multo potius quam ego sim restio. 25

9. [*tergum doleat*], this seems to have been first suggested by Hermann.
The Vulg. has *tergum exsinceratum fuit*, which is due to Camer., but the
word *exsinceratus* does not occur elsewhere.

11. *Sincerum* CDFZ. *Sicerum* B; the *n* a correction by c. *votem*
BCD. *votem* FZ. *verberari*, so Pylad. *verberare* the MSS.

12. *tectum* CDFZ. *trcum* B; the *t* not by first hand. *imperabo* BD.

13. *inpluit* C. *impluat* DFZ. *in pluit* B.

15. This line is very corrupt in the MSS., and no satisfactory emendation has been proposed. We have given the Vulg., which is due to Camer.
Bonis sum improbis sunt malus fuit B, though the true reading may possibly
be *Bonis sunt*. *Boni sum improbi sunt malus fuit* CDFZ. W gives *Bonus
cum probis 'st*. ¶ *Malus cum malis*.

16. *vivont* the MSS.

17. *advorsum* B, so v. 21, and *adversus* v. 37.

18. *Vocantur* CDFZ. *vocatur* B, the *n* being an old correction.

19. *quo* Z. *quod* the MSS. *pastum foras* Pylad. R.

20. *pretium* B. *inde abstuli : abii*, so Camer., who, however, has *ita
abii—unde abstultabi* BD. *unde abstult abi* C.

21. *die crastini*, so Pylad., but this is in reality the reading in B, which
has *di crastini* ; the *e* in black ink, the *a* older. *di crastini* CDF.

23. *exuviis* CDFZ. *exuviis* B, with a dot below the *s* ; written
bubulisex.

24. There is a space in B after *prodo*, but the sense is complete. The
two last letters of *prodo* and the *t* of *tergum* are in black ink.

25. B assigns this line to the Danista, and line 26 to Tranio, but

K

PHANISCVS. SERVVS. ALIVS.

SE. Mane tu atque adsiste ilico,

Phanisce, etiam respice. PH. Mihi molestus ne sis.

SE. Vide ut fastidit simia. PH. Mihi sum : lubet esse :
  quid id curas ?

SE. Manesne ilico, inpure parasite ?

PH. Qui parasitus sum ? SE. Ego enim dicam, cibo
  perduci poteris quovis ;   30

Ferocem facis quia te herus tam amat. PH. Vah,

Oculi dolent. SE. PH. Cur ? PH. Quia fumus molestus.

SE. Tace, sis, faber qui cudere soles plumbeos numos.

PH. Non potes tu cogere me ut tibi maledicam,

Novit herus me. SE. Suam quidem pol culcitullam
  oportet.   35

PH. Si sobrius sis male non dicas. SE. Tibi optem-
  perem quom tu mihi nequeas!

PH. At tu mecum, pessume, i advorsus. SE. Quaeso
  hercle apstine

Iam sermonem de istis rebus. PH. Faciam, et pultabo fores.

these marks are omitted in CD. B has no farther indications of a division
in the dialogue throughout the remainder of the scene, nor are there any
blanks left for the insertion of names ; the text runs on continuously. In
FZ, however, we find the whole dialogue distributed between Tranio and
the Danista.

26. *ilico* B and v. 29.,

28. *Mibi* FZ. *Milis* B, corrected by an old hand. *Milis* CD.

30. *poteris*, so Camer. *poterrs* BCD. *patires* F.

31. *quia te herus tam amat* . *Vah*, so Camer. The MSS. are very
corrupt. *quia te cratusamatuba* B. The writing appears to have been in
the first instance *cratus atuba* ; the letters *am* are inserted in a different but
old hand, and a perpendicular line after the *s* was probably inserted at the
same time. *cratus* CDF. *amatu ba* C. *amant vrí* D.

32. *qur* C.

33. *Tace sis* CDFZ. *Tace si* B. *mummos* DFZ. *mummos* C.
numbusnos B, with a line after *plumbeos* as if to mark a stop, so —. So in
the next line, after *tibi*. All these in ink darker than the original.

36. *Si sobrius* CDFZ. B has an erasure of a letter after *Si* . — a sort
of stop (;) after *sis*, by a late hand in black ink, and another in same ink,
thus, | after *mihi*. *neqveas* FZ. *neq cas* B.

37. *prissume i*, so Camer. *prisimi iu* BCD. *prishume* FZ. *queso*
the MSS.

38. *fores* (acc.) all.

Heus! ecquis hic est maxumam qui his iniuriam
Foribus defendat? ecquis, ecquis huc exit atque aperit? 40
Nemo hinc quidem foras exit: ut esse addecet nequam
    homines ita sunt:
Sed eo magis cauto est opus, ne huc exeat qui male me
    mulcet.

ACTVS IV.   SCENA II.

TRANIO. THEVROPIDES.

TR. Quid tibi visum est mercimonii?   *TH.* Totus
    gaudeo.
TR. Num nimio emptae tibi videntur?   *TH.* Numquam
    edepol ego me scio
Vidisse umquam abiectas aedes, nisi modo hasce.   *TR.* Ec-
    quid placent?
TH. Ecquid placeant, me rogas?   Imo hercle vero
    perplacent.
TR. Quoiusmodi gunaeceum! quid porticum?   *TH.* In-
    sanum bonam.   5
Non equidem ullam in publico esse maiorem hac exis-
    tumo.

---

39. *ecquis, ecquis* FZ.   *hrcquis, ecquis* B.   *hrcquis hrcquis* D.   *harc quis harc quis* C.   *maximam* the MSS.
40. *hrcquis ecquis* B, certainly.
41. Some of the MSS. have *mulcet,* others *multet.*

---

1. *est mercimonii,* so the MSS.   *est hoc mercimoni* Pylad. Vulg. W. *visumst mercimoni [hoc esse]* R.
2. *empte* C.   *edepol ego* CDFZ.   B omits *ego,* and so Vulg. *scio,* so Plus.   *scito* the MSS.
3. . *umquam* the MSS.   Most edd., following Dousa, have *usquam. abiectas* Dc.   *abiectas* BbCDZ, and so Scaliger.   *ablactas* Ba.   *aedes* (acc.) the MSS.   *Ecquid.* The MSS. present a series of corrupt forms.   *Hacquid* Ba.   *Acquid* Bb.   *Hare quid* C, but D has *Hrcquid.*
4. *Ecquid placeant,* so Camer.   The MSS. have *placent.*
5. *gynaeceum* B.

K 2

TR. Quin ego ipse et Philolaches in publico omnis
porticus
Sumus commensi. TH. Quid igitur? TR. Longe omnium
longissuma est.
TH. Di immortales, mercimonii lepidi! [Si] hercle nunc
ferat
Sex talenta magna argenti pro istis praesentaria,   10
Numquam accipiam. TR. Si hercle accipere cupias, ego
numquam sinam.
TH. Bene res nostra conlocata est istoc mercimonio.
TR. Me suasore atque inpulsore id factum audacter
dicito,
Qui subegi, faenore argentum ab danista ut sumeret,
Quod isti dedimus arraboni. TH. Servavisti omnem
ratem.   15
Nempe octoginta debentur huic minae? TR. Haud numo
amplius.
TH. Hodie accipiat. TR. Ita enimvero, ne qua causa
supsiet,
Vel mihi denumerato; ego illi porro denumeravero.
TH. At enim ne quid captioni mihi sit, si dederim tibi.
TR. Egone te ioculo modo ausim dicto aut facto
fallere?   20
TH. Egon' aps te ausim non cavere, ne quid committam
tibi?

8. *Summus* BaCDa, an evident blunder.
9. *Si hercle*, so Camer. The MSS. omit *Si*, and it is, perhaps, not
necessary. *mercimonii*, so the MSS.
11. *accipiam*, so Camer. BCDF have *accipiem*, which may be an
ancient form. Again, *cupias* Camer. *cupies* the MSS. *Si hercle*, so
the MSS. of Pylad. The best MSS. are corrupt. *Sierrie* B. *Si erele* C.
Si errete D.
12. *conlocata* BD.
13. *inpulsare* BC. *impulsore* D.
16. *minæ* C. *hau numme* CD. *haunummo* Ra.
19. *tit*, so B is corrected by an old hand. *sed* BCDF.
20. *te ioculo* Bb and the MSS. of Pylad. *Ie loculo* BaDFZ. *celo
culo* C.
21. *cavere* so F and the MSS. of Pylad. *cavere si* BCD, and
so R.

TR. Quia tibi umquam quicquam, postquam tuus sum,
   verborum dedi ?
TH. Ego enim cavi recte.   *TR.* Eam [mihi] debes gra.
   tiam, atque animo meo.
TH. Sat sapio, si aps te modo uno caveo.   *TR.* Tecum
   sentio.
TH. Nunc abi rus: dic, me advenisse, filia.   *TR.* Faciam,
   ut voles.   25
TH. Curriculo iube in urbem veniat iam simol tecum.
   TR. Licet.
Nunc ego me illac per posticum ad congerrones conferam :
Dicam, ut hic res sint quietae atque ut hunc hinc
   amoverim.

ACTVS IV.   SCENA III.

PHANISCVS. ALIVS SERVOS. THEVROPIDES.

Hic quidem neque convivarum sonitus itidem ut antehac
   fuit,
Neque tibicinam cantantem, neque alium quemquam audio.

22. *Quia tibi umquam,* so BCDZ, except that in B we have ˉumquam,
and hence *Quia tibi numquam* F.   *Quian' tibi umquam* W.   *Quid ! tibin'*
umquam R.
23. *Eam [mibi] debes.* We have printed this line as it appears in B,
with the addition of *mibi,* which is a conj. of Camer.   *debes,* in B, was
originally written *debis,* but corrected.   *rete eam debis* CD.   W, following Acidalius and the Vulg., gives the whole line to Theuropides, and reads
Eam mihi debeo.   R supposes that we have here the fragments of two
lines combined into one in B, but at the same time admits that there is
no trace of more than one line in A.   There is a space in B between *rete*
and *eam.*
25. *Nunc* Bb.   *Non* Ba.   ABIRVS, so A and FZ.   *abi i rus* BCD
(*babi* C).
26. CVRRICVLOIVBE, so A.   *Curriculo . ibi,* with an erasure, B.
Curriculo ubi iube CFZ.   *Curriculo tibi iube* D.   *Curriculo i iube* W.
27. ILLAC, so A.   *illa* the rest of the MSS. Vulg. W.   *et con-*
gerrones BaC.
28. *ut hunc hinc,* so the MSS.   *hunc ut hinc* Guyet RW.

1. *itidem,* so the MSS.   *item* Both. WR.

TH. Quae illacc res est? quid illic homines quaerunt
 apud aedis meas?

Quid volunt? quid introspectant? *PH.* Pergam pultare
 ostium.

Heus, reclude, heus, Tranio! Etiamne aperis? *TR.* Quae
 haec est fabula?   5

PH. Etiamne aperis? Callidamati nostro advorsum venimus.

TH. Heus vos, pueri, quid istic agitis? quid istas aedis
 frangitis?

PH. Herus hic noster potat.   *TH.* Herus hic voster
 potat?   *PH.* Ita loquor.

TH. Puere, nimium delicatus es.   *PH.* Ei advorsum
 venimus.

TH. Quoi homini?   *PH.* Hero nostro.   Quaeso, quoties
 dicundum est tibi?   10

TH. Puere, nemo hic habitat: nam te esse arbitror
 puerum probum.

PH. Non hic Philolaches adulescens habitat bisce in
 aedibus?

---

3. *illic homines* BFZ.   *illis ehomines* CD.   *illice homines* W.   *illisce homines* R.   *querunt* BC.   v. 10 *queso* BC.   v. 21 *pergreeari* BC.
v. 42 *preditas* BC.   v. 49 *questum* BaCD.

4. *pultare* B.   *pultari* CDZ.   *bultium* DFZ.

5. ETIAMNE, so, apparently, A.   *etiam* C and v. 39.   *etiamne* C v. 6.
Etiam the rest of the MSS. and Vulg.   *que lrr* C.

7. *edis* C.   After v. 7 there follow in A six lines which do not
appear in other MSS., but the traces of the original writing in the
Palimpsest are so faint, that not above four words in all can be decyphered. A *fac simile* of this portion of A is given by Ritschl. In his
Parrrg., p. 447.

8. *herus* twice BCD ("*prorsus praeter morem*" R).

9. PUERE, so A.   *Puer* the rest of the MSS.   *adelicatus* BCD.
FZ have *delicatus*, which is, perhaps, equivalent to *delicatu's*, and so
Pylad. R.   *es delicatus* Camer. Vulg. W.

10. *cui* the MSS.   *dicendum* the MSS.

11. *Puere* R, but not the MSS.   NEMOHIC, so A.   *hic nemo* the
rest of the MSS.

12. *Nam hic* B.   *adulesrens* B.   HISCINAEDIBVS B.   The rest
of the MSS. omit *in*.   *bisce in aedibus* Pylad. Camer.   *edibus* nearly all.
There are in A the remains of a line after v. 12 not found in other MSS.,
but the traces are very indistinct, except at the close, where we read
HISCEAEDIBVS. See Ritschl. *Parrrg.*, p. 448.

Se. Hic senex cerebrosus est certe. *Ph.* Erras pervorse,
   pater :
Nam nisi hinc hodie emigravit aut heri, certo scio
Hic habitare. *Th.* Quin sex menses iam hic nemo habitat.
   Se. Somnias.   15
   Th. Egone? *Se.* Tu. *Th.* Tu ne molestus. Sine me
   cum puero loqui.
   Ph. Nemo habitat? Hem! *Th.* Ita. *Ph.* Profecto :
   nam heri et nudiustertius,
Quartus, quintus, sextus usque, postquam hinc peregre
   eius pater
Abiit, numquam hic triduom unum desitum est potarier.
   Th. Quid ais? *Ph.* Triduom unum est haud inter-
   missum hic esse et bibi,   20
Scorta duci, pergraecari, fidicinas, tibicinas
Ducere. *Th.* Quis istaec faciebat? *Ph.* Philolaches.
   Th. Qui Philolaches?
   Ph. Quoi patrem Theuropidem esse opinor. *Th.* Hei,
   hei, occidi,

13. *cerebrosus est* BbCDFZ.   *cerebro . us* Ba.   Some critics have
asserted that the reading in A is ELLEBOROSUSESTCERTE.   W has *certe
est*, but gives no authority.   *pervorse* BaCD.
   14. HINC, so A and Camer.   *hic* the rest of the MSS.
   15. *menses*, so the MSS.
   16. *Egone tu tu ne* BCD.   R has *Egone?* PH. *Tu ne.* TH. *Ne molestu's.*
   17. *Nemo habitat.* PH. *Hem ita* B.   *Nemo habitat bare tat* CD.
Nemo habitat.   DA. *Habitat* FZ.   The arrangement, as given in the
text, is due to Camer.   R has *Nemo habitat.* PH. *Habitat profecto.
nam;* A is said to have IAM.   *eri* B, but not R.
   18. *hinc peregre eius,* so the MSS., except A, which has PEREGREILLIUS.
peregre hinc eius R.
   19. *triduom unum* BbDFZ, and also, it is said, A.   *triduom numum*
BaC, which, perhaps, indicates *triduom in umom.*   See next line.   DE-
SITUMESTPOTARIER A.   *desitumust* R.   *desitum esse et bibi est* CDF.
desitum est esse et bibi Bb, and so Vulg. W.   Ba is somewhat mutilated
and corrupt here, but the same reading as in CD is clearly indicated.
   20. *Quid ais,* so Bb and the MSS. of Pylad.   The rest have *Quid agis.*
R has *Quid ais tandem,* but *tandem* is not found in the MSS.   Ba has
Triduom in umom.   R has *haud esse intermissum hic bibi,* but the reading
of the MSS. is that given in the text.   W has *haud intermissum est.*
   21. *Ducere,* so the MSS.   *Conduci* R.   *ista bre* BaD.   *ista bare* C.
fatirbat B.   *Qui Philolaches,* so B.   The rest of the MSS. *Quid* P.
   23. A is said to have CUIUS.   *Hei, hei,* so Gruter.   *opinor . occidi,*
with an erasure, B.   *opinor et occidi* CD.   *Hei mihi* Camer. R.

Si haec hic vera memorat.   Pergam porro percontarier.
Ain' tu, istic potare solitum Philolachem istum, quisquis
    est,   25
Cum hero vostro? *PH.* Hic, inquam. *TH.* Puere, praeter
    speciem stultus es;
Vide, sis, ne forte ad merendam quopiam devorteris,
Atque ibi melius quam satis fuit, biberis. *PH.* Quid est?
TH. Ita dico: ne ad alias aedis perperam deveneris.
PH. Scio, qua me ire oportet, et, quo venerim, novi locum. 30
Philolaches hic habitat, quoius est pater Theuropides,
Qui, postquam pater ad mercatum abiit hinc, tibicinam
Liberavit. *TH.* Philolachesne ergo? *PH.* Ita: Philem-
    atium quidem.
   TH. Quanti?   *SE.* Triginta talentis.   *PH.* Μὰ τὸν
       Ἀπόλλω, sed minis.
   TH. Ain', minis triginta amicam destinasse Philo-
       lachem?   35

24. *bre* B.
25. *istic*, so the Vulg. and most edd.   *istuc* BCD.   *istoc* Camer.
potare Vulg.   *portare* BaCD, an obvious blunder.
26. *vostro* Bb.   *vestra* BaCD, an obvious blunder.   *His* BbFZ.
Hec Ba.   *Haec* CD.
27. *Videsis—Vnsis* Ba.   *Vnsis* Bb.   *quopiam* Vulg.   *copiam* BCD.
28. *ibi . . . eliusquam* A.   *ibi melius quam* FZ.   *ibi melius cuiquam*
BaC.   *ibi melius cuiquam* Bb.   *ibi melius culiquam* Da, whence *meliuscule*
quam Camer. Vulg. W.   *ibi ne plus quam satis* R.   *Quid est?* so the
MSS.   *Quid [ita nam? quid] est?* R.
29. *ad alias edis* BbDcFZ.   *abalias sedis* Ba.   *ab alia sedis* C.   *ab*
alias edis Da.   *deveneris*, so Camer.   *neveneris* B.   *ne eveneris* CFZ.
ni veneris D.
30. *me ire* BbFZ.   *me rire* is probably the reading of BaCD.   *mentre*
BaCD.   *et* is omitted in B.   *locum*, so A.   *loqui* BDFZ. Vulg.
loquiqur C.   *loci* Gulielm. W.
31. *abiit* BbFZ.   *babit* Ba.   *abit* CD.   A is said to have *obiit*.
bine BCDF.   *hic* ZW.
33. *Philolachesne*, so A.   *ne* omitted by the rest of the MSS.
34. A has Matonapollosed, and so FZ.   BCD have *sex* instead of
sed.   Some critics have imagined that they can decypher a new line
here in A to the following effect—
       Th. Liberavit.   *Ph.* Liberavit illamce triginta minis,
but it seems very doubtful.
35. *destinasse Philolachem*, a plausible conj. of R.   *destinatum Philo-*
lachem the MSS.   *destinatam Philolachi* Gulielm. Vulg. W; but A has
distinctly Philolachem.

PH. Aio.   *TH.* Atque eam manu emisisse ?   *PH.* Aio.
   TH. Et postquam eius hinc pater
Sit profectus peregre, perpotasse adsiduo
Tuo cum domino?   *PH.* Aio.   *TH.* Quid? is aedes emit
   hic proxumas ?
PH. Non aio.   *TH.* Quadraginta etiam dedit huic, quae
   essent pignori ?
PH. Neque istud aio.   *TH.* Hei, perdis!   *PH.* Imo
   suum patrem illic perdidit.   40
TH. Vera cantas! Vana vellem!   *PH.* Patris amicus
   videlicet.
TH. Heu, edepol patrem eum miserum praedicas!
   PH. Nihil hoc quidem est,
Triginta minae, prae quam alios dapsiles sumptus facit.
Perdidit patrem. Vnus istic servos est sacerrumus,
Tranio; is vel Herculi conterere quaestum possiet.   45
Edepol nae me eius patris misere miseret; qui quom
   istaec sciet

---

36. *emisisse* BbCDbZ, *emisit* BaF. *misisse* Da.
37. So the MSS., except that Ba has *atsiduo.* R, following some
obscure traces in A, gives—
   Sit profectus peregre, tum perpotasse assiduo hic simul,
while W has—
   Sit profectus peregre, perpotasse hic assiduo tuo
   Cum domino!
38. *Aio,* so Vulg. *Alio* BaCD, an obvious blunder.   *Quid? is aedes
emit hie,* so B.   *edis* C.   A is said to have HAS for *hic.*   *Quid? is bas
aedis emit* R.   *Quid? aedes emit bie is* W.   *praximas* BC.
39. *aio; agio* BaD, an obvious blunder.   HVICQVAERSSENT A, and
so Camer. conj.   *huc quae sit* BaCD.
40. *istud* CDFZ.   *illud* B.
42. *patrem manom* BD.   *cum merito miserum,* throwing *Heu* out of the
verse, R.
43. *prae quam* Lamb.   *praterquam* the MSS.   *dapsiles* FZ.   The
word appears under a corrupt shape in BCD, but there is no doubt as to
the correction.
44. R assigns the words *Perdidit patrem* to Theuropides.   SERVVS A.
EST SACERRIMVS, so A and F.   *si acerrimus* BCD.
45. *rredi* C.   *conterere* BbF.   *conterre* Ba.   *conterre* CD.
possiet Camer.   *potest* the MSS.
46. NEMEEIVSPATRISMISEREMISERET, so distinctly A.   The rest of
the MSS. omit *miseret,* and so the Vulg.   W adopts the reading of our
text, omitting *nae.*   R adds *now* before *misere.*   *cum* BCDZ.

L

Facta ita, amburet misero ei corculum carbunculus.

Tu. Si quidem istaec vera sunt.   *Ph.* Quid mercar,
   quamobrem mentiar?

Heus vos? ecquis aperit has?   *Se.* Quid istas pultas, ubi
   nemo intus est?

Ph. Alio credo comissatum abisse: abeamus nunc iam. 50

Tu. Puere, iamne abis? Libertas pnenula est tergo tuo.

Ph. Mihi, nisi ut herum metuam et curem, nihil est,
   qui tergum tegam.

ACTVS IV.   SCENA IV.

THEVROPIDES. SIMO.

Tu. Perii hercle! quid opus est verbis? Vt verba audio,
Non equidem in Aeguptum hinc modo vectus fui,
Sed etiam in terras solas orasque ultumas
Sum circumvectus: ita, ubi nunc sim, nescio.
Verum iam scibo: nam eccum, unde aedis filius   5
Meus emit. Quid agis tu?   *Si.* A foro incedo domum.

---

47. *misero ei* the MSS.   *ei misero* WR.
49. APERITHAS A.   *haste aperit* BCDW.   R omits *has.*   ISTAS,
so A and Camer.   *istae* B and Vulg.   *ista* CD.   *ita* FZW.
50. COMISATVM A.   *cōmissatum* BaC.   *cōmessatum* Bb.   *cōmes-*
sati D.   *abeamus* FZ.   *abemus* BaCD, an obvious blunder.   *mor-*
tiam BaCD for *nunc iam.*   After this verse, traces of a line appear in A, not
found in BCD, but unfortunately only two detached words are legible—

   PVRRE . . Q . . . . HACMB ——————

51, 52. These two lines are regarded as spurious by W.
52. NISIVTHRRVM is apparently the reading in A.   The rest have *nisi*
herum ut.

---

1. *Perii* Bb.   *Prri* BaFZ.   . *eri* C.   *Heri* D.   *verba,* so Camer.
verbera B.   *verbarra* C.   *verberit* D.
3. *boras* B.   v. 7 *odie* Da for *bodie.*
4. *circumvectus* Z.   *circumventus* BCDF.
5. *ardis* (acc.) all.
6. *agu,* so Ald.   *ais* the MSS.

Th. Num quid processit ad forum [tibi] hodie novi?
Si. Etiam. *Th.* Quid tandem? *Si.* Vidi efferri mort-
uom. *Th.* Hem,
Novom! *Si.* Vnum vidi mortuom efferri foras.
Modo eum vixisse aiebant. *Th.* Vae capiti tuo! 10
Si. Quid tu otiosus res novas requiritas?
Th. Quia hodie adveni peregre. *Si.* Promisi foras
Ad cenam, ne me te vocare censeas.
Th. Haud postulo edepol. *Si.* Verum cras, nisi [quis]
prius
Vocaverit me, vel apud te cenavero. 15
Th. Ne istuc quidem edepol postulo. Nisi quid
magis
Es occupatus, operam mihi da. *Si.* Maxume.
Th. Minas quadraginta accepisti, quas sciam,
A Philolachete. *Si.* Numquam numum, quod sciam.
Th. Quid? a Tranione servo? *Si.* Multo [hercle] id
minus. 20
Th. Quas arraboni tibi dedit? *Si.* Quid somnias?

7. *forum* [*tibi*] *hodie*, so Camer. The MSS. omit *tibi*. Gullelm.
suggests *ibi*. R has *hic*.
8. *etiam* C. v. 11 *eriam* all. *mortuom* BbFZ. *mortuom* BaCD,
an evident blunder.
9, 10. These lines appear thus in B. R supposes that one line has
been here expanded by interpolation into two, and reads—
       Novom. *Si.* Modo vixisse aibant. *Th.* Vae capiti tuo.
10. *modo eum* B. *modo rai* C. *modo vixisse eum* DFZ. *Vae
capiti tuo*, so BbF. *Tuae capiti tuo* BC (*tuae* D).
11. *Quid tu otiosus* ZRW. *Quid tu ut otiosus* the MSS., and so the
Vulg.
13. *ne me te vocare*, so Camer. *ne me tue vocare* BCD. *ne me tu
evocare* F.
14. *nisi quis prius* Camer. The MSS. omit *quis*.
16. *istuc* BbFZ. *iste* BaCD.
17. *maxime* the MSS. v. 3 *ultumas* most of the MSS.
18. *quadraginta*, so Pylad. *triginta* the MSS. *quas sciam* B.
quassciam CD. *quod sciam* Guyet. RW.
20. So the line appears in BCDFZ, with a blank in BD, where
hercle is inserted, according to the conj. of R, who, however, prints
the line—
       Quid, ain tu a Tranione? *Si.* Multo hercle id minus.
servo meo. *Si. Multo id minus* Camer. W. F has *nimis* for *minus*.

L 2

TH. Egone ? At quidem tu, qui istoc te speras modo
Potesse dissimulando infectum hoc reddere.
   Si. Quid autem ?   *TH.* Quod me apsente [tecum] hic
   filius
Negoti gessit.   *Si.* Mecum ut ille hic gesserit,   25
Dum tu hinc abes, negoti ? quidnam, aut quo die ?
   TH. Minas tibi octoginta argenti debeo.
   Si. Non mihi quidem hercle ; verum, si debes, cedo.
Fides servanda est.   Ne ire infitias postules.
   TH. Profecto non negabo debere, et dabo.   30
Tu cave, quadraginta accepisse hinc ne neges.
   Si. Quaeso edepol, huc me aspecta et responde mihi.
Te velle uxorem aiebat tuo gnato dare :
Ideo aedificare hoc velle aiebat in tuis.
   TH. Hic aedificare volui ?   *Si.* Sic dixit mihi.   35
   TH. Hei mihi, disperii ! vocis non habeo satis!
Vicini, perii, interii !   *Si.* Numquid Tranio
Turbavit ?   *TH.* Imo exturbavit omnia.
Te ludificatus est et me hodie indignis modis.
   Si. Quid tu ais ?   *TH.* Haec res sic est, ut narro
   tibi :   40

23. *Potes sedis simulando* C.
24. [*terum*] *hic* ; Camer. supplied *tecum*, which is not found in the MSS.
26. So the MSS. R imagines that there ought to be three lines here,
which he has reconstructed according to his own fancy.
31. *ar neges*, so the MSS. *te neges* Lamb. R.
32. *queso* CD. *quoso* B.   *bus me aspecta* BCDZ, *ad me huc
sperta* R.   R supposes that there is a great gap after v. 32, and has
written 23 lines to supply the deficiency.
33. *airbat* Vulg. RW. *agrbat* BaCD, an obvious blunder.
34. *edificarr*, and again v. 35 BC.   *bor* the MSS., and so Vulg.
hic Camer. W.
35. *voluit* B.
37. *Vicini* the MSS. *Vicine* Acidal. R.
38. BaC have *turbabit*, an obvious blunder. *immo mi* Both. R, but *mi*
is not in the MSS.
39. *Te ludificatus est et me hodie indignis modis.* This seems to be the
reading of B, and is adopted by Camer. and Vulg. CD are corrupt here.
R and W have—

      Deludificatus est me hodie indignis modis.

40. *bre* B (nom. sing.) *bre* (acc. plur.) C, v. 43.   *ais* Z. *agis*
the MSS.

Deludificatus est me hodie in perpetuom modum.
Nunc te opsecro, ut me bene iuves, operamque des.
  Sr. Quid vis?   *Th.* I mecum [hac] opsecro [te] una
    simul.
  Sr. Fiat.   *Th.* Servorumque operam et lora mihi cedo.
  Sr. Sume.   *Th.* Eademque opera haec tibi narravero, 45
Quis me exemplis hodie eludificatus [est].

ACTVS V.   SCENA I.

TRANIO.

Qui homo timidus erit in rebus dubiis, nauci non erit;
Atque equidem, quid id esse dicam verbum, nauci, nescio.
Nam herus me postquam rus misit, ut filium suum arces-
    cerem:
Abii illa per angiportum ad hortum nostrum clanculum.
Ostium quod in angiportu est horti patefeci fores; 5
Eaque eduxi omnem legionem, et maris et feminas.

---

41. *Deludificatust me hodie* BCD.   R has [*Disperdidit me ille*] *hodie.*
42. *Nunc* Vulg.   *Non* BaCD, an evident blunder.
43. The MSS. omit *hac* and *te*, which are supplements by Camer.
R has *I mecum, te obsecro, una mecum simul.*
45. *Sume eademque opera* CD.   *Sume eademque operam* B.   *Sume eadem
ego opera* Camer. WR.   *hare tibi* the MSS.   *hare intus tibi* R.
46. This is the reading of BCD, omitting *est*.   W has—
    Quis med exemplis hodie [ille] ludificatus est.
R has—
    Quis me hodie exemplis ille ludificatus est.

---

1. *dubiis,* so Priscian, who quotes this line at p. 682.   The MSS. are in
some confusion.   *dubii...s* Ba.   *dubiisis* Bb.   *dubii sis* C.   *dubiis is* D.
2. R believes that there is a blank after v. 2.
3. *ut filium* the MSS.   *filium ut* Both. RW.   *accerserem* the MSS.
arcesserem most edd.
4. *Abii illa,* so Camer.   *Abilla* BCD.   *Ab illo* FZ.
5. *orti* BCD.   *horti* the rest.   *eius* R.   *foris* Camer.   *fores*
the MSS.

Postquam ex opsidione in tutum eduxi maniplares meos :
Capio consilium, ut senatum congerronum convocem ;
Quem quom convocavi, atque illi me ex senatu segregant.
Vbi egomet video vorti rem in meo foro, quantum potest,   10
Facio idem, quod plurimi alii, quibus res timida aut tur-
      bida est :
Pergunt turbare usque, ut ne quid possit conquiescere.
Nam scio equidem, nullo pacto iam esse posse clam
      senem.
Sed quid hoc est, quod foris concrepuit proxuma vicinia?
Herus meus hic quidem est.   Gustare ego eius sermonem
      volo.   15

ACTVS V.   SCENA II.

THEVROPIDES.   TRANIO.

TH. Ilico intra limen astate illic : ut, quom extemplo
      vocem,

7. *obsidione* FZ.   *opsidionem* BaCDa, an evident blunder.
8. *congerronum* Bb.   *congerronum* Ba and the rest of the MSS.

9. *Quem cum convocavi* Camer.   *Quom convocavi* B.   *Qm convocavi*
CD.   *Quom cum convocavi* R.   EXSENATV is said to be the reading
of A.   *e* the rest of the MSS.   *senatu* F.   *senatus* or *sarnatus* BCD,
an obvious blunder.   *segregant* C.
    10. This line is entirely omitted in B.   *egomet* Z.   *ego me*
CDF.   *rem verti* Pylad.   *verti rem* F, Vulg.   *veruri* CD.
    11. *facio* B.   *plurimi* the MSS.   v. 14 *proxima* the MSS.   *alii*
quibus Camer.   *aliquibus* BCD.   *quibus* FZ.
    12. *ut ne quid possit* Camer.   *ut ne quid sit* B.   *ut quid sit* the rest of
the MSS.
    13. *Nescio* Ba, an evident blunder.   After this line there are traces
in A of seven lines altogether omitted in BCDFZ, but of these only three
disjointed words can be decyphered—XET or AVT at the beginning of the
third, PRO at the beginning of the fourth, and ILLE at the beginning of
the fifth.
    14. *Sed quid* BbFZ.   *Sed qui* BaCD.   *proxima vicinia* ABDFZ.
proxima vicina C, an obvious blunder.   *proxume viciniae* R.
    15. *Seruus meus* B, an evident blunder.   QVIDEMST A.   *quidem est*
the rest.

1. *Ilico* AFZ.   *illico* 'praeter morem' BCD.   *limen astate illic ut*
cum, so the MSS.   *limen ista state ut quom* R.   The traces in A are too

Continuo esiliatis.   Manicas celeriter conectite.

Ego illum ante aedis praestolabor ludificatorem meum,

Quoius ego hodie ludificabor corium, si vivo, probe.

   TR. Res palam est.   Nunc te videre melius est, quid

     agas, Tranio.   5

   TH. Docte atque astute mihi captandum est cum illoc,

     ubi huc advenerit.

Non ego illi extemplo ita meum ostendam sensum: mittam

   lineam;

Dissimulabo me horum quicquam scire.   *TR.* O mortalem

   malum!

Alter hoc Athenis nemo doctior dici potest.

Verba illi non magis dare hodie quisquam, quam lapidi,

   potest.   10

Adgrediar hominem; appellabo.   *TH.* Nunc ego ille huc

   veniat velim.

   TR. Si quidem pol me quaeris, adsum praesens praesenti

     tibi.

   TH. Euge, Tranio, quid agitur?   *TR.* Veniunt ruri

     rustici;

---

doubtful to be accepted as a guide.   *extemplo* Vulg.   *exemplo* BaCa,
an obvious blunder.

   2. *Manicas* Vulg.   BCD have *Maxilas.*   *conectite* ABCDa.   *con-nectite* DcFZ.

   3. PRAESTOLABOR A.   *praestabor* B.   *praestabo* the rest of the
MSS.

   4. *quoius* B.   *cuius* the rest, including A.   HO ... LUDIFICABOR A.
hodie ludificabor R.   *hic ludificabor* Ba.   *hic ludificabo* Bb and the rest of
the MSS. Vulg. W.

   6. *astute mihi* the MSS.   *astu* Both. R.   W omits *mihi.*   *illoc,*
so the MSS.   *illo* Camer. R and perhaps A.

   7. So the MSS., except that B has *mum* and *sens*, but these are corrected in Bb.   *extemplo iram ostendam: sensim* R.   Camer. omits *ita,*
and so Vulg. W.   EXTEMPLO .. AM . MOSTEN ———— A.

   8. *mortalem,* so Plus.   *mortale* the MSS.

   9. *Aliter* Ba, an evident blunder.

   10. ILLINONMAGISDAREHODIE A.   *illi non magis hodie* the MSS.
dare illi non magis hodie Camer. Vulg. W.   Da entirely omits this
line.

   11. R omits *ille* against all the MSS.

   12. *quaeris* BC.   *praesens* B.   *praesenti* BC.   So v. 37 *praesente* B.
praesente Dc.   v. 34 *quaestioni* BC, vv. 29 and 31 BCD.   v. 32 *quaestio* all.

Philolaches iam hic aderit. · *TH.* Edepol mihi opportune
  advenit.
Nostrum ego hunc vicinum opinor esse hominem audacem
  et malum.   15
  TR. Quidum ? *TH.* Qui negat novisse vos. *TR.* Negat ?
  TH. Nec vos sibi
Numum umquam argenti dedisse. *TR.* Abi, ludis me,
  credo. Haud negat.
  TH. Quid iam ? *TR.* Scio, iocaris nunc tu : nam ille
  quidem haud negat.
  TH. Imo edepol negat profecto ; neque se hasce aedis
  Philolachi
Vendidisse. *TR.* Eho, an negavit, sibi datum argentum,
  opsecro ?   20
  TH. Qui iusiurandum pollicitus est dare se, si vellem,
  mihi,
Neque se hasce aedis vendidisse, neque sibi argentum
  datum esse.
Dixi ego istuc idem illi. *TR.* Quid ait ? *TH.* Servos
  pollicitus est dare
Suos mihi omnes quaestioni. *TR.* Nugas ! numquam edepol
  dabit.

14. C entirely omits this line.   *opportune mi* R against the MSS.
opurtune B.   *advenit* Z.   *advenies* BD.   *advenit* F.
15. *buou* Vulg.   *bic* Z.   *buc* BCF.   *boc* D.
16. *Quia negat* Both. R, against the MSS.   *novise* BaC.
17. *Nononiquam* BaC.   *Numoniquam* Bb.   *Numquam* Da.   *Nonquam* Dc.   *argenti* FZ.   *argentei* BbCD.   *argeiti* Ba.
18. This line is found in B, but is omitted in the rest of the MSS.
W brackets it.   *locaris* Ba.   R has *baut edepol negat.*   *baut negat* Ba.   *baud negat* Bb.
19. *hasce aedis* DbFZ.   *bas credis* CDa.   *bas . aedis*, with an erasure B.
bas aedis Vulg. W.
21. *Qui* BCD.   *Quin* most edd. RW.
22. *aedis* (acc.) all (C *edis*).   *datum esse* BbDcFZ.   *datum est*
BaCDa.   *datum* Pylad. Vulg.   *esse argentum datum* W.   *sibi argentum datum* R.   R, following Acidalius, supposes that a line is wanting after
v. 22.
24. *omnes* (acc.) all.

TH. Dat profecto.   TR. Quin et illum in ius iube ire.
TH. Iam mane :   25
Experiar, ut opinor; certum est mihi.   TR. [Mihi] [huc]
    hominem cedo!
TH. Quid, si igitur ego accersam homines ?   TR. Factum
    esse iam oportuit.
Vel hominem iube aedis mancupio poscere.   TH. Imo hoc
    primum volo:
Quaestioni accipere servos.   TR. Faciundum edepol censeo.
Ego interim hanc aram occupabo.   TH. Quid ita ?   TR. Null-
    am rem sapis: 30
Ne enim illi huc confugere possint, quaestioni quos dabit,
Hic ego tibi praesidebo: ne interbitat quaestio.
TH. Surge.   TR. Minume.   TH. Ne occupassis, opsecro,
    aram.   TR. Cur ?   TH. Scies:
Quia enim id maxume volo, ut illi istoc confugiant. Sine :
Tanto apud iudicem hunc argenti condemnabo facilius.   35
    TR. Quod agis, id agas. Quid tu porro vis serere
    negotium ?

25. *in ius iube ire.* TH. *Iam mane,* so Camer. on conj., and so Vulg. W.
BC are very corrupt in v. 25. This and the four following lines appear
thus in BCD—

    Tr. Dat profecto quin et illum in iussi veniam mane
    Experiar ut opinor. Tb. Certum est mihi hominem cedo.
    Quid si igitur ego accersam homines? Tr. Factum esse iam oportuit.
    Vel hominem iube aedis mancipio poscere. Immo hoc primum volo.
    Tb. Quaestioni accipere servos. Tr. Faciundum edepol censeo.

From which it will be seen, that scarcely any changes are required, except
in v. 25, although R has thought it necessary, "*dubitanter,*" however, to
recast the whole passage. In v. 26, *but* is a conj. addition by Camer., and
the second *mihi* by W. In v. 28, CDFZ omit *hoc.*
  27. *homines* (acc.) all.
  28. *aedis* (acc.) all.
  30. *aram bone* R against the MSS.
  31. *but* Saracenus. *hic* the MSS.
  32. *Hic ergo* R against the MSS.   *praesidebo ne* Vulg.   *preside
bone* BF.   *praeside bone* CD.   *interbitat* B.
  33. *minime* all, and v. 34 *maxime* all.   *aram* Pylad.   *arma* BCD.
  34. *illi istor* R against the MSS.
  35. *but* BbFZ.   *bint* BaCD.   *condemnabo* D.
  36. *Quod agis* Pylad. *Quod agas* the MSS.   *serere vis* Both. RW
against the MSS.

M

Nescis quam meticulosa res sit ire ad iudicem.

TH. Surgedum huc: est consulere igitur quiddam quod
tecum volo.

TR. Sic tamen hinc consilium dedero: nimio plus sapio
sedens.

Tum consilia firmiora sunt de divinis locis.   40

TH. Surge! ne nugare! aspicedum contra me! *TR.* Aspexi.
TH. Vides?

TR. Video, huc si quis intercedat tertius pereat fame.

TH. Quidum? *TR.* Quia nihil quaesti siet, mali hercle .
ambo sumus.

TH. Perii! *TR.* Quid tibi est? *TH.* Dedisti verba.
TR. Qui tandem? *TH.* Probe

Med emunxti. *TR.* Vide, sis, satine recte: num mucci
fluont?   45

TH. Imo etiam cerebrum quoque omnem e capite
emunxisti meo.

Nam omnia malefacta vostra reperi radicitus;

37. *Nescis tu* Camer. W against the MSS. See Priscan, p. 617.
meticulosa B.   *res sit ire; resistire* BaCDa.

38. *Surgedum hinc* Both. R against the MSS.   *consulerest* R against
the MSS.

39. *Sic tamen, so* Plus. *Si tamen* the MSS.

40. *Tum* B. *Tunc* the rest of the MSS.

41. *intercedat* Vulg. *intercedas* BaC.   *terrius* C.   v. 46 *etiam* C.

43. *Quia nibil quaesti siet, mali,* so Camer. *quia nibil quo estis id mali*
BCD (*quaestis id* C), which, when properly arranged, Is the reading of
Camer., with the change of one letter, viz., *id* into *it.* W has *quia nibil
quaesti sit; quia mali.* R has *quia nibil quaesti sit ei, ita mali,* both of which
are more remote from the MSS.

44. *Probe,* so the MSS. of Pylad., Camer. *Probi* the MSS., except that
BbZ have *Probri.*

45. *Med emunxti,* so Pius, Botb. WR, *Me emunxisti* Db. *Me emunxit*
BaCDFZ. *Vide sis, satine recte* B (*Vide sis satin recte*). *Vide si satin
recte* CD. *num mucci fluont* BC. *numma fluunt* D. *nummi huc*
fluunt FZ.

46. *omnem e capite emunxisti meo,* so Pylad., from MSS., as he says.
omnem e capite munxit muro Ba. *omne e capite munxti meum* Hb. *omnem
e capite uxti muro* C. *omnem e capiem uexi muro* D, and so FZ, which,
however, have *uxvi.* W has the same as our text, except *muum* for *muo.*
R has *omnu* and *muo.*

47. *Nam omnia iam male facta* R against the MSS.   *vostra*
the MSS.

Non radicitus quidem hercle, verum etiam eradicitus.
Numquam edepol haec hodie inultus destinaveris. Tibi
Iam iubebo ignem et sarmen, carnufex, circumdari.   50
  TR. Ne faxis: nam elixus esse, quam assus, soleo
  suavior.
  TH. Exempla edepol faciam ego in te. TR. Quia placeo,
  exemplum expetis.
  TH. Loquere: quoiusmodi reliqui, quom hinc abibam,
  filium?
  TR. Cum pedibus, manibus, cum digitis, auribus, oculis,
  labris.
  TH. Aliud te rogo. TR. Aliud ergo nunc tibi re-
  spondeo.   55
Sed eccum tui gnati sodalem video huc incedere,
Callidamatem : illo praesente mecum agito, si quid voles.

---

48. *eradicitus* the MSS., not *exradicitus*, as R has it.
49. *numquam* B, and perhaps the rest.
49, 50. These lines appear in a confused and corrupt form in the MSS.
B has—

  Tr. Numquam edepol hodie inditus destinant tibi.
  Tb. Iam iubeo ignem et sarmen carnifex circumdari,

where the other MSS. omit Tr. and Tb. Instead of *inditus* CD have
invitus. *haec* is due to Acidalius; *inultus* to Pius; *destinaverit* to Camerarius; *iubebo* to Pylades. Different editors have adopted various emendations, R, as usual, the least probable of all.   W has—

  Nunquam edepol hoc hodie inultus destinaveris. Tibi
  Iam iubebo ignem et sarmenta, carnufex, circumdari.

51. *Ne faxis, nam* BbZ. *Ne faxis iis nam* BaDF. *faxis iis nam* C.
iole Vulg. *iolie* BaCDa.
52. *faciam* D. *Quia placeo,* so the MSS. *placeo, eo* R, omitting
quia.
53. *quoiusmodi* C. v. 53 *quom* B.
54. *digitis* Vulg. *dicitis* Ba. *dititis* Da.
55. *ergo nunc* CDF. *ego nunc* BZ. *ergo nunc ego* R.
56. *eccum tui gnati* FZ. *haec cum tui gnatis* B (*gnati* Bb). *hic cum
tu ignati* C. *hectum i gnat'* D. *video huc* the MSS. of Pylades.
video huic BCD. *video hic* FZ. *videod hus* W (!). *huc ad eas
video* R.
57. *agite* CD.

ACTVS V. SCENA III.

CALLIDAMATES. THEVROPIDES. TRANIO.

CA. Vbi somnum sepelivi omnem, omnem atque obdorm-
   ivi crapulam,
Philolaches venisse mihi suum [narravit] peregre huc
   patrem,
Quoque modo hominem ad[venientem] servos ludificatus sit ;
Ait, se metuere in conspe[ctum illius] occedere.
Nunc ego de sodalitate solus sum orator datus,   5
Qui a patre eius conciliarem pacem. Atque eccum optume.
Iubeo te salvere, et, salvos quom advenis, Theuropides,
Peregre, gaudeo. Hic apud nos hodie cenes. Sic face.
   TH. Callidamate, di te ament. De cena facio gratiam.
   CA. Quin venis ?   *TR.* Promitte : ego ibo pro te, si
   tibi non lubet.   10
   TH. Verbero, etiam inrides ?   *TR.* Quian' me pro te
   ire ad cenam autumo ?

1. *somnum* Z.   *omnium* BaCD (the correction in Bb is doubtful). *somnium* F.   *somno meam* R.   *omnem atque* BCD.   *omnemque* FZW.   *obdormivi*, so the MSS. *edormivi* Camer. RW.
2. *suum* [*narravit*] *peregre huc patrem*, so Camer. The MSS. omit *narravit*, without any indications of a blank. WR place *narravit* before *suum*. C has *huic* instead of *huc*.
3. *ad*[*venientem*] *servos*, so Aldus. BCD have *ad . . . . . . servos*, with a blank between *ad* and *servos*.
4. *conspe*[*ctum illius*], so Pylad. Camer. There is a blank in BCD between *conspe* and *occedere*, which R fills thus—[*ctum sui patris*]. *occedere* CD. *accedere* B. *accedere* Pylad. *procedere* Camer. R.
6. *optime* or *optimi* all. v. 23 *maxime* all.
7. *advenis Teuropides* FZ.   *advenisset bruropides* Ba.   *advuminisarte bruropides* Bb.   *advenisset bruropides* CD.
9. *Calidamate* the MSS. *Callidamates* R.   *fatio* B.   *gracis* C.
10. *libet* the MSS.
10, 11. *si tibi . . . . quiane me pro te*, these words are omitted in C.   *si tibi* BDb.   *sibi* Da.   *si ire* FZ.
11. *irrides* FZ.   *inridens* BD.   *quian* BaD.   *qaia* Bb.   *quin* FZ. *te ire;* B omits *ire.*   *autumo* FZ.   *aut bumo* BaC.   *aut . umo* Bb. *autbumo* D.

TH. Non enim ibis: ego ferare faxo, ut meruisti, in
    crucem.

CA. Age mitte ista ac ito ad me ad cenam.   *TR.* Dic
    venturum, quid taces?

CA. Sed tu istuc quid confugisti in aram inscitissumus?

TR. Adveniens perterruit me. — Loquere nunc, quid
    fecerim.   15

Nunc utrisque disceptator, eccum, adest: age, disputa.

TH. Filium corrupisse aio te meum.   *TR.* Ausculta
    modo.

Fateor peccavisse; amicam liberasse; apsente te

Faenori argentum sumpsisse; id esse apsumptum praedico.

Numquid aliud fecit, nisi quod *faciunt summis gnati
    generibus?   20

TH. Hercle mihi tecum cavendum est: nimis qui es
    orator catus.

---

13. This line appears thus in B—

    Ca. Age mitte ista acto ad me ad cenam.   *Tr.* Dic ventu quid taces?

while in CD we have *ista acto*, a blank after *cenam*, followed by two
contracted words, which have been decyphered *dicuntur umquid*. In FZ
we have—

    Tr. Age mitte ista hęc et me ad coenā dic Ituiū . quid taces?

and so W. Camer. and Vulg. have—

    Ca. Age mitte ista et ito ad me ad coenam.   *Tr.* Dic venturum
        quid taces?

while R gives—

    Ca. Age mitte istaec: te ad me ad cenam dic venturum.
    Tr. Quid taces?

It will be observed that B has *cenam*, and this appears to be the usual
orthography.

14. *aram bine* R. *aram banc* Pylad., but the MSS. have neither *bine*
nor *banc*. *inscitissimus* all.

18. *peccavisse*, so the MSS. *potavisse* Acidal. R. *absente te* B.
The rest of the MSS. omit *te*.

19. *praedico* B.

20. *fecit* B. *feci* CD. *nisi quod fatiunt* B. *nisi quod feci* CD.
faciunt is bracketed by W, and omitted by R. Both. omits *aliud*.
summis BbF. *sum* Ba. *summi* CDZ. *gnati* so B.

21. *Hercle*, so Plus. *Erile* BCD. *Hcrile* FZ. *qui es*; the MSS.
have *quis*. R, following Gifan., prints *qui's*. Camer. has *quam es*, and so
Vulg. W.

CA. Sine me dum istuc iudicare.   Surge : ego isti
adsedero.

TH. Maxume.   Accipito hanc ad te litem.   *TR.* Enim
istic captio est.

Fac, ego ne metuam, [igitur, et] ut tu meam timeas
vicem.

TH. Iam minoris [omnia fa]cio, prae quam quibus
modis   25

Me ludificatus est.   *TR.* Bene hercle factum, et factum
gaudeo.

Sapere istac aetate oportet, qui sunt capite candido.

TH. Quid ego nunc faciam, si amicus Demipho aut
Philonides . . . ,

TR. Dicito iis, quo pacto tuus te servos ludificaverit :

Optumas frustrationes dederis in comoediis.   30

    CA. Tace parumper : sine vicissim me loqui.—Ausculta.
    TH. Licet.

    CA. Omnium primum sodalem me esse scis gnato tuo.

Is adiit me : nam illum prodire pudet in conspectum tuum

22. *iti* BCD.   *istic* F.   *istuc* Z.
23. *Accipito* Bb.   *Accipite* Ba and the rest of the MSS.   There is
a blank in BD between *hanc* . . . . *ad*, but not in C.   Hence R has *hanc*
[*tute*] *ad*.   *istic*, so the MSS.   *istarc* Both. W.
24. *metuam* [*igitur et*] *ut tu*, so Camer.   There is a blank in BCD
between *metuam* . . . . *ut tu*.   D has *tu*, and hence W *tu ut*.   R has
metuam [*mibi atque*] *ut tu*.
25. *minoris* [*omnia fa*]*cio*, so Camer.   There is a blank in BCD
between *minoris* . . . . *cio*.   R has *minoris* [*omnia alia fa*]*cio*.   W adopts
the conj. of Camer., but has *quibus me modis*, omitting *me* at the commencement of the following line.   *pre* BCD.
26. *Me ludificatus est*, so the MSS.   *Ludificatust me* R.
27. *qui sunt*, so Camer.   *quis* the MSS.
28. *Demipho aut Philonides*, so Camer.   The MSS. have *Dephilo aut*
Philomontes, except that Ba has *phino montes*.   R supposes that a line
has fallen out after v. 28.
29. *pacto*, so Vulg.   *capto* BCD.   *servus* Ba.
30. *frustraciones* C.   *in comoediis* Z.   *in commodiis* BCD.   *in-*
commodus F.
31. *parumper sine* DcFZ.   *parum persine* BaC.   *parum persine* Bb.
praumper sine Da.   *vicissim me loqui* Acklal. WR.   *me vicissim loqui*
DFZ.   *me vicissim lo qui* B.   *me vicissimio qui* C.   *Licet*, so Vulg.
Lucet BaCD).
33. *adiit me*, so the MSS.   *me adiit* Guyet. R.

Propterea, quia fecit, quae te scire scit. Nunc te opsecro,
Stultitiae adulescentiaeque eius ignoscas. Tuus est ;   35
Scis, solere illanc aetatem tali ludo ludere ;
Quidquid fecit, nobiscum una fecit ; nos deliquimus :
Faenus, sortem, sumptumque omnem, qui amica [empta]
    est, omnia
Nos dabimus, nos conferemus, nostro sumptu, non tuo.
  TH. Non potuit venire orator magis ad me inpetra-
    bilis,   40
Quam tu : neque illi sum iratus, neque quicquam suc-
    censeo ;
Imo me praesente amato, bibito, facito quod lubet.
Si hoc pudet, fecisse sumptum, supplicii habeo satis.
  CA. Dispudet.   *TR.* Dat istam veniam. Quid me fiet
    nunc iam ?
  TH. Verberibus, lutum, caedere pendens ! *TR.* Tamenetsi
    pudet ?   45

---

34. *Propterea quia fecit quae te* CDFZ (*facit* C). *Propterea qui fecit
quam . te,* with the erasure of one letter, Ba. *Propterea qui fecit quam-te* Bb.
Propter ea quae fecit quom te R. *Propterea quae fecit quia te* W.
  35. *stultitia* BaF. *stultitiae* BbC. *adolescentiaeque,* or *adulescentiaeque*
the MSS. *adulescentiaeque* R. *ignoscat* Ba, an evident blunder.
  36. *illunc* Ba, an evident blunder. *etatem* C.
  37. *nobiscum una* Camer. *una nobiscum* the MSS. *nos,* so Camer.
non, or *ñ,* the MSS. *deliquimus,* so Pius. *delinquimus* the MSS.
  38. *qui amica [empta] est,* so WR. *empta* is not found in the MSS.
quanti amica est Camer.
  39. *conferimus* B.
  41. *illi sum iratus,* so the MSS. (. su . , ratus Ba . . su . iratus Bb).
illi iam sum iratus R. *illi sum [iam] iratus* W. *quidquam succenseo,*
so the MSS. *quicquam ei succenseo* R.
  43. *pudet* C, an evident blunder. *supplici iam* R.
  44. So Acidal. Vulg. W. The MSS. are corrupt. Thus B has—
    Tr. Dispudetis tam veniam quid me fiet. *Tb.* Nuntiam
(*Nuntiam* Bb). CDFZ have—
  Tr. Dispudet istam veniam quid me fiet nunc iam,
except that CD omit *Tr.* R has—
  Ca. Dispudet. *Tr.* Si istam das veniam, quid me fiet nunc iam.
  45. *lutum caedere* Guyet. RW. *caedere lutum* BaC. *cedere lutum*
DFZ. *caedere visum* Bb. *Tamenetsi,* so Gruter. *Taminest si* Ba.
Taminest si Bb. *Tam inest si* C. *Taminestsi* D. *Tametsi* F. *Tam
et si* Z.

TH. Interimam hercle [te] ego, si vivo! *CA.* Fac
    istam cunctam gratiam:
Tranioni remitte, quaeso, hanc noxiam causa mea.
  TH. Aliud quidvis inpetrari a me facilius perferam,
Quam ut non ego istum pro suis factis pessumis pessum
    premam.
  CA. Mitte quaeso, istunc. *TH.* Hem, viden', ut restat
    furcifer?   50
  CA. Tranio, quiesce, si sapis. *TH.* Tu quiesce hanc
    rem modo
Petere; ego illum verberibus, ut sit quietus, subegero.
  CA. Nihil opus est profecto. Age iam, sine ted ex-
    orarier.
  TH. Nolo ores. *CA.* Quaeso hercle. *TH.* Nolo, in-
    quam, ores. *CA.* Nequiquam nevis:

---

46. *interremam* Ba.   *hrcle te,* so Both. RW. The MSS. omit *te.*
ego si vivo. CA. *Fac istam,* so Camer. *ego suibo.* CA. *Facistam* Ba
(but Bb has *suibo*). *ego suibo facis tam* C. *ego suibo farista* D. *ego
iubro fac istam* FZ.
  47. *Tranioni remitte quaeso* BFZ. *Tranioni remitte remitte quaeso* CD.
Tranioni iam remitte, omitting *quaeso* R.
  48. *a me facilius perferam,* so the MSS. *perferam a me facilius*
Both. R.
  50. So Camer. Vulg. The MSS. are very corrupt, thus—*Mitte quae sis
tum . vident ut restat furcifer* Ba. *Mitte quaepis tume . viden . ut restat
furcifer* Bb. *Mitteq; sis tume viden ut restat furcifer* C. *Mitte quesis tu
me viden ut restat furcifer* Da (*quesis tu me* Dc). TB. *Mitte quepo tu me.*
TB. *Viden ut restat furcifer* FZ (*Videm* Z). R has—
    Ca. Mitte quaeso istum. *Th.* [Illum ut mittam] viden ut astat
        furcifer?
W has—
    Tr. Mitte, quaeso, sis, tu med. *Th.* Hem, viden' ut restat furcifer.
  51. So Camer. Vulg. W. Here again the MSS. are corrupt. *Tranio
qui esse sapis.* TH. *Tu qui esse* B. *Tranio quiesse sapis tu quiesse* C.
Tranio quie re sapis tu quiesce D. R has CA. *Tranio, si sapis, quiesce.*
TH. *Tu quiesce.*
  52. *ego illum* B. *verberibus ut sit quietus,* so the MSS. *ut sit
quietus verberibus* Acidal. R. *verberibus ut quietus sit* W.
  53. *Nil opus est profecto,* FZR assign these words to Tranio. *ted,*
so Guyet. *te* the MSS.
  54. *inquam ores* BC. *inquam ores* D. *inquam oras* FZ.

Hanc unam noxiam unam, quaeso, fac causa mea.   55

   TR. Quid gravaris? Quasi non cras iam commeream
     aliam noxiam:

Ibi utrumque, et hoc et illud, poteris ulcisci probe.

   CA. Sine te exorem.   TH. Age, habe; abi inpune!

   Hem, huic habeto gratiam.

Spectatores, fabula haec est acta: vos plausum date.

   55. So BCD, B having *quæso. Hanc modo noxiam unam quæso missam fac* R. *Hanc modo unam noxae un.iam quæso fac* Both. W.

   56. *non cras iam*, so Camer., and this is the corrected reading of B, which has *non cras iam. non gratiâ* CF. *non grūm* D. *gratiam non* Z.

   57. *Ibi tu utrumque* R, but *tu* is not in the MSS.

   58. *Age, abi, abi* Bb. *Age, ab* .. with an erasure Ba. *Age abe abi* CD. *Age, habe, abi* FZW.   *em* B. *hem* the rest of the MSS. *em* R.

NOTES.

I. i. 1. *Exi ... foras.*] Of the two forms of the word signifying a door, *fora* of the first declension, and *foris* of the third, the former is found only in the accusative plural *foras*, and the ablative plural *foris*, and these are by some grammarians designated as adverbs. We may say a few words upon each.

FORAS.—1st. In the great majority of cases in which *foras* is employed it is combined with a verb which implies the movement of the person or thing addressed or spoken of from the interior of a house to the door. The verbs generally used are, *foras ire, abire, exire, exsurgere, effugere, efferre, educere, seducere, deferre, excludere, extrudere, excire, excitare, eicere, vocare, evocare, egredi, progredi, pellere, edere se, proruere se*[*], *prosequi*, and the like. Less common but still conveying the same idea, Trin. II. ii. 1, *Quo illic homo foras se penetravit ex aedibus?* Eun. II. iii. 66, *Homo quatitur certe cum domo foras*, 'hurled, kicked out.' Sometimes the expression is figurative without reference to a door, as in Rud. I. ii. 82, *fluctus eiecit foras*, 'the wave has cast her forth;' and Truc. I. i. 18, *Pisces .. eduxit foras*, of drawing fish out of a pond in a net; and in Most. III. i. 68 (64), *abire foras* is 'to go to a foreign land;' and still stranger, Phor. V. vii. 65, *Vides peccatum tuum esse delatum foras*, 'carried out,' i.e. 'has been hinted abroad, has been disclosed.' 2nd. The idea of motion outwards, although always implied, is in one or two phrases much less direct. Thus since *vocari ad cenam foras* means 'to be invited out to dinner,' so *promittere foras ad cenam* means 'to accept such an invitation,' 'to promise to go out to dinner.' Thus Rud. V. iii. 64, *Neve adeo vocatos credam vos esse ad cenam foras;* and Most. IV. iii. 12 (iv. 12), *Promisi foras Ad cenam, ne me te vocare censeas;* and Stich. IV. ii. 16,

[*] In Eun. III. v. 31, *Foras simul omnes proruunt se* is used with reference to persons hurrying out of a room in the interior of a house in order to proceed into another apartment.

Ad cenam hercle alio promisi foras ; while in Men. I. ii. 15 we have the singular phrase *ad cenam aliquo condicam foras.* Still more remarkable are the expressions *vendere foras, numerare argentum foras,* and *locitare foras.* The first of these occurs in Stich. I. iii. 66, *Foras necessum est quidquid habeo vendere,* i.e. 'to sell off.' The second in Pers. IV. iii. 62 (70), *quamobrem ego argentum numerem foras,* i.e. 'why should I pay out money?' The third in Adel. V. viii. 26, *Agelli est hic sub urbe paulum quod locitas foras,* i.e. 'which you are in the habit of letting to a tenant.' All of these convey the notion of an object *passing out* of the hands or immediate control of the owner to an external holder.

FORIS.—*Foris* is used in direct opposition to *intus* and to *domi.* When opposed to *intus* it signifies the outside of a house as opposed to the inside; when opposed to *domi* it signifies in a more general sense 'abroad,' as opposed to 'at home.' *Intus* and *domi* are sometimes expressed and sometimes omitted. Thus, Capt. I. ii. 6, *Sinito ambulare si foris, si intus volent ;* Cist. IV. ii. 20, *Nam et intus parvo et foris formido ;* Merc. III. iv. 2, *Si domi sum foris est animus, sin foris sum animus domi est ;* Cas. II. ii. 8, *Domi et foris aegre quod sit, satis semper est ;* Hec. II. i. 21, *Ideo quia ut vos mihi domi eritis, proinde ego ero fama foris.* Again, *intus* being omitted, Most. II. i. 58, *hisce ego aedes occludam hinc foris,* i.e. 'I shall lock up the house from hence on the outside ;' and III. i. 153 (150), *Ego hic tantisper, dum exis, te opperiar foris,* i.e. 'I shall wait for you outside ;' again, *domi* being omitted, II. ii. 21, *Foris ambulatis, natus nemo in aedibus,* i.e. 'you are walking abroad, not a living soul is in the house ;' and so Phor. II. i. 78, *D. Antipho ubi nunc est ? P. Foris,* i.e. 'not at home ;' so in Eun. V. iv. 12, *Quae dum foris sunt,* 'who while not at home ;' *domi* being opposed in line 16. We have seen above that *promittere foras ad cenam* signifies 'to accept an invitation to dine out ;' in like manner *cenare foris* is 'to dine out ;' thus Most. II. ii. 53, *Vt foris cenaverat Tuus gnatus* (one night) 'when your son had dined out ;' and Stich. I. iii. 36, *Vocem te ad cenam, nisi egomet cenem foris ;* and IV. ii. 16, *G. Quid ais Pamphilippe ? P. Ad cenam, hercle, alio promisi foras. G. Quid? foras ? P. Foras hercle vero. G. Qui, malum, tibi lasso lubet Foris cenare ? P. Virum tu censes ? G. Iube domi cenam coqui ;* and in Men. I. ii. 17 we have *nam si foris cenat.* In Heaut. V. i. 50, *Nonne id flagitium est, te aliis consilium dare, Foris sapere, tibi non posse auxiliarier,* i.e. 'that you are wise for other people, but cannot help yourself.' In Phor. V. i. 18, *ne vos forte imprudentes foris Effutiretis,* means, 'lest you unawares might blab, when from home,' where *foras* might be substituted for *foris*, and *effutire foras* would signify ' blab out the secret.' *Foris*, In the sense of *from without*, does not appear in the earliest Latin writers, but is so used by Lucretius V. 544 and by Cicero.

2. *exhibes argutias*] i.e. ' playing off your quips on me.' Comp. Bac. I. ii. 19, *Etiam me adversus exordire argutias?* The root *arg* seems to have conveyed the idea of *brilliant light*, and hence the words into which it enters denote something *shining*, or *white*, or *piercing*. Passing from the Greek ἀργός, ἀργεννός, ἀργύριον, we have in Latin *argentum*, ' the brilliant white metal;' *argilla*, ' white clay ;' and the verb *arguo*, which properly signifies to ' pierce' or ' penetrate,' and when applied to the mind, ' prove' or ' convince.' Hence *argutus*, in reference to sounds, signifies strictly ' sharp,' ' shrill ;' in reference to the mind of man, ' acute,' ' penetrating ;' and *argutiae* are ' subtleties,' and in a bad sense ' sophisms,' ' verbal tricks.' According, then, as we select the literal or the figurative meaning, *argutus homo* may signify either a shrewd, sharp fellow (as opposed to ' a flat'), or simply one who is ' a noisy chatterer.' In Truc. II. vi. 12, *arguti* are clever talkers, *Strenui nimio plus prosunt populo quam arguti et cati. Facile tibi facunditatem virtus argutam invenit, Sine virtute argutum circum mihi habeam pro praefica.** In Trin. I. ii. 163, which will be quoted in the note on v. 14, *argutus* is applied to ' garrulous gossipers.' For *argutus* see also Merc. III. iv. 44, Pseud. II. iv. 56; *arguti*, Trin. IV. ii. 132; *argutarier*, ' to quibble,' Amph. I. i. 193. In Amph. III. ii. 2, *argutam* is the participle, and means ' charged,' ' accused.'

3. *herilis pernicies*] ' thou that art thy master's bane.' There is for the most part little difficulty in determining the force of the epithet *herilis* in Plautus. Thus no doubt can exist with regard to *herilis filius, filia, amica, concubina, res, patria; herile imperium, negotium.† Herilis metus* (Amph. V. i. 17) signifies ' the alarm which I felt for the safety of my mistress ;' *custos herilis* (As. III. iii. 65), ' thou that art the guardian of thy master.' In Poen. I. ii. 73, *Nam pro herili et nostro quaestu satis bene ornatae sumus* signifies, ' in so far as regards our master's profit and our own ;' but the most difficult combination is

* See frag. Frivol, *Superaboque omnes argutando praeficas*, where *argutando* means ' with piercing cries.'
† Aul. II. iii. 8, IV. i. 13; Bac. II. i. 1, II. iii. 117, 132, IV. ix. 7; Capt. II. i. 5; Cist. II. iii. 8, IV, ii. 83; Epid. I. i. 18, I. ii. 61; Men. V. vi. 1; Mil. II. i. 37, 44, II. iii. 3, 66, II. v. 6, 48, 60, II. vi. 1, 28, 68; Most. I. i. 20, 79, II. 1, 2; Pseud. I. iv. 2, 20, II. iii. 7; Stich. II. ii. 2; Trin. III. i. 1; Truc. II. ii. 42, III. ii. 1.

in Pers. II. ii. 11, *Scio fidei hercle herili ut soleat impudicitia oppro-*
brarier, where *fidei herili* means 'honesty of a slave (i. e. when a slave
is honest) in the service of his master;' and the import of the passage
is, 'I know that it is usual for a slave who is honest in the service of
his master to be twitted with impure motives.' In so far as the
sentiment of the passage is concerned, it is repeated below, IV. i.
3, 5. Weise, who explains "Sensus debet esse: scio heros non
stare solere promissis," has entirely mistaken the meaning, which
was correctly apprehended by Acidalius.

4. *le . . . ulciscar probe.*] We have the same words in Poen. V. iv. 58,
Nunc pol ego te ulciscar probe. *Vlciscor,* in Plautus and Terence, is
generally construed, as here, with the accusative of the person on
whom vengeance is to be taken.* Sometimes we have in the
ablative the kind of punishment, as Cas. II. i. 8, *Flagitium illud*
hominis! ego illum fame, ego illum Siti, maledictis, malefactis, amatorem
Vlciscar: but it is also construed with the accusative of the thing on
account of which vengeance is taken, as in this play, the third line
from the end, *Ibi utrumque, et hoc et illud, poteris ulcisci probe;* so also
Poen. V. v. 1, *Si ego minam non ultus fuero probe, quam lenoni dedi*
Tum profecto me sibi habento scurrae ludificatae; and Trin. V. ii. 49,
Miserum est male promerita, ut merita, si mihi ulcisci non licet, i. e. 'It
is very provoking if I am not allowed to inflict upon evil deeds the
punishment they have deserved.' This is the speech of Charmides
after he had unwillingly agreed to forgive his son. Welse appears
to have mistaken the meaning when he says, "Sensus: miserum est
si mihi non licet et filium punire, et amicum remunerare aut gratias
referre ei;" and he seems to have had some misgiving, for he adds,
" Sed haec sententia aliquanto plus iusto perplexa est."

5. *Exi, inquam, nidor, e culina*] i. e. 'come forth, you stinking
scullion.' The reading is very doubtful, and was probably suggested
to Pylades or some other early corrector by the line in Juvenal S.
V. 162, *Captum te nidore suae putat ille culinae,* and that in Martial
I. xciii. (xcii.) 9, *Pasceris et nigrae solo nidore culinae.* *Nidor* properly
signifies the smell, smoke, or vapour proceeding from some object
when burned, and generally indicates a rank, foetid, or suffocating

---

* So Amph. IV. III. 9; As. I. ii. 22; Cas. II. iv. 20; Bac. III. iv. 9, *istanc*
ulciscar multis modis; Bac. V. 2, 69; Epid. II. ll. 84; Men. I. ii. 17, IV. ii.
72; Pers. IV. vii. 16; Pseud. V. ii. 26; Rud. III. iii. 36; Trin. III. i. 18;
As. V. ii. 53, where the accusative of the person is understood, not expressed: and so And. III. v. 18; Eun. IV. vi. 24; Hec. I. i. 15; Phor.
V. vii. 69. *hunc nostro modo ulcisci.*

odour. It is applied by Lucretius to the stench proceeding from a recently extinguished lamp (VI. 792, *acris nidor*), by Virgil to fumigations with galbanum to drive away snakes (G. III. 415, *galbaneo nidore*) and to the burning beard of Ebusus (Æn. XII. 301, *nidoremque ambusta dedit*), by Livy to burning feathers (XXXVIII. 7, *foedo quodam nidore ex adusta pluma*), by Ovid to the entrails of a victim consumed on the altar (Met. XII. 153, *Dis acceptus nidor*),* and by Pliny to the fumes of sulphur (XXXV. 15, § 50, *tanta vis est ut morbos comitiales deprehendat nidore imposito igni*).

6. *aedis.*] For spelling compare I. i. 77, *Periere, et aedis et ager:* I. ii. 18, *Aedes quom extemplo,* &c.; 20, *Laudunt fabrum atque aedes probant;* iii. 9, *periere hae oppido aedes;* the MSS. often read *edis:* see critical notes throughout.

8. *Abi rus, abi dierecte.*] Cf. Cas. I. 15, *Abi rus, abi dierectus tuam in provinciam;* Most. III. ii. 163, *Vbi canis est? T. Abi dierecta: si, abin' hinc in malam crucem.* Rud. IV. iv. 126, *Quin tu i directa cum sucula et cum porculis.* That *abi dierecte, abi dierecta, abi dierectus, i hinc dierectus, abin dierectus, recede hinc dierecte,* phrases not uncommon in Plautus, are equivalent to *abi in malam crucem,* 'go to the mischief,' 'be hanged to you,' seems certain, but the etymology of the word is very doubtful, and it is found in Plautus only, with the exception of the passage quoted by Nonius from the Eumenides of Varro. (See below.) The most plausible explanation is that which represents it as a compound of *erigo, di-erectus,* and makes it refer to the outstretched limbs of a malefactor when hoisted up and nailed on a cross or gibbet. Thus Poen. I. ii. 134, *I dierecte in maxumam malam crucem;* the passage from Most. III. ii. 163, quoted above; and Capt. III. iv. 103, *Quin quiescis dierectum cor meum! I ac suspende te, Tu supsultas, ego miser vix asto prae formidine;* and, as a sort of commentary or illustration, we may take Mil. II. iv. 6, *Credo ego istoc exemplo tibi esse eundem actutum extra portam, Dispessis manibus patibulum quom habebis.* When we read in the Men. II. iii. 87 (92), *Periit probe Ducit lembum dierectum navis praedatoria,* the expression must mean 'the piratical galley is leading (or towing) the skiff to destruction,' but in Curc. II. i. 21, *P. Sed quid tibi est? C. Lien necat, renes dolent. Pulmones*

---

* Since the vapour arising from meat while cooked is by no means necessarily disagreeable, we find Martial VII. xxvii. 5, when speaking of the roasting of a wild boar, *Pinguescant madidi lardo nidore penates,* where, however, several MSS. have *madido* and *lardi,* and in any case *lardus* is equivalent to the *Dis acceptus nidor* quoted above.

distrahuntur, cruciatur iecur, Radices cordis pereunt, hirae omnes dolent.
P. Tum te igitur morbus agitat hepatarius.   . . . .
C. Lien dirrectus est, the word seems to be, taken literally, ' my spleen
is bursting with distension.' The reading *diruptus est* is evidently
a gloss. For other passages in Plautus where *dierectus, &c.,* occur,
see Bac. IV. l. 7, *Recede hinc dierecte;* Cas. I. 15, *Abi rus abi dierectus
tuam in provinciam;* Merc. l. 72, *I hinc dierectus;* Merc. IV. iv. 16,
Abin dierectus; Poen l. i. 32, *Abi dierectus; Quin tu i dierecta,* Rud.
IV. iv. 126; *Abin hinc dierecte,* Trin. ll. iv. 56. Nonius (p. 49) explains the word, giving an example from Varro, '*Dierecti* dicti cruci-
fixi, quasi ad diem erecti. Varro Eumenidibus; *Apage in dierectum
a domo nostra istam insanitatem.*' The interpretation given in Paulus
Diaconus (p. 69, ed. Müll.) seems founded on the etymology adopted
by Nonius, "*Dierectum* dicebant per antiphrasin, volentes significare
malum diem." On the prosody of *dierectus* see note of W. on
Men. ll. iii. 92.

9. *En, hoccine volebas*] 'There's for you' (giving him a blow), 'is
that what you were wanting?' *Hem,* although not found in the
MSS., is probably the true reading. At least elsewhere we find this
word employed to mark that a blow has been given, e. g. Poen. I. ii.
168, where Agorastocles, enraged with Milphio, who had addressed
Adelphasium in terms of the most tender endearment (the lines are
quoted below, in the note on v. 14), flies upon him, exclaiming, *Non ego
homo trioboli sum, nisi ego illi mastigiae Exturbo oculos atque dentes: hem
voluptatem tibi! Hem mel! hem cor! hem labellum! Hem salutem! hem
suavium!* where a blow accompanies each repetition of the word
hem, and so Men. V. vii. 29.
  - *Perii* is here an exclamation of pain and anger. In Plautus,
generally, *perii* signifies 'I am lost, I am undone,' and *perire* 'to be
lost, to be ruined, to ruin oneself.' So below, ll. i. 2, *Iupiter . .
me perisse . . cupit;* and v. 6, *perii Tranio; perii,* ll. ii. 78 (77); and
in a multitude of passages. We cannot have better examples than
As. I. iii. 80, *Non omnino iam perii: est reliquom quo peream magis.*
Truc. I. i. 24, *Extemplo et ipsus periit, et res, et fides;* and in the
lines which immediately follow, *Bis periit amator, ab re atque animo
simul, idem perit, ab animo perit, res perit, aurum periit, aliquid
semper est quod pereat.* In the same play, IV. i. 9, *Salvus sum quia
perro, si non peream plane interram,* i. e. 'because I am going to
the dogs, because I am ruining myself,' where we may remark the
jingle between *per-eam* and *inter-ram,* a device to which we shall
afterwards call attention.

– *haccine*] So *haeccine*, acc. pl. neut. *v.* 24; *hoccine*, acc. sing. neut. *v.* 26; *hoccine modo*, *v.* 25.

12. *frutex*] i. e. 'you dunderhead.' *Frutex* properly signifies 'a shrub' or 'dwarf tree,' also 'the stalk of a plant.' There is a line in Terence, Heaut. V. i. 4, which may serve as a commentary, *In me quidvis harum rerum convenit Quae sunt dicta in stultum, caudex, stipes, asinus, plumbeus*, and we ourselves talk of a fellow as being 'a poor stick' or 'a perfect stick.'* R. has adopted the conjecture of Guyetus and has introduced *rupex* into his text, a word quoted by Festus (s. v. *Squarrosa*, p. 329, ed. Müll.) from Lucilius, and which, as we gather from Aul. Gell. (xiii. 9) and Tertullian (De Pall. 4, with note of Salmasius, Apol. 21, De Anima, 6), signifies 'an ignorant boor.' Since all the best MSS. agree in *frutex*, no change is necessary.

14. *deliciae popli.*] This in the English edition of Forcellini is rendered, 'the sport and diversion of the people,' but it means rather 'the darling of the people,' i.e. 'of society.' This is the sense of *deliciae* in Catull. II. 1, *Passer deliciae meae puellae*; and so in Plautus, Poen. I. ii. 152, we find it in a string of endearing appellations, *Mea voluptas! meae deliciae! mea rita! mea amoenitas! Meus ocellus! meum labellum! mea salus! meum suavium Meum mel! meum cor! mea colostra! meus molliculus caseus!* and so in Pseud. I. ii. 47, *quibus deliciae estis; v.* 90, *Phoenicium .. deliciae summatum virum;* Pers. II. ii. 22, *Paegnium, deliciae pueri, salve* ('you darling, darling boy'); and Stich. V. v. 1, *Morem vobis geram, meae deliciae!* and we have several examples in Cicero. We shall have occasion to say more about this word in the note on IV. iii. 9 in this play. In Asin. V. ii. 35, *Subripiam in deliciis pallam quam habet*, i. e. 'which she loves so much.'

15. *Rus mihi tu obiectas*] i. e. 'do you cast the country in my teeth?' The Scotch phrase, 'to cast up a thing to any one,' i. e. 'to reproach any one with a thing,' is still more close. Below, in III. ii. 121, *Ah! cave tu illi obiectes nunc in aegritudine Te has emisse*, 'do not taunt him' (remind him). The phrase is varied in Truc. II. ii. 25, *Rus tu mihi opprobras? ut nacta es hominem quem pudeat probri.* With regard to the contemptuous use of *rus* we may compare Truc. II. ii. 14, *Rus merum hoc quidem est*, 'this is rustic coarseness in perfection,' 'this is a pure specimen of a coarse country clown.'

* *Lapis* is used in the same sense, Merc. III iv. 46, *egomet credidi Homini docto rem mandare, is lapidi mando maxumo.*

17. *Cis, hercle, paucas tempestates*] i. e. 'within a brief period.' We have *cis* employed in the same manner in Truc. II. iii. 27, *cis dies paucos;* and in Merc. I. 42, *paucas cis menses.* In the latter passage, however, *cis* is not found in the MSS. but was inserted on conjecture by Acidalius, and has been admitted by the best editors. *Tempestates paucas* is here equivalent to *breve tempus.* *Tempestas* in the singular is used in the sense of *tempus* in Truc. II. iv. 29. *Verum tempestas nemini quom quandam fuit,* 'I remember when there was a time;' and in the Prologue (not by Plautus) to the Cas. v. 18, *Ea tempestate flos poetarum fuit.* Elsewhere in Plautus, *tempestas, tempestatem, tempestate, tempestatibus,* signify bad weather, a storm, either with or without a qualifying epithet. In Cicero *tempestas,* both with and without a qualifying epithet, is used in several passages to signify 'fine weather.' *Tempestas,* weather (bad weather), Amph. II. ii. 58: *liquida tempestas,* Most. III. ii. 64 (62): *tempestas,* a storm, I. ii. 27 (24), 57 (52), iii. 6; Rud. II. iii. 38, IV. i. 10, iii. 3: *tempestatibus,* storms, Merc. I. 83; Stich. III. i. 2: *tempestate,* storm, Rud. IV. ii. 12, iv. 143: *tempestatem (importunam),* Trin. II. iii. 8.

18. *Ferratilis* is an ἅπ. λεγ.

20. *Corrumpis herilem filium.*] So v. 27, *corrumpat et rem et filium,* i. e. 'is leading to ruin,' and vv. 28, 80, V. ii. 17 (iii. 17). Cf. Merc. III. ii. 1, *Tandem impetravi ut egomet me corrumperem. Empta est amica clam uxore mea et filio.* In the whole of the following passages the word is applied to leading the young astray, undermining their principles: *corrumpatur,* Bac. IV. x. 3, V. ii. 72; *corrumpi,* III. iii. 15, IV. x. 3; *corrupto,* III. iii. 16; *corruptelae,* 'ruin,' As. v. ii. 17; *corruptela,* Truc. III. ii. 3; *corrumpit,* Epid. II. ii. 83, &c., &c. Amph. I. iii. 32, *ne corrumpe oculos,* 'do not spoil;' Merc. III. i. 3, *oculos corrumpis;* Amph. V. i. 6, *corrupta sum,* 'I am undone;' Men. IV. ii. 33 and 31, *diem corrupit* and *corrupi,* 'wasted, lost the day;' Epid. I. i. 86, *plane hoc corruptum est caput,* 'I am utterly undone;' Pseud. III. ii. 102, *corrumpitur iam cena;* Trin. II. i. 14, *hominum corruptor;* Pers. V. ii. 3, *corruptor,* 'that villain.'

21. *pergraecamini*] i. e. 'play the profligate.' The stern and austere old Romans, when they first became acquainted with the Greeks in Southern Italy, would naturally be shocked by a mode of life so repugnant to their own habits and prejudices, and hence when they wished to express that a man was indulging in dissolute practices and embarked on a profligate career, they said that he was 'playing the Greek.' The word occurs again in this scene, v. 61,

and in IV. ii. 44 (iii. 21). See also Bac. IV. vii. 15, Poen. III. ii. 26, Truc. I. i. 69. *Congraccere*, from an active form, *congraucco*, was introduced by Aldus and Camerarius into the text of Bac. IV. iv. 91, where the MSS. give *congregem*, but so the MSS. have *pergregetur* in IV. vii. 15, where *pergraecetur* is undoubtedly true.

22, 23. *pascite Parasitos.*] See IV. ii. 6 (i. 29), *S. Manesne ilico, impure parasite? P. Qui parasitus sum? S. Ego enim Dicam: cibo perduci poteris quovis.*

23. *opsonate polluribiliter.*] *Opsono*, the active form, and *opsonor*, the deponent form, seem to be used indifferently; thus Aul. II. iv. 1, *Postquam opsonavit herus et conduxit cocos;* and a few lines lower down, *v.* 16, *Quid? hic non poterat de suo Senex opsonari filias in nuptiis?* so also Adel. I. ii. 37, *Opsonat, potat, olet unguenta, de meo;* and And. II. vi. 20, *Vix, inquit, drachmis opsonatus est decem;* the active form, however, is the more common. As to the orthography, see Proleg. ὄψον or ὀψώνιον denotes in Greek any article of food except bread and wine—generally, anything eaten with farinaceous food to give it a relish, especially ' fish,' the favourite dainty among the Athenians. So in Latin, *pulmentum* denotes properly anything eaten with *puls* to give it a relish; hence ' a dainty,' and hence *pulmentaria* are rich-dressed dishes, but occasionally simply a relish. *Tu pulmentaria quaere Sudando,* Hor. S. II. ii. 20.

— *polluribiliter.*] The verb *pollucere* was used in connection with religious observances, and seems to have been a priestly term signifying ' to present as an offering to a god.' Thus Festus (p. 253, ed. Müll.), *Pollucere merces [quas cuivis deo] liceat, sunt far, polenta, vinum, panis fermentalis, ficus, pasta, suilla, bubulina, agnina, casei, ovilla, alica, sesama, et oleum, pisces quibus est squama praeter squarum (scarum): Herculi autem omnia esculenta, poculenta.* Cassius Hemina, as quoted by Plin. H. N. xxxii. § 2, § 10, *Numa constituit ut pisces qui squamosi non essent ni polluerent, parsimonia* commentus, ut convivia publica et privata cenaeque ad pulvinaria facilius compararentur, ni qui ad polluctum emerent, pretio minus parcerent eaque praemercarentur.* Again, Cato R. R. 132, *Dapem hoc modo fieri oportet. Iovi dapali culignam vini quantum vis polluceto. . . Cum pollucere oportebit sic facies. Iupiter dapalis, quod tibi fieri oportet, in domo familia mea culignam vini dapi, eius rei ergo macte hac illace dape pollucenda esto.* So also Stich. I. iii. 80, *Haec venisse iam opus est, quantum potest I?*

---

* *Parsimonia* is a conj. of Scalig., the MSS. have *patrimonia*.

decumam partem Herculi * *polluceam.* We find also the participle in
Rud. II. iv. 11, *Non ego sum pollucta pago. Potin' ut me apstineas
manum?* which must mean, 'Hands off! I am no tit bit for the
bumpkins of the parish,' i.e. 'I am meat for your masters.' The
application of this word in Curc. I. iii. 37, *Tun' meam l'enerem vituperas? Quod quidem mihi polluctus virgis servos sermonem serat!* which
must signify 'a slave who has been entertained with a liberal allow-
ance of stripes:' for the verb *polluceo* signifying 'to offer in sacrifice,'
and the custom being to present the most choice objects of each
kind to the gods, the derivatives of *polluceo* frequently convey the
notion of sumptuousness, magnificence, unsparing liberality; thus
we find in Macrob. S. II. 13, *pollucibilis cena* in the sense of a
sumptuous banquet, and in the passage before us *opsonate pollucibiliter*
mean, 'make your market without stinting yourself.' So also we
have seen above, in the passage quoted from Cassius Hemina,
polluctum used in reference to a banquet prepared in honour of the
gods without regard to price; and Macrob. S. II. 12 mentions
specially a *polluctum Herculis;* in the Rud. V. iii. 63 we read,
*Spectatores, vos quoque ad cenam vocem, Ni daturus nil sim, neque sit
quicquam pollucti domi,* i.e. 'anything dainty;' and finally, in Stich.
V. iv. 6, *hinc quidem Hodie polluctura, praeter nos, iam dabitur nemini,*
i.e. 'good cheer.' The modification in meaning which *polluceo* and
its derivatives assumed in the later writers may be seen by referring
to the Lexicons. The etymology is uncertain, but it has been
conjectured with some plausibility that it is connected with *porricio,*
which also is a sacrificial word. See Priscian IX. p. 874, and
quotation from the Colax of Naevius. See also Bentley's Terence,
ed. Volbehr, p. xxvi.

24. *quom peregre hinc iit.*] The young scholar will observe that
peregre signifies, 1. 'to' a foreign land; 2. 'from' a foreign land;
3. 'in' a foreign land; according to the verb with which it is constructed. 1. The words in our text yield an example of the first,
and so *abiit peregre* in IV. ii. 41 (iii. 18). 2. In II. i. 6, *herus
advenit peregre, periit Tranio;* and so *peregre advenit, advenisse, adveni
advenis, venit, venisse,* in II. i. 27, III. i. 83 (79), III. ii. 54, 118 (116),
IV. iii. (iv.) 12, V. ii. (iii.) 2, V. ii. (iii.) 8. 3. In Pers. I. i. 30,
*T. Basilice agito eleutheria. S. Quid iam? T. Quia herus peregre
est. S. Ain tu, peregre est?* So *peregre ablegavit,* Cas. Prol. 62;
p. profectus est, Trin. I. ii. 112; *p. gestandus clupeus,* Trin. II. iv. 195;

* Compare omnino Bac. IV. iv. 15.

p. vendidit, Pseud. I. i. 49; *p. advenientem*, Trin. II. iv. 21, IV. ii. 155, Truc. II. vi. 34; *p. rediisse*, Stich. IV. ii. 7.

31. *in aliam partem*] i.e. 'moving in a different direction, towards a different goal.' The young scholar must remember that *in* is followed by the accusative not only when it denotes actual physical motion towards a person, place, or thing, but also when it denotes an action tending towards some definite result, or a movement of the mind in the direction of or towards any particular object. So below, *v.* 64, *in vesperum*, 'against evening,' i.e. 'with a view to my evening repast;' and so I. ii. 38 (41), *in firmitatem*, 'with a view to secure strength;' and in the next line, *in usum*, 'with a view to their being practically serviceable;' *in speciem*, 'with a view to fair appearance,' &c.

33. *Quid tibi, malum, nu, aut quid ego agam, curatio*] i.e. 'what business have you, confound you, to look after me or my proceedings?' The construction *quid curatio est tibi me*, in which the accusative is put after the verbal substantive in *io*, is by no means uncommon in Plautus. *Quid tibi hanc curatio est rem, verbero, aut mutitio?* Amph. I. iii. 21; *Sed quid tibi, nos mendice homo, tactio est?* Aul. III. ii. 9; *Quid tibi ergo meam, me invito, tactio est?* Aul. IV. x. 14; *Quid tibi huc receptio ad te est meam virum?* As. V. ii. 70; *Quid tibi istunc tactio est?* Cas. II. vi. 54; *Quid tibi tactio hunc fuvit*, ib. 56; *Quid istum tibi tactio est?* Curc. V. ii. 27; *Quid me vobis tactio est?* Men. V. vii. 27; *Quid tibi hanc digito tactio est?* Poen. V. v. 29; *Quid tibi huc ventio est? Quid tibi hanc aditio est? Quid tibi hanc notio est, amicam meam?* Truc. II. vii. 61. In all the above examples, with the exception of that from Amph. I. iii. 21, where *rem* is in reality equivalent to *me*, we have the accusative of a person; when a place is introduced, sometimes a preposition is supplied before the accusative, as *Quid tibi ad hasce accessio aedes est prope aut pultatio?* Truc. II. ii. 3 (cf. *Quid illi ex utero exitio est?* Truc. II. vi. 30); and sometimes the accusative is expressed by an adverb, *Quid illi reditio huc etiam fuit?* Most. II. i. 30; *Quid tibi interpellatio aut in concilium huc accessio est?* Trin. III. ii. 83; and so in the example quoted above from Truc. II. vii. 61. We find the dative after *auscultatio*, Rud. II. vi. 18. *Quid mihi scelesto tibi erat auscultatio, Quidve hinc abitio, quidve in navem inscensio?* It will be observed that in all the above examples, 1. the clause is interrogative with *quid*, the verb *sum*, and the dative of a pronoun (*tibi, mihi, vobis, illi*); 2. the verbal substantive ends in *io*; 3. there is uniformly an expression of impatience, indignation, remonstrance, or anger. Hence such constructions as

the following, *Opulento homini hoc servitus dura est*, Amph. I. i. 12;
imperator Numidis, Sall. Iug. 14; *Is tibi imperatorem aliquem quaerit*,
ib. 85; can scarcely be regarded as analogous, although sometimes
adduced in illustration. The line quoted from Amph. prol. 34,
Nam iusta ab iustis iustus sum orator datus, where *iusta* is regarded
as under the government of *orator*, would be remarkable, but *iusta*
is not found in the best MSS., all of which seem to have *iuste*,
and so Vulg.

35. *scorta ducere*.] *Scorta ducere, ductare, ductitare circumducere*,
&c., are established phrases denoting 'to keep loose company.'
So below, IV. ii. 43 (iii. 21); cf. Asin. I. iii. 12, 13, 17, V. ii. 13;
Men. I. ii. 15, IV. iii. 20, V. iv. 62; Poen. I. ii. 60, IV. ii. 46;
Stich. V. iv. 48; Truc. III. ii. 10. Compare especially Poen. Prol.
108, *Dat aurum, ducit noctem;* Stich. IV. l. 65, *Vt iam nunc scelestus sese ducit pro adolescentulo;* Poen. IV. ii. 46, *Neque triobulum
ullum amicae das, et ductas gratiis;* Merc. IV. iv. 46, *Na pol ego
patiar, sic me nuptam tam male Measque in aedes sic scorta obductarier.*

37. *fui.*] This denotes an eructation on the part of Grumio.
We have a coarse jest on the same theme in Pseud. V. ii. 5, where
Pseudolus staggers in drunk and is greeted by Simo with—*Di te
ament Pseudole!* to which Pseudolus replies by hiccuping in Simo's
face, who expresses his disgust, *Phui—in malam crucem;* and then,
*P. Cur ego me afflictor? S. Quid tu, malum, ergo in os mihi ebrius
inructas?* again, on a repetition of the offence, *Pergin' ructare in os
mihi?* to which Pseudolus retorts, *Suavis ructus mihi est, sic tine modo.*

38. *oboluisti allium.*] On *olere* with acc. see Madvig § 223. 2.

39. *Germana iniuvies*] i. e. 'pure, unalloyed filth;' so in Rud.
III. iv. 32, *ex germana Graecia* means of 'pure Greek parentage;'
and in Cas. III. iv. 25, *Nunc tu mihi amicus es, in germanum modum*,
i. e. 'a true, sincere friend.' In Capt. II. ii. 38, *Nam ille quidem
Theodoromedes fuit, germano nomine*, means, 'his own real name was
Theodoromedes,' in opposition to the nickname of Thesaurochru-
sonicochrusides; and so *fratrem geminum germanum meum*, Men. II.
i. 7. Elsewhere in Plautus *germanus* and *germana* are used to denote
the relationship of brother and sister. We have *germana, germana
soror, gemina germana soror, germanus, germanus frater, gemini germani
fratres*, &c., &c., over and over again. So Mil. II. ii. 83, *Vt Philocomasio
hanc sororem geminam germanam alteram;* iv. 30, *Mea soror gemina
germana*, and so II. v. 31; ib. 64. *germana huius;* Men. V. ix. 43.
fratres germanos duos Geminos, una matre natos, et patre uno, uno die;
Truc. II. iv. 84, *Germanae quod sorori non credit soror.*

41. *Olere.*] The verse requires that we should shorten the penultimate syllable. Priscian p. 838 recognises the double form of this verb, and quotes the line before us as an example, 'Oleo, oles, et olo olis.' Plautus in Mostellaria, *Non omnes possunt olere unguenta exotica* nam nisi corripias penultimam Iambus stare non potest.' He quotes also a line of Afranius and repeats his observation in p. 866. So Nonius (p. 147, s. v. *olat*) quotes the same line from Afranius as an example of *olat, Non potest quin illa stacta longeque et multis olat ;* and *olant* is found in Poen. I. ii. 56. On the other hand, the common form of the verb occurs in the next line, *oles,* and in I. iii. 121, *Quid oleant nescias nisi id unum ut male olere intellegas,* we must have penultimate *long,* otherwise the trochaic measure would be vitiated.

43. *Neque tam facetis, quam tu vivis, victibus*] i. e. 'delicate.' The idea originally involved in *facetus* has nothing to do with wit or humour, but, supposing it to be derived from *facio,* is 'dextrous,' 'handy,' 'clever,' 'agreeable,' and it seems to be properly applied as an epithet to anything done gracefully, indeed 'graceful' would in a great number of cases accurately represent the meaning. We see this force of the word exemplified in Hor. S. I. x. 44, *molle atque facetum Virgilio annuerunt gaudentes rure Camenae ;* in Ep. I. vi. 55 it is equivalent to 'affable' or 'courteous,' *Frater, Pater, adde ; I't cuique est aetas, ita quemque facetus adopta ;* and in the sense of 'graceful, delicate pleasantry' with strong irony in Sat. I. ii. 26, *Malthinus tunicis demissis ambulat : est qui Inguen ad obscaenum subductis usque facetus ;* but when in Sat. I. iv. 7 he characterises Lucilius as *facetus, Emunctae naris,* the meaning will be 'clever' or 'witty and keen scented.' Even when applied directly to conversation *facetus* by no means always implies humour; thus, when Cicero De Off. I. 29 divides humour into two species (*duplex iocandi genus*), he characterises one of them as *elegans, urbanum, ingeniosum, facetum,* where *facetus* must signify 'delicate' or 'graceful.' So also Iustin. XXXIX. 25, speaks of *faceti ioci.* In like manner *facete* in Plautus frequently signifies simply, 'cleverly,' 'agreeably,' 'aptly,' 'to the purpose.' Thus, Asin. III. ii. 35, *Ut adsimulabat Sauream med esse, quam facete !* Capt. II. ii. 26, *Ut facete orationem ad servitutem contulit ;* I. ii. 73, H. *Quia mi est natalis dies, Propterea te vocari ad cenam volo.* E. *Facete dictum !* (somewhat different in Poen. III. iii. 24, where it means 'a well-expressed sentiment ;') Mil. I. i. 39, *Facete advortis animum tuum ad animum meum ;* and II. vi. 58, III. iii. 33, IV. iv. 5, 25. Pers. II. v. 22, *S. Dominus me boves mercatum Eretriam misit,*

Nunc mihi Eretria erit haec tua domus. T. Nimis tu facete loquere
i. e. 'to the purpose.' Indeed, it is doubtful whether *facetus* in
Plautus ever strictly denotes 'humour.' There seem to be two
meanings; handy, dextrous, clever, agreeable, apt, to the purpose;
and the other expressed by the English 'dainty.' Thus Cist. II.
i. 16, *Eo facetus es, quia tibi alia est sponsa locuples Lemnia?*
i. e. 'proud, uplifted' 'give yourself airs and graces.' The context
will not admit the sense 'merry.' Mil. III. i. 47, *Vel cavillator
facetus, vel convica commodus,* agreeable raillery. Pers. II. v. 6,
*T. Propera, abi domum. S. Nunc ego huic graphice facetus fiam;
Subnixis alis me inferam, atque amicibor gloriose. T. Sed quis hic
ansatus ambulat. S. Magnifice conscreabor.* Here again *facetus*
must mean, 'I will bear myself proudly, daintily,' or 'like an ex-
quisite of the first water.' Poen. I. ii. 25, *Miror, quidem, soror, te
istaec sic fabulari, Quae tam callida, et docta sis et facta,* i. e. 'clever,'
'sharp;' Truc. V. 38, *Qui, malum, bella aut facete es, quae ames
hominem istiusmodi,* i. e. 'either handsome or clever, witty;' Asin.
II. ii. 84, *Extemplo facio facetum me atque magnificum virum,* i. e.
'proud and haughty,' 'majestic;' Mil. IV. ix. 8, *Facetum puerum!*
i. e. 'a clever lad, he speaks to the purpose;' in the passage before
us, *Neque tam facetis quam tu vivis victibus,* 'dainty, lordly viands;'
Mil. II. i. 69, *Ei nos facetis fabricis et doctis dolis Glaucomam ob oculas
obicimus,* i. e. 'cleverly contrived.' For *facete* in the same senses,
compare Asin. III. ii. 35; Capt. I. ii. 73, II. ii. 26; Cas. III. v. 64;
Men. I. ii. 22; Pers. II. v. 22, &c. Stich. V. ii. 7, *fecisti hrre
facetias,* you have acted 'most agreeably.'

45. *alliato.*] Whether we read *alliato,* which is a near approach
to the *aleato* of the best MSS., or adopt *alliatum,* the conjecture of
Saracenus, the meaning will be much the same. In the former case,
alliato may form a substantive. *alliatum,* 'allow me living on my
garlick-seasoned fare;' In the latter, we must regard *alliatum* as an
adj. and translate, 'allow me all be-garlicked as I am;' *alliatus* or
alliatum is an ἅπ. λεγ.

55. *istuc*] nom. sing. neut. So II. ii. 47. *istuc,* acc. sing. neut.,
ib. 70. 67, 68, iii. 51, 95. III. i. 99 (95); *istanc,* acc. sing. fem., I. iii.
19; *istaec,* nom. sing. fem., iii. 27; *istaec,* nom. plur. fem., iii. 117;
istoc modo, abl. sing. masc., iv. 8; *istic* (there, adv.), II. i. 25, III. i. 71;
istaec, acc. plur. neut., II. i. 41, IV. ii. 69 (iii. 46); *istaec,* nom.
plur. neut., II. i. 48, IV. ii. 71 (iii. 48); *istic,* nom. sing. masc., III. i.
40 (36); *istunc,* acc. masc., i. 139 (136).

57. *compendiface*] i. e. 'save yourself the trouble of further talk,'

may be written as two distinct words, *compendi face*, for the component parts are frequently separated. The phrase *facere aliquid compendi* properly signifies, 1. 'to save;' 2. 'to abridge;' and hence 'to cut short.' Thus, Bac. II. ii. 6, *Compendi multa verba iam faciam tibi*, i. e. 'I shall make a long story short for you,' 'I shall save you the trouble of making a long speech.' So Pseud. IV. vii. 42, *Quisquis es, adulescens, operam fac compendi quaerere*, 'save yourself the trouble.' Again, Truc. II. iv. 26, *Si quid tibi Compendi facere possim, factum edepol velim*, i. e. 'if I can make any saving for you;' and Pers. IV. iii. 2, *Nam ego hodie compendi feci binos panes indies*, i. e. 'I have made a saving of two loaves per day.' The passive of *facio* is also used, As. II. ii. 41, *Verbivelitationem fieri compendi volo*, i. e. 'I wish this skirmishing of words to be cut short.' Sometimes *compendium* is put in the accusative, followed by a genitive or dative, Rud. I. ii. 90, *Si ad saxum quo capessit,* ea deorsum cadit Errationis fecerit compendium*, i. e. 'she will have brought her wanderings to an abrupt termination,' 'save herself from all further wandering.' In Stich. I. iii. 39, *Haec verba subigunt me mores ut barbaros Discam, atque ut faciam praeconis compendium, Itaque auctionem praedicem, ipse ut vendidtem*, the reading, as far as the last word is concerned, is very doubtful. The Palatine MSS. are corrupt, but the Palimpsest has preserved the true reading, and the meaning is tolerably clear. The parasite says that he is about to have a sale of his property by auction after the Roman fashion, and that he *will save the expense* of an auctioneer by acting in that capacity himself. So *facere compendium pultandi*, 'to cease from,' Pseud. II. ii. 11. Again, in Capt. V. ii. 12, with the dative, *Satis facundus es, sed iam fieri dictis compendium volo*. A verb different from *facere* is occasionally employed, Mil. III. i. 186, *Quam pote tam verba confer maxume ad compendium*. And we have *ponere ad compendium* in Cas. III. i. 3, 5, where *ponito ad compendium* means 'cut short by leaving that out.' See the passage. Finally, since, according to the proverb, what is saved is gained, we find *facere compendium* signify 'to make an acquisition;' Bac. I. ii. 51, *Compendium, edepol, haud aetati optabile, Fecisti, cum istanc nactus es impudentiam;* where it must be regarded as opposed to *dispendium*. And indeed this seems to lead to the true meaning of the phrase, which seems to be, 'to make a saving of,' and hence, to 'spare,' 'cut short,' *compendium* signifying a saving or contraction of expenditure, just as *dispendium* signifies a lavish outlay.

---

* See note of W, who appears to be quite wrong.

P

58. *Nisi te mala re magna mactari cupis.*] The verb *macto* deserves particular notice. It seems to be derived from the same root as *magis* and *magnus*, and to be a frequentative form of an obsolete verb, *mago*, of which the participle *mactus* remained in use. 1. The original signification of *macto* was 'to magnify,' 'to glorify,' in the sense of paying homage to a deity by offerings or sacrifices, and thence was applied to men when exalted by honour. In this sense it is constructed with the accusative of the object to which homage is paid, and the ablative of the object employed to testify homage. Thus, Cic. in Vat. VI. § 14, *Volo ut mihi respondeas . . . quae te tanta pravitas mentis tenuerit, qui tantus furor, ut, quum inaudita ac nefaria sacra susceperis, quum inferorum animas elicere, quum puerorum extis Deos Manes mactare soleas,* &c.; and De Rep. 1. 43, *Eos autem, qui in magistratu privatorum similes esse velint, eosque privatos, qui efficiant nequid inter privatum et magistratum differat, ferunt laudibus et mactant honoribus.* So also Enn. Ann. IX. frag. II. ed. Vahlen, *Livius inde rediit magno mactatus triumpho.* 2. Hence *macto* signifies simply, 'to offer in sacrifice,' and is constructed with the accusative of the thing offered, to which the dative of the object to which the sacrifice is offered is sometimes added. Examples are very common, e. g. Lucret. III. 52, *Et nigras mactant pecudes et Manibus divis Inferias mittunt;* Varro ap. Non. p. 341, *Quod Kalendis Iuniis et publice et privatim favatam pultem Diis mactat;* again, passively, Hor. C. I. xix. 16, *Mactata veniet lenior hostia;* and in Liv. X. 28, Decius exclaims, *Iam ego mecum hostium legiones mactandas Telluri ac Diis Manibus dabo.* 3. We now come to that sense which is exemplified in our text, the sense in which it is used almost invariably by Plautus,*—to magnify with a bad or ironical force, 'to load a person with misfortune,' and is then constructed with the accusative of the person and the ablative of the word denoting misfortune. Thus we have in Aul. III. v. 61, *Dotatae mactant et malo et damno viros;* and in a fragment of the Amph., *At ego certe cruce et cruciatu mactabo: exi, O, foras, mastigia.* The expression is very frequently couched in the form of an imprecation, e. g. Trin. IV. ii. 151, *Ego ob hanc operam argentum accepi; te macto infortunio;* and Bac. IV. viii. 45, *Et ego te et ille mactamus infortunio;* and so Curc. IV. iii. 5, Bac. II. iii. 130, Poen. III. 1. 14. This use of the word is by no means peculiar to Plautus, for we read in Ennius (frag. Teleph. V. ed. Vahlen), *qui illum dii deaeque magno*

---

* We can scarcely consider Rud. I. II. 8 an exception, *Si sapiam, her, quod me mactat, consumrem intum,* where *mactat* means, is 'tormenting me,' is 'playing the deuce with me.'

mactassint malo; In Afranius (Privig. frag. XVI. ed. Ribbeck), *Ah, fulica, bene peristi, di te mactassint malo;* and in Pomponius (Praeco post. frag. V. ed. Ribbeck), *At te di omnes cum consilio, cahv, mactassint malo.* Occasionally we find a play upon the double meaning of *macto*, as in Novius (Gallinaria frag. III. ed. Ribbeck), where the speaker is addressing some deity, *Macto te his verbenis, macta tu illanc infortunio;* and in Plaut. Amph. IV. ii. 14, *M. Sacrufico ego tibi. A. Qui? M. Quia enim te macto infortunio.* 4. Nonius, who enlarges on the different meanings of *macto*, and quotes a great number of the passages adduced above, adds yet another signification, *praecipitare,* which may be connected with the preceding as denoting 'to consign to destruction;' he gives as his authority a passage from Accius (Antenoridae frag. V. ed. Ribbeck), *qui aut illorum copias Fundam in campo, aut navis uram, aut castra mactabo in mare.*

The use of *mactus* is peculiar. It is generally employed in the vocative singular, *macte*, and when a deity is addressed signifies, 'be thou honoured or glorified;' examples are common in Cato de R. R. Thus (cap. 132), *Iupiter dapalis . . . macte hac illace dape polluecenda esto . . . macte vino inferio esto;* again (cap. 134), *Iupiter, macte fercto esto;* and (cap. 141), *Mars pater . . macte his suovetaurilibus lactentibus esto.* When *macte* is addressed to a human being it is generally coupled with *virtute,** or some word expressing a good quality, and is a sort of complimentary formula implying a prayer that the person addressed may prosper and make constant additions to his stock of worth. That *mactus* implies the notion of making honourable additions to what we possess is seen in a line quoted from Lucilius by Serv. on Virg. Æn. IX. 641, *Macte, inquam, virtute simulque his versibus esto.* In the passage in the Æn. we have *Macte nova virtute, puer, sic itur ad astra;* and Liv. X. 40, *Tu quidem macte virtute diligentiaque esto;* in the line of Accius (Neoptol. frag. IX. ed. Ribbeck), *Tu, uti dixi, macte his armis, macta virtutem patris, macta* must mean simply 'add to' or 'transcend.' Occasionally, we find *macti* in the vocative plural, as in Liv. VII. 36, *Macti virtute, inquit, milites Romani, este.* Lastly, but rarely, *mactus* is employed to mean 'loaded,' 'overwhelmed,' 'hard pressed,' 'violently assailed;' in Lucret. V. 1339, *Et nunc saepe boves Lucae ferro male mactae Diffugiunt, fera fata suis cum multa dedere;*

---

* In the later writers *macte* is followed by a genitive, e. g. Mart. XII. vi. 7, *Macte animi, quem rarus habet, morumque tuorum Quos Numa quos hilaris posset habere Cato.* And so Stat. Theb. II. 495. In these cases some might consider *bonis* or some equivalent word understood, which is actually expressed in Stat. Sil. I. iii. 106.

and the force of *macte* in a fragment of Accius (Diomed. frag. XVI.
ed. Ribbeck), *Maneas, his ante exilio macte Pelopiis Ex terris*, must
be 'violently driven forth.' The note of Serv. on Æn. IX. 641 is
worth reading. It begins, '*Macte*, magis aucte, adfectatae gloriae. Et
est sermo tractus a sacris: quotiens enim aut tus aut vinum super
victimam fundebatur, dicebant, mactus est taurus vel vino vel ture,
hoc est, cumulata est hostia et magis aucta. Macte ergo, pro
mactus esto, vocativum pro nominativo posuit ut Persius, *Stemmate
quod Tusco ramum millesime ducis Censoremve tuum vel quod trabeate
salutas*.'

59. *ervom*.] *Ervom* was a sort of vetch, or lentile, the same
probably with the French *ers*, used for feeding cattle. See Col.
II. xl. § 11, VI. 3, § 4, XI. 2, § 10, and comp. Virg. Ed. III. 100,
Heu! Heu! quam pingui macer est mihi taurus in ervo.

60. *agite, porro pergite*] i.e. 'drive on, proceed in your career.'
Porro, which is identical with πόρρω, the later Attic form of πρόσω,
always conveys the idea of 'progress' or 'movement forwards,' and
is employed with reference to, I. Place; II. Time; III. Actions
and Ideas. I. *Place*. Rud. IV. iii. 95, *T. Vbi tu hic habitas?
G. Porro illic longe, usque in campis ultimis*, i.e. 'on there, in that
direction, far away,' &c.; Trin. IV. ii. 97, *C. Sed quid ais? quo inde
isti porro? S. Si animum adverlas eloquar*, i.e. 'whither did you
proceed from thence in your onward course?' and so in v. 103,
Deinde porro. II. *Time*. Phor. V. viii. 33, *Sed quid sperem? aetate
porro minus peccaturum putem?* 'but what can I hope? can I think
that he will improve as his years advance?' and in v. 36, *Quid mihi
nunc adferes, quamobrem expectem aut sperem porro non fore*, i.e. 'that
the same will not happen hereafter;' Hec. V. i. 38, *Fac eadem ut sis
porro: nostra utere amicitia ut voles*, i.e. 'be the same for the future
as you are now,' 'persevere in your present conduct;' so in Heaut. I.
i. 107, *at porro recte spero*, 'for the future;' and Phor. III. l. 10,
Ecquid spei porro est; so also *porro* signifies 'forthwith,' 'straight-
way,' in V. vii. 28–30, *Sed transi sodes ad forum, atque illud mihi
Argentum rursum iube rescribi, Phormio. P. Quodve ego descripsi
porro illis quibus debui?* and Most. III. iii. 18 (IV. ii. 18).
III. *Porro* is also used in what may be called a figurative sense
with reference to actions and ideas, and may in very many cases be
represented by the English expressions, 'to proceed,' 'in the next
place,' 'furthermore,' 'in addition;' thus, Heaut. IV. v. 23, *Sed
porro, ausculta, quod superest fallaciae*, i.e. 'but to proceed, to listen
to what,' &c.; Adel V. iv. 14, *Duxi uxorem, quam ibi miseriam vidi!*

nati filii, Alia cura! porro autem illis dum studeo, &c., 'but to proceed,'
'in the next place;' Adel. V. ix. 22, *M. Syre, processisti hodie pulcre.
D. Si quidem porro, Micio, Tu tuum officium facies,* i. e. 'if you will
proceed onwards in doing your duty;' Hec. IV. iv. 12, *turbent porro,*
'let them go on,' 'let them make confusion right on;' and Most. V.
i. 51 (ii. 36); again, Adel. IV. iv. 23, *nunc porro, Aeschine, expergiscere,*
'now, Aeschines, get on,' 'wake up,' 'be alive;' Andr. Prol. 22, *Dehinc ut
quiescant, porro moneo, et desinant Maledicere.* According to this punctuation, *porro moneo* is 'furthermore I warn these persons;' or if we
take *quiescant porro,* 'let them keep quiet for the future.' Heaut. III.
iii. 30, *Censen vero? quid illum porro credis facturum, Chreme?* i. e.
'what do you believe that he will do next?' III. i. 84, *Cedo dextram:
porro te idem oro ut facias, Chreme,* i. e. 'in the next place;' Hec. IV.
iv. 99, *Et te oro porro, in hac re adiutor sis mihi,* i. e. 'and furthermore I implore you;' Heaut. IV. vii. 10, *Porro haec talenta dotis
adposcunt duo,* i. e. 'furthermore,' 'in addition;' and Rud. III. ii. 39.
The student may examine the following examples for himself: Poen.
IV. i. 3, V. iii. 34; Trin. I. ii. 125, III. ii. 56, iii. 47, IV. ii. 97,
103; Epid. V. ii. 61; Curc. III. 83; Men. V. ix. 51; Mil II. iv. 33,
III. i. 202, IV. i. 13, ii. 57, 99, iv. 8.

62. *saginam caedit.*] This expression is very embarrassing. Let
us first examine the meaning of the word *sagina.* In the writers upon
rural affairs it signifies the act or process of fattening domestic animals.[*]
Thus Varro R. R. III. 10 says that five points must be attended to
in the management of geese—*de genere, de fetura, de ovis, de pullis, de
sagina,* i. e. 'the breed,' 'the propagation,' 'the eggs,' 'the goslings,' and
'the process of fattening;' and Columella VIII. 14 tells us that when
the goslings are four months old the largest are to be selected and set
aside for fattening, *furturae maximus quisque destinatur;* and then
goes on, *et est facilis harum avium sagina,* i. e. 'the process of fattening
these birds is easy;' so also Plin. H. N. IX. 56, § 82 informs us, on
the authority of Varro, that Fulvius Lupinus, a short time before the
civil war, was the first who kept snails in a preserve (*coclearum vivaria
instituit*), and proceeds, *quin et saginam earum commentus est sapa et
farre aliisque generibus,* &c. In the above passages the word *sagina*
denotes the 'art' or 'process of fattening,' and hence it easily
passed into the signification found in Tacitus, Juvenal, &c., of the
'materials used for fattening,' 'nourishing, rich food,' and hence 'food'
in general. This use is not, however, confined to the writers who

---

[*] Gesner, in his Index to the R. R. Scriptores, would connect the word
with the Greek verb σάττω.

flourished after Augustus, as Freund asserts in his Lexicon, for Varro
R. R. III. 17 says that Hortensius kept a body of fishermen in his
pay to furnish the precious inhabitants of his ponds (*piscinae*) with
little fishes, and that when the weather was so tempestuous that they
could not bring to shore in their nets *vivam saginam*, then he supplied
them with morsels of salted fish (*salsamenta*), where *vivam saginam*
must signify 'living food,' in contradiction to the *salsamenta* or
pickled tunny.* Hence we have the verb *saginare*, 'to fatten,' *sagi-
natus* and *saginandus;* and Varro R. R. III. 10 supplies us with the
term *saginarium* for a 'fattening coop.' This being premised we
may pass on to examine the three passages in Plautus, in addition
to that before us, where the word is found. 1. Most. I. iii. 78 (77),
*Iam ista quidem apsumpta res erit, dies noctesque estur, bibitur Ne-
que quisquam parsimoniam adhibet; sagina plane est,* which the older
commentators explain, 'the place is a regular fatting coop,' making
sagina = saginarium. But this is quite unnecessary, and we may keep
to the strict sense, 'it is a clear case of stuffing and cramming.'
Again, 2. Trin. III. ii. 96, where Stasimus, speaking of his master as
about to enter the service of some foreign prince, says, *Aut aliquem
ad regem in saginam herus se coniecit meus,* i. e. 'in order that he may
grow fat at his cost;' and we have a parallel to this in Cicero pro
Flacco VII., *Nuper epulati, paullo ante omni largitione saturati, Per-
gameni, quod Mithridates, qui multitudinem illam non auctoritate sed
sagina tenebat, se velle dixit, id sutores, id zonarii conclamarunt.* Cf.
also Tacit. H. II. 71. 3. The third example is in Mil. III. ii. 31,
where a drunken slave, who had been stealing wine, says that if his
misdeeds are discovered, *Posita sagina ego ciciar cellaria,* where the
term *sagina cellaria,* being evidently a whimsical phrase coined to
raise a laugh, must not be pressed too closely. But none of these
throw any light upon the phrase before us. B has *saginam caedit,*
the rest *cedit.* Lambinus adopts *cedite* and explains it *date,* that is,
give me food for my oxen. But this would involve a false quantity,
for in that case *cedite* must be regarded as equivalent to *cette* and
connected with *cedo,* 'give me,' and then it would be impossible to
scan the line. Weise renders the words by *cibos comedit,* than which
nothing could be more tame. Forcellini finds a way out of the difficulty
by assigning a special meaning to *sagina,* of which this passage affords
the only example, viz. *ipsum animal sagina pinguefactum,* in which
case we might render the line, 'eat, cram yourselves, slay the fatted

* The passage in Propert. IV. viii. 35 is not decisive.

calf.'* Upon the whole, although I feel no confidence, I am inclined to consider that *cardite* is here equivalent to *concidite*, and is used with reference to *effercite, farcio* signifying properly to stuff a sausage, 'eat, stuff yourselves out like sausages, chop up the good things.'

63. *ire . . . parare*] i. e. 'to go to the Piraeus for the purpose of procuring.' This use of the infinitive to denote a purpose or design, especially after a verb of motion, is extremely rare in the writers of the Augustan age, but is by no means uncommon in Plautus, as will appear from the following examples: thus, Amph. I. i. 106, *Nunc pergam heri imperium exsequi, et me domum capessere;* Bac. II. iii. 120, *Senex in Ephesum ibit aurum arcessere;* IV. iii. 18, *Parasitus modo venerat aurum petere;* IV. viii. 69, *Illa autem in arcem abivit aedem visere Minervae;* Curc. I. iii. 50, *Minume: nam parasitum misi nudius quartus Cariam Petere argentum;* Rud. I. ii. 6, *Nunc huc ad Veneris fanum venio visere;* iv. 4, *Omnia iam circumcursavi atque omnibus in latebris perreptavi Quaerere conservam voce, oculis, auribus, ut pervestigarem;* Truc. V. 1, *Eo mihi amare* (a very strange phrase); Trin. IV. iii. 6, *Ecce hominem te, Stasime, nihili ! satin in thermopolio Condalium es oblitus. postquam thermopotasti gulturem ! Recipe te, et recurre petere, re recenti;* Pseud. II. ii. 47, *Reddere hoc non perdere herus me misit.* IV. v. 4, quoted by W, is not an example according to the common reading. Nor do I think that Amph. I. i. 106, quoted above, falls under this head. See example of constructions of *pergo.*

64. *piscatum.*] *Piscatus* must here signify 'a dish of fish.' So below, III. ii. 41, *piscatu probo,* 'excellent fish;' and in Cic. de Fin. II. 8, *piscatu, aucupio, venatione,* signify 'the produce of fishing, fowling, and the chase.' The meaning varies in different passages: in Bac. I. i. 69, *bonus piscatus* is 'a good take or haul of fish;' and so Rud. IV. ii. 6, *piscatu novo me uberi compotivit* (sc. Neptunus), while in the next line *piscatus* seems to be the 'act of fishing,' *Miroque modo atque incredibili hic piscatus mihi Lepide evenit,* i. e. 'this fishing of mine,' but it may mean here also, 'this haul of fish;' in Rud. IV. l. 7, *abiit piscatum ad mare* must mean, 'he went away a-fishing to the sea;' and so it is used by Plin. H. N. VIII. 16, § 17, *omnium quos venatus aucupia piscatusque alebant.* *Piscatus,* like *gemitus, senatus, sumptus, tumultus,* and many others, belonged also to the second declension in the earlier form of the language, and Non. s. v. *piscati,* p. 488, quotes from Pomponius *omne piscati genus,*

* The translation given in the English ed., 'chew your mast,' 'exercise your grinders,' is vague and quite wide of For.'s meaning.

i. e. 'all kinds of fish;' and from Turpilius, *si flabat Aquilo aut Auster inopia tum erat piscati*, i. e. 'there was a scarcity of fish.' We may remark that we use the word *fishing* in a double sense in English, when we say 'he is gone a-fishing,' and 'he has had a good fishing,' meaning 'a good haul of fish;' but we cannot with any accuracy employ the word *fishing* to denote the *fish* captured.

66. *optuere.*] The verse requires that the penultimate should here be short, and hence the verb is *optuor;* but in III. ii. 151 (150), *optuere* from *optueor;* and in III. ii. 154, *opturrier;* and so again in Amph. III. ii. 19; *opturre* in Bac. IV. iv. 18, but the text and scansion of the line are doubtful; *optuetur*, Mil. IV. vi. 56. The simple *tuor* is in the received text of Trin. III. ii. 82, *Etiam ob stultitiam tuam te tueris? multam abomina,* where *tueris* is an anapaest; and in Lucret. IV. 449, *Omnia quae tuimur fieri tum bina tuendo;* and again IV. 362. So *contui* is found below III. ii. 152 (151), and in As. I. i. 111, III. i. 20; *contuor*, As. II. iii. 23, Pers. II. ii. 26; *intuor*, Most. III. ii. 150 (149); *intuor*, Rud. II. iv. 28; *intuetur*, Capt. III. iv. 25, Truc. II. vii. 40; *intuentur*, Bac. V. ii. 12; *intueri*, Truc. I. ii. 58; *intuens*, Eun. III. v. 32; *intuitur*, Heaut. II. iv. 23. Festus, although his text is here imperfect, seems distinctly to recognise the double form, *tuor* and *tueor,* and says that when he wrote they were used indifferently; but we find nothing in the old writers to support his notion that *tuor* originally was equivalent to *video* and *tueor* to *defendo.* See Fest. and Paul. Diac. pp. 354, 355, ed. Müll.

67. *G. Pol tibi istuc credo nomen actutum fore. T. Dum interea sic sit, istuc "actutum" sino.*] So L iv. 24 (25), Philolaches says, *Iam revortar;* to which Philematium replies, *Diu est "iam" id mihi.*

72. *Ne tu erres, hercle, praeterhac mihi non facies moram.*] So *antehac*, III. ii. 42; *Imo vita antehac erat*, and *antidhac*, Amph. II. ii. 79, Cist. I. i. 1.

73. *Satin abiit.*] *Satin* is frequently employed by Plautus, not merely as a simple interrogative, but also to express strong emotion, anxiety, surprise, and indignation. It is used both alone and also in combination with *ut* and *si.* We shall give examples, explaining as we go along. 1. Simple interrogation: Stich. IV. i. 13, *Sed satin ego tecum pacificatus sum, Antipho?* i. e. 'have I made my peace with you sufficiently?' Most. I. iii. 10, *Contempla, amabo, mea Scapha, satin haec me vestis deceat?* i. e. 'look and tell me, Scapha, whether this dress becomes me well enough?' and similar examples will be found in Most. I. iii. 125; Pers. I. i. 18; Merc. II. iv. 27; Men. IV. ii. 51, V. i. 41. In Men. IV. ii. 38, *Satin audis?* is a very earnest question,

NOTES. I. i. 66–73.

113

and still stronger, Trin. V. ii. 53, *L. Satine salve? dic mihi. C. Recte.*
'Is all well? speak. C. All right.' 2. Delight, wonder, perplexity;
Poen. IV. ii. 97, *Satine, prius quam unum est iniectum telum, tum instat
alterum*, i. e. 'is it not famous to see that before one dart has been
fairly launched a second follows close upon its heels?' In the two
following examples astonishment and perplexity are indicated. Trin.
IV. iii. 63, *Mare, terra, caelum, Di vostram fidem, Satin ego oculis
plane video? estne ipsus, an non est?* Merc. IV. i. 16, *Satin tu sana es,
opsecro?* In Truc. II. vii. 2, *Satine qui amat nequit quin nihili sit Atque
improbis se artibus expoliat?* the meaning is, 'is it not strange that
a man in love cannot avoid being good for nothing?' Here, and in
many other passages, W considers that *satin* and *satin est* are equivalent to *nonne*, but the full force of *satin* would in this case be quite
lost. 3. Wrath and indignation, mingled with surprise, real or
affected—this is the force of *satin* in the line of our text, *Satin abiit,
neque quod dixi, flocci existumat?* i. e. 'is it possible that he has gone
off?' &c.; and so in Mil. II. vi. 1, which is exactly parallel, *Satin
abiit ille, neque herile plus negotium Curat, quam si non serviulem
serviat?* so also Pseud. V. ii. 19, *Satin ultro et argentum aufert et me
irridet?* In Trin. IV. iii. 6, *satin* implies self-reproach. Cf. Men.
V. v. 42, Cist. I. iii. 2. We now pass on to the combination *satin ut*,
with respect to which we must distinguish two cases—(a) when *satin
ut* is followed by the indicative; (b) when *satin ut* is followed by the
subjunctive. (a) When *satin ut* is followed by the indicative it is
equivalent to *nonne vides ut*, i. e. 'mark how,' as in Pers. IV. iv. 106,
Satin ut meminit libertatis? Dabit haec tibi grandes bolos, and may,
according to circumstances, indicate admiration or contempt or surprise. It indicates admiration in Stich. I. iii. 114, *Sed eccum Dinacium
eius puerum! Hoc vide! Satin ut facete atque ex pictura adstitit?*
contempt, in Men. I. ii. 67, *Mane, mane, opsecro, herele: ab ss, ecca,
exit. Ah! solem vides. Satin ut occaecatus est, prae huius corporis
candoribus!* surprise, Merc. II. iv. 13, *E. Tute heri ipsus mihi nar-
rasti. C. Satin ut oblitus fui Tibi me narravisse?* i. e. 'is it not wonderful how I forgot that' etc.; surprise and pleasure in Mil. IV. iii. 41.
There is a slight difference in the combination of the following
passage, where *ut* is followed by *ita*, Men. III. ii. 56, *Quid hoc negoti
est? Satin ut quemque conspicor Ita me ludificant?* 'What does this
mean? Is it not possible for me to see any one without being
mocked by him?' (b) When *satin ut* is followed by the subjunctive,
as in Bac. III. iii. 87, *Satin ut quem tu habeas fidelem tibi, aut quoi
credas, nescias?* i. e. 'is it to be endured that,' 'is it not abominable

Q

to think that,' it indicates strong indignation. In this and in many
other cases, where *satin* and *satin ut* occur, Weise considers that they
may be expressed by the simple *nonne*; but it will be found upon examination that in many places *nonne* would very inadequately express
the force, and in others it is altogether out of place. Lastly, we have
satin si; thus Rud. IV. v. 3, *Satin, si quoi homini dei esse benefactum
volunt Aliquo illud pacto optingit optatum piis?* i.e. 'is it not manifest
that if the gods,' &c.; while in Pseud. I. i. 110, *Satin est si hanc
hodie mulierem efficio tibi Tua ut sit?* I.e. 'are you content if?'

– *Satin' abiit, neque quod dixi, flocci existumat?*] Compare V. i. 1,
*Qui homo timidus erit in rebus dubiis, nauci non erit Atque equidem
quid id esse dicam verbum nauci, nescio;* Men. II. IIi. 69, *Neque ego
illum maneo, neque floccifacio;* V. vii. 5, *Cave quisquam, quod illic
minitetur, vostrum floccifecerit;* Cas. II. v. 24, *Tu istos minutos cave
Deos floccifeceris;* Stich. II. i. 12, *Cave quemquam floccifeceris;* Trin.
IV. ii. 73, *Neque adeo edepol floccifacio; v.* 150, *Di te perdant, etsi
floccifacio an perisses prius; v.* 152, *Ceterum qui sis, qui non sis,
floccum non interduim;* Truc. IV. ii. 56, *De nihilo illi est irasci, quae
te non floccifacit;* Rud. Prol. 47, *flocci non fecit fidem.* Compare
further Trin. I. ii. 174, Truc. II. vii. 46, Rud. III. v. 16.

I. ii. 2. *Argumenta.*] *Argumentum* is properly (see note on I. i. 2)
'something which pierces and carries conviction with it,' hence 'a
proof,' hence 'reasoning,' hence 'a discussion' or 'dissertation' in
which *argumenta* are adduced, and hence the 'subject or theme of a
discussion or dissertation.' It is from the idea of movement implied
in reasons which 'pierce and carry conviction with them,' that *in* is
here followed by *pectus* in the accusative: 'I have raised discussions
and adduced proofs which might penetrate into my breast.' To say,
with Lambinus, that *in pectus* is put for *in pectore* "antiquo more," is
little better than an attempt to conceal ignorance. Observe that in
the following line we have *in corde* not *in cor;* after the discussions,
reasonings, and proofs had made their way into his breast, he then
turned them over and arranged them "*in corde.*" In *v.* 9, *Ei rei
argumenta dicam* means, 'I will adduce proofs of what I assert,' and
so *v.* 15, 37, while in *v.* 9 we have the same meaning expressed by *ad*
with the accusative, *Auscultate argumenta dum dico ad hanc rem.* In
Trin. II. iv. 121 we find nearly the same words, *Ei rei argumentum
dicam*, which there signify, 'I will prove to you that you ought to
follow my advice;' and in Truc. I. ii. 68, *Amator similis est oppidi
hostilis. D. Quo argumento est?* 'How do you make that out?' 'How
do you prove that?' The transition is easy from *a discussion* to the

'subject or theme of a discussion,' and thus *argumentum* is used specially for the 'plot or story of a drama.' Thus Amph. Prol. 51, 96, *Post argumentum huius eloquar tragoediae;* and Trin. III. ii. 81, *Facile palmam habes; hic victus. Vicit tua comoedia Hic agit magis ex argumento et versus meliores facit,* i. e. 'he keeps more closely to the story;' hence, in a still more general sense, *argumentum* signifies the representation of story in a work of art. Thus Virgil calls the representation of the story of Io on the shield of Turnus, *argumentum ingens;* and Cicero Verr. Act. II. iv. 56, when describing the famous doors of the Temple of Minerva in the Insula at Syracuse, *Ex ebore diligentissime perfecta argumenta erant in valvis.* We have *argumentari* in the Vulg. of Truc. IV. ii. 23, but the reading is more than doubtful. Examples of *argumentum,* in the sense of 'reasonings,' 'proofs,' 'arguments,' may be found in Amph. I. i. 267, 277, II. i. 45, II. ii. 174, V. i. 35; As. II. ii. 36; Cas. IV. iii. 13; Mil. IV. ii. 11, 24; Rud. IV. iii. 84; Truc. II. vi. 26; in the last passage *argumenta* are the tokens by which the paternity of a child is proved. In the sense of 'the plot of a play' in As. Prol. 8; Cist. I. iii. 7; Men. Prol. 5, 11, 13, 16; Mil. II. i. 7, 20; Merc. Prol. 2; Poen. Prol. 46, 56, 57; Rud. Prol. 31; Trin. Prol. 16; And. Prol. 6, 11; Heaut. Prol. 6; Adel. Prol. 22.

5. *Similis*] with genitive. So in vv. 5, 8, 38 (35), 47 (43).

7. *Id reperi iam exemplum.*) The modifications of meaning which *exemplum* undergoes are worthy of attention. There can be little doubt that *exemplum* is derived, like *eximius,* from *eximo,* and it seems properly to signify an object picked out or selected from others of the same kind on account of its excellence. Hence it means 'a model,' something set up to be copied or imitated. Of this meaning we have an instance a few lines lower down v. 21 (19), *inde exemplum expetunt,* and again, III. ii. 75, 76, 86 (73, 74, 84). Hence figuratively, Men. V. vi. 27, *Eo exemplo servio, tergi ut in rem esse arbitror,* i. e. 'keeping the interest of my hide steadily in view,' as an artist who copies from a model; and Bac. III. vi. 11, *Multi more isto atque exemplo vivont,* i. e. 'making that manner of life their model.' Hence in Trin. IV. ii. 76, Charmides, when endeavouring to bring a name to the recollection of the Sycophanta, *Quod ad exemplum est? coniectura si reperire possumus. S. Ad hoc exemplum est, Char. C. An Chares? An Charidemus. An Charmides?* i. e. 'What is it like? ... It is like Char.' Moreover *exemplum* may be used in a bad as well as in a good sense, and may signify an object selected not as a model but as a warning to others, as we talk in English of *making an example*

of an offender. So Rud. III. ii. 3, *Ferte opem inopiae atque exemplum pessumum pessumdate.* Plautus takes advantage of the double meaning in this play, V. i. 67 (ii. 52), *T. Exemplum edepol faciam ego in te. C. Quia placeo, exemplum expetis;* cf. Rud. III. ii. 6. In Epid. I. i. 7, *exemplum* signifies an object to be looked at or contemplated, *E. Quid tu? agis ut velis? T. Exemplum adest;* i. e. 'look at me and judge.' *Exemplum* may also signify *the copy* as well as *the model;* thus Poen. V. iv. 102 it occurs in both senses, *O Apella, O Zeuxis pictor Cur numero estis mortui? hinc exemplum ut pingeretis. Nam alios pictores nil moror huiusmodi tractare exempla;* while in Pseud. II. ii. 56 *exemplum* is the impression of a portrait (*expressa imago*) made from a seal. The transition is easy to such expressions as the following: Rud. III. i. 2, *Ego ad hoc exemplum simiae respondeo;* and II. vi. 3, *Nam si quis quid cum eo rei commiscuit Ad hoc exemplum amittit ornatum domum;* and As. II. iii. 9, *Si istoc exemplo tu omnibus qui quaerunt respondebis,* in which *ad hoc exemplum* and *istoc exemplo* signify 'in this (that) manner,' 'after this (that) fashion.' Hence *exemplum* is frequently employed as identical with *modus,* as in Rud. III. i. 1, *Miris modis Di ludos faciunt hominibus Mirisque exemplis somnia in somnis danunt,* where *modis* and *exemplis* might be interchanged without affecting the meaning; so also Truc. I. i. 5, *Quot amans exemplis ludificetur, quot modis Pereat, quotque exoretur exorabulis;* so in the Pers. I. iii. 77, Toxilus tells the parasite Saturio . . . . *Tu gnatam tuam Ornatam adduce lepide in peregrinum modum;* and in a subsequent part of the play, III. i. 7, Saturio having brought in his daughter dressed up tells her, *Ea causa ad hoc exemplum te exornavi ego;* so also in this play, IV. iii. 39 (iv. 39), Theuropides says, *Deludificatus est me hodie indignis modis;* and in r. 46 he says, *tibi narrarero Quis me exemplis hodie ille ludificatus est.* Lastly, we have the phrases, Most. I. iii. 35, *Di Deaeque omnes pessumis exemplis interficiant;* and v. 55, *Perii hercle ni ego illam pessumis exemplis enicasso;* also Bac. III. iv. 6, *Nam mihi divini numquam quisquam creduat Ni ego illam exemplis plurimis plurisque amo;* and Rud. II. iii. 40, *nos ventisque fluctibusque iactatae exemplis plurimis miserae perpetuam noctem,* in both of which *exemplis* may be rendered by 'manner' or 'way.' We can however easily trace the proper and original force of *exemplum* in this and in all cases where it is regarded as equivalent to *modus.* Thus, *interficere pessumis exemplis* is to put to death, 'taking the most cruel kinds of death as a model;' and *amare plurimis exemplis* is to love, 'taking as a model all kinds and varieties of love;' and so *iactatae plurimis exemplis,* &c., &c.

16. *gnarures . . . hanc rem.*] We cannot draw any distinction as
to meaning between *gnarus* and *gnaruris.* The latter occurs again
in Poen. Prol. 47, *Ad argumentum nunc vicissatim volo Remigrare,
atque ut mecum sitis gnardres,* but it is not found elsewhere until we
come down to Arnobius and Ausonius. Forcellini marks the penultimate long, *gnarūris.* The versification in the passage before us
is so uncertain that it cannot be employed in evidence, while in the
line from the Poenulus, which is an Iambic Trimeter, the penultimate
must be short; and so also in Auson. Epp. XXII. 19, *Non cultor
instans non arator gnarūris,* which line also is an Iambic Trimeter.
The young scholar will remark the accusative after *gnarures* governed,
we must suppose, by the verb implied in the adjective.

18. *examussim*] i.e. 'true to rule and plummet.' While, strictly,
regula signifies 'a straight rule,' *norma* 'two straight rules joined at
right angles,' that is, 'a square,' *perpendiculum* 'a plumb-line,' *libella*
'the combination of a rule and plummet,' and *rubrica* 'the chalked
cord' used by masons, *amussis* would seem to denote a carpenter's or
mason's 'level,' that is, an instrument used to ascertain that a surface
is perfectly horizontal. This at least seems to be the meaning of
Varro, as quoted by Nonius (s.v. *Examussim* p. 9), *amussis est aequa-
men levamentum, id est apud fabros tabula quaedam qua utuntur ad saxa
coagmentata;* and of Paul. Diac. (s.v., p. 6, ed. Müll.), who explains it
as *regula ad quam aliquid exaequatur,* although, in all probability, the
whole of the above words were employed indifferently when technical
language was not required.* See Auson. Eidyll. XVI. 11, where we
have the nominative *amussis.* *Ad amussim,* or, in one word, *Adamus-
sim,* is found in Varro R. R. II. 1, *Si inquam, numerus non est ut sit
ad amussim,* which means, if the number given is not 'precisely
exact;' and in Aul. Gell. I. 4, XX. 1, Macrob. S. I. 4, it means in like
manner, 'to a nicety, exactly.' *Examussim* is found again in Plaut.
Amph. II. ii. 213, *Nae ista edepol, si haec vera loquitur, examussim est
optima,* i.e. 'is absolutely perfect;' and Men. Prol. 50, *Ut hanc rem
vobis examussim disputem,* i.e. 'with perfect accuracy and distinctness;'
and reappears later in Apuleius. In Mil. III. i. 38 we have *amussitata,* the participle of a verb *amussito, Inest in hoc amussitata sua
sibi ingenua indoles,* i.e. 'a liberal disposition squared and balanced
according to the nicest rule of right.'

25. *tegulas imbricesque.*] *Imbrex* is probably the gutter or open

* Sisenna, quoted by Charis. p. 178, makes *amussis* an instrument for
determining that a wall is built perpendicularly.

channel which receives the rain as it drops from the tiles, and carries
it from the roof in a single stream. Such seems to be the explanation of Isidorus XIX. 10 and of Pliny H. N. XXXV. 12, § 43, who,
when recounting the inventions of Dibutades of Sicyon, says, *primusque
personas tegularum extremis imbricibus imposuit*, although his words
are by no means clear. *Imbrex* occurs again in connection with
tegulae in Mil. II. vi. 24, *Quod meas confregisti imbrices et tegulas;* and
in Sisenna Histor. III., *dissipatis imbricum fragminibus ac testis tegularum*, quoted by Non. p. 125, s. v. *Imbrices ac tegulas*. From the
curved form of the *imbrex* it is used by Virgil in connection with an
arched roof (*imbrice tecti*, G. IV. 296); in Martial Epp. II. xxxvii. 2
it denotes some portion of a pig, *Mammas suminis imbricemque porci*,
but what portion we cannot tell; while from the sound of water
rushing through a narrow channel it was applied to one of the forms
of theatrical applause executed by bodies of men trained for the
purpose (*bombos et imbrices et testas vocabant*), perhaps something
like our *Kentish fire*. See the very curious passage in Sueton.
Ner. 20.

26. *Nevolt.*] Observe that *ne* was the original form of the Latin
negative. Compare *ne parcunt = non parcunt*, *ne quidem*, *nedum*, and
such words as *neglego*, *negotium*, *necopinatus*.

27. *Perpluont Tigna.*] The verb *perpluo* is used by Plautus in
two ways, transitively and intransitively. Here it is used intransitively:
perpluont tigna, 'the beams let in the water,' i. e. 'the water makes
its way into the beams.' In iii. 8 we have it in the transitive sense:
*Haec illa est tempestas mea, mihi quae modestiam omnem Detexit tectus
qua fui quam mihi Amor et Cupido In pectus perpluit meum*, i. e.
'rained through into my heart;' and in Trin. II. ii. 41, *Benefacta bene-
factis aliis pertegito ne perpluant*, i. e. intransitively, 'lest they let the
water through.' *Perpluit* is generally used impersonally, 'to let rain
or liquid in through a crevice;' but see Most. IV. i. 16, *Malum quom
impluit ceteros, non impluat mihi*, and observe the change of construction.
For other examples of the use of *perpluere* see Fest. p. 250, ed. M.,
"*Patram perplovere* in sacris quum dicerent, significabant pertusam
esse," i. e. 'leaks, lets out the liquid,' where we see the ancient form
plovo, whence *pluvius* (cf. *fluo-fluvius*); Cato R. R. 155, *In villa cum
pluit, circumire oportet, sicubi perpluat, et signare carbone, cum desierit
pluere, uti tegula mutetur*, i. e. 'water makes its way in.' Quint. VI.
ii. § 64 relates a witticism of Galba, who, when a person asked the
loan of a cloak, replied, "*Non possum commodare, domi maneo*," and
then Quint. adds the explanation, *cum cenaculum eius perplueret.*

i. e. 'let in water through the roof;' Apul. Met. X. 236. *Tum de summo montis cacumine per quandam latentem fistulam in excelsum prorumpit vino crocus diluta, sparsimque defluens pascentis circa capellas odoro perpluit imbre,* l. e. 'wets them through,' transitively, as in Most. I. iii. 8.

31. *si quid numo sarciri potest.*] So in the parallel r. 68 (62), *non vidcor mihi Sarcire posse aedes meas.*

32. *Vsque mantant*] 'they keep putting off, procrastinating.' *Manto* is a frequentative from *maneo.* The word occurs again in Poen. I. ii. 52, *Acrus nos apud 'aedem Veneris mantat,* i. e. 'is waiting for us;' and Pseud. I. iii. 49, *aliquot hos dies manta modo,* i. e. 'only wait for a few days;' and in the same scene, r. 23, *vah, manta,* 'pooh, stop;' and again, Rud. II. iv. 26; it is quoted from Caecilius by Fest. s. v. *mantare,* p. 133, ed. Müll.; and by Non. a. v. *mantat,* p. 505. There is another frequentative form *mansito,* which appears in the Post-Augustan writers.

38. *Extollunt, parant sedulo in firmitatem, Vt et in usum boni et in speciem populo Sint;* but in r. 60, *ego sum in usu Factus nimio nequior;* here W reads *usum,* but is wrong. For this use of *in* with the accusative see note on l. 31, and compare Ampb. I. i. 25, *numero mihi in mentem fuit. Ecquid te pudet? S. Omnia quae tu vis. C. Vbi in lustra iacuisti. S. Egone in lustra!* Trin. III. iii. 38, *Is homo exornetur graphice in peregrinum modum;* Rud. I. iv. 1, *Quid mihi melius est, quid magis in rem est quam,* &c.; IV. ii. 31, *Magnas res hic agito in mentem instruere;* Pseud. I. i. 126, *edico . . . In hunc diem a me ut caveant;* r. 121, *De istac re in oculum utrumvis conquiescito. C. Oculum utrum, anne in aurem? T. At hoc percolgatum est minus.*

47. *Igitur tum*] 'thereafter;' and again III. i. 159 (156). (In the latter of these the Vulg. gives *Igitur dum,* in opposition to all the MSS.) Whatever may be the etymology of *igitur*—and nothing can be more unsatisfactory than the one proposed by Hand, in which scholars seem, for the most part, to have acquiesced—it is certain that in the older forms of the language *igitur* uniformly signifies 'then' or 'thereafter,' and denotes that an event follows after another previously mentioned, either simply in time or both in time and as a result; the use of *igitur,* denoting a logical result, belongs to a late period. We cannot have a better example than the Law of the XII. Tables quoted by Porph. on Hor. S. I. ix. 76, and cleverly restored by Carrio and Dirksen, *Si. in. ius. vocat. ni. it. antestator. igitur. em.capito. Igitur* in Plautus sometimes stands alone, and sometimes

is combined with *tum*, *demum*, or *deinde*. 1. *Igitur* alone, Cas. II. ii.
39, C. Abro. *M. Mox magis quom otium mihi et tibi erit, Igitur tecum
loquar; nunc vale.* C. *Valeas*—where *igitur* signifies simply 'then;'
in Amph. I. i. 55. where Sosia is giving an account of the propositions made by his master to the Teleboi, *sin aliter sient animati
neque dent quae petat Sese igitur summa vi virisque eorum oppidum
expugnassere, igitur* is not 'therefore' but 'thereafter' or 'thereafter
the result will be,' and so in Mil. III. i. 177. Another very good
example occurs in Epid. III. iii. 1-4, where *ut igitur* signifies 'in
order that thereafter.' 2. *Igitur tum;* in addition to the line before
us we have *tum igitur* in Trin. III. ii. 50, and in Bac. III. iv. 19,
*Igitur mihi inani atque inopi subblandibitur Tum, quom mea illud nihilo
pluris referet Quam si ad sefulcrum mortuo dicat iocum,* i. e. 'Thereafter
... at a time when.' 3. *Igitur demum*, in Amph. I. ii. 11, *Igitur
demum omnes scient Quae facta,* i. e. 'then (or thereafter) at length;'
and III. i. 16, *Post igitur demum faciam res fiat palam;* so also
below, II. i. 33. and Rud. IV. ii. 25. In Merc. III. ii. 9 we have
Demum igitur quom senex sis, &c.; and Trin. III. iii. 52, *Tum
tu igitur demum id adulescenti aurum dabis Vbi erit locata virgo in
matrimonium.* 4. *Igitur deinde*, Stich. I. ii. 27, *Sic faciam: adsimulabo,
quasi culpam aliquam in sese admiserint; Perplexabiliter eorum hodie
perperefaciam pectora: Post id agam igitur deinde: ut animus meus
erit, faciam palam.* Such is the punctuation adopted by modern
editors, but I prefer the Vulgate, *Post id agam igitur: deinde, ut animus meus erit,* &c., i. e. 'thereafter I shall press that scheme: then, (at
a later period,) as I shall feel inclined. I shall disclose the truth;'
where *deinde* will denote a stage in the progress of events beyond
that indicated by *igitur*. We have *igitur* signifying 'then,' with the
force of 'in that case,' Epid. III. iv. 63, *Quid tibi negoti est meae
domi igitur*, which is the nearest approach to the late force of
igitur.

51. *Perdidi operam ... oppido.*] *Oppido* was used extensively in
conversation and familiar composition, and the force of the word
may, in most cases, be conveyed by 'thoroughly,' 'entirely,' 'completely.' 1. With verbs we have above *perdidi oppido;* in Aul. IV. ix.
18, Amph. I. i. 143, *oppido interii;* in Bac. IV. viii. 12, As. II. ii. 21,
Aul. III. i. 5, IV. x. 70, Merc. IV. iii. 10, Most. III. i. 27 (23),
Pers. IV. ix. 4, and Rud. II. vi. 66, *peri oppido;* in Most. I.
iii. 9, *periere hae oppido aedes;* III. ii. 44, *oppido occidimus;* Pseud.
I. v. 10, *oppido opsepta est via;* Merc. II. i. 21, *oppido bene velle;*
Bac. IV. viii. 28, *animam amborum exsorbebo oppido.* 2. With

participles and adjectives; As. V. ii. 33, *corruptum oppido;* Curc. I. ii. 44, *Ego oppido servatu;* Epid. III. ii. 3, *hoc oppido politum est;* Mil. III. i. 33, *oppido Acheruuticus;* Merc. II. i. 15, *oppido mirum;* Phor. V. i. 36, *animo iniquo oppido;* Heaut. IV. ii. 2, *angustum oppido;* iii. 26, *iustam rem oppido;* iv. 12, *oppido invitam;* Hec. II. i. 41, *lassam oppido;* so also with an adverb, Adel. III. ii. 14, *oppido opportune te optulisti mihi obviam;* in all of which *oppido,* joined to the positive, gives it the force of a superlative. In one case *oppido* is used with a superlative, Rud. I. iii. 25, *Hoc quod indula sum summae opes oppido,* i. e. 'the clothes upon my back form the entire amount of my wealth.' 3. More rarely *oppido* qualifies a conjunction; thus Most. III. ii. 122 (120), *Qualibet perambula usdes oppido tamquam tuas,* i. e. 'completely as if it was your own;' and Mil. III. i. 40, *Nam benignitas quidem huius oppido ut adulescentuli est;* in the first of these, however, we may, if we please, place a comma after *oppido* and connect it with *perambula.* In Liv. XXXIX. 47 and Vitruv. VIII. 3 we have the combination *oppido quam,* 'exceedingly.' 4. Lastly, *oppido* is used by itself, in dialogue, as a strong affirmative, 'exactly so,' 'precisely so.' Thus Bac. IV. iv. 30, *C. Reddidisti* (sc. *peruniam*)? *M. Reddidi. C. Omnemne? M. Oppido.* i. e. 'exactly so, the whole.' So Phor. V. vii. 12, *C. Estne ea, ita ut dixi, liberalis? D. Oppido.* i. e. 'Is she not, as I said, quite the lady?' 'Yes, decidedly; very much so;' and II. ii. 1, *P. Itane patris ais conspectum veritam hinc abisse? G. Admodum. P. Phanium relictam solam? G. Sic. P. Et iratum senem? G. Oppido,*—where *admodum* (for another example of *admodum* in this sense see Hec. III. v. 8), *sic,* and *oppido* are all equivalent to 'exactly so.' In each of the above examples we may, if we please, supply the preceding adjective after *oppido, oppido omnem, oppido liberalis, oppido iratum.* With regard to the origin of *oppido,* grammarians have, for the most part, acquiesced in the explanation given by Paulus Diaconus after Festus (s. v. *oppido,* p. 184, ed. Müll.), although the canon laid down as to the correct use of the word is not supported by the practice of the best writers: " *Oppido* valde multum. Ortum est autem hoc verbum ex sermone inter se confabulantium quantum quisque frugum faceret, utque multitudo significaretur saepe respondebatur, *quantum vel oppido satis esset.* Hinc in consuetudinem venit ut diceretur *oppido* pro valde multum. Itaque, si qui in aliis rebus eo utuntur, ut puta si qui dicant Oppido didici, spectavi, ambulavi, errant; quia nulli eorum subiici potest, vel quod satis est." I feel little hesitation in repudiating this etymology, and entertain little doubt that from the root *ops,* pl. *opes,* was formed an adjective, *opidus* or

R

oppidus, signifying 'abundant,' to which *oppidum*, 'a town,' and *oppido*,
both belong, and that the true meaning of *oppido* is 'abundantly,'
which we ourselves use as equivalent to 'very,' when we speak
of a matter as 'abundantly clear,' 'evident,' 'ridiculous,' and so
forth. There is a very obscure passage in Quintilian VIII. 3, § 25,
with regard to this word; "*Satis* est vetus: quid necesse est, quaeso,
dicere *oppido?* quo sunt usi paululum tempore nostro superiores:
vereor ut iam nos ferat quisquam." Are we to understand that Quintilian here condemns altogether the use of the word *oppido*, or that he
merely disapproves of the use of *oppido* in the sense of *satis*, or does
he mean something different from either of these explanations?

52. *Venit ignavia*] I. e. 'dissipation.' *Ignavus* is the opposite of
gnavus, 'energetic,' 'vigorous,' 'active,' 'strenuous,' and since idleness
is the mother of mischief, *ignavia* and *ignavus* are employed to
denote various phases of moral turpitude. Thus in our text *ignaria*
signifies profligacy, dissipation, extravagance; and so in Trin. I. ii.
95, Megaronides bitterly reproaches Callicles with having given a
supply of money to Lesbonicus, *Qui exaedificaret suam inchoatam
ignaviam*, i. e. 'build up to the summit the structure of his profligacy already commenced;' so too Poen. IV. ii. 24, where *ignavus* is
opposed to *frugi bonae*, 'respectable,' *Proinde habel hic orationem quasi
ipse sit frugi bonae Qui ipsus hercle ignaviorem potis est facere ignaviam.*
Ignavia signifies carelessness, want of activity, in Merc. III. iv. 77.
In I. 23, *Nusquam est disciplina ignavior*, 'nowhere is household
discipline more lax.' The most common meaning is 'worthless,
good-for-nothing;' *ille ignavos*, 'that profligate,' Trin. I. ii. 128;
ignavom, 'a coward,' Most. III. ii. 169; *ignavi*, 'cowards in war,'
Capt. II. ii. 12; *mea ignavia*, 'thou that art the monument of my
folly,' Pers. V. ii. 68; *is ignavissumus* (in wrath), 'that rascal,' Poen.
V. v. 3; *ignavi homines*, 'these rascals,' Rud. III. v. 49; and so
ignavis and *ignavia*, in Men. V. vi. 8, 11; *ignavi*, 'idle scoundrels'
(to slaves), Pseud. I. ii. 1; *ipsi ignavi*, 'the worthless, good-for-
nothing,' Bac. III. vi. 15, and *me esse dicito ignavissumum*, 'call me
utterly worthless,' v. 27; *ille ignavissumus*, 'that most worthless of
men,' Trin. IV. ii. 81; and so *homo ignavissume*, Men. V. v. 25;
ignave, 'you good-for-nothing old profligate,' Cas. II. iii. 23; *igna-
riorem* in the same sense, v. 28; and so *ignavissumis vervecibus*,
'these good-for-nothing worn-out old wethers,' III. ii. 4. Compare *indiligens* in vv. 23, 29.

54. 55. 56.] Compare iii. 6, *Haec illa est tempestas mea, mihi quae
molestiam omnem Detexit, tectus qua fui.*

62. *quin totae Perpetuae ruant*] 'tumble down, with a crash, from top to bottom,' the fall being uninterrupted, no portion being left standing. *Perpetuus* properly conveys the idea of unbroken continuity; it is seldom, if ever, equivalent to the English *perpetual*, in the sense of 'lasting for ever,' but the meaning may generally be expressed by 'uninterrupted.' Thus *perpetua iuga*, applied by Pliny (H. N. III. v. 7) to the course of the Apennines from the Alps to the extremity of Italy, denotes that the ridge was continuous or uninterrupted; *perpetuae mensae* (Virg. Æn. VII. 176) are long tables stretching in a straight line up and down, uninterrupted or unbroken by a transverse piece like the *tricliniuum; perpetuae quaestiones* were the courts for the trial of certain criminal offences, which sat from year to year 'without interruption,' unlike the special commissions appointed from time to time. *Perpetuus* and the adverb *perpetuo* are often employed by Plautus and Terence, uniformly with the force above explained. Thus *perpetuom diem*, Most. III. ii. 78 (76); *perpetuam noctem*, Rud. II. iii. 40; *triduom perpetuom*, Adel. IV. i. 4; *biennium perpetuom*. Hec. I. ii. 12; *perpetuos decem annos*, Stich. I. iii. 14, require no explanation. *Solida et perpetua fides* (Merc. II. iii. 44) is 'truth or honour, firm and uninterrupted.' When Laches says (Hec. II. ii. 10), *Si perpetuam vis esse affinitatem hanc*, he means, 'if you desire that this connection between our families should remain unbroken;' and the same phrase recurs IV. iv. 14. The sentiment expressed by Auxilium in Cist. I. iii. 46, *Vt sunt humana, nihil est perpetuom datum*, is, 'nothing goes on steadily without interruption;' with which compare Hec. III. iii. 46. The expression *perpetuus modus* is peculiar to Plautus; thus Most. IV. iii. 41 (iv. 41), *Te ludificatus est et me hodie in perpetuom modum*, means, 'he has befooled you and me this day one after the other, without interruption;' and again III. i. 5, *Nunc pol ego perii plane in perpetuom modum*, means, 'now am I evidently undone, and must be ruined without a pause,' 'without anything to break or arrest or interrupt my downward career.' In like manner with regard to the adverb *perpetuo*, the expression in Amph. Prol. 60, *Nam me perpetuo facere ut sit comoedia*, denotes, 'for me to bring it about that this piece should be a comedy from beginning to end.' Again in Epid. I. i. 15, when the slave inquires, *Quid ais? perpetuon, valuisti?* he means, 'have you enjoyed uninterrupted good health?' and so again, Merc. II. iii. 53, *D. Vsquene valuisti? C. Perpetuo recte, dum quidem illic fui*, i. e. 'I enjoyed uninterrupted good health as long as I was there;' Heaut. IV. viii. 11, *perfice hoc mihi perpetuo, Chreme*, i. e. 'without interruption.' In

Most. III. i. 23 (19), *Metuo ne technae meae perpetuo perierint*, 'I am afraid that my schemes have been and will be upset one after another without a pause;' and so *perpetuo perire* signifies the same as *perire in perpetuom modum*, 'to go to destruction headlong;' Pers. II. iv. 10, Adel. II. iv. 19, Eun. V. iii. 13. The phrase *in perpetuom* is sometimes equivalent to 'always,' and may be used with reference to the period of a whole life: Heaut. IV. v. 33; Cic. Cat. I. 12; Liv. VII. 37. The verb *perpetuare* occurs once in Plautus, Pseud. I. III. 72, *Non est iustus quisquam amator nisi qui perpetuat data*, 'unless one who makes presents uninterruptedly,' and is found in Cicero also. For other examples of *perpetuus* and *perpetuo*, see Amph. Prol. 6; Poen. I. ii. 82; Pers. III. i. 2; Eun. V. iv. 11; Adel. V. ix. 15; And. III. iii. 32; Adel. IV. i. 6; Hec. III. iii. 46.

64. *Cor dolet*] i. e. 'my heart aches,' from which is formed the substantive *cordolium*, 'the heart-ache,' found twice in Plautus; Cist. I. i. 67, Poen. I. ii. 86; and revived by Apuleius Met. IX. 190. It has been adopted into Italian as *cordoglio*.

68. *Discipulinae aliis eram*] i. e. 'I was a pattern (or model) to others.' The original unsyncopated form of the word is here preserved in the Palatine MSS. In this passage *discipulinae* is equivalent to *exemplo*, 'I was a model from which others might learn their duty,' but it assumes many shades of meaning, which may however be easily connected with each other. Thus in Ad. L. iii. 49, *eadem disciplina utimur* means, 'we follow the same system;' in Cas. III. v. 24, *Atticam disciplinam*, 'the laws and usages of Athens;' and in v. 28, *Malarum malum disciplinam*, 'the evil example or customs of bad women;' in Cist. I. i. 18, *disciplina* is 'the ways and rules of a family;' in Bac. I. ii. 27, *tua disciplina* is exactly represented by 'your discipline,' viz., that of a teacher towards a pupil, and so III. ii. 17; in Mil. II. ii. 30, *paret disciplinam*, 'let her school herself;' in Merc. I. 6, *haec disciplina*, 'this fashion or custom;' in Truc. I. i. 30, *ita est disciplina*, 'thus are matters ordered;' in I. ii. 29, *ea est disciplina*, 'so was I trained to be.'

— *Parsimonia et duritia discipulinae aliis eram.*] *Discipulinae* may be either the genitive after *parsimonia* and *duritia*, signifying 'training,' in which case the construction will be *eram exemplo aliis*, or the dative, *eram discipulinae aliis*, i. e. 'I was a lesson to others.'

I. iii. 9. *Periere haec oppido aedes.*] This is the reading of B, which has *hae*, and was adopted by Camerarius; the rest of the MSS. have *hae*. There can be no doubt however that *haec* was used occasionally by the older writers as the feminine nom. pl., and it is

evident that it was much more likely to be changed by transcribers
into the common form *hur* than the reverse. Thus in AuL III. v. 58,
*Hace sunt atque aliae multae in magnis dotibus Incommoditates sump-
tusque intolerabiles*, is the reading of the best MSS. and is retained
in the Vulg.; so Eun. III. v. 34, *Abducit secum ancillas: paucae, quae
circum illam essent, manent Novitiae puellae: continuo hace adornant ut
latet*, where the reading is, apparently, not disputed; so also Phor.
V. viii. 23, where however the reading is doubtful; so *istae*, nom.
pl. fem. (=*istae hace*); Hec. IV. ii. 17, S. *Nihil pol iam istaec res
mihi voluptatis ferunt.*

11. *meo ocello*] 'the apple of my eye.' Catullus employs the same
term when addressing his beloved Sirmio, *Peninsularum, Sirmio,
insularumque Ocelle.* For a collection of terms of endearment see
Excursus.

14. *sapit scelesta multum*] 'the cunning jade is very knowing.'
Scelestus in the dramatists bears two significations, which must be
kept distinct.   1. It is used in the strict literal sense of *villainous;*
thus below, II. ii. 72 (71), *Scelestus, auri causa,* 'the villain (did it)
for the sake of gold;' and vituperatively, below, *v.* 26, *Quid ais,
scelesta,* 'what's that you say, you wretch?' and Rud. IV. i. 4, *Sed
uxor scelesta,* 'but that jade, my wife,' where Weise is quite mistaken.
In this sense the epithet may be applied to things as well as persons,
as in the line immediately following the one quoted above, *Scelestae
hae sunt aedes,* 'guilt attaches to this mansion;' and in III. i. 1, *Scelestiorem ego annum*, &c., 'never did I see a more villainous year for
lending out money;' and this use of *villainous* is common in our own
language.   *Scelestus* is also employed to denote craft or subtlety
rather than actual guilt, as in Trin. II. iv. 126, *etsi scelestus est At mi
infidelis non est,* 'although the fellow is a cunning rogue, yet he is
not unfaithful to me;' it is used also playfully, as in the line before
us, and so *sceleste*, Most. II. ii. 47, where the reading is doubtful, means
'you rascal,' but without any serious emphasis.   2. As if to indicate
the due connection between crime and misery, *scelestus* passes into
the sense of *miserable*, and is used without necessarily implying guilt
at all, in the sense of 'unhappy' or 'unfortunate.'   So below, III. l. 36
(33), *nae ego sum miser, Scelestus, natus dis inimicis omnibus.*   One who
was unlucky or unfortunate might be regarded as punished by the
gods for some crime; and this seems to be indicated in the above
passage, and also in Capt. III. v. 104, Eun. II. iii. 34, and As. V.
ii. 6, *At scelesta ego praeter alios meum virum fui rata Siccum, frugi,
continentem, amantem uxoris maxume,* 'wretched beyond others;'

so *scelestus*, 'unlucky wretch that I am,' Rud. III. v. 22; *scelestius*, 'more unfortunate,' Men. III. i. 2; *scelestissumum*, 'most wretched,' Cas. III. v. 34; *me infelicem et scelestam*, Cist. IV. ii. 17; cf. Rud. IV. iv. 123; *mihi scelesto*, Rud. II. vi. 18; and advantage is sometimes taken of the double meaning, as in As. II. iv. 69, *Age, impudice, Sceleste. L. Non audes mihi scelesto subvenire.* There is a close analogy between the use of *scelestus* and the English adjective *wretched*, which is ambiguous, since it may be applied to a man who is simply unhappy, or to a man in an unhappy position from guilt. So also 'you wretch' and 'he is a wretch' are vituperative, while both may be employed playfully; not so, however, 'wretch that I am!' So we talk of *wretched weather*, a *wretched harvest*, a *wretched year for farmers*, and the like.

23. *aut meam speciem alios inridere.*] Cf. III. ii. 125 (123), *Ergo inridere ne vidrare et gestire admodum* (here absolutely); V. ii. 11 (iii. 11), *Verbero, etiam inrides?* again absolutely. Examples of *in-ridere* with the accusative may be found in Pseud. V. ii. 19; Poen. V. ii. 71; Pers. V. ii. 26; Merc. II. i. 26.

29. *Catus.*] For *catus* Cf. V. ii. 21 (iii. 21), *Hercle mihi tecum cavendum est: nimis quam es orator catus.*

32. *illi Morem praecipue sic geras.*] *Morem gerere alicui* denotes that a person suits his or accommodates his or her ways and wishes to those of another, and hence signifies generally, 'to comply with,' 'to obey.' We have several examples in this play; I. iii. 43, 69; II. i. 51; III. i. 50 (51); ii. 36 (37): see also Pers. IV. iv. 55; Capt. II. iii. 44; Curc. I. ii. 62; Men. V. ii. 37. Sometimes the phrase is applied to one who indulges his own inclinations, e. g. Amph. Prol. 131, *Pater nunc intus suo animo morem gerit.* From the combination *morem gerere* are formed the adjective *morigerus* and the verb *morigero* or *morigeror*; so below, II. i. 51, *Morigerae tibi erimus ambae;* and in Cist. I. iii. 27, *Ea diem suum obiit, facta morigera est viro,* i. e. 'she did what her husband wished her to do—she died;' and I. i. 86, *de ea re gessit morem morigerat mihi,* i. e. 'in that matter my mother yielded to me, who in other matters was obedient to her;' and with *moribus* in Men. I. iii. 19, *Cape tibi hanc* (sc. *pullam*): *quando una ribis meis morigera moribus.* See also Cas. II. viii. 39; Curc. I. ii. 70; Amph. III. iii. 26; Epid. V. i. 1. The verb is less common, but is found in both the active and deponent form; Amph. III. iii. 26, *Volo deludi illum, dum cum hac usuraria Uxore nunc mihi morigero;* and Capt. II. i. 4, *Nunc servitus si evenit, ei ros morigerari mos bonus est.* The simple word *mos* is occasionally

found in Plautus in the sense of 'will,' 'wish,' 'favour;' thus Bac.
III. iii. 55, *Opsequens obediensque est mori atque imperiis patris;* also
below, *v.* 128, *Nam amator meretricis mores sibi emit auro et purpura.*

33. *unum inservire amantem.*] Plautus constructs *inservire* with
the accusative here and below, *v.* 59, *si illum inservibis solum;* in
Terence it is followed by the dative, Heaut. III. I. 9, *Ita ut filium
meum amico aequae aequali suo Video inservire, et socium esse in negotiis,*
and this is the practice of Cicero, Caesar, Livy, Tacitus, &c., in whose
writings we find *inservire honoribus, omnibus rebus, artibus, famae,* &c.
Occasionally it is used without a case, as in Poen. IV. II. 105, *Nam
et hoc docte consulendum, quomodo concreditum est Et illud autem inser-
viendum est consilium vernaculum,* i.e. 'and on the other hand that
scheme of our own must be zealously prosecuted;' and so also
Cic. Epp. ad Fam. VI. 12, *Sed nihil est a me inservitum temporis
causa.* *Praeservire* is found once in Plautus, and takes the dative;
Amph. Prol. 126, *Vt praeservire meo amanti possem patri.* The word
does not occur elsewhere until we come down to Aulus Gellius
I. 7. § 3.

51. *Inscita . . . es*] i.e. 'you are a simpleton.' 1. The meaning
of *scitus* in colloquial language may, in many cases, be correctly
represented by the English 'knowing.' Thus Pseud. I. iii. 151, *Ad
eam rem usus est hominem astutum, doctum, scitum et callidum;* also
Amph. I. iii. 8, *Nimis hic scitus est sycophanta,* i.e. 'a very knowing
rogue is this fellow;' and so Cas. III. i. 8, *nimium scite scitus es,* and
v. 11, *te demum nullum scitum scitius.* The pun implied in the last
example is more fully developed in Pseud. II. iv. 58, *P. Ecquid is
homo scitus est? C. Plebiscitum non est scitius;* so also Merc. III.
i. 28, *tondetur nimium scite,* 'that old ewe will be very cleverly
shorn.' So *scite* in Bac. II. iii. 69, Mil. IV. ii. 74, Trin. III. iii. 53,
56, V. ii. 23; *scitissume,* in Stich. I. iii. 116; *satis scite,* Trin. III.
iii. 56. Below, *v.* 104, *scita tu es quidem,* 'a very knowing one art
thou,' is ironical. Nor is the epithet confined to animate objects,
for we have in As. IV. i. 47, *Pulcre scripsti! scitum syngraphum!*
'you have written well! a clever bond!' and in Amph. I. i. 132,
Haec nox est scita, 'this night is suitable, convenient (jolly).' *Inscitus*
being the opposite of *scitus,* signifies 'simple,' 'green,' 'foolish,' as in
the line before us; so *inscitus,* Men. II. iii. 88; *verum esse in-
sciti credimus.* 'we in our folly believe it to be true,' Truc. I. ii. 90;
and so Mil. III. i. 141, *Qui deorum consilia culpet, stultus inscitusque
sit;* and so Merc. V. iv. 59, *inscitum arbitrabimur,* 'we shall look
upon him as an old idiot;' in Rud. III. i. 5, *inscitum somniari*

somnium means, 'I have dreamed a senseless (unmeaning) dream.'[*] In
like manner *inscitia* is 'folly,' as in Curc. I. iii. 29, *male mereri de im-
merenti inscitia est;* and so Mil. II. vi. 61, Poen. IV. ii. 99, Truc. IV.
iii. 71. Paul. Diac. p. 111, ed. Müller, explains "*Inscitia*, stultitia."
2. *Scitus* signifying, as we have seen above, 'knowing,' 'clever,' 'smart,'
is occasionally employed to denote personal attractions, and may be
rendered 'nice-looking;' thus in Merc. IV. iv. 15, *Satis scitum filum
mulieris* means, 'not a bad-looking slip of a girl;' and so again in
v. 17. The diminutive *scitulus* bears the same meaning; thus Rud.
II. vii. 7, *L. Qua sunt facie? S. Scitula.* 'L. What sort of looking
girls are they? S. Pretty.' And again, Rud. IV. i. 3, *iam eluentlas
reperi Atque ambas forma scitula atque aetatula.* In Bac. II. ii. 31,
Scitum istuc! is spoken ironically, 'that's very pretty;' and in Stich.
I. iii. 30, *Oratio scitissuma* means, 'a most sensible and agreeable sort of discourse.' *Scitamenta,* if the reading be correct, in
Men. I. lii. 26, signifies 'dainties,' 'tit-bits,' *Iube igitur nobis apud te
prandium adcurarier Atque aliquid scitamentorum de foro opsonarier.*
The text is so uncertain in Cist. IV. ii. 12 and in Truc. V. 42, where
scitior and *scitus* appear in the Vulgate, that it is useless to discuss
these difficult passages.

54. *pro capite tuo*] i. e. *pro te, pro tuo corpore;* and so below, vv. 85
and 142, and Rud. IV. ii. 24. The head being the principal member
of the body, and according to the popular belief of the ancients the
seat of life, is frequently put for the whole body, the whole individual.
Thus *hoc caput* is frequently equivalent to *ego* or *me.* This is the
force of *caput* in such phrases as Pseud. II. iv. 33, *G. Egone? P. Tute.*
G. Ego? P. Ipsus, inquam, siquidem hoc vivet caput, i. e. 'if I live;'
and so Epid. I. i. 86, *plane hoc corruptum est caput,* i. e. *ego;* again,
suum caput means *se ipsum* in Epid. III. ii. 33; and in Pseud. I. i. 129,
Atque ipse egreditur, penitus periurum caput; Stich. V. v. 10, *fugit hoc
libertas caput,* i. e. 'me.' *Caput* is also frequently used in such exclamations as *O lepidum caput,* 'what a jolly cove!' Mil. III. i. 131;
Ridiculum caput, 'you absurd fool!' Andr. II. ii. 34; *Festivom
caput,* 'what a trump!' Adel. II. iii. 8; and in the vituperative, *Vae
capiti tuo!* with which cf. Poen. III. iii. 32, Rud. III. vi. 47. So also
the diminutive *capitulum* in Eun. III. iii. 25, *O capitulum lepidissumum,*
'O you darling old boy!' *Capitulum* is used in the sense of *caput,
coperto capitulo,* Curc. II. iii. 14; and in As. II. iv. 89, *huic capitulo*
is *mihi,* 'to this humble individual.'

83. *Nec recte si illi dixeris*] i. e. 'to speak evil of him,' as opposed to *in illum bene loqui* of the preceding line. The expressions, *Nec recte dicere alicui* or *in aliquem, Inclementer dicere alicui* or *in aliquem, Male loqui alicui, Nec recte loqui alicui, Male dicere alicui*, are all used in the sense, 'to speak reproachfully of a person,' or, 'to address reproach or rebuke to a person.' Festus s. v. *Nec*, p. 162 ed. Müll. quotes, *Nec recte si illi dixeris* from the Phasma of Plautus, and, *Nec recte dici mihi, quod iamdudum audio* from the Demetrius of Turpilius. Thus As I. iii. 3, *Nec recte quae tu in nos dicis aurum atque argentum merum est;* II. iv. 65, *Malo hercle iam magno tuo nunc isti nec recte dicis;* Bac. I. ii. 11, *Mali sunt homines qui bonis dicunt male, Tu Dis nec recte dicis: non aequom facis;* Poen. III. i. 13, *Si nec recte dicis nobis, dives de summo loco, Divitem audacter solemus mactare infortunio;* Pseud. IV. vi. 23, *Nam quanti refert te nec recte dicere Qui nihili faciat quique infitias non eat?* where there is an ellipse of *illi* after *nec recte dicere;* Amph. II. ii. 110, *Iterum iam hic in me inclementer dicit, atque id sine malo?* Poen. V. v. 43, *Quid tibi lubido, opsecro, Anthemonides, Loqui inclementer nostro cognato et patri?* Rud. I. ii. 26, *Aut qui inclementer dicat homini libero;* III. iv. 29, *Tun, trifurcifer, mihi audes inclementer dicere?* Truc. II. vii. 44, *cur ausus inclementer Mihi dicere?* Pseud. I. i. 25, *Cur inclementer dicis lepidis literis, Lepidis tabellis, lepida conscriptis manu;* again, As. II. iv. 71, *Quae res? Tun libero homini Male servos loquere?* so also Bac. IV. iv. 83, *Chrysalus mihi usque quaque loquitur nec recte pater;* and below, IV. ii. 12 (i. 34), *Non potes tu cogere me ut tibi maledicam;* and so Ampl. II. i. 22; Curc. I. ii. 30, IV. ii. 27; Men. II. ii. 35, 40; Pers. II. iv. 8, 20; Poen. V. ii. 76; Rud. III. ii. 25 (without a case); Stich. I. ii. 57; Trin. IV. ii. 149; Truc. IV. iii. 1.

91. *Speculum.*] The material of which the mirror was made we discover from r. 110: S. *Linteum cape, atque exterge tibi manus.* P. *Quid ita, opsecro?* S. *Vt speculum tenuisti, metuo ne oleant argentum manus.*

101. *Cerussa*] 'white lead,' the ψίμυθος or ψιμμύθιον of the Greeks. The process of manufacture is described by Plin. H. N. XXXIV. 18, § 54. *Psimithium quoque, hoc est cerussam, plumbariae dant officinae, laudatissimam in Rhodo: fit autem ramentis plumbi tenuissimis super vas aceti asperrimi impositis atque ita destillantibus. . . . Fit et alio modo, addito in urceos aceti plumbo opturatos per dies decem derasoque ceu situ ac rursus reiecto donec deficiat materia.* He also (l. c.) notices its employment as a cosmetic: *Vis eius eadem quae supra dictis, lenissima tantum ex omnibus, praeterque ad candorem feminarum.* See also Ovid

s

Medic. fac. 73, *Nec cerussa tibi, nec nitri spuma rubentis Detit, et Illyrica quae venit iris humo*, but here it forms part of a complicated recipe. We find the word *cerussatus* quoted from Cic. in Pison. XI. (*cerussatasque buccae*, when describing the general appearance of Gabinius), but all the MSS. here are corrupt, and present *pultatae*; It occurs, however, in Martial VII. xxv. 2, *Dulcia cum tantum scribas epigrammata semper Et cerussata candidiora cute*. There is another Ep. of Mart. in which *cerussa* is mentioned, X. xxii., *Cur spleniato saepe prodeam mento Albove pictus sana labra cerussa, Philaeni, quaeris? basiare te nolo*.

102. *Atramentum*] when used to denote a black pigment, is what we call *lamp-black*, and the mode in which it was usually prepared is distinctly described in Plin. H.N. XXXV. 6, § 25, *Fit enim e fuligine pluribus modis, resina vel pice exustis, propter quod etiam officinas aedificavere fumum cum non emittentes*. Cf. Vitruv. VII. 10. Apelles and Micon are said to have used *atramentum* made from the charcoal of grape-stones, while Apelles also employed bone-black obtained from ivory. (Plin. l.c.) *Atramentum librarium*, or writing-ink, was composed by mixing *atramentum* with gum, while in *atramentum tectorium*, for stuccoing the walls of rooms, glue was the vehicle. (Vitruv. l.c.) Totally distinct from the *atramentum* described above was what the Romans called *atramentum sutorium*, and the Greeks χάλκανθον. This, as is evident from the description of Pliny (H.N. XXXIV. § 32), was sulphate of iron, which, when applied to tanned leather, would stain it black, forming exactly the compound which constitutes the common writing ink of modern times.*

– *postules*] i.e. 'you may as well try (expect) at the same time to whiten ivory with lamp-black.' It is commonly set down in books upon Latin Synonyms that *postulo* is the strongest of all the verbs which signify 'to seek' or 'to ask for,' and that it denotes that the person employing it peremptorily demands something to which he has an unquestionable right. This is however by no means the common force of the word when used colloquially. We shall find a great number of passages in the dramatists where it means simply 'to desire,' 'to want,' or 'to try to do something,' and 'to expect to be able to do;' in addition it sometimes conveys the idea that a

---

* When Cic. Epp. Fam. IX. 21, speaking of Cn. Carbo the partizan of Marius says, *Iam pater eius, accusatus a M. Antonio, sutorio atramento absolutus putatur*, he probably means that he poisoned himself with this substance, but the explanation is uncertain. Galen reckons it among poisons. Consult Pereira.

person wishes or endeavours to do something from a conviction that
he is discharging a duty, or at all events seeking to do something
which is desirable or right or fair,* and conversely it is frequently
employed in a half-ironical sense, when one person desires to represent the wishes or expectations of another as altogether unreasonable
or unjust, ridiculous or impossible, as in the line now before us. A
few examples will make this plain: thus below, IV. iii. 29 (iv. 29),
ne ire infitias postules, 'do not attempt to draw back;' and so in
III. i. 85 (81), and in IV. iii. 14 (iv. 14), *haud postulo,* 'I don't want
you;' in III. i. 15, *ita haec res postulat,* 'so the circumstances of
the present case demand;' Epid. III. iv. 8, 9, *Non repperisti, adulescens, tranquillum locum ubi tuas virtutes explices ut postulas,* 'as
you think proper or reasonable;' Amph. II. ii. 137, *Nam haec quidem
nos delirantes facere dictis postulat,* 'wants to make us out to be mad;'
Men. V. ii. 42, *Quae haec, malum, impudentia est? Una opera prohibere
ad cenam me promittat postules, Neve quemquam accipiat alienum apud
te: servire tibi Postulas viros? Dare una opera pensum postules,
Inter ancillas sedere iubeas, lanam carere,* i.e. 'can you ask,' 'do you
think it reasonable to ask?' the meaning of *postulare* being, 'to
require a thing which is fair and reasonable;' Rud. IV. iv. 106, *Si
hercle tantillum peccassis quod posterius postules Te ad verum convorti,
nugas, mulier, magnas egeris;* IV. iii. 4, *Nihil habeo, adulescens, piscium:
ne tu mihi esse postules,* i.e. 'I say this in case you may wish
that I had some,' 'may insist that;' III. iv. 4, *Tune legirupionem
hic nobis cum Dis facere postulas?* Trin. II. iv. 40, *Ego quoque volo
esse liber, nequiquam volo: Hic postulet frugi esse, nugas postulet;
IV. iii. 15, Inter eosne homines condalium te redipisci postulas,* i.e.
'is it reasonable to want (to think that)?' Truc. IV. ii. 17, *Stultus
es qui facta infecta facere verbis postules.* For other examples see
Rud. Prol. 17; II. vi. 59; II. iii. 63; Trin. II. i. 11; IV. ii.
130; Truc. IV. iv. 9, 10; &c., &c.   In some of the following
passages *postulo* may fairly be translated 'I demand,' but even
then it seldom carries with it a peremptory force.   In the great
majority of cases 'to ask' is the proper translation: Amph. III.
ii. 10; As. I. iii. 37; Aul. II. vi. 12, 13, IV. i. 3, x. 27; Capt. I. ii.
83, II. ii. 89, III. v. 81, V. i. 18, 21; Cas. II. ii. 22, v. 3, V. iv. 1;
Men. II. iii. 88, V. ii. 17 (*expect*), ix. 21; Mil. IV. v. 6, II. iii. 31;
Poen. I. ii. 187 (*expect*), III. i. 41, v. 11, 31, vi. 14, V. ii. 122;

---

* Of this latter meaning we have good examples in Pers. I. i. 42;
Pseud. III. ii. 62; Mil. II. v. 37.

Pseud. I. i. 99. Observe that in Mil. II. vi. 35, *postulare tecum* signifies 'to complain of you,' 'to accuse you;' and so *postulatio*, Cas. III. ii. 26. See also Bac. III. iii. 38, 45.

104. *Purpurissum.*] 'Rouge.' It was made by boiling fine chalk with the purple dye obtained from the murex. Plin. H. N. XXXV. 6, § 26, *E reliquis coloribus quos a dominis dari diximus propter magnitudinem preti ante omnes est purpurissum. Creta argentaria cum purpuris pariter tinguitur bibitque eum colorem celerius lanis.* Cf. XXXV. 6, § 12. The form *purpurissa* is quoted by Non. p. 218, from the Sanniones of Naevius, *Inlino cretam, cerussam, purpurissam.* Plautus uses also the participial adjective *purpurissatus*, Truc. II. i. 35, *Quia adeo fores nostras unguentis uncta es ausa accedere, Quiaque istas buccas tam belle purpurissatas habes.*

105. *Interpolare.*] This verb is found only in the form of a compound, but we can scarcely doubt that the simple *polo* is derived from the same root as *polio.* The true meaning of the word seems to be 'to renovate,' 'to furbish up,' 'to change the appearance of an object,' the idea being usually implied that this is effected by the addition of something which enters into combination with the original object. It is said to have been properly a term describing the operations performed by *fullones* in cleaning woollen garments, and this explanation is supported by a passage in Cic. Epp. ad Q. F. II. xii. 2, when speaking of Antiochus of Commagene ; *Quod vult, inquam, renovare honores eosdem, quominus togam praetextam quotannis interpolet, decernendum nihil censeo,* i. e. 'to save him from furbishing up his old toga praetexta ever year.'* *Vestimenta interpola* in the Digest XVIII. 1, § 45 are opposed to *nova.* Cf. XXI. i. 37. Hence it signifies 'to clean' simply, without the notion of adding anything, as in Plin. H. N. XII. 14, § 32, *At, Hercules, Alexandriae, ubi tura interpolantur.* The meaning of the expression in Aul. IV. ix. 6 is very doubtful. Of the word used in the general or figurative sense of 'to invest an object with a new aspect,' we have a good example in Amph. I. l. 160, where Mercury, addressing his own clenched fist, observes, *Alia forma oportet esse, quem tu pugno legeris;* to which Sosia rejoins, *Illic homo me interpolabit, meumque os finget demuo ;* and in Cic. in Verr. Act. II. i. 61, § 158, *Hoc modo iste sibi et saluti suae prospicere didicit, referendo in tabulas et privatas et publicas*

_____
* It is well known that *togae* were cleaned and whitened by rubbing in chalk or pipe-clay ; hence the phrases (Livy IV. 25) *album in vestimentum addere petitionis . . . causa,* and (Pers. V. 177) *cretata ambitio.* Compare Plin. H. N. XXXV. 17 § 57.

quod gestum non esset; tollendo quod esset, et semper aliquid demendo, mutando, interpolando. In the passage before us *interpolare* may be translated 'you seek to beautify a most charming work of art by daubing it over with (i.e. by the addition of) fresh colours.' See also Plin. H. N. XXXV. 16, § 56. *Est in medicaminibus et Chia terra candicans, effectus eiusdem, qui Samiae. Vsus ad mulierum maxime cutem: idem et Selinusiae. Lactei coloris est haec et aqua dilui celerrima: eadem lacte diluta tectoriorum albaria interpolantur,* i. e. 'the white plaster on walls is renovated' (by the addition of this whitewash). See also Q. Curt. VI. 2, § 5, speaking of Alexander, *Igitur quum intempestivis conviviis dies pariter noctesque consumeret, satietatem epularum ludis interpolabat,* i. e. 'diversified by the introduction of.' See also IV. 6, § 28, where the reading is doubtful. Below, I. iii. 117, we have the adjective *interpoles,* i. e. 'painted Jezebels,' a word which occurs only in this passage and twice in Pliny: H. N. XIX. 2, § 8, speaking of spartum, so extensively used for cordage, he remarks, *Est quidem eius natura interpolis, rursusque quam libeat vetustum novo miscetur,* i. e. 'is susceptible of renovation,' i. e. as explained by what follows, 'the old fibre may be worked up again with new to any extent without injuring the quality of the product.' Again, II. N. XXIX. 1, § 5, speaking of medicine, *Mutatur ars quotidie totiens interpolis et ingeniorum Graeciae flatu impellimur,* i. e. 'changing its aspect daily.' Holland thus paraphrases the expression, 'Thus you see how often this art from time to time hath been altered, and daily still it is turned like a garment new dressed,' &c.

107. *Melinum*] sc. pigmentum, a fine white earth, named from the island of Melos in which it was found. Plin. II. N. XXXV. 6, § 19, *Melinum candidum et ipsum est, optimum in Melo insula; in Samo quoque nascitur: eo non utuntur pictores propter nimium pinguitudinem;*[*] *accubantes effodiunt ibi inter saxa venam scrutantes.* It was used also as a medicine. (Plin. l. c.) The young student must be careful to distinguish this adjective from another the quantity and spelling of which are the same, viz. *mēlīnus,* derived from μῆλον, an apple or quince.[†] It is used by Plautus to denote some colour,

---

[*] And yet he tells us that *melinum* was one of the four colours used exclusively by Apelles, Echion, Melanthius, and Nicomachus, the others being lamp-black (*atramentum*), the red of Sinope, and the yellow ochre (*sil*) of Athens. Plin. H. N. XXXV. 6, § 32.

[†] In Plin. H. N. XXIII. 6, § 54, *fit et oleum ex bis, quod melinum vocavimus,* and in XIII. 1, § 2, we have *melinum* denoting a perfume (*unguentum*) particularly valued in Cos; and lower down he gives the mode in which it was compounded by the admixture of various substances with *melinum oleum.*

perhaps apple-green, in his long catalogue of dresses of, different forms and shades, Epid. II. ii. 49, *Cumatile aut plumatile, cerinum aut melinum;* again Plautus uses *mēlina* to denote a purse or wallet made of sheepskin (μῆλον) or badger-skin (*meles*); Epid. I. i. 20, *Sed ubi est is? T. Adveni simul. E. Vbi is ergo est? nisi si in vidulo, Aut si in melina attulisti;* and in another passage *mēlina* is employed for a wine sweetened with honey (μέλι), Pseud. II. iv. 51, *Quid, si opus sit, ut dulce promat indidem? ecquid habet? C. Rogas? Murrhinam, passum, defrutum, melinam, mel quoiusmodi. Quin in corde instruere quondam coepit thermopolium.*

107, 118. *Offuciam. Fuco.*] *Fucus,* according to Pliny H. N. XIII. 25, § 48, is a general term for marine shrubs, and he tells us that the Latin language has no word equivalent to the Greek φῦκος, *quoniam alga herbarum magis vocabulum intelligitur, hic autem est frutex.* He goes on to describe three species growing on the rocks by the sea shore, one of these a native of Crete,[*] and elsewhere speaks of it as communicating a very fast red colour to wool. There can be little doubt that Pliny, or at least his authorities, intended to indicate by the word *fucus* some of the tinctorial lichens, of which a considerable number are found upon maritime rocks in the Mediterranean, and even on our own shores, especially those which yield the red or purple colours, and form the principal constituents of the dye stuff known as *archil.* The most celebrated of these is the *roccella tinctoria,* which many modern writers have supposed to be identical with the πόντιον φῦκος of Theophrastus, the φῦκος θαλάσσιον of Dioscorides, the *phycos thalassion* or *fucus* of Pliny. Dioscorides denies that the paint used by women was made from this plant, and asserts that it was a root bearing the same name, and hence in our dictionaries we find it frequently stated that *fucus* means the *anchusa tinctoria* or alkanet root. A German botanist (Endlicher) has recently maintained that the *fucus* of the ancient was obtained from one of the algae, the *cyliphlaea tinctoria,* from which a red colour can be extracted.[†] Hence the word *fucus* is used to signify generally a dye or pigment, chiefly red, from whatever source obtained, as in the passage before

---

[*] And yet in XXXII. 6, § 22, he terms this very plant an *alga—Laudatissima (alga maris, &c.) quae in Creta insula iuxta terram in petris nascitur, tingendis etiam lanis ita colorem adligans, ut elui postea non possit;* and in XXVI. 10, § 66, he mentions the medicinal properties of the same plants, which he comprehends under the name of *phycos thalassium id est fucus marinus,* describing the three varieties and alluding to Crete as the *habitat* of that used in dyeing.

[†] See Pereira, vol. II. pt. 1, p. 28.

us, (see also Hor. C. III. v. 28, Epp. I. x. 27,) and even colour in the abstract; thus Lucretius, when arguing that the ultimate atoms are destitute of colour, points out that blind men can distinguish bodies by touch, and goes on (II. 743), *Scire licet nostrae quoque menti corpora posse Vorti in notitiam nullo circumlita fuco.* Again, since paint conceals the surface of those objects to which it is applied, *fucus* is used figuratively to denote deception, fraud, trickery, as in Capt. III. iii. 6, *Nec subdolis mendaciis mihi usquam integumentum est mei: Nec sycophantiis nec fucis ullum mantellum obviam est ;* and Cic. Epp. ad Att. I. 1, *Prensat unus P. Galba. Sine fuco ac fullariis, more maiorum, negatur,* and hence the proverbial phrase *fucum facere,* i. e. 'to humbug a person.' See also Hor. S. I. ii. 83 and Q. Cic. de pet. cons. 9. In reference to style *fucus* is used to denote a tawdry ornament. See Cic. de Orat. II. 45, III. 52; Quintil. VIII. 3, § 6; cf. II. 15, § 25. In this last passage Quint. alludes to a practice prevalent among *mangones* of painting the slaves they had for sale, which may be regarded as an illustration of the passage before us, and the object was, evidently, *ut vitia corporis occulerent,* &c.

Offucia is employed both literally and figuratively. Here literally to denote paint. Figuratively in Capt. III. iv. 123, *Ita mi stolido sursum vorsum as sublevere offuciis ;* and in Aul. Gell. N. A. XIV. 1, § 2, who reports the views of Favorinus to the effect, *Disciplinam istam Chaldaeorum tantae vetustatis non esse, quantae videri volunt : neque eos principes eius auctoresque esse, quos ipsi ferunt : sed id praestigiarum atque offuciarum genus commentos esse homines aeruscatores, et cibum quaestumque ex mendaciis captantes.*

118. *Edentulae*] i. e. 'toothless from age.' See Martian. Capell. lib. IV. p. 116, Grot. Plautus uses the word in exactly the same sense in Cas. III. iii. 20, *Quid ego nunc faciam ? Flagitium maxumum feci miser Propter operam illius hirci improbi atque edentuli ;* and in Men. V. ii. 111, *Vt ego hunc proteram leonem vetulum, olentem, edentulum;* while in Poen. III. iii. 87 it is applied to wine which has lost all harshness from age, *Vbi tu Leucadio, Lesbio, Thasio, Coo, Vetustate vino edentulo aetatem irriges.* He uses also the verb *edentare,* 'to knock out or deprive of teeth,' in Rud. III. ii. 48, *Nimis velim improbissumo homini malas edentaverint.*

132. *si morata est male*] i. e. 'if her habits (or ways) are bad;' so below, I. iv. 8, *istoc modo moratus. Moratus,* derived from *mores,* signifies "moribus praeditus sive bonis sive malis;" and so Hec. IV. iv. 21, *sed quid mulieris Uxorem habes ? aut quibus moratam moribus ?* it occurs in this sense in As. III. i. 3, *isto more moratam ;*

Capt. I. ii. 22, *eius moratus moribus;* Merc. II. iii. 58, *ut morata est?*
Pers. IV. iv. 6, *si incolae bene sunt morati;* As. II. iii. 10, *ita haec
morata est ianua;* Aul. II. ii. 62, *morata recte;* Stich. I. ii. 52, *prius
moratam;* Truc. I. ii. 5, *ita adulescentes morati sunt;* Aul. Prol. 22
(*filium pariter moratum*), and is not uncommon in Cicero. In Hor.
A. P. 319, *morataque recte Fabula,* is correctly explained by the old
commentator, "in qua mores singularum personarum optime ex-
primuntur."

142. *Triginta minas*] and so again III. ii. 136. The price of an
accomplished and attractive female slave seems to have varied from
20 to 60 minae. Thus Stratippocles, Epid. I. I. 50, is represented
as having paid 40 minae for a beautiful captive girl; in the Curc. I.
i. 63, Phaedromus complains of the leno who was the proprietor of
Planesium, *Alias me poscit pro illa triginta minas Alias talentum
magnum.* He at one time asks 30 minae, at another 60, and in II.
iii. 65 she is represented as having been sold for 30, with the addition
of 10 for her apparel and ornaments. In Merc. II. iii. 93, 20 minae
are spoken of as a reasonable price for a handsome female slave,
and 30 minae were paid by Philolaches for Philematium, and by
Pleusidippus for Palaestra, Rud. Prol. 45. The same price was fixed
for the attractive Pamphila in the Phormio, III. iii. 24. In Pseud.
I. i. 51, iii. 110, Phoenicium is represented as having been sold
for 20 minae; and in Adel. II. i. 37, IV. vii. 34, 20 minae is the
price paid by a leno for a psaltria. In Pers. IV. iv. 113, a maiden
believed by the purchaser to be a slave is sold without a warranty
for 60 minae, the seller having at first asked 100: *Tuo periculo sexaginta haec datur argenti minis.* In Poen. IV. ii. 75, two little girls,
one five, the other four years old, were sold to a dealer by a Sicilian
pirate for 18 minae (it seems doubtful whether the nutrix who was
sold along with them was included in the above sum). Phaedria tells
Thais, Eun. I. ii. 89, that he gave 20 minae for a little black girl
(*ex Aethiopia ancillulam*) and an eunuch, both of which he had presented to her. As to men, Hegio (Capt. II. ii. 103, iii. 4, 20) values
Philocrates, whom he regards as a young able-bodied slave, at 20
minae; and in the same play we are told that a little boy was kidnapped when four years old and sold for 6 minae (Capt. V. ii. 21,
iii. 2, iv. 15). In the As. (I. iii. 77, II. ii. 97) Cleaereta agrees to
make over her daughter Philenium to Argyrippus exclusively for one
year (*hunc annum*) for 20 minae.

144. *Nec quicquam argenti locavi iam diu usquam atque bene.* Cf.
III. i. 4, *Locare argenti nemini numum quero.*

I. iv. 1. *Advorsum venire mihi.*] Cf. IV. i. 19 (18), *ubi advorsum ut Eant vocantur hero; v.* 24 (21), *Nunc eo advorsum hero ex plurimis servis;* ii. 16 (i. 36), *At tu mecum, pessume, i advorsus;* ii. 29 (iii. 6), *Callidamati nostro advorsum venimus;* ii. 32 (iii. 9), *ei advorsum venimus.*

17. *Iacentes, &c.*] So in Pseud. V. i. 1, where Pseudolus staggers in drunk, *Quid hoc? siccine hoc fit? pedes, statin an non? An id voltis ut me hic iacentem aliquis tollat?*

18. *Madet homo*] 'the man's drunk,' spoken aside, but overheard by Callidamates. *Madidus* like *Vvidus* in Horace (C. II. xix. 18, IV. v. 39) is an euphemism for *ebrius,* and so *madere mero,* or, absolutely, *madere.* Thus in Truc. IV. iv. 2, *Si alia membra vino madeant, cor sit saltem sobrium;* Pseud. V. ii. 7, *Molliter siste nunc me, cave ne cadam, non vides me ut madide madeam;* and we find opposed to each other in Aa. V. ii. 7 and 9, *Siccum, frugi, continentem, amantem uxoris maxume,* and *Madidum, nihili, incontinentem, atque osorem uxoris suae;* while in Amph. III. iv. 18, Mercury, playing on the double meaning of *madidus,* says that when Amph. arrives, *De supero, quom huc accesserit, faciam ut sit madidus sobrius,* i.e. 'I'll moisten his clay for him without making him tipsy.' From the same root probably comes the word *madulsa* found in Pseud. V. i. 7, *Profecto edepol eo nunc probe abeo madulsa,* with regard to which we read in Paul. Diac. s.v., p. 126, ed. Müll, " *Madulsa* ebrius, a Graeco μαδᾶν deductum, vel quia madidus satis a vino."

25. *Pistol. Iam revortar. Philem. Diu est 'Iam' id mihi,* 'I shall be back directly.' 'That "Directly" is an age to me;' so in Amph. I. iii. 32, *I. Ne corrumpe oculos; redibo actutum. A. Id 'actutum' diu est;* Merc. II. iv. 25, *C. Invenietur, exquiretur, aliquid fiet. E. Enicas, Iam istuc 'Aliquid Fiet' metuo;* and Poen. I. ii. 50, *M. Taceo. A. Si tacuisses iam istuc 'Taceo' non natum foret.*

33. *eumpse.*] We find in Plautus the nominative fem. *eapse* (Cist. I. ii. 17; Curc. I. iii. 4; Mil. II. i. 63; Rud. II. iii. 80; Truc. I. i. 3, II. vi. 15), the accusatives *eampse* (Aul. V. i. 7; Cist. I. iii. 21; Men. V. ii. 22; Mil. IV. ii. 77; Poen. I. ii. 60; Rud. IV. viii. 14) and *eumpse* (Most. I. iv. 32 (33); Truc. I. ii. 68, IV. iv. 37), and the ablatives *eapse* (Trin. IV. ii. 132, *in eapse occasiuncula*) and *eopse* (Curc. IV. iii. 6, *eapse illo* sc. *infortunio*), which seem to be colloquial abbreviations for *ea ipsa, eum ipsum, eam ipsam, ea ipsa,* and *eo ipso;* at least this is a more reasonable account of the words than to dismiss them with the observation that *pse* is a "syllabica adiectio," and receives support from Truc. I. ii. 31, *Quia te adducturum huc dixeras*

T

eum ipsum, non eampse (see *v.* 18 preceding, and also IV. iv. 37, *Sine eum ipsum adire huc: sine si is est modo. Sine eum ipsum adire ut cupit*), and from the word *reapse*, which occurs not only in Plautus, Truc. IV. iii. 41, *De istoc ipsa, etsi tu taceas, reapse experta intellego*, but also in Cicero, and is explained by Festus p. 278, ed. Müll. s.v. *Reapse*, "*Reapse* est *Reipsa:* Pacuvius in Armorum iudicio, *Si non est ingratum reapse quod feci bene*." Lucretius divides *reapse* into two halves in II. 658, but the reading is doubtful.

II. i. 1. *summis opibus atque industriis*] 'with all his might and main.' So in Merc. l. 1, *Ex summis opibus viribusque usque experire, nitere.* The plural of *industria* is so rare that lexicographers quote no example except that before us. It is possible that Tranio employs it designedly to raise a laugh, as a strange word or a piece of bad grammar is sometimes introduced for that purpose in our own comedies.

4. *Nec Salus nobis saluti iam esse*, &c.] It is obvious that *Salus* ought to be printed with a capital, and *saluti* without, as the first is intended as the personification of the second. There is an exact parallel in Capt. III. iii. 14, *Neque iam Salus servare, si volt, me potest: nec copia est;* and in Adel. IV. vii. 43, *ipsa si cupiat Salus Servare prorsus non potest hanc familiam.* Compare As. III. iii. 123, *Atque ut Deo mihi hic immolas bovem, nam ego tibi Salus sum;* and *v.* 137, *Vt consuevere, homines Salus frustratur et Fortuna.* In Hec. III. ii. 3, *Salus* is the goddess of health, and is paired with Æsculapius.

5. *mali maeroris montem.*] So in Epid. I. 77, *Tantae in te impendent ruinae, nisi subfulcis firmiter, Non potes supsistere, itaque in te inruont montes mali;* and in Merc. III. iv. 32, *Montes tu quidem mali in me ardentes iamdudum iacis.*

– *ad portum.*] It will be remembered that in the first scene (*v.* 63) Tranio announced his intention of going down to the Piraeus.

6 *peregre*] 'from abroad.' See note on I. i. 24.

7. *lucri* is in opposition to *argenti*, 'Is there any one who may wish to make some money, clear gain.'

8. *excruciari meam vicem.*] *Vicem*, when used adverbially with a genitive or a personal pronoun, signifies 'instead of,' 'in exchange for.' Thus below, V. iii. 24, *Fac ego ne mutuam igitur et ut tu meam timeas vicem;* so Capt. III. iii. 10, *Omnis res palam est, neque de hac re negotium est quin male Occidam, oppetamque pestem, heri vicem meamque;* Mil. II. i. 72, *Et mox, ne erretis, haec, duarum hodie vicem, Et hic et illic mulier feret imaginem;* Rud. III. v. 34, *Vos respondetote istine istarum vicem;* Truc. I. ii. 56, *A. Quae in nos illosque ea omnia tibi*

diris, Dinarche, Et nostram et illorum vicem. This use of *vicem* is not however confined to Plautus, but is found in Cicero, Livy, and other writers.

9. *Plagipatidae*] i. e. *qui plagas patiuntur:* vox Plautina. It occurs again in Capt. III. i. 12, where it is applied to parasites, *Nil morantur iam Laconas, imi supselli viros, Plagipatidas, quibus sunt verba sine pœnu et pecunia,* i. e. 'men of Spartan endurance.' The word is in form a patronymic, like *rapacidae* in Aul. II. vii. 8, *Rapacidarum ubi tantum siet in aedibus,* i. e. 'children of the lash.' Plautus uses two other words bearing the same meaning : *plagiger,* Pseud. I. ii. 21, *Huc adhibete aures, quae ego loquar, plagigera genera hominum,* and *plagigerulus,* below IV. L 19, q. v. *Plagiger* and *plagigerulus* are both ἅπ. λεγ.

— *Ferritribax,* a hybrid compound from *ferrum* and τρίβω; the pure Latin word is *ferriterus,* Trin. IV. iii. 14, *Oculicrepidae, cruricrepidae, ferrikeri, mastigiae. Ferriterium,* below III. ii. 55 q. v. is equivalent to *Ergastulum,* a place which is described in As. I. i. 21 as *Apud sustitudinas ferricrepinas insulas Ubi vivos homines mortui incursant boves.* All the words given above, *ferritribax, ferriterus, ferriterium, ferralilis, ferricrepinus,* seem to be ἅπ. λεγ.

10. *Fala.*] This word is thus explained by Non. p. 114; "*Falas* turres sunt ligneae (Ennius Lib. XV., '*Malos defindunt, fiunt tabulata falaeque.*') haec sunt in circo, quae apud veteres propter spectatores e lignis erigebantur." Again, Paul. Diac. p. 88, ed. Müll, "*Falas* dicta ab altitudine, a falando, quod apud Etruscos significat caelum;" and again, ib., "*Falarica* genus teli missile, quo utuntur ex falis, id est locis exstructis, dimicantes." The *falae* in the Circus are alluded to by Juv. S. VI. 590, *Consulit ante falas delphinorumque columnas;* and appear to have been not, as we might infer from the words of Nonius, elevated wooden structures from which the spectators viewed the shows, but a row of seven wooden pillars which were ranged along the spina, and on which were placed the *ova,* which marked the courses. See the commentators on the passage. The *falarica* is well known from the description given by Livy XXI. 8 (see too XXXIV. 14). See also Enn. Ann. 534, ed. Vahlen; Virg. Æn. IX. 705, and note of Servius; Lucan. VI. 196; Sil I. 351, &c. There is another word which some suppose to be derived from the same source, viz. *falere,* found in Varro R. R. III. 5, § 14 seqq., but the meaning of this term as there employed is very doubtful. With regard to the etymology proposed by Festus it is difficult to offer an opinion, but we can scarcely doubt that the same root appears in

the Greek φίλαι, which Hesychius interprets Ὄρα, σαόται, corrected
by Scaliger Ὄρη, σασπίαι, and by others Ὄρᾳ σκοπιαί.

10. For explanation of this line see Excursus on "Terms used
in reference to money," &c.

15. *curro curriculo.*] Cf. Pers. II. ii. 17, *T. Vola curriculo. P. Istuc
Marinus Passer per Circum solet.*

30. See *quid . . . curatio,* I. i. 33; *quid clamitatio . . .* I. i. 6.

33. *miserum est opus, Igitur demum fodere puteum, ubi sitis fauces
tenet.*] Cf. Amph. I. ii. 11, *igitur demum;* Stich. I. ii. 29, *igitur deinde;*
Most. III. i. 159 (156), *Igitur tum accedam hunc, quando quid agam
invenero,* i.e. *tum demum;* Epid. III. iii. 4, *Igitur,* 'then' or 'thereafter;' As. II. i. 3, *Iam diu est factum quam discesti ab hero atque
abiisti ad forum Igitur inveniundo argento ut fingeres fallaciam:* some
interpret it 'idcirco, ea gratia,' but I prefer 'then,' 'thereafter,' 'forthwith;' Amph. III. i. 16, *Post igitur demum faciam res fiat palam.*

37. *Cedo soleas mihi.*] It was the practice to throw off the slippers
before reclining on the triclinium, and hence when any one wished to
rise from table he called for his slippers. So in Truc. II. iv. 12,
Dinarchus, when feigning that he was banqueting with Phronesium
and wished abruptly to break up the party, exclaims, *Cedo soleas mihi
Properate, auferte mensam,* and then, as if he had been propitiated,
Deme soleas. Cedo bibam.

39. *matula.*] This word is used in a peculiar sense in Pers. IV.
iii. 64, *Tacen an non taces? numquam ego te tam esse matulam credidi,*
which seems to mean, 'I never took you for such a blockhead.'

41. There are several colloquial phrases in which *nullus* is equivalent to *non* or *ne.* 1. (as in the passage before us) *Nullus sum,* i.e. *Perii,*
'I am undone,' 'I have ceased to exist.' This phrase is common in
Plautus and Terence, e.g. Merc. I. 104, II. iii. 130 (*nullus sum, occidi*),
V. iv. 17; Hec. III. i. 39, IV. iv. 31; And. III. iv. 20; Ph. V. vii. 49;
and in Cas. II. iv. 26, *ni id factum est, ecce me nullum senem,* i.e. 'I am
an undone elderly.' *Nulla sum,* Hec. IV. i. 6. There is an analogy
between the above and an expression in Pseud. I. i. 35, *C. At te Di
Deaeque quantus es . .* he was about to add *perduint,* but is interrupted
by Pseud., who adds, *serrassint quidem.* 2. With the subjunctive
nullus is equivalent to *nullo modo,* or simply to *ne* or *non,* 'upon no
account.' Bac. I. i. 67, *tu nullus adfueris si non lubet;* Trin. III. i. 5,
C. Non credibile dicis. S. At tu edepol nullus creduas; Rud. IV. iv. 91,
where Palaestra is speaking of the contents of the cistella, *Ibi ego
dicam quidquid inerit nominatim: tu mihi Nullus ostenderis;* Hec. I.
ii. 4, *si non quaeret, nullus dixeris.* In all the above there is an

injunction or command, but not in the following: Eun. II. i. 10, *Memini tametsi nullus moneas.* In the phrase *nullus venit,* As. II. iv. 2, *Libanum in tonstrinam ut iusseram venire, nullus venit, nullus* is certainly equivalent to the simple *non; nullus venit* again, Rud. I. ii. 55, II. ii. 17; and so, perhaps, *neque ullus* in II. iii. 10; compare also Men. V. v. 27; to which add Cas. IV. ii. 16, *Qui amat, tamen hercle si esurit, nullum esurit* 'not at all.' There is a remarkable use of *nullus* in And. II. ii. 33, which we may notice here; *C. Libratus sum hodie, Dave, tua opera. D. Ac nullus quidem,* i. e. 'and yet you are not so,' 'you are not out of the wood.'

46. *non hoc longe, Delphium.*] *Hoc* is deictic, 'not so far as the breadth of this nail,' pointing perhaps to the nail of his finger. Cf. Trin. II. iv. 80, *Decedam ego illi de via, de semita, De honore populi; verum quod ad ventrem attinet Non hercle hoc longe, nisi me pugnis vicerit;* and Bac. III. iii. 19, *Nego tibi hoc annis viginti fuisse primis copiae, Digitum longe a paedagogo pedum ut efferres aedibus.*

47. *Nam intus potate.*] The words *intus* and *intro* are found again and again in Plautus, chiefly in reference to the interior of a house, and for the sake of the young scholar we may explain the force of each.—1. INTUS. *Intus* has two distinct meanings. It is equivalent sometimes to the Greek ἔνδον, 'within,' no motion being implied, and sometimes to the Greek ἔνδοθεν, 'from within,' motion from within outwards being indicated. 1. Of the first we have an example in the line before us, 'For drink away inside the house;' and in vv. 54, 55, *Intus cave multire quemquam siveris. P. Curabitur. T. Tamquam si intus natus nemo in aedibus,* 'Beware of permitting any one to whisper inside,' ... 'just as if no living creature was dwelling inside;' and in III. ii. 12, *Nam et cenandum et cubandum est intus male.* 2. Of the second also this scene will afford an example, v. 57, *clarum mi harunce aedium Laconicam Iam iube efferri intus,* i. e. 'to be brought out from within;' and again, III. i. 145 (142), *evoca aliquem intus;* so *exit intus,* Truc. II. i. 43; *exit foras intus,* Cas. II. v. 42; *arcessit intus,* Bac. IV. vi. 26; *evocate intus,* Men. I. iii. 35. For other examples see Amph. II. ii. 138; Cist. III. 8; Cas. II. v. 43; Epid. III. ii. 44, iv. 45, &c.—II. INTRO. *Intro,* on the other hand, has only one meaning, and invariably denotes motion from without inwards; thus Most. II. i. 50, *Omnium primum, Philematium, intro abi,* 'go away into the house;' and again, III. ii. 161, *ergo intro eo sine perductore.* So *Redi nunc iam intro atque intus serva,* Aul. I. ii. 3; *sequere tu intro,* Epid. II. ii. 120; *remeabo intro,* V. i. 55; *vise intro,* ii. 47; *recortamur intro,* Bac. V. ii. 21; *illicere intro, v. 32, &c.*; almost every

page will supply examples. The only passage in any classical writer in which *intro* does not imply motion is in Cato R. R. 57 § 7, who, when descanting on the virtues of pickled cabbage, declares, *Et si bilis atra est, et si lienes turgent, et si cor dolet, et si iecur, aut pulmones, aut praecordia, uno verbo omnia sana faciet intro quae dolitabunt*, although he had said in the previous sentence, *Si quid antea mali intus erit.* Forcellini quotes a passage from Palladius I. 40, *ut si pilam miseris, intro stare non possit*, where, however, the difficulty is removed by a slight change in the punctuation, which ought to be, *si pilam miseris intro, stare non possit.*

48. *eveniant.*] So the MSS. Nonius (p. 509) quotes a line from the Hecuba of Ennius in which he employs *evenat* for *eveniat*, and hence Both. and R would here read *evenant*, but the introduction of this form here is altogether uncalled for. Cf. Curc. I. i. 39; Epid. II. ii. 105, III. i. 2; Trin. I. ii. 3; in some of which the change may be made with propriety. See also *pervenant*, Rud. III. ii. 12; Trin. I. ii. 56.

54. *mutire*] 'to speak even in a whisper.' *Mutio* or *muttio* signifies properly 'to speak through compressed lips,' and hence 'to speak in a whisper,' and sometimes 'to mutter' or 'grumble,' as in Amph. I. i. 225, *M. Etiam mutis? S. Iam tacebo.* Occasionally it is used humourously with regard to inanimate objects, as in Curc. 1. i. 20, of a door (*ostium*), *Bellissumum hercle vidi et taciturnissumum, Numquam ullum verbum mutit: quom aperitur, tacet;* and again, *v.* 93, *Vide! ut aperiuntur aedes festivissumae! Non mutit cardo:* so also *neu virgae mutiant*, Poen. Prol. 18. Other examples of *mutire* will be found in Amph. I. iii. 22; Bac. IV. vii. 2; Men. V. i. 11; Mil. II. vi. 83; Pers. V. ii. 46; Andr. III. ii. 25. In one passage in Terence, Hec. V. iv. 26, *mutire* must signify 'to be silent:' *P. Dic mihi, harum rerum num quid dixti iam patri? B. Nihil. P. Neque opus est: Adeo mutito: placet non fieri hoc itidem, ut in comoediis Omnia omnes ubi resciscunt:* &c., where *adeo mutito* must mean 'be silent then' or 'remain silent.'* We have also a substantive *mutitio* in Amph. I. iii. 21, a line which we have quoted above in the note on I. i. 33. The frequentative form *musso* is found in Aul. II. i. 12, *Neque occultum id haberi neque*

* Freund takes this quite differently; he seems to suppose that *mutito* is the ablative of the participle, and would construe *neque opus est adeo mutito*, 'there is no need of whispering it about;' but if that were the construction it would rather mean, 'there is no need of speaking about it in a whisper,' i.e. 'you may speak openly if you please,' which is directly the reverse of the obvious sense of the passage.

per metum mussari, where *mussari* must signify 'be suppressed;' in Merc. Prol. 49 the common reading *mussans* is uncertain.* *Mussito* also is employed by both Plautus and Terence, and is generally equivalent to *reticere*.† Thus Pseud. I. v. 86, *Non a me scibas pistrinum in mundo tibi Quom ea mussitabas ?* i.e. 'when you maintained silence with regard to those matters;' and Mil. II. v. 65, *S. Quid propius fuit Quam ut perirem, si locu'us fuissem hero ? P. Ergo, si sapis Mussitabis;* also Truc. II. ii. 57, *Egone haec mussitem ?* 'can I keep silence on these matters?' Adel. II. i. 53, *Accipiunda et mussitanda iniuria adulescentium est;* lastly, in Cas. III. v. 33 it means simply 'to keep still,' without the idea of withholding the knowledge of something, *Ita omnes sub arcis sub lectis latentes Metu mussitant :* i.e. 'keep still,' 'do not utter a word.' On the other hand, the context in Mil. II. iii. 40 seems to require that we should translate *mussitabo* 'I shall whisper the truth;' and again, Mil. III. i. 120, *Ego haec mecum mussito* is equivalent to 'says I to myself.' See also Liv. I. 50.

63. *Quamvis desubito*] i.e. 'on however short a notice.' Cf. II. ii. 57, *Atque ille exclamat derepente maxumum.*

69. *Profecto ut liqueant omnia et tranquilla sint.*] Cf. III. ii. 64 (62), *Tam liquidus est, quam liquida esse tempestas solet,* i.e. 'clear and serene.'

II. ii. 1-2. We have a similar address in Stich. III. i. 1, *Quom bene re gesta salvos convortor domum Neptuno grates habeo et tempestatibus;* and at greater length in Trin. IV. i. 1-22, *Salsipotenti et multipotenti Iovis fratri et Nerei ! Neptuni Laetus, lubens, laudes ago, et grates gratiasque habeo, et fluctibus salsis Quos penes mei potestas bonis meis quid foret et meae vitae, Quom suis me ex locis in patriam urbisque moenia reducem faciunt; Atque ego, Neptune, tibi ante alios Deos gratias ago atque habeo summas.* Cf. also Rud. IV. ii. 1. *Quom,* 'since,' 'inasmuch as,' is constantly used in thanksgivings and congratulations

---

* *Musso* is used in the sense of 'to speak with hesitation' by the writers of a somewhat later period, e.g. Lucr. VI. 1179, *mussabat tacito medicina timore;* Virg. Aen. XI. 345, *sed dicere mussant;* XII. 657, *mussat rex ipse Latinus Quos generos vocet;* and in the sense of 'to mutter,' 'grumble,' Liv. VII. 25, *mussantesque inter se rogitabant;* and XXXIII. 31, *sub Actoli decretum decem legatorum clam mussantes carprbant. Musso* is also quoted by Festus p. 144 from Ennius, but the reading is somewhat doubtful. *Mussati* (deponent) is quoted by Non. from Varro.

† See note of Donatus on Adel. II. i. 53.

‡ The best MSS. agree in this reading, which presents the obvious difficulty that Nereus is nowhere spoken of as the son of Neptune. R and others have adopted the conj. of Both., *Iovis fratri aetherei Neptuno,* which is ingenious but not convincing.

in order to point out the cause of the gratitude expressed. Thus, in addition to the examples we have given above, we may quote Rud. IV. viii. 6, *P. Quid? patri etiam gratulabor, quom illam invenit? T. Censeo;* cf. Rud. IV. ii. 3, iv. 134, vi. 3; Trin. II. iv. 104; Truc. II. vi. 36.

3. *Verum si posthac me pedem latum modo Scis inposisse in undam.*] So Rud. V. ii. 7, *cubitum hercle longis literis signabo iam usque quaque.*

11. *expectatus*] i. e. 'looked for with eagerness.' Thus Amph. II. ii. 26, *Certe enim me illi expectatum optato venturum scio. S. Quid? me non rere expectatum amicae venturum meae?* so also II. ii. 47, Amphitruo asks, *expectatusne advenio?* to which Sosia replies ironically, *Haud vidi magis Expectatum: eum salutat magis haud quisquam quam canem;* and in Trin. II. iv. 173, *expectatus filius* is a son whose birth had long been eagerly looked for.

18. *Here, salve: salvom te advenisse gaudeo: Vsque invaluisti?*] i. e. 'have you been quite well up to the present time?' This was the ordinary salutation when the person addressed had been absent for a considerable time; sometimes it is *perpetuone valuisti?* i. e. 'have you kept your health without interruption?' Thus Amph. II. ii. 47, *Valuistin usque?* and in v. 83 Alcumena says, *Et salutavi, et valuissesne usque, exquisivi simul, Mi vir:* and Bac. II. iii. 14, *N. Benene usque valuit? C. Pancratice atque athletice* (like a prize-fighter); and we have an address of this kind in its most formal shape in Ep. I. ii. 27, *Adgrediar hominem: advenientem peregre herum suum Stratippoclem Salva impertit salute servos Epidicus. S. Vbi is est? E. Adest. Salvom te gaudeo huc advenisse. S. Tam tibi istuc credo quam mihi. E. Benene usque valuisti?* again, I. i. 15, *Quid ais? perpetuom, valuisti?* and Merc. II. iii. 53, *D. Vsquene valuisti? C. Perpetuo recte, dum quidem illic fui.* Cf. Trin. I. ii. 12, where there is a cordial reciprocation of compliments between two friends; Curc. I. i. 16; Pers. I. i. 23.

23. 25. The words generally employed by the dramatists to denote the outer door of a dwelling-house are *Ianua, Ostium,* and *Foris* or *Fores.* Of these the second occurs more frequently than the first, and the third more frequently than either of the two others, the plural *Fores* being more common than the singular *Foris,* which may be accounted for by supposing that doors were usually in two pieces, or folding doors. When the door was closed, and a person was desirous of obtaining admission, he knocked, which is expressed sometimes by such verbs as *percutere* (vv. 84, 88), *pellere* (Adel. IV. v. 4, V. iii. 2), but the *vox signata* is

Pultare (*pulta dum fores,* Most. III. i. 144; *Quis ostium pultavit,*
Adel. IV. v. 3; *Ibo et pultabo ianuam hanc,* Poen. III. iv. 30; *Quid si
recenti re aedes pultem?* v. 18, &c.). This operation, when the visitor
became impatient, was performed with great violence with the feet;
thus, in the passage before us, Theuropides complains, *Pultando pedibus pene confregi hasce ambas;* and again, v. 25, *Quin pultando, inquam,
pene confregi fores;* so Eun. II. ii. 53, Parmeno to Gnatho entering
the house of Thais, *Qui mihi uno digitulo fores aperis fortunatus Nas
tu istas saxo calcibus saepe insultabis frustra;* and Merc. I. 20, *At
etiam asto? at etiam cesso foribus facere hisce assulas?* i.e. 'to kick
these doors to splinters.' Cf. Most. IV. ii. 19. But the young scholar
must carefully avoid confounding *pultare ostium s. fores* with the
phrases into which the verbs *crepo* and *concrepo* enter, viz. *crepuit
s. concrepuit ostium s. foris, crepuerunt fores,* and the like. These are
employed exclusively to denote that some one is opening the door in
order to come forth from the interior of a house, and they constantly
serve to herald the appearance on the stage of one of the characters;
thus Pseud. I. i. 127, *C. St! tace, opsecro hercle! P. Quid negoti est?
C. Ostium Lenonis crepuit. P. Crura mavellem modo. C. Atque ipse
egreditur penitus periurum caput;* Amph. I. ii. 34, *crepuit foris, Amphitruo subditivus, eccum, exit foras;* so Cas. V. i. 17; Aul. IV. v. 5;
Phor. V. v. 12, *P. Sed ostium concrepuit aps te. A. Vide quis egre-
diatur. P. Geta est;* Hec. IV. i. 6; Cas. II. i. 15, *Sed foris
concrepuit atque ea ipsa, eccam, egreditur;* Most. V. i. 14; and in
Andr. IV. 1. 59, the entrance of Mysis is thus announced, *D. Hem!
St! mane, concrepuit a Glycerio ostium;* in like manner Mil. II. i.
76, *Foris concrepuit hinc a vicino sene, Ipse exit;* Curc. IV. i. 25,
Sed interim fores crepuere, linguae moderandum est mihi; Poen. III.
iv. 31, *Tacendi tempus est nam crepuerunt fores.* In these phrases we
remark the idiomatic use of *a* or *abs: ostium concrepuit aps te—concrepuit a Glycerio ostium—hinc a vicino sene;* and so *fores crepuere ab
ea,* Eun. V. vii. 5; *crepuerunt fores hinc a me,* Heaut. I. i. 121; *quid
est quod tam a nobis graviter crepuerunt fores,* III. iii. 52; where the
word following the preposition indicates *what* door is rattling.* It
has been supposed that the noise thus spoken of must refer merely
to the grating of the hinges, and this opinion receives support from
Curc. I. i. 20, where Phaedromus formally salutes the *ostium* of his
mistress, on which Palinurus asks, *P. Quid tu ergo, insane, rogitas,*

* The same idiom occurs, but more rarely, in reference to knocking
from the outside; Adel. V. iii. 2, *quisnam a me pepulit tam graviter fores;*
compare also Truc. IV. iii. 78, *acer ab sese egreditur foras.*

*valeatne ostium ? Pɪɪ. Bellissumum hercle vidi et taciturnissumum, Num-
quam ullum verbum mutit, quom aperitur, tacet; Quomque illa noctu
clanculum ad me exit, tacet;* and at the end of the same scene, v. 93.
*Vide! ut aperiuntur aedes festivissumae! Nem mutit cardo. Est lepidus.
P. Quin das suavium?* and again in the same play, I. iii. 1, *Placide
egredere, et sonitum prohibe forum, et crepitum cardinum;* and Trin V.
i. 8, *sed fores Hae sonitu suo mihi moram iniciunt incommode.* Some
of the older commentators however imagine that the doors of the
dwelling houses opened outwards directly upon the street, so that
every one who issued forth rattled the door before opening it, in
order to give warning to passers by. According to this view, when,
in *v.* 75, Tranio is endeavouring to frighten Theuropides and to
make him believe that the outraged ghost is about to sally forth, he
exclaims, *Concrepuit foris! Hiccine percussit?* i.e. 'the door rattles!
was it he (the ghost) who smote on it?'

42. *Sermonem nostrum qui aucupet.*] Plautus is fond of the metaphor derived from the watchful stillness and artifices of a bird-catcher;
so As. V. ii. 31, *Aucupemus ex insidiis clanculum quam rem gerant;*
Mil. IV. i. 43, *Viden tu illam oculis venaturam facere, atque aucupium
auribus;* so ii. 6; Men. IV. l. 12, *Huc concedamus: ex insidiis aucupa;*
Rud. IV. iv. 49, *Viden scelestus ut aucupatur,* 'is playing off his lures;'
Truc. V. 72, *Lepide mecastor aucupavi,* 'I have had capital sport.'

44. *Capitalis caedis facta est*] i.e. 'an atrocious murder was
committed.' *Caedis* is another form of the more common nomi-
native *caedes,* as we find *aedis* for *aedes, torquis* for *torques,* and *canis*
and *canes.* The epithet *capitalis* is emphatic, since *caedes* or *caedis*
would not, taken alone, necessarily imply murder. Young scholars
are apt to be embarrassed by the word *capitalis.* As there is a want
of distinctness in some even of our best dictionaries in regard to the
modifications of meaning assumed by this word, and their connection
with each other, we shall say a few words on the subject. *Caput*
signifies* (1) 'the head.' (2) The head being regarded by many
ancient physiologists as the seat of the vital principle, *Caput* denoted
'the life.' (3) *Caput* was used by the jurists to designate 'the political life' of a Roman citizen, and comprehended the whole amount
of his privileges as a free man, as a member of a family, and as a
civis optimo iure. Hence when an individual from any cause suffered
the loss of these privileges, or of any portion of them, he was said

* We notice here those leading meanings only of *caput* which are
necessary for our present purpose. For others see notes on I. iii. 54,
III. i. 60.

to undergo *Capitis Deminutio.* This being premised, the adjective *Capitalis* when employed with reference to (2) and (3) may be applied to what affects the *physical life,* or to what affects the *political life.* 1. As affecting the physical life it signifies literally 'deadly' or 'dangerous to life,' and in this sense it occurs in Mil. II. iii. 23, *Tuis nunc cruribus capitique fraudem capitalem hinc creas,* i. e. 'you are raising up a deadly injury to limb and life;' so *capitali ex periculo,* Rud. II. iii. 19; *rectus capitali periculo,* Trin. IV. iii. 81; and figuratively, Poen. IV. ii. 57, *Scin tu herum tuum meo hero esse inimicum capitalem,* i. e. 'a deadly enemy;' so *ira capitalis* in Hor. S. I. vii. 13; and *odium capitale* in Cicero de Am. i. Hence *Capitalis* signifies 'terrible,' 'atrocious,' as in the passage now before us, and in Adel. IV. vii. 3, *D. Fero alia flagitia ad te ingentia Boni illius adulescentis. M. Ecce autem. D. Nova, Capitalia,* i. e. 'atrocious;' and so in Cicero we have *capitalis oratio, capitalis iniustitia, capitalem et pestiferum Antonii reditum,* and even *capitalis homo.* 2. As affecting the political life *capitalis* is extensively employed with regard to criminal proceedings. Since the punishment for some criminal offences was death, but for a much larger class was some penalty which entailed *capitis deminutio,* the phrases *res capitalis, causa facinus crimen capitale, iudicium capitale, poena capitalis,* taken by themselves, are ambiguous, and their force must in each case be determined by the context. They *may* signify a 'capital' charge trial or punishment, according to the English force of the term in such cases, but much more frequently they indicate merely a charge trial or punishment affecting the political privileges but not the life of the person implicated. 3. Since anything which affects either the physical or political life of an individual is of serious importance to him, *capitalis* occasionally signifies 'of paramount importance;' and so we may take Stich. III. ii. 46, *Eam auspicavi ego in re capitali mea,* 'upon her I depended for an omen when all my best interests were at stake.' 4. Occasionally, *Capitalis* is found in the sense of 'excellent,' as when we talk of 'a capital speech,' 'a capital dinner,' or the like; thus Ovid. Fast. III. 839; Cic. ad Q. F. II. 13; Trebell. Poll. XXX. Tyrann. 10; all of which are quoted in Forcellini.

Before quitting *Capitalis* we must notice *Capital,* which is used as a substantive, but appears to be merely the abbreviated form of the neuter *capitale.* It is used 1. with *linteum, vestimentum, velum* or some such word understood, to signify a napkin worn upon the head by priestesses. "Item texta fasciola qua capillum in capite alligarent dictum *Capital* a capite, quod sacerdotulae in capite etiam nunc solent habere," Varro L. L. V. § 130, ed. Müll. (iv. 29); and so Paul. Diac. p. 57, ed. Müll., "*Capital* linteum quoddam quo in sacrificiis utebantur." 2. with *facinus* understood, Paul. Diac. p. 48, "*Capital*, facinus quod capitis poena luitur." Plautus has it twice; Men. I. L 16, *Nunquam edepol fugiet, tametsi capital fecerit;* and Merc. IV. iv. 26, *C. Eutuche capital facis. E. Qui? C. Quia aequalem et sodalem, civem liberum, enicas.* See also Lucil. ap. Non. s. v. *capital,* I. 175 (p. 38).

In the passage now before us, Weise, following the Ed. Prin. in opposition to the best MSS., reads *capitalis aedis facta est,* which he explains, "Capitalis autem hic est, propter crimen in ea commissum quasi interdicta," but he adduces no authority for such a meaning of *capitalis.* We find indeed in Paul. Diac. p. 66, ed. Müll., "*Capitalis lucus,* ubi, si quid violatum est, caput violatoris expiatur," but this can have no place here.

57. In the well known passage in Virgil G. L 203, *Non aliter quam qui,* &c., Aulus Gellius (X. 29) and Servius (ad. loc.) agree that *atque* is equivalent to *statim,* and in the line now before us scholars propose to translate *atque* by 'forthwith.' I do not however see that this is necessary, and would render it simply 'and then,' i. e. 'the next thing that happened was.' There are however several passages in Plautus where the latter of two events connected by *atque* is represented as following so immediately upon the former that the conjunction may fairly be translated 'forthwith;' thus Bac. II. iii. 45, *Dum circumspecto, atque ego lembum conspicor;* Epid. II. ii. 33, *Quom ad pestum venio, atque ego illam illic video praestolarier;* Merc. II. iii. 17, *Nunc si dico, ut res est, atque illam mihi me Emisse indico, quemadmodum existumet me? Atque illam apstrahat, trans mare hinc venum asportet;* Capt. III. i. 19, *Salvete inquam, Quo imus una, inquam, ad prandium? atque illi tacent;* to which we may add Merc. II. iii. 17, i. 35; Trin. III. ii. 43; but scarcely Poen. III. iii. 38. In Cas. Prol. 48 *at* seems to be equivalent to *statim;* and in Amph. III. ii. 74 *atque* is most conveniently translated by 'but.'

62. *Mirum quin vigilanti diceret*] 'It is wonderful that the man who was murdered sixty years ago did not tell his tale to my master when wide awake,' the force being 'It is a very likely story, is it not, that (the ghost of) a man who was murdered sixty years ago would tell his tale to one who was wide awake!' *Mirum quin* implies strong irony, and is employed to evince the impatient contempt felt by the speaker for some statement or observation made or implied by the person with whom he is conversing. Thus Amph. II. ii. 118,

Mirum quin te advorsus dicat, i. e. 'it is very likely that he (your own slave) will contradict you!'* Aul. I. ii. 7, *Mirum quin tua nunc me causa faciat Iuppiter Philippum regem aut Darium, trivenefica!* i. e. 'it is very likely, is it not, that Iupiter, for your sake, will make us rich as king Philip or Darius!' Cist. IV. ii. 67, Halisca, when inquiring for the cistella which she had lost, says, *Non edepol praeda magna,* 'it would be no great prize to any one who has found it,' to which Lampadiscus replies, *Mirum quin grex venalium in cistella infuerit una,* i. e. 'it is very likely, is it not, that there should be a troop of slaves (or anything else of value) in that box of yours!'† Merc. I. 91, *Mirum quin me subagitarel!* 'it's very likely, isn't it, that he would take liberties with me!' and so exactly Pers. III. i. 11, iii. 28; Rud. V. iii. 37; Trin. IV. ii. 125.   There is a passage in Pers. III. iii. 37, in which *mirum* is followed by *quin,* but they are disconnected by a long stop, and hence the meaning is different; *T. Fortasse metuis in manum concredere. D. Mirum: quin citius iam a foro argentarii Abeunt, quam in cursu rotula circumvortitur,* i. e. 'you are perhaps afraid to trust her in my hands (without payment down),' to which Dordalus replies with a sneer, 'that is wonderful, isn't it! why I tell you that now-a-days (even) bankers levant more rapidly than a wheel turns round when rolling along.'   The phrases *mirum ni, mira sunt ni, mira sunt nisi,* are altogether distinct; they express real surprise or wonder, and mean literally, 'I shall be surprised if so and so is not the case,' but generally may be correctly expressed by our 'I shouldn't wonder if so and so is the case;' thus Amph. I. i. 163, *Mirum ni hic me quasi muraenam exossare cogitat,* 'I shall be surprised if this fellow is not thinking of boning me as if I were a muraena,' i. e. 'I believe that this fellow is,' 'I shouldn't wonder if he were;' *v.* 127, *Mira sunt nisi invitabit sese in cena plusculum,* i. e. 'I shouldn't wonder if he had been taking a drop too much last night;' and again, *v.* 275, *Mira sunt nisi latuit intus illic in illac hirnea,* i. e. 'I shouldn't be surprised if that fellow was lying concealed in that wine jar;' Bac. III. iii. 46, *Mira sunt ni Pistoclerus Ludum pugnis contudit,* 'I shouldn't wonder if P. had been giving L. a beating;' Cas. III. ii. 24, *Atque edepol mirum ni subolet iam hoc huic vicinae meae,* 'indeed I shouldn't wonder if the lady my neighbour had got an inkling of this already;' Trin. IV. ii. 19, *Quam magis specto, minus placet mihi hominis facies: mira sunt Ni illic homo est aut dormitator, aut sector zonarius,* 'I

---

* Welse quite misunderstood the force of this when he renders it *velim cum advorsus te idem edicere, h. e. repetere quod modo dixit.*
† Here again W. has completely misunderstood the meaning.

shouldn't wonder if that fellow were either a robber or a cut-purse.'
In Trin. II. iv. 94, after Philto had been moralising upon the lot of
man, and declaring that rich and poor after they had passed into the
nether world were upon a complete equality as far as wealth was concerned, Stasimus, according to the Vulgate text, is made to say, *Mirum
ni tu illuc tecum divitias feras*, which cannot be explained according to
the view we have given of *mirum ni*. But the Milan Palimpsest gives
here AXMIRUMQUINTU, and the Pall. MSS. (BCD) *An mirum inito* or *an
mirum ini tu*, while *mirum ni* is found only in the interpolated MSS.
and Ed. Prin. Hence there can be little doubt that R has restored
the true reading, *Mirum quin tu illo tecum divitias feras*, i. e. 'it is very
likely, isn't it, that you could carry your riches to the other world,'—
a contemptuous sneer, which is quite appropriate and in character.

70. *Defodit insepultum clam.*] *Clam* and *Palam* are employed as
adverbs in the sense of 'secretly' and 'openly,' and are often directly
opposed to each other; thus Merc. V. iv. 63, *Si quis prohibuerit plus
perdet clam, quam si prohibuerit palam.* *Clam* is sometimes combined
with another adverb, as Poen. III. iii. 49, *At enim hic clam furtim esse
volt.* *Clam*, moreover, is in very many passages used as a preposition
governing the accusative, or the ablative, or, more rarely, the genitive,
and in this case signifies 'without the knowledge of' or 'concealed
from the knowledge of;' thus Cas. Prol. 61, *Pater filiusque clam alter
alterum*, 'the one without the knowledge of the other;' Most V. i. 13,
Nam scio equidem nullo pacto iam esse posse clam senem, 'that in no
way can the truth be concealed from;' Merc. III. ii. 2, with the ablative, *Empta est amica clam uxore mea et filio ;* Merc. Prol. 43, with the
genitive, *Res exulatum ad illam abibat clam patris.* So *clam me*, Cas.
I. i. 7, Rud. I. ii. 45, Heaut. I. i. 46, 66, Hec. II. ii. 10, III. iv. 10,
IV. ii. 1 ; *clam te*, Andr. I. v. 52, Eun. IV. vii. 25, Hec. IV. iv. 59,
Phor. V. viii. 15 ; *clam illum*, Merc. II. iii. 26 ; *clam uxorem*, As. IV. ii.
6, Cas. Prol. 54, II. viii. 15, 32 ; *clam virum*, Amph. Prol. 107, Cas.
II. ii. 27. The choice of case seems quite arbitrary, for we have
clam uxorem and *clam viro* in the same sentence, Merc. IV. vi. 3, 5,
11 ; and no distinction of meaning can be drawn between *clam patrem*,
Merc. II. iii. 8 ; *clam patre*, Truc. II. i. 37 ; and *clam patris*, Merc.
Prol. 43. *Palam* is not used as a preposition, but both *clam* and
palam, especially the latter, appear as indeclinable adjectives, signifying respectively 'secret' and 'evident' or 'open;' thus Adel. I. i.
46, *Dum id rescitum iri credit, tantisper cavet; Si sperat fore clam,
rursus ad ingenium redit*, i. e. 'if he hopes that what he does will be
secret ;' and hence *facere aliquid palam* signifies not 'to do something

openly,' but to 'make something evident,' ' to reveal or disclose something, as in Poen. Prol. 126, *Quod restat, restant alii qui faciant palam,* i. e. ' who will disclose' or ' make clear ;' and Truc. IV. iii. 77, *ipsa haec ultro, ut factum est, fecit omnem rem palam,* 'revealed the whole matter ;' so Heaut. IV. iii. 43, *C. Metuo quid agam. S. Metuis? quasi non ea potestas sit tua Quo velis in tempore ut te exsolvas, rem facias palam;* and Hec. I. ii. 30, *PA. Non est opus prolato: hoc percontarier Desiste. PH. Nempe ea causa ut ne id fiat palam,* i. e. ' that the thing may not be revealed ;' and Adel. IV. iv. 16, *Sensi ithco id illas suspicari; sed me reprehendi tamen, Ne quid de fratre garrulae illi dicerem, ac fieret palam;* and so Trin. I. ii. 106, with *clam* opposed in the preceding clause.

84. *Quae res te agitat, Tranio?*] Theuropides says this observing the anxiety and alarm, partly real and partly affected, exhibited by Tranio. So in Men. II. ii. 47, *Quod te urget scelus?* in Bac. IV. ii. 2, *Quae te mala crux agitat?* cf. also Aul. I. i. 32, *Quae illunc hominem intemperiae tenent?* and Epid. III. iv. 39, Mil. II. v. 24, *Quae te intemperiae tenent?*

95. Compare IV. ii. 68 (iii. 45), *is vel Herculi conterere quaestum possiet,* and note.

III. i. 39. *pilum iniecisti mihi.*] We have a similar expression in Epid. V. ii. 25, *Tragulam in te inicere adornat: nescio quam fabricam facit,* but in the latter case the phrase represents the perpetration of some fraud or trick.

40. *Hic homo certe est ariolus*] i. e. 'this man is assuredly a wizard.' *Ariolus* seems to signify ' a diviner,' one who knows the truth with regard to the past, the present, and the future, without reference to the source from which his knowledge is procured. Thus Amph. V. ii. 2, *Nil est quod timeas: ariolos, aruspices, Mitte omnes: quae futura et quae facta eloquar;* and so Cas. II. vi. 4. Terence also classes together *ariolí* and *aruspices* in the general sense of ' diviners,' Phor. IV. iv. 27, *interdixit ariolus Aruspex retulit ante brumam aliquid novi Negoti incipere.* Sometimes the word signifies emphatically ' a true prophet;' thus Poen. III. v. 46, *Eheu quam ego habui ariolos aruspices,* i. e. ' alas, how I have found the Aruspices turn out true prophets,' referring to the words which he had used at the commencement of the scene; and so also Rud. II. ii. 20. Sometimes, as in the passage before us, it is used contemptuously, as when we call a man ' a wizard' or ' a conjuror.' Sometimes, since a prophet when he uttered his predictions was supposed to be excited to frenzy by the direct influence of a present God, *ariolus* signifies ' one possessed,'

'a madman;' thus Truc. II. vii. 41, *Truxit ex intimo ventre suspirium, hoc vide, dentibus Frendit, icit femur: num obsecro nam ariolus, qui ipsus se verberat?* Plautus employs *superstitiosus* in the same sense as *ariolus;* thus Amph. I. i. 167, *Illic homo superstitiosus est,* i. e. 'that man's a conjuror;' and again, Curc. III. 27, with exactly the same force, *Superstitiosus hic quidem est, vera praedicat;* while in Rud. IV. iv. 95 we find the two words combined: Palaestra having offered to give an exact account of the contents of the cistella enclosed in the vidulus, Gripus, fearful of losing his booty, interferes, *Quid si ista aut superstitiosa, aut ariola est, atque omnia, Quidquid insit, vera dicet? anne habebit ariola? D. Non feret nisi vera dicet, nequiquam ariolabitur,* where we have the feminine *ariola,* which occurs again in Mil. III. i. 99, *Praecantatrici, coniectrici, ariolae atque aruspicae;* and the verb *ariolor,* which is found again in As. III. ii. 33. Cist. IV. ii. 80, Rud. II. iii. 17, Phor. III. ii. 8, in all of which *ariolare* simply signifies 'you are right,' 'you have divined the truth;' and so *ariolare vera,* As. V. ii. 74. In Rud. II. iii. 46, *Capillum promittam optumum est, occipiamque ariolari,* i. e. 'the best thing I can do is to let my hair grow long and begin to play the prophet.' In Mil. IV. vi. 41 *ariolari* and *divinare* are identical, *Ariolatur. Quia me amat, propterea Venus fecit eam ut divinaret;* and so As. II. ii. 50. In Adel. II. i. 48, *sed ego hoc ariolor* means simply 'but this I predict.' It will be seen from the above passages that *Ariolus* and *Ariolor,* although sometimes used loosely in the sense of prediction or prophesy, generally speaking imply that what is said is absolutely true, and this seems to be in the mind of Cicero when he says, Epp. ad Att. VIII. 11, Προθεσπίζω igitur, noster Attice, non hariolans ut illa (sc. Cassandra) cui nemo credidit, sed coniectura prospiciens, i. e. 'I predict what will happen, not speaking with the certainty of an inspired prophet like Cassandra, but looking into the future by drawing inferences (from the present and the past) (*coniectura*).' In another passage, De N. D. I. 20, he classes together among the professors of μαντική or Divinatio, *haruspices, augures, harioli, vates et coniectores.* Plautus uses *coniector* in the sense of 'a prophet' Amph. V. i. 76, *Ego Tiresiam coniectorem advocabo;* and in Curc. II. i. 33 it is 'a professional diviner,' *l'ah! solus hic homo est, qui sciat divinitus: Quin coniectores a me consilium petunt;* and in Poen. I. iii. 34 it means 'a skilful interpreter,' *Nam isti quidem hercle orationi Oedipo Opus est coniectore qui Sphingi interpres fuit.* The feminine *coniectrix* has been quoted above from Mil. III. i. 99.

41. *Quin tu istas mittis tricas*] Anglice 'tricks,' 'shufflings.' The word *Tricae* deserves notice. It occurs in Plautus in the following

passages: Curc. V. ii. 15, *Quod argentum, quas tu mihi tricas narras?*
Pers. V. ii. 17, *Quid ais, crux, stimulorum tritor? quomodo me hodie
vorsavisti! Ut me in tricas conieristi!* In Rud. V. ii. 36, *Tricas!* means
'pshaw,' 'nonsense,' 'mere trash;' Pers. IV. iii. 61, *nihil mihi opus
est Litibus neque tricis,* i. e. 'quibbles.' Cicero uses the word in
the sense of 'embarrassments,' 'hindrances:' *domesticas tricas,* ad Att.
X. 8, sub. fin. See also Caelius in ad. Fam. VIII. 5. The original
and proper meaning of *tricae* seems to have been 'threads,' and from
the passage quoted above from Pers. V. ii. 17 compared with IV. I. 9,
it is clear that it denoted 'a noose' or 'snare;' hence the transition
is easy to 'a trick' or 'deception,' and hence, as in Pers. IV. iii. 61,
it means 'paltry legal tricks' or 'quibbles,' and hence in Rud. V.
ii. 36 the exclamation *tricas!* is one of contempt,—'what you offer
is a paltry subterfuge;' and it may be observed that the expression
of contempt used by Gripus in the next clause is *tramas putridas.*
Lexicographers have sought a different origin and explanation of the
word, referring to Pliny II. N. III. ii. § 16, where he is discussing
the geography of Apulia. He mentions *Arpi* as having been founded
by Diomedes and named Argos Hippium, which was subsequently
corrupted into Argyrippa, and then goes on, *Diomedes ibi delevit gentes
Monadorum Dardorumque et urbes duas quae in proverbi ludicrum
vertere, Apinam et Tricam.* The proverb itself is to be found in
Martial XIV. i. 7, who, when about to write a series of distichs
descriptive of the small gifts interchanged by all classes at the
Saturnalia, says, *Sunt apinae tricaeque et si quid vilius istis,* 'they are,
I admit, trash and trumpery;' and again, I. cxiv. 2, *Quaecumque lusi
iuvenis et puer quondam Apinasque nostras, quas nec ipse iam novi,* &c.
Now although the Romans may have been unable to explain the
origin of the proverbial expression *Apinae Tricaeque,* and although
we may find it difficult to give any account of *Apinae,* no sober-
minded philologist will be willing to accept and rest satisfied with
the story of Pliny about the two towns destroyed by Diomedes.
Non. Marcellus p. 8, seems to consider that *tricae* is the same
word as the Greek τρίχες, "*Tricae* sunt impedimenta et Implicationes
dictae quasi tericae quod pullos gallinaceos involvant et impediant
capilli pedibus implicati." *Trico-onis* In the sense of 'a shuffling knave'
or 'cheat' is quoted twice by Nonius (s. v. *Tricones,* p. 22) from Lucilius, *Luciu' Cotta senex, Crassi pater huiu' Panaeti Magnus trico fuit
nummariu' solvere nulli, Lentus;* and again (s. v. *Tricae,* p. 338), *Nec
mihi amatore hoc opu' nec tricone vadato:* and the word reappears
again in the Augustan Historians (Capitolin. Ver. 4.) in the sense

of 'a drunken brawler.' *Tricosus*, which is quoted from Lucilius,
is a conj. emend. for *sitricosus*, which is the reading of the MSS.
in Non. s. v. *Bovinator* (or *Boviator*) p. 79. Cf. Aul. Gell. xi. 7.
Tricor the verb is found twice in Cicero, Ad Att. XV. 3, XIV. 19, in
both cases in the sense of shuffling, equivocating. We have also
in Plautus the verbs *extrico* and *intrico*: Epid. 1. ii. 48, *S. Quid de
illa fiet fidicina igitur? E. Aliqua reperibitur, Aliqua ope exsolvam,
extricabor aliqua. S. Plenus consili es.* Pers. IV. i. 9, *Nunc ego lenonem ita hodie intricatum dabo Vt ipsus sese qua se expediat nesciat.*
Extrico and *extricatur* are used by Cicero and Horace in the sense
of 'to disentangle.' *Intrico* is quoted from Afranius, from a frag.
of Cicero, and is used by Ulpian in the Digest.

43. *Magis opportunus advenire quam advenis.*] So Merc. V. iv. 3,
Optuma opportunitate ambo advenistis.

55. *D. Iam hercle ego illunc nominabo.*] Plautus here alludes, in
all probability, to a privilege accorded by the laws of the XII. Tables
to creditors. In virtue of this any one who had a claim against
another might, if the legal evidence were defective, proceed to the
house of his debtor and publicly demand payment in loud and abusive
language, so as to bring shame upon the defaulter among his neigh-
bours. Thus Festus s. v. *Vagulatio*, p. 375, ed. Müll., "*Vagulatio* in
L. XII. significat quaestionem cum convicio. *Cui testimonium defuerit,
is tertiis diebus ob portum obvagulatum ito;*" and again, s. v. *Portum*,
"*Portum* in XII. pro domo positum omnes fere consentiunt; *Cui
testimonium defuerit, his tertiis diebus ob portum obvagulatum ito.*"
This *Vagulatio* seems to be equivalent to what Plautus elsewhere
terms *Pipulum* (Aul. III. ii. 32), *Ita me bene amet Laverna, te iam,
nisi reddi Mihi vasa iubes, pipulo hic differam ante aedes.* With regard
to *Pipulum* the student may consult Varro L. L. VII. § 103, ed. Müll.
See also Aul. Gell. XX. 9, where however some edd. consider the
passage as an interpolation. The words *Flagitare, Flagitator, Flagitium*, are also frequently employed to denote a clamorous demand
by creditors for payment; thus Poen. III. i. 34, *Est domi quod edimus,
ne nos tam contemptim contras: Quidquid est pauxillulum illuc nostrum,
illud omne intus est Neque nos quemquam flagitamus, neque nos quisquam
flagitat:* Pseud. IV. vii. 46, *Sed tu, bone vir, flagitare saepe clamore
in fore, Quom libella nusquam est;* 1. v. 143, *edepol si non dabis
Clamore magno et multum flagitabere;* and Men. Prol. 45, *Propterea
illius nomen memini facilius Quia illum clamore vidi flagitarier.* So
for *flagitator*, Cas. Prol. 24, *Nequis formidet flagitatorem suum, Ludi
sunt; ludus datus est argentariis;* and below, Most. III. ii. 80 (78), *Sol*

semper hic est usque a mani ad vesperum Quasi flagitator astat usque ad ostium; and for *flagitium*, Epid. III. iv. 77, *F. Fides non reddis? P. Neque fides, neque tibias. Propera igitur fugere hinc, si te Di amant. F. Abiero. Flagitio cum maiore post reddes tamen.* The same practice is alluded to in I. ii. 15, where a debtor exclaims, *Quin edepol egomet clamore defetigor, differor;* and Curc. V. iii. 5, *Postquam nihil fit, clamore hominem posco;* and in a more general sense Truc. IV. ii. 46, *Iam hercle ego tibi, illecebra, ludos faciam clamore in via Quae advorsum legem accepisti a plurimis pecuniam.*

62. *te extentatum*] 'to exhaust yourself with bawling,' i.e. 'to stretch your lungs till they crack.' The verb *extento*, a frequentative from *extendo*, occurs again in Bac. IV. ii. 1, *Quid istuc? quae istaec est pulsatio? Quae te mala crux agitat? ad istunc qui modum Alieno vires tuas extentes ostio?* and in Lucr. III. 489, where he is describing a man seized with a fit, *Concidit et spumas agit, ingemit et tremit artus, Desipit, extentat nervos, torquetur, anhelat;* but it is not found in any other Latin author till we come down to Ammianus Marcellinus.

63. *Νέ γρυ quidem.*] γρυ, as will be seen from the various readings, is a conjecture of Acidalius. The MSS. have *nec erit quidem*, which is quite unintelligible. There are several passages in Plautus where Greek words are brought in, and these, as might be expected, appear in most cases in a very corrupt form in the MSS. Below, in IV. iii. 46, Μὰ τὸν Ἀπόλλω is written correctly in Latin characters in the Palimpsest; in Bac. V. ii. 43, Hermann has probably hit the truth when he substitutes Ναὶ γὰρ for the *necar* of the Palatine MSS., which appears in interpolated MSS. and the Vulgate as *neras:* so in Trin. II. iv. 17 we cannot doubt that *oechele* or *oe che te* of the MSS. has been correctly interpreted by οἴχεται, and that in Poen. I. i. 9 *lyracline* stands for λῆρος λῆρος; so in Cas. III. vi. 9, 10, the reading πράγματά μοι παρέχεις, μέγα κακὸν, 'Ω Ζεῦ, rests upon satisfactory traces; in Truc. V. 36 φλυαρεῖν may be accepted, but in Pseud. II. iv. 22 the χάρω τούτῳ ποιῶ of Scaliger, the χάρω οἰκοῦν ποιῶ of Camerarius, the χαῖρε, οἰκοῦν ποιῶ of Lambinus, and the χαίρειν Χαρῖνον volo of Acidalius, although all ingenious, are mere guesses, for the characters in the MSS. are so obscure that they cannot be deciphered with any approach to certainty.

81. *Ne inconciliare quid nos porro postules.*] The word *inconciliare* is found three or four times in Plautus, but is not found in the extant writings of any other classical author. Looking to the etymology, since *conciliare* signifies 'to join together,' 'to bring into close union,' and hence 'to act the part of a go-between or broker' in

matrimonial and mercantile transactions, we might naturally suppose
that *inconciliare* denoted 'to separate,' 'to set at variance,' 'to disturb,'
a meaning which would suit the passage before us. But it has been
objected that this interpretation is contrary to analogy,—that although
in has frequently a negative force when compounded with adjectives
or participles, it never has this force when compounded with verbs.
The old grammarians seem to have been in doubt as to the meaning
of *inconciliare*; thus Festus, or rather Paulus Diaconus, p. 107, ed.
Müll, "*Inconciliasti*, comparasti, commendasti, vel, ut antiqui, per dolum
decipere," where it is supposed that *antiqui* is intended to indicate
Plautus. The passages in which the word occurs are the following:
1. Bac. III. vi. 21, *Ille, quod in se fuit, adcuratum habuit quod posset
mali Facere et in me inconciliare copias omnes meas.* This is the reading
of the MSS. Camer. proposes *facere et*, while R retains *faceret* and
reads *inconciliaret;* the former connects *in me* with *inconciliare*, the
latter with *faceret.* It must be observed that the change proposed
by R is more violent than that introduced by Camer., indeed the
substitution of *facere et* for *faceret* cannot be regarded as a change
at all—according to either reading, 'to set at variance with me,' 'to
disturb or throw into confusion,' 'to stir up against me,' would be
a satisfactory meaning. 2. The line in the Mostellaria, now before
us. 3. Trin. I. ii. 99. *Inconciliastin cum qui mandatus est tibi, Ille qui
mandarit, cum exturbasti ex aedibus? Edepol mandatum pulcre et curatum
probe!* Here the sense given by Paul. Diac., 'decipere per dolum,' would
be more applicable. Goeller renders it, 'malam rem ei et damnum
conciliare.' Lastly, in the Persa, V. ii. 53, *inconciliavit* appears in the
printed editions, but the MSS. here are so corrupt that it is hard to
say whether the word *inconciliavit* is indicated at all, and therefore
we can found nothing upon this passage.* On the whole, if we
admit that *inconciliare* cannot signify to 'disunite,' there is no reason
why it should not mean 'to unite against,' 'to stir up opposition,'
and so 'to bring trouble upon any one,' which will suit the passage
from the Mostellaria, and hence, ultimately, 'to injure' or 'deceive.'

87. *Obici argentum* &c.] If we adopt the reading given in our
text the meaning will be 'Order, I beseech you, the mouth of this
unclean brute to be plugged (gagged) with silver.' *Os* is here used
in its proper signification, but it is frequently employed by Plautus
to signify 'the face' or 'the whole head.' Thus Capt. IV. ii. 11,

* Compare the word *inconciliare*, Curc. III. 30, and Festus on the
word.

Eminor interminorque, ne quis mi opstiterit obviam Nam qui opstiterit ore sistet: with which compare Curc. II. iii. 5, *Nec quisquam sit tam opulentus, qui mi opsistat in via . . . . . . Quin cadat, quin capite sistat in via de semita,* in which it is manifest that *ore sistere* and *capite sistere* are equivalent to each other; so in Amph. 1. i. 161, *S. Illic homo me interpolabit, meumque os finget denuo. M. Exossatum os esse oportet quam probe percusseris ;* Pers. II. iv. 12, *Non hercle si os perciderim tibi, metuam, morticine ;* and Epid. III. iii. 1, *Non oris causa modo hominis aequom fuit Sibi habere speculum, ubi os contemplarent suum ;* see also Rud. III. iv. 5 and Mil. II. ii. 56.

87. *illic.*] Compare III. i. 78 (82), *Quid illuc est faenus, opsecro, quod illic petit ? v.* 55 (59), *Iam, hercle, ego illunc nominabo. T. Euge, strenua !* IV. iii. 3 (ii. 26), *Quas illaec res est ? quid illi homines quaerunt apud aedes meas ?*

109. *Quid ? eas quanti destinat ?*] See below, IV. ii. 58 (iii. 35), V. i. 64 (ii. 49). The etymology of *destino* is uncertain, although it may possibly be connected with *sisto* and *lordve.* It signifies 1. 'to fix' or 'fasten down,' in a direct material sense, as when Caesar B. G. III. 14 speaks of *funes qui antennas ad malos destinabant:* and B. C. 1. 27, *Has* (sc. *rates duplices) quaternis ancoris ex quatuor angulis destinabat, ne fluctibus moverentur.* 2. 'To fix' in a figurative or mental sense, 'to mark out,' 'to determine,' 'resolve,' 'assign,' as in the phrases, *Quin eum* (sc. *Papirium Cursorem) parem destinant animis Magno Alexandro ducem, si arma, Asia perdomita, in Europam vertisset,* Liv. IX. 16; so Liv. VI. 6, the colleagues of Camillus are represented as acknowledging *regimen omnium rerum, ubi quid bellici terroris ingruat, in viro uno esse: sibique destinatum in animo esse Camillo submittere imperium;* so also Hor. S. II. iii. 83, *Danda est hellebori multo pars maxima avaris Nescio an Ant.cyram ratio illis destinet omnem;* and Virg. Æn. II. 129, *Composito rumpit vocem et me destinat arae.* 3. The word as it occurs in Plautus is generally employed in the sense of 'to fix upon some object for purchase,' or 'to fix the price which one is willing to give for an object,' hence 'to bargain for the purchase,' and hence simply 'to purchase.' Thus Rud. Prol. 45, *Minis triginta sibi puellam destinat Datque arrabonem;* and Pers. IV. iii. 72, *Etiam tu illam destinas ? D. Vidram modo Mercimonium. T. Aequa dicis;* and again, iv. 115, *S. Tuo periculo sexaginta haec datur argenti minis. D. Toxile, quid ago? T. Di deaeque te agitant irati, seclus, Qui hanc non properes destinare.* The reading in Most. IV. ii. 68 (iii. 35) is doubtful, and also in V. ii. 64 (49). We have in Non. p. 289, "*Destinare* dicitur parare. Destimare,

emere. Lucilius lib. XXVII : *facio, ad lenonem venio, tribus in libertatem milibus Destiner.*" Cic. Epp. Fam. VII. xxiii. § 3, when speaking of the purchase of several works of art, *Quod tibi destinaras* τραπεζοφόρον, *si te delectat, habebis ; sin autem sententiam mutasti, ego habebo scilicet.* Plautus uses also the verb *Praestino*, manifestly connected with the same root as *Destino*, in the sense of 'to purchase.' Thus Paul. Diac. p. 233, ed. Müll., "*Praestinare* apud Plautum prae-emere est, id est emendo tenere ;" thus Capt. IV. ii. 66, *Iuben an non iubes astitui aulas ? patinas elui ? Laridum atque epulas foveri foculis fer-ventibus ? Alium pisces praestinatum abire ?* Epid. II. ii. 90, *E. Quasi tu cupias liberare fidicinam animi gratia, Quasique ames vehementer tu illam. P. Quam ad rem istuc refert ? E. Rogas ? Vt enim praestines argento, priusquam veniat filius ;* Pseud. I. ii. 36, *Ego eo in macellum ut piscium quidquid est pretio praestinem.* The word seems to occur in no other author until it was revived by Apuleius, who employs it repeatedly : Met. I. 5, 24, IV. 15, VII. 9, VIII. 23, 24, IX. 6, 10; Apol. 101. See note of Hildebrand on VII. 9.

111. *arraboni.*] See also III. iii. 15 (IV. ii. 15), IV. iii. 21 (iv. 21). The word *arrabo*, which appears also under the shape of *arra*, is taken directly from the Greek ἀρραβών, which again is taken from a Hebrew verb signifying 'to promise,' 'to become security.' Both words are frequently found written with an aspirate *arrha* and *arrhabo*, but these forms probably belong to a period of the language subsequent to the age of Plautus. Technically an *arrabo* was a partial payment made by a purchaser when he concluded a bargain, in security that he would not repudiate his engagement. The French word *les arrhes* is identical in meaning, and in Scotland the earnest-penny given to a servant when hired is called *the arles.* Thus Rud. Prol. 45, *Minis tri-ginta sibi puellam destinat Datque arrabonem et iureiurando adligat ;* and so again, in reference to the same transaction, II. vi. 71, III. vi. 23, from which it is evident that when a seller received an *arrabo* he was bound to abide by his bargain. In Poen. V. vi. 22 it is used more loosely to denote an object seized as security or compensation for a debt, *Leno arrabonem hoc pro mina mecum fero ;* and in Heaut. III. iii. 42 an object (a girl) left as security for money borrowed, *Ea* (sc. *filia adulescentula*) *relicta huic arraboni est pro illo argento.* In Mil. IV. i. 11 it is used figuratively : Palaestrio, presenting a ring to the soldier, says, *Hunc arrabonem amoris primum a me accipe ;* and in Truc. III. ii. 22 there is an elaborate joke in consequence of a slave having by design or accident said *rabonem* instead of *arrabonem : A. Perii ! Rabonem, quam esse dicam hanc belluam ? Quin tu arrabonem*

dicis? S. ar facio lucri Vt Praenestinis conia est ciconia. There are some remarks upon this word in Aul. Gell. XVII. 2, who quotes a passage from Claudius Quadrigarius, and adds "nunc *arrabo* in sordidis verbis haberi coeptus, ac multo rectius videtur arra, quamquam arra quoque veteres saepe dixerunt, et compluriens Laberius."

116. *Apsolve hunc, quaeso, vomitum.*] Unless *comitus* be taken here in a general sense to signify 'filth,' it must mean 'an emetic,' 'something causing sickness;' usually, however, it is employed to denote the act of vomiting or the result. Thus Merc. III. iii. 14, *Senex hircosus, tu osculere mulierem? Vtine adveniens vomitum excutias mulieri?* and Rud. II. vi. 26, *L. Perii, animo male fit! contine, quaeso, caput. C. Pulmoneum edepol nimis velim vomitum vomas,* i. e. 'it is all over with me, I am sick, hold my head I beseech you.' ' Very much should I like it if you were to retch up your lungs.' Bothe and Ritschl, offended apparently by this use of *vomitus*, have proposed a correction which is no improvement. Weise in his index seems to explain *vomitus* in this passage by *argenti numeratio.* Does he mean 'disgorge the money,' 'up with it?'

120. *Adulescens*] i. e. 'young man,' is constantly employed by dramatists in addressing and describing a person without reference, at least emphatically, to his age. It is not employed when one person accosts another ceremoniously, and occasionally, although by no means uniformly, implies that the person addressed is in a social position somewhat inferior to that of the speaker. It may thus be often correctly represented by our phrase 'my lad,' 'my man,' or 'my friend.' In like manner *puer* is the common term applied to a slave, whatever his age may be; so in French a waiter is called *garçon* although he may be old and decrepit, and among ourselves the same takes place with regard to post-*boys*. In our early writers *Childe* is applied to knights and squires, and in the plays and novels of the last century *child* is frequently used by ladies when addressing full-grown women of a lower grade. The following examples of this use of *adulescens* will suffice to illustrate what we have said: As. II. ii. 70, III. iii. 44; Epid. I. i. 1, III. iv. 4, 8, 23; Men. II. ii. 11, 15, III. ii. 29, 33, 41; Pers. IV. iv. 108; Poen. V. v. 28; Pseud. II. ii. 21; Rud. IV. iii. 4; Trin. IV. ii. 47, 126.

144. *ad unum saxum.*] "Abundat *unum*," and on Aul. I. ii. 11 "Vox *unam* pleonastice adiecta ut saepius in Plauto," says Weise, a most unsatisfactory explanation, one which ought ever to be regarded with extreme distrust. There can be no doubt that in the older forms of the language *unus* denoted not merely 'one' with numerical

emphasis, but was equivalent in many cases to the indefinite article *a*
or *an*, which is in reality *ane* or *one*, and was anciently employed
just as *un, uno, ein*, etc. are in modern languages. Plautus will afford
several examples: in this play, IV. ii. 67 (iii. 44), we have *Vnus istic
servos est sacerrumus;* and IV. iii. 9 (iv. 9), *Vnum ridi' mortuom
efferri foras;* so Capt. III. i. 22, *unum ridiculum dictum;* Epid. III. iv.
17, *Pol ego magis unum quaero,* i. e. 'I seek (some) one.' In Trin. IV.
iv. 11. *Curre in Piraeum, atque unum curriculum face,* which Weise
explains by saying "*unum* pleonastice ut saepius," *unum* is highly
emphatic, 'run to the Piraeus and make *one* course of it,' i. e. 'do
not halt for a moment.' In Pseud. I. i. 52 (q. v.), *nunc unae quinque
remorantur minae* may signify 'a matter of five minae,' but *unae* is
here rather equivalent to *solae* or *solum,* 'now the balance of five minae
alone detains me here;' and so *tres unos passus,* Bac. IV. vii. 34.

147. *Ducere, Ductare, Circumducere, Perductare, Perductor,* all
occur in the same sense in the course of this play. In Pers. IV.
iv. 85, *Omne ego pro nihilo esse ducto quod fuit quando fuit,* the MS.
reading *ducto* in this sense is an ἅπ. λεγ. W reads *duco.*

III. ii. 10. *Tota turget mihi uxor*] i. e. 'is all in a ferment.'
There is a line in Cas. II. v. 17 which may serve as a commentary,
Nunc in fermento tota est, ita turget mihi.

12. *cubandum est male.*] The same expression in As. IV. ii. 87,
Male cubandum est: iudicatum me uxor adducit domum.

79. *Quasi flagitator*] i. e. 'like a dun.' See note on v. 55.

110. *Sibi quisque ruri metit.*] A proverbial expression equivalent
to 'every one for himself in this world' or 'charity begins at home.'
Compare Epid. II. ii. 80, *Mihi istic nec seritur nec metitur,* i. e. 'I
have no interest in that matter, it does not concern me.'

111. *Redhibere* is a technical legal term employed when a
purchaser returns the article purchased upon the hands of the seller
on account of some defect. The explanation of Ulpian is perfectly
distinct (Digest. XXI. 1, § 21), "*Redhibere* est facere ut rursus habeat
venditor quod habuerit;" and so Festus p. 270, ed. Müll., where
however the text is somewhat corrupt. The act of returning an
object under these circumstances was called *Redhibitio,* and a suit
brought to compel the seller to receive the object and to return
the price was *Actio Redhibitoria,* and so *Iudicium Redhibitorium.* See
Digest. XXI. 1, § 18, 48, 54, 60; see also Quintil. I. O. VIII. 3,
§ 14; Aul. Gell. IV. 2, XVII. 6. Plautus employs the word again,
Merc. II. iii. 84, *Dixit se redhibere si non placeat,* i. e. 'he (the
purchaser) said that he would return her if she did not give

satisfaction.'* In the Vulgate text of Men. V. vii. 49 we find *redhibebo*, but there the true reading is probably *reddibo* for *reddam*. See Non. s. v. *reddibo*, pp. 476 and 508. The word is generally used in reference to the purchase and sale of slaves, as may be seen by consulting the authorities referred to above, and from Cic. de Off. III. 23, *In mancipio vendendo dicendam vitia, non ea, quae nisi dixeris, redhibeatur mancipium iure civili, sed haec, mendacem esse, aleatorem, furacem, ebriosum.*

141. *pultiphagus opifex . . . barbarus*] i. e. 'no clumsy porridge-eating Roman workman.' Plautus, when translating or adapting his Greek originals, often loves to assume the position of an Athenian writer, and to raise a laugh by designating himself and his countrymen as *barbari*: of this we have several examples, e. g. As. Prol. 11, *huic nomen Graece Onagos fabulae, Demophilus scripsit, Marcus vortit barbare*; and again, Trin. Prol. 18, *Huic nomen Graece est Thesauro fabulae, Philemo scripsit, Plautus vortit barbare.* In Capt. III. i. 32, *barbarica lege* is probably 'Roman law;' in the same play, IV. ii. 102, Ergasilus swears by Cora, Praeneste, Signia, Frusino, and Alatrium, upon which Hegio asks, *Quid tu per barbaricas urbes iuras?* in Mil. II. ii. 56, *poetae barbaro* is Naevius; in Poen. III. ii. 21, and in a fragment of the Faeneratrix quoted by Festus s. v. *Vapula Papiria*, p. 372, ed. Müll., *barbaria* is Italy; in Stich. I. iii. 49, *mores barbaros* are Roman customs. On the other hand, *barbarum hospitem*, Rud. II. vii. 25, is simply 'a foreign guest;' and there is nothing in the phrase or the context which would justify us in asserting that *barbarico ritu* in Cas. III. vi. 19 refers especially to Roman customs. In Curc. I. ii. 63, *ludii* is *Ludii*, i. e. Lydians, who were not properly Greeks, and therefore are termed *Ludii barbari.* In Bac. I. ii. 13, *Nimium quam, O Lude, es barbarus Quam ego sapere nimio censui plus quam Thalem, I, stultior es barbaro Potitio: barbarus* is used in the general sense of 'illiterate,' and then *barbaro Potitio* signifies 'that ignorant savage, the Roman Potitius.' The epithet *pultiphagus* (*pultifagus*) which is an ἅπ. λεγ. ties down the *barbarus* to a Roman workman, for *puls* or porridge made of *far* was the ancient national dish among the Roman peasants, as *polenta* was among the rustic Greeks. See Val. Max. II. 5, § 5, and Plin. H. N. XVIII. 8, who,

---

* In Forcellini and Freund this is explained to mean, 'he, the seller, said that he would take her back;' but this is contrary to the established use of the word, and is quite unnecessary, indeed it is inadmissible, for Demea replies, *nihil istac opus est Litigare ego nolo vos*,—whereas, if the seller had agreed to take her back, there was no room for litigation.

speaking of *far*, says, *Primus antiquis Latio cibus, magno argumento
in adoreae donis, sicuti diximus; pulte autem non pane vixisse longo
tempore Romanos manifestum, quoniam et pulmentaria hodieque dicuntur
. . . . Et hodie sacra prisca atque natalium pulte fritilla conficiuntur,
videnturque tam puls ignota Graeciae fuisse quam Italiae polenta.*
Respect for a great name must not allow us to hesitate in rejecting
the explanation of Scaliger, who would make the *pultiphagus opifex
barbarus* a Carthaginian artificer, because mention is frequently made
in the Roman writers of carpentry work executed by the Cartha-
ginians. See notes on Varr. R. R. III. 7.

IV. i. 5. *Exercent sese ad currurram*] i. e. 'they train themselves in
running.' Cf. Stich. II. l. 34, *Simulque ad cursuram meditabor me
ad ludos Olympias;* see also As. II. ii. 61, Bac. I. i. 34, Merc. I. 10,
Trin. IV. ii. 164, iii. 9.

17. *Plagigerulus* and *Plagiger* are ἅπ. λεγ., each being found once
in Plautus. The latter occurs Pseud. 1. ii. 20, *Huc adhibete auris,
quae ego loquar, plagigera genera hominum.* *Plagipatida*, which also
is a vox Plautina, occurs twice: above, II. l. 9, *Vbi sunt isti plagipatidae, ferritribaces viri;* and again, Capt. III. i. 12, *Nil morantur
iam Lacones, imi supelli viros, Plagipatidas, quibus sunt verba sine
pernu et pecunia.*

22. *die crastini*] i. e. *die crastino, cras.* Aulus Gellius, X. 24,
states that the forms *die quarti, quinti, noni, pristini* (for *pridie*),
crastini, proximi, and the like were employed exclusively by Cicero
and his predecessors instead of *die quarto, quinto, nono, pristino,* &c.,
which afterwards came into general use, and that the older combination was frequently used by Augustus in his letters. He adds that
the ancients said indifferently *die quarti* or *quarte, quinti* or *quinte,* the
words *die quarti,* &c., being pronounced as one, and regarded as an
adverb with the second syllable short. He quotes from the *Mimiambi*
of Cn. Matius, whom he characterises as 'impense doctus,' two lines
to prove that *die quarto* was considered by him equivalent to *nudius
quartus,* and arrives at the conclusion that *die quarto* properly refers
to past time, and *die quarti* or *quarte* to future time. See also
Macrob. S. I. 4. In Plautus we find, Men. V. ix. 94, *Mea Vis con-
clamari auctionem fore? Quodie? Ms. Die septimi. Mea. Auctio fiet
Menaechmi mane sane septimi;* and Pers. II. iii. 7, *Nam herus meus me
Eretriam misit, domitos boves uti sibi mercarer Dedit argentum: nam
ibi mercatum dixit esse die septimi.*

24. *Postremo.*] It is a little difficult to catch the precise force of
this word in dialogue; here it seems to be equivalent to 'Well, well;

be that as it may,' or 'Well, well, at all events,' generally after a pause
of reflection before the word *postremo*, as if the speaker were thinking
over the position of affairs. So also we may render it in Cist. IV. ii.
40, Trin. III. i. 12. It may be translated 'in short' in As. I. iii. 85,
Cas. II. vi. 24, III. iv. 19, Truc. I. ii. 55 ('to sum the whole'), Trin.
V. ii. 36, Bac. III. vi. 41 ('to conclude,' 'to make a long story short'),
Epid. IV. ii. 21, Trin. III. ii. 36; 'well, at all events,' with a
distinct pause before *postremo* in Aul. IV. iv. 30, Cist. II. i. 56, Most.
I. iii. 41; 'after all' will give the meaning in Stich. I. i. 52, Merc.
III. ii. 15 (*Verum hercle postremo ut ut est*), Epid. V. ii. 43, As. I. i. 35.
See note of W on Most. IV. i. 24 and his index.

25. *Bucaidae*] an ἅπ. λεγ. from *bos* and *caedo*. There is no
doubt, apparently, as to the reading. *Restio* is found in this passage
and in Sueton. Octav. 2. *M. Antonius libertinum ei* (sc. *Octavio*)
proavum exprobrat, restionem, e pago Thurino: avum argentarium.
Casaubon, on the above, quotes "Glossarium: Σχοινοπλέκος, *restitu-*
larius, restio;" and in Cornelius Fronto *De differentiis vocabulorum*,
p. 2201 ed. Putsch., we find "*Restiarium* et *Restionem. Restiarius* qui
facit: *Restio* qui vendit." *Restio* was the title of one of the mimes
of Laberius; thus Aul. Gell. X. 17, "Laberius poeta in mimo quem
scripsit Restionem;" and again, XVI. 7, "Laberius .... in Restione
calabarriunculos dicit quos vulgus *calabarriones.*"

35. *culcitullam*] 'a pillow.' This is the form in which the word
appears in BCDF (D has *culcitulla*, F has *culcit ullam*), other MSS.
have *culcitellam.* It is an ἅπ. λεγ. *Culcitula* is quoted by Non.
(s.v. *privum*) from Lucil. lib. XXX. *Culcitulae accedunt privae cenion-*
ibus binis. The simple *culcita* signifies 'a stuffed cushion' or 'bed:'
Varro L. L. V. 167, "Postea quam transierunt ad culcitas, quod in eas
acus aut tomentum aliudve quid calcabant, ab inculcando *culcita* dicta;"
Paul. Diac. p. 50, ed. Müll., "*Culcita* quod tomento inculcatur appellata."
In Mil. IV. iv. 42, *culcitam ob oculos lanam* is a 'woolen pad;' in
Cas. II. iv. 28, Stalino exclaims in tragic vein, *Si sors autem decollassit,*
gladium faciam culcitam, 'my sword shall be my couch,' 'I shall fall
upon my sword.' We have *culcita plumea* in Sen. Epp. 87.

IV. ii. 19. *At enim ne quid captioni mihi sit, si dederim tibi.*] So
below, V. ii. 23 (ii. 23), *Enim istic captio est;* and V. i. 21 (ii. 6),
Docte atque astute mihi captandum est cum illoc. Since the verb *capere*
is frequently used with reference to the catching of game by the
hunter or fowler, both the simple verb and its frequentative *capto*
and the substantive *captio* denote 'to lie in wait for prey,' and hence
'to entrap,' 'to deceive.' In addition to the examples given above

from this play, the following will serve to illustrate the origin of these phrases and the manner in which they are used: Capt. III. iv. 120, *Satin me illi hodie scelesti capti ceperunt dolo*, where there is a sort of pun on *capti* (prisoners) and *ceperunt;* so Bac. V. ii. 88, *Lepide ipsi hi sunt capti, suis qui filiis fecere insidias: ii;* and Pseud. IV. iii. 11, *Metuo autem, ne herus redeat etiam dum a foro, Ne capta praeda capti praedones fuant;* Epid. III. ii. 23, *iam ipse cautor captus est.* *Capio* signifies 'to lie in wait for;' Amph. I. i. 266, *Quid me captas, carnufex?* i.e. 'why are you trying to catch me by your questions?' II. ii. 163, *Me captas,* 'you are trying to ensnare me;' and in v. 189, *capto* is distinguished from *capio, Tu si me impudicitiae captas, non potes capere,* i.e. 'if you are endeavouring to lead me into a snare, and convict me of unchastity, you are not able to entrap me;' and in Epid. II. ii. 31, *eos captabant* signifies 'they were watching to ensnare them;' in v. 112, *Verum, si plus dederis, referam: nihil in ea re captio est.* So *captio est,* Truc. II. vii. 65, 'that is not fair;' and As. IV. i. 45, *captiones metuis,* 'you are afraid of having tricks played off upon you.'

27. *Nunc ego me illac per posticum ad congerrones conferam.*] There seems to be no doubt that the word *congerrones* signifies 'jolly companions,' 'mates,' or something equivalent. It occurs again below, V. i. 8, *Capio consilium ut senatum congerronum convocem;* and in Pers. I. iii. 9, *Iam pol ille hic aderit, credo, congerro meus.* Non., p. 118, quotes the line from the Persa and explains it, 'ut conlusor meus qui easdem exerceat nugas.' *Gerro* is found in Heaut. V. iv. 10, *gerro, iners, fraus, helluo Ganeo, dammosus.* Observe also the word *gerres* denoting 'sprats' or some small, worthless fish. The etymology is altogether uncertain. Varro, L. L. VII. 55, who also quotes this line, says, "*Congerro* a gerra et Graecum est, et in Latina cratis." The Greek form with which we are acquainted is γέρρον, and signifies 'anything made of wicker-work,' thus answering closely to *cratis,* but the connection with *congerro* is by no means obvious. *Gerrae* is used several times by Plautus in the sense of 'stuff and nonsense,' 'bosh,' 'trash;' e. g. Poen. I. i. 8, *Nam tuae blanditiae mihi sunt, quod dici solet, Gerrae germanae, atque edepol λῆροι λήρων*; and so *gerrae maxumae,* in Epid. II. ii. 49: frequently it is simply an exclamation, as in Trin. III. iii. 31, and As. III. iii. 10. The word reappears in Ausonius, in the preface addressed to Symmachus, prefixed to Eidyll. XI. *Misi itaque ad te frivola gerris Siculis raniora,* where by the epithet *Siculis* he evidently alludes to the foolish story told in Paul. Diac. (s.v. *Gerrae,* p. 94, ed. Müll.) to explain how *gerrae,* supposing it to

be the same with γίλλο, came to bear the same meaning as *nugae*. The same grammarian supplies us with the word *cerrones* (p. 40), which he interprets by *leves et inepti*, repeating the story about the Sicilians and the Athenians, and *cerrones* is evidently the archaic form of *gerrones*, of which *congerro* is a compound. But a different explanation is suggested by Nonius, p. 118, who has "*Gerrae*, nugae, ineptiae; et sunt gerrae fascini, qui sic in Naxo insula Veneris ab incolis appellantur." In corroboration of this, one of the interpretations given to the Greek γίλλον is αἰδοῖον. For the form *congerra* we are referred to Fest. s.v. *Sodalis*, p. 297, and s.v. *Tappulam*, p. 363, but in both the reading is so doubtful that nothing can be founded on it. Fulgentius (p. 566), under the title *Quid sit congerro*, would derive the word from *gero*, and make it equivalent to 'robbers,' 'marauders:' "*Congerrones* dicuntur qui aliena ad se congregant. Unde et apud Romanos gerrones Brutiani dicti sunt." But the true reading is probably *Congerones*, and this word is found in the Vulg. text of Truc. I. ii. 6, *Vt semel advenium ad scorta congerones*, where 'thieves' is an appropriate translation.

IV. iii. 9. *Puere, nimium delicatus es*] i.e. 'you are a great joker,' at least this seems to be the meaning, although this force of *delicatus* has been little noticed. We find however the phrase *delicias facere*, in the sense of 'to jest,' 'to turn into ridicule,' in several passages of Plautus, e.g. Poen. I. ii. 67, *A. Milphio, heus, Milphio, ubi es? M. Assum apud te, eccum. A. At ego elixum volo. M. Enimvero, here, facis delicias*, and again v. 83; so Cas. III. i. 14, *S. Fac habeant linguam tuae aedes. A. Quid ita? S. Quom veniam, vocent. A. Attatae, caedundus tu homo es: nimias delicias facis. S. Quid me amare refert, nisi sim doctus et dicax nimis;* and Men. II. iii. 30, which is exactly parallel to the passage in the Most., *M. Vbi tu hunc hominem novisti? E. Ibidem, ubi hic me iam diu, In Epidamno. M. In Epidamno? qui huc in hanc urbem pedem Nisi hodie, numquam intro tetuli. E. Eia, delicias facis, Mi Menaechme.* In Rud. II. v. 8, where Sceparnio thinks that Ampelisca has hidden herself, he exclaims, *Sed ubi tu es, delicata? Cape aquam hanc sis. Vbi es?* i.e. 'where are you with your tricks?' and this may be the meaning of *delicatus* in Mil. IV. i. 37, *Pr. Placet, uti dicis. Sed, ne istanc amittam et hanc mulet fidem Vide modo. PA. Vah delicatus! quae te tamquam oculos amet!* where however I would rather give the meaning 'fanciful,' 'over scrupulous,' to *delicatus*. In Men. I. ii. 10, *Nimium ego te habui delicatam*, the meaning must be 'I have been too indulgent,' 'have humoured you too much.'

27. *Vide, sis, ne forte ad merendam quopiam divorteris.*] The
grammarians who explain this word seem to have relied more on
what they believed to be its etymology than upon passages to which
they could refer. Thus Paul. Diac. p. 123, ed. Müll., " *Merendam* antiqui dicebant pro prandio, quod medio die caperetur;" and in p. 69
we read, " *Cyprio boni merendum* Ennius sotadico versu quum dixit,
significavit id, quod solet fieri in insula Cypro, in qua boves humano
stercore pascuntur." Non. Marcell. p. 28, " *Merenda* dicitur cibus post
meridiem qui datur. Afranius, Fratris: *Interim Merendam occurro:
ad cenam cum veni iuvat.*" Isidor. XX. 2, § 12, " *Merenda* est cibus, qui
declinante die sumitur, quasi post meridiem edenda et proxima cenae.
Vnde et Antecenia a quibusdam vocantur. Item *Merendare* quasi
medio die edere." Again, XX. 3, § 3, " *Merum* dicimus, cum vinum
purum significamus. Nam merum dicimus quidquid purum atque sincerum est, sicut et aquam meram, nulli utique rei admixtam. Hinc et
Merenda, quod antiquitus id temporis pueris operariis quibus panis
merus dabatur aut quod *meridiens* eodem tempore, id est soli ac sepa-
ratim, non utique in prandio aut in cena ad unum mensam. Inde
credimus etiam illud tempus, quod post medium diem est, *meridiem*
appellari, quod purum sit." Calpurnius Siculus is the only writer
who speaks distinctly, and his evidence cannot carry much weight,
as we know not the period to which he belongs, Ecl. V. 60, *Verum
ubi declivi iam nona tepescere sole Incipiet, seraeque videbitur hora
merendae, Rursus pasce greges et opacas desere lucas.* In Seneca Controv.
V. 33, some copies have the word *merendarios*, which must mean
' beggars who went about collecting scraps,' but others read *merce-
narios.* In Plautus we should conclude that the *merenda* was taken
about the time of or soon after the *prandium*, as Simo a short way
before speaks of having finished his *prandium.*

43. *prae quam*] i. e. ' in comparison with;' and so below, V. ii. 25
(iii. 25), *prae quam quibus modis me ludificatus est;* and so Amph.
II. ii. 3, Aul. III. v. 33, with precisely the same meaning. In
Merc. Prol. 23 the use is, at first sight, different; *Nec pol profecto
quisquam sine grandi malo, Praequam res patitur, studuit elegantiae,*
i. e. ' to a greater extent than is compatible with his means,' which
means, when a man indulges in show or luxury too great ' when
compared with' or ' in comparison with his means.' The combination *prae quod* is found in Stich. II. ii. 38, *Imo res omnes relictas
habeo prae quod tu velis,* ' no, no, I consider all things as of secondary
importance in comparison with what you may wish;' so also *prae ut,*
Amph. I. i. 218, *S. Perii. M. Parum etiam, prae ut futurum est*

praedicas, i.e. 'what you say is a trifle, in comparison with what will befall you;' so Men. II. iii. 25, with an aposiopesis, *Dixin ego istaec solere fieri? folia nunc cadunt Prae ut si triduom hoc hic erimus, tum arbores in te cadent*, i.e. 'the leaves are falling now, but that is a trifle in comparison with what will happen if we shall remain here for the next three days, for then the trees themselves will fall upon you;' so Men. V. v. 33, *Imo modestior nunc quidem est de verbis, praeut dudum fuit;* and Merc. II. iv. 2, *Pentheum diripuisse aiunt Bacchas, nugas maxumas Fuisse credo, praeut quo pacto ego divorsus distrahor.* In Epid. III. iv. 85 *prae* is construed regularly with the ablative of a pronoun, *Ac me minoris facio* *prae illo, qui omnium Legum atque iurium fictor, conditor, cluet.*

– *prae quam alios dapsiles sumptus facit.*] Although *dapsiles* appears under a corrupt form in BCD,† it is found elsewhere in Plautus in its proper shape, e.g. Pseud. I. iv. 3, *Quid nunc acturus, postquam herili filio Largitus dictis dapsilis? ubi sunt ea?* although the passage is by no means free from difficulty; and again, in the same play, V. i. 21, *Vnguenta atque odores, lemniscos, corollas dari dapsiles;* again, in Truc. I. i. 34, *Aut vasum aenum aliquod, aut lectus dapsilis*, the reading is not doubtful, although some MSS. have *laptilis* or *leptilis;* and the word occurs again, Aul. II. i. 45, *Istas magnas factiones, animos, dotes dapsiles.* *Dapsilis* is found also in Columella III. 2, § 27, *Spionia* (a kind of vine) *dapsilis musto;* and IV. 27, § 6, *dapsili proventu fatigata vitis;* and also in Apuleius. The adverbial forms *dapsile, dapsilius, dapsiliter*, are quoted by the grammarians from Pomponius, Lucilius, and Naevius, and of these *dapsile* reappears in Suet. Vesp. 19.

44. *unus istic servos est sacerrumus Tranio*] i.e. 'a cursed scoundrel.' The force of *sacer* as here employed is distinctly explained by Festus p. 318, ed. Müll., "*Homo sacer* is est quem populus iudicavit ob maleficium, neque fas est eum immolari, sed, qui occidit, parricidi non damnatur, nam lege tribunicia prima cavetur si quis eum qui eo plebi scito sacer sit occiderit, parricida ne sit, ex quo quivis homo malus atque improbus *sacer* appellari solet." The phrase is given more fully in the fragment of a law ascribed to Numa, quoted by Paul. Diac. s.v. *Aliuta* p. 6, ed. Müll., *Si quisquam aliuta* (i.e. *aliter*) *faxit, ipsos Iovi sacer esto;* and so Liv. III. 55, in the law passed B.C. 449 immediately after the abdication of Appius and his colleagues it was enacted, *Vt qui tribunis plebis, aedilibus, iudicibus, decemviris nocuisset,*

* W. reads *factum*.
† *dapsillies* B2C, *dapsillies* Bb, *dapsiles* D.

*rius caput Iovi sacrum esset: familia ad aedem Cereris, Liberi, Liber-
aeque, venum iret,* on which Livy remarks, *Hac lege iuris interpretes
negant quenquam sacrosanctum esse, sed eum qui eorum cuiquam nocuerit
sacrum sanciri.* See also Law of XII. Tables quoted by Serv. ad
Virg. Æn. VI. 609, and Hor. S. II. iii. 181, *is intestabilis et sacer esto.*
The theory seems to have been that any man who was solemnly made
over and devoted to a God was thereby placed beyond the pale of
human sympathy and protection. It is commonly asserted that an
individual under these circumstances was *sacer dis inferis,* but in both
quotations given above where a God is named it is Iupiter. See
Macrob. S. III. 7. *Sacer* in the general sense of 'worthless,' 'good-
for-nothing,' 'vile,' was originally, as might be expected, applied to
persons only, and this is the case uniformly in Plautus and the earliest
writers (Dac. IV. vi. 14, Poen. Prol. 90, Rud. I. ii. 69), but Catullus
applies the epithet to a book, XIV. 12, *Di magni, horribilem et sacrum
libellum,* and to a rank smell, LXXXI. 1, *Si quoi, Virro, bono sacer
alarum obstitit hircus,* while the *auri sacra fames* of Virgil (Æn. III.
57) has passed into a proverb. With regard to the use of *unus* in
the line before us we have an exact parallel in Truc. II. i. 39, *Sed est
huic unus servos violentissumus.*

45. *is vel Herculi conterere quaestum possiet.*] The wealth of
Hercules was proverbial among the Romans. 1. He was regarded
as the guardian of hidden treasures, and those who discovered
such hoards were wont to ascribe their good fortune to the favour
of the God; thus Hor. S. II. vi. 10, *O si urnam argenti fors quae
mihi monstret, ut illi Thesauro invento qui mercenarius agrum Illum
ipsum mercatus aravit, dives amico Hercule;* and Pers. S. II. 10, *O
si Sub rastro crepet argenti mihi seria, dextro Hercule.* Indeed it
would appear that, according to popular belief, Hercules was looked
upon in the same light as those spirits who in Eastern and Northern
mythology are supposed to dwell beneath the earth, brooding over
and watching hidden gold; thus Acron explains the allusion in
Horace, *Ideo quia thesauris praeest, et sunt qui eundem Incubonem esse
velint,* to which we may add the following curious notice in the tract
known to writers on Roman topography as *Curiosum Vrbis Romae.**
Among the remarkable objects in the Regio XIV, the Transtiberina,

---

* The title at full length as it appears in the Vatican MS. is—*Incipit
Curiosum vrbis Romae Regionum XIIII cum Brebiariis suis.* It will be found
in Muratori, Thes. Inscrip. T. IV., and is given at the end of the first
volume of Becker's Handbuch der Römischen Alterthümer. See also
Bunsen, Beschreibung der S. R. Tom. I. p. 175. It probably belongs to
the early part of the fourth century.

is placed *Herculem sub terram mediam cubantem : sub quem plurimum aurum positum est.* 2. But the power of the God was by no means restricted within the narrow limits indicated above, for we learn from Diodorus Siculus and Dionysius of Halicarnassus, who enter into minute details, that he was worshipped generally as the bestower of wealth, and that those who had accumulated great riches were wont, in gratitude or in the fulfilment of a vow, to dedicate to him a tithe of all their possessions. It will be seen from the quotations given at length below, that both authors carry back the origin of this practice to a remote mythical epoch—to the period when Hercules passed over into Italy from Spain—and both distinctly state that it still prevailed when they wrote. The former states specifically that Lucullus, having calculated the amount of his fortune, consecrated a tithe of the whole to Hercules, and expended the amount in a long series of costly banquets, and this statement is corroborated by Plutarch, who relates the same of Sulla and of Crassus, and proposes as the subject of one of his Roman Problems (15), Διὰ τί τῳ Ἡρακλεῖ πολλοὶ τῶν πλουσίων ἐδεκάτευον τὰς οὐσίας; These passages are so important that they deserve to be quoted. After having narrated the hospitable reception of Hercules by the aborigines who had a town upon the Palatine, Diodorus proceeds (IV. 21), Ὁ δ' οὖν Ἡρακλῆς ἀποδεξάμενος τὴν εὔνοιαν τῶν τὸ Παλάτιον οἰκούντων, προείπεν αὐτοῖς, ὅτι μετὰ τὴν ἑαυτοῦ μετάστασιν εἰς θεούς, τοῖς εὐξαμένοις ἀποδεκατεύσειν Ἡρακλεῖ τὴν οὐσίαν, συμβήσεται τὸν βίον εὐδαιμονέστερον ἕξειν. ὁ καὶ συνέβη κατὰ τοὺς ὕστερον χρόνους διαμεῖναι μέχρι τῶν καθ' ἡμᾶς χρόνων. πολλοὺς γὰρ Ῥωμαίων, οὐ μόνον τῶν συμμέτρους οὐσίας κεκτημένων, ἀλλὰ καὶ τῶν μεγαλοπλούτων τινὰς, εὐξαμένους ἀποδεκατεύσειν Ἡρακλεῖ, καὶ μετὰ ταῦτα γενομένους εὐδαίμονας, ἀποδεκατεῦσαι τὰς οὐσίας οὔσας ταλάντων τετρακισχιλίων. Λεύκολλος γὰρ ὁ τῶν καθ' αὑτὸν Ῥωμαίων σχεδόν τι πλουσιώτατος ὤν, διατιμησάμενος τὴν ἰδίαν οὐσίαν, κατέθυσε τῷ θεῷ πᾶσαν τὴν δεκάτην, εὐωχίας ποιῶν συνεχεῖς καὶ πολυδαπάνους. κατεσκεύασαν δὲ καὶ Ῥωμαῖοι τούτῳ τῷ θεῷ παρὰ τὸν Τίβεριν ἱερὸν ἀξιόλογον, ἐν ᾧ νομίζουσι συντελεῖν τὰς ἐκ τῆς δεκάτης θυσίας—where, it must be remarked, Diodorus speaks of facts within his own knowledge and observation. In like manner Dionysius (A. R. I. 40) after recounting the legend of the erection of an altar in honour of Hercules by Evander and of the sacrifice of a tithe of his spoils by the hero himself, concludes with these words: Ὁ δὲ βωμὸς, ἐφ' οὗ τὰς δεκάτας ἐπέθυσεν Ἡρακλῆς, καλεῖται μὲν ὑπὸ Ῥωμαίων Μέγιστος, ἔστι δὲ Βοαρίας λεγομένης ἀγορᾶς πλησίον, ἁγιστευόμενος εἰ καί τις ἄλλος ὑπὸ τῶν ἐπιχωρίων. ὅμοια τε γὰρ ἐπ' αὐτῷ καὶ συνθήκας τοῖς βουλομένοις βεβαίως τι διαπράττεσθαι, καὶ δεκατεύσεις χρημάτων γίνονται συχναὶ κατ' εὐχάς. Τῇ

Z

μέντοι αστασευή πολὺ τῆς δόξης ἐστὶ απαθείστερος. So too Plutarch,
Vit. Sullae, c. 35: Ἀποδύων δὲ τῆς οὐσίας ἀπέστη ὁ Σύλλας τῷ Ἡρακλεῖ
δεκάτην, ἰστιάσεις ἐποιεῖτο τῷ δήμῳ πολυτελεῖς. καὶ τοσοῦτον περιττὴ ἦν ἡ
παρασκευή τῆς χρείας, ὥστε παμπληθῆ καθ᾽ ἑκάστην ἡμέραν εἰς τὸν ποταμὸν
ὄψα ῥιπτεῖσθαι, πίνεσθαι δ᾽ οἶνον ἐτῶν τεσσαράκοντα, καὶ παλαιότερον. And
he goes on to tell how this banquet lasted for many days. The same
author again, Vit. Crassi, c. 12, when speaking of the discord between
Pompeius and Crassus in their first consulship, says that they effected
nothing worth notice. ... πλὴν ὅτι Κράσσος Ἡρακλεῖ μεγάλην θυσίαν
ποιησάμενος, εἰστίασε τὸν δήμον ἀπὸ μυρίων τραπεζῶν, καὶ σῖτον ἐμέτρησεν εἰς
τρίμηνον. The form in which these offerings were presented—that of
costly public banquets—while it exhibited the piety of the donors in
a shape eminently calculated to extend their popularity, probably
had some reference to the gluttony ascribed to this deity by the
Greeks, under the epithet βούφαγος. (See Preller II. M. p. 653.) The
appropriate term for a feast of this description appears to have been
polluctum, a word to which we have already referred when discussing
polluribiliter (I. l. 23). 3. The following passages in Plautus refer to
the practice of offering tithes to Hercules: Stich. I. iii. 80, *Haec
remisse iam opus est, quantum potest, Vti decumam partem Herculi
polluceam;* Bac. IV. iv. 15, *Sed lubet scire, quantum aurum herus sibi
dempsit, et quid suo reddidit patri. Si frugi est, Herculem fecit ex
patre : decumam partem ei Dedit, sibi novem apstulit ;* Truc. II. vii. 10,
Nam iam de hoc opsonio de mina una diminui Modo quinque numos :*
mihi detraxi partem Herculaneam; Stich. II. ii. 62, *non vendo logos,
Iam non facio auctionem : mihi optigit hereditas. Malevoli perquisitores
auctionum perierint: Hercules, decumam esse adauctam, tibi quam vovi,
gratulor;* and to these we may add an inscription found near
Capua:—P. ATEIVS. P. L. REGILLVS. FECIT. SIBI. ET. P. ATEIO.
P. L. SALVIO. PATRON. POMARIO. IB. TER. HERCVLI. DECVMAM.
FECIT. Mommsen n. 3578.

47. *amburet misero ei corculum corbunculus.*] *Corculum* occurs in
Cas. II. vi. 9, *C. ... stimulus ego nunc sum tibi : Fodico corculum :
adsultasti iam ex metu ;* and again, IV. iv. 14, *meum corculum, melliculum, Verculum,* where it is a term of endearment equivalent to
'sweetheart.'

IV. iv. 10. *Vae capiti tuo !*] i. e. 'confound you and your jokes!'
This is a formula employed when a speaker feels disgusted by being
made the object of an ill-timed jest. So *Vae aetati tuae,* Capt. IV.

* Therefore the coin here spoken of must have been a *didrachm.*

ii. 105, Stich. IV. ii. 14; *Vae capiti tuo*, Amph. II. ii. 109, Curc. II. iii.
35, Men. III. ii. 47, Mil. II. iii. 55; *Vae tibi*, Epid. I. i. 26, III. ii. 12,
Aa. II. ii. 40, Merc. I. 49; *Vae tibi nugator*, Mil. IV. ii. 86; *Vae capiti
atque aetati tuae*, Rud. II. iii. 44. But *vae tibi* is employed also in
the sense of 'confound you!' where there is no question of a jest,
e. g. Cas. I. 27, III. v. 12, Truc. II. ii. 2; so *Vae illi*, Pers. II. iii. 18;
to indicate real sorrow, as *vae misero mihi*, Capt. V. i. 25, Truc. II. iii.
21; *vae miserae mihi*, Amph. V. i. 5; *Vae mihi* (terror), v. 28; *Vae
illis virgis miseris* (humorous), Capt. III. iv. 117; *Vae misero illi*,
IV. II. 26.

V. i. 1. *Qui homo timidus erit in rebus dubiis, nauci non erit; Atque
equidem, quid id esse dicam verbum nauci, nescio.*] The ignorance of
Tranio with regard to the real meaning of the word *Naucus* seems to
have been shared by the Roman philologists: thus Fest. s.v., p. 166,
ed. Müll., "Naucum ait Ateius Philologus poni pro nugis. Cincius,
quod in oleae nucis quod intus sit.* Aelius Stilo, omnium rerum puta-
men. Glossematorum autem scriptores fabae grani quod haerent in
fabulo. Quidam ex Graeco, quod sit *val kal ouχl*, levem hominem
significari. Quidam nucis iuglandis, quam Verrius iuglandam† vocat,
medium velut dissepimentum." Festus then quotes the latter of the
two lines of our text, and other passages from Plautus, Naevius, and
Ennius. There are one or two other examples of the word in
Plautus, and one in the line quoted by Cicero from Ennius (De
Divin. I. 58), *Non nauci facio Marsum augurem. Nauci* is found in
the genitive only, accompanied by *non*, except in the line quoted by
Festus from Naevius, in which *nauci* occurs without the negative.

4. *Abii illa per angiportum ad horeum nostrum clanculum.*] *Angiportus* or *Angiportum* was a narrow lane or passage which separated
two adjacent houses or blocks of building (*insulae*), analogous to
what is termed a *close* in the older portions of Scottish towns. It is
thus explained in Paul. Diac. p. 17, ed. Müll.: "*Angiportus* est iter
compendiarium in oppido, eo quod sit angustus portus, id est, aditus ad
portum." Varro is less distinct, and while he proposes two etymo-
logies, seems to prefer that which is erroneous: thus L. L. V. § 145,
ed. Müll, "*Angiportum* sive quod id angustum, sive ab agendo et
portu;" and again, VI. § 41, "Qua vix agi potest, hinc *angiportum.*"
It must be observed that according to the express testimony of
Festus (p. 233) *portus* was anciently used as synonymous with *domus:*
"*Portum* in XII. pro domo positum omnes fere consentiunt" (see above

* Müll. corrects *quod oleae nucisque intus sit.*
† In the text *iugulandam*, corrected by Müll. *inglandum.*

z 2

note on III. l. 55); and so Donat. ad Terent. Adel. IV. ii. 39, after giving one absurd etymology (quasi anguiportus, i.e. angusta et curva via), goes on, "Alii, quod inter portus sit locus angustus, hoc est inter domos. Nam *domos*, vel *portus* vel *insulas* veteres dixerunt."

4, 5. If the reading be correct, these lines contain an anacoluthon, indicating the hurry and confusion of the narrator.

V. ii. 6. *Docte atque astute mihi captandum est cum illoc*] i.e. 'I must skilfully and craftily lay a trap to ensnare him.' The construction *mihi captandum est cum illoc* is remarkable. On the force of *capto* see note on IV. ii. 19.

23. *servos pollicitus est dare Suos mihi omnes quaestioni. Th. Nugas! numquam edepol dabit. Tu. Dat profecto.*] Cf. v. 29, *Imo hoc primum volo Quaestioni accipere servos.*

28. *Vel hominem iube aedis mancupio poscere.*] Since *hominem* in v. 26 refers to Simo, it might appear harsh to make *hominem* in this line refer to Philolaches, and to translate 'order Philolaches to demand;' but we may regard *hominem aedis* as the double accusative after *poscere*, 'order (your son) to make a demand upon the man (Simo) for the house.' The emendation *posci*, proposed by Dousa and adopted by Bothe and Weise, is not sanctioned by any MS., and is unnecessary. In any case the meaning of the passage is 'make a demand to have the house legally conveyed under a clear title.' Plautus here, as in many other places, altogether forgets that a Greek is speaking who would not employ the technical phrases of Roman law. Since houses were *Res Mancupi*, the *Dominium* or absolute right of property could in ancient times be conveyed to a purchaser by the ceremony of *Mancupatio* only, and hence the phrases *mancupio promittere, dare mancupio, accipere mancupio, poscere mancupio.* There is a good illustration in Trin. II. iv. 19, *Minas quadraginta accepisti a Callicle, Et illi aedis aps te accepit mancupio.* Slaves also were *Res Mancupi*, and when a slave was made over to a new master by *mancupatio* it was held as a guarantee that the seller possessed *dominium*, or absolute right of property in the slave, and if, under any circumstances, it afterwards turned out that he did not really possess any such right, then he was bound to reimburse the purchaser.[*] If however the slave was sold without *mancupatio*, then the buyer made the purchase *suo periculo*, at his own risk, and had no recourse upon the seller. Thus in the Persa, where the plot turns upon the fraudulent

---

[*] Hence *Manceps* signifies one who becomes security, Curc. IV. ii. 29, *Ego mancipem te nihil moror nec leronem alium quemquam.*

sale of a free Greek damsel to a leno under the pretext that she had been kidnapped and brought from the most remote regions of Arabia, the terms on which she is offered for sale expressly exclude *mancupatio* (IV. lii. 55), *Ac suo periclo is emat, qui eam mercabitur, Mancupio neque promittet, neque quisquam dabit,* and therefore Dordalus at first objects to the proposal, *Nihil mihi opus est Litibus neque tricis: quamobrem ego argentum numerem foras? Nisi mancupio accipio, quid eo mihi opus mercimonio?* but when he is at last persuaded he is reminded (iv. 40), *Prius dico hanc mancupio nemo tibi dabit,* and after the price has been settled, *v.* 113, *Tuo periculo sexaginta haec datur argenti minis;* and when eventually the trick is disclosed he is obliged to acquiesce in the loss of his money, glad to escape a prosecution for trafficking in free maidens. So in Merc. II. iii. 112, Charinus endeavours to avoid selling Pasicompsa by urging that he has no legal title, *Non ego illam mancupio accepi.* See Curc. IV. ii. 8, V. ii. 19; Bac. I. I. 59 *tibi me emancupo,* 'I make myself over to you absolutely;' and so Mil. I. 23.

32. *Hic ego tibi praesidebo: ne interbitat quaestio*] i. e. 'lest the examination should fall through,' i. e. 'should fail,' where *interbitat* is equivalent to *intereat.* The simple verb *bito,* which seems to have the same force as *eo,* both as a simple verb and in composition, is found once or twice in Plautus. Thus Curc. I. ii. 51, *Qui me in terra aeque fortunatus erit, si illa ad me bitet;* and Merc. II. iii. 117, *Ad portum ne bitas, dico iam tibi. C. Auscultabitur. Bitat* in Mil. IV. ii. 7 is a conj. emend.; so also *bitere* in Pseud. I. iii. 23. We find also several compounds; Capt. II. iii. 30, *Si non rebitas huc, ut viginti minas Dem pro te (rebitas=redeas);* III. iv. 72, *Namque edepol si adbites propius os denasabit tibi (adbites=adibis);* Rud. II. vi. 11, *Vtinam te prius quam oculis vidissem meis, Malo cruciatu in Siciliam perbiteres (i. e. perires);* Stich. IV. ii. 28, *Non it, non it, quia tanto opere suades ne ebitat,* where *ebitat* would be admissible; Pseud. III. i. 12, *Eum cras cruciatu maxumo perbitere (perbitere=periturum esse);* Poen. V. iii. 44, *A. Quid, si eamus illis obviam? H. At ne inter vias Praeterbitamus, metuo,* where *praeterbitamus* would be admissible. In all the above passages except two the penultimate of *bito* must be long; in the two excepted the long quantity is equally admissible, and therefore there can be no doubt as to the quantity.* Nonius,

* There is yet another example in Plautus, viz. *abitat,* which is quoted by Freund as *abito:* the line is in Rud. III. iv. 72, *Hunc quoque adservo ipsum, ut quo abitat, nam promisimus,* which is a Troch. Tetr. Cat., and scansion demands that we should pronounce *abitat.*

p. 77, presents the words under the form of *beto:* "*Betere*, id est, ire:" and quotes from Varro, *mulierem foras betere iussit;* and from Pacuvius, *si ire conor, prohibet betere.* There is a second quotation from Pacuvius, but it is so corrupt as not to be available. Etymologists would connect *bito* or *beto* with βῆμι βαίνω, etc.

37. *Nescis quam meticulosa res sit ire ad iudicem.*] *Meticulosus,* 'full of fear,' from *metus.* The word is found again in Amph. I. i. 137, *Nullus est hoc meticulosus aeque;* and reappears in the writings of Apuleius Florid. I. 2, § 2. Observe that in the Most. the word signifies 'causing fear,' in the Amph. 'feeling fear,' in Apuleius it is applied as an epithet of the hare (*leporem meticulosum*).

V. iii. 1. *Vbi somnum sepelivi omnem atque obdormivi crapulam.*] *Crapula,* which is identical with the Greek κραιπάλη, signifies properly the headache and nausea which follow a drunken debauch. Plautus employs it again in Pseud. V. i. 35 and in Rud. II. vii. 28: in the latter passage we read, *Quin abeo hinc in Veneris fanum, ut edormiscam hanc crapulam,* whence many edd. substitute *edormivi* for *obdormivi* in our text. *Crapula* is found also in Cicero, Livy, and Pliny. The adjective *crapularius* appears in Stich. I. iii. 74, *Vel unctiones Graecas sudatorias Vendo, vel alias malacas crapularias:*[*] *crapulentus* and *crapulosus* occur in late writers only.

9. *De cena facio gratiam*] i.e. 'thank you, excuse me.' This was the formula when a person wished politely to decline an invitation, and is exactly represented by the French *je vous remercie* and the Italian *grazia,* which, when used in reply to an offer or invitation, always signify 'no, I thank you.' The phrase is varied in Men. II. iii. 36, *E. Eamus intro, ut prandeamus. M. Bene vocas: tam gratia est,* i.e. 'you are very kind'—'(I must decline, but) I am obliged to you all the same;' and so again in Stich. III. ii. 17, *Cenabis apud me, quoniam salvos advenis. E. Vocata est opera nunc quidem: tam gratia est,* 'I am engaged, but I am obliged to you all the same;' in Trin. II. ii. 14, *Hi mores maiorum laudant, Eosdem lutulant, quos collaudant, hisce ego te artibus gratiam Facio, neu colas, neu imbuas ingenium:* i.e. 'from following such practices I excuse you.'

23. *enim istic captio est.*] *Enim* here indicates an aposiopesis. We must supply, 'no, I thank you, for there is fraud in that proposal of yours.' The same words occur in the same sense in Epid. V. ii. 36. For the word *Captio* see note on IV. ii. 19.

[*] This at least is the reading of the Ambrosian Palimpsest. BCD have *vel alias mala rastra pallarias.*

36. *illunc oetatem*] I. e. 'youth;' so Bac. III. iii. 5, *Minus mirandum est, illaec aetas si quid illorum facit, Quam si non faciat : feci ego istaec itidem in adulescentia.*

41. *neque quicquam succenseo*] 'nor do I retain any lurking grudge on any account;' so Bac. III. iv. 27, *Eadem exorabo, Chrusalo causa mea Pater ne noceat, neu quid ei succenseat;* and in IV. iv. 39 Mnesilochus assures Chrysalus that he had prevailed upon his father . . . *tibi ne noceat, neu quid ob eam rem succenseat.* The full construction is *succensere alicui aliquid* or *ob aliquam rem*, but it is frequently used with one case only, or without a case, and frequently signifies simply 'to be angry.' Thus As. I. ii. 20, II. ii. 87, 105, iv. 53 ; Bac. III. vi. 4; Capt. III. v. 11, 22, V. l. 23 ; Men. V. vii. 58; Merc. II. ii. 46, V. iii. 15, iv. 52 ; Mil. III. i. 102 ; Pers. III. iii. 26 ; Poen. I. ii. 157; Pseud. I. v. 56, 57 ; Stich. IV. ii. 20 ; Trin. V. ii. 40, 42, 60 ; Truc. V. 6.

47. *Tranioni remitte, quaeso, hanc noxiam.*] Cf. Poen. I. ii. 191, *Verum etiam tibi hanc amittam noxiam unam, Agorastocles, Non sum irata.*

EXCVRSVS.

I.—*ADEO*.

This word, as exhibited in some of our best dictionaries, presents a somewhat formidable aspect. In that of Freund, for example, what with classifications and divisions and subdivisions, the meanings are distributed under seventeen or eighteen heads, and no pains have been taken to connect them by a common bond. Let us endeavour to simplify the matter.

It cannot reasonably be doubted that *adeo* is compounded of *ad* and *eo*. The Roman grammarians, while admitting this etymology, were embarrassed by the consideration that *ad*, a preposition governing the accusative, should be followed by an ablative *eo*. Thus Paulus Diaconus s. v., p. 19, ed. Müll., while distinguishing *adeo* the verb from *adeo* the adverb, remarks with regard to the latter—" idem (significat) quod *usque eo*, non quidem secundum rationem, quia *ad* praepositio accusativis accommodata est, sed vetusta quadam loquendi consuetudine"—a practice, as Müller observes, similar to that which prevails in the words *praeterea, propterea, hacpropter, quoad, adquo,*[*] &c. Avoiding all etymological speculations as to the form *eo*, but taking it for granted that *adeo* is made up of *ad* and *eo*, it will be necessary, in the first place, to examine the meanings of *eo*. These, although at first sight various, may all be reduced to two.

I. *Eo* signifying 'to that.'

II. *Eo* signifying 'by that.'

I. *Eo* signifying 'to that' is used directly with reference to place in such phrases as *eo se recipere coeperunt*, i.e. 'they began to betake themselves thither (to that place);' and so *eo pervenire, eo reverti*, &c. —it is used with reference to time in *eo usque me vivere vultis donec; eoque usque dum ea nascantur ad Casilinum sessurus sum*—it is used

---

[*] See Non. Marc. s. v. *adquo*, p. 76.

A 2

generally in *eo accessit*, ' to that was added.' So *eodem* may mean ' to the same place' and ' to the same person.'

Since *eo* may signify ' to that place,' the place may, in certain cases, be regarded as the extreme point or limit of progression, and hence, when followed by *ut*, it frequently signifies ' to that (such a) point,' ' to that (such a) pitch,' ' to that (such an) extent,' &c., as in the phrases, *urbs eo crevit ut magnitudine laboret sua*, ' the city has increased to that point,' or ' to such an extent;' *eo rem adducam ut*, &c., ' I will bring the matter to that (such a) point;' *eo furoris processit*, ' he advanced to that point (such a pitch) of phrenzy,' &c.

From the idea of moving or travelling towards a certain place or point, the transition is easy to the notion of ' keeping an object in view.' Hence, figuratively, *eo* denotes the direction in which the thoughts or actions move, and hence ' a purpose, ' an intention,' ' a design,' being in this case followed by *quo*, *ut*, *ne*, *quin*, or the like. This is clearly brought out in the expressions—*eo scripsi quo plus auctoritatis haberem*—*literas ad te eo misi ut*—*eo te non interpellavi ne*—*non eo hoc dico quin quae tu vis ego velim et faciam lubens*. So *eodem* signifies ' to the same purpose' in the phrase *eodem pertinere*.

II. *Eo* signifying ' by that.' When we read in Livy—*Nocte et mittebantur et perveniebant : eo custodias hostium fallebant*—*eo* signifies ' by that,' ' by that mode of procedure,' ' by doing that,' and it serves to explain a previous statement. Hence *eo* is frequently equivalent to ' thus' or *hoc modo*, ' for this reason,' ' therefore;' and when Cicero says, *frater es, eo terreor, eo* is explanatory, and means ' for that reason,' ' therefore;' and again, *dederam triduo ante literas ad te, eo ero brevior*. So *eo* when joined with a comparative signifies ' by that' in the sense of *tanto—eo gravior est dolor, quo culpa maior*—and so *eo magis, eo minus*, ' by that (so much) the more,' ' by that (so much) the less.'

This being premised with regard to *eo*, it will be found, as might have been expected, that *adeo* resembles it very closely in meaning. Indeed, in many cases, *eo* might be substituted for *adeo* and vice versa, without the sense being perceptibly changed. The different meanings of *adeo* may be ranged under three heads.

1. *Adeo* equivalent to *praeterea*, and signifying simply ' in addition to that.'

II. *Adeo* signifying ' up to that point.'

III. *Adeo* signifying ' thus,' ' in that way,' ' therefore.'

We shall select some of the most striking examples of the multifarious meanings ascribed by Freund and others to *adeo*, and

endeavour to show that the whole can, without violence, be arranged
under one or other of the above three heads.

I. *Adeo* equivalent to *ad ea*, *praeterea*, 'in addition,' 'besides,'
'moreover,' 'also.'* Rud. IV. iv. 122, *Qui te Di omnes perdant, qui
me hodie oculis vidisti tuis, Meque adeo scelestum qui non circumspexi
venties*, i.e. 'and me also;' Amph. II. ii. 44, *Amphitruo uxorem
salutat laetus speratam suam, Quam omnium Thebis vir unam esse
optumam diiudicat, Quamque adeo cives Thebani vero rumificant pro-
bam*, i.e. 'and whom the citizens of Thebes also;' Eun. I. ii. 124, *Et
quidquid huius feci, causa virginis Feci: nam me eius spero fratrem
propemodum Iam repperisse, adulescentem adeo nobilem*, i.e. 'for I
hope that I have discovered her brother, a young man moreover of
good family;' Andr. III. iii. 47, *Tute adeo iam eius verba audis,*
'and you yourself moreover,' 'more than that, you with your own
ears shall hear his words;'† Hec. II. i. 42, *Tuae esse ego illi mores
morbum magis quam ullam aliam rem arbitror Et merito adeo, nam, &c.*,
i.e. 'and with good reason too.' Such seems to be the force of *adeo*
in a fragment of the *Medea Exsul* of Ennius, quoted by Probus on
Virg. Ecl. VI. 31, *Iuppiter, tuque adeo summe Sol, qui omnes res inspicis*,
i.e. 'thou Jove, and thou also Sol, high above all;' and in the invocation at the beginning of the first Georgic, where the poet, after
addressing the gods of the sky, of earth, and of ocean, turns his
prayer to Caesar (*v.* 24), *Tuque adeo quem mox*, 'and on thee also
do I call.' We may, perhaps, place under the same head, Virg. Ecl.
IV. 11, *Teque adeo, decus hoc aevi, te consule, inibit, Pollio : et incipient
magni procedere menses*, i.e. 'and in addition to all the other propitious
combinations of this happy epoch, the boy will enter upon his career
in thy consulship, O Pollio,' &c. Virg. Ecl. II. 25 is more doubtful;
Nec sum adeo informis, which we may translate, 'and besides, I am
by no means unshapely,' but we may refer this example to the next
section, an ellipse being implied, 'and I am not so (to such an extent)
ugly (as to make me repulsive).'

II. *Adeo* equivalent to 'up to that point or limit,' 'to that (such a)
degree or extent,' 'to that (such a) pitch or pass,' meanings, as

* Freund says that *adeo* occurs in this sense in the comic writers only.
He quotes two examples—Pseud. I. ii. 80, where, according to my view, it
signifies 'thus,' 'in this way,' and Most. III. i. 101 (97), where, whatever
it may denote, it cannot possibly mean *ad bene* or *praeterea*. See note
on the passage. It will appear from the quotations which we shall give
that *adeo* in this sense is found not only in the comic writers, but in the
tragedies of Ennius and in Virgil.

† Here Donatus says " παρέλκεται *adeo*, modo et abundat."

explained above, belonging to *eo* when it means 'to that.' *Adeo* in this sense is sometimes used absolutely; it is frequently followed by *ut*, by adverbs of time as *dum*, *donec*, and in combination with *usque*.

1. Absolutely, in Heaut. I. i. 61, *Postremo adeo res rediit, adulescentulus Saepe eadem et graviter audiendo victus est*, i. e. 'at last the matter came to this point;' Phor. I. ii. 4, *G. Amo te, et non neclexisse habeo gratiam. P. Praesertim ut nunc sunt mores, adeo res redit, Si quis quid reddit, magna habenda est gratia*, i. e. 'things now-a-days have come to such a pass;' V. vii. 39, *I in malam rem hinc cum istac magnificentia, Fugitive: etiam nunc credis te ignorarier Aut tua facta adeo?* i. e. 'to such an extent.'

2. *Adeo* followed by *ut*, signifying 'as:' Epid. IV. i. 38, *Ille eam rem adeo sobrie et frugaliter Adcuravit, ut alias res est inpense inprobus*, i. e. 'to the same extent (or, in the same degree) as he is in other matters utterly good-for-nothing,' 'he was praiseworthy in this matter to the same extent as he is the reverse in other matters;' Andr. I. v. 10, *Adeone hominem esse invenustum aut infelicem quemquam ut ego sum!* 'lives there the man hateful to Venus and unfortunate to such an extent as I am!'

3. *Adeo* followed by *ut*, signifying 'that:' Capt. Prol. 65, *Ego faciam ut pugnam inspectet non bonam Adeo ut spectare postea omnes oderit*, 'to such an extent that;' Bac. II. iii. 49, *Adione me fuisse fungum ut qui illi crederem!* 'to think that I should have been such a mushroom (blockhead) that I believed him,' 'a blockhead to such an extent that,' &c.; Andr. I. i. 93, *Si. Forte unam adspicio adulescentulam Forma— So. Bona fortasse. Si. Et voltu, Sosia, Adeo modesto, adeo venusto, ut nihil supra;* Hec. II. i. 24, *Iampridem equidem audivi, accepisse odium tui Philumenam, Minumeque adeo mirum: et, ni id fecisset, magis mirum foret: Sed non credidi adeo ut etiam totam hunc odisset domum.* The first *adeo* means 'so far,' 'to that extent,' *adeo ut* in the next line 'to such a degree that,' or 'to such an extent that.'

4. *Adeo* followed by *usque*, *dum*, *donec*, &c.: Bac. III. iv. 10, *Adeo ego illam cogam usque ut mendicet meus pater*, 'I will press (my gifts) upon her even to the extent that I will make a beggar of my father;' Merc. Prol. 77, *Adeo dum, quae tum haberet, peperisset bona*, 'up to the point (of time) when,' &c.; and so III. iv. 72; Amph. I. ii. 10, *Adeo usque satietatem dum capiet frater Illius, quam amat;* Andr. IV. i. 38, *numquam destitit Instare, ut dicerem me esse ducturum patri; Suadere, orare, usque adeo donec perpulit.*

We have *usque adeo quoad* in Cic. pro Sest. XXXVIII. § 82, and *usque adeo quo*, 'up to the point where,' in Cato R. R. XI. § 13.

5. Again, *adeo ut*, like *eo ut*, frequently refers to an object kept in view, a design, a purpose : Rud. V. iii. 31, *dandum huic argentum est probum, Id ego continuo huic dabo, adeo me ut hic emittat manu,* i. e. 'with the intent that;' Stich. V. iv. 15, *Atque adeo ut tu scire possis, factum ego tecum divido,* 'and with the intent that you may be able to trust in my sincerity,' &c.; Aul. III. ii. 27, *Adeo ut tu meam sententiam iam iam noscere possis,* i. e. 'to the intent that you may be able to become acquainted forthwith with my views,' &c.; IV. x. 8, *Fateor precarisse. et me culpam commeritum scio, Id adeo te oratum advenio ut animo aequo ignoscas mihi.* The combination here is somewhat more complicated, but this may be designed to express the confusion and agitation of the speaker; the general meaning is, 'I have come with the intention of entreating your forgiveness.'

III. *Adeo* equivalent to *eo modo, ea ratione,* is used for the most part with an explanatory force, 'in that way,' 'thus,' 'such being the case,' 'therefore,' 'then.'

When *adeo* is translated by 'therefore' or by 'then,' the former of these is not to be regarded as necessarily denoting a strict logical deduction, nor the latter as denoting with emphasis a particular point of time, but both are used like the Greek οὖν to indicate a sequence of events, or the continuation of an action or of a narrative, as when we say, 'after many dangers therefore Hannibal descended from the Alps into the plains of Italy,' 'let reason then at her own quarry fly,' 'we first leave childhood behind us, then youth, then the years of ripened manhood, then' &c. *There* is properly an adverb of place, *then* of time, but they are not unfrequently regarded as equivalent. Thus in the Gospel of St. John, cap. ii. 18, the words ἀπεκρίθησαν οὖν οἱ Ἰουδαῖοι are translated in our authorized version, 'then answered the Jews and said unto him,' but in Wicliffe's Bible, 'therfor the Jewis answerden and seiden to him;' and this brings us round to what may be regarded as the original etymological meaning of *adeo,* viz. *adea, praeterea,* 'besides,' 'moreover.'

The meanings of *adeo* which belong to head III. must be illustrated by several examples, for they have in many cases embarrassed lexicographers and commentators, and have led to useless complications, or, not seldom, to the despairing remark, "*adeo* abundat," i. c. 'means nothing :' Epid. V. ii. 38, *P. Dedin tibi minus triginta ob filiam ? E. Fateor datas, Et eo argento illam me emisse amicam fili fidicinam, Pro tua filia : istis adeo te lelgi triginta minis,* 'in that way,' 'thus,' *eo (hoc) modo;* As. II. iii. 22, Libanus having given a minute description of the personal appearance of Saurea, the

mercator exclaims, *Non potuit pictor rectius describere eius formam,
Atque hercle ipsum adeo contuor, quassanti capite incedit,* 'and, by
Hercules, I see the man himself as you describe him' (*adeo=eo modo
quo*); Hec. IV. iv. 68, *Cui tu opsecutus, facis huic adeo iniuriam,*
'yielding to her, you in this way do wrong to your own wife;' and
so Epid. II. i. 2; Amph. l. i. 98, *Hoc adeo hoc commemini magis, quia
illo die inpransus fui,* 'this event, in this way, upon this account, have
I described the more minutely because on that day I went without
my breakfast;' Aul. IV. ii. 15, *Multi congialem plenam faciam tibi
fideliam, Id adeo tibi faciam, verum ego mihi bibam, ubi id fecero,* 'the
cup will I thus compound in honour of you, but I will drink it in
honour of myself;' Curc. V. iii. 1, *Argentariis male credi, qui aiunt,
nugas praedicant, Nam et bene et male credi dico, id adeo hodie ego
expertus sum,* 'and thus have I found the matter to be this day by
experience;' Aul. II. iv. 12, *Cuius ducit filiam? S. Vicini huius
Euclionis e praximo, Ei adeo opsoni hinc dimidium iussit dari,* where
adeo='thus,' 'for this reason;' Poen. I. ii. 56, speaking of females
of the lowest class, *Miseras, schoeno delibutas, servicolas sordidas, Quas
tibi olant stabulum, statumque, sellam et assibulum merum, Quas adeo
haud quisquam umquam liber tetigit, neque duxit domum,* 'whom,
thus,' 'for that reason;' Stich. I. iii. 59, *Quot adeo cenas, quas deflevi,
mortuae!* and c. 62, *Prae maerore adeo miser atque aegritudine
Consenui,*—in both cases *adeo*='thus,' 'in this way,' *hoc modo;* and
so also in Eun. II. ii. 16, *Hoc novom est aucupium: ego adeo hanc
primus inveni viam,* and then follows a description of the *novom
aucupium;* Epid. I. i. 51, Epidicus having extracted from Thesprio
the fact that Stratippocles had paid a large sum for a female captive,
Thesprio goes on, *Id adeo argentum ab Danista apud Thebas sumpsit
faenore In dies minasque argenti singulas numis:* here *adeo* may be
regarded as serving to continue and connect the details of the story,
'and that money then;' or *adeo* may refer to the terms upon which the
money was borrowed, 'and that money he obtained from a money-
lender thus (*hoc modo*), upon condition of paying a numus a-day for
each mina;' Andr. II. vi. 7, *S. Num illi molestae quidpiam hae sunt
nuptiae, Propter huiusce hospitae consuetudinem? D. Nihil, hercle: aut,
si adeo, bidui est aut tridui Haec sollicitudo,* 'no, he does not mind
it at all, or if he feels at all thus, if he has any feeling of this sort,
the annoyance will be an affair of two days, or three (at most);' Cas.
V. iv. 22, *Si umquam posthac aut amasso Casinam, aut occepso modo
Ne ut eam amasso, si ego umquam adeo posthac tale admitero;* here
adeo seems to explain or connect. 'if ever then,' 'if ever, I say.'

Heaut. I. i. 1, *Quamquam haec inter nos nuper notitia admodum est Inde adeo quod agrum in proxumo hic mercatus es;* here *adeo* is explanatory, 'arising in this way;' and in the same sense *v.* 57, *Nulla adeo ex re istuc fit, nisi ex nimio otio,* 'from no other cause do matters go on thus,' 'in this way;' Amph. Prol. 72, *Sive adeo aediles perfidiose quoi duint,* 'or whether in this manner (i.e. from influence, and not on account of merit) the aediles have corruptly bestowed the prize on any competitor;' Merc. V. iv. 33, *Si, Hercle, scivissem, sive adeo ioculo dixisset mihi Se illam amare,* 'if he had thus (to this effect) spoken to me in jest;' Truc. IV. iii. 1, *Egone tibi male dicam, aut tibi adeo male velim?* 'is it possible that I should abuse you, or wish you evil after this fashion;' Hec. IV. i. 9, *Vir ego tuus sum? Tun virum me, aut hominem deputas adeo esse,* 'am I your husband? do you regard me as your husband? or, (treating me) in this way, do you behave towards me as to any ordinary man?' Andr. IV. iv. 20, *D. Adeone videmur vobis esse idonei In quibus sic inludatis? C. Veni in tempore. D. Propera adeo puerum tollere hinc ab ianua:* here the first *adeo* signifies 'to such an extent,' the second 'then' or 'therefore,' and expresses impatience, 'make haste, then, can't you.'

Nunc adeo is a very common combination, and in this phrase *adeo* must be generally translated 'therefore' or 'such being the case:' Mil. II. ii. 4, *Nunc adeo edico omnibus,* 'now then,' 'now therefore,' 'now, this being the case;' Merc. II. ii. 67, *Quin mihi quoque etiam est ad portum negotium, Nunc adeo ibo illuc,* 'now therefore,' 'now, such being the case;' Rud. III. iv. 23, *Do tibi argentum? Nunc adeo ut scias meam sententiam,* 'I give you money? now therefore,' &c.; and *adeo* three lines lower down may also be translated 'therefore,' or 'such being the case.' So As. III. i. 29, Men. I. ii. 11, Pseud. I. ii. 52, Truc. II. ii. 12, Andr. IV. iv. 36.

Less common is *adeo quasi:* Heaut. V. i. 12, *C. Quid ait? Gaudere adeo coepit quasi qui cupiunt nuptias,* 'he began to rejoice in the same manner as those (eo modo quo) who are eager for,' &c.; here *adeo* might be referred to our second head, 'to the same extent,' 'in the same degree as if he were one of these,' &c.

We find also *numquam adeo quin:* Adel. II. ii. 13, *Credo istuc melius esse: verum ego numquam adeo astutus fui Quin, quidquid possem, mallem auferre potius in praesentia,* 'I never attained to such a pitch of cunning as to refrain,' &c.

The following deserve attention: Amph. I. ii. 4, *Iam ille illuc ad herum quom Amphitruonem advenerit, Narrabit servom hinc sese ex foribus Sosiam Amovisse. Ille adeo illum mentiri sibi Credet, neque credit huc profectum ut iusserat:* here *adeo* is explanatory, 'In this way,' 'thus,' 'thus it will come to pass that Amphitruo will believe that Sosia is telling him a falsehood.' Bac. IV. vii. 30, *Tum libertatem Chrusalo largibere Ego adeo numquam accipiam:* here *adeo* continues, connects, and to a certain degree explains the narrative, 'upon that you will generously bestow freedom upon Chrysalus; I then (thereafter, upon that), you understand, will refuse to accept it.' So Mil. IV. iv. 55, *Ille iubebit me ire cum illa ad portum: ego adeo, ut tu scias Prorsum Athenas protinus abibo tecum:* this example closely resembles the preceding, 'he will order me to go along with her to the harbour, I then (thereafter), you understand, will depart with you,' &c.; Truc. IV. iii. 73, *Cetrum uxorem, quam primum potest, abduce ex aedibus, Ego adeo iam illi remittam nuntium adfini meo:* precisely similar to the two preceding.

We believe that the examples quoted above, if carefully examined, will enable a young scholar to give a satisfactory explanation of *adeo* in the writings of the Latin Classics, to whatever period they belong.

II.—*DVM.*

Dum is strictly an adverb of time, and may be regarded as in all cases equivalent to one of two English words.

I. 'Now,' 'at this present time.'

II. 'While,' applied generally to time, with its compounds 'whilst,' 'until,' 'till' (while-es, unto-while, to-while?).

1. *Dum* signifying 'now:' Trin. V. ii. 1, *Neque fuit, neque erit, neque esse quemquam hominum in terra dum arbitror,* 'nor do I believe that there is at this present time on earth,' where, however, it must be remarked that *in terra dum* is an emendation of Camerarius, for the MSS. exhibit *interdum,* which is not intelligible; Epid. III. iii. 7, *Vel quasi egomet qui dum fili causa coeperam Ego me excruciare animi,* 'I who at this very time had begun;' iv. 68, *P. Vbi habitat* (sc. *Acropolistis)? F. Postquam libera est, ubi Habitet dum, incerto scio,* 'where she may be living now, at this time, since she became free:' here again the text exhibits variations.

In the following examples we have *etiam dum* in negative propositions, 'not even now,' 'not even yet,' 'not even now at this present time:' Truc. II. ii. 66, *Tristis exit; haud convenit etiam hic dum Phronesium,* 'not even now has he had an interview with Phronesium;' Pseud. IV. ii. 2, *nihil etiam dum harpagavit praeter cuathum et canthorum,* 'nothing even at this present time (i. e. as yet) has be stolen except,' &c. In Merc. II. iii. 14, 15, we have a double *dum*, signifying 'now' and 'now again,' like *modo* .... *modo* or *nunc* .... *nunc*, *Dum servi mei perplacet mihi consilium, Dum rursum haud placet*.

Very frequently *dum* is subjoined to the imperative, and in that case may always be rendered by 'now;' thus Most. III. i. 144 (141), *pulta dum fores*, 'knock at the door now;' v. 149 (146), *evoca dum aliquem*, 'call some one out now;' V. i. 56 (ii. 41), *aspice dum contra me*, 'look me now in the face.' So Heaut. II. iii. 8, *Abi dum*; Rud. V. ii. 45, *Accede dum huc*; Men. II. iii. 35, *Accipe dum hoc*; Andr. I. i. 2, *Ades dum*; Stich. I. i. 9, *Sed hic, mea soror, adsis dum*, 'come beside now for a while; Rud. III. v. 6, *et passim Age dum*; Bac. IV. iv. 93, *Adscribe dum*; Rud. IV. iv. 133, *Capedum*; Men. II. i. 40, *Cedo dum mihi huc marsupium*; Trin. IV. ii. 126, *Cedo dum istuc aurum mihi*; Hec. V. iii. 5, *Die dum*; Rud. IV. iii. 84, *Fac dum ex te sciam*, 'come, tell me now;' Cas. III. i. 9, Heaut. III. ii. 39, *Facito dum memineris*, 'see now that you recollect;' Rud. III. v. 7, *Iube dum*; Cas. II. vi. 32, *Mane dum*; Bac. IV. vi. 24, *Mane dum parumper*; Truc. II. vii. 67, *Sine dum*; or with *me* interposed, Most. V. ii. 22 (iii. 22), *Sine me dum istuc iudicare*, 'permit me now at present;' Men. II. iii. 27, *Sed sine me dum hanc compellare*; ii. 73, *Tace dum parumper*; Rud. III. v. 17, *Tange dum*, 'touch them now' (if you dare). So *Qui dum* signifies 'how now?' 'how so?' 'why so?' and is generally introduced when an explanation is required: thus Most. II. ii. 20, *Quid vos? insanin estis? T. Qui dum?* 'how now?' i.e. 'what do you mean by that?' See also III. ii. 44, V. i. 58 (ii. 16); As. III. iii. 30; Bac. III. iii. 62; Epid. II. ii. 114; Men. I. ii. 51; Trin. I. ii. 129; Truc. IV. ii. 19; Eun. II. ii. 42; Hec. III. i. 39.

Dum signifying 'now' is frequently subjoined to other adverbs; thus Most. I. ii. 39, *Primum dum*, 'first of all now,' 'to begin now;' and so Rud. Prol. 32, Trin. I. ii. 61. In Pseud. II. iv. 40, *Nec dum exiit ex aedibus*, 'nor (even) now has he gone out of the house,' 'nor as yet;' and in much the same sense, *nihil etiam dum*, in Pseud. IV. ii. 2; *haud etiam dum*, in Truc. II. ii. 66. See also Mil. IV. ii. 2, Eun. III. v. 22.

Non dum properly signifies 'not now,' and so 'not yet.'

Ne dum, which generally implies a comparison, is, for the most part, used elliptically; thus Heaut. III. i. 43, *Satrapes si siet Amator, numquam subferre eius sumptus queat, Ne dum tu possis*, 'if a Persian potentate were her lover, he would never be able to support her

extravagance, (therefore) do not you now imagine that you are able.' *
Eho dum dic mihi, 'hearken now, tell me,' in Eun. II. iii. 68; Andr.
III. v. 10. *Vix dum* is 'scarcely now.' *Dum* in *interdum* belongs
rather to the next head, 'between whiles,' &c.

II. *Dum* signifying 'while.'

The meaning of 'while' is variously modified.

1. 'While' often signifies 'at the time when,' 'during the time that ;'
thus in English, 'while you are reading I shall take a walk ;' Andr. I.
v. 31, *Dum in dubio est animus, paulo momento huc vel illuc inpellitur*,
'while (at the time when) the mind is in a state of hesitation ;' Eun. II.
iii. 49, *Dum haec dicit, abiit hora ; rogo num quid velit*, 'while (during
the time that) he was saying these things, time slipped away ;' Epid.
III. iv. 65, *Conducta veni ut fidibus cantarem seni Dum rem divinam
faceret*, 'while (during the time that) he might be offering sacrifice ;'
and so Pseud. V. i. 33, *dum enitor*.

2. 'While' is employed when an event is represented as resulting
from the time spent or pains bestowed in doing something else : thus
in English, 'while attending to the affairs of others I sacrificed my
own interests,' where 'while' implies 'in consequence of' or 'in consequence of the time I spent ;' Andr. V. i. 3, *Dum studeo opsequi tibi,
paene inlusi vitam filiae ;* Adel. V. vii. 1, *Occidunt me quidem dum nimis
sanctas nuptias Student facere ;* Phor. I. ii. 26, *Seni fideli dum sum,
scapulas perdidi';* V. ii. 2, *Nostrapte culpa facimus, ut malos expediat
esse, Dum nimium dici nos bonos studemus et benignos*.

3. 'While' meaning 'till' or 'until.' Whether we accept or reject
the etymology of Horne Tooke, who regards *till* as *to while*, and
until as *unto while*, there can be no doubt that in the earlier forms
of our language 'while' was used as equivalent to 'until :' thus, *Then
he commanded her to be bounden to a wylde horse tayle by the here
of her hedde, and so to be drawen whyle she was dede ;* and in some
provincial dialects such phrases as *I will stay while evening* are said
to be still current.† For instances of *dum* in this signification, see
Rud. II. ii. 22, *Nunc quid mihi melius est, quam ilico hic opperiar,
herum dum veniat ;* Trin. I. ii. 133, *Lupus opservavit dum dormitaret
canes ;* Eun. III. iii. 28, *At tu apud nos hic mane Dum redeat ipsa ;*
Andr. II. i. 28, *Saltem aliquot dies Profer, dum proficiscor aliquo, ne
videam ;* Heaut. IV. iii. 39, *Vnus est dies, dum argentum eripio : pax :*

---

* *Ne* has this force without the addition of *dum*, e.g. Aul. III. ii. 20,
Cas. V. iv. 15.

† See Horne Tooke, Diversions of Purley, Part 1. chap. 9, p. 142,
ed. 1819.

nihil amplius. The following combination is unusual: Heaut. III. ii.
32, *Et nunc quid expectas, Syre? an dum hinc denuo Abeas, quom
tolerare huius sumptus non queat?* 'is he waiting until.'

Perhaps, wherever *dum*, standing alone, signifies 'until,' there may
be an ellipse of *usque* or some such word, and this is sometimes
supplied; Pers. 1. i. 53, *Vsque ero domi dum excoxero lenoni malum,*
'up to the time when;' Merc. Prol. 77, *Adeo dum, quae tum haberet,
peperisset bona,* 'he said that he had persevered in this course, up to
the time when (until) he had acquired the property of which he was
then in possession.' See this line quoted above, under *adeo* (p. 180).

4. 'While' indicating duration of time, 'as long as,' 'so long as,' as
in English, 'I shall love him while he lives,' i.e. 'as long as he
lives;' Truc. II. i. 23, *Dum habeat tum amet; ubi nihil habeat, alium
quaestum coepiat;* Rud. II. vi. 73, *Quid, stulte, ploras? tibi quidem edepol
copia est, Dum lingua vivet, qui rem solvas omnibus;* Eun. IV. v. 2,
*Atat! data hercle verba mihi sunt: vicit vinum quod bibi; At, dum
adcubabam, quam videbar mihi esse pulcre sobrius! Postquam surrexi,
neque pes, neque mens satis suum officium facit,* 'as long as I was
reclining at table;' Heaut. V. v. 14, *Haec dum incipias gravia sunt,
Dumque ignores, ubi cognoris, facilia:* the first *dum* may be rendered
'until' or 'while,' the second 'so long as.'

Dum when used in this sense is sometimes preceded by *tantisper,*
and thus is closely connected with 'until;' Truc. Prol. 11, *Athenae
istae sunto, ita ut hoc est proscenium, Tantisper dum transigimus hanc
Comoediam;* Heaut. I. i. 54, *Ego te meum esse dici tantisper volo,
Dum quod te dignum est facies;* and so again, v. 95, *Decrevi tantisper
me minus iniuriae, Chreme, meo gnato facere, dum fiam miser;* and so
paulisper dum, Cic. pro Mil. 10.

In like manner *usque adeo* sometimes precedes *dum;* Eun. IV. vi. 4,
*Vsque adeo ego illius ferre possum ineptias et magnifica verba, Verba
dum sint; verum enim si ad rem conferentur vapulabit.*

For other examples of *dum* signifying 'as long as,' see Eun. V.
iv. 12; Phor. V. viii. 41; Heaut. II. iii. 104, IV. iii. 36, V. i. 78;
Andr. III. iii. 24, V. i. 13.

5. It frequently happens that when 'while' means 'as long as,' a
condition is implied, and hence the transition to 'provided that' is
easy: thus when we say, 'while the child is obedient he will not be
punished,' it is much the same as 'provided that the child be obedient' &c. *Dum* is common with this force, and is in this case always
followed by the subjunctive; Pers. 1. iii. 66, *Quaeso, hercle, me quoque
etiam vendas, si lubet, Dum saturum vendas,* 'provided always that you

sell me with a well-filled stomach;' Trin. IV. ii. 137, *Dum ille ne sis, quem ego esse nolo, sis, mea causa, qui lubet;* Andr. IV. i. 53, *Ego, Pamphile, hoc tibi pro servitio debeo, Conari manibus, pedibus, noctesque et dies, Capitis periculum adire, dum prosim tibi,* 'provided only that I can be of service to you;' and so in V. i. 6, *Dum efficias id quod cupis.*

With *modo,* Eun. II. iii. 28, *Hanc tu mihi vel vi, vel clam, vel precario Fac tradas; mea nihil refert dum potiar modo;* and so again, Adel. III. ii. 15, *Dum illos ulciscar modo.* In Heaut. IV. iii. 36, 37, *Nam dum amicam hanc meam esse credet, non committet filiam. Tu fortasse quid me fiat parvi pendis, dum illi consulas* the first *dum* signifies 'as long as,' strictly with reference to time; the second *dum* signifies 'provided that.' Other examples of *dum* signifying 'provided that,' in Cas. Prol. 76; Merc. Prol. 83; Epid. III. ii. 12, V. ii. 14. In Pers. IV. iv. 105, *D. Vin mea esse? V. Dum quidem ne nimis diu tua sim, volo, dum quidem* is 'provided always that.' In Merc. II. iii. 53, *D. Vsquene valuisti? C. Perpetuo recte dum quidem illic fui, dum quidem* is 'as long, at least, as.'

III.—ETIAM.

Although *Etiam,* in Plautus, appears at first sight to bear several meanings differing widely from each other, it will be found that it is, in very many instances, equivalent to the English 'even now,' and perhaps we ought in all such cases to resolve *etiam* into its component parts and write them separately, as *et iam.* It must be borne in mind that the force of 'even now' is variously modified according to the general sense of the passages into which these words enter. Thus,

1. 'Even now' signifies 'at this present time,' 'directly,' 'without delay,' in such phrases as 'the battle is even now going on,' 'I must leave you even now,' and the like.

2. With a negative 'even now' may signify 'yet,' 'as yet,' 'up to this time,' in such phrases as 'even now the boy cannot write,' 'even now I have never employed him in such work.'

3. The expression 'is the man even now awake?' may imply 'is the man, having been for some time awake, still awake?' and hence it appears that 'even now' may indicate that things are continuing without interruption in the same state in which they have been for some time previously. So, when we say 'he is even now beating his slave,' or 'he is even now mocking me,' these words may indicate that the person spoken of is continuing an action previously com- menced—that he is inflicting fresh punishment or heaping up fresh

ridicule, and thus the idea of addition is connected with 'even now,' as it is with 'still' and 'yet,' in such phrases as 'give me still (or yet) another volume,' that is, a volume 'in addition to' those previously given. All these words may denote the repetition of an action, and hence *etiam atque etiam* means 'again and again.'

4. But the expression 'is the man even now awake?' may imply 'is the man, having been for some time asleep, yet awake?' and hence 'even now' may indicate that things having continued in one particular state for some time, this state has been or is likely to be interrupted. Questions such as the above are frequently put with some degree of surprise or impatience, and this is often rendered emphatic in English by the introduction of a negative. Thus, 'is the man not even now awake?' 'is the man not going even now to hold his tongue?' and hence 'even now' is often equivalent to 'at last.'

We may proceed to give examples of *etiam* under each of the above heads.

1. 'Even now,' 'at this present time,' &c.; Amph. I. i. 47, *Sed quo modo et verbis quibus me decet fabularier, Prius ipse mecum etiam volo hic meditari,* i. e. 'even now, at this present time;' Aul. IV. iv. 6, *Verbera-bilissume, etiam rogitas? non fur, sed trifur,* 'do you even now heap questions on me when I have detected you in the very act of trying to rob me?' Most. III. i. 19, *Etiam fatetur de hospite?* 'does he even now (after being accused by you) confess about his guest?' Pers. IV. iii. 72, *Etiam tu illam destinas? D. Videam modo Mercimonium,* 'are you going to buy her even now—on the spot?' In both of the last quoted examples we should in English have inserted a negative: 'does he not even now confess?' and 'ar'nt you going to buy her on the spot?' V. ii. 66, *D. Malum vobis dabo. T. At tibi nos dedi-mus dabimusque etiam. D. Hei nates percellit!* It is evident from the exclamation of Dordalus that the threat of Toxilus was instantly exe-cuted. I would therefore translate, 'we have brought misfortune upon you, and we will do the same even now' or 'directly,' rather than render *etiam* by 'again' or 'in addition.' Cas. II. viii. 86, Stalino says to Olympio, 'be off with you (*abi*), I do not wish money to be spared, purchase liberally,' and then adds, with reference to *abi, Nam mihi vicino hoc etiam convento est opus,* 'for I must have a meeting with this neighbour of mine even now (directly).' Pseud. I. v. 153. Pseudolus, addressing his audience, says, 'I dare say you suppose that I have promised to perform all these achievements merely to keep you amused, and that I have not really any intention of carrying them out,' *Non demutabo: atque etiam [quod] certum sciam, Quo sim facturus*

pacto, nil etiam scio, 'I will not shrink from my engagement, and (yet
with reference to) that which at this present moment I know will assuredly come to pass, I do not know at this present moment (as yet)
how I shall bring it about.' Such seems to be the meaning of this
difficult passage. The first of the two lines appears under a different
form in almost every different edition. We have inserted *quod*, without which the line cannot be scanned, but in other respects have
adhered to the best MSS., which do not exhibit any variation.

2. 'Even now' with a negative, 'as yet,' 'up to this time;' Pers. I.
iii. 48, *Numquam edepol quoiquam etiam utendam dedi*, 'never as yet,'
'never up to this time have I' &c.; II. ii. 49, Sophoclidisca says to
the boy Paegnium, *Tu quidem haud etiam es octoginta pondo*, 'not yet do
you weigh six stones;' IV. iv. 4, Toxilus having asked Dordalus if he
had not been struck by the wisdom displayed by the maiden as soon
as she opened her mouth, the leno replies coolly, *Haud potui etiam
in primo verbo perspicere sapientiam*, 'I have not been able as yet, on
hearing the first word she uttered, clearly to discern her wisdom.'
Sometimes, to make the meaning more clear and emphatic, *adhuc* is
added: thus Amph. I. i. 92, *Numquam etiam quicquam adhuc verborum
est probentus perperam*, 'not one word even now (as yet) up to the
present moment has he uttered contrary to truth.'

3. 'Even now,' implying that an action is continued without interruption. This is distinctly expressed in Amph. II. i. 21, *Rogasne,
improbe, etiam qui ludos facis me?* 'you who are even now (still)
making game of me,' 'continuing to make game of me;' in I. i. 213,
Mercury says to Sosia, *At mentiris etiam,* 'you are lying even now,'
'you are continuing to tell falsehoods,' having previously said *compositis mendaciis advenisti;* As. V. ii. 73, *At etiam cubat cuculus! Surge,
amator, i domum,* 'but that old cuckoo is even now (still) roosting
there,' 'is continuing to roost there;' Cas. II. vi. 16, *Iam dudum,
hercle, fabulor.* C. *Pol tu quidem, atque etiam facis,* 'I have been
prating here ever so long.' 'There's no mistake about that, and you
are doing so even now,' 'you are continuing to prate;' Bac. IV. iv.
93, *M. Loquere porro. C. Adscribe dum. M. Etiam loquere,* where
etiam loquere is the same as *loquere porro,* 'go on,' 'continue.' Other
examples of *etiam* in this sense may be found in Amph. I. i. 225; As.
II. ii. 61; Capt. III. iv. 24; Curc. I. iii. 40; Men. IV. iii. 23, V. i. 10;
Merc. IV. iv. 23; Mil. III. i. 45; Pers. V. ii. 46; Trin. II. iv. 171.

Etiam implies addition in such combinations as the following:
Mil. V. 8, Cario says to his master, *Iam in hominem involo?* to which
Periplectomenes replies, *Imo, etiam prius verberetur fustibus,* 'no, not

yet, let him first be beaten even now again,' 'beaten in addition to
the beating which he has already received;' so in v. 25. *Verberetur
etiam, post tibi amittendum censeo;* and again, in v. 31, *Verberone
etiam antequam amittis?* Capt. Prol. 53. *Sed etiam est paucis ros quod
monitos voluerim,* 'but there is something even now,' 'something in
addition;' and the same again in As. I. iii. 79; Most. V. ii. 11 (iii. 11),
Verbero, etiam inrides? '(not satisfied with betraying me) do you in
addition laugh at me, you scoundrel?' Pers. IV. iv. 117, *Heus tu!
etiam pro vestimentis huc decem accedunt minae,* 'ten minae in addition,
for the lady's wardrobe;' Men. V. v. 23, *Mane modo: etiam perconta-
bor,* 'I will question him yet further,' 'I will put additional questions
to him;' Trin. V. ii. 12, *Sed maneam etiam opinor,* 'but I ought, I think,
to wait even now,' i. e. 'to wait longer,' 'to wait an additional time,'
'to continue to wait;' and so Men. I. ii. 63, III. ii. 68; As. L. i. 27,
*L. Age, age, usque exserta. D. Etiamne? L. Quaeso hercle usque
ex penitis faucibus. D. Etiam. L. Amplius. L.* 'Come, come, spit
still.' D. 'What, more?' L. 'Spit, I beseech you, from the very
depths of your gullet.' D. 'More still?' L. 'Yes, more.' Bac. IV.
iv. 41, *C. Quid vis curem? M. Vt ad senem etiam alteram facias
viam,* 'that you construct yet a second road by which you may gain
access to the old man,' 'a new road in addition to the former;' Aul.
II. iv. 46, *Tun trium literarum homo Me vituperas? fur, etiam fur
trifurcifer,* 'thief, and more than thief.'

Etiam, from this notion of addition, may occasionally be rendered
by 'yes.' In Amph. I. iii. 46, Amphitruo says to Alcumena, *numquid
vis? Al. Etiam, ut actutum advenias. Am.* 'You wish nothing
further, do you?' Al. 'Yes, I wish also,' 'I wish this in addition.'
Pseud. I. iii. 119, *C. Iuravistin te illam nulli venditurum nisi mihi?
B. Fateor. C. Nempe conceptis verbis. B. Etiam, consultis quoque,*
'yes, and more than that.' There is a remarkable example in Most.
IV. iii. 7 (iv. 7), *T. Num quid processit ad forum hodie novi? S. Etiam.
T. Quid tandem? S. Vidi ecferri mortuom.* T. 'Nothing new upon
Change to-day, was there?' S. 'Yes, there was,' where *etiam* stands
by itself for 'yes, there was,' at least this is more natural than the
interpretation 'even now something new did happen.'

4. 'Even now,' implying that an action which has continued for
some time has been or is likely to be interrupted. *Etiam* with this
force is generally found in interrogatory clauses, and the full force
must, in most cases, be brought out in English by the addition of
a negative. Thus in Most. II. i. 36, Callidamates having again
dropped over into a drunken sleep, Philematium, endeavouring to

rouse him, bawls into his ear, *Etiam vigilas?* 'are you (not) going
to wake up even now, (yet)?' In As. I. i. 95, Demaenetus having announced to Libanus, *Ego eo ad forum, nisi quid vis*, instead of walking
away still lingers, upon which Libanus urges him, *I! etiamne am-
bulas?* 'be off with you! are you (not) going to mizzle yet?' so Most.
IV. ii. 28, 29 (iii. 5, 6), *etiam aperis . . . . etiamne aperis?* 'are you
(not) going to open the door even now, yet, at last? are you (not)
going to open the door yet, I say?' so Pers. II. iv. 4, *etiam respicis,*
v. 7, etiamne dicis; Bac. V. ii. 48, *etiam redditis;* Pers. I. iii. 72.
Curc. I. i. 41, Trin. II. iv. 113, *etiam taces* or *etiamne taces*, 'are you
(not) going to hold your tongue even now,' 'yet,' 'at last;' Curc. I.
iii. 33, *etiam dispartimini*, 'are you (not) going to separate yet,' 'even
now;' Rud. II. v. 12, *etiam acceptura es urnam hanc*, 'are you (not)
going to take this jar at last?' We have the imperative in Most. IV.
ii. 3 (i. 27), *etiam respice*, 'look round at last, won't you.'

Occasionally we find one *etiam* closely followed by another, each
exhibiting a different modification of meaning: thus in Amph. I. i.
220, Sosia bawls for help, *Proh fidem! Thebani cives! M. Etiam
clamas, carnufex?* i.e. 'do you dare, in addition to the rest of your
villainy, to shout for help against me?' but a few lines lower down,
v. 225, M. Etiam muttis? S. Iam tacebo: signifies 'are you even now,
still, venturing to murmur;' so in As. I. i. 95, a portion of which we
gave above, *D. Ego eo ad forum nisi quid vis. L. I, etiamne am-
bulas? D. Atque audin etiam? L. Ecce.* L. 'Be off, are you not
away yet?' 'And, do you hear this besides?' L. 'Well' &c. See also
Pers. V. ii. 46.

Sometimes *nunc* is added to *etiam* to give additional emphasis:
thus Amph. I. i. 173, *Lassus sum hercle e navi, ut vectus huc sum,
etiam nunc nauseo,* 'even now, at this present time, I am sick;' Cas.
III. v. 50, *Sed etiamne habet Casina, etiam nunc, gladium?* 'but has
Casina still got, even at this present time, a sword?' Mil. IV. viii. 29,
Etiam nunc saluto te, Lar familiaris, priusquam eo, 'and now once
more I greet thee,' having previously rendered this homage; Men. I.
ii. 48, *M. Concede huc a foribus. P. Fiat. M. Etiam concede huc.
P. Licet. M. Etiam nunc concede audacter ab leonino cavo;* and so
exactly Aul. I. i. 16, *Apscede — etiam nunc — etiam nunc — etiam —
Ohe! Illic astato.* In both passages *etiam* signifies 'further,' 'an
additional space,' and *etiam nunc* is 'further still.' Amph. V. i. 30,
*Scin me tuum esse herum Amphitruonem? B. Scio. A. Viden etiam
nunc? B. Scio,* 'even now when you look again steadily.' In Truc.
I. ii. 104 we have *etiam iam nunc : Nam tu edepol noster es etiam iam*

nunc, Dinarche, where *iam* is added in order to give the utmost possible
emphasis: 'for we consider you as ours, Dinarchus, even now at this
very time, critical as the conjuncture is.' We have *etiam atque etiam
nunc* in Aul. IV. ii. 7, conveying the idea of intense anxiety; *Vide,
Fides, etiam atque etiam nunc, salvam ut aulam aps te auferam*, 'again
and again now in this hour of peril do I implore thee.' *Etiam
tunc;* Rud. III. vi. 8, *Etiamne in ara tunc sedebant mulieres Quom ad
me profectus ire? Etiam dum;* Mil. IV. ii. 2, *Dissimulabo, hos quasi
non videam, neque esse hic etiam dum sciam*, 'even now at this present
time.' See also Truc. II. 66, *haud . . . etiam . . . dum.*

Etiam is not seldom subjoined to *quoque*: Pers. I. iii. 65, *Quaeso hercle
me quoque etiam vendas, si lubet*, 'sell me also even now,' 'on the spot;'
Merc. II. ii. 56, *Quin mihi quoque etiam est ad portum negotium*, 'why,
for that matter, I also even now have business at the harbour;' Amph.
Prol. 30, *Atque ego quoque etiam qui Iovis sum filius Contagione mei
patris mutuo malum*, 'I also even now;' Truc. I. i. 77, *Cum ea quoque
etiam mihi fuit commercium*, 'with her also, even now (i. e. already, on
a previous occasion) I have had dealings.' Other examples of *quoque
etiam* in Amph. Prol. 81, II. ii. 85, 121; Epid. II. ii. 50, IV. ii. 19;
Men. V. ix. 98; Poen. Prol. 40; Truc. IV. ii. 18.

Quoque and *etiam* sometimes occur in the same clause, but not
linked together, and in this case may qualify different words. Thus
in Amph. I. i. 125, where Sosia is speaking of the miraculous length
of the night, *Eam quoque edepol etiam multo hace vicit longitudine*,
where *etiam* may be connected with *multo;* so II. ii. 70, *etiam tu
quoque;* and so As. II. iv. 95; III. ii. 21, *etiam tua quoque malefacta;*
Curc. I. ii. 40, *etiam mihi quoque;* Pseud. I. iii. 119, quoted above;
i. 120, *etiam matrem quoque;* Trin. IV. iii. 41, *illis quoque abrogant
etiam fidem.* In As. I. iii. 79 we have *etiam priusquam;* In Cist. II. iii.
43, *etiam prius, Sed illaec se quamdam aiebat mulierem Suam benevolentiam
convenire etiam prius*, 'even now before fulfilling her promise to me.'

Etiamnum is found in the text of some edd. of Truc. II. vi. 53, but
rests upon no MS. authority: again, in v. 68, the words *etiamnum mali
pendit*, although the reading of the Palatine MSS., are on all hands
regarded as corrupt. In Men. III. ii. 15, *Ibo, etiamnum reliquiarum
spes animum oblectat meum*, the true reading is probably *etiamdum.*

It is not easy, however, in every case to determine with certainty
the precise force of *etiam*, or to fix on the word which it qualifies:
thus when, in Curc. I. iii. 16, Planesium says to Phaedromus,
*Pl. Tene me, amplectere, ergo. Ph. Hoc etiam est quamobrem cupiam
vivere*, I cannot agree with Weise that *etiam* qualifies *cupiam vivere:*

C C

"Hoc est, quare adhuc (etiam) cupiam vivere," but rather, 'this is an additional motive for making me desire to live.' In the same scene, Planesium having used the word *odium* in reference to Palinurus, he, in wrath, rejoins, v. 34. *Quid ais, propudium! Tun etiam cum noctuinis oculis 'odium' me vocas?* where the meaning may be 'do you, even now (standing there before us), with those owl-eyes of yours, call me an abomination?' (With respect to the use of the word *odium* in this passage, we may observe that although we can talk in English of a person being 'a love,' we can scarcely term any one 'a hate,' probably because we have no familiar personification of Hate.)

IV.—*IMO.*

Imo or *Immo* (for the etymology and orthography are alike uncertain*) occurs very frequently in the dramatic writers, and no word is more likely to puzzle a young scholar, in consequence of the conflicting opinions expressed by lexicographers, grammarians, and commentators. According to some high authorities *imo* properly signifies 'no,' according to others 'yes,' according to others either 'yes' or 'no.'†

I feel no difficulty in asserting that wherever *imo* occurs in the dramatists it always denotes dissent on the part of the speaker from some statement made, or from some opinion or idea enunciated previously. This dissent, however, comprises every modification, from a direct and vehement contradiction to a slight correction of or improvement upon what has been said, such correction or improvement tending, in many cases, not to overthrow but to strengthen and confirm the assertion to which it refers.

There is no doubt that *imo* may sometimes be translated fairly by 'yes,' but in those cases only where, according to our idiom, 'yes' is intended to rebut a negation, and is in reality equivalent to 'on the contrary.' Thus, when A says to B, 'You can sing.' B. 'No I cannot.' A. 'Yes you can'—'yes' is intended to contradict the 'no' of B, and really means, 'on the contrary, you can sing, what you say is not true.' In what follows we shall give a series of examples for

* E.g. Scheller and Freund would connect it with *imus*, Doederlein with ἔτυμος. Mr. Long (in Cic. Verr. Act. II. i. 1) considers that it stands for *in modo*.

† See the dictionaries of Forcellini and Freund, the grammars of Ramshorn, Zumpt, Madvig and Key; the note of Long on Cic. Verr. Act. II. I. i, and of Macleane on Juvenal XVI. 9. Ramshorn says distinctly that *imo* is to be rendered "bald durch *Ja wohl* bald durch *O nein*."

the purpose of illustrating the doctrine laid down above, and we shall endeavour to include several passages which might, at first sight, appear inconsistent with the view which we have taken of the true force of *imo*.

It will be observed that such words as *hercle, edepol, vero, enimvero, etiam*, &c., are not unfrequently combined with *imo* to render it more emphatic.

1. *Imo* frequently signifies plain 'no,' more or less forcible according to circumstances; frequently it conveys a direct contradiction equivalent to 'the very reverse is true,' and this contradiction is often indicative of strong emotion on the part of the speaker. On the other hand, *imo* may imply merely a polite disclaimer or gentle remonstrance, in which case it may be rendered by 'nay' or 'nay, nay not so.'

1. Plain 'no;' Adel. IV. iii. 13, *H. Egomet narrabo quae mihi dixti. M. Imo, ego ibo. H. Bene facis*, 'no, I will go in person;' Andr. I. i. 2, *Si. Adesdum, paucis te volo. So. Dictum puta, Nempe ut curentur recte haec. Si. Imo, aliud. So. Quid est?* 'no, a different matter;' Hec. V. iii. 10, *B. Parmeno, opportune te obfers: propere curre ad Pamphilum. P. Quid eo? B. Dic me orare ut veniat. P. Ad te? Imo, ad Philumenam*, 'no, not to my house, to the house of Philumena;' Curc. II. iii. 44, *P. Pernam, abdomen, sumen, suis glandium. C. Ain tu omnia haec? In carnario fortasse dicis? P. Imo, in lancibus. C.* 'You mean perhaps that all these dainties are in the larder?' *P.* 'No, not at all, upon dishes ready to be served up;' Andr. III. ii. 41, *D. Postremo id mihi da negoti: tu tamen idem has nuptias Perge facere ita ut facis: sed id spero adiuturos deos. S. Imo abi intro, ibi me opperire, et quod parato opus est para*, where *imo* is 'no,' in reply to *id mihi da negoti;* v. 10, *P. Ehodum, bone vir, quid ais? viden me tuis consiliis Miserum inpeditum esse? D. At iam expediam. P. Expedies? D. Certe, Pamphile. P. Nempe ut modo. D. Imo, melius spero.* Pamphilus says bitterly, 'I suppose you will get me out of this scrape after the same fashion you did just now.' *D.* 'No, no, better this time, I hope;' Heaut. V. i. 62, *Quid hoc, quod volo, ut illa nubat nostro? nisi quid est Quod mavis. C. Imo, et gener et adfines placent:* here *imo* is in reply to the supposition implied by the words *nisi quid est quod mavis*, viz. that Chremes was not satisfied with the alliance, 'no, by no means, both the son-in-law and his relations are agreeable to me.'

2. Repudiating an idea or proposal in anger; Andr. V. iii. 15, *Sed quid ego? cur me excrucio? cur me macero? Cur meam senectutem*

huius sollicito amentia? An ut pro huius peccatis ego subplicium subferam?
Imo habeat, valeat, vivat cum illa, 'no, rather than suffer such misery,
let him have her,' &c.; and so in Heaut. V. i. 55, Chremes in wrath
rejects the proposal of Menedemus regarding his son, *Imo, abeat
multo malo quovis gentium,* 'no, let him go to the mischief rather;'
and again, Phor. IV. iii. 38, *G. Quid? nimium quantum libuit. C. Dic.
G. Si quis daret Talentum magnum. C. Imo malum hercle,* 'give him
a talent? No, give him damnation rather!'

3. Contradiction, with various degrees and kinds of emphasis.

(a) Direct contradiction: in Most. III. ii. 80 (77), Tranio having
told Simo that Theuropides had been informed that the architectural
arrangements of Simo's house were so skilful that those who lived
in it could enjoy shade all day long, Simo replies, *Imo edepol vero,
quom usquequaque umbra est, tamen Sol semper hic est usque a mani ad
vesperum,* 'no, the very reverse of what you state is the truth,' &c.; so
Heaut. IV. iii. 27, *C. Et scilicet iam me hoc voles patrem exorare, ut
celet Senem vostrum. S. Imo, ut recta via rem narret ordine omnem,*
'no, on the contrary,' &c.; Hec. III. v. 13, *P. Quidquid est id quod
reliquit, profuit. L. Imo, obfuit,* 'no, on the contrary.'

(b) Earnest contradiction: Epid. III. iv. 48, Periphanes having
purchased by mistake a fidicina on the supposition that his son was
in love with her, the Miles endeavours to make him comprehend that
he had not got hold of the right person, then Periphanes, who is still
obstinate, urges, *P. Equidem hercle argentum pro hac dedi. M. Stulte
datum Reor, atque peccatum largiter. P. Imo, haec ea est,* 'no, I tell
you, this is the very person.'

(c) Vehement contradiction: Capt. III. iv. 34, *H. Quem vides, eum
ignoras: illum nominas quem non vides. A. Imo, iste eum sese ait, qui
non est, esse, et qui vero est negat,* 'no, I tell you, he is telling a falsehood,' &c.

(d) Stern prohibition and contradiction: Bac. I. ii. 37, *L. Tu
amicam habebis? P. Quom videbis tum scies. L. Imo, neque habebis,
nec sinam: iturus sum domum,* 'no, I tell you, you shall not have
one, nor will I suffer it.'

(e) Jeering contradiction: Curc. I. iii. 11, *Ph. Est lepida. Pa. Nimis lepida. Ph. Sum Deus. Pa. Imo, homo non magni preti.* 'I am a
God,' exclaims Phaedromus in his rapture. 'No,' rejoins Palinurus,
'nothing of the sort, you are a mean man of no great worth.'

(f) Kindly contradiction: Capt. V. i. 12, *H. Philocrates, numquam
referre gratiam possim satis Proinde ut tu promeritus es de me et filio
meo. P. Imo potes Pater. et poteris, et ego potero,* 'nay, not so, father.'

(g) Courteous contradiction: Capt. IV. ii. 77, *H. Egone? E. Tute. II. Tum tu mihi igitur herus es. E. Imo, bene volens,* 'no, not your master, your well-wisher.'

4. Remonstrance: Phor. IV. iii. 34, *D. Quis te istuc iussit loqui? C. Imo non potuit melius pervenirier Eo quo nos volumus. Imo* refers to the angry tone assumed by Demipho, 'nay, you ought not to blame me upon that account, for in no way could the point we have in view be better reached:' so also in Heaut. IV. v. 49, *C. Haud faciam. S. Imo, aliis si licet, tibi non licet: Omnes te in lauta et bene acta parte putant. C. Quin egomet iam ad eam deferam. S. Imo, filium Iube potius:* the first *imo* is used in a tone of complimentary remonstrance, 'no, no, you must not act thus, such conduct would be inconsistent with the high reputation you enjoy;' the second *imo* is simply 'no, no, a better plan will be to desire your son to convey it.' Again, IL iv. 20, *Sure, vix subfero. Hoccine me miserum non licere meo modo ingenium frui? S. Imo, ut patrem tuum vidi esse habitum, diu etiam duras dabit,* i. e. 'nay, be not so impatient, for as far as I have seen the temper of your father he will yet for a long time make it hard lines for you;' Andr. V. i. 2, *C. Satis pericli coepi adire: orandi iam finem face, Dum studeo obsequi tibi, pene inlusi vitam filiae. S. Imo enim nunc quam maxume apte postule atque oro, Chreme,* 'nay, say not so, for now above all,' &c.; Heaut. V. ii. 29, *C. Inrides in re tanta, neque me quicquam consilio adiuvas? S. Imo, et tibi nunc sum, et utque id qi dudum, dum loquitur pater,* 'nay, say not so, you wrong me,' &c.

5. Polite disclaimer: Phor. II. ii. 23, *G. Non potest satis pro merito ab illo tibi referri gratia. P. Imo enim nemo satis pro merito gratiam regi referet,* 'nay, not so, for no one in my position (i. e. a parasite) can ever show sufficient gratitude to his protector.'

6. Deprecating the anger of another: Heaut. IL iii. 108, *S. Concaluit, quid vis? C. Redi, redi. S. Adsum, dic, quid est? Iam hoc quoque negabis tibi placere. C. Imo, Sure, Et me, et meum amorem et famam permitto tibi,* 'nay, speak not so, Syrus.'

II. *Imo* is used to correct the statement of a speaker, or to qualify or modify some expression which he has employed, and which is regarded by the other speaker as inaccurate or inappropriate, such qualification or modification being frequently introduced for the purpose of strengthening the phrase to which it applies. It will be seen from some of the examples which follow that in order to catch the full force of *imo* it is necessary to attend closely to the train of thought passing through the minds of those who support the dialogue, and occasionally to fill up gaps.

1. Correction of a positive blunder: Cist. II. i. 37, *A. Itaque me Iuno regina et Iovis supremi filia, Itaque me Saturnus patruus eius. M. Ecastor, pater. A. Itaque me Ops opulenta illius avia. M. Imo, mulier quidem,* 'no, no, Ops was his mother, not his grandmother:' here the correction of the first mistake is introduced by *Ecastor.*

Simple correction: Cist. II. iii. 22, *P. An, amabo, meretrix illa est, quae illam sustulit? L. Imo meretrix fuit.* The last words must not be translated 'yes, she was,' but the emphasis depends upon the change of tense from the present *est* to the past *fuit.* Phanostrata asks, 'what, tell me, I beg, is that woman who brought him up an hetaera?' to which Lampadius replies, 'no, she is not, but she was: she is an old woman now.'

The use of *imo* in the following passage must be ranked under this head; Eun. III. i. 17, Thraso is boasting of the confidence reposed in him by the *Rex* whom he served, and goes on, *T. Tum me conviram solum abducebat sibi. G. Hui! Regem degantem narras. T. Imo sic homo est Perpaucorum hominum. G. Imo nullorum arbitror, Si tecum vivit:* here, in each case, *imo* introduces a correction: G. 'You describe a king fastidious in the choice of his associates,' to which Thraso, all unconscious of the contemptuous irony of Gnatho, replies, T. 'Nay (you must not suppose that he has many associates), such as he is towards me (although treating me with the highest distinction), he is one who bestows his friendship on very few men,' on which Gnatho remarks aside, 'nay, (say rather) on none at all, if he lives with you,' the emphasis being on *nullorum hominum,* 'on none who deserve the name of men, if you are a sample of his favourites.'

2. Again, *imo* is often used to correct and improve some expression, the correction frequently consisting in the substitution of a strong word for a weak one; Eun. IV. vii. 41, *T. Quid nunc agimus? G. Quin redeamus: iam haec tibi aderit supplicans Vltro. T. Credin? G. Imo certe, novi ingenium mulierum:* here *imo certe* does not mean 'yes, assuredly,' but *imo* is introduced with reference to the word *credin,* which implies a certain degree of doubt. The true translation is, therefore, T. 'Do you believe that?' G. '(Believe it!) no, no, ('believe' is too weak a word,) I am sure of it;' Phor. I. ii. 95, *D. Non multum habet Quod det fortasse. G. Imo nihil, nisi spem meram,* which we must render, D. 'Perhaps he has not much to give.' G. 'No, ('multum' is not the word,) he has nothing;' Eun. II. iii. 36, *C. Is, dum sequor hanc, fit mihi obviam. P. Incommode, hercle. C. Imo enimvero infeliciter, Nam incommoda alia sunt dicenda, Parmeno. Imo* refers to *incommode.* 'No, 'incommode' is not the word, you should have

said '*infeliciter*;' Adel. V. viii. 2, *D. Ego vero iubeo, et in hac re, et aliis omnibus Quam maxume unum facere nos hanc familiam, Colere, adiuvare, adiungere. A. Ita quaeso, pater. M. Haud aliter censeo. D. Imo hercle ita nobis decet:* here *imo* indicates an exception taken to the word *censeo* as too feeble: M. '*My sentiments are the same.* D. '*Nay,* ('*censeo*' is not the word, this is not a matter of opinion or sentiment,) it is our duty;' Eun. V. ii. 33, *C. At nunc dehinc spero aeternam inter nos gratiam Fore, Thais: saepe ex huiusmodi re quapiam et Malo principio magna familiaritas Conflata est: quid si hoc quispiam voluit Deus? T. Equidem pol in eam partem accipioque et volo. C. Imo ita quaeso:* here *imo* refers to the words *accipio et volo* as contrasted with the more earnest *quaeso.* We may thus paraphrase the passage: T. 'Assuredly I am ready to view the matter under this aspect (i. e. as intended by the Gods to establish '*aeterna gratia*' between us) and I am willing that such may be the result.' C. 'Nay, ('ready and willing' are not the words) I implore the Gods that this may come to pass.'

When *imo* is employed to correct and strengthen, it may frequently be translated by 'nay, more;' Adel. III. iv. 36, *H. Hunc abduce, vinci, quaere rem. G. Imo hercle extorque,* 'nay, more (take stronger measures still), wrench the truth out of him by torture;' Eun. III. v. 14, *A. Narra istuc, quaeso, quid sit. C. Imo ego te opsecro hercle ut audias,* 'nay, more, (not only will I tell you as you request, but) I implore you to listen;' Phor. V. viii. 58, *N. Satis tibi est? P. Imo vero pulcre discedo et probe Et praeter spem:* here *imo* refers to *satis:* 'nay, more than that (not only am I content, but) I come off gloriously and beyond my expectations;' Heaut. IV. viii. 11, *M. Erravi: res acta: quanta de spe decidi! C. Imo, haec quidem, quae apud me est, Clitophonis est Amica,* 'nay (that is not all), more than that;' so in Phor. V. viii. 54, *imo* means 'nay, more, I have not done yet;' Aul. IV. x. 51, *L. Filiam ex te habes. E. Imo, eccillam domi:* here, at first sight, we might suppose that *imo* was equivalent to simple 'yes,' but the true force is 'nay, more than that, not only have I a daughter, but she is there in my house even now;' Hec. V. iv. 29, Pamphilus (v. 26) enjoins silence upon Bacchis (*neque opus est adeo muttito*), who replies, *Imo etiam hoc qui occultari facilius credas, dabo,* 'nay, more, (not only will I keep the secret) but I will supply you with information,' &c. See other examples of *imo etiam* in Andr. IV. i. 31, 50, ii. 25, Phor. V. vi. 37, in all of which 'nay more' is the proper translation.

This force of *imo* is well developed in the Bacchides II. ii. 27.

Pistoclerus having pointed out to Chrysalus the residence of Bacchis, the latter exclaims, *'t istuc est lepidum! proxumae viciniae Habitat: et quidnam meminit Mnesilochi? P. Rogas? Imo unice unum Plurumi pendit. C. Papae! P. Imo ut eum, credis, misera amans desiderat! C. Scitum istuc. P. Imo, Chrusele, hem, non tantulum Vmquam intermittit tempus quin eum nominet. C. Tanto hercle melior Bacchis. P. Imo ... C. Imo, hercle abiero Potius. P. Num invitus rem bene gestam audis heri?* which may be translated, C. 'How jolly that is! she is actually living next door—and does she retain any recollection of Mnesilochus?' P. 'Do you ask? Nay, more, not only does she remember him, but she prizes him as one without a rival.' C. 'You don't say so!' P. 'Nay, more, how eagerly does she (do you believe me?) pining in love long for him absent!' C. 'That's capital!' P. 'Nay, more, she never suffers any time, however short, to elapse without speaking about him.' C. 'So much more to the credit of Bacchis.' P. 'Nay, more,' ... —but here Chrysalus getting bored by the repetition of *imo* interrupts Pistoclerus with—'Nay, more, I tell you that I'll take myself off rather than listen to any more of your 'Nay mores.''

Imo may also be translated by 'nay, rather' when used to correct a statement which might give rise to a false impression, or when advice is given at variance with some previous proposal; Phor. III. ii. 19, *P. O fortunatissime Antipho! A. Egone? P. Cui quod amas domi est: Nec cum huiusmodi umquam usus venit ut conflictares malo. A. Mihin domi est? imo, id quod aiunt, auribus teneo lupum: Nam neque quomodo a me amittam invenio, neque uti retineam scio,* '(there is no cause to congratulate me,) nay, rather, I may apply to myself the proverb, I have hold of a wolf by the ears (I have caught a Tartar);' Adel. V. iii. 55, *D. ... rus cras cum filio Cum primo luci ibo hinc. M. Imo de nocte censeo,* 'nay, rather, I advise you to go at nightfall.'

Sometimes a whole sentence must be supplied mentally in order to bring out clearly the force of *imo*; thus Andr. III. iii. 15, *C. Sed si ex ea re plus mali est quam commodi V'rique, id oro te, in commune ut consulas, Quasi illa tua sit, Pamphilique ego sim pater. S. Imo ita volo, itaque postulo ut fiat, Chreme:* here *imo* refers to the tone of entreaty assumed by Chremes, and especially to the word *oro*, 'it is unnecessary for you to use words of entreaty as if my wishes were different from your own; no, no, on the contrary, *ita volo, ita postulo:'* so also IV. i. 1, *Hoccine est credibile aut memorabile, Tanta vecordia innata quoiquam ut siet, Ut malis gaudeant atque ex incommodis Alterius sua ut comparent commoda? Ah! Idne est verum? imo id est genus hominum pessumum In denegando modo quis pudor paululum adest,* 'is it really true, (you will ask, that there are such persons. Yes, there are, but bad as these are whom I have described, they are not the worst sort of people:) no, the worst are those who' &c., and then he proceeds to characterize a class.

III. In certain cases *imo* may be translated 'yes,' but this happens only when *imo* is used in reply to a negative proposition, and where 'yes' is in reality equivalent to 'on the contrary;' Aul. III. vi. 9, *E. Neque, pol, Megadore, mihi neque cuiquam pauperi Opinione melius res structa est domi. M. Imo est, et Di faciant uti siet,* &c.: here *imo* contradicts the negative proposition introduced by *neque,* 'yes it is (i.e. on the contrary, it is, &c.);' Bac. II. iii. 81, *N. Sed vos nihilne adtulistis inde auri domum? C. Imo, etiam, verum quantum adtulerit nescio:* here *imo* refers to *nihil,* 'have you not brought any gold home from thence?' 'Yes, we have (i.e. on the contrary, we have), even now, but how much I know not;' Hec. II. i. 31, *S. Non mea opera, neque pol culpa evenit. L. Imo maxume:* here *imo* refers to *non . . . neque,* 'yes, (i.e. on the contrary) it did, in the highest degree;' Adel. II. ii. 39, *S. Num quid vis quin abeam? Imo hercle hoc quaeso, Sure:* 'You don't want anything, do you, to hinder me from going away?' S. 'Yes, (on the contrary, I do want something,) I have to beg of you' &c.; Hec. V. iv. 35, *PAM. Nescis, Parmeno, Quantum hodie profueris mihi, et ex quanta aerumna extraxeris. PAR. Imo vero scio: neque hoc inprudens feci:* 'You don't know.' 'Yes, (on the contrary,) I do know very well:' or we might translate, 'no, I am not ignorant, I do know well;' Cas. II. vi. 30, Stalino, Chalinus, and Olympio are wrangling before proceeding to cast lots: *S. Quod bonum atque fortunatum mihi sit. O. Ita vero et mihi. C. Non. O. Imo hercle. C. Imo mihi hercle.* Stalino having prayed that the result may be fortunate for himself, Olympio adds, 'be it so, and for me also,' upon which Chalinus interposes, 'no (not for you);' Olympio retorts, with reference to the *non* of Chalinus, 'yes, (on the contary,) for me, I say,' and then Chalinus, 'no, not for you, but for me:' here, in the same line, we may translate the first *imo* by 'yes' and the second by 'no,' but there is, in reality, no inconsistency, for in each case *imo* is employed to contradict the preceding speaker.

In the following passage *imo* conveys dissent from the form in which the preceding speaker expresses himself, but assent to the substance of his proposal; Epid. II. ii. 95, *E. Vbi erit empta, ut aliquo ex urbe amoveas: nisi quid tua Sieus sententia est. P. Imo, docte.* Epidicus says, 'this is the plan which I recommend,' and then adds

politely, 'unless your opinion is in aught at variance with mine,' to
which Periphanes replies, 'no, (I do not differ from you, on the contrary) you have contrived cleverly.'

Imo si scias is a combination in which *imo* is said to have sometimes the force of 'yes' used as a direct affirmative. But if we
examine carefully the passages referred to, it will be found that they
have not been interpreted correctly: thus Eun. II. iii. 61, Parmeno
is describing to Chaerea the gift presented to Thais, *C. Quis is est
tam potens cum tanto munere hoc? P. Miles Thraso Phaedriae rivalis.
C. Duras fratris partes praedicas. P. Imo enim si scias quod donum
huic dono contra comparet, Tum magis id dicas :* C. 'According to what
you state my brother has a hard part to play.' P. 'No, no, (it is
too soon for you to speak of that, what I have mentioned is a
mere trifle,) for if you were to know what gift your brother is
providing in opposition to this gift, you would have better grounds
for saying so.' 'Yes' is, at first sight, the natural translation of
imo in this passage, but *enim* is introduced to explain why Parmeno
says 'no' when 'yes' might have been expected. Exactly similar
is Heaut. III. iii. 38, *S. Pessuma haec est meretrix. C. Ita videtur.
S. Imo si scias. Vah ! vide quod inceptet facinus,* 'nay, (it would be
time enough for you to say so,) if you were to know all;' and
again, IV. v. 22, *C. Probe. S. Dic sodes. C. Nimium inquam.
S. Imo si scias, Sed porro ausculta quod superest fallaciae,* 'nay, (not
so fast, say not so yet,) if you were to know all (you might say so),
but listen,' &c.

The following passage from the Andria, IV. ii. 25, presents considerable difficulty, and is quoted as an example of *imo* signifying
plain 'yes.' Davus having announced to Pamphilus and Charinus
that he had hit upon a scheme which would extricate the former from
his embarrassments, Pamphilus asks (v. 22), *P. Quid facies? cedo.
D. Dies mihi hic ut sit satis vereor Ad agendum: ne vacuom esse me
nunc ad narrandum credas, Proinde hinc vos amolimini: nam mihi
impedimento estis. P. Ego hanc visam. D. Quid tu ? Quo hinc te agis ?
C. Verum vis dicam ? O. Imo etiam Narrationis incipit mihi initium.
C. Quid me fiet ?* It will be seen that Davus declares that he has so
much to do that he has no time for explanations, and tells the young
men to take themselves off, as they are in his way. On this Pamphilus says that he will go and pay a visit to Glycerium; Charinus
lingers, and Davus turning to him sharply asks, 'and whither are you
going?' Charinus, instead of making a short direct reply, asks, *Verum
vis dicam.* Davus from these words anticipates that the young man

is about to begin a long story to which he has no time to listen,
replies quickly, 'certainly not:' and then adds testily, 'even now (at
this critical time) he is entering upon some history or other.' The
punctuation ought to be, *Imo: etiam narrationis incipit initium.*
The common punctuation is *Imo etiam* : and the translation given is
'yes, certainly:' which is manifestly altogether inconsistent with the
impatient haste of Davus.

V.—*MODO*.

Although *Modo* does not present the same complications as *Adeo*,
we nevertheless find the discussions with regard to this word overlaid
with perplexing and useless distinctions and refinements.

The fact is that *modo* employed as an adverb has two, and not
more than two, separate meanings, which are represented in English by

I. 'Only' or 'provided only.'

II. 'Just now.'

These have no obvious connection, although in reality the second
is only a particular case of the first, but both flow directly and easily
from the proper signification of *modus*. We shall examine them
separately.

I. *Modo* signifying 'only' or 'provided only.' The primitive
meaning of *modus* is 'a measure,' and hence 'a definite quantity'
of any object.* Thus *modo* conveys the idea of something definite,
bounded, and therefore limited; Most. L iii. 43, *Nihilo ego, quam
nunc tu, amata sum, atque uni modo gessi morem*, 'I devoted myself to
one person only,' or, in other words, 'I limited my affections to a
single lover;' Pseud. I. iii. 30, *Potin at semel modo, Ballio, huc cum
lucro respicias*, 'once only,' 'limiting yourself to this single occasion;'
il. 88, *Tu autem quae pro capite argentum mihi iam iamque saepe numeras,
Ea pacisci modo scis, sed quae pacta es non scis solvere*, 'you know only
how to make a bargain, but do not know how to keep it,' 'your
knowledge is limited to making a bargain;' As. II. ii. 8, *Aetatem velim
servire Libanum ut conveniam modo*, 'I would be content to remain
a slave for ever could I only meet Libanus,' 'provided only,' 'with
this limitation;' Phor. I. ii. 9, *D. Quid istuc est? G. Scies Modo ut
tacere possis*, 'provided only,' 'with this limitation, that you can hold
your tongue;' Cic. de Off. III. 19, § 77, *Huic igitur viro bono, quem
Fimbria etiam, non modo Socrates noterat*, 'an acquaintance with whom

---

* Cf. *medius, modulus, modulor, modulamen.*

was not limited to Socrates but extended to Fimbria also;' Cic. de
Div. I. 39, § 36, *Nemo aliter philosophus sensit, in quo modo esset
auctoritas*, 'provided only he were a man of weight.' Cicero wishes
to qualify the expression *Nemo philosophus* as too comprehensive, and
to limit his assertion to those whose names carried *auctoritas* with
them. Cic. de Senect. VII. § 22, *Manent ingenia senibus, modo per-
maneat studium et industria*, 'provided only:' here again *modo* fixes
a limit to the proposition *manent ingenia senibus*, which would not be
true unless thus restricted. Phor. I. li. 17, *is senem per epistulas
Perlexit, modo non monies auri pollicens*, 'only not promising,' 'promising everything short of whole hills of gold,' 'the only limit to his
promises was' &c. This is the Greek μόνον ουχί. Cf. Tibull. I. i.
25. *Modo* is frequently used after an imperative, in dialogue, when
a certain amount of impatience or indignation is implied; so As. V.
ii. 19, *Tace modo*, 'only hold your tongue,' 'I limit my request to
this,' 'all I ask is, hold your tongue;' Men. IV. i. 4, *Quin tu taces ...
sequere hac modo*, 'only follow me,' 'I limit my request to this,' 'all
I ask is;' Rud. III. iii. 29, *Sedete hic modo;* Men. I. iii. 32, *Propera
modo;* Trin. II. iv. 182, *Quin tu i modo ... i modo ... quin tu i modo
... abi modo ... i modo ... i modo ..., i modo ... i modo, i modo, i
modo.*

II. *Modo* signifying 'just now' or 'this moment.' *Modus*, as
stated above, signifies generally 'a measure,' specially it denotes 'a
measure of time,' 'an unit of time,' and is employed with reference
to the unit of time immediately preceding an event; or, during which
an event is taking place; or, immediately following an event. So in
English we say, 1. he *was* here just now, this moment, this instant;
2. he *is* here just now (this moment, this instant); 3. he *will be* here
just now, this moment, this instant.

1. Past time: As. V. ii. 76, *D. Iam opsecro, uxor. A. Nunc
uxorem me esse meministi tuam? Modo quom dicta in me ingerebas,
odium, non uxor, eram;* Andr. I. ii. 2, *Ita Davom modo timere sensi,
ubi nuptias Futuras esse audivit.*

2. Present time: Adel. III. i. 1, *S. Opsecro, mea nutrix, quid nunc
fiet? C. Quid fiat rogas? Recte edepol spero. S. Modo dolores, mea tu,
occipiunt primulum:*—on which Donatus observes, "Evidenter hic *modo*
temporis praesentis est adverbium." On Hec. III. v. 8 the same
grammarian remarks, "Difficile invenitur praesentis temporis *modo*."

3. Future time: Andr. III. iv. 15, *Domum modo ibo.* We frequently find a double *modo*, in which case the first signifies 'at one
moment,' the second 'at another moment,' and hence 'sometimes

... sometimes:' so Eun. IV. iv. 47, *modo ait, modo negat,* 'at one
moment he says "yes," and the next moment he says "no."' In
the poets and later writers various adverbs are substituted for the
second *modo,* such as *nunc, aliquando, interdum, ac statim, saepe, nonnumquam, rursus,* &c., but these constructions are hardly to be found
in the dramatic writers.

VI.—*NAM, ENIM, ENIM VERO, &c.*

Every one has felt that in animated conversation or eager discussion
the thoughts of a speaker not unfrequently outstrip the powers of
utterance, and hence single words or even whole clauses are suppressed, and must be supplied by the hearer.

The same thing happens in vehement declamation, sometimes
unintentionally and sometimes designedly on the part of the orator,
and, generally, such an omission may naturally take place whenever
a speaker is, or wishes to appear to be, under the influence of great
eagerness or strong passion. The words which indicate a chasm of
this kind, in the dramatic writers, are for the most part *nam* and
enim, which serve to introduce an explanation of some difficulty
suggested by what goes before, although the connecting link must
often be mentally supplied.

I. *Nam.* Amph. Prol. 104. Mercury, in the Prologue to the Amphitruo, seeks to startle the audience by announcing that Jupiter will
appear in person on the stage, and take part in the action of the play.
He then informs them that the scene is laid in Thebes, proceeds to
give an account of Amphitruo and Alcumena, and tells us how the
former had some time previously gone forth in command of the Theban
army to war against the Teleboans: *Is* (sc. *Amphitruo) priusquam
hinc abiit ipsemet in exercitum, Gravidam Alcumenam uxorem fecit suam.
Nam ego vos novisse credo iam ut sit pater meus, Quam liber harum rerum
multarum siet, Quantusque amator quom quid complacitum est semel : Is
amare occepit Alcumenam clam virum,*—where the *nam* is introduced
most abruptly, and we must supply the train of thought somewhat
after this fashion : 'having mentioned the beautiful Alcumena, you
will no longer feel any surprise that Jupiter should be mixed up with
this business, for, I doubt not, you are all by this time well aware of
what sort of person my father is,' &c. ; Truc. IV. iv. 3, *Blitea et lutea
est meretrix, nisi quae sapit in vino ad rem suam. Si alia membra vino
madeant, cor sit saltem sobrium. Nam mihi dividia est, tonstricem meam
sic mulcatam male,* 'I am led to make this remark, for I am annoyed,'

&c.; Poen. V. iii. 1, *G. Quis pultat? M. Qui te proximus est. G. Quid vis? M. Eho Novistin tu illunc tunicatum hominem, qui siet? G. Nam quem ego adspicio! Proh supreme Iupiter!* here great wonder is expressed, 'can I believe my eyes! I am amazed, for whom do I see?'

II. *Enim.* *Enim* is more common under such circumstances, and this use of the word has, in very many cases, been overlooked by commentators, who, in such examples as those which follow, assert that *enim* is equivalent to *enim vero,* assuming that *enim vero* is equivalent to the simple *vero,* and may signify merely 'truly' or 'indeed,' being little better than an expletive. But we maintain that in the earlier writers *enim vero* always signifies 'for in truth,' as *enim* always signifies 'for,' and that both are uniformly employed to introduce an explanation. Frequently the blank is very easily supplied, an affirmation or negation only being suppressed: thus Pers. II. v. 16, *S. Quia boves bini hic sunt in crumena. T. Emitte sodes, ne enices fame, sine ire pastum. S. Enim metuo ut possim in bubilem reicere ne vagentur,* 'nay, not so, for I am afraid that I shall not be able to drive them back again to their stall, and that they will stray;' Most. III. iii. 23 (IV. ii. 23), *Tr. Quia tibi unquam quicquam, postquam tuus sum, verborum dedi! Tr. Ego enim cavi recte,* 'no, you have not, for I have been well on my guard.'

Sometimes the suppressed clause is less simple, but, in general, it may be very easily deduced from the context: thus Epid. V. i. 41, *S. Accipe argentum hoc, Danista: hic sunt quadraginta minae, Si quid erit dubium inmutabo. D. Beneferisti: bene vale. S. Nunc enim tu mea es:* here, in all probability, the *enim* is explanatory of an action or gesture—Stratippocles having paid the money proceeds to lay hold of the slave whom he had purchased, and upon her shrinking back he exclaims, 'I have a right to take possession of you, for you are now my property;' Bac. IV. iv. 51, *M. Nunc quid nos vis facere? C. Enim nihil, nisi ut ametis inpero:* 'Now what do you want us to do?' 'Be easy as to that, for I bid you do nothing except' &c. Cas. II. iv. 1, *S. Qui illum Di omnes Deaeque perdant! C. Te uxor aiebat tua Me vocare. S. Ego enim vocari iussi,* 'she said truly, for I ordered you to be called;' Pers. IV. iv. 59, *T. Sequere me: adduco hanc, si quid vis ex hac percontarier. D. Enim volo te adisse,* 'by all means will I question her now, for I wish you to be present;' Most. V. ii. 11 (iii. 11), *Tr. Verbero, etiam inrides? Tr. Quian' me pro te ire ad cenam autumo? Tu. Non enim ibis, ego ferare saxo, ut meruisti, in crucem,* 'you need say nothing about going to supper, you shall not go, I will cause you to be carried to quite another place—to the gibbet;' so v. 23, Th. *Maxume accipito hanc ad te litem. Tu Enim istic captio est,* 'by no means' or 'no, I thank you, for there is a trick in that;' and the same words are repeated in Epid. V. ii. 36; Men. II. i. 25, *Mex. Molestus ne sis: non tuo hoc fiet modo. Mex Hem, Illoc enim verbo esse me servom scio,* 'I am done for by that expression, I am reminded that I am a slave;' Cas. II. vi. 19. *C. Quid est? S. Dicam enim, mea mulsa:* 'What does all this mean?' 'Listen (or, *soyez tranquille*), for I will tell you, my sweet one;' Trin. V. ii. 8, *C. Est ita ut tu dicis: sed ego hoc nequeo mirari satis, Eum sororem despondisse suam in tam fortem familiam, Lusiteli quidem Philtonis filio. L. Enim me nominat. C. Familiam optumam obcupavit. L. Quid ego cesso hos conloqui?* Lysiteles has not yet shown himself, but is listening to the conversation of Charmides and Callicles: on hearing his own name he makes a step forward—'I had better appear, for he names me,' and in the next line expresses himself more fully, *Quid ego cesso, &c.*; I. ii. 23, *C. Vin commutemus? tuam ego ducam et tu meam? Faxo haud tantillum dederis verborum mihi. M. Numquam enim tu, credo, mihi inprudenti obrepseris,* 'do not crow so loud, for I don't believe that you will ever catch me asleep.' The text however is not certain. The MSS. have all *namque enim,* for which Camerarius substitutes *numquam enim,* Ritschl *nempe enim,* others *neque enim;* Poen. IV. ii. 31,. *M. Habe rem pactam. S. Si futurum est, do tibi operam hanc. M. Quomodo? S. Vt, enim, ubi mihi vapulandum est, tu corium subferas:* here *enim* refers to the words *si futurum est.* Syncerastus agrees to aid Milphio, *si futurum est . . .* 'if what I stipulate for is promised . . .' Milphio asks for an explanation, *Quomodo?* 'how, what mean you, what do you require?' and Syncerastus replies, 'I shall aid you if my terms are complied with; and I say this, for I bargain that when I am to be beaten you are to supply the hide (your own) to be walloped,' i. e. 'I am ready to help you if you relieve me from all risk of the consequences.'

In the following passage *enim,* at first sight, is equivalent simply to 'indeed' or 'truly;' Most. III. i. 24 (20), Tranio having heard, to his consternation, that Theuropides had met the man who sold the house and had questioned him about the truth of the pretended murder, exclaims, *Metuo ne technae meae perpetuo perierint. Tu. Quid tute tecum? Ta. Nihil enim: sed dic mihi.* The difficulty here arises solely from defective punctuation. We ought to write, *Tu. Quid tute tecum? Ta. Nihil—enim—sed dic mihi.* Theuropides perceiving that Tranio, absent and distracted, was talking to himself, says sharply,

Quid tute tecum? ' what's that you're muttering to yourself?' Tranio
starts and replies in confusion, *Nihil*, ' O nothing, I was speaking
for . . .' and then breaks off abruptly in order, before committing
himself, to ascertain exactly what Theuropides had heard from the
seller. The broken sentences are a mark of confusion and embarrassment.

On the same principle we explain Cas. II. vi. 11. The *sortitio*
which is to decide the fate of Casina is about to take place in the
presence of Stalino and his wife Cleostrata. Stalino who, for his own
ends, is eager on behalf of Olympio, says, *S. Adpone hic sitellam,
sortes cedo mihi : animum advortite Atque ego censui aps te posse hoc me
inpetrare, uxor mea. Casina ut uxor mihi daretur, et nunc etiam censeo.
C. Tibi daretur illa ! S. Mihi enim—ah ! id non volui dicere, Dum
mihi volui huic dixi : atque adeo dum mihi cupio perperam Iamdudum
hercle fabulor. C. Pol tu quidem : atque etiam facis.* Stalino is so
eager and agitated that he becomes thoroughly confused, and unawares discloses the real state of his feelings. He begins by saying,
' I thought, my dear wife, that I might have obtained from you this
favour, that Casina should be made over as a wife to—,' and then
mihi slips out instead of *Olympioni.* On this Cleostrata very naturally
exclaims in wonder, ' She given to you !' Stalino, carried away by
his excitement, does not at first perceive his blunder, and continues,
' yes, to me, for—,' and then, becoming aware of what he had said,
interrupts himself, ' no, no, I did not mean to say that,' and then, in
his terror, he gets hopelessly involved, and plunges deeper and deeper
at every step. We ought therefore to punctuate, *C. Tibi daretur
illa ! S. Mihi, enim—ah ! id non volui dicere, Dum mihi volui huic
dixi, atque adeo dum mihi cupio—perperam Iamdudum, hercle, fabulor,*
&c., making another abrupt stop after *cupio,* where Stalino becomes
sensible that he is still floundering, and endeavours to get out by
adding, ' by Hercules, I have been talking nonsense for some time.'
To this Cleostrata dryly assents, ' yes, you have been and you are
still talking nonsense.'

III. *Quia enim.* The combination *Quia enim* seems to be represented
correctly by the idiomatic English phrase 'for why,' signifying 'because;'
Cas. II. vi. 33, *C. Quid tu id curas ? O. Quia enim metuo ne in aqua
summa natet;* Amph. II. iii. 34, *A. Qui tibi istuc in mentem venit ?
S. Quia enim sero advenimus;* Mil. IV. ii. 11, *PA. Quo argumento ?
PY. Quia enim loquitur laute et minume sordide;* Truc. IV. ii. 19,
*D. Non ego nunc intro ad vos mittar ? A. Quidum quam miles magis ?
D. Quia enim plus dedi.* In all of the above *quia enim* introduces

a direct answer, accompanied by an explanation, to a direct question, and may be translated 'because.'

It will be unnecessary to examine the following passages at length. We shall merely give the references, and suggest the clauses to be supplied.

Amph. I. l. 175. Mercury, in order to play upon the fears of Sosia, pretends to be groping about doubtfully in the dark : ' I cannot be mistaken, *certe enim*,' &c., and then in the next line but one he continues, ' there is no doubt about it, *hinc enim*,' &c.; Aul. III. v. 26, ' I have a just claim, *enim mihi quidem*,' &c.; V. l. 4, ' I cannot be mistaken, *certo enim*,' &c.; Bac. III. iii. 53, Lydus having exclaimed (*v.* 51), *Fortunatum Nicobulum qui illum produxit sibi !* is interrupted, but continues in the next line but one, ' well may I say so, *hic enim*,' but in fact it is not absolutely necessary to supply anything ; Capt. III. iv. 36, ' you expect to be believed, I suppose, *tu enim repertus*,' &c.; IV. ii. 80, ' just so, *nam enim*,' &c.; Cas. II. v. 15, ' she is in a fine rage, *negavi enim*,' &c., see *v.* 17; III. i. 11, Stalino having quoted a line from Naevius, Alcesimus replies, *Meminero*, on which Stalino sneeringly rejoins, ' doubtless you do, *nunc enim te*,' &c.; Men. I. ii. 52, the parasite exclaims, ' what do I say ? you may be easy upon that score,' or ' it is quite unnecessary to ask such a question, *id enim*,' &c.; Mil. II. v. 19, Sceledrus is in a state of bewilderment, Palaestrio asks, *Quid metuis ?* on which Sceledrus, *Enim—ne nos perdiderimus uspiam*, ' I am afraid, for I fear lest,' &c.; iii. 12, ' no, no, *non enim*,' &c.; III. i. 215, ' be easy, *ego enim*,' &c.; IV. ii. 27, ' you need say no more, *enim cognovi*,' &c.; Most. III. ii. 143 (141), it is scarcely necessary to supply anything here, ' the pillars are good enough if coated with pitch,' *non enim*, &c., ' for the workmanship is excellent ;' Pers. II. ii. 54, Sophoclidisca, in answer to a question, says, ' what's your business ?' to which Paegnium retorts, ' I'll let you see that it's my business, *enim non ibis . . . nisi*,' &c; Truc. I. ii. 27, I would punctuate *At, enim amabo, sine me ire quo eas*, and not *At enim, amabo* &c.; II. ii. 54, *enim* refers to what Stratilax had said previously, ' I shall report your proceedings to the old gentleman, . . . for he is one who,' &c.

IV. *Enim vero*. The words *enim vero* signify 'for in sooth,' and serve to explain or illustrate some preceding statement. It is often necessary, as in the case of the simple *enim*, to supply a connecting clause, but this is, for the most part, easy and obvious; Capt. Prol. 22, *Hic nunc domi servit suo patri, nec scit patr, Enim vero Di nos quasi pilas homines habent*, ' this may appear strange, but need not excite our wonder, for in sooth the Gods toss us men about as if we were balls in their hands;' III. iv. 3, *H. Quo illum nunc hominem proripuisse foras se dicam ex aedibus? T. Nunc enim vero ego occidi: eunt ad te hostes, Tyndari, quid loquar?* 'what will become of me? for now in very sooth I am undone: the enemy is upon thee, Tyndaris!' *v.* 75, *A. Verum si quid metuis a me, iube me vinciri, volo, Dum istic itidem vinciatur. T. Imo, enim vero, Hegio, Istic qui volt vinciatur,* 'nay, not so, for in truth this would be unfair; let him be cast into chains who is willing;' and *v.* 94, *H. Quid tu ais? T. Me tuom esse servom, et te meum herum. H. Haud istuc rogo. Fuistin liber? T. Fui. A. Enim vero non fuit, nugas agit,* 'it is false, for in truth he was not, he is deceiving you;' Cas. II. viii. 39, Chalinus overhears the conversation between Stalino and Olympio, and discovers the plan of the old man with regard to Casina; he then exclaims, *Nunc pol ego demum in rectam redii semitam, His ipsus Casinam deperit: habeo viros:* the dialogue goes on between Stalino and Olympio, and further disclosures are made, upon this Chalinus, *Enim vero huc aures magis sunt adhibendae mihi, Iam ego uno in saltu lepide apros capiam duos,* 'I must keep quiet, for in truth I must employ my ears rather than any other members;' Curc. I. iii. 19, *Enim vero nequeo durare quin ego herum accusem meum,* 'I must interfere, for in truth I can no longer refrain,' &c.; Men. V. ii. 92, *S. Ibo adducam qui hunc hinc tollant et domi devinciant, Priusquam turbarum quid faciat amplius. M. Enim vero misi Occupo aliquid mihi consilium, hi domum me ad se auferent,* 'I must take some decided step, for in truth unless I am before-hand in forming some plan for myself,' &c. We need not examine Cist. II. i. 43, for the discourse of Alcesimarchus is designedly incoherent; he is raving. Amph. I. i. 109, Mercury declares his intention of be-fooling Sosia, *Quando imago est huius in me, certum est hominem eludere. Et enim vero quoniam formam cepi huius in me et statum, Decet et facta moresque huius habere me similes item,* 'and so I ought to do, for in sooth since,' &c.; *v.* 188, *M. Ain vero? S. Aio enim vero. M. Verbero, mentiris nunc iam,* 'say you so in truth?' S. 'I do say so, for in very sooth . . .' and then he is interrupted by Mercury, who does not permit him to finish; II. ii. 89, *A. Verum tu magnum malum habebis, si hic suum officium facit: Ob istuc omen, ominator, capies quod te condecet. S. Enim vero praegnanti oportet et malum et malum dari,* 'you say well, for in truth,' &c., and then he proceeds to pun upon *malum* and *malum; v.* 126, *AM. Tun' me heri adveniisse dicis? AL. Tun' te abisse hodie hinc negas? AM. Nego enim vero, et me advenire nunc primum aio ad te domum,* 'I do deny it, for in very truth I must deny it;' *v.* 139, *A. Secede huc tu, Sosia, Enim vero illud praeter alia mira*

miror maxume, 'I am perplexed, for in truth,' &c.; As. III. iii. 97,
P. *Amandone exorarier vis te, an osculando? L. Enim vero utrumque,*
'not by either singly, for in truth I desire both.' The above examples comprise the whole of the references to *enim vero* in the index
of Weise. We may add Capt. III. iv. 60: Aristophontes, provoked
beyond endurance by Tyndaris, exclaims, *Enim vero iam nequeo con-
tineri,* 'I must fly at the fellow, for in truth I can no longer restrain
myself.'

V. *Verum enim.* Eun. IV. vi. 3. *Vsque adeo ego illius ferre possum
ineptias et magnifica verba, Verba dum sint, verum enim si ad rem conferentur, vapulabit,* 'I can endure his folly and grandiloquent words
provided they are words only, but there my forbearance ends; for, to
tell the truth, if he shall attempt to put in practice what he says, he
shall be trounced.'

VII.—*QVI.*

Most. I. i. 55, *Qui scis,* i. e. 'how do you know?'
The use of *Qui* for *quomodo* or *qua ratione* in direct questions is
familiar to us from Horace, who employs it repeatedly in that sense,[*]
as do Cicero and Persius. When the word is used in this manner
many grammarians call it an adverb, but it is in reality an old form
of the ablative of *quis,* and it stands for the ablative of the relative
in all genders.

Thus it is masculine in Most. V. ii. 38 (iii. 38), *Famus, sortem,
sumptumque omnem qui amica [empta] est;* and so Cas. III. vi. 21,
Most. I. iii. 109, III. ii. 26, Pseud. I. iii. 115, Trin. I. ii. 92, 95,
III. ii. 61, Eun. IV. vii. 9.

It is feminine in Trin. III. ii. 50, *Tum igitur tibi aquae erit cupido
genus qui res tinguastuam;* and so As. III. i. 36, II. 43, Most. I. iii.
101, Trin. I. ii. 98, III. ii. 52, Rud. II. vii. 74, Andr. II. iv. 5.

It is neuter in Most. III. i. 7, *Danista adest qui dedit argentum faenori
Qui amica est empta;* and so Pers. IV. iv. 41, *Indica minumo daturus
qui sis, qui duci queat,* 'name the lowest price at which you will
dispose of her, at which she may be taken away by the purchaser,'
pretio being understood, which occurs frequently in the preceding
lines. In the same scene, v. 109, *Tum tu pauca in verba confer: qui
datur, tanti indica;* cf. Merc. II. iv. 20, Hec. V. i. 23.

[*] F. g. S. 1. L 1, Ul. 128, II. II. 19, III. 108, 241, 260, 275, 311, vII. 96, 103,
Epp. I. vi. 42, xvi. 63, Ad. Pis. 462.

Quicum is the ablative singular masculine in Cas. II. v. 9, Most. II.
ii. 86 (85), Poen. III. vi. 3, Eun. IV. iv. 31, Heaut. I. ii. 4, IV. i. 2,
Phor. V. i. 32; and so *quicumvis*, Stich. IV. ii. 47.

Quicum is the ablative singular feminine in Trin. IV. ii. 3, Stich.
IV. i. 41, 42, Adel. III. iv. 31, IV. vii. 32.

Qui in the ablative neuter is frequently equivalent to 'wherewithal;'
thus Trin. II. iv. 160, *Nam qui riramus nihil est;* L. ii. 151, *Occlusti
linguam, nihil est qui respondeam;* Truc. II. vii. 24, *Valeo et venio ad
minus valentem, et melius qui valeat fero;* Eun. III. ii. 34, *Nam hercle,
nemo possel, sat scio, Qui haberel, qui pararet alium, hunc perpeli;* other
examples in Trin. Prol. 14, II. ii. 73, III. ii. 27, 74, Phor. V. ii. 5.

This form of the ablative is found in some compounds also, e. g.
quivis, in Adel. II. iii. 1, *Aps quivis homine, quom est opus, beneficium
adcipere gaudeas; quiqnam*, in As. IV. i. 9, *neque cum quiquam alio
quidem;* and Pers. IV. iii. 8, *Nec satis a quiquam homine accepi;
aliqui*, in Most. I. iii. 18, *Ergo hoc ob verbum te, Scapha, donabo ego
hodie aliqui;* and Truc. V. 30, 31, *Quamquam ego tibi videor stultus,
gaudere aliqui me volo: Nam quamquam es bella, malo tuo es, nisi terum
aliqui gaudeo;* cf. Mil. IV. iv. 45, Stich. I. ii. 10.

It being thus established that *qui* is an ablative, and that it may
be used elliptically, we now readily understand how *qui*, standing for
quo modo or *qua ratione*, is employed in direct questions. This use
of the word is so common in the dramatists that examples may be
easily accumulated, e. g. Andr. I. i. 26, III. ii. 21, 22, Merc. I. 71,
Most. IV. ii. 7 (i. 30), III. i. 111 (107), Rud. I. iii. 37, Stich. II. i. 29,
Trin. I. ii. 50, II. ii. 49. *Qui scis*, which we have in our text, occurs
several times in the Andria alone, e. g. II. i. 2, ii. 15, III. iii. 33, 43.

Sometimes no verb follows, and then *qui* is equivalent to 'how
so?' thus Phor. V. vii. 22, *P. Satin superbe inluditis me? D. Qui?
P. Rogas?* and so Andr. V. iv. 51, Eun. IV. vi. 7.

Sometimes *qui* is followed by *cedo*, as Andr. I. i. 123, *Qui, cedo?*
or by *dum*, as Most. II. ii. 20, *T. Quid vos, insanin' estis? Tu. Qui
dum?* 'how now?' 'what do you mean?' and again III. ii. 44, Hec.
III. i. 39: or by *iam*, Stich. I. i. 37, *Tace sis! cave sis audiam ego
istuc, Cave, posthac ex te. P. Nam qui iam?* 'for why?' 'how now?'
asking an explanation. Cf. Rud. I. ii. 63, II. vi. 38, 54. In Eun. I.
ii. 41 we find *Qui istuc?*

But *qui* is used as equivalent to *quo modo*, 'how,' 'in what way,'
where there is no direct question; thus Heaut. II. iii. 121, *At hoc
demiror qui tam facile potueris Persuadere illi;* and so Trin. IV. iii. 43,
Hoc qui in mentem venerit mihi, reipsa modo commonitus sum; and

Andr. II. i. 7, *Ah! quanto satius est, te id dare operam qui istum amorem ex animo amoveas tuo.* For other examples see Most. II. i. 41, Trin. I. ii. 126, Andr. II. i. 34, 35, Eun. V. iii. 2, 11, Heaut. III. i. 83, Hec. II. iii. 6, III. i. 8, V. iv. 29, Phor. I. ii. 80, II. iii. 49, 51, V. vi. 15, 49; to which we may add Merc. II. i. 34, *Conlubitum est illud mihi nescio qui vivere,* i. e. *nescio quo modo,* 'somehow or other.'

Qui is used in a direct question not only as equivalent to *quo modo, quo ratione,* but also for the simple *cur* or *quare (perché)*; Curc. II. ii. 27, *Heus Phaedrome, exi, exi, exi, isquam, ocius. P. Qui istic clamorem tollis?* Merc. II. iv. 18, *E. Visne tam ad portum? C. Qui potius quam voles? E. Atque eximam Mulierem pretio? Qui potius quam auro expendas?* see also Rud. III. ii. 25, Stich. I. ii. 4, Trin. I. ii. 40.

As in the case of *quo modo, qui* may be used for *cur* or *quare* when there is no direct question, and is in this case equivalent to *propter quod;* thus Poen. I. ii. 64, *Quid habetis qui mage inmortales vos credam esse quam ego siem;* Truc. III. i. 19, *Quid istuc alienum est, amabo, mi Strabax, Qui non extemplo intres:* but in this last example we might regard *qui* as the nominative.

In like manner as *quis* or *qui* in the nominative is occasionally equivalent to *aliquis,* so *qui* in the ablative is employed for *aliquo modo* or *ullo modo;* thus Rud. III. iv. 31, *Fateor, ego trifurcifer sum: tu es homo adprime probus. Num qui minus hasce esse oportet liberas?* 'I confess it, I am a triple-dyed scoundrel; you are a man among the foremost in worth; but ought these damsels to be in any way less free on that account?' again, Truc. II. i. 27, *Probus est amator, qui relictis rebus rem perdit suam, At nos male agere praedicant viri solere secum, Nosque esse avaras: quaeso num qui male nos agimus tandem?* 'I should like to know, do we, after all, in any way treat them ill?' In the above examples *qui* is preceded by *num,* but this is not the case in Trin. I. ii. 83, *Quin eum restituis? quin ad frugem corrigis? Ei rei operam dare te fuerat aliquanto aequius, Si qui probiorem facere possis,* 'If, in some way or other,' (or, 'in any way,') 'you may be able to make him more respectable.'

Not only is *qui* used as the ablative singular of the relative, but there are a few passages in which, according to the natural and obvious construction, it must represent the ablative plural *quibus;* thus Stich. II. i. 20, *Sed tandem, opinor, aequius est heram mihi esse supplicem, Atque oratores mittere ad me, donaque ex auro, et quadrigas Qui vehar: nam pedibus ire non queo;* Rud. I. ii. 35, *Quin tu in paludem is, exsiccasque arundines Qui peragamus villam, dum sudum est;* IV. iv. 66, *Cistellam istic inesse oportet caudeam in isto vidulo, Ubi sunt signa*

qui parentes noscere haec possit suos; with which compare II. iii. 69,
A. *Quia leno ademit cistulam ei, quam habebat, ubique habebat Qui suos
parentes noscere posset: eam veretur Ne perierit.* T. *Vbinam ea fuit
cistellula?* A. *Ibidem in navi Conclusit ipse in vidulum, ne copia esset
eius Qui suos parentes nosceret;* compare also Cist. IV. ii. 48, *H. Disperii misera: quid ego meae herae dicam? quae me opere tanto Servare
iussit, qui suos Silenium parentes Facilius posset noscere,* where the
antecedent to *qui* is *cistellam cum crepundiis* (*v.* 43), or simply *cistellam*
(*v.* 46). If we read with all the best MSS. in As. II. iii. 135, *Viginti
argenti commodus minas, huius quidem matri,* it might appear that *qui*
was here equivalent to *quas,* but in this, and perhaps in some of the
preceding examples, it may be held that *qui=ut,* 'in order that.'

VIII.—*QVIN.*

Quin occurs perpetually in the dramatic writers, and modifies the
clauses with which it is combined in so many different ways that it
demands close attention. We may perhaps class the different meanings under three heads. Of these, two are simple and distinct, but
the third is somewhat complicated.

1. *Quin* is employed in direct interrogations, in which case it is
followed by the indicative, and is equivalent to *cur non.* We may
fairly regard *quin* here as representing *qui non* or *qui ne.* (On *qui*
see preceding Excursus.) *Quin* is not unfrequently followed by the
second person of the imperative, but in this case it has in reality
the force of a direct Interrogation, as we shall point out below.

2. *Quin* is employed in negative propositions, or in propositions
in which a negation is implied, as equivalent to *ut non,* and is followed
by the subjunctive. Here *quin,* in most cases, represents *qui non,*
i.e. *ut is non.*

3. *Quin* is employed very frequently in dialogue to introduce an
explanation of some statement or remark made previously, either by
the speaker himself or by the person with whom he is conversing.
It must be borne in mind that a speaker may repeat the remark of
another in different words, for the purpose of ascertaining that he
has correctly understood the remark in question, seeking an explanation, as it were; or he may repeat a remark previously made
by himself, for the purpose of making his meaning more clear, thus
giving an explanation, and all this may be done without emotion,
or with an expression of anger or of impatience, and the emotion may
in many cases be indicated by the tone of the speaker, and hence not

meet the eye in a written conversation. Again, the speaker may
affirm what has been said, but with a qualification; this qualification
may be such as to strengthen the remark previously made, or it may
call in question the accuracy of a portion of the remark, and the
qualification may in certain cases be so important as to amount to
a contradiction.

The force of *quin*, when explanatory, may generally be rendered
by one or other of the English expressions 'well, then,' 'why, I tell
you,' 'but,' 'nay,' 'nay, for that matter,' but the full force would in
many cases be conveyed by the tone or gestures of the speaker. It
will be seen from some of the quotations that *quin* and *imo* are
occasionally equivalent.

What we have said will be more easily understood from the
following examples.

1. *Quin* equivalent to *cur non* in a simple direct interrogation
followed by the indicative: Most. I. ii. 12, *Quin tu te exornas moribus lepidis quom lepida tota es?* Trin. III. iii. 73, *Quid nunc stas? quin
te hinc amoves et te moves?* Merc. I. 77, 78, *Eho tu, eho tu, quin cavisti',
ne eam videret, verbero? Quin, scelesle, apstrudebas, ne eam conspiceret
pater?* The last example is specially remarkable because it is said
to be the only passage in Plautus in which *quin*, in the sense of *cur
non*, is followed by a past tense.

Sometimes the question is put in an indignant tone; e. g. Trin. I.
ii. 81, *Quin cum restituis? Quin ad frugem corrigis?* or denotes impatience, as Men. IV. ii. 76, *Quid id est? quid taces? quin dicis quid
sit?* or conveys a remonstrance or entreaty, Pers. III. i. 69, *Quin tu
me ducis, si quo ducturus, pater? Vel tu me vende, vel face quod tibi
lubet;* and so Men. V. vii. 11, *Epidamnienses, subvenite, cives! quin
me millitis?*

Quin is frequently followed by the imperative, and in this case the
expression may always be regarded as elliptical; thus Most. I. iii. 16,
Quin me aspice et contempla, is equivalent to *Aspice et contempla me, quin
aspicis?* i. e. 'look at me, why don't you look?' and so again, v. 30,
Quin mone, quaeso, si quid erro . . . Mone, quaeso, quin mones? i. e.
'advise me, I beg, why don't you?' In III. i. 45 (41) we have a
good example, in the same line, of *quin* in a direct interrogation, and
also followed by the imperative; *D. Quin tu istas mittis tricas?
T. Quin quid vis cedo. Quin* followed by the imperative may imply
encouragement; thus Adel. IV. ii. 4, *C. Perii! S. Quin tu animo
bono es,* i. e. 'cheer up, can't you?' and in the previous scene, v. 17,
Quin otiosus es, 'be easy, can't you!' There is an ellipse of the

verb in Stich. IV. ii. 12, *E. Edepol te vocem lubenter, si superfiat locus.
G. Quin tu : stans optruxero aliquid strenue : E.* 'I would willingly
invite you if there was a place vacant.' G. 'Why not (invite me then):
I shall cram down something vigorously, although standing:' here we
may supply *vocas*, making it a direct question, or *vora*, 'invite me
then, why don't you?'

2. *Quin* equivalent to *ut non* in negative propositions: thus Most.
I. ii. 68 (62), *Non vidsor mihi Sarcire posse aedis meas, quin totae
Perpetuae ruant, quin cum fundamento Perierint;* Andr. I. ii. 1, *Non
dubium est quin uxorem nolit filius;* so Trin. III. ii. 14, *nec depellor
quin;* Men. II. i. 28, *nequeo continere quin;* Trin. III. iii. 2, *non potest
fieri quin;* Most. II. ii. 5, *haud causa est quin,* &c.

The same takes place occasionally in interrogative sentences where
a negation is implied but not directly expressed; thus Men. V. ix. 85,
Numquid me morare, quin ego liber, ut iussisti, eam? i.e. 'you are not
going to hinder me, are you?' so Adel. II. ii. 39, *Numquid vis quin
abeam?* i.e. 'you don't want anything, do you, to prevent me from
going away?' Cist. I. i. 119, *Numquid me vis, mater, intro quin cam?*
Eun. V. viii. 13, *Numquid, Gnatho, tu dubitas quin ego nunc perpetuo
perierim?*

In the above examples the negative character of the sentence is
clearly indicated by *numquid*, but in most cases we rely on the general
sense of the passage; thus Heaut. I. ii. 19, *Quid reliqui est quin habeat
quae quidem in homine dicuntur bona?* i.e. *nihil reliqui est;* so Eun. I.
ii. 100, *quam ioco Rem voluisti a me tandem quin perfeceris?* i.e. *nullam
rem voluisti;* and Phor. III. iii. 3, *Itaue hunc patiemur, Geta, Fieri
miserum qui nec dudum, ut dixti, adiuvit comiter, Quin, cum opus est,
beneficium rursum ei experiemur reddere?* i.e. 'surely we will never
suffer' &c.; and Andr. III. iv. 21, *Quid causae est quin hinc in pistrinum
recta proficiscar via?* i.e. *nulla causa est;* and exactly parallel, Rud.
III. iv. 53, *Quid causae est quin virgis te usque ad saturitatem sauciem?*
in Poen. I. i. 65 *quid tu dubitas quin* means 'you cannot doubt but
that;' and on the same principle we explain Trin. II. iv. 187, *O pater,
Aequom videtur, quin quod peccarim . . . potissumum mihi id opsit?* i.e.
'is it not just that' &c.

The following is less distinct: Eun. IV. vii. 41, *T. Quid nunc
agimus? G. Quin redeamus, iam hace tibi aderit supplicans Vltro,*
where we may explain the construction either by supposing an
ellipse, *nulla causa est quin redeamus,* or by considering *redeamus* as
an imperative, 'let us return, why should we not?'

In like manner *quin* is employed in sentences where prevention or prohibition are expressed or implied; thus Most. I. iii. 46, *Vix comprimor quin involem illi in oculos stimulatrici*, i. e. 'I can scarcely restrain myself from' &c.; and, exactly parallel, Eun. V. ii. 20, *Vix me contineo quin involem in Capillum;* so Epid. III. iv. 1, *Cave praeterbitas ullas aedes quin roges, Senex ubi habitat Periphanes Platenius;* and Trin. I. ii. 67, *Est atque non est mihi in manu, Megaronides: Quin dicant, non est: merito ut ne dicant, id est,* i. e. *prohibere quin dicant.*

3. *Quin,* followed by an indicative, is sometimes explanatory or affirmative; Epid. II. iii. 1, *Nullum esse opinor ego agrum in agro Attico, Aeque feracem quam hic est noster Periphanes; Quin ex occulto atque opsignato armario Decutio argenti tantum quantum mihi lubet,* where *quin* is introduced to explain the metaphor employed in the two preceding lines, 'why, I tell you,' or, 'for you see;' Rud. III. iv. 62, *L. Ignem magnum hic faciam. D. Quin ut humanum exuras tibi,* where *quin* is equivalent to *videlicet.* Daemones pretends to interpret or explain what Latrax had said, 'for the purpose, I presume, of offering a sacrifice to the dead in honour of yourself,' i. e. 'in order to burn yourself;' Cist. I. ii. 1, *Idem mihi magnae quod parti est vitium mulierum. Quae hunc quaestum facimus : quae ubi saburratae sumus, Largiloquae extemplo sumus : plus loquimur quam sat est. . . . . Quin ego nunc, quia sum onusta mea ex sententia, Quiaque adeo me complevi flore Liberi, Magis libera uti lingua conlubitum est mihi.* The old woman remarks that persons of her class, when well ballasted with liquor, forthwith become talkative, and talk more than is convenient; she then proceeds to disclose a piece of secret history, and interrupting herself goes on, *quin ego,* 'why, for example, I at this time, having got a heavy cargo of wine on board, to my heart's content, feel inclined to use my tongue more freely than is expedient.' In Cas. II. iv. 6 we have *quin* twice in the same line in different senses; *C. Quin, si ita arbitrare, emittis me manu? S. Quin, id volo,* where the first *quin* is equivalent to *cur non,* the second is explanatory, 'why, I tell you, I am willing to do that.'

Quin may frequently be rendered by 'why, I tell you,' or 'why, to be sure,' when the speaker manifests eagerness, impatience, or indignation. Eagerness: Heaut. IV. iv. 16, *S. Perii hercle ! Bacchis, mane, mane : quo mittis istanc? quaeso, Iube maneat. B. I. S. Quin est paratum argentum. B. Quin ego maneo,* 'stop, stop, bid her stop;' 'why, I tell you, the money is all ready,' where the first *quin* is spoken in eager excitement, and the word is repeated in mockery by Bacchis, 'then, I tell you, I stop.' Impatience: Men. V. iv. 4 ; the physician

asks with what malady the patient to whom he had been called is
affected, on which the old man replies testily, *Quin ea te causa duco
ut id dicas mihi,* 'why, I tell you, I am taking you to him for this
very reason, that you may tell me what his malady is.' Impatience
and indignation: Men. V. viii. 2, *Mes. Men' hodie usquam convenisse te,
audax, audes dicere, Postquam advorsum mihi imperavi ut huc venires?
Mes. Quin modo Eripui,* 'met you! why, just now I rescued you.'
Great indignation: Cas. II. ii. 22, *Vir me habet pessumis despicatam
modis. . . . . Quin mihi ancillulam ingratis postulat,
quae mea est, Quae meo educata sumptu est, villico suo se dare,* 'why, he
even goes the length of insisting,' &c.

Quin is affirmative in Merc. II. iii. 77, *Hercle, quin tu recte dicis et
tibi adsentior ego,* 'by Hercules, but thou sayest well:' we have the
same phrase again, V. iv. 47, Men. II. iii. 74, and, slightly varied,
in V. ix. 33, *Hercle quin tu me admonuisti recte, et habeo gratiam.*
It denotes strong affirmation in Poen. IV. ii. 86, *S. Profecto ad in-
citas lenonem rediget si eas abduxerit. M. Quin prius disperibit, faxo,
quam unam calcem civerit. Ita paratum est,* 'but I am determined
that he shall be utterly destroyed before he shall have made a single
move: I have taken measures to that effect.'

Frequently *quin* is not a simple affirmative, but adds something
which gives greater force or emphasis to the question or remark of
the preceding speaker; thus Most. II. ii. 25, *Ta. An tu tetigisti has
aedes? Tu. Cur non tangerem? Quin pultando, inquam, paene confregi
fores,* 'not only have I touched the door, but, more than that, I tell
you that I have almost smashed it to pieces by battering it;' so Cas.
III. i. 7, *S. Fac vacent aedes. A. Quin, edepol, servos, ancillas, domo
Certum est omnes mittere ad te,* i. e. 'not only will I see to that, but,
more than that, I have resolved' &c.; Men. V. iv. 7, *S. Magna cum
cura ego illum curari volo. M. Quin suspirabo plus sexcenties in die:
Ita ego illum cum cura ego magna curabo tibi.* The commentators have
missed the sense of this passage; there is a pun on the double
meaning of *cura,* which may signify, as in English, either simply
'diligence' or 'mental anxiety:' S. 'I wish him to be cared for with
great care.' M. 'Why, for that matter, I will heave sighs of care
more than six hundred times a day, so great shall be the care with
which I will take care of him for you.'

When *quin* is used in this sense it is sometimes followed by *etiam;*
thus Most. II. i. 74, [*Herus*] *iussit maxumo Opere orare, ut patrem
aliquo apsterreres modo Ne introiret aedis. T. Quin etiam illi hoc
dicito Facturum ut me etiam aspicere aedis audeat,* i. e. 'tell him that

I will not only scare his father from entering the house, but, more than that, that I will deal with him in such a manner that he will not venture even to look at it, but' &c.; so Men. V. ii. 55, *S. Male facit, si istuc facit; si non facit, tu male facis, Quae insontem insimules. M. Quin etiam nunc habet pallam pater, Et spinther, quod ad hanc detulerat: nunc, quia rescivi, refert,* i. e. 'not only do I not falsely accuse him of having carried off my property, but, more than that, at this very time he has in his possession a dress and a broach,' &c., where, however, *etiam* may, if we please, be connected with *nunc*. We have the expression still more fully in Eun. IV. iii. 3, *Quin etiam insuper serivi,* &c.

The form of *quin* in the following passages may be conveyed by the words 'well' or 'nay,' 'for that matter, assuredly,' and it serves to introduce an explanation of the feelings or actions of the speaker: Adel. IV. vii. 14, after Demea has reproached his brother for his indifference and indulgence in the matter of Aeschinus and Pamphila, Micio asks—*M. Quid faciam amplius? D. Quid facias? si non ipsa re istuc tibi dolet, Simulare certe est hominis. M. Quin iam virginem Despondi: res composita est: fiunt nuptiae: Dempsi metum omnem: haec magis sunt hominis,* 'nay, for that matter, (in so far as my duty as a right-minded man is concerned,) I have already settled the marriage of the maiden with my son; the affair is arranged; the wedding is in progress:' here *quin* introduces an explanation and conveys, perhaps, a tone of indignation, 'why I tell you;' Andr. IV. ii. 20, *P. Scio quid conere. D. Hoc ego tibi profecto effectum reddam. P. Iam hoc opus est. D. Quin iam habeo. C. Quid est?* 'well, then, for that matter, I have already a scheme;' Heaut. IV. iii. 23, Clinia is discussing with Syrus how the real state of affairs may best be concealed from his father—*C. Num quo ore appellabo patrem? Tenes quid dicam? S. Quidni? C. Quid dicam? quam causam adferam? S. Quin, nole mentiare. Aperte, ita ut res sese habet, narrato,* 'nay, for that matter, I do not want you to tell a lie,' 'do not suppose that I want you:' here *quin* is explanatory, as Syrus wishes to guard against a misapprehension; Merc. III. iv. 43, *C. Deos apsentes testes memoras: qui ego istuc credam tibi? E. Quin tibi in manu est, quod credas: ego quod dicam id mihi mea in manu est,* 'well, for that matter, you have the power of believing what you°please; I have the power of saying what I please;' Most. III. i. 86 (82), *Vide, num moratur? D. Quin feram, si quid datur,* 'nay, for that matter,' or 'assuredly, you may be sure of this, that' &c.; Heaut. V. i. 71, *Id mirari te simulato, et illum hoc rogitato simul, Quamobrem id faciam. M. Quin ego vero quamobrem id facias nescio*, 'why, for that matter, in sooth, I do not know why you are doing that.'

Sometimes the qualification introduced by *quin* is so strong that it must be translated 'nay, on the contrary:' Trin. IV. iL 87, *C. Lubet audire, nisi molestum est. S. Quin discupio dicere* : here *quin* refers to the foregoing *molestum*—'(disagreeable!) nay, on the contrary, I am most eager to tell you;' Merc. I. 43, *Egon' ausim tibi usquam quicquam facinus falsum proloqui? Quin iam priusquam sim elocutus, scis, si mentiri volo*, 'do you think it possible that I would dare to tell you a falsehood? No, on the contrary, before I open my lips, you know' &c.; Most. IV. ii. 38 (iii. 15), *P. Nam nisi hinc hodie emigravit, aut heri, certo scio Hic habitare. T. Quin sex menses iam hic nemo habitat*, 'why, on the contrary, I tell you,' &c.; Merc. II. ii. 54, *L. Ad portum proparo : nam ibi mihi negotium est. D. Bene ambulato. L. Bene valeto. D. Bene sit tibi* : here Lysimachus quits the stage and Demipho continues, *Quin mihi quoque etiam est ad portum negotium, Nunc adeo ibo illuc:* Demipho replies to his own thoughts as it were, 'dare any one suppose that I am going to remain here? No, on the contrary, I also have business at the harbour, and therefore I will now repair thither.'

The use of *quin* in the following passages may, at first sight, cause some embarrassment, but they may be referred to one or other of the classes examined above: Stich. IV. ii. 44, *G. Quid igitur? E. Dixi equidem in carcerem ires. G. Quin, iusseris, Eo quoque ibo*, 'well, then,' 'nay, for that matter,' or simply 'but, if you give the order, I shall go even thither' (to prison); where *quin* qualifies *eo quoque ibo*. Many editors read *si iusseris*, but *si* is not found in the best MSS., and is unnecessary, in so far as the construction is concerned, the perfect of the subjunctive being frequently employed to indicate an hypothesis; thus Iuv. S. III. 77, *omnia novit Graeculus esuriens, in caelum, iusseris, ibit:* Trin. II. ii. 60, *Non eo hoc dico quin, quas tu vis, ego velim et faciam lubens*, 'I do not say this for the purpose of implying that I am not willing to accommodate myself to your wishes, and to do cheerfully what you desire,' where *quin* is equivalent to *ut non;* Merc. II. iii. 93, the father and son are disputing about Pasicompsa, Demipho says, *Viginti minis. opinor, posse me illam vendere. C. At ego si velim, iam dantur septem et viginti minae. D. At ego ... C. Quin, ego, inquam ... D. At nescis quid dicturus sim, tace:* *quin* here marks an eager interruption—Demipho says, 'But I (would give).' C. 'No, but I, I tell you, (would give more);' IV. Iv. 25, *D. Palam istaec fiunt, te me odisse. L. Quin nego*, 'no, no, I deny it;' Pers. I. i. 40, *Qua confidentia rogare te a me argentum tantum audes Impudens? quin si egomet totus veneam, vix recipi potessit Quod tu me rogas, nam tu aquam a pumice nunc postulas* : here a contradiction is implied—'why (far from having such a sum at my disposal), if I were to be sold bodily, bag and baggage,' &c.; Eun. II. i. 6, Phaedria having given an order to Parmeno which calls forth a sort of reproof from the slave, Phaedria adds, *Ne istuc tam iniquo patiare animo. Par. Minume: quin effectum dabo,* 'do not be so much distressed by that piece of extravagance.' Par. 'By no means: on the contrary, I shall carry out your wishes;' Trin. II. iv. 63, *L. Oculum ego effodiam tibi Si verbum addideris. S. Hercle, quin dicam tamen*: here we may suppose an ellipse of *non deterrebis me quin dicam*, or, if we regard *dicam* as the future, we may translate 'nay, but speak I will, in spite of your threats;' Merc. IV. iii. 25, Lysimachus is being cross-questioned by his wife, and knows not what answer to give; Dorippa repeats her interrogation, *D. Quin dicis? L. Quin si liceat . . . D. Dictum oportuit,* 'why do you not speak out?' upon which Lysimachus in his embarrassment catches up the *quin*, 'nay, for that matter, if you would let me,' . . . —there was probably a pause of hesitation between *quin* and *si liceat*, which ought to be indicated by the punctuation, *Quin . . . si liceat . . .*; Eun. V. ii. 63, *Quin, Pythias, Tu me servato: quin* may seem here to imply expostulation or remonstrance, 'nay, come now, Pythias, help me,' but we may regard it simply as a case of *quin* followed by the imperative, 'save me, Pythias, why do you not aid me?' Heaut. III. iii. 20, *C. Sure, pudet me. S. Credo, neque id iniuria. Quin mihi molestum est,* 'I well believe that you are ashamed, and you have good reason. Why, I tell you (more than that) that even I am annoyed by this business,' with a strong emphasis on *I;* IV. v. 51, Chremes, convinced by the arguments of Syrus, agrees to pay the money to Bacchis, *Quin egomet iam ad eam deferam,* 'well, then, not only am I willing to pay the money, but, more than that, I shall carry it to her in person;' Phor. V. viii. 25, *Ego, Nausistrata, esse in hac re culpam meritam non nego, Sed tam, quin sit ignoscenda,* 'I do not deny that guilt has been incurred in this matter, but I do deny that the guilt has been such (*tam=talem*) as to be unpardonable,' where *quin* is equivalent to *ut non*. If, with many MSS., we read *ea*, we must place a comma or hyphen after *sed*—(*nego culpam esse talem*) *ut ea non sit ignoscenda*, but in this case the ellipse is somewhat violent.

The examples given above, although numerous, by no means

222   PLAVTI MOSTELLARIA.

exhaust the delicate modifications of meaning conveyed by *quin*, but
enough has been said to guide the student in his investigations.
We may conclude by quoting a passage from the *Casina* III. iv.
9, seqq. in which *quin* is used in a wrangle, and, except in the first
line, where it is equivalent to *cur non*, must be rendered by ' why,
I tell you' and 'nay, more than that:' *A. Quin tu suspendis te?*
Nempe tute dixeras, Tuam arcessituram esse hinc uxorem meam.
S. Ergo arcessivisse ait esse, et dixisse te Eam non missurum. A. Quin
ea ipsa ultro mihi Negavit eius operam se moraritr. S. Quin ea ipsa
me adlegavit, qui istam arcesserem. A. 'Quin' nihili facio. S. Quin me
perdis. A. Quin bene est. Quin etiam diu morabor: quin cupio tibi,
Quin aliquid aegre facere, quin faciam lubens. Numquam tibi hodie
'quin' erit plus quam mihi. Quin hercle di te perdant postremo quidem.

IX.—*VT.*

We shall confine our remarks to those uses of this word which,
although not peculiar to the dramatic writers, occur more frequently
in dialogue than in ordinary composition.

The different meanings of *Vt* may be conveniently arranged under
two heads.

1. *Vt* signifying 'how,' 'as,' 'when,' meanings which may easily
be deduced from each other, and may in many cases be represented
by *quo modo*, or *eo modo quo* or *modum quo*, *quam*, *quantum*, *quanto*,
qualis. In this case *ut* in direct propositions is generally followed
by the indicative mood.

II. *Vt* signifying 'that' or 'in order that.' This meaning also
may be deduced from 'how,' but the transition is not so obvious.
In this case *ut* is followed by the subjunctive mood.

I. *Vt* signifying 'how,' 'as,' 'when.'

1. *Vt*, 'how,' indicating a simple direct interrogation, as in the
English phrases 'how does she look?' 'how are you?' 'how goes
it?' Merc. II. iii. 56, *D. Sed quis ais? ecquam tu advexti tuae matri*
ancillam Rhodo? C. Advexi. D. Quid? ea ut videtur mulier?
C. Non edepol mala. D. Vt morata est? C. Nullam vidi melius mea
sententia, 'what sort of appearance has the woman?' 'how does she
look?' 'how is she in disposition?' or 'how is she in manners?'
(i.e. 'is she well-bred?') so Most. III. ii. 28, Rud. V. ii. 17, *ut vales?*
'how are you?' and Truc. II. vii. 23. *quid agis, uti vales?* Pers. IV.
iv. 5. *ut moenitum muro tibi visum est oppidum?* Rud. II. ii. 6, *quid*
agitis? ut peritis? where *ut peritis* is a pleasantry σὺν ἰρωνείᾳ, *ut*

valuis being expected; As. III. iii. 115, *ut tu iuredis?* 'what kind of stepping is that?' When the question is direct, *ut* is followed by the indicative, as in the above examples, but in a dependent clause it is, of course, followed by the subjunctive: Aul. I. iii. 29, *Rogitant me ut valeam, quid agam, quid rerum geram.*

2. *Vt*, 'how,' indicating emotion, the character of the emotion being determined by the circumstances of the case or by the words with which it is combined, as in English, 'how he struggles!' 'how he runs!' 'how his eyes sparkle!' Thus we have (a) Eager interest and excitement: Rud. I. ii. 66, *Homunculi quanti estis! eiecti ut natant!* and v. 82, *Viden alteram illam? ut fluctus eiecit foras!* (b) Alarm: Men. V. ii. 76, 77, 80, *Viden tu illi oculos virere? Vt viridis exoritur colos Ex temporibus atque fronte! Vt oculi scintillant! vide! . . . . Vt pendiculans oscitatur! Quid nunc faciam, mi pater?* (c) Admiration: Truc. II. iv. 3, *Ver vide! Vt tota floret! ut olet! ut nitide nitet!* As. III. ii. 35, *Vt adsimulabat Sauream med esse! quam facete!* and so Cas. II. iii. 25, *ut cito commentatus est!* Poen. V. iv. 27, *ut sapit!* 'how wise she is!' Bac. IV. viii. 57, *ut iurat!* 'how famously he swears!' (d) Merriment: Mil IV. ii. 74, *Vt ludo! . . Vt subleclo os!* (e) Indignation: Cas. II. iii. 30, *Vnde is, nihili? ubi fuisti? ubi lustratus? ubi bibisti? Id est, mecastor: vide! palliolum ut rugat!* and so Pseud. II. iv. 17, *ut paratragoedat carnufex!* 'how the hang-dog struts and rants!' Rud. III. vi. 31, *viden me! ut rapior!* (f) Joy: Stich. III. ii. 12, *Epignome, ut ego te nunc conspicio lubens! Vt prae laetitia lacrumae prosiliunt mihi!* (g) Ironical sneer: Truc. II. ii. 25, *Rus tu mihi obprobras? ut nacta es* * *hominem quem pudeat probri!* 'dost thou flout me with the country? how successful you are in finding a man who is ashamed of the taunt!'

3. *Vt*, 'how,' in the sense of 'to what extent,' 'to what degree' (*quam*), 'how much' (*quantum*), as in English, 'how good he is,' 'how I love him;' Amph. V. i. 51, *Sed puer ille quem ego laui, ut magnus est et multum valet!* i.e. 'how high he is, and how strong!' Men. I. iii. 7, *Vt ego uxorem, mea voluptas, ubi te aspicio, odi male!* i.e. 'how I detest my wife!' Rud. Prol. 10, *Is nos per gentes alium alia disparat, Hominum qui facta, mores, pietatem et fidem Noscamus, ut quemque adiuvet opulentia,* i.e. 'to what extent;' Capt. II. ii. 41, *Ad rem divinam quibus est opus Samiis vasis utitur, Ne ipse Genius subripiat. Proinde aliis ut credat, vide,* 'judge from that how far—to what extent—he will trust others;' Trin. IV. ii. 68, the Sycophanta

* Weise is quite mistaken when he explains *ut* here by "postquam nacta es."

having forgotten the name of Charmides, from whom he pretended
to be the bearer of a letter, Charmides, who is playing with him, says
ironically—*C. Vide, homo, ut hominem noveris. S. Tamquam me,* 'see
you now then, my good fellow, how far—to what extent—you are
acquainted with this person,' to which the Sycophanta replies, ' I
know him as well as I know myself.'

This is probably the force of *ut* in Bac. II. ii. 30, *Imo ut cum,
credis, misera amans desiderat:* all the MSS. have *eam,* for which
recent editors, following Acidalius, substitute *eam,* but if we punctuate
as above the change is unnecessary. We have already quoted this
line under *imo,* p. 199 sub fin.

In Most. III. ii. 146 (144) *ut* is equivalent to *quanto; T. Vt
quicquid magis contemplor, tanto magis placet.*

4. *Vt,* 'how,' in the sense 'of what kind' (*qualis*), as in the
English phrase, 'how is he as to temper?' thus in Stich. I. ii. 55,
where Antipho and Pinacium are discussing *mulierum mores,* the
latter says—*P. Scio ut oportet esse si sint ita ut ego aequom censeo.
A. Volo scire ergo, ut aequom censes. P. Vt per urbem quom ambulent,
Omnibus os opturent ne quis merito maledicat sibi,* where the first and
second *ut* are equivalent to *quales;* so in Curc. I. i. 59, *Imo ut illam
censes?* it is clear from the context that these words are equivalent
to *qualem illam censes esse;* so Amph. Prol. 104, *Nam ego vos novisse
credo iam ut sit pater meus, Quam liber harum rerum multarum siet,*
' I take it for granted that you know what kind of person my father
is, how he conducts himself,' &c.

This force of *ut* may, not unfrequently, be represented by the
English 'as.' Amph. III. iii. 4, *Atque ita servom par videtur frugi
sese instituere, Proinde heri ut sint, ipse item sit,* where *Proinde ut,*
'just as,' is equivalent to *quales;* so Capt. II. i. 32, *Ero, ut me voles
esse,* 'I shall be as you wish me to be,' i.e. 'such as' *talis qualem;*
and again, v. 39, *Nunc ut te mihi volo esse, esse autumo;* Truc. II. vii.
16, *meretricem ego item esse reor mare ut est,* 'such as is the sea,'
talem quale.

In Men. II. iii. 78, *MES. Quid ergo? MEN. Opus est. MES. Quid
opus est? MEN. Scio, ut me dices. MES. Tanto nequior es :* the text
is probably corrupt.

5. *Vt,* 'how,' has frequently an explanatory force in dependent
clauses; thus in English, 'I will tell you how it happened,' 'let us
consult how we may best assist him,' and the like. In all such cases
ut, in Latin, must be followed by the subjunctive: Poen. I. i. 66,
Abeamus intro ut Collubiscum villicum Hunc perdoceamus ut ferat

fallaciam; Truc. II. ii. 43, *S. Scio ego plus quam me arbitrare scire. A. Quid id est, opsecro, Quod scias? S. Herilis noster filius apud vos Strabax Vt pereat, ut eum inliciatis in malam fraudem;* Epid. III. ii. 41, *Haec scitis iam ut futura sint, abeo;* Truc. IV. iii. 50, *Neque ut hinc abeam, neque ut hunc adeam scio, timore torpeo.*

6. *Vt,* 'as,' *eo modo quo;* so in English, 'I tell you the story as I heard it,' followed by the indicative: As. III. ii. 30, *Num male rdata est gratia? ut contegam contaudari? L. Vt meque teque maxume atque ingenio nostro decuit,* where *ut* in the direct interrogation is equivalent to *quomodo,* and *ut* in the correlative clause to *eo modo quo;* II. ii. 100, *Nunc tu abi ad forum, ad herum, et narra haec ut nos acturi sumus,* L e. *narra haec eo modo quo nos,* &c.; *v.* 109, *I.x. Dico ut usus fieri. Lt. Dico, hercle, ego quoque ut facturus sum,* where in both clauses *ut* is equivalent to *eo modo quo.*

7. *Vt,* 'as,' equivalent to *ita ut,* 'according to,' 'according as,' 'just as:' so in English, 'as I understand the matter,' i. e. 'according to my understanding of the matter;' 'he will act as his inclination prompts him,' i. e. 'according as,' 'just as,' &c.: Cist. I. i. 5, *ut meus est animus,* Truc. IV. iii. 1, *ut animus meus est,* 'according to my view;' Bac. II. ii. 40, *ut rem hanc gnatam esse intellego;* Truc. V. 70, *ut rem gnatam video,* 'according to my understanding of the matter;' Most. III. ii. 47, *ut voluimus riximus,* 'we have lived just as we wished, according to our wishes;' Cist. IV. ii. 51, *Hanc scire oportet, filia tua ubi sit, signa ut dicit,* i. e. 'according to the tokens which she mentions,' 'judging from the tokens' &c.; Trin. II. iv. 146, *Sed iste est ager profecto, ut te audivi loqui, Malos in quem omnes publice mitti decet,* i. e. 'according to what you say,' 'judging from what you say;' Cas. II. viii. 56, *Abi atque opsona, propera, sed lepide volo: Mollirulas escas, ut ipsa mollirula est,* 'viands soft and tender, just as (in like manner as) she herself is soft and tender.'

8. *Vt,* 'as,' explanatory, equivalent to 'inasmuch as:' so in English, 'the inn was crowded, as a number of travellers had arrived,' 'he was much looked up to, as holding a high office:' Men. Prol. 30, *Mortales multi, ut ad ludos, convenerant:* here *ut* is used to explain *multi,* 'a great crowd had assembled, inasmuch as they had flocked together to behold the games,' 'there was a great crowd, as was to be expected, inasmuch as' &c.; Truc. II. vii. 22, *Atat eccam, adest propinque, credo audisse haec me loqui; Pallida est ut peperit puerum:* here *ut* is used to explain the epithet *pallida,* 'she is pale, inasmuch as she has given birth to a boy.'

9. *Vt,* 'as,' used with reference to time, and signifying 'when:'

G g

so in English 'as' and 'when' are frequently convertible—we may say, 'he came as I was at dinner' or 'when I was at dinner,' 'I saw him as I was sitting in a shop' or 'when I was sitting:' so Merc. Prol. 99, *Discubitum noctu ut imus, ecce ad me advenit,* i. e. 'as we were going to bed,' or 'when we' &c.; As. II. ii. 76, *Verum in tonstrina ut sedebam, me infit percontarier,* i. e. 'as I was sitting,' or 'when I was sitting.' *Vt semel* signifies 'as soon as:' Truc. I. ii. 6, *Vt semel adveniunt ad scorta congerrones.*

Vt with a perfect tense must often be rendered as if it were *postquam,* as in the following examples: Most. I. iii. 63, *Eumdem animum oportet nunc mihi esse gratum ut impetravi, Atque olim, priusquam,* i. e. *postquam impetrari;* Capt. III. i. 18, *Nam ut dudum hinc abii, adcessi ad adulescentes in foro;* Men. IV. ii. 71, *Quin ut dudum divorti aps te, redeo nunc demum domum;* Epid. IV. ii. 30, *Quid ego? qui illam ut primum vidi, numquam vidi postea;* Most. I. iii. 111, *Vt speculum tenuisti, metuo ne oleant argentum manus.* We may compare the well-known line in Virgil, Ecl. VIII. 41, *Vt vidi, ut perii, ut me malus abstulit error!*

Vt followed by *quemque* signifies 'when' in the sense of 'as soon as:' As. I. iii. 93, *Supplicabo, exopsecrabo, ut quemque amicum videro;* Men. III. ii. 56, *Quid hoc negoti est? Satin ut quemque conspicor, Ita me ludificant?*

II. *Vt* signifying 'that.'

1. *Vt,* 'that,' is occasionally used in what we may term a rhetorical question, that is, a question not put for the sake of obtaining information, but as a mode of expressing the indignation, scorn, contempt, or ridicule entertained by the speaker for some statement or opinion expressed by another. In all such cases there is an aposiopesis before *ut,* and the blank must be mentally supplied: thus Truc. II. iv. 87, *Egone illam ut non amem! egone illi ut non bene velim!* '(is it possible) that I should not love her? (is it possible to believe) that I should not wish her well?' IV. ii. 28, D. *Illine ut inimici mei Bona istic comedant? Mortuom, hercle, me quam ut id patiar malelim,* '(is it to be endured) that those my enemies should eat up in that house my good things?' Trin. III. iii. 21, *Vt ego nunc adulescenti thesaurum indicem Indomito, pleno amoris ac lascitiae? Minume, minume hercle vero,* '(what I do you advise) that I should reveal the hoard,' &c.; Men. IV. iii. 9, *Mihi ut tu dederis pallam et spinther? Numquam factum reperies,* '(what, have you the assurance to assert) that you gave me a shawl and a buckle?' Pers. I. iii. 51, *T. Hic leno neque te novit neque gnatam*

tuam. S. Me ut quisquam norit nisi illa qui praebet cibum? '(it isn't
very likely, is it) that any one should be acquainted with me except'
&c.; Most. IV. iii. 25 (iv. 25), *S. Mecum ut ille gesserit, Dum tu hinc
abes, negoti? quidnam? aut quodie?* '(it's a very likely story) that he
transacted business with me while you were away! what was it?
when was it?' Poen. I. ii. 103, *Vt tu quidem huius oculos inlotis manibus tractes aut teras?* '(what I do you dare) to handle or rub the
eyes of this my love with unwashed hands?' As. V. ii. 34, *D. Egon'
ut non domo uxori meae Subripiam in deliciis pallam quam habet, atque
ad te deferam?* '(do you think that I will hesitate) to filch from my
wife,' &c.; Curc. V. ii. 17, *P. Virgo haec libera est. T. Meane ancilla libera ut sit! quam ego numquam emisi manu,* '(do you mean to
say) that my female slave is a free woman?'

We find the same construction in Cicero, in rhetorical passages:
thus in Cat. I. 9, *Quamquam quid loquar? Te ut ulla res frangat?
Tu ut umquam te corrigas? Tu ut ullam fugam mediteris? Tu ut
ullum exsilium cogites?*

2. *Vt,* 'that,' is occasionally used elliptically in prayers and
imprecations, the word *precor,* or *quaero,* or the like, being omitted:
so in English we say, 'O that ruin may overtake him!' i.e. 'O, I
pray that' &c.; Pers. II. iv. 19, *S. Quid hoc? P. Quid est? S. Etiam,
scelus, male loquere? P. Tandem ut liceat, Quom servos sis, servom tibi
male dicere! 'O* that at length I might be allowed!' Cas. II. iii. 20,
*Teneor: cesso caput pallio detergere? uti te bonus Mercurius perdat,
muropola, qui hanc mihi dedisti!* Adel. IV. vi. 1, *Deferxus sum ambu-
lando: ut, Sure, te cum tua Monstratione magnus perdat Iupiter!* Aul.
IV. x. 55, *Vt illum Di inmortales omnes Deaeque, quantum est, perduint!*
exactly parallel, Heaut. IV. vi. 7, *Vt te quidem omnes Di Deaeque,
quantum est, Sure, Cum tuo istoc invento cumque incepto perduint!* and
Eun. II. iii. 10, *Vt illum Di Deaeque senium perdant, qui me hodie
remoratus est!*

All are familiar with *utinam* in this sense, and here also there is
a similar ellipse. Sometimes the ellipse is supplied, as in Cas. II. vi.
37, *O. Tace, Deos quaeso. C. Vt quidem tu hodie canem et furcam
feras! O. Mihi ut sortitio eveniat. C. Vt quidem, hercle, pedibus pendeas. O. At tu ut oculos emungare ex capite per nasum tuos!*

3. *Vt,* 'that,' is used elliptically in the sense of 'on condition of,'
'provided only that:' thus Men. I. iii. 34, *Neque hodie, ut te perdam,
meream Deorum divitias mihi,* 'nor would I this day seek to earn the
wealth of the Gods on the condition of losing sight of you;' As. II.
ii. 8, *Aetatem velim servire, Libanum ut conveniam modo,* 'I would be

content to remain a slave for ever, provided only that I could meet
with Libanus just now.'

4. *Vt*, 'that,' is used very elliptically in the following passage,
where a threat is conveyed: Pers. V. ii. 9, *Quem pol ego ut non in
cruciatum atque in compedes cogam si vivam*, 'nor shall anything prevent me from consigning this fellow to chains and torture,' where *ut
non cogam* is equivalent to *nec possum prohiberi quin cogam*.

There is yet another elliptical use of *ut*, which may however be
ranked under (2): Poen. IV. ii. 90, *Valeas, beneque ut tibi sit*, where
we might supply *precor*, but the ellipse seems to be *cura*, which
appears in the next line, in the reply of Sincerastus, *Vale, et haec cura
clanculum ut sint dicta*; so again, Stich. I. ii. 48, *Discipulus venio ad
magistras: quibus matronas moribus, Quae optumae sunt, esse oportet?
sed utraque ut dicat mihi*, where it is more natural to supply *cura*
than *precor*, 'see that each of you two answer me.'

In a few cases it is open to us to translate *ut* either by 'how' or
by 'in order that:' thus Cist. I. i. 95, *G. Mihi istum hominem vellem
dari, Vt ego illum vorsarem!* which we may render, according to the
punctuation we select, either 'in order that I might turn him over
and over,' or, putting a comma after *dari* and a note of admiration
after *vorsarem*, 'how I would turn him over and over!' the idea being
perhaps taken from a cook grilling meat, or tossing an omelette in
a frying pan. The English phrase of 'turning a person round one's
finger' implies the same amount of absolute control on one side, and
helplessness on the other.

In Epid. II. ii. 40 we may translate *ut* either by 'as' or 'how:'
*P. Quid erat induta? an regillam induculam, an mendiculam Implu-
viatam? ut istae faciunt vestimentis nomina*, where *ut* may be either
'as they call their dresses,' or, making it an exclamation, 'how they
call,' i.e. 'what strange names, to be sure, they give their dresses!'

In the following passages, which are all difficult, *ut*, if the true
reading, must be equivalent to *utut*: Poen. IV. ii. 9, *Quodvis genus
ibi hominum videas, quasi Achirontem veneris, Equitem, peditem, libertinum, furem ac fugitivom velis, Verberatum, vinctum, addictum, qui
habet quod det, ut homo est*, i.e. 'be who has money to spend, whatever
kind of man he is,' where Bothe and others adopt *utut*, the conj. of
Gulielm.; Merc. Prol. 81, *Avorus, amansque, ut animum obfirmo meum,
Dico esse iturum me mercatum, si velit*, where *ut* must signify 'as best
I may,' or 'when I steel my resolution, I then say to my father,' &c.:
Pylades here reads *utut*, Ritschl conj. *actutum*; Phor. V. iv. 1, *Laetus
sum, ut meae res sese habent, fratri optigisse quod volt*: the best MSS.

here give *ut*, which the verse requires, and not *utut* of the Vulg. text: the meaning will be 'however (bad) the condition of my own affairs;' but Bentley renders it, 'I rejoice in so far as the condition of my own affairs permits me to rejoice.' The combination *utut* occurs several times in Plautus, where the reading is not doubtful, e. g. Most. III. i. 14, *Verum utut rese sese habet, Pergam turbare porro : ita haec res postulat.*

X.—FRVGI, NEQVAM.

That *frugi* is frequently used as an indeclinable adjective by writers of all epochs is unquestionable, and it is equally certain that it is the dative case of *frux, frugis*. In Plautus it is frequently construed with *sum*, and may in that case be regarded as a real dative : As. II. iv. 91, *quamquam ego sum sordidatus, Frugi tamen sum ;* Pers. IV. i. 5, *Si malus aut nequam est, male res vortunt quas agit; Sin autem frugi est, eveniunt frugaliter,* and as if to mark the word more distinctly as a substantive the epithet *bonae* is often added ; Pseud. I. v. 53, *Cupis me esse nequam, tamen ero frugi bonae ;* As. III. iii. 12, *Numquam bonae frugi sient, dies noctesque potent,* while the accusative *frugem* is occasionally found in the same sense ; thus Trin. I. ii. 81, *Quin ad frugem corrigis ?* II. i. 34, *Certum est ad frugem adplicare animum ;* Poen. IV. ii. 70, *Herus si haec velit facere frugem ;* but in many instances it must be regarded as indeclinable, as may be observed in some of the examples given below.

The true meaning of *frugi* is clearly indicated by the etymology— it is used to denote that a person is 'profitable' or 'useful' either to himself or to others. Thus it assumes many modifications of meaning.[*]

1. When used with reference to one who is profitable to himself it may signify 'economical' or 'thrifty,' as in the following lines, where it is opposed to *benignus :* Truc. I. i. 13, *Tentat benignusne an bonae frugi sies ; v.* 20, *si id quod oratur dedit, Atque est benignus potius quam frugi bonae :* or 'prudent,' Capt. II. ii. 44, *Philocrates hic fecit hominem frugi ut facere oportuit :* or 'respectable,' Curc. IV. ii. 16, *Nec vobiscum quitquam in foro frugi consistere audet ;* and so Aul. IV. ix. 6, *Quid ait ? quid ridetis ? novi omnes : scio fures esse hic complures*

[*] Cic. Tusc. III. 8, § 17 has a disquisition on the meanings of *frugalitas* and *frugi.* Cf. IV. 16, § 36 ; Pro Fonteio, XVII. § 39 (XIII. § 29); Pro Deiot. IX. § 26.

Qui reditus et creta occultant sese atque sedent quasi sient frugi; and
again, Cas. III. ii. 32, Trin. IV. iii. 11, and, generally, 'of good moral
character;' thus As. V. ii. 7, *Siccum, frugi, continentem, amantem uxoris
maxume;* and *v.* 11, *Ego quoque hercle illum antehac hominem semper
tum frugi ratus :* also, however, 'discreet' or 'worldly wise,' without
implying moral rectitude; Bac. IV. iv. 10, *Nullus frugi esse potest
homo nisi qui et bene et male facere tenet; Improbis cum improbus sit,
harpaget, furibus furetur quod queat : Versipellem frugi convenit esse
hominem, prelus quoi sapit. Bonus sit bonis, malus sit malis : utcumque
res sit, ita animum habeat;* and, still more strongly, Capt. II. ii. 19,
where it must mean 'if he is worth anything,' 'if he has his wits
about him,' while in As. I. iii. 23 it is applied to a *lena* who attends
to her own interests. In Poen. V. ii. 3, *si frugi esse vis, Eat liberali
iam adseres causa manu,* we must translate, 'if you wish to do your
duty,' 'to do what is right and proper.'

2. *Frugi* may be used also with reference to one who is profitable
to others, and hence it is the characteristic epithet for an honest,
steady, thrifty, respectable slave, who studies his master's interest :
Cas. II. iii. 50, *Vt enim frugi servo detur potius quam servo inprobo.*
Compare Hor. S. II. vii. 2, *Davus, amicum Mancipium domino, et
frugi, quod sit satis.*

3. In writers of the decline *frugi* is applied to inanimate objects :
thus Iuv. S. III. 167, *frugi cenula;* Mart. XIII. xxxi. 1, *irnacula
frugi;* Quintil. I. O. V. 10, § 27, *Sicut victus luxuriosus, an frugi, an
sordidus quaeritur;* and in a letter from Cicero's son, Epp. ad fam.
XVL 21, § 4, to Tiro we find, *Nam quid ego de Bruttio dicam . . .?
cuius quum frugi severaque est vita, tunc etiam iucundissima convictio.*

The word directly opposed to *frugi* is *nequam,* which signifies
'good-for-nothing.' This contrast is expressed in the line quoted
above from Pseud. I. v. 63, and in Cicero pro Fonteio, XVII. § 39.

Horace frequently employs *frugi,* e. g. S. I. iii. 49, II. v. 77,
A. P. 207. See also Terent. Heaut. III. iii. 19.

XI.—PROBVS, PROBE.

Probus, when applied to persons, properly denotes moral goodness,
absolute worth; as Trin. II. ii. 39, *It probus est, quem poenitet quam
probus sit et frugi bonae; Qui ipsus sibi satis placet, nec probus est nec
frugi bonae;* and so in Most. IV. ii. 34 (iii. 11) *puerum probum* is
'a respectable slave.' But occasionally the epithet *probus* signifies

that the person spoken of is merely 'good of his kind;' as Poen. V.
iii. 6, *Praestigiator hic quidem Poenus probus est,* 'this Carthaginian
is a capital juggler;' and Most. I. iii. 86, *Oh probus homo sum, Quae
pro me causam diceret patronum liberavi,* 'I am a knowing fellow.'

Probus, when applied to inanimate objects, denotes that they are
'good of their kind:' thus Most. III. ii. 41, *Vinu et victu piscatu probo
electili;* and Rud. III. v. 19, *D. I dum, Turbalio, curriculo adfer huc
foras Duas clavas. L. Clavas? D. Sed probus,* 'but see that they
are good (stout) ones.'

Probe, the adverb, is applied to any act or work performed in a
satisfactory manner: Most. I. ii. 19 (18), *Factae* (sc. *aedes*) *probe,
examussim,* i. e. 'well-constructed;' so Men. III. ii. 1, *Potin ut
quiescas, si ego tibi hanc* (sc. *pallam*) *hodie probe Lepideque concinnatam
referam temperi?* again, As. IV. i. 10, *scribas vide plane et probe,*
'see that you write it distinctly and correctly;' and Most. III. ii. 47,
Nos profecto probe, ut voluimus, viximus, 'we have lived well,' that is,
'lived a pleasant life;' and in the same play, I. iv. 29, *Probe quin amabo
accubas, Delphium mea,* 'place yourself comfortably—at your ease.'

There is however a modification of the meaning of *probe* which
deserves especial notice, since it occurs very frequently in the
dramatists. It is employed to denote that an action has been or
will be performed *completely and in the best manner,* while the action
itself may or may not be praiseworthy, and in this sense the force
of the word may frequently be correctly conveyed by the English
'thoroughly:' thus Amph. III. iii. 20, *Qui me Amphitruonem rentur
esse, errant probe,* 'are thoroughly or completely mistaken;' so Trin.
III. iii. 88, *Eumque huc ad adulescentem meditatum probe Mittam,*
'thoroughly schooled;' again, Most. I. i. 4, *Ego pol te ruri, si vivam,
ulciscar probe;* and V. i. 19 (ii. 4), *Quoius ego hic ludificabo corium, si
vivo, probe;* and Bac. III. iii. 94, *Adfatim est, Mnesiloche, cura et con-
castiga hominem probe;* and Cas. I. 36, *Ita te adgerunda curvom aqua
faciam probe, Vt postilena possit ex te fieri,* 'I will render you so
thoroughly crooked that a saddle-tree (frame of a packsaddle) may
be made out of you;' so Bac. IV. iv. 50, *Emungam hominem probe
hodie,* 'I will befool;' Most. V. i. 59 (ii. 44), *probe me emunxti;*
Trin. IV. ii. 51, *ludam hominem probe;* Amph. III. iv. 14, 22, *faxo
probe iam hic deludetur;* and in the passage referred to from Capt.
II. ii. 19, *usque admutilabit probe.*

Plautus uses also the form *adprobe* in Trin. IV. ii. 115, *Mihi con-
crederet, nisi me ille et ego illum nossem adprobe,* but it seems to be an
ἅπ. λεγ. The word is mentioned by Aul. Gell. VII. 7.

XII.—*NIMIS, NIMIVS, NIMIVM, NIMIO.*

These words convey the idea of 'excess.' But it must be borne in mind that excess may be of two kinds. The word may denote that the object spoken of transcends the limits of what is right, proper, or convenient, in which case censure is conveyed, or it may denote that the object spoken of transcends the limits by which such an object is usually bounded, and in this case censure or praise, or neither, may be conveyed, according to circumstances. The former meaning is usually expressed in English by the word 'too,' the latter by 'excessively,' 'most,' 'very,' and is equivalent to a superlative. Thus when we say that a person or thing is *too long*, or *too short*, *too rich*, or *too poor*, we wish to indicate that the proper limit, in each case, has been passed; but when we say that a person or thing is *excessively long*, or *excessively short*, *excessively rich*, or *excessively poor*, we do not necessarily imply anything except that the usual or ordinary limit has been passed. In Latin, *Nimis, Nimius*, are used in both senses, and we must, in each case, be guided by the context in determining which of the two is applicable. The same takes place in our own language with 'too,' but to a very small extent, in such colloquial phrases as *that is too good, too delightful, too charming, too ridiculous, too absurd.* The following examples will illustrate what we have said.

1. *Nimis.* In such passages as the following, *nimis* must signify 'too much:' Epid. III. iii. 23, *Docte et sapienter dicis: non nimis potest Pudicitiam quisquam suae servare filiae,* i.e. 'too closely,' 'too carefully;' and Andr. I. i. 34, *id arbitror Adprime in vita esse utile ut ne quid nimis;* cf. Heaut. III. ii. 8, *nihil nimis.*

On the other hand it has the force of ἄγαν, *valde,* 'excessively,' in Most. I. iii. 109, *Nimis velim lapidem qui ego illi speculo diminuam caput,* i.e. 'very much should I like to have a stone,' &c.; so *nimis velim* in Aul. IV. vi. 4, Pseud. II. ii. 4, Rud. II. vi. 27; *nimis vellem* in As. III. ii. 43, Stich. II. i. 40, V. iv. 31; and *nimis nolo,* Bac. IV. x. 8, 'I am excessively unwilling;' so again, Most. I. iii. 134, *S. Nam si pulcra est* (sc. *mulier) nimis ornata est. P. Nimis diu apstineo manum,* where *nimis ornata est* means 'she is abundantly decorated,' and *nimis diu* means 'too long;' Cas. III. i. 15, *Quid me amare refert, nisi sim doctus dicax nimis;* Truc. II. i. 36, *Nimis pol mortalis lepidus, nimisque probus dator.* In Epid. II. ii. 25 *Nimis factum bene!* is an exclamation, 'capital!' 'excellent!' and in Merc. I. 15, where a slave out of breath exclaims, *Perii, animam nequeo vortere, nimis nihili tibicen siem; nimis nihili* means 'utterly good-for-nothing;' and so in Rud. IV. ii. 14, *nimis homo nihili.*

Before quitting *nimis* we must remark that it is occasionally combined with *quam :* thus Truc. II. v. 15, *Nimis quam paucas sunt defessae, male quae facere occeperunt. Nimis quam paucas efficiunt, si quid occeperint bene facere;* so Most. II. ii. 79 (78), *Nimis quam formido ne manufesto hic me opprimat;* and V. ii. 21 (iii. 21), *Hercle mihi locum cavendum est, nimis quam es orator catus :* the simple interpretation of this combination seems to be 'how very few,' 'how very much I fear,' 'how very crafty (shrewd) a pleader you are.' *

For other examples of *nimis* followed by adjectives, adverbs, and verbs, we have *nimis sanctas,* Adel. V. vii. 1 ; *nimis doctus,* Epid. III. ii. 42 ; *nimis inepta,* Rud. III. iii. 19 ; *nimis longo,* Trin. III. iii. 77 ; *nimis truculentus,* Truc. II. ii. 10 ; *nimis iracunda,* Amph. III. ii. 22 ; *nimis lenis,* Men. I. l. 18 ; *nimis tardus,* Merc. III. iv. 10 ; *nimis pulcris,* Amph. I. i. 63 ; *nimis bella,* As. III. iii. 84 ; *vehemens nimis,* Heaut. III. i. 31 ; *nimis iracunde,* Bac. IV. ii. 12, Men. IV. iii. 22 ; *nimis stulte,* Men. I. l. 5, Merc. III. i. 3, Pers. I. i. 19 ; *nimis lepide,* Cas. IV. i. 15, Rud. II. iii. 30, Poen. III. iii. 53 ; *nimis bene,* Men. V. vii. 30, Stich. II. ii. 50 ; *nimis nequiter,* Men. V. v. 61 ; *nimis facete,* Pers. II. v. 22 ; *nimis argute,* Trin. IV. ii. 132 ; *nimis ferociter,* Amph. I. i. 58 ; *nimis astute,* Epid. II. ii. 96 ; *nimis longum,* III. ii. 40, Pers. I. iii. 87 ; *nimis diu,* Epid. III. i. 2, Merc. I. 54, Pers. IV. iv. 105, V. ii. 41 ; *nimis metuo et formido male,* Pseud. IV. iii. 3 ; *nimis odi male,* Rud. IV. ii. 14 ; *nimis placent . . . dant,* Poen. V. iv. 34 ; *nimis sancte pius,* Rud. IV. vii. 8 ; *nimis paene inepta,* v. 14 ; *nimis paene mane,* Pers. I. iii. 34 ; *misere nimis cupio,* Adel. IV. i. 6.

2. *Nimius :* Poen. I. ii. 29, *Modus, omnibus in rebus, soror, optumum est habitu : Nimia omnia nimium exhibent negotium hominibus ex se,* where *nimia omnia* must signify 'all things when carried to excess,' and *nimium negotium* 'excessive trouble;' so Heaut. I. i. 57, *Nulla adeo ex re istuc fit nisi ex nimio otio,* i. e. 'too much leisure;' so III. i. 96, *gaudio nimio;* Adel. I. l. 38, *vestitu nimio.*

On the other hand, Poen. V. iv. 35, *Nimiae voluptati est, quod in extis nostris portentum est, soror, Quodque haruspex de ambabus dixit,* where *nimiae voluptati* must mean 'it is a source of very great

---

* We find *nimium* followed by *quam* in Bac. I. ii. 13 in the Vulgate text. But *nimium* is here a conjecture of Gruterus without any MS. authority.

pleasure,' &c.; so *nimia est voluptas*, Stich. IV. i. 18; *nimio periculo*
is 'very great danger,' in Men. I. iii. 16.

3. *Nimium* as an adverb: Bac. I. I. 40, *P. Apage a me, apage !*
B. Ah ! nimium ferus es. P. Mihi tum. B. Malacissandus es.
Equidem tibi do hanc operam. P. Ah ! nimium pretiosa es operaria,
'you are too savage,' 'you are too costly a workwoman;' and so
Adel. II. i. 13, *Accede illuc, Parmeno, Nimium istoc abisti, hic propter*
hunc adsiste, 'you have gone too far in that direction.' On the
other hand, Trin. IV. ii. 86, *C. Quos locos adisti? S. Nimium miris*
modis mirabiles, i. e. 'most wonderful places;' and Truc. II. vi. 24,
S. Sed peperitne, opsecro, Phronesium? A. Peperit puerum nimium
lepidum, i. e. 'a remarkably fine boy.'

For other examples of *nimium* see Cas. II. iii. 32, III. i. 8, IV. i.
13; Cist. I. i. 20; Epid. I. i. 2, V. i. 24; Men. I. ii. 10; Merc. III.
i. 28, IV. i. 20, ii. 4; Most. IV. ii. 32 (iii. 11); Pseud. III. ii. 99, IV.
iii. 15; Rud. II. iv. 6; Stich. II. ii. 36, 55, V. v. 7; Trin. I. i. 6, IV.
ii. 86, 91, iii. 53; Truc. IV. iii. 78, V. 4; Adel. I. i. 38, IV. v. 50,
V. iii. 49, viii. 31; Andr. II. vi. 24; Heaut. IV. viii. 20; Hec. V. iv.
13; Phor. V. ii. 2.

. The following passages from Terence may, at first sight, cause
some embarrassment: Eun. V. vi. 16, *P. Hem, quid dixti, pessuma?*
an mentita es? etiam rides? Itane lepidum tibi visum est, scelus, nos
inridere? Pr. Nimium. P. Siquidem istuc inpune habueris. Pr. Ve-
rum. P. Reddam, hercle. Pr. Credo : here *lepidum* must be supplied
after *nimium*, 'just so, very amusing;' and so in Heaut. IV. ii. 22,
Nimium, inquam, where *probe* is to be repeated after *nimium*, 'capital,
I say.' In Phor. IV. iii. 38 the Vulgate text gives, *G. A primo homo*
insanibat. C. Cedo, quid postulat? G. Quid? nimium quantum lubuit.
C. Dic, &c., which it is very hard to understand; but if we punctuate,
G. Quid? Nimium. Quantum lubuit, the sense will be 'what did he
demand? Too much. A fancy sum;' and *nimium* occurs exactly in
this sense a few lines farther on, *v.* 59, *Nimium est*, &c. This passage, it must be observed, was a theme of controversy among the
old grammarians (see Charis. p. 185, ed. Puts.), and modern editors
have not been able to agree either as to the reading, the punctuation,
or the distribution of the words among the speakers.

Terence uses *pernimium* once, in Adel. III. iii. 38, *D. Fratris me*
quidem Pudet pigetque. S. Nimium inter vos, Demea, ac Non quia ades
praesens dico hoc, pernimium inturest : indeed, the word is found in
this passage only, and in the Digest. XLVIII. iii. 2. *Sed haec inter-*
pretatio perdura et pernimium severa est in eo, &c.

4. *Nimio* as an adverb. *Nimio* is used adverbially in clauses in which comparison is expressed or implied.

(a) In the great majority of instances it is combined with the comparative degree of an adjective or adverb: thus Most. I. i. 69, *nimio celerius*, 'more quickly by far;' ii. 66 (60), *nimio nequior*, 'worse by far;' II. ii. 12, *nimio expectatior*, 'looked for with far greater pleasure;' V. i. 54 (ii. 39), *nimio plus sapio*, 'I am wiser by a great deal;' so *nimio aequius*, Merc. III. ii. 6; *nimio citius*, Trin. II. ii. 106; *nimio docilior*, Bac. I. ii. 56; *nimio facilius*, Pseud. I. iii. 47; *nimio lubentius*, Men. V. vi. 15; *nimio melius*, Pers. I. iii. 31, Truc. II. v. 17; *nimio minus*, Rud. I. ii. 1, II. v. 3, Truc. II. v. 3; *nimio ocius*, Stich. V. v. 5; *nimio plus*, Bac. I. ii. 14; *nimio pluris*, Trin. I. i. 12; *nimio rectius*, Bac. II. iii. 80; *nimio satius*, I. ii. 42, Trin. II. ii. 30.

(b) Sometimes *nimio* is connected with a verb which implies comparison: thus Bac. III. ii. 12, *Nimio praestat ingeniosum te quam ingratum dicier;* Poen. I. ii. 90, *Bonam ego quam beatam me esse nimio dici mavolo.* Into the following also the idea of comparison enters: Truc. IV. i. 6, *Quom hoc iam volupe est, tum hoc nimio magnae mellinae mihi;* that is, 'while, on the one hand, this circumstance (viz. that my gifts have been graciously received by Phronesium) is a source of pleasure, on the other hand, this other circumstance (viz. that the gifts of my rival have been scorned) is more sweet by far:' *mellinis* is an ἅπ. λεγ., and is generally understood to mean some sweet drink. In Men. V. ii. 69, *S. Tu negas. Ms. Nego hercle vero. Mv. Nimio haec inpudenter negas :* the meaning is clearly 'these denials are more shameless by far than your previous falsehoods.' More difficult is the line at the commencement of the 6th Scene of the 4th Act of the Bacchides: Nicobulus enters saying, *Nimio illaec res est magnae dividiae mihi, Supterfugisse sic mihi hodie Chrusalum :* but we may regard this as intended to be the continuation of a soliloquy commenced by Nicobulus before he appeared on the stage, in which, after having mentioned some annoyance, he goes on, 'far more am I incensed by the circumstance that Chrysalus,' &c.

(c) Sometimes the emphasis is increased by the addition of *multo :* Bac. I. ii. 42, *Video nimio iam multo plus quam volueram, Vixisse nimio satius est iam quam vivere;* and again in the same play, IV. iv. 20, *M. Chrusale, occidi. C. Fortassis tu auri dempsisti parum. M. Qui, malum, parum? imo vero nimio minus multo parum;* while we find in Stich. II. ii. 15, *Nimio inpertior multo tanto plus quam speras.* In Most. III. iii. 2 (IV. ii. 2), *Num nimio emptae tibi videntur ?* (sc. aedes).

nimio is not an adverb, but the ablative of *nimius* with *argento* or some such word understood, 'the house does not appear to you to have been purchased at too long a price, does it?'
Nimio used as an adverb seems not to occur in Terence.

XIII.—*SODES, SIS* pl. *SVLTIS, AMABO, QVAESO, OBSECRO.*

These five words are employed by the dramatists in the sense of 'pray,' 'prithee,' 'if you please,' 'I beg of you,' 'I beseech you,' 'I implore you.' We may make a few remarks upon each.

I. *Sodes* was regarded by the Romans themselves as a contraction of *si audes* : thus Cic. Orat. XLV. § 154, *Libenter etiam copulando verba iungebant, ut 'sodes' pro 'si audes,' 'sis' pro 'si vis;'* and Festus, s. v. *sultis*, p. 343, ed. Müll., *"Sultis, si voltis* significat, composito vocabulo, ita ut alia sunt, *sodes, si audes, sis, si vis,'* &c.

The uncontracted form is found Trin. II. i. 17, *Da mihi hoc, mel meum, si me amas, si audes;* and in Aul. II. i. 48, as the line is quoted by Priscian, p. 960, ed. Puts., *Dic mihi, si audes, quis ea est quam vis ducere uxorem?* where however our MSS. of Plautus give *quaeso* instead of *si audes.*

Generally speaking, *sodes* is used without much emphasis: thus Bac. IV. vii. 39, *C. Novistine hominem? N. Novi. C. Dic sodes mihi, Bellan' videtur specie mulier? N. Admodum,* i.e. 'pray, tell me,' or 'tell me, if you please;' and so Men. III. iii. 21, Trin. II. iv. 161, Pers. II. v. 17.

It is a formula of civility in Hec. V. i. 27, *sed scin quid volo potius sodes facias?* i.e. 'if it so please you;' and so Heaut. IV. iv. 16, Phor. V. vii. 28.

There is considerable earnestness in Adel. IV. v. 9, *dic sodes, pater,* 'tell me, I entreat you;' and in Hec. V. iv. 1, *Vide, mi Parmeno, etiam sodes,* i.e. 'pray, be careful;' while there is something soothing or deprecatory in Phor. V. iii. 10, *Parce sodes;* and coaxing in Poen. III. v. 12, *Mitte ad me sodes,* &c., and in Trin. II. i. 17. For other examples of *sodes* see Adel. IV. i. 1, Andr. I. i. 58, Heaut. III. i. 50, iii. 19, IV. iv. 16, v. 22, Hec. III. ii. 23, V. iv. 4, Phor. V. i. 14. See also Catull. CIII. 1, Cic. Epp. ad Att. VII. 3, Hor. S. I. ix. 41, Epp. I. i. 62, vii. 15, XVI. 31, Ad Pisones 438.

It will be observed from the above examples that *sodes* usually follows an imperative, but this is not the case invariably, as may be seen by referring to Heaut. IV. iv. 16, Hec. V. l. 27. In Horace, S. I, ix. 41, although the imperative is not expressed it is implied from the preceding clause.

II. *Sis* and *Sultis* stand for *si vis* and *si vultis*: see passages from Cicero and Festus quoted under *Sodes*. We find *sis*, although rarely, in the uncontracted form: thus Adel. II. i. 30, *Si satis iam debacchatus es, leno, audi, si vis, nunc iam,* &c.

Sis is generally subjoined to an imperative, and is frequently connected with it so closely that the two words were, probably, in the more familiar combinations, pronounced as one, and are so printed: thus we find *videsis, caves is, apagesis, abisis,* and the like. *Sis* however is occasionally separated from its imperative by a word: thus, Cas. II. vi. 27, *Accipe hanc sis;* and sometimes placed before the imperative, as Pers. IV. iv. 104, *Ne, sis, plora,* and V. ii. 15, *Ne sis me uno digito attigeris.*

According to the circumstances under which it is employed, and to the tone of voice in which it is uttered, *sis* may express feelings of a varied description, just as the words 'if you please,' 'I'll thank you,' 'I'll trouble you,' in English, may express a civil request, a peremptory command, anger, scorn, contempt, and many other emotions.

Thus it denotes ordinary conventional civility in Cas. III. vi. 20, II. vi. 27, Epid. III. iv. 39, Merc. III. i. 45, Pers. II. v. 20, IV. iv. 58, Pseud. III. ii. 50, Rud. II. vii. 18: advice, warning, reproof, Pseud. I. i. 46, *vide sis quam tu rem geras,* 'you had better take care what you are about;' Curc. IV. ii. 35, *fac sis bonae frugi sies,* 'see now that you behave like a good girl;' Cas. II. ii. 31, *tace sis,* 'hold your tongue, will you;' so Epid. V. ii. 3, Pers. II. v. 15, III. i. 61, V. ii. 54, Poen. III. v. 16: threat, Pers. V. ii. 15, *Ne sis me uno digito attigeris, ne te ad terram, scelus, adfligam,* 'you'd better not lay a single finger upon me;' Trin. IV. i. 19, *Apage me sis,* 'keep clear of me, if you please;' and so Curc. V. iii. 9: angry command to a slave, Cas. IV. ii. 14: anger, impatience, Poen. I. ii. 162, Stich. I. i. 36: a sneer, Truc. IV. iii. 35, *Vide sis facinus muliebre,* 'there's a woman's trick for you!' and so Adel. V. i. 4: contempt, scorn, Merc. I. 67, Pseud. III. ii. 102: insolent tone, Pers. III. iii. 8, 9, 17, 32, *Accipe sis argentum, Tene sis argentum, Cedo sis mihi argentum, Cape hoc sis,* 'take the money, confound you!' so Merc. IV. iv. 37: deprecatory tone, Merc. II. ii. 49, Pseud. I. iii. 10: wonder, Pers. IV. iv. 45: coaxing tone, Pers. V. i. 12, Truc. II. vi. 44: triumph, Epid. III. ii. 9: eagerness, Poen. III. iv. 3: bitterness, Bac. I. ii. 29: demand, Poen. V. ii. 124.

The student may classify for himself the following examples:
Merc. II. ii. 52, Pers. IV. iv. 104, Poen. I. ii. 79, 102, III. ii. 1,
Rud. IV. ii. 29, 44, Trin. II. i. 31, iv. 112, 154, Eun. II. iii. 19, IV.
vi. 18, vii. 29, Heaut. I. ii. 38, II. iii. 128, 133, Phor. I. ii. 9.

Sultis occurs less frequently. In Poen. III. vi. 19 it means 'if
you like,' without any emphasis; in Stich. I. iii. 67, 'pray,' simple
invitation; in Pers. V. ii. 52, *agite, sultis, hunc ludificemus*, there is
some eagerness; in Men. II. ii. 75 it is employed in addressing
slaves; in Stich. I. ii. 8, Rud. III. v. 40, it is addressed to slaves in
an accent of stern command.

Sis is found, although rarely, in the sense of *si vis*, 'if you wish,'
as in As. III. iii. 93, *Quaeso hercle, Libane, sis herum tuis factis sospitari, Da mihi istas viginti minas;* and in the same play, II. ii. 43, *Sis
amanti subvenire familiari filio;* but in the latter passage the punctuation and the arrangement of the speakers in the dialogue are
doubtful.

III. *Amabo*, it is evident, strictly means '(if you will do what I
ask) I shall love you (in return),' and this is fully expressed in Poen.
I. ii. 40, *AD. Soror, parce amabo: tal til istuc alios dicere nobis, Ne
nosmet nostra etiam vitia loquamur. AS. Quiesco. AD. Ergo amo te:*
compare with this Men. II. iii. 71, *Sed scin quid te amabo ut facias?*
and Truc. IV. iv. 26, *Multum amabo te ob istam rem, mecastor.* Hence
in Phor. I. ii. 4 *Amo te* may be rendered 'many thanks;' and so in
Heaut. IV. vi. 21, *Desmo te;* and in Phor. III. i. 14, *Omnes vos amo.*
Cf. Eun. I. ii. 106, III. ii. 3.

Amabo occurs very often in Plautus, and is sometimes followed by
an accusative, but is generally without a case. It passes through
the same modifications of meaning as *sis*. It is frequently a mere
expression of ordinary civility or simple inquiry, 'pray, if you please,'
'have the goodness,' although a certain degree of earnestness may
be implied: thus Most. I. iii. 10, *Contempla, amabo, mea Scapha, satin
haec me vestis deceat?* and in *v.* 140, *Cedo, amabo, decem:* and II. i. 38,
Tace, amabo, 'I beg and pray;' see also I. iv. 29 (30), II. ii. 36, Bac.
I. i. 19, 28, 67, Cas. II. ii. 6, vi. 34, 41, Cist. I. i. 19, Curc. I. ii. 18,
Merc. III. i. 5, Pers. II. ii. 63, III. i. 8, *Qui, amabo*, 'how so, pray?'
V. ii. 68, Poen. I. ii. 31, 189, Eun. I. ii. 50, III. iii. 28, 31, IV. iv. 7:
it implies argumentative inquiry, Bac. V. ii. 76: anxious inquiry, Cist.
II. iii. 22: inquiry and surprise (real or pretended), Bac. V. ii. 3, 30,
Cist. I. i. 18: eager exclamation, wonder, Rud. I. iv. 33, Heaut. II. iv.
24, Merc. III. i. 41: anxiety and alarm, Cist. III. 12, *amabo, accurrite,
Ne se interimat*, 'in the name of heaven, haste, lest he kill himself:'

earnest request, 'I beseech you,' 'I implore you,' Bac. I. i. 10, Cas.
II. ii. 38, III. v. 13, 14, 16, IV. iv. 11, Cist. I. i. 106, 112, 115, III.
12, IV. ii. 42, Men. IV. iii. 4, Poen. I. ii. 123, 137, Truc. IV. iv. 19,
20, V. 66, 74, Eun. I. ii. 70, IV. iii. 21: earnest adjuration, Poen. V.
iv. 87, 95: curiosity, Cist. IV. ii. 62: coaxing, Bac. V. ii. 80, Cas. I.
49, Curc. I. ii. 47, Men. II. iii. 31, III. iii. 17, Pers. III. i. 8, V. i. 13,
Truc. III. i. 19, ii. 19, 28: reproach, Cist. I. i. 21, Truc. II. iv. 1:
indignation, contempt, Cas. II. iii. 19, Men. II. iii. 54, Poen. I. ii. 187,
Truc. V. 49, Hec. I. i. 13: expostulation and entreaty, As. III. iii. 117,
Curc. I. iii. 41, Poen. I. ii. 51: despair, Rud. I. iv. 29.

IV. *Quaeso* is an old form of *Quaero*, and was identical with it in
signification: thus Festus, s.v., p. 258, ed. Müll., "*Quaeso* ut significat idem quod *rogo*, ita *quaesere* ponitur ab antiquis pro *quaerere*, ut
est apud Ennium l. II. *Ostia munito est; idem loca navibus pulcris
mundo* (leg. *mundi*) *facit, nautisque mari quaesentibus vitam* et in
Chresponte (leg. *Cresphonte*) *ducit me uxorem liberorum sibi quaesendum gratia*, et in Andromeda *liberum quaesendum causa familiae
matrem huae*."

In dialogue *quaeso* signifies 'I beg,' 'I request,' 'I beseech,' and
in the majority of cases conveys the idea of considerable earnestness
on the part of the speaker: thus Capt. V. iv. 28, *Compedibus, quaeso,
ut tibi sit levior filius;* sometimes accompanied by tenderness, Amph.
I. iii. 2, *Atque imperce, quaeso*, 'take care of yourself, I beseech you.'
It is frequently rendered more emphatic by the addition of *edepol* or
hercle, 'I implore you,' as in Most. II. i. 29, *Quaeso edepol exsurge,
pater adveni;* and As. III. iii. 93, *Quaeso, hercle, Libane, sis harum
tuis factis sospitari'.* It implies a solemn entreaty in Capt. II. iii. 72,
*Sed te quaeso, cogitato hinc mea fide mitti domum Te aestimatum, et
meam esse vitam hic pro te positam pignori.*

It sometimes assumes the form of an actual prayer to heaven:
Cas. II. vi. 37, *Taceo: Deos quaeso;* Adel. II. iv. 11, *Deos quaeso ut
istaec prohibeant;* Amph. II. ii. 88, *Equidem sana sum et Deos quaeso
ut salva pariam filium;* Aul. II. viii. 24, *Apollo, quaeso, subveni mihi
atque adiuva;* Poen. IV. iv. 15, *Iupiter du diem hunc sospitem quaeso;*
and accompanies an imprecation in Rud. II. vi. 15. It indicates
impatience in Most. I. i. 34: indignation in Curc. III. 22: it is
deprecatory or soothing in Most. V. ii. 47, 50: supplicatory in Mil.
II. vi. 16, 85, Pseud. V. ii. 23, Rud. II. vi. 26, III. v. 34: it implies
remonstrance, Truc. II. i. 27, Andr. I. ii. 33, *Bona verba quaeso:* surprise, Pseud. I. i. 20, Trin. IV. ii. 144, Phor. V. vii. 42: surprise and
remonstrance, Hec. IV. ii. 12. It asks for an explanation, Mil. IV.

vii. 23: and conveys a civil request, Rud. IV. iv. 9: it is quite devoid
of emphasis in Pers. IV. vi. 6, Poen. V. ii. 80: sometimes it is little
more than an exclamation, as in Mil. II. iv. 46, *At, Sceledre, quaeso,
I't ad id exemplum somnium quam simile somniavit!* (= 'I say!') and
IV. vi. 38, *I't, quaeso, amore perdita est haec misera!* see also Mil. IV.
viii. 1, Truc. II. viii. 5.

Generally it is used absolutely, but we have Capt. II. ii. 90, *Te
quaeso;* Trin. I. ii. 153, *Te quaeso ut;* Cas. II. vi. 37, *Deos quaeso;*
Adel. II. iv. 11, *Deos quaeso ut;* Curc. III. 62, *Tecum oro et quaeso . . .
ut;* V. ii. 30, *Quaeso ut mihi dicas;* Rud. III. il. 15, *Teque oro et
quaeso . . . ut;* Aul. IV. ii. 4, *Verum id te quaeso ut prohibessis, Fides.*

V. *Obsecro,* looking to the etymology, ought to be much more
forcible than any of the preceding words, since it must signify, properly, 'I adjure you by things holy,' 'in the name of Heaven.'
Sometimes it is a direct prayer addressed to a deity, as Adel. III. iv.
41, *Iuno Lucina, fer opem, serva me, obsecro:* sometimes it conveys
an earnest appeal to the person or persons addressed, as II. i. 1,
Obsecro, populares, ferte misero atque innocenti auxilium; Poen. I. iii. 8,
*Nunc obsecro te, Milphio, hanc per dexteram, Perque hanc sororem
lacrymam, perque oculos tuos, Perque meos amores,* &c.; Curc. II. iii. 28,
ubi sunt spes meae? Eloquere, obsecro, hercle. C. *Eloquere, te obsecro,
ubi sunt meae?* and so vv. 31, 34, 35, V. iii. 18, 19.   Sometimes it
is an exclamation of horror, Eun. IV. iii. 22, *Perii, obsecro, tam
infandum facinus, mea tu, ne audivi quidem:* or of alarm, Andr. IV.
iv. 46, C. *Audivi, inquam, a principio.* D. *Audistine obsecro!* or of
wonder and agitation, Rud. I. iv. 15, *Num Ampelisca, obsecro, est?* 'in
the name of heaven, surely that is not Ampelisca, is it?' and so
Andr. IV. v. 5, *Obsecro, quem video?* or of great astonishment, Eun.
IV. iii. 14, *Au, obsecro, mea Pythias, quid istuc nam monstri fuit?*
or of joy and excitement, Heaut. IV. iii. 6, *O mi Sure, audistine,
obsecro?* or it may indicate that the feelings of the speaker have been
offended or shocked, Hec. IV. i. 12, P. *Peperit filia? hem! taces?
ex quo?* M. *Istuc patrem rogare est aequom? Perii! ex quo censes,
nisi ex illo, cui data est nuptum, obsecro?*

But although, in the above and many other passages, it denotes
emotions of the strongest kind, it is in many cases identical with
amabo: thus in Cas. II. iii. 16 we find, C. *Obsecro, satun' es?* and
in Truc. II. iv. 13. *Amabo, satun' es?* and it passes through the same
varieties of meaning: simple inquiry, civil request, more or less
earnest, Bac. I. i. 68, Cas. II. ii. 18, Curc. I. ii. 25, Hec. III. i. 38:
very earnest request or inquiry (I beseech, I implore), Cas. II. ii. 24,

Adel. IV. ii. 11, v. 63, Andr. IV. iii. 6, V. iv. 52, Eun. IV. iv. 18,
Heaut. II. iii. 26, 98, Phor. II. ii. 5, III. iii. 20: coaxing, Truc. V.
57, Eun. I. ii. 15: wonder, impatience, contempt, Adel. IV. v. 21, 27,
Andr. IV. iii. 10, iv. 8, Eun. IV. iv. 12, Hec. IV. i. 41, Phor. I. iv. 19,
Poen. I. ii. 122, V. iv. 22. It will be seen from the above examples
that *obsecro*, like *amabo*, is not unfrequently followed by the accusative of the person appealed to, but more frequently does not take
a case, and is in many instances a mere exclamation. In Heaut.
IV. i. 31 it is construed with a double accusative, *Mi Chreme, peccavi,*
fateor, vincor, nunc hoc te obsecro; and in Pers. I. i. 49 the entreaty is
strengthened by the addition of *resecro—Opsecro te, resecro, operam da*
hanc mihi fidelem.

Perhaps it is scarcely worth remarking that while *amabo* recurs
again and again in Plautus, *obsecro* is found in comparatively few
passages, while Terence evinces a decided preference for *obsecro* over
amabo; quaeso is more common, in proportion, in Plautus than in
Terence; *sodes* is used upwards of a dozen times in the six plays of
Terence, and not more than five or six times in the twenty plays
of Plautus. *Sultis* does not occur in Terence; it is quoted by Festus
(pp. 301, 343, ed. Müll.) from Plautus, Cato, and Ennius.

XIV.—TERMS EMPLOYED WITH REFERENCE TO MONEY.

TALENTVM, MINA, DRACHMA, OBOLVS, PHILIPPVS s. NVMVS PHILIPPEVS, NVMVS s. NVMVS ARGENTI.

1. *Talentum, Mina, Drachma, Obolus.* As might be expected,
considering the source from which the works of Plautus and Terence
are derived, the sums of money mentioned in their plays are, for
the most part, calculated according to the Greek system of Talents,
Minae, and Drachmae.

We may remind the young scholar that these terms all denoted
certain weights, and that although the absolute value of each differed
in different states, their mutual relation was invariable. *Mina* may
be represented in all cases by the English word *Pound*, but as the
Avoirdupois Pound differs from the Troyes Pound, and both from
the Italian Pound, so the Mina of Athens was different in absolute
weight from the Mina of Ægina, and both differed from the Mina

1 i

of Alexandria. But in these and in all other places where the same
denominations were employed,

1 Talent	=	60 Minae.
1 Mina	=	100 Drachmae.
1 Drachma	=	6 Obols.

Moreover, throughout Greece and her colonies in Asia and Africa,
when money was concerned, a Talent denoted sixty pounds' weight
of silver,* a Mina one pound weight of silver, and a Drachma
1/80th of a pound weight of silver; but since the absolute weight of
the Mina varied in different districts, the actual money value of a
Talent, a Mina, and a Drachma varied in like proportion. Of these
three denominations the Drachma alone was a coin; no piece of the
weight of a Talent or even of a Mina was ever minted for circulation.
The heaviest Greek coin known is a Decadrachm, the most common
are Tetradrachms and Didrachms,† and the Athenians coined silver
pieces as low as a quarter-obol, or 1/24th of a Drachma.

In the works of the Latin dramatists all computations in Greek
money must be referred to the Attic standard, and wherever moderate sums are named we shall not commit any grave error if we
consider the value of the

Attic Drachma	=			9d.	sterling.
— Mina	=	£3	15	0	,,
— Talent	=	£225	0	0	,,
and the — Obolus	=			1½	,,

Since the Athenians employed silver as the standard of their
currency, wherever we find the words *Talentum* or *Mina* in Plautus
or Terence they uniformly denote respectively a sum of 6000 and
and 100 Drachmae, the word *argenti* being sometimes added and
sometimes omitted. Thus when we read in Merc. IV. iii. 4, *Hem
quoi decem talenta dotis detuli;* and in Heaut. V. I. 67, *Duo talenta
pro re nostra ego esse decrevi satis,* the same Talent is indicated as
when it is said, Phor. V. iii. 6, *ex his praediis talenta argenti bina
Statim capiebat;* and in Merc. Prol. 88, *Talentum argenti ipsus sua
adnumeral manu:* in the latter passage it is clearly implied that the
value of a Talent was counted out in silver coin; and so As. I. iii. 41,
Si mihi dantur duo talenta argenti numerata in manum.

But the expression *Talentum magnum*, which occurs frequently in

---

* If this does not hold good universally, the exceptions are not such
as require to be noticed here.
† This is to be understood of the Greek coinage in general—the Didrachms of Athens are extremely rare.

the Latin dramatists,* and also *Talentum magnum argenti,*† proved for
a considerable period a source of embarrassment to scholars until
Gronovius (De pecun. vet.) demonstrated that these terms, like the
simple *Talentum* or *Talentum argenti,* denoted the ordinary Attic
Talent,‡ and that the epithet *magnum* was occasionally employed by
the Roman writers, for by them only is it used, because they first
became acquainted with the word *Talentum* in their intercourse
with the Greeks of Sicily and of some cities of Magna Graecia,
who, like the old Italians, had adopted copper as the standard of
their currency, and whose money Talent was therefore a Talent
of copper, and equivalent to a very small sum. Hence when the
Romans, at a subsequent period, first became acquainted with the
Attic Talent, they would naturally seek to distinguish it from the
small Sicilian talent by attaching to it the epithet *magnum.* §

In like manner as *Talentum* and *Talentum argenti* are used indif-
ferently, so are *Minae* || and *Argenti minae,* ¶ and likewise *Drachmae*
and *Drachmae argenti* a. *argenteae.*** When in one passage, Truc.
V. 8, we read, *Ego, mea voluptas, si quid peccavi prius, Subplicium ad
te habet minam fero auri,* we must understand *minam auri* to signify
not 'a pound of gold' but 'the value of a Mina, or pound of silver,
in gold.'

We have said that wherever mention is made of Greek money in
the Latin dramatists we must refer it to the Attic standard. To this
there is one exception, where however the distinction is carefully
marked, Trin. II. iv. 23, *Trapezitae mille drachumarum Olumpicum,
Quas de ratione dehibuisti, redditae.* What these Olympic Drachmas
may have been we cannot tell, for, as far as I am aware, they are
not named in any other passage in the Classics.

One or two phrases connected with money and money payments require some explanation.

(a) *Commodus* denotes that a sum mentioned is 'of full weight;' Rud. V. ii. 31, *Talentum argenti commodum magnum inerat in crumena;* and As. III. iii. 135, *Quid ego aliud exoptem amplius, nisi illud quoius inopia est, Viginti argenti commodas minas huius quas dem matri?* and Merc. II. iii. 101, where the father and son are bidding in opposition, each pretending to be the agent of a friend, *D. Etiam nunc admutat: addam sex minas. C. Septem mihi (Numquam edepol me vincet hodie) commodis poscit, pater.*

Modicus seems to be employed in the same sense, Pseud. IV. vii. 130, *B. Perdidit me. S. At me viginti modicis mulctavit minis.*

(b) *Probatus* again indicates that the purity of the metal in the coin or bullion had been tested; thus Pers. IV. vi. 1, *Probati hic argenti sunt sexaginta minae,* with which compare III. iii. 33.

(c) When Labrax says, Rud. III. iv. 21, *Tu, senex, si istas amas, huic arido argento est opus,* the phrase is probably equivalent to 'hard cash:' the explanations given by the older commentators are fanciful, not to say ridiculous.

(d) Among the smaller denominations the *Triobolum* is frequently mentioned, generally indefinitely for a very small sum, as in Rud. V. ii. 43, when Gripus is asked how much he demands for giving the information sought, he replies, *Talentum magnum, non potest triobolum hinc abesse,* 'a talent, not a farthing less;' and lower down, *v.* 67, *Non illi ego hodie debeo triobolum,* 'I don't owe him a farthing:' see also Bac. II. iii. 26, Poen. IV. ii. 46, Rud. IV. iii. 100, V. iii. 11: in like manner Poen. I. ii. 168, *Non ego homo trioboli sum, nisi ego illi mastigiae Exturbo oculos atque dentes,* 'I am a man not worth a farthing if' &c.; and the same expression recurs, II. 17.

(e) *Diobolaris,* an adjective, is found in Poen. I. ii. 58, and Frag. Cistell. ap. Varr. L. L. VIII. 64, ed. Müll. See also Paul. Diac. s. v., p. 74, ed. Müll.

II. *Philippus s. Numus Philippeus.* The coinage of Athens and of the rest of Greece may be said to have consisted of silver and copper exclusively up to 350 B.C., for although gold was occasionally minted before that period, it was issued in very small quantities, and the circulation was necessarily extremely limited. About the time however indicated above, Philip II of Macedon, the father of Alexander the Great, obtained such large supplies of gold from the mines of Thrace that during the remainder of his life he struck enormous numbers of gold coins, which were speedily dispersed all over the world. These were known as Gold Philips, they were up to a recent period to be found in circulation on the eastern borders of Europe, they are still frequently discovered in large hoards, and numerous specimens are to be seen in all collections of ancient Greek medals.* They are mentioned frequently in Plautus,† and must have been a common medium when the authors of the New Comedy flourished.

We may enumerate the different names by which they are designated. In the Poenulus we find three hundred spoken of as, I. i. 37, *aurei trecenti numi Philippei;* III. iv. 3, *aurei trecenti numi qui vocantur Philippei;* iii. 57, *trecentos numos Philippos;* I. iii. 6, *trecentos Philippos.* In the Bacchides we find two hundred spoken of, IV. viii. 41, *ducentos numos aureos Philippos probos;* ii. 7, *ducentos Philippos aureos;* cf. ix. 45, 87, 103, *ducentos numos Philippos;* viii. 27, *ducenti Philippi;* cf. v. 38, ix. 127, and simply r. 10, *ducenti numi;* cf. IV. iv. 55, 58, viii. 32. In the Trinumus, a thousand, V. ii. 34, *mille auri Philippum;* v. 15, *mille numum aureum;* cf. IV. ii. 112, where the reading is doubtful; see also As. I. iii. 1, Trin. I. ii. 115.

When Agorastocles says, Poen. I. ii. 132, *Sunt mihi intus nescio quot numi aurei lumphatici,* he means 'gold Philips struggling to make their escape,' as if they were madmen under restraint.

There is a puzzling passage in Rud. V. ii. 26: Labrax is describing the contents of the Vidulus; we read in the Vulgate Text, *Numi octingenti aurei in marsupio infuerunt, Praeterea centum denaria Philippea in pasceolo scorsus,* but the word *denaria* is altogether destitute of support from any good MS. The Vetus Codex of Camerarius gives, *Praeterea centum mna philippia,* which may mean 'a hundred Minae in Philips,' if we suppose that there was a familiar idiom by which the singular could be substituted for the plural, as when we talk of 'a hundred pound.'

It would appear that Philips, in consequence of the ease with which they could be procured, and the purity of the metal, were commonly employed as bullion by artificers who executed works in gold; hence the allusion in Curc. III. 70, *ibi nunc statuam volt dare auream Solidam faciundam ex auro Philippeo.*

---

* They passed into Gaul and from thence to Britain, and the whole of the early gold coinage of these countries "may be said to consist of imitations more or less rude and degenerate of the Macedonian Philippus." See the admirable work of Mr. John Evans on the Coins of the Ancient Britons. Lond. 1864, p. 24.

† Never in Terence, who adhered more closely than Plautus to his Greek originals. The name of Philip may not have been agreeable to an Athenian audience.

III. *Numus s. Numus argenti.* It will be seen from the examples quoted above that the word *Numus* is occasionally used with reference to the *Philippus*, but in this case the adjective *aureus* (or *Philippeus*) is usually combined with it, and where these are omitted, as in Bac. IV. iv. 55, 58, viii. 27, 32, ix. 110, Poen. III. ii. 17, Trin. IV. ii. 128, 161, the context is such as to leave no doubt that the *Philippus* is meant.

But there are several passages in Plautus in which *numus* cannot mean the *numus aureus* or *Philippus*, indeed the designation *numus argenti* is by no means uncommon, e. g. As. II. iv. 80, *argenti numum;* Aul. I. ii. 30, *argenti numos:* cf. v. 34; Pseud. I. i. 95, *numus argenti;* iii. 65, *numum argenti.*

In such cases it is difficult to discover what sum is indicated. Moreover doubts have arisen whether the same sum or coin is uniformly indicated by *Numus*, and also whether the word is employed with reference to Greek or to Roman currency.

1. It is used for money in general, or pieces of money, without special reference to any particular sum or coin: thus Bac. IV. iv. 17, *Num qui numi exciderunt, here, tibi, quod sic terram Optuere?* 'you have not dropped some pieces of money, master, have you?' and so As. II. iv. 34, *adducit* (sc. *trapezitam*) *domum etiam ultro, et scribit numos,* 'draws a bill upon him.'

2. *Numus* or *Numus argenti* is used to denote a trifling sum: thus Capt. II. ii. 82, *Eum si reddis mihi, praeterea unum numum ne duis,* 'if you restore to me my son, do not give me a single shilling in addition (for your ransom). In Pers. IV. iv. 111 *numus abesse hinc non potest* means, 'I won't take a shilling less;' just as we had above quoted from Rud. V. ii. 43, *non potest triobolum hinc abesse;* so also in Most. I. ii. 34 (31), *si quid numo sarciri potest,* 'if any defect can be repaired for a trifle;' cf. Pseud. 1. i. 79, iii. 122, v. 91, II. ii. 49, V. ii. 24; in Epid. V. ii. 35, where the slave offers to take heavy odds, he says, *ni ergo matris filia est, In meum numum, in tuum talentum, pignus da,* 'I bet you a numus to a talent;' and so III. i. 9.

3. But there can be no doubt that *Numus* is frequently used to indicate a piece of money of definite value: thus in Epid. I. i. 52 Stratippocles is represented as having borrowed a sum of money at Thebes from an usurer, for which he was to pay at the rate of a *numus* per day for each *mina;* in Men. II. ii. 16, 37, a *numus* is named as the price of a young pig fit for sacrifice (*porci sacres sinceri*); in Epid. III. ii. 36 Epidicus proposes to hire the services of a *fidicina* for a *numus;* in Pers. IV. vi. 2, when a sum of sixty

minae are paid over, two *numi* are deducted as the value of the bag (*crumena*); in Men. I. iv. 1 Erotium gives Cylindrus three *numi* to purchase viands for a *prandium;* in Trin. IV. ii. 1 the Sycophanta says, *Huic ego dici nomen trinummo faciam, nam ego operam meam Tribus numis hodie locavi ad artes nugatorias,* with which compare *1v.* 6, 163. The passage in Most. II. i. 10 will be examined below.

There is nothing in any of the above examples from which we could with certainty infer the precise value of the *Nummus.* Some light however is thrown upon the inquiry by the speech of the cook, in Pseud. III. ii. 20, who complains that when people went to the market to hire a cook, they looked out not for the best artiste but for the cheapest: hence, he exclaims, *Hoc ego fui hodie solus opsessor fori, Illi drachmis* * *issent miseri, me nemo potest Minoris quisquam numo†ut surgam subigere;* cf. Aul. III. ii. 34. Pseud. III. ii. 58, 87. This proves conclusively that the *Nummus* was more in value than the *Drachma.* But we can go farther; in Truc. II. iv. 91 Dinarchus declares that he will expend a *Mina* on viands for Phronesium, *Praeterea opsonari dumtaxat ad minam,* and in vii. 11, Geta, who had been employed to lay out the money, gives, in a soliloquy, an account of his stewardship, rejoicing that he had not failed to take good care of himself, *Num iam de hoc opsonio de mna una deminui Modo quinque numos, mihi detraxi partem Herculaneam.* But the *Pars Herculanea* (see note on Most. IV. iii. 45) was a tithe, therefore five *numi* were one-tenth of a *Mina,* and since a Mina = 100 Drachmae, five *numi* must have been equal to 10 *Drachmae,* and hence a *Nummus* was equal to two *Drachmae* or a *Didrachm.*

This value of the *Nummus* will suit perfectly the passages quoted above, and those also in which considerable sums are mentioned. In Rud. V. iii. 50 Labrax says that he paid a thousand *Numi* (*mille numos denumeravi*) for Ampelisca, but according to the above computation 1000 *Numi* would be 20 *Minae,* which was an ordinary price for a female slave (see note on Most. I. iii. 142), and so 600 *Numi,* or 12 *Minae,* is the price of a female slave of an inferior description in Pers. I. i. 37, iii. 37. III. iii. 32, V. ii. 70. *Mille numos* is found in Rud. V. ii. 40, where the context proves that the sum was considerably less than a talent; and *mille numum* occurs in Merc. II. iv. 23, but here the context does not enable us to fix even an approximate value for the amount indicated.

---

* In Merc. IV. iv. 37 a cook demands a drachma as his hire for a day.

† It is almost unnecessary to observe that the explanation given by some of the older commentators " numo aureo Romano " is altogether absurd.

Although *Nummus* must mean a *Didrachm* in the passage quoted
above from the Truculentus, there are two others in which commentators have believed that it clearly denotes a different sum, and
these we must examine.

In Heaut. III. iii. 38 Syrus fabricates a story to the following
effect: that an old woman of Corinth had borrowed 1000 drachmae
(*drachumarum argenti mille*) from Bacchis, and, having died without
paying her debt, that her young daughter Antiphila had been left as
security in the hands of Bacchis, *Ea relicta huic arraboni pro illo
argento*. Everything is distinct up to *v.* 43, but unfortunately the
text of the two lines which follow (44, 45), as they appear in the
older editions, is admitted by all to be corrupt, and has been variously
emended by different editors. In these lines the words *mille numum*
are found, and the sense is taken to be that Bacchis now wishes
Clinias to pay her 1000 *numi*, in consideration of which she will give
up Antiphila. It is taken for granted that the *mille numum* are
identical with the *drachumarum argenti mille* previously mentioned,
and hence it is inferred that *numus* is here used as equivalent to
drachma. Now although it might be fairly urged that a passage in
which the text is avowedly corrupt and the meaning uncertain cannot
be received in evidence at all, yet, even admitting the interpretation
to be generally correct, it by no means follows that the conclusion
is inevitable. Syrus, to answer his own ends, had just characterised
Bacchis as a *pessuma meretrix*, and what is more likely than that he
should represent such a person as not satisfied with having the mere
principal of the sum which she had lent repaid, but as seeking a large
addition for interest, and as taking advantage of the passion of Clinias
to demand double the original loan, that is, according to the view
given above, 1000 *Numi* or 2000 *Drachmae*. Terence uses *numus*
in one other passage only, Phor. I. i. 3, 4, where the phrase introduced, *pauxilulum numerum*, decides nothing.

The second passage is in Most. II. i. 10, *Vel isti qui [hastis] trium
numorum causa subeunt sub falas*, where Lipsius and others interpret
tres numi to mean *tres asses*, and to refer to the daily pay of a Roman
soldier. It is urged that this explanation is corroborated by the
well-known passage in Polybius (VI. 37), where he informs us that
the Roman legionary received two obols a day, which, if we adopt the
common practice of the Greek and Roman writers, and reckon the
drachma and the *denarius* as equivalent, would amount to 3⅓ asses. But
there are various considerations which render this opinion untenable.

1. The word *Numus*, when employed by Roman writers definitely

with reference to their own currency, signifies *κατ' ἐξοχήν*, the *Numus Sestertius*. But the daily pay of the Roman soldier was certainly not three *Sestertii* at this period.

2. Plautus, Pseud. I. i. 95, makes Calidorus say, *Quid ego ni fleam Quoi nec paratus numus argenti siet, Neque cui libellae spes sit usquam gentium;* from which we naturally infer that the *numus argenti* is something different from the *libella*. But the *Libella*, according to Varro (L. L. V. § 174, ed. Müll.), was a small silver coin equal in value to the copper *As*. Hence we may translate, 'I, who have not got a shilling in my pocket, and have no hope of procuring a penny anywhere.' It is quite true that *libella* is employed elsewhere (as it is indeed here) by Plautus in the same sense as *triobolum* and *numus*, to denote indefinitely a trifling sum, as in Cas. II. v. 8, *Quod si tu nolis, filiusque etiam tuus, Vobis invitis atque amborum ingratiis Vna libella liber possum fieri;* * and that when Hegio says, Capt. V. i. 27, *At ob eam rem mihi libellam pro eo argenti ne duis*, the meaning is precisely the same as when he says, II. ii. 81, *Eum si reddis mihi, praeterea unum numum ne duis;* but our object at present is to ascertain whether the value of the *numus*, when used by Plautus to denote a specific sum or coin, is constant or variable.

3. Lastly, as to the passage Most. II. i. 10. When Lipsius and others assert that the words *trium numerum causa* refer to the daily pay of the Roman soldier, even if we were to admit that the words really allude to the pay of the Roman soldier, it is a pure assumption to take it for granted that his *daily* pay is meant. Supposing the *tres numi* equivalent to six *drachmae* or six *denarii* (for, as we remarked above, the Roman writers are wont to regard the *drachma* and the *denarius* as equivalent), the *tres numi* would be equal to 60 *asses*, or two *asses* per day for a month. That this may have actually been the pay of the Roman soldier when Plautus wrote is by no means improbable, since it was only two obols or 3½ asses per day in the time of Polybius, although the wealth of Rome and the importance of her armies had increased enormously during the interval. This is a mere conjecture, and may be taken for what it is worth, but we must bear in mind that we have no proof whatsoever that the words of Tranio refer to the pay of a Roman soldier. That three *numi* were occasionally given

* So again, Pseud. II. ii. 34, *Tibi libellam argenti nunquam credam*. No specimen of the *Libella* having ever been found, some numismatologists have most unreasonably maintained that there never was such a coin; but the words of Varro (l. c.) are perfectly distinct—"Numi denarii decuma libella, quod libram pondo aeris valebat, et erat ex argento parva."

in Greece for a day's work appears from Trin. IV. ii. 1, quoted above, p. 247.

There is another passage in Plautus which may throw some light upon the subject; in Men. III. iii. 17 Erotium's maid says to Menaechmus, *Amabo, mi Mrnacchme, inaureis da mihi Faciundas pondo duum numum, stalagmia,* 'please, Menaechmus dear, give the jeweller (gold) to the weight of two numi to make for me a pair of drop-earrings.' If we suppose that a *numus* weighed two drachmae, i. e. about 131 or 133 Troy grains, the quantity here asked for would be appropriate, but the weight of a *libella* in silver, say six Troy grains, would be greatly too small, and the weight of a *libella* in copper absurdly large.

It will be observed also that the gold *Philippus* weighed two Attic Drachms, and hence the term *numus* denoting Didrachm was naturally applied to each, the epithet *aureus* being employed to distinguish the golden Didrachm from the silver Didrachm.

There is still another consideration which, although hypothetical, may possibly bear upon this question. No attempt to coin silver was made at Rome until 269 B.C. When we consider the stormy and critical character of her history for nearly a century after that date, it is not probable that the mint would be very active until the spoils of Macedonia and Asia were poured into the Treasury. Hence during the life of Plautus the silver currency must have consisted chiefly of foreign coins, those in circulation among the Greeks of Magna Graecia and Sicily. But, judging from the medals which have come down to modern times, the Didrachm was more common than any other piece in these regions, and vast numbers have been preserved belonging to Tarentum, Velia, and Syracuse. These do not, in most cases, exactly correspond to the weight of the Attic Didrachm, but Plautus might give the name of *numus* or *numus argenti* to the pieces with which he was most familiar.

We may now briefly recapitulate the different propositions which we have endeavoured to prove.

1. The *Numus* of Plautus, when the word is used to designate a particular coin or specific sum, refers to the Greek monetary system exclusively.

2. When the epithet *aureus* is added, or distinctly implied, it denotes the *Philippus*.

3. When the epithet *aureus* is not expressed, and not evidently implied, then the simple *numus*, sometimes termed *numus argenti*, invariably represents a Greek Didrachm of silver.

Before quitting this subject we may advert to the circumstance that a great deal of bad money was in circulation, and hence, when a sum was paid, not only was it customary to assure the receiver that the coin was good, but it was submitted to some skilled person in order that it might be scrutinized and tested; thus Pers. III. iii. 32, *Numi sexcenti hic erunt Probi numerati, fac sit mulier libera, Atque huc continuo adduce. D. Iam faxo hic erit, Non, hercle, cui nunc hoc dem spectandum, scio;* and again, IV. vi. 1, *Probati hic argenti sunt sexaginta minae.*

That forgeries were common we might infer from the number of counterfeits, many of them executed with great ingenuity, which are preserved in the cabinets of collectors. There are the *numi plumbei* of Plautus; thus Cas. II. iii. 40, *Cui homini hodie peculi numus non est plumbeus,* 'a fellow whose savings do not amount to a bad shilling;' so also Most. IV. ii. 12 (i. 33). *Tace sis, faber, qui cudere soles plumbeos Numos;* and Trin. IV. ii. 120, *sine aurum crederem, Cui, si capiti res siet, numum numquam credam plumbeum?* 'is it likely that I would trust that fellow with gold, whom, were his all at stake, I would never trust with a bad shilling?'

XV.—*PUNISHMENTS INFLICTED UPON SLAVES.*

Since the tricks and deceptions which so often form the staple of the New Comedy are for the most part contrived and executed by cunning slaves, and since their own masters are not seldom represented as the victims of these frauds, it is not surprising that the works of the dramatists should abound in words and phrases applied as taunts to those who had paid the penalty of previous offences. The expressions employed are curiously varied, by Plautus especially, and a multitude of terms seem to have been coined for the purpose.

The common punishment for an ordinary offence was the scourge (*flagrum*) applied to the naked back (*dorsus* s. *dorsum*—*tergus* s. *tergum*) and shoulders (*scapulae*), often with such severity as to produce livid marks, scars, and wheals (*cicatrices*—*offerrumentae*), and even to flay off the skin. The instrument employed was a cat made of ropes (*restes*), or strips of ox-hide (*terginum*—*lora*), or bundles of rods (*virgae*) in which elm twigs (*virgae ulmeae*) generally took the place of our own national birch.

The following examples will be rendered intelligible by what has been said: Most. IV. L 12 (10), *Vt adhuc fuit, mihi corium esse oportet Sincerum, atque ut volem verberari;* cf. I. i. 36, IV. l. 27 (24), V. i. 19 (ii. 4), Pers. III. i. 33, *Herus si minatus est malum servo suo, Tamenetsi id futurum non est, ubi captum est flagrum, Dum tunicas ponit, quanta adficitur miseria!* Capt. III. iv. 117, *Vae illis virgis miseris quae hodie in tergo morientur meo!* As. III. ii. 28, *Vbi saepe ad languorem tua durilia dederis octo Validos lictores ulmeis adfectos lentis virgis;* Pseud. I. ii. 20, *Huc adhibete aures, quae ego loquar, plagigera genera hominum, Numquam edepol vostrum durius tergum erit, quam terginum hoc meum;* Epid. I. i. 84, *corium perdidi: nam ubi senex senserit Sibi data esse verba, virgis dorsum despoliet meum; v. 25, T. At unum a praetura tua, Epidice, abest. E. Quidnam? T. Scies: Lictores duo, duo viminei fasces virgarum;* Most. IV. ii. 26 (23), *Mane castigabit eos bubulis exuviis;* Poen. I. i. 10, *Nunc mihi blandidicus es, heri in tergo meo Tris facile corios contrivisti bubulos;* and hence Aul. IV. i. 15, *censio bubula;* Trin. IV. iii. 4, *bubuli collabi;* Pers. II. iv. 11, *Caedere hodie tu restibus;* Phor. I. ii. 26, *Seni fidelis dum sum, scapulas perdidi;* and so Trin. IV. iii. 2, *ne metus exoriatur scapulis;* Poen. I. i. 25, *meae istuc scapulae sentiunt;* Pers. I. i. 32, *Vah! iam scapulae pruriunt, quia te istuc audivi loqui,* with which compare Mil. II. iv. 44, *Timeo quid rerum gesserim, ita dorsus totus pruruit;* Pers. IV. viii. 1, *Transcidi loris omnes, adveniens, domi;* and so Adel. II. i. 28, *usque ad necem obperiere loris;* Truc. IV. iii. 19, *Iam livorem tute scapulis istoc concinnas tuis;* Pseud. I. ii. 12, *Ita ego vostra latera loris faciam ut valide varia sient;* Rud. IV. iii. 60, *Tu hercle opinor in ridulum te piscem comvortes, nisi caves, Fiet tibi puniceum corium, postea atrum denuo;* As. III. ii. 7, *Qui saepe ante in nostras scapulas cicatrices indiderunt;* Rud. III. iv. 48, *Contende ergo uter sit tergo verior. Ni obserrumentas habebis plures in tergo tuo Quam ulla navis longa clavos, tum ego ero mendacissumus; Postea adspicito meum, quando ego tuum inspectavero: Nisi erit tam sincerum ut quivis dicat ampullarius, Optumum esse opere faciundo corium, et sincerissumum; Quid causae est quin virgis te usque ad saturitatem sauciem?*

The general idea of flogging is made to assume a number of whimsical forms.

Sometimes the scourgers are represented as painters who execute a drawing with elm-tree pigments on the hide: Epid. V. i. 19, *Ex tuis verbis meum futurum corium pulcrum praedicas: Quem Apelles atque Zeuxis duo pingent pigmentis ulmeis.*

Sometimes the rods are parasites who shave close the person to

whom they attach themselves: Epid. II. iii. 6, *Quod pol ego metuo, si
senex resiverit, Ne ulmos parasitos faciat quae usque adtondeant.*

Sometimes they are pens, the back of the culprit being the
copy-book: Pseud. I. v. 131, *Quasi in libro quom scribuntur calamo
literae, Stulis me totum usque ulmeis conscribito.*

Sometimes they are catapults hurling darts and death: Pers. I. i.
28, *Vide modo ulmeae catapultae tuum ne transfigant latus.*

Sometimes the victim is a bottomless abyss of rods: Amph. IV.
ii. 9, *Verbero, etiam quis ego sim me rogitas? ulmorum Acheruns, Quem
pol ego hodie ob istaec dicta faciam ferventem flagris.*

Sometimes he will absorb so many elm rods that he will be
changed into their substance: As. II. ii. 96, *Mihi tibique intermiatus
est nos futuros ulmeos.*

Sometimes he is an anvil: Amph. I. i. 7, *Quasi incudem me miserum
homines octo validi caedunt: ita Peregre adveniens hospitio publicitus
accipiar.*

Sometimes he is a solid melted by the fervent heat engendered
by the rods: Cas. II. vi. 48, *Tu ut liquescas, ipse actutum virgis
calefactabere.*

Sometimes he is a garden well watered by blows: Epid. I. ii. 18,
Quem quidem ego hominem inrigatum plagis pistori dabo.

Sometimes he is a farmer who may look for an abundant vintage,
not of grapes but of rods—a rich harvest of misfortune: Rud. III. ii.
21, *At ego te per crura et talos tergumque optestor tuum, Si tibi ulmeam
uberem esse speras virgi demiam, Et tibi eventurum hoc anno uberem
messem mali, Vt . . . mihi dicas . . . &c.*

Sometimes he is a debtor who defers the day of payment by
contracting fresh loans, with the certainty of having a heavier account
to settle eventually: Phor. V. ii. 15, *Quid fiet? in eodem luto haesitas:
versura solves* [*], *Geta, praesens quod fuerat malum in diem abiit,
plagae crescunt.*

[*] Salmasius and Gronovius proved long ago that the mercantile term
versura denoted the expedient of paying off a debt by contracting a fresh
loan, the creditor being thus changed. But whenever a plan of this kind
is resorted to, the new loan must be equal to the sum originally borrowed,
together with the interest due upon it, so that, on each repetition of the
process, an addition is made to the debt, just as at the present day, when
a bill of exchange is renewed instead of being paid, the new bill must
always be for a larger sum than that for which it is substituted. Geta
having committed an offence which exposed him to punishment, staves off
the evil hour by a fresh piece of knavery, but by so doing the number of
stripes due by him is increased (*plagae crescunt*).

The technical phrase for renewing a loan in this manner is *Versuram
facere*, and hence *Versura solvere* means 'to pay off an old loan by a new'

Sometimes he is to be tied round with rods, as a nosegay of myrtles is bound with rushes: Rud. III. iv. 26, *Vos adeo, ubi ego innuero vobis, si ne ei caput exoculassitis Quasi murteta iuncis, ita ego vos virgis circumvinciam.*

Sometimes he is to be required to quaff a draught expressed from the *fructus fullonius,* i. e. the staves with which cloth-scourers beat and thumped the woollen garments consigned to them: Pseud. III. i. 15, *Nunc nisi lenoni munus hodie mixero, Cras mihi potandus fructus est fullonius.*

Sometimes an entertainment is provided, scot-free, for his shoulders: Epid. I. ii. 22, *Sine meo sumptu paratae iam sunt scapulis sumbolae.*

Sometimes a well-flayed back is compared to a richly-embroidered carpet: Pseud. I. ii. 12, *Ita ego vostra latera loris faciam ut valide varia sint, Vt ne peristromata quidem aeque picta sint Campanica, Neque Alexandrina belluata conchuliata tapetia.*

We talk in familiar English of 'giving a fellow a good dressing;' exactly the same idea is expressed in Heaut. V. i. 77, *C. Sed S. . . . . rum— M. Quid eum? C. Egone? si vivo, adeo exornatum dabo, Adeo depexum, ut dum vivat, meminerit semper mei.*

When it was wished to make the punishment more severe, the culprit was manacled and drawn up to a beam, from which he was suspended by the wrists while a heavy weight was attached to his feet. In this way he was rendered incapable of wincing or struggling:[*] Phor. I. iv. 43, *Ego plectar pendens nisi quid me fefellerit;* Eun. V. vi. 20, *Tu iam pendebis qui stultum adulescentulum nobilitas Flagitiis;* Poen. I. i. 18, *Suspende, vinci, verbera, auctor sum, sino;* Most. V. ii. 45 (iii. 45), *Verberibus, lutum, caedere pendens;* As. III. ii. 18, *Vbi saepe causam dixeris pendens advorsus octo Astulos, audaces viros, valentes virgatores;* see also Truc. IV. iii. 3.

We find occasionally the expression *pendere per pedes,* which, according to the natural force of the words, would lead us to infer that the slaves were sometimes hung up by the feet, head downwards. But it seems doubtful whether this is really the meaning of the phrase: thus As. II. ii. 33. *Le. Quot pondo led esse census nudum? Li. Non edepol scio. Le. Scibam ego te nescire; at pol ego, qui ted expendi, scio: Nudus vinctus centum pondo es, quando pendes per pedes. Li. Quo argumento istoc? Le. Ego dicam quo argumento et quo modo. Ad pedes quando adligatus es, aequom centupondium, Vbi manus manicae complexae sunt atque adductae ad trabem, Nec dependis, nec propendis, quin malus nequamque sis.** Although the interpretation of some portions of the above lines is by no means certain, it is quite evident that when Leonidas says *pendes per pedes* he means 'suspended by the hands with the feet hanging down weighted,' and hence when we find in Cas. II. vi. 38, *O. Mihi ut tortitio eveniat. C. Vt quidem hercle pedibus pendeas*, the signification is probably the same.

Sometimes goads (*stimuli*), that is, long poles with sharp iron spikes, used for driving cattle, were employed to prick the flesh, under the pretext that the skin of habitual malefactors had become so indurated as to be insensible to the lash: Pseud. I. ii. 4. *Neque ego homines magis asinos unquam vidi, ita plagis costae callent, Quos dum ferias, tibi plus noceas, eo enim ingenio hi sunt flagritribae;* As. II. iv. 12, *L. Vtinam nunc stimulus in manu mihi sit. M. Quiesce, quaeso. L. Qui latera conteram tua quae occalluere plagis;* Cas. II. viii. 10, *At candidatus cedit hic mastigia, Stimulorum loculi,* 'whose body is a sheath for goads.'

The goad might be applied to one hanging up: Men. V. v. 48. *At ego te pendentem fodiam stimulis triginta dies;* or to one bearing about the *furca* or *patibulum* (see below); Most. I. i. 52, *O carnuficium cribrum, quod credo fore, Ita te forabunt patibulatum per vias Stimulis, si huc revenial [quam primum] senex.*

In the lines last quoted reference is made to a form of torture to which we find numerous allusions. A heavy log of wood was employed, forked at the extremity (*furca*), or with a cross piece like a gibbet (*patibulum*); the hands of the slave were attached to the limbs of the log, which he dragged about, and was flogged or goaded as he staggered painfully under the load: Pers. V. ii. 72, *T. Satis sumpsimus supplici iam. D. Fateor, manus vobis do. T. Et post dabis Sub furcis;* Men. V. v. 40, *Et ob eam rem in carcerem ted esse compactum scio, Et postquam es emissus, caesum virgis sub furca scio;*

---

* *Adligatus es, dependis, propendis* are the readings of the best MSS., which have been corrected plausibly *adligatum est, dependes, propendes.*

Cas. II. viii. 2, *Sine modo rus veniat, ego remittam ad te virum Cum
furca in urbem, Tamquam carbonarium*, i. e. 'as black with blows
as if he were a charcoal burner;'* vi. 37, *O. Taceo, Deos quaeso.
C. Vt quidem tu hodie canem † et furcam feras. O. Mihi ut sortitio
eveniat. C. Vt quidem hercle pedibus pendeas.*

A thief was sometimes branded with the three letters FVR, and
hence was called in derision *literatus* or *trium literarum homo*: Cas.
II. vi. 48, *C. Tu ut liquescas, ipse actutum virgis calefactabere. S. Hoc
age sis, Olumpio. O. Si hic literatus me sinat;* Aul. II. iv. 46, *Tun'
trium literarum homo Me vituperas? fur, etiam fur trifurcifer.* ‡

When a slave belonging to the *Familia Vrbana* had committed
some unpardonable offence, or was found to be of habits incorrigibly
bad, he was transferred to the *Familia Rustica*, and was sent to the
country, where he was hardly used, frequently worked in chains, and
was employed in the most severe and distasteful labour. The sort
of toil most frequently referred to is working in the mills where the
corn was husked and ground (*pistrinum—mola*), and this task was
probably generally assigned to refractory town slaves because no
more skill was necessary than is required in turning a modern
tread-mill or prison-crank: Most. I. i. 18, *Angebis ruri numerum,
genus ferratile;* Andr. L. ii. 28, *Verberibus caesum te, Dave, in pistrinum
dedam usque ad necem Ea lege atque omine ut, si te inde exemerim, ego
pro te molam;* Phor. II. i. 18, *Herus si redierit, Molendum usque in
pistrino, vapulandum, habendae compedes, Opus ruri faciundum;* see
also Andr. I. iii 9, III. iv. 21, Heaut. III. ii. 19, Bac. IV. vi. 11,
Most. I. i. 15; Pseud. I. v. 84, *P. Pistrinum in mundo §‖ scibam, si*

---

* It is not impossible that there may be a double meaning here, and
that charcoal burners may have carried their burdens on a frame similar
to what French porters call a *fourchette*.

† *Canem* seems to be the reading of the MSS., and if it is correct the
meaning must be left to conjecture. Meursius would substitute *Camum*
(the Greek κημός, a muzzle or twitch for a horse), which is supposed to
mean a 'collar' or 'chain' in a passage quoted from Accius by Nonius,
p. 200.

‡ *Stigmatias* is used to denote a branded slave in Cic. de Off. II. 7, § 25,
O miserum, qui fideliorem et barbarum et stigmatiam putaret quam coniugem!
a passage quoted by Nonius (41). *Stigmosus* is found in Petronius Arbiter,
c. 109, and in Plin. Epp. I. v. quoted from M. Regulus.

§ The expression *in mundo* occurs elsewhere in Plautus, Cas. III. ii. 3,
*Stultitia magna est, mea quidem sententia, Hominem amatorem ullum ad forum
procedere In eum diem, quoi quod amet in mundo siet;* Epid. V. i. 12, *S. Habe
bonum animum. E. Quippe ego qui libertas in mundo sita est;* Pers. I. i. 46,
*T. Quaesivi (sc. argentum), nusquam repperi. S. Quaeram equidem si quis
credat. T. Nempe habeo in mundo.* It is explained by Paul. Diac. p. 109,
ed. Müll., "*In mundo* dicebant antiqui, quum aliquid in promptu esse

id faxem, mihi. S. Non a me scibas pistrinum in mundo tibi, Quom ea mussitabas?

We have an elaborate exposition in Aa. I. i. 16, *L. Nam me illuc ducis ubi lapis lapidem terit?* . . . . . . *Vbi fiunt nequam homines qui polentam pronritant.* . . . . . . *Apud fustitudinas ferricrepinas insulas, Vbi vivos homines mortui incursant boves. D. Modo pol percepi, Libane, quid istuc sit loci, Vbi fit polenta, et fortasse dicere;* and a complicated jest on the same subject in Pers. I. i. 21, where a slave is excusing himself for not having·visited his friend, *S. Negotium edepol. T. Ferreum fortasse. S. Plusculum annum Fui praeferratus apud molas, tribunus vapularis. T. Vetus iam istaec militia est tua: S.* 'I was occupied by business, I assure you.' T. 'Something connected with the iron trade perhaps?' S. 'For somewhat more than a year I was in the midst of iron at the mills, a captain in the beating (hammering) department.'

In Pseud. IV. vi. 38 the convict is spoken of as one who enrols himself as a settler in a 'mill-colony:' *Bene hercle factum: quid ego censo Pseudolum Facere ut det nomen ad molarum coloniam?*

Other kinds of severe coarse labour, such as hewing wood and drawing water, were exacted: Poen. V. iii. 33, *quos ego iam detrudam ad molas, Inde porro ad puteum atque ad robustum codicem,* on which Pseud. L. ii. 24 may serve as a commentary.

In Cas. I. i. 32 we find a sort of catalogue of the hardships inflicted on a refractory slave, at the Villa. Labour in stone quarries (*lautumiae*) was especially dreaded: Poen. IV. ii. 5, *Ita me Di ament! vel in lautumiis, vel in pistrino mavelim Agere aetatem, praependitus latera forti ferro mea;* but it is in the Captivi that the horrors of this punishment are chiefly dilated on, e. g. III. v. 63, *ducite Vbi ponderosas, crassas capiat compedes, Inde ibis porro in latomias lapidarias. Ibi quom alii octonas lapides effoderint, Nisi cotidianus sesquiopus conficeris, Sexcentoplago nomen indetur tibi.* . . . . *v. 71, Nam noctu nervo vinctus custodibitur, Interdius sub terra lapides eximet. Diu ego hunc cruciabo, non uno apsoloam die. A. Certumne est tibi istuc? H. Nom moriri certiust. Abducite istum artutum ad Hippolytum fabrum: Iubete huic crassas compedes impingier. Inde extra portam ad meum libertum Cordalum, In lapicidinas facite deductus sit, Atque hunc ita me velle, dicite, curarier, Ne qui deterius huic sit, quam quoi pessume est; V. iv. 1, Vidi ego multa saepe picta, quae*

volebant intelligi;" and by Charis. p. 180. ed. Puts., "*In mundo pro palam et in expedito ac cito,*" who quotes the above passage from the Pseudolus, and also Caecilius and Ennius.

Acherunti fierent, Cruciamenta: verum enimvero nulla adaeque est Acheruns, Atque ubi ego fui in lapicidinis. . . . .

v. 7, Itidem haec mihi advenienti upupa,* qui me delectet, data est.

It must not be supposed that these various forms of torture were by any means confined to male slaves, for women also seem to have been treated by brutal masters with the same merciless severity. This will appear from the terms in which Callicles addresses his ancillae in Truc. IV. iii. 1 seqq., and the cruelty of Roman ladies to their attendants has been forcibly depicted by Juvenal in his sixth Satire. There is a curious passage in Terence, Adel. V. iii. 60, where Demea declares that he will carry off to the country the beautiful Psaltria, who had fascinated his son, and compel her to perform the labours of a rustic drudge: *M. Modo facito ut illam serves. D. Ego istuc videro: Atque illi favillae plena, fumi, ac pollinis, Coquendo sit faxo et molendo: praeter haec Meridie ipso faciam ut stipulam conligat: Tam excoctam reddam atque atram quam carbo est;* cf. Merc. II. iii. 78.

Although tortured in a vast variety of ways, slaves were rarely put to death by their masters, because such vengeance would have entailed the loss of valuable property. Crucifixion however is frequently spoken of, and is used as a threat, or a taunt, or a jest: Most. V. ii. 12 (iii. 12), *Non enim ibis: ego ferare faxo, ut meruisti, in crucem;* Andr. III. v. 15, *P. An non dixi hoc esse futurum? D. Dixti. P. Quid meritus? D. Crucem;* Mil. II. iv. 19, *Noli minitari: scio crucem futuram mihi sepulcrum, Ibi mei maiores sunt siti: pater, avos, proavos, abavos, Non possunt mihi minaciis tuis hisce oculi fodiri.*

In Mil. II. iv. 6 there is an allusion to the practice of making the criminal carry the cross or gibbet to which he was to be nailed through the streets to the spot outside the walls where the execution took place: *Credo ego istoc exemplo tibi esse eundum actutum extra portam,†Dispessis manibus patibulum quom habebis;* on which a fragment from the lost play of the Carbonaria ‡ serves as a commentary, *Patibulum ferat per urbem deinde adfigatur cruci.*

---

* We talk of *a crow (bar)*, the Romans called it *an owl*. The joke in *delectet* refers to the practice of boys keeping sparrows, owls, and other birds as pets.

† We are told that this gate was called the *Porta Metia* on the authority of Cas. II. vi. 2: *Cl. Face, Chaline, me certiorem, quid meus vir me velit. Ch. Ille edepol videre ardentem te extra portam Metiam;* and Pseud. I. III. 97, *Iam bis ero: verum extra portam Metiam currendum est prius;* but in both passages the word *Metiam* is totally destitute of MS. authority.

‡ Nonius s. v. *Patibulum*, p. 221.

The nailing of the feet and hands is alluded to in Most. II. i. 12 : *Ego dabo ei talentum primus qui in crucem excucurrerit, Sed ea lege, ut adfigantur bis pedes, bis brachia;* and perhaps the breaking of the legs in Poen. IV. ii. 64, where Sinceratus says, *Si herus meus med esse locutum quoiquam mortali sciat, Continuo is me ex Sincerato crurifragium fecerit.* See other allusions to crucifixion in Aul. I. i. 20, Mill. II. ii. 28, iii. 29, Most. III. ii. 56, Pers. II. iv. 24, Rud. IV. iv. 26, Stich. IV. ii. 45.

In the great majority of instances, however, in which the word *Crux* is introduced by the dramatists, it means either,

1. 'Pain,' 'evil,' 'mischief,' 'anxiety,' 'torment' in general: Aul. III. v. 48, *Aut aliqua mala crux semper est quae aliquid petat,* 'some torment or other is always pestering one for something;' and so IV. iv. 4; Bac. IV. ii. 2, *Quae te mala crux agitat?* 'what phrenzy (fury) is exciting you?' and Cas. II. vi. 64, *mala crux ea est quidem,* 'that is indeed torture.' In Phor. III. iii. 11, *Ni etiam nunc me huius causa quaerere in malo iubeas crucem,* signifies 'unless you wish me, who am involved in a scrape, to seek in it a worse one—to jump from the frying pan into the fire.' In Eun. II. iii. 91 we have the plural *crucibus* in the same sense.

2. 'An imprecation:' *I in crucem, I in malam crucem,* 'go to the mischief,' 'go to the deuce.' Of this we shall speak more fully hereafter. The curse is not always confined to persons: Capt. III. i. 9, *Ilicet parasiticae arti maxumam in malam crucem!* 'thrice accursed be the trade of the parasite!' The phrase *ire in malam crucem* is found where there is no imprecation, in the sense of 'to go to the mischief,' 'to go to destruction,' 'to come to a bad end:' Pseud. I. iii. 101, *In malam crucem istic ibit Iupiter lenonius;* and so Rud. I. ii. 87, and Trin. II. iv. 197. So with *abstrahere,* Men. Prol. 66, *Rapidus* (sc. *fluvius*) *raptori pueri subduxit pedes, Apstraxitque hominem in maxumam malam crucem;* and *fugere,* Poen. III. v. 44, *Sed quid ego dubito fugere hinc in malam crucem?*

Carnufex is the general term for one employed to administer punishment: Bac. IV. iv. 36, *Istoc dicto dedisti hodie in cruciatum Chrusalum: Nam ubi me adspiciet, ad carnuficem rapiet continuo senex;* As. II. ii. 45, *Omnes de nobis carnuficum concelebrabuntur dies;* Poen. I. ii. 156, *Nisi ego illum iubeo quadrigis cursim ad carnuficem rapi;* V. v. 23, *Iam hercle ego illum excruciandum totum carnufici dabo;* so Rud. II. ii. 16, III. iv. 73, vi. 19. Other words are used humourously in the same sense as *virgatores,* As. III. ii. 19; *elatabor,* Rud. III. v. 25; but each of these occurs once only.

The occupation itself was called *Carnuficina*, Cist. II. i. 1; and those who practised it were said *carnuficinam facere*, Capt. I. ii. 29, equivalent to which is *facere quaestum carcerarium*, v. 26. The employment was by no means honourable nor popular, and hence no term of vituperation is more common than *carnufex*.

The word *Lorarii* is found in the *Dramatis Personae* and stage directions of some plays, but does not occur in the text of any classical author. Aulus Gellius (N. A. X. 3) tells us that, after the departure of Hannibal from Italy, the Romans refused to acknowledge the Bruttii as *socii*, or to enrol them as soldiers, but employed them to discharge servile duties for provincial governors—" Itaque hi sequebantur magistratus, tamquam in scenicis fabulis qui dicebantur *lorarii*, et quos erant iussi vinciebant et verberabant."

Sometimes fantastic terms are used: thus Truc. IV. iii. 8, *Nisi si ad tintinnaculos vos voltis educi viros*, where the *tintinnaculi viri* are the floggers who make the scourge sing or whistle about the ears of the sufferers: in like manner Pseud. I. iii. 98, *Lanios inde arcessam duos cum tintinnabulis. Eadem duo greges virgarum inde ulmearum adegero;* with which compare Rud. III. v. 25, *D. Ehem! optume edepol, eccum clavator advenit. L. Illud quidem edepol tinnimentum est auribus;* while in Pers. II. iii. 12 we have another expression for the sound of the lash upon the flesh, *Diu quod bene erit die uno apsolvam, tax tax tergo meo erit.*

We may conclude by quoting some lines from As. III. ii. 1, which give a sort of summary of the tortures inflicted upon slaves; *Perfidiae laudes gratiasque habemus merito magnas, Quom nostris sucophantiis, dolis, astutiisque, Scapularum confidentia, virtute ulmorum freti, Qui advorsum stimulos, laminas, crucesque, compedesque Nervos, catenas, carceres, numellas, pedicas, boias, Indoctoresque acerrimos, gnarosque nostri tergi, Qui saepe ante in nostras scapulas cicatrices indiderunt;* and with these we may compare Men. V. vi. 8, *Recordetur id, qui nihili sunt, quid iis preti Detur ab suis heris, ignavis, inprobis Viris: verbera, compedes, molae, magna Lassitudo, fames, frigus durum, Haec pretia sunt ignaviae.* A few of the words given above may require explanation, in addition to what has been said already.

Laminae were thin plates of metal raised to a red heat and applied to the flesh: they are spoken of by Lucretius, III. 1029, *Verbera, carnufices, robur, pix, lamina, taedae;* by Cicero, In Verr. Act. II. v. 63, *Quid quum ignes ardentesque laminae ceterique cruciatus admovebantur?* and by Horace, Epp. I. xv. 36, *Scilicet ut ventres lamna candente nepotum Diceret urendos corrector Bestius.*

Numella 1. Numellus seems to signify a combination of a collar
for the neck with stocks for the feet. Similar contrivances were
employed for confining cattle and dogs. See Nonius (144), "*Nu-
mellae* machinae genus ligneum ad discruciandos noxios paratum,
quo et collum et pedes inmittunt. Plautus Aulularia, *nervas, catenas,
carcerem, numellas, pedicas, boias,*" where "Aulularia" is a mistake
for "Asinaria." Paul. Diac. p. 172, ed. Müll., "*Numella* genus
vinculi quo quadrupedes deligantur." See also Colum. R. R. VI.
19, VII. 8.

Boia. That this was a collar would be proved by a passage in
Prudent. Psychom. Praef. 33, *attrita boiis colla,* if we could depend
upon the text, but the reading is very doubtful. Plautus has a pun-
ning joke upon the word in Capt. IV. ii. 108, and it will be observed
that in the passage which we are discussing *numellas, pedicas, boias*
are placed together.

Nervus 1. Nervum is explained by Festus, p. 165, ed. Müll.:
"*Nervum* appellamus etiam ferreum vinculum quo pedes inpedi-
untur: quamquam Plautus eo etiam cervices vinciri ait *perfidiose
captus eo epol nervo cervices probat.*" The word occurs again in Aul.
IV. x. 13, Capt. III. v. 71, Curc. V. iii. 12, 40, 45, Poen. V. iv. 99,
Rud. III. vi. 34, 38, 51. In the last there seems to be a direct
reference to the neck: *Credo alium in aliam beluam hominem tortier,
Illic in columbum, credo, leno tortitur, Nam in columbari collum haud
multo post erit, In nervom ille hodie nidamenta congeret;* where *colum-
bare* must mean a collar, and is introduced in connection with
columbus in consequence of its resemblance to *columbarium.* In
many passages *nervus* is equivalent to a chain, hence may signify
a prison, and this may be the meaning in the line just quoted. Cf.
Curc. V. iii. 40. In Phor. II. ii. 10 the expression *O vir fortis atque
amicus! verum hoc saepe, Phormio, Verror, ne istaec fortitudo in nervom
erumpat denique,* seems to be equivalent to our 'should come to
grief.' In the same play, IV. iv. 15, *In nervom potius ibit* probably
means 'he will go to gaol first.' It would appear that the original
meaning of *nervus* or *nervum,* which is probably identical with the
Greek νεῦρον, was not, as lexicographers insist, 'a muscle' or 'sinew'
or 'tendon,' but 'a thong or strap made of hide,' and hence 'a
cord' or 'string,' the anatomical application being figurative and
secondary. In all the oldest Latin writers it is generally equivalent
to *vincula,* either in the sense of a collar, or of bonds, or of a place
of confinement. In the Laws of the XII. Tables, as quoted by
Aul. Gell. XX. 1, with regard to insolvent debtors, the creditor is

empowered—SECVM DVCITO VINCITO AVT NERVO AVT COMPEDIBVS QVINDECIM PONDO NE MINORE AVT SI VOLET MAIORE VINCITO; and in a speech of the elder Cato, quoted also by Aul. Gell. XI. 18, *Fures privatorum furtorum in nervo atque in compedibus aetatem agunt : fures publici in auro atque in purpura.* In one passage of Plautus it may signify 'a strap' or 'cord:' Curc. V. iii. 12, *Atque ita te nervo torquebo itidem uti catapultas solent;* and here there is probably a pun. Freund is certainly mistaken when he quotes, as an example of *nervus* in the sense of a 'sinew' or 'muscle,' the line from the Poenulus V. iv. 99, where Hanno says to his newly-discovered daughter, *Condamus alter alterum ergo in nervom brachialem :* he means, 'let us shut up each other in the prison of our arms,' or, if we choose to take *nervus* to mean 'a collar,' it will be, 'let us encircle each other's necks in the collar of our arms.' We find it in the metaphorical sense of 'mental strength,' 'power,' 'energy,' for the first time in Eun. II. iii. 21, *Sive adeo digna res est ubi tu nervos intendas tuos;* but it may be fairly doubted whether there is here any figurative allusion to an anatomical term.

When a slave had been detected in any serious offence, he was usually seized upon the spot, and bound hand and foot to prevent him from running off,[*] or from taking refuge in some sanctuary,[†] and was frequently kept in prison until his fate was decided. Handcuffs were called *manicae* or *copulae:* thus Most. V. i. 17 (ii. 2), *Continuo exsiliatis: manicas celeriter conectite;* Capt. III. v. 1, *Inicite huic manicas mastigiae;*[‡] Epid. V. i. 11, *Quaeritant me, in manibus gestant copulas sesuncias.* Fetters for the feet were *compedes* or *pedicae,* and were riveted on: Aul. IV. i. 15, *Qui ea curabit apstinebit censione bubula, Nec sua opera rediget umquam in splendorem compedis;* Capt. III. iv. 118, *H. Verba mihi data esse video. T. Quid cessatis, compedes, Currere ad me, meaque amplecti crura, ut vos custodiam?* Pers. IV. iv. 24, *Ferreas tute tibi inpingi§ iubeas crassas compedes;* Poen. III. i. 10, *Nam iste quidem gradus subereetus est cribro pollinario, Nisi*

<hr>

[*] Sceledrus in Mil. II. vi. 99, *Nam iam aliquo aufugiam, et me occultabo aliquot dies, Dum haec consilescunt turbae atque irae leniunt.*

[†] So Tranio, Most. V. i. 45 (II. 30), seats himself upon an altar.

[‡] We have *manicae* again in As. II. ii. 38. *Manicula* in Plautus signifies 'a little hand:' Rud. IV. iv. 125, Pseud. V. i. 16. By Varro L. L. V. 31, § 135, it is explained to mean the cross-bar passing through the *stiva* of a plough, which was grasped by the ploughman, 'the handle of the plough.'

[§] Cf. Men. I. i. 9, *Tum compediti anum lima perterunt, Aut lapide excutiunt clavum,* where *anum,* if this reading is correct, must be equivalent to *anulum,* and *clavom* must be the riveting-bolt.

cum pedicis condidicistis sic hoc grassari gradu.* There seems to be
a distinction drawn, in Men. I. i. 3, between *catenae* and *compedes,*
the former being a more general term: *Homines captivos qui catenis
vinciunt, Et qui fugitivis terris induunt compedes;* cf. *vv.* 8, 9, 10.

Catellus is also used by Plautus as a diminutive of *catena,* as well
as a diminutive of *catulus:* Curc. V. iii. 13, where Phaedromus is
addressing the leno Cappadox, *Delicatum te hodie faciam cum catello
ut accubes, Ferreo ego dico.* *Catellus* in the sense of 'a puppy,' Stich.
IV. ii. 40; and *catellum,* As. III. iii. 103.

The works of Plautus and Terence, of the former especially, are
full of words and phrases applied as taunts to those who had undergone the punishments above described; some of these recur perpetually, others seem to have been coined on the spot as it were,
and are *ἅπ. λεγ.* Such are *Verbero, Mastigia, Flagritriba, Plagipatida,
Bucaeda, Restio, Crux, Sexcentoplagus, Furcifer, Trifurcifer, Verberea
Statua, Stimulorum Tritor, Carnuficium cribrum, Genus ferratile,
Ferritribaces viri, Plagigera genera hominum, Vimorum Acheruns.*

Whole lines are found composed of such titles, as in Trin. IV.
iii. 14, *Oculicrepidae, cruricrepidae, ferritri, mastigiae;* and sometimes two wranglers reciprocate a series of such compliments: As. II.
ii. 31, *Le. Gumnasium flagri salveto. Li. Quid agis, custos carceris?
Le. O catenarum colone! Li. O virgarum lascivia!*

A large collection of such terms of abuse will be found in Pseud.
I. ii. 1 seqq. and in Pers. III. iii. 13 seqq.

XVI.—*TERMS AND PHRASES DENOTING ROGUERY, DECEPTION, &c.*

Since the plot in most of the specimens of the New Comedy,
which have been transmitted to us through the medium of the Latin
dramatists, turns upon some trick or mystification, played off generally by a crafty slave, we might anticipate that the vocabulary of
Plautus and Terence would be well stored with words and expressions denoting roguery.

Accordingly, we shall find the idea of deception presented to us
under a great variety of different forms, many of them highly
ingenious, lively and amusing.

Several of the words which convey the simple notion of craft or

* *Pedicas* again in As. III. ii. 5.

falsehood require no illustration. Such are *Astutia, Dolus, Fallacia, Fraus, Technae, Tricae* (see note on Most. III. i. 45 (41)), *Calliditates* (Heaut. V. i. 14); others however may demand some explanation.

1. *Fabrica.* Since any roguish device requires art, contrivance, and skill, the verbs *Fabricari*, 'to construct or manufacture;' *Fingere*, 'to mould;' *Consuere*, 'to sew together;' *Conglutinare*, 'to cement;' *Machinari*, 'to apply mechanical power;' and such like, together with the substantives connected with them, are frequently employed: thus Cas. V. i. 6, *nec fallaciam Astutiorem ullus fecit poeta, atque Vt haec est fabre facta a nobis;* Heaut. III. ii. 34, *Nonne ad senem aliquam fabricam fingit?* Epid. V. ii. 25, *Tragulam in te inicere adornat, nescio quam fabricam facit;* Mil. II. i. 69, *Ei nos facetis fabricis et doctis dolis Glaucomam ab oculos obiciemus;* Pers. V. ii. 4, *Ita me Toxilus perfabricavit, itaque meam rem divexavit,* where *perfabricare* seems to be an ἅπ. λεγ.; Bac. IV. iv. 43, *Compara, fabricare, finge quod lubet, conglutina, Vt senem hodie doctum docte fallas, aurumque auferas;* Capt. Prol. 47, *Ita compararunt et confinxerunt dolum;* Cas. I. 7, *Sequi decretum est: dehinc conicito celerum, Possisne necne, clam me, tutelis tuis, Praeripere Casinam uxorem, proinde ut postulas,* i.e. 'by falsehoods tacked together and patched up;' so Capt. III. v. 34, *Atque ob tutelas tuas te morti misero;* Amph. I. i. 210, *Nae tu istic hodie, malo tuo, compositis mendaciis Advenisti, audaciae columen, consutis dolis. S. Imo equidem tunicis consutis huc advenio, non dolis;* Bac. II. ii. 54, *Inde ego hodie aliquam machinabor machinam, Vnde aurum efficiam amanti·herili filio,* 'I will construct some engine by means of which' &c.

2. *Fucus.* Since paint conceals the real appearance of objects, *fuci* and *obfucia* denote 'tricks and deceit,' and *facere fucum alicui* is 'to deceive a person:' thus Capt. III. iii. 5, *Nec mendaciis subdolis mihi usquam mantellum est meis: Nec sucophantiis nec fucis ullum mantellum obviam est;* Eun. III. v. 41, *animus gaudebat mihi Deum sese in hominem convortisse, atque in alienas tegulas Venisse clanculum per impluvium, fucum factum mulieri.*

3. *Sycophanta,* from which we have the substantive *Sycophantia,* the verb *Sycophantor,* and the adverb *Sycophantiose,* is taken directly from the Greek συκοφάντης, a word of doubtful etymology, which, in Aristophanes, is employed to denote those pests of Athenian life, the public informers. The transition from this to the more general meaning of 'liar,' 'rogue,' 'scoundrel,' is simple and easy. In this latter sense alone is it found in the Roman writers, while, curiously enough, in modern English it is restricted to that species of lying

which consists in flattery: thus in Pseud. IV. vii. 103, *Purus putus hic sucophanta est*, 'this fellow is an unalloyed, unmitigated swindler (scoundrel),' to which Harpax, who is the person addressed, replies, *v.* 113, *Ego nec sucophantiose quicquam ago nec malefice;* II. iii. 5, *Nam haec adlata cornucopia est, ubi inest quidquid volo, Hic doli, hic fallaciae omnes sunt, hic sunt sucophantiae:* As. III. ii. 1, *Perfidiae laudes gratiasque habemus merito magnas, Quom nostris sucophantiis, dolis, astutiisque,* &c.   See too Aul. IV. iv. 22, Bac. IV. vii. 7, Poen. I. iii. 16, III. iii. 41, Pseud. I. v. 70, 113.   We find the combinations, *Sucophantias struere*, As. I. i. 66; *instruere et comparare*, Pers. II. v. 24; *componere*, Bac. IV. iv. 88; *concenturiare*, Pseud. I. v. 169; *sistere*, Trin. IV. ii. 25.

As an example of the verb we have Trin. III. iii. 67, *hoc me aetatis sucophantari pudet*, 'I am ashamed, at my time of life, to play the deceiver.'

For examples of *Sycophanta*, see Amph. I. iii. 8, *scitus sucophanta;* Pseud. IV. vii. 107, *sucophanta nequam;* Trin. III. iii. 86, *sucophantam iam conduco de foro;* IV. ii. 18, *plane sucophantam; v.* 47, *hic homo solide sucophanta est;* see also Pseud. IV. vii. 100, Poen. I. ii. 162.

4. *Nugari*, with the substantive *nugator* and the combination *artes nugatoriae*, in the writings of Cicero and those who followed him, convey the idea of 'to trifle,' 'a trifler,' 'a simpleton,' &c., but in Plautus are frequently synonymous with *sycophantor, sycophantia, sycophantiae*, as will appear evident from the following quotations: Curc. IV. i. 1, *Edepol nugatorem lepidum lepide hunc nactus est Phaedromus, Holophantam an sucophantam hunc magis esse dicam nescio;* in Trin. IV. ii. 116 Charmides says, *Enimvero ego nunc sucophantae huic sucophantari volo*, 'I should like to beguile this rascal,' but on making the attempt the Sycophanta retorts, *v.* 130, *Abi sis, nugator, nugari nugatori postulas*, 'Be off with you, you rascal, you've met your match;' again, *v.* 55, *Mihi quoque edepol, quom hic nugatur, contra nugari lubet*, i.e. 'plays the deceiver;' and in the same play, V. ii. 14, *Modo mihi advenienti nugator quidam accessit obviam, Nimis pergraphicus sucophanta;* and again in the same play, IV. ii. 1, the Sycophanta, who had been hired to personate a false character, says, *Huic ego dui nomen Trinummo faciam, nam ego operam meam Tribus nummis hodie locavi ad artes nugatorias*, 'to carry out schemes of roguery.'   The same personage (*v.* 94), when asked his name, replies that his every-day name was *Pax*, on which Charmides rejoins, *Edepol nomen nugatorium*, 'by Pollux, a rascal's name.'   In Mil. IV. ii. 86, *Vae tibi, nugator*, 'go along with you, you impostor;' Most.

III. i. 57 (53), *Quid hic nugamini?* 'why are you trying to play off your tricks?' and again V. i. 56 (ii. 41); Epid. III. iv. 42, *non mihi nugari potes,* 'you cannot deceive me.'

We may remark that although Plautus occasionally uses the simple word *nugae* in the sense of 'tricks,' yet in the great majority of instances, and these are very numerous, he employs it to mean ' trifles,' 'nonsense,' and not unfrequently as an exclamation of impatience.

Nugae must signify 'tricks' or 'roguish devices' in Trin. IV. ii. 14; the Sycophanta speaks, *Ille qui me conduxit, ubi conduxit, abduxit domum; Quae voluit, mihi dixit: docuit, et praemonstravit prius, Quomodo quidque agerem: nunc adeo, si quid addidero amplius, Eo conductor melius de me nugas conciliaverit;* and again, in Pseud. IV. vii. 107, *Non confidit: sucophanta hic nequam est: nugis meditatur male;* in Truc. IV. iv. 8 also, *P. Quid agitur, voluptas mea? D. Non voluptas: aufer nugas: nihil ego nunc de istac re ago,* where, although we may translate *aufer nugas* 'none of your tricks and cajoleries,' we may with equal propriety render the words by 'come, none of that nonsense.' It would be difficult to find many examples of *nugae* in Plautus in the sense of 'tricks,' but it is very common with the force of 'trifles,' 'nonsense,' and the like: thus Merc. II. iv. 1, *Pentheum diripuisse aiunt Bacchas, nugas maxumas fuisse credo, praeut quo pacto ego divorsus distrahor,* 'I believe that what befell him was an absolute trifle in comparison with' &c.; Trin. II. iv. 40, *Hic postulet frugi esse —nugas postulet!* 'let him desire to become respectable — desire nonsense!' Most. V. i. 38 (ii. 24), *Tu. Servos pollicitus est dare Suos mihi omnes quaestioni. Th. Nugas! numquam edepol dabit,* 'stuff and nonsense! he will never give them, be sure of that.' In Capt. III. iv. 80 *nugas ludificabitur* may mean 'he will give utterance to the most ridiculous ravings.' In Pseud. IV. vi. 19 we have, *S. Quid ait? quid narrat, quaeso? quid dicit tibi? B. Nugas theatri, verba quae in comoediis Solent lenoni dici, quae pueri sciunt: Malum et scelestum et periurum aibat esse me,* 'trash such as you hear upon the stage;' so Amph. II. i. 57, *Quas, malum, nugas,* 'what nonsense are you talking, confound you?' v. 79, *nugas blatis;* Curc. V. ii. 6, *nugas garris,* and so Aul. V. 21; Bac. III. vi. 40, *loqueris nunc nugas sciens;* Aul. IV. iv. 24, *nugas agis,* and so Men. IV. ii. 57, 58, 59, 60, 61, Aul. IV. iv. 11, As. I. i. 78, Cist. II. iii. 39, Poen. III. v. 31, Men. Prol. 54, 55, Poen. Prol. 81, Merc. I. 11, Rud. IV. iv. 107; Aul. V. 19, *non potes probasse nugas;* Capt. III. iii. 17, *nugas ineptiasque incipisso;* Curc. V. iii. 1, *nugas praedicant;* other examples in As. IV. i. 63, Capt. V. ii. 16, Pseud. I. iii. 9, Bac. IV. iii. 25, Pers. IV. vii. 8, Curc. I. iii. 36,

43, Poen l. ii. 135, Cas. II. v. 25, V. iii. 15, Men. I. i. 10, Merc. V. ii. 101, Stich. II. i. 22, Truc. II. i. 21, IV. ii. 55.

Although, on the other hand, *nugari* generally signifies 'to deceive,' it must mean 'to Jest' or 'to trifle' in Merc. I. 72, *C. Qui potuit videre? A. Oculis. C. Quo pacto? A. Hiantibus. C. I hinc dierectus: nugare in re capitali mea. A. Qui, malum, ego nugor, si tibi quod me rogas, respondeo?*

Nugigerulis is found in Aul. III. v. 61, in the sense of 'venders of women's trumpery,' but in this passage Nonius reads *Nugivendis*, which is found in some MSS. *Nugipoluloquides*, 'babbler of trash,' is found in Pers. IV. vi. 21, among a bunch of fictitious names. Although *nugae* and its derivatives occur so frequently in Plautus, there is but one example in Terence, Heaut. IV. i. 8, *Nae ista hercle magno iam conatu magnas nugas dixerit*, i.e. 'a pack of nonsense.'

5. *Tangere.* Some common words seem to have been employed, in what may be termed *slang* language, to express deceit or cheating. Among these we may place the verb *tangere*: thus Pseud. I. i. 118, *Si neminem alium potero, tuum tangam patrem;* Pers. IV. iv. 82, *Tactus est leno qui rogarat, ubi nata esset, diceret;* Epid. V. ii. 40, *istis adeo te tetigi triginta minis*, 'I did you out of those thirty minae;' so Pseud. V. ii. 13, *ut probe tactus Ballio est;* Poen. V. v. 7, *aere militari teligero lenunculum.* Nonius (p. 408) gives this as one of the meanings of *tangere*: "*Tangere* etiam *circumvenire.* Turpilius Demetrio: *at etiam ineptus meus mihi est iratus pater, Quia se talento argenti tetigi;*" and Cicero (De Orat. II. LXIV. 257) quotes, apparently from Caecilius Statius, *Sentin' senem esse tactum triginta minis?* How *tangere* came to bear this force it is not so easy to determine; from Bac. V. ii. 39, *Tactus sum vehementer visco: cor stimulo foditur*, we might suppose that the idea was taken from a bird entrapped by bird-lime;[*] while from Poen. Prol. 101 we might conclude that the notion of 'catching fish by casting a net' was involved: *Quia amare cernit, tangere hominem volt bolo;*[†] with which compare True. I. i. 10,

---

[*] Cf. Petron. Arb. c. 109, Ecce etiam per antennam pelagiae connederant volucres, quas textis arundinibus peritus artifex *tetigit*, illae viscatis infligatae viminibus deferebantur ad manus.

[†] *Bolus*, the Greek βόλος. The pure Latin word is *iactus*. It signifies 1. 'A cast of the dice,' Curc. V. ii. 13. 2. 'A cast of a net;' Plautus, Rud. II. iii. 30, turns the double meaning to account—*Ob Neptune lepide, salve! Nec te aleator ullus est sapientior: profecto Nimis lepide iesusti bolum, periurum perdidisti.* 3. 'A good haul,' and hence generally 'gain,' 'profit,' Pers. IV. iv. 106. 4. Equivalent to *iactura*, 'damage,' 'loss,' True. IV. iii. 70, *verum hoc ego te mulctabo bolo.* In True. I. i. 10 Plautus probably means to play upon this meaning and that of 'a cast with a net.'

where the metaphor of a damsel catching her lovers in a net like
a fisherman is worked out at length.

Terence uses *tangere* in a different sense: in Eun. III. i. 30
Thraso asks the parasite, *Quid illud, Gnatho, Quo pacto Rhodium
tetigerim in convivio Nunquam tibi dixi?* 'did I never tell you how
I touched up a Rhodian at a banquet—what a sharp cut I gave
him?'

6. *Intervortere* seems properly to signify 'to come between an
object and its proper destination, and turn it to one's own profit,'
and hence is used by Plautus in the general sense of 'to defraud'
or 'cheat.' Thus As. II. i. 10, *Vnde sumam? quem intervortam? quo
hanc celocem conferam?* and again, ii. 92, *L. Hem, istuc ago, Quomodo
argentum intervortam et adventorem et Sauream.* Observe the construction of this verb in the passage last quoted and in Pseud. III.
ii. 110, *Vt me, si posset, muliere intervorteret;* and Rud. V. iii. 44, *Non
hercle istoc me intervortes, si aliam praedam perdidi:* in all of these
we have a double accusative.

7. *Admordere,* 'to gnaw close,' has a like force: Pers. II. iii. 14,
*Nam id demum lepidum est, triparcos homines, vetulos, avidos, aridos,
Bene admordere, qui salinum serro opsignant cum sale,* i. e. 'to get a
good bite out of them.' This is illustrated by Pseud. IV. vii. 24,
*Habet argentum. Iam admordere hunc mihi lubet. S. Iamne illum
comesurus es? B. Dum recens est, Dum datur, dum calet, devorari
decet.*

8. *Pugnare* or *Dare pugnam* or *Pugnam edere,* 'to make a hit:'
thus Adel. V. iii. 57, *D. Et istam psaltriam Vna illuc mecum hinc
apstraham. M. Pugnaveris. Eo pacto prorsum illic adligaris filium,*
'if you do that you will have made a good hit;' cf. Epid. III. iv. 57,
which we shall quote afterwards; Eun. V. ii. 60, *Dabit hic aliquam
pugnam denuo;* Capt. III. iv. 53, *Atque, ut perspicio, profecto iam aliquid
pugnae edidit,* 'he has succeeded in making a stroke.'

9. *Obrepere,* 'to creep up to,' 'to take by surprise,' 'to take at
a disadvantage,' 'to overreach:' thus Trin. I. ii. 22, *C. Faxo haud
tantillum dederis verborum mihi. M. Namque enim tu, credo, mihi
inprudenti obrepseris:* C. 'I shall take care that you shall not have,
to ever so small an extent, the best of the bargain.' M. 'You make
the proposal, I suppose, because you calculate upon taking me by
surprise (overreaching me).' *Namque* is the reading of the MSS.;
Ritschl has *Nempe,* Weise *Numquam,* but no change is necessary.

10. *Dare verba alicui.* Of all the numerous phrases which signify
'to deceive,' 'to impose upon by falsehood,' this is perhaps the most

common, and is generally equivalent to our 'to humbug:' thus
Pseud. IV. i. 5, *Dedit verba mihi, hercle, ut opinor, malus cum malo
stulte cavi;* Rud. II. ii. 19, *Data verba hero sunt; leno abiit scelestus
exsulatum;* Phor. IV. v. 1, *Quictus esto, inquam, ego curabo ne quid
verborum duit;* other examples in Aul. I. i. 23, Bac. IV. vi. 25, Capt.
V. ii. 25, Epid. I. i. 85, III. iv. 84, V. i. 8, Men. I. ii. 22, Mil. II. vi.
93, Pseud IV. v. 7, Rud. IV. iii. 57, iv. 28, Trin. I. ii. 22, Adel. IV.
iv. 13, Andr. I. iii. 6, III. ii. 25, Eun. Prol. 24, IV. v. 1, V. i. 17,
iv. 28, Heaut. IV. iv. 13, V. i. 41.

11. *Manum adire alicui*, 'to disappoint,' 'to frustrate,' 'to befool,'
'to deceive,' 'to play a trick upon.' This phrase was probably
suggested by the play among children of stretching out a hand containing some object as if to present it to a person, and then, when
the victim of the joke is about to take the object, suddenly with-
drawing the hand: thus Aul. II. viii. 8, *Ita illis impuris omnibus adii
manum*, 'I disappointed all those filthy fellows—frustrated their
designs;' Cas. V. ii. 54, *Quid nunc? satin lepide adita est vobis manus?*
'haven't you been cleverly jockeyed?' Poen. II. 11, *Eo pacto avaras
Veneri pulcre adii manum;* and v. 16, *Quom scribunt, Veneri ut adierit
leno manum;* Pers. V. ii. 18, *Vt me in tricas conieristi! Quomodo de
Persa manus mihi adita est!* In the last-quoted example we have
conicere in tricas, 'to entangle in a net;' and so IV. i. 9, *Nunc ego
lenonum ita hodie intricatum dabo, Vt ipsus sese qua se expediat nesciat.*
(See note on Most. III. i. 45 (41).)

12. *Circum.* Verbs compounded with *circum* frequently imply
that a person is 'led round,' that is, not straight to, but away from,
an object which he wishes to reach, or, that one person 'gets round'
another, that is, takes him at disadvantage by coming upon him from
behind. Such verbs are frequently used in the general sense of 'to
deceive,' 'to cheat:' thus *circumducere*, construed with the accusative of the person cheated, to which is generally added the ablative
of the thing out of which he is cheated: thus As. I. i. 83, *Qua me, qua
uxorem, qua tu servom Sauream Potes, circumduce, aufer;* Truc. IV.
iv. 21, *Triduum hoc saltem, dum aliquo miles circumducitur;* Pseud. II.
ii. 39, *Quasi tu dicas me te velle argento circumducere;* Bac. V. ii. 64,
Quadringentis Philippis filius me et Chrusalus circumduxerunt. In
Poen. V. v. 7 *circumducere* and *tangere* are combined: *Sic dedero:
aere militari tetigero lenunculum; Nactus est hominem, mina quem
argenti circumduceret:* other examples of *circumducere* in Pseud. I. v.
16, Trin. IV. ii. 17. There is a curious anacoluthon with *circum-
ducam* in Pseud. I. v. 115, but perhaps the passage is corrupt.

The substantive *circumductio* is found in the same sense: Capt. V.
Cal. 3, *Nec pueri suppositio, nec argenti circumductio.*

Circumvenire: Hec. Prol. 46, *Ne eum circumventum inique iniqui
inrideant.*

Circumire: Phor. IV. iii. 9, *Tun dixeras huic? facinus indignum,
Chreme, Sic circumiri.**

Circumvertere: Pseud. I. v. 125, *Quid si hice inter se consenserunt,
Callipho, Aut de compacto faciunt consultis dolis, Qui me argento circum-
vortunt?* Here the idea may be similar to that expressed in familiar
English when we talk of 'one person twisting another round his
finger,' and this leads us to observe that a great number of curious
phrases, which express fraud and trickery, represent the person
deceived as an object animate or inanimate, as the case may be,
under the absolute control of the deceiver, who can deal with him
as he pleases.

13. *Vendere. Venalis.* Thus he is sometimes said 'to be sold,'†
as a master might dispose of a slave: Bac. IV. vii. 16, *C. O stulte,
stulte, nescis nunc venire te? Atque in eo ipso adstas lapide, ubi praeco
praedicat. N. Responde, quis me vendit?* When slaves were sold by
auction they were made to stand upon a stone, to elevate them above
the crowd, so that they might be distinctly seen by intending pur-
chasers. Cicero refers to this practice (In Pison. 15) when he calls
Serranus and Numerius *duos de lapide emptos tribunos.* Again, Mil. II.
vi. 97, *Me habent venalem: sensi et iamdudum scio, Numquam hercle
ex ista nassa ego hodie escam petam,* 'they are selling me; assuredly
I shall not nibble the bait out of that trap to-day.'

14. *Sublinere s. Oblinere os.* According to a favourite figure, he
is represented as a helpless drunkard who falls asleep at a banquet
and has his face blackened by his companions—a practical joke by
no means unknown in our own day.‡ Thus Merc. II. iv. 17, *Vin
patri sublinere pulcre me os tuo?* 'to befool your father handsomely;'
Aul. IV. vi. 1, *Fidei censebam maxumam multo fidem Esse, ea sublevit*

---

* *Circumire* is sometimes quoted from Pseud. III. ii. 109 in this sense,
but upon referring to the passage it will be seen that here it may simply
mean 'he is going about.'

† Mark the identity with English modern slang, to say nothing of the
Shakespearian: 'It would make a man as mad as a buck *to be so bought
and sold,*' Comedy of Errors, III. i.; *'bought and sold* Lord Talbot,' K. Hen.
VI. Part I. Act IV. iv.; and 'Diccon, thy master is *bought and sold,*'
Richd. III. Act V. iii.

‡ A short time ago the Police Reports contained the case of some
young men who were brought up before a magistrate for blackening the
face of an old woman whom they found lying drunk on London Bridge.

os mihi pensisume, 'she has thoroughly played me false ;' Capt. III.
iv. 123, *Ita mihi stolido sursum rorsum os subleuere obfuciis;* Curc. IV.
iv. 33, *Quid ego faciam? mancam an abeam? siccine mihi esse os
oblitum?* Epid. III. iii. 48, *Ego si adtegissem aliquem ad hoc negotium
Minus hominem doctum, minusque ad hanc rem callidum, Os sublitum
esset: itaque me albis dentibus Meus derideret filius meritissumo:* other
examples, Epid. III. iv. 55, Capt. IV. ii. 3, Merc. III. iv. 19, 46, Mil.
II. i. 32, 75, v. 57, Pseud. II. iv. 29, Trin. II. iv. 157.

15. *Admutilare. Adtondere.* Sometimes he is a man in the hands
of a barber—that most helpless of all conditions. This notion is
elaborately developed in Capt. II. ii. 16, *Nunc anex est in tonstrina:
nunc iam cultros adtinet. Ne id quidem inuoluere inicere uoluit, reskm
ut ne inquinet. Sed utrum strictimne adtonsurum dicam esse, an per
pectinem, Nescio: uerum si frugi est, usque admutilabit probe;* Mil. III.
i. 172, *Ego inueni lepidam sucophantiam, Qui admutiletur miles usque
caesariatus;* Pers. V. ii. 48, *Iam taceo hercle: atque tu Persa es, qui
me usque admutilauisti ad cutem.*

16. *Emungere.* Sometimes he is an infant or paralytic old man
who cannot wipe his own nose, and hence the phrase *emungere
aliquem,* sometimes followed by the ablative of the thing obtained
by fraud: thus Bac. IV. iv. 50, *Emungam hercle hominem probe hodie,
ne id nequiquam dixerit;* Phor. IV. iv. 1, *A. Geta! G. Hem! A. Quid
egisti? G. Emunxi argento senex;* Epid. III. iv. 57, *Euge, frugi,
Epidice, frugi es, pugnasti, homo es Qui me emunxti mucidum, minumi
preti;* Most. V. i. 60 (ii. 45), *Tu, Perii. Tr. Quid tibi est? Tu. Dedisti uerba. Tr. Qui tandem? Tu. Probe Med emunxti. Tr. Vide sis
satine recte: num mucci fluont? Tu. Imo etiam cerebrum quoque omnem
e capite emunxisti meo.* In Bac. V. i. 14 we have a variety of different
figures, this among the others, *Hoc, hoc est quod peracescit, hoc demum
est quod percrucior, Me hoc aetatis ludificari, imo edepol sic ludos factum
Cano capite, atque alba barba, miserum me auro esse emunctum! Chrusalus me hodie lacerauit, Chrusalus me miserum spoliauit, Is me, scelus,
usque adtondit doctis dolis.*

17. *Ducere. Ductare.* Sometimes he is a horse bridled, bitted,
and led about by means of the tricks played off upon him: thus
Capt. III. v. 97, *Quod apsque hoc esset, qui mihi hoc fecit palam, Vsque
obfrenatum suis me ductarent dolis:* hence the verb *duco* and the
frequentatives *ducto* and *ductito* signify 'to lead by the nose;' IV. ii.
7, *Hic ille est senex ductus, quoi uerba data sunt;* Most. III. ii. 26,
*Hoc habet: reperi qui senem ducerem, Quo dolo a me dolorem procul
pellerem;* Capt. III. iv. 109, *nae, ut lubitum est, ductauit dolis;* Epid.

III. ii. 13. *E. Ego tuum patrem faciam perenticidam. S. Quid istuc est verbi? F. Nihil moror vetera et volgata verba, Peratim ductare: at ego follitim ductitabo.*＊ *Perductor* in Cicero (In Verr. Act. II. l 12, cf. Lact. VI. 17) signifies a pander or profligate of some sort, and Plautus in Most. III. ii. 157 takes advantage of the double meaning of *ductare, circumducere, perducere, perductor.*

18. *Inponere sarcinam.* Sometimes he is a mule or other beast of burden, who may be overloaded without scruple: Most. II. i. 82, *Concedam a foribus huc, hinc speculabor procul, Vnde advenienti sarcinam inponam seni;* Bac. II. iii. 115, *Ille est oneratus recte † et plus iusto vehit;* but the most full developement of the idea will be found in Most. III. ii. 91 (89), *Vehit hic clitellas, vehit hic autem alter senex, Novitium mihi quaestum institui non malum: Nam muliones mulos clitellarios Habent; ego habeo homines clitellarios, Magni sunt oneris, quidquid inponas, vehunt.*

19. *Intendere fallaciam. Tragulam inicere.* Sometimes he is a butt at which the arrows or javelins of roguery may be aimed: Heaut. III. ii. 2, *Huc illuc circumcursa, inveniundum est tamen Argentum: intendenda in senem est fallacia;* ‡ cf. Epid. V. ii. 25, *Tragulam in te inicere adornat.*

20. *Tondere.* Sometimes he is an innocent sheep in the hands of the shearers: Bac. II. iii. 7, *Adibo hunc, quem quidem ego hodie faciam hic aridem Phruxi, itaque tondebo auro usque ad vivam cutem;* and in V. ii. 3 seqq., where Nicobulus and Philoxenus are compared to old sheep, the verbs *adtondere, detondere, tonsitare* are applied with the double meaning, and so again Merc. III. i. 28 and Bac. V. i. 9, *usque adtondit dolis doctis.*

21. *Concidere articulatim. Delacerare. Deartuare. Exenterare.* Sometimes he is a dead carcase in the hands of a butcher: Epid. III. iv. 51, *M. Hem! istic homo Articulatim te concidit, senex, tuus Serras. P. Quid? concidit? M. Nihil—sic suspicio est. Nam pro fidicina huic subposita est tibi. Senex, tibi os est sublitum plane et probe:* the rest of the passage has been already quoted, p. 271; again, Capt.

＊ *Perenticida, Peratim, Follitim,* seem to have been coined by Plautus for the occasion, and are not found elsewhere. *Perenticida* was evidently fabricated to resemble *Parenticida,* and in order to give a meaning to the following line, we must suppose that *Pera,* when used to denote 'a purse,' was of smaller capacity than *Follis.*

† *Onustus* is applied in a very different sense in Epid. III. ii. 39, *Eam permeditatam meis dolis, astutiisque onustam Mittam.*

‡ The metaphor here may be taken from the toils stretched to wild animals, or from the nooses for entrapping birds.

III. v. 13, *Tuis scelestis fallidicis fallaciis Delaceravisti, deartua-vistique opes.* *Deartuare* occurs again in III. iv. 108, and *lacerare* in Bac. V. i. 8.

Deartuare may signify either 'to cut up into joints,' as a butcher, in which case it will be equivalent to *concidere articulatim*, or it may mean 'to put out of joint,' 'to dislocate.' The former is the interpretation of Nonius, p. 95, who quotes the two passages from Plautus in which alone the word is found.

The metaphor is taken from the butcher's trade in Epid. II. ii. 2, *acutum cultrum habeo, senis qui exenterem Marsupium;* and again, III. iv. 73, *planissume Meum exenteravit Epidicus marsupium;* and V. ii. 7, *Vt illic autem exenteravit mihi opes argentarias.*

22. Sometimes he is a pigeon or thrush enticed into a snare by the fowler: Poen. III. iii. 63, *Nos tibi palumbem ad aream usque adduximus;* Pers. IV. iii. 11, *Hunc ego hominem hodie in transennam doctis ducam dolis;* Bac. IV. vi. 22, *Nunc ab transenna hic turdus lumbricum petit, Pendebit hodie pulcre, ita intendi tenus;* Poen. III. iv. 35, *Quin, si voles, Operire capita, ne nos leno noverit, Qui illi malae rei tantae fuimus inlices,* where *inlices* are 'decoy-birds.' There are some lines in As. I. iii. 63 which will serve as a commentary on the above quotations: *Non tu scis? hic noster quaestus aucupi simillumus est. Auceps quando concinnavit aream, obfundit cibum, Aves adsuescunt: necesse est facere sumptum, qui quaerit lucrum. Saepe edunt: semel si captae sunt, rem soluunt aucupi: Itidem hic apud nos: aedis nobis area est, auceps sum ego, Esca est meretrix, lectus inlix est, amatores aves.*

23. Sometimes he is a fortified town which is to be formally besieged: Mil. II. ii. 111, *Si invenio qui vidit, ad eum vineas pluteosque agam, Res parata est, vi pugnandoque hominem capere certa res est.*

24. Sometimes he is a lump of clay which a potter can mould into any shape: Heaut. V. i. 25, *Sed ille tuum quoque Surus idem mire finxit filium.*

25. Sometimes he is a log which a carpenter fashions with his adze or his plane according to his fancy: Mil. III. iii. 11, *Tibi dixi miles quemadmodum potis esset deasciari;* and IV. iv. 6, *Vt lepide deruncinavit militem!* while in Capt. III. iv. 108 we have a combination of three of the forms illustrated above, *Tum ego deruncinatus, deartuatus sum miser Huius scelesti technis, qui me ut lubitum est ductavit dolis.* The trade of the carpenter suggested also the following figurative expressions: Mil. IV. iv. 20, *Quot apud nos fallaciarum est excusum,* which is used with reference to the preceding *ad rem video silvae esse satis;* again, v. 38, *satin est si tibi Meum opus ita dabo*

N n

expolitum ut inprobare non queas? and again, III. iii. 64, *si hodie hunc dolum dolamus,* where we remark the play on *dolum* and *dolamus.*

26. Sometimes he is an anvil on which a deceiver is, like a smith, to hammer out his tricks: thus Pseud. II. ii. 20, Pseudolus says of Harpax, *Nam haec mihi incus est: procudam ego hodie hinc multos dolos.*

27. *Versare.* Sometimes he is a piece of meat or a lentil in a frying-pan, which is tossed and turned over by the cook until ' done brown :' Bac. IV. v. 6, *Vorsabo* ego illum hodie, si vivo, probe, Tam frictum ego illum reddam quam frictum est cicer,* 'until he is done brown;' Pers. V. ii. 17, *Quid ais, crux, stimulorum tritor? quomodo me hodie vorsavisti! Ut me in tricas coniecisti! quomodo de Persa manus mihi adita est.*

28. *Extexere.* Sometimes he is a piece of old cloth or rope which is pulled down or unravelled for the sake of the thread: Bac. II. iii 5, *Extexam ego illum pulcre iam, si Di volunt,* where *extexo* is a *der.* key.

29. This is the proper place to notice a set of words which are frequently, although by no means uniformly, employed by the dramatists to denote 'fraud,' 'deceit,' and 'imposture.' They are *Ludus, Ludi, Ludibrium, Ludo, Ludifacio, Ludifico, Deludo, Inludo,* and some other compounds of *Ludo.*

i. *Ludus.* In so far as the substantive *ludus* is concerned we must carefully distinguish the singular *ludus* from the plural *ludi. Ludus,* in the singular, signifies in Plautus and Terence, as in other authors, 'play,' 'sport,' 'fun,' 'amusement,' and also 'a place of instruction,' 'a school.' Thus, in the sense of 'play,' 'sport,' &c.; Rud. II. iv. 13, *Otium ubi erit, tum tibi operam ludo et deliciae dabo;* Capt. IV. i. 2, *Maxumas opimitates opiparasque obfers mihi, Laudem, lucrum, ludum, iocum, festivitatem, ferias;* As. Prol. 13, *Inest lepos ludusque in hac Comoedia;* so Bac. I. ii. 8, Pseud. I. i. 63, *Iocus, ludus, sermo;* Truc. I. ii. 11, *per ioculum et ludum.* In Pseud. V. i. 32 the drunken slave, after telling that he had had a tumble, adds, *id fuit naenia ludo,* which means, 'that (tumble) brought my fun to a melancholy end,' 'turned my merriment into wailing.' *Ludus* in the sense of 'a school' occurs in Rud. Prol. 43, *Eam vidit ire e ludo fidicino domum;* and Pers. II. i. 6, *Nam equidem te iam sector quintum*

---

* On the other hand *Versutus* signifies one who is 'versatile,' who can turn his wits to anything, and therefore 'subtle,' 'crafty:' As. I. i. 105, *Non esse servos prior hoc quisquam potest, Nec magis versutus, nec ab quo caveas magis;* Epid. III. ii. 35, *Versutior es quam rota figularis.*

hunc annum, quom interim credo, Cuculus ni in ludum iret, potuisset iam fieri ut probe literas sciret; while in Bac. 1. ii. 21 and Aa. 1. iii. 73 the word, perhaps designedly on the part of the poet, may bear either meaning.

Two peculiar, apparently proverbial, expressions occur in Plautus: Poen. I. ii. 83, *Enimvero, here, meo me lacessis ludo, et delicias facis;* and Pseud. II. iv. 53, *Eugepae, lepide, Charine, me meo ludo lamberas;* * both of which seem to signify, 'you are attacking me with my own weapons.'

We may notice also the phrase *dare ludum*, meaning 'to indulge,' 'to give full play or scope:' Bac. IV. x. 7, *Ego dare me ludum meo gnato institui ut animo obsequium Sumere possit: aequom esse puto: sed nimis nolo desidiae Ei dare ludum;* so Hor. C. III. xii. 1, *Miserarum est neque Amori dare ludum;* and Cic. pro Caelio XII. § 28, *Datur enim concessu omnium huic aliquis ludus aetati*, i.e. 'some amount of indulgence.' In a passage to be quoted below from Cas. Prol. 25, *ludus datur est* signifies 'a holiday has been given.'†

ii. *Ludi.* *Ludi* is the technical word for 'Public Games,' such as the Olympic Games, the Ludi Circenses, the Ludi Romani, and the like. In this sense it occurs frequently in Plautus, e.g. Cist. I. iii. 9, Men. Prol. 29, 30, *Tarenti ludi forte erant;* Pers. III. iii. 31, Poen. Prol. 36, 41, V. ii. 52, v. 12, Stich. II. i. 34, *ludos Olumpiae;* Fr. 1. 53, 81; and so Cas. Prol. 27, 28, *Ludi sunt: ludus datus est argentariis*, 'the games are going on—this is a Bank-Holiday.' *Facere ludos* signifies 'to exhibit public games,' and hence we have the phrase common in Plautus, *facere aliquem ludos*, which means, 'to make an exhibition of a person,' 'to hold up a person as an object of public amusement,' 'to make game of,' 'to deceive and befool:' Amph. II. i. 21, *Rogasne, inprobe, etiam, qui ludos facis me?* Men. II. iii. 54, *Iam me, amabo, desine ludos facere;* Capt. III. iv. 47, *Vt scelestus, Hegio, nunc is te ludos facit;* Bac. V. i. 14, *Hoc, hoc est quod peracescit, hoc est demum quod percrucior, Me hoc aetatis ludificari, imo edepol sic ludos factum;* Pseud. IV. vii. 71, *S. Exploratorem hunc faciamus ludo subpositicium. B. Adeo donicum ipsus sese ludos fieri senserit;* see also Aul. II. ii. 75, Bac. V. i. 4, Pers. V. i. 19, V. ii. 83, Rud. II. v. 13. The expression in Rud. III. v. 12 is peculiar, *Numquam hercle quisquam me lenonem dixerit, Si non te ludos pessumos dimisero*, which is interpreted as equivalent to *si non te ludos pessumos fecero et dimisero*,

---

* "*Lamberat* scindit ac laniat." Paul. Diac. p. 118, ed. Müll.

† So Scottice, when a schoolmaster gives his boys a holiday, he is said 'to give them the play.'

'if I do not send you about your business after I have made you cut
a miserable figure.' In Pseud. I. iii. 135 we have the phrase, to be
noticed again below, *operam ludere*, 'to lose one's labour,' *In pertusum
ingerimus dicta dolium, operam ludimus;* and this in Rud. IV. I. 9
appears under the form, *Nam nunc et operam ludos facit* * *et retia*, 'he
is losing his labour and spoiling his nets.'

We must carefully distinguish the phrase *ludos facere aliquem*, 'to
make a show of a person,' from *ludos facere alicui*,† which properly
signifies 'to exhibit games in honour of one deceased,' and is used
by Plautus in the ironical sense, 'to exhibit a spectacle for the
amusement of others in honour of a living man, who is as powerless
in the hands of the exhibitors as if he were a corpse on the funeral
pyre.' The origin of the expression is clearly indicated in Most. II.
i. 80, *Ludos ego hodie vivo praesenti hic seni Faciam, quod credo mortuo
numquam fore*, 'I will exhibit games in honour of this old gentleman
alive and looking on—a distinction which, I fancy, will never be
accorded to him when dead;' so Cas. IV. i. 1, *Nec pol ego Nemeae
credo, neque ego Olumpiae, Neque usquam ludos tam festivos fieri, Quam
hic intus fiunt ludi ludificabiles Seni nostro, et nostro Olumpioni villico;*
and so Truc. IV. ii. 46, where Dinarchus exclaims, *Iam hercle ego tibi,
intecebra, ludos faciam, clamore in via*, he does not mean, 'I will make
game of you,' or 'I will make a fool of you,' but says ironically, 'I
will make an exhibition in honour of you by shouting out your name
in the public street,' referring to the *pipulum*, which is fully explained
in the note on Most. III. i. 59 (55).

We find the following couplet twice in Plautus, Merc. II. i. 1 and
Rud. III. i. 1, *Miris modis Di ludos faciunt hominibus, Mirisque
exemplis somnia in somnis danunt*. We must not suppose that the
speaker intends to say, 'the Gods make sport of men,' that is,
'befool or deceive or hold them up to ridicule,' which would by no
means accord with the belief then prevalent with regard to dreams,
but, 'after a marvellous fashion do the Gods exhibit spectacles for
men,' that is, 'for the interest and instruction of men, by warning
them of coming events by strange appearances exhibited to them in
dreams.' Observe that the forms used by Plautus are invariably
ludos facere aliquem or *ludos facere alicui*, never *ludum*, the phrases
being derived from *ludi* in the sense of Public Spectacles; the only

---

* Here the MSS. have *ludos das*, but Priscian in quoting the passage
gives *ludus facit*.
† Ritschl, Parerg. Plaut. I. p. 477-10, seems to regard them as synonymous.

apparent exceptions are Bac. V. i. 4, where the Vulgate text has *Hoccine me aetatis ludum bis factum esse indigne*, but the best MSS. give *ludos;* and Pseud. IV. vii. 71, *Exploratorem hunc faciamus ludo subpositicium*, where however there can be no doubt that *ludos* is the true reading, the *s* having been lost in consequence of the next word beginning with the same letter.

Advantage is sometimes taken of the double meaning with which *ludi* is thus invested to enlarge the metaphor: Mil. IV. ii. 1, *Iam est ante aedes Circus, ubi sunt ludi faciundi mihi;* and so in a fragment of the Cornicularia (Varro L. L. V. 153, ed. Müll.) *Circus* is applied to a soldier who is made a butt, *Quid cessamus ludos facere? Circus noster, ecce, adest;* so also Poen. I. i. 78, *Heus! i foras, Agorastocles, Si vis videre ludos iucundissumos;* and Pseud. I. i. 133, *Indice ludos nunc iam quando lubet;* and *v.* 139, *Lubido est ludos tuos spectare, Pseudole.*

In the MSS. of Andr. III. i. 21 we read, *S. Hiccine me si imparatum in veris nuptiis Adortus esset, quos mihi ludos redderet?* where Bentley unhesitatingly corrects *quos me ludos redderet*, considering *reddere* as equivalent to *facere*. But it may be doubted whether we could substitute *reddere* for *facere* in this phrase, and *quos mihi ludos redderet* may perhaps signify 'how he would pay me off,' or something of that sort.

iii. *Ludibrium. Ludificatus. Ludibrium* in Plautus and Terence is uniformly in the dative with the verb *habere*, followed by the accusative of a person—*habere aliquem ludibrio*, signifying 'to make a laughing-stock of any one,' and hence 'to deceive' or 'defraud:' Cas. III. v. 19, *Cerebrum dispercutiam, excetra tu, ludibrio pessuma adhuc Quae me habuisti;* Epid. V. ii. 1, *Satin ille hic homo ludibrio nos vetulos decrepitos duos Habet?* so Cas. V. i. 13, Men. II. iii. 45, V. ii. 32 (*ludibrio, pater, habeor*). In Hec. I. ii. 74 *eam ludibrio haberi* has a graver meaning, 'that she should be ill-treated.' Instead of *ludibrio* we read in Poen. V. v. 2, *Tum profecto me sibi habento scurrae ludificatui.* If the reading is correct, *ludificatus* is a *dr. λεγ.*

iv. *Ludere. Lusitare. Deludere. Inludere. Ludere* signifies 'to sport' or 'play,' and is used (a) absolutely, Curc. II. iii. 76, *Provocat me in aleam, ut ego ludam: pono pallium;* Poen. V. ii. 114, *Signum esse oportet in manu laeva tibi, Ludenti puero quod momordit simia*, 'the mark of a bite which a monkey gave you when you were a boy at play;' and so Stich. V. iv. 20, *nos volo tamen ludere inter nos*, 'to disport ourselves;' Cas. V. iv. 11, Curc. II. iii. 17. (b) With the accusative or ablative of the cognate substantive, Eun. III. v. 38, *et quia consimilem luserat Iam olim ille ludum;* Most. V. ii. 36 (iii. 36), *Scis solere illanc aetatem tali ludo ludere.* (c) With the ablative of the thing played with, Adel. IV. vii. 21, *Ita vita est hominum, quasi quom ludas tesseris;* and so Mil. II. iii. 54, *ludo ludo.*

But when *ludo* is construed with the accusative of a person, it signifies 'to make game of the person,' and hence 'to beguile,' 'to deceive :' Cas. III. v. 46, *Ludo ego hunc facete;* Eun. II. ii. 38, *Nebulonem hunc certum est ludere;* Adel. IV. v. 68, *Opsecro, non ludis tu nunc me ...?* so also As. III. iii. 140, Bac. IV. iv. 3, Capt. IV. ii. 97, Curc. II. iii. 47, Mil. II. iii. 53, Most. V. i. 32 (ii. 17), Trin. IV. ii. 51, Truc. IV. ii. 7, but in the last passage the reading is doubtful. Observe the form, Pseud. I. i. 22, *Ludis me ludo tuo,* 'you are laughing at me.' The accusative is rarely omitted, as in Pers. IV. iv. 82, *Lepide lusit,* 'she made game of him cleverly.' The line in Rud. IV. vii. 22, *Ego mihi quom lusi nihil moror ullum lucrum,* is probably corrupt.

In Mil. IV. ii. 74, and again v. 81, *Vt ludo* may signify either 'what a fool I am making of him,' or the words may be regarded as an exclamation, 'what fun!'

Ludere is construed also with the accusative *operam,* signifying 'to lose one's labour :' Pseud. I. iii. 135, *In pertusum ingerimus dicta dolium, operam ludimus;* Capt. II. ii. 94, *At nihil est ignotum ad illum mittere, operam luseris;* Phor. II. ii. 18, *Quia enim in illis fructus est, in illis opera luditur.*

Lusito is found in Capt. V. iv. 6, *quasi patriciis pueris aut monedulae, Aut anates, aut coturnices dantur quicum lusitent;* but nowhere else except Aul. Gell. XVIII. 13, *Saturnalibus Athenis alea quadam festiva et honesta lusitabamus huiuscemodi.*

Deludere requires scarcely any explanation. It is used either absolutely, or, more frequently, with the accusative of the person played upon : Amph. V. i. 45, *Quaeso apsolvite hinc me extemplo quando satis deluseris;* II. ii. 62, *Te ut deludam contra, lusorem meum;* see also I. i. 139, III. iii. 25, iv. 14, 15, 22, As. III. i. 24, Iii. 56, 87, 121, Cas. III. ii. 30, Cist. II. i. 9, Pseud. II. iii. 25.

Inludere is not found in Plautus. Terence has it five times, and varies the construction four times : Andr. IV. iv. 18, *Adeone ridemur vobis esse idonei In quibus sic inludatis?* Heaut. IV. iv. 19, *Dignam me putas quam inludas?* Andr. V. i. 3, *Dum studeo opsequi tibi, pene inlusi vitam filiae;* Eun. V. iv. 20, *Ego pol te pro istis dictis et factis, scelus, Vlciscar: ut ne inpune in nos inluseris* (some MSS. omit *in*); Phor. V. vii. 22, *Satis superbe inludistis me.*

v. *Ludifacio. Ludifico. Ludificor. Ludifacio* is found once in Plautus, probably in no other writer: Epid. V. ii. 41, *Quomodo me ludifecisti de illa conductitia Fidicina!*

The most common verb in this sense is *ludifico*, while *ludificor* is employed sometimes as a passive, sometimes as a deponent: Cist. II. i. 8, *Ita me amor lassum animi ludificat, fugat, agit, adpetit, Raptat, retinet, lactat, largitur, quod dat non dat, deludit;* Amph. IV. iii. 7, *Numquam edepol me inultus istic ludificabit, quisquis est;* Eun. IV. iv. 50, *Actum est, siquidem tu me hic etiam, nebulo, ludificabere;* Amph. II. L 15, *Tun me, verbero, audes herum ludificari?* Bac. IV. iv. 3, *Herum maiorem meum ut ego hodie lusi lepide! ut ludificatus est!* Mil. II. vi. 57, *Numquam edepol hominem quemquam ludificarier Magis facete vidi.* Although *ludifico* and the deponent *ludificor* are generally followed by an accusative of the person befooled, we have, Most. V. i. 19 (ii. 4), *Quoius ego hic ludificabo corium, si vivo, probe,* which may be regarded as a piece of humour; and also Capt. III. iv. 80, *H. Quid ais? quid si adeam hunc insanum? T. Nugas ludificabitur,* which could only mean 'he will rave ridiculously;' but perhaps we ought, with some editors, to punctuate, *Nugas! ludificabitur,* 'nonsense! he will make a fool of you.'

Ludifico is used also in the sense of 'to insult:' thus Mil. II. vi. 8, *Non hercle hice homines me marem, sed feminam Vicini rentur esse servi militis, Ita me ludificant: meamne hic in via hospitam Tractatam et ludificatam, ingenuam et liberam;* and again, v. 15, *Meam ludificasti hospitam ante aedes modo?* In Eun. IV. iii. 3 *ludificatus est virginem* has the same force as *eam ludibrio haberi* in Hec. I. ii. 74.

We find in Rud. I. ii. 59 *Deludifico,* which seems to be a ἅπ. λεγ., *Deludificavit me ille homo indignis modis.* For other examples of *ludifico* and *ludificor* see Amph. II. 1. 38, III. ii. 71, IV. iii. 13, Bac. III. iv. 28, IV. iv. 3, Capt. III. i. 27, 30, Cas. III. ii. 28, 30, iv. 2, Cist. II. i. 25, Epid. III. ii. 37, Men. III. ii. 57, Merc. II. ii. 36, V. ii. 79, Mil. III. iii. 53, IV. iv. 25, Most. III. ii. 147 (145), V. ii. (iii.) 3, 26, Pers. V. ii. 52, Pseud. IV. vii. 18, Stich. IV. i. 72, Truc. I. i. 5, II. viii. 6; *ludificabilis,* Cas. IV. i. 3, ἅπ. λεγ.; *ludibundus,* Pseud. V. i. 30; *lusor,* Amph. II. ii. 62; *ludius,* Aul. II. ix. 6; *ludificator,* Most. V. i. 18 (ii. 3), a ἅπ. λεγ.

XVII.—*TERMS OF ENDEARMENT AND ABUSE; IMPRECATIONS; EJACULATIONS.*

1. *Terms of endearment.* The vocabulary of the dramatists, especially Plautus, is extremely rich in this department, more so indeed by far than the works of the amatory poets. We find lovers addressing each other as *Mama, Mamilla, Deliciae, Anime mi, Mi Animule, Mea Vita, Meus Oculus, Meus Ocellus, Meum corculum, Mea Amoenitas, Mea Commoditas, Mea Salus, Mea Suavitudo, Mea Voluptas, Mi Lepos, Mea Mulsa.* Sometimes such expressions are grouped together in doublets and triplets, as in Cas. IV. iv. 14, *Meum corculum melliculum verculum!* and v. 19, *Corpusculum melliculum! mea uxorcula!* Stich. V. iv. 54, *Mea suavis amabilis amoena Stephanium!* while occasionally they are showered down as thick as hail: thus Poen. I. ii. 152, *Mea voluptas! meae deliciae! mea vita! mea amoenitas! Meus ocellus! meum labellum! mea salus! meum suavium! Meum mel! meum cor! mea colostra! meus molliculus caseus!* Pseud. I. il. 46, *Natalem scitis mihi diem esse hunc: ubi isti sunt quibus vos oculi estis? Quibus vitae? quibus deliciae estis? quibus suavia? mamillae? mellitae?* Cas. I. 46, *Mi animule, mi Olumpio, Mea vita, mea mellilla, mea festivitas, Sine tuos ocellos deosculer, voluptas mea; Sine, amabo, te amari, meus festus dies, Meus pullus passer, mea columba, mi lepus (lepos?)!* As. III. ill. 74, *P. Da meus ocellus, mea rosa, mi anime, da mea voluptas, Leonida, argentum mihi: ne nos deiunge amantes. L. Dic igitur me tuum passerculum, gallinam, coturnicem, Agnellum, haedillum me tuum dic esse, vel vitellum;* and again v. 101, *P. Mi Libane, ocellus aureus, donum decusque amoris, Amabo, faciam quod voles, da istuc argentum nobis. L. Dic igitur me anaticulam, columbam, vel catellum, Hirundinem, monedulam, passerculum, putillum.*

2. *Terms of abuse.* These are for the most part addressed to slaves and *lenones.* Such characters frequently interchange whole vollies of the coarsest Billingsgate. When treating of the punishments inflicted upon slaves we have already adverted to such expressions as *Verbero, Mastigia, Furcifer, Carnufex,* which constantly recur, also to the more recondite *Carnuficium cribrum, Stimulorum tritor, Vlmorum Acheruns, Gymnasium flagri, Catenarum colone, Virgarum lascivia,* and many others which specially refer to corporal punishment.

The following are more general in their application:

Scelus, Scelesk, 'you incarnation of villainy.'
Scelerosus, 'lump of iniquity.'
Impius, 'godless one.'
Sceleris semen, 'devil's brat.'
Carcer, Custos carceris, 'gaol-bird.'
Stabulum flagiti, 'den of infamy.'
Flagiti flagrantia, 'blazing fire of scandal.'
Fons viti et periuri, 'well-spring of guilt and falsehood.'
Penitus periurum caput, 'unmitigated scoundrel.'
Capuli decus, 'hoary-headed villain.'
Silicernium, 'dead-alive old reprobate.'
Legum contortor, 'perverter of the laws.'
Bonorum extortor, 'robber.'
Perfassor parietum, 'burglar.'
Veneficus, 'poisoner.'
Impurissime, Impuratissume, 'foulest of men.'
Labes populi, Pestis, 'plague-spot of the community.'
Luteus, Luteum lenonium,
Caeno conlitus, Caenum conmistum, } 'filthy blackguard.'
Sterquilinium, Sterquilinium publicum, 'common dunghill.'

In Rud. III. iv. 16 Tranio thus assails the leno Labrax, *Extemplo hercle ego te follem pugillatorium* * *Faciam, et pendentem insursabo pugnis, periurissime;* and again *v.* 47 addresses to him the challenge, *Contende ergo, uter sit tergo verior, Ni offerumentas habebis plures in tergo tuo, Quam ulla navis longa clavos, tum ego ero mendacissumus.* But the most prolonged series of colloquial amenities is to be found in Pseud. I. iii. 125, *C. Ingere mala multa. P. Iam ego te differam dictis meis, Impudice. B. Ita est. P. Sceleste ! B. Dicis vera. P. Verbero ! B. Quippini ? C. Bustirape ! B. Certe. C. Furcifer. B. Factum optume. C. Sociofraude ! B. Sunt mea haec ista. P. Parricida ! B. Perge tu. P. Sacrilege ! B. Fateor. C. Periure ! B. Vetera raticinamini. C. Legirupa ! B. Valide. P. Pernicies adulescentum ! B. Acerrume. C. Fur ! B. Babae. P. Fugitive ! B. Bombax. C. Fraus populi ! B. Planissume. P. Fraudulente ! C. Impure leno ! P. Caenum ! B. Cantores probos !* &c.; so also Pers. III. iii. 2, *D. Toxile, quid agitur ? T. Eho ! lutum lenonium, Commictum caenum, sterquilinum publicum ! Impure ! inhoneste ! iniure ! illex ! labes populi ! Pecuniae accipiter ! avide atque invide ! Procax ! rapax !*

---

* This can scarcely be a 'boxing-glove,' as some imagine, but rather an inflated or stuffed cushion to box against.

trahax ! trecentis versibus Tuas impuritias traloqui nemo potest; and
again, Poen. V. v. 31, *A. Ligula, i in malam crucem ! Tune hic
amator audes esse, hallex viri ? Aut contrectare quod nares homines
amant ? Deglupta maena, Sarrapis sementium, Mastruga, Ðe ἀγορᾶς
ἀμα· tum autem plenior Alli, ulpicique, quam Romani remiges,* and
compare Pseud. I. ii. 1. sqq.

Nor are such compliments addressed to men alone, women also
come in for their share: *Pessuma, Scelesta, Sacrilega, Merx mala,
Merces malae, Venefica, Sexungula* (' six-clawed '), *Colubrino ingenio*
(' double-tongued '), and the like, are freely poured upon them,
and we have already referred to the lines, Truc. IV. iii. 1, where
Callicles hurls threats and abuse at his ancillae.

3. *Imprecations.* The most common of these is the word *malum,*
generally used interjectionally, which may be fairly represented by the
English 'mischief,' 'confusion,' 'confound you :' Most. I. i. 6, *Quid tibi,
malum, hic ante aedes clamatio est ?* ' what are you bawling here for,
in front of the house, confound you ?' and so again v. 53, II. i. 21.
Cf. Rud. II. vi. 8, Adel. IV. ii. 18, Eun. IV. vii. 10, Heaut. IV. iii. 38,
Phor. IV. v. 11, V. vii. 55 ; so also Most. III. i. 122 and Phor. V. vii.
83, *Malum—quod isti di deaeque omnes duint !* ' confusion—and may
all the gods and goddesses bring it (i. e. confusion, mischief) upon
the head of that fellow !' and so again, Amph. II. i. 13, *Malum—quod
tibi di dabunt atque ego hodie Dabo.* The expressions, *I in malam rem*
(Poen. I. ii. 82), *Malam rem his et magnam,* ' bad luck to them, and
plenty of it' (Truc. V. 45), *Quae res tibi vortat male* (Adel. II. i. 37),
I in crucem (As. V. ii. 91), *I in malam crucem* (Poen. I. ii. 59), *I in
malum cruciatum* (Pers. IV. iv. 25, Rud. II. vi. 10), *Abi dierectus,* ' you
be hanged' (Poen. I. i. 32, note on Most. I. i. 8), *Quin tu is hinc a
me in maxumam malam crucem* (Rud. II. vi. 34, Pers. III. i. 24), *I
dierecte in maxumam malam crucem* (Poen. I. ii. 134), and the like,
need no explanation, for the English equivalents will suggest themselves to every one. Our characteristic national imprecation is fully
represented by the phrases, *Quod di te omnes advenientem peregre
perdant, Charmides !* Trin. III. iii. 155 ; *At te di deaeque perduint
cum isto odio Lache !* Hec. I. ii. 59 ; and *Vt te quidem omnes di deaeque, quantum est, Sure, Cum istoc invento cumque incepto perduint !*
Heaut. IV. vi. 7 ; so also Adel. IV. vi. 1, Eun. II. iii. 10.

Sometimes the curse assumes a whimsical form; thus Rud. II. vi.
27, *L. Perii, animo male fit ! contine quaeso caput. C. Pulmoneum
edepol nimis velim vomitum vomas !* L. ' I am sick, pray hold my head.'
C. ' I wish, with all my heart, that you would retch up your lungs !'

and Cas. II. vi. 37, *O. Taceo: Deos quaeso . . . C. Vt quidem tu hodie canem et furcam feras ! O. Mihi ut sortitio eveniat. C. Vt quidem, hercle, pedibus pendeas ! O. At tu ut oculos emungare ex capite per nasum tuos !* 'but I pray that you may blow your eyes out through your nose !'

4. *Adjurations.* No one can fail to be struck by the multitude of adjurations with which the dialogue in Plautus and Terence is interlarded, and which are, for the most part, mere expletives, destitute of any particular emphasis, corresponding to the 'Gad,' 'Bedad,' 'Faith,' 'By Jove,' and a host of others, with which many of our dramatists were wont to season the discourse of their characters.

The words of this kind which appear to have been most in favour with the Romans were, as might be anticipated, appeals to their popular deities, the Great Twin Brethren and Hercules, expressed by *Pol, Edepol, Mecastor, Ecastor, Hercle,* &c.

Pol is manifestly an abbreviation of *Pollux,* and is used either as an independent ejaculation or in connection with verbs and such adverbs as *certe, sane, profecto.* The combination *Per pol,* found in Hec. I. i. 1, *Per pol quam paucos reperias meretricibus Fidles evenire amatores, Syra,* is so strange that commentators have sought to explain it by *tmesis,* conjoining the *per* with *quam.*

Edepol has been held to be a contraction for *per aedem Pollucis,* and hence is sometimes printed *aedepol,* but it is probably merely another form of *Epol,* which is found occasionally in the MSS. of Plautus. *Pol* and *Edepol* in the extant Latin writers are freely used by men and women alike.

Mecastor, we cannot doubt, stands for *me, Castor, iuva,* or *me Castor iuvet,* 'so help me, Castor,' as *Mehercules* or *Mehercule* stand for *me, Hercules, iuva,* or *me Hercules iuvet,* and *Mediusfidius* for *me, Dius Fidius, iuva,* or *me Dius Fidius iuvet,* 'so help me, God of Truth.'

Ecastor, although explained like *Edepol* to be a contraction for *per aedem Castoris,* seems to be simply the name *Castor* with the ejaculatory particle *e* prefixed, as in *Equirine* (Paul. Diac. p. 81, ed. Müll.), *Eiuno* (Charis. p. 183, ed. Puts.), and *Epol,* noticed above.

Hercule or *Hercle* * are the forms in which the invocation of this deity generally appears in Plautus and Terence ; *Mehercle,* although not without example, is rare—Eun. I. i. 22, III. i. 26. The following passage from Aulus Gellius, XI. 6, is curious : "In veteribus scriptis

---

* Cic. Orat. XLVII. § 157, "Et *pomeridianas quadrigas* quam *postmeridianas* libentius dixerim, et *mehercule* quam *mehercules*."

neque mulieres Romanae per Herculem deiurant, neque viri per Castorem. Sed cur illae non iuraverint Herculem, obscurum non est. Nam Herculaneo sacrificio abstinent. Cur autem viri Castorem iurantes non appellaverint, non facile dictu est. Nusquam igitur scriptum invenire est apud idoneos quidem scriptores, aut *mehercule* feminam dicere, aut *mecastor* virum. *Aedepol* autem, quod iusiurandum per Pollucem est, et viro et feminae commune est. Sed M. Varro asseverat antiquissimos viros neque per Castorem neque per Pollucem deiurare solitos; sed id iusiurandum fuisse tantum feminarum ex Initiis Eleusiniis acceptum: paulatim tamen, inscitia antiquitatis, viros dicere *aedepol* cepisse; factumque esse ita dicendi morem: sed *mecastor* a viro dici, in nullo vetere scripto inveniri."

This doctrine has been called in question by scholars, and the following passages have been quoted to prove that men did swear by Castor, and women by Hercules, but they will be found to present no real difficulty. We must bear in mind the circumstance, to which we have already adverted in the Prolegomena, that the distribution of the dialogue among the different characters rests in many cases solely upon the discretion of the mediaeval transcriber or modern editor, for it appears certain that in the MS. which was the archetype of those now existing, the change from one speaker to another was indicated merely by a blank space, the name of the speaker not having been inserted. Indeed, in the best existing MS. of Plautus, the *Vetus Codex* of Camerarius, the space for the names is left blank in some of the plays. This being premised, we may proceed to examine the examples which have been adduced in opposition to the clearly expressed and positive assertion of Varro.

In As. V. ii. the persons on the stage are Artemona, the wife of Demaenetus, Demaenetus himself, his son Argyrippus, Philenium, and a parasite. Artemona and the parasite, unseen by the rest, overhear the conversation of the father, the son, and Philenium; at *v.* 44 the text of the Vulgate is as follows. *Pu. Dic, amabo, an foeki anima uxoris tuae? D. Nautam Bibere malim, si necessum est, quam illam oscularier. Art. Miser ecastor es. Pa. Mecastor dignus est:* but it would be more appropriate to put the words *Miser ecastor es* into the mouth of Philenium, and to make the observation *Mecastor dignus es* proceed from the angry and insulted wife instead of from the parasite.

The next example is to be found in the same scene, *v.* 80, *D. Totus perii! A. Quid tandem? anima foekt ne uxoris tuae? D. Murrham clet. A. Iam subripuisti pallam quam scorto dares?*

A 20. *Ecastor quin subrepturum pallam promisit tibi:* but it will be seen, on referring to the passage, that the last line might proceed quite as naturally from Philenium as from Argyrippus.

A third example is given from Cas. V. iv. 13, where the words *Times ecastor* are assigned to Olympio; but it is not worth while to discuss this, for the whole of the concluding portion of the play is so mutilated that no reliance can be placed on the text, and a large blank commences in this very line.

Again, in order to prove that women sometimes swear by Hercules, we are referred to Merc. IV. iii. 22, where the words *Cupio hercle scire* are given to Dorippa; and to Truc. V. 29, where Phronesium is made to exclaim, *Hercle vero serio.*

In the former passage, Ritschl, following Bothe, slightly alters the arrangement of the lines, and attaches *Cupio hercle scire* to the previous speech of Lysimachus; *Quid autem urbani deliquerunt? dic mihi, Cupio hercle scire. D. Sic tu me temptas sciens:* which, upon studying the passage, will be found to be a much better arrangement.

In the latter there is no reason to prevent us from considering that the words in question are an indignant exclamation proceeding from Stratophanes, and nothing can be more probable, *a priori*, than that some confusion should arise in the distribution of the dialogue from the circumstance that the first four letters in the names *Strabax* and *Stratophanes* are identical.

It is very possible that some other apparent exceptions may be found, but we have little doubt that they may be disposed of as easily as the foregoing.

INDEX.

INDEX.

—:❖Ⅸ❖:—

www.ingramcontent.com/pod-product-compliance
Lightning Source LLC
Chambersburg PA
CBHW032307280326
41932CB00009B/732